Freedom of Information

The International Library of Essays in Law and Legal Theory
Second Series
Series Editor: Tom D. Campbell

Titles in the Series:

Freedom of Speech, Volumes I and II
Larry Alexander

Privacy
Eric M. Barendt

Comparative Legal Cultures
John Bell

Contract Law, Volumes I and II
Brian Bix

Corporate Law
William W. Bratton

Legal Positivism
Tom D. Campbell

Administrative Law
Peter Cane

International Trade Law
Ronald A. Cass and Michael S. Knoll

**Sociological Perspectives on Law,
Volumes I and II**
Roger Cotterrell

Intellectual Property
Peter Drahos

Family, State and Law, Volumes I and II
Michael D. Freeman

Natural Law
Robert P. George

Commercial Law
Clayton P. Gillette

Competition Law
Rosa Greaves

Chinese Law and Legal Theory
Perry Keller

International Law, Volumes I and II
Martti Koskenniemi and David Kennedy

Constitutional Law
Ian D. Loveland

Interpretation of Law
D. Neil MacCormick and Fernando Atria

Human Rights
Robert McCorquodale

Anti-Discrimination Law
Christopher McCrudden

Medical Law and Ethics
Sheila McLean

Mediation
Carrie Menkel-Meadow

Environmental Law
Peter Menell

Criminal Law
Thomas Morawetz

Law and Language
Thomas Morawetz

Law and Anthropology
Martha Mundy

Gender and Justice
Ngaire Naffine

Law and Economics
Eric A. Posner

Japanese Law
J. Mark Ramseyer

Justice
Wojciech Sadurski

The Rule of Law
Frederick Schauer

Regulation
Colin Scott

Restitution
Lionel D. Smith

Company Law
David Sugarman

Freedom of Information
Robert G. Vaughn

Tort Law
Ernest J. Weinrib

Rights
Robin West

Welfare Law
Lucy A. Williams

Freedom of Information

Edited by

Robert G. Vaughn

American University, USA

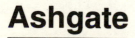

Ashgate

DARTMOUTH

Aldershot • Burlington USA • Singapore • Sydney

Published by
Dartmouth Publishing Company Limited
Ashgate Publishing Limited
Gower House
Croft Road
Aldershot
Hants GU11 3HR
England

Ashgate Publishing Company
131 Main Street
Burlington
Vermont 05401-5600 USA

Ashgate website: http://www.ashgate.com

British Library Cataloguing in Publication Data
Freedom of information. – (International library of essays
   in law and legal theory. Second series)
   1. Freedom of information 2. Freedom of information –
   Political aspects 3. Freedom of information – United States
   4. Whistle blowing – Law and legislation – United States
   I. Vaughn, Robert G.
   342'.0853

Library of Congress Cataloging-in-Publication Data
Freedom of information / edited by Robert G. Vaughn.
         p. cm. — (International library of essays in law and legal theory. Second series)
      Includes bibliographical references.
      ISBN 0-7546-2081-6 (HB)
         1. Freedom of information. 2. Government information. 3. Public records—Law and
   legislation. 4. Freedom of information—United States. 5. Government records—United
   States. 6. Public records—Law and legislation—United States. I. Vaughn, Robert G. II.
   Series.

   K3476 .F74 2000
   342.73'0853—dc21   00-030628

ISBN 0 7546 2081 6

Printed and bound by Athenaeum Press, Ltd.,
Gateshead, Tyne & Wear.

Contents

Acknowledgements

The editor and publishers wish to thank the following for permission to use copyright material.

ABA Publishing for the essays: Michael E. Tankersley (1998), 'How the Electronic Freedom of Information Act Amendments of 1996 Update Public Access for the Information Age', *Administrative Law Review*, **50**, pp. 421–58; James T. O'Reilly (1998), 'Expanding the Purpose of Federal Records Access: New Private Entitlement or New Threat to Privacy?', *Administrative Law Review*, **50**, pp. 371–89; Thomas M. Devine (1999), 'The Whistleblower Protection Act of 1989: Foundation for the Modern Law of Employment Dissent', *Administrative Law Review*, **51**, pp. 531–79. Reprinted by permission.

American University for the essay: Debra L. Silverman (1997), 'Freedom of Information: Will Blair be Able to Break the Walls of Secrecy in Britain?', *American University International Law Review*, **13**, pp. 471–551.

Cato Institute for the essay: Antonin Scalia (1982), 'The Freedom of Information Act Has No Clothes', *Regulation: AEI Journal on Government and Society*, **14**, pp. 15–19.

Harvard Law Review for the essay: Thomas O. McGarity and Sidney A. Shapiro (1980), 'The Trade Secret Status of Health and Safety Testing Information: Reforming Agency Disclosure Policies', *Harvard Law Review*, **93**, pp. 837–88. Copyright © 1980 Harvard Law Review.

University of California Press for the essay: James Boyle (1992), 'A Theory of Law and Information: Copyright, Spleens, Blackmail, and Insider Trading', *California Law Review*, **80**, pp. 1413–540. Copyright © 1992 California Law Review, Inc.

Wisconsin Law Review for the essay: Thomas O. Sargentich (1984), 'The Reform of the American Administrative Process: The Contemporary Debate', *Wisconsin Law Review*, pp. 385–442.

Preface to the Second Series

The first series of the International Library of Essays in Law and Legal Theory has established itself as a major research resource with fifty-eight volumes of the most significant theoretical essays in contemporary legal studies. Each volume contains essays of central theoretical importance in its subject area and the series as a whole makes available an extensive range of valuable material of considerable interest to those involved in research, teaching and the study of law.

The rapid growth of theoretically interesting scholarly work in law has created a demand for a second series which includes more recent publications of note and earlier essays to which renewed attention is being given. It also affords the opportunity to extend the areas of law covered in the first series.

The new series follows the successful pattern of reproducing entire essays with the original page numbers as an aid to comprehensive research and accurate referencing. Editors have selected not only the most influential essays but also those which they consider to be of greatest continuing importance. The objective of the second series is to enlarge the scope of the library, include significant recent work and reflect a variety of editorial perspectives.

Each volume is edited by an expert in the specific area who makes the selection on the basis of the quality, influence and significance of the essays, taking care to include essays which are not readily available. Each volume contains a substantial introduction explaining the context and significance of the essays selected.

I am most grateful for the care which volume editors have taken in carrying out the complex task of selecting and presenting essays which meet the exacting criteria set for the series.

TOM CAMPBELL
Series Editor
The Faculty of Law
The Australian National University

Introduction

Freedom of information laws permit individuals and organizations to obtain government documents and records as well as other information. Although these laws have a long lineage in some Scandinavian countries,[1] in the United States, Canada and Australia, freedom of information provisions of general applicability are features of the later third of the Twentieth Century. In the United States, the federal Freedom of Information Act[2] (FOIA) dates from 1966, although some states passed laws before that date and some common-law access to public documents dated from the formation of the country. Now, every US state as well as the federal government has a freedom of information provision giving access to government documents and records. Canada[3] and Australia[4] joined the United States in 1982.

These laws, however, are becoming more common. Recently Great Britain[5] has considered and Japan[6] has enacted broadly applicable laws. European Union provisions provide access to the documents of EU institutions[7] and one directs national governments to make available certain types of government documents and records regarding the environment.[8] The structure and content of this latter directive is reminiscent of the US FOIA. The advocates of transparency in international organizations, such as the World Bank, propose reforms incorporating principles contained in national freedom of information laws. Thus, freedom of information laws now affect the world's major industrial nations and increasingly are given international scope. Most of the literature in English describing and analyzing these laws addresses the United States, Canada and Australia but this literature suggests methods for examining and evaluating freedom of information laws generally.

Freedom of information provisions address similar issues. This similarity reflects the commonality of the problems that any such law must consider. These common issues concern the scope and coverage of the law, exemptions from disclosure, the obligations of government officials, the methods of enforcement and the rights of those persons and groups that submit information to the government. The federal Freedom of Information Act in the United States provides one example of the resolution of these common issues.

Under that law *any person* may request government documents and records; a person need not give a reason for a request because government documents and records are presumed to be available to any requester. Moreover, certain types of documents and records, such as agency rules and regulations, opinions resolving agency adjudications, and portions of manuals and guides that affect members of the public must be made available, without request, in public reading rooms. Not every government agency, however, is necessarily subject to the law. For example, in the United States, the Executive Office of the President, including the National Security Council, are not agencies covered by the law.

Because the law applies to *government* documents and records, it does not cover private records of government officials, narrowly defined. Recently, Congress has proposed a law that would expand the federal FOIA to include the documents and records of government contractors relating to government contracts performed by them.[9] This expansion would bring a substantial number of organizations within the ambit of the law.

All access laws must address exemptions from disclosure, including the substance and generality of the exemptions. These exemptions can be mandatory, requiring withholding of the indicated documents, or discretionary, authorizing but not requiring an agency to claim an exemption. The exemptions can be very broad – as in the EU code of conduct regarding the European Commission providing that its documents may be withheld in 'the public interest'[10] – or they can be quite specific, detailing dozens of specific exemptions – as is the case in the freedom of information law of the State of Virginia in the United States.[11]

The federal FOIA contains nine exemptions. These include ones for documents:

1. properly classified in the interests of national defense or foreign policy,
2. that are internal guides or directives discussing enforcement strategies, the release of which would risk evasion of the law,
3. the disclosure of which is specifically prohibited by other laws,
4. containing confidential or privileged commercial or financial information,
5. protected by certain litigation privileges, including the attorney–client, work product and deliberative process privileges,
6. the release of which would constitute a clearly unwarranted invasion of personal privacy,
7. complied for law enforcement purposes, the release of which would, or in some instances could reasonably be expected to, create the risk of certain harms,
8. contained in or related to oversight of financial institutions by an agency charged with regulation or supervision of such institutions,
9. containing geophysical and geological information regarding oil wells.[12]

Just because a document contains information which would be exempted from disclosure is an insufficient basis for an agency to withhold the entire document. The federal FOIA obligates the agency to release all portions of the document that can be reasonably segregated from those portions of the documents that are exempt. Thus, a requester is not automatically denied a document because part of it would be exempt.

Generally, the exemptions only authorize, but do not require the withholding of documents by an agency. Some of the exemptions, however, do address types of documents which may not be disclosed. The two principal examples are the exemptions protecting properly classified national security information and personal privacy. The mandatory character of these exemptions results from related laws that restrict the discretion provided by the FOIA. The personal privacy exemption and a similar one in the exemption regarding law enforcement records are the only ones that require a balancing of the interests harmed by disclosure against the interests served by access.

Freedom of information statutes articulate administrative procedures for requests, including periods for response and agency obligations to provide reasons for the denial of a request. The federal FOIA specifies these administrative procedures and several amendments to the law have concerned them. Many statutes place enforcement on administrative officials, such as ombudspersons, with the courts playing a limited or complementary role. The federal FOIA relies upon judicial enforcement through the federal courts in which the requester may sue for redress from a denial. In this suit, no deference is given to the agency's decision or to the agency's findings of facts. Rather, the court conducts a *de novo* review of the agency's decision. In that review, the agency has the burden of persuasion to demonstrate that its withholding of the requested documents is authorized by law.

Much of the information contained in government documents is not generated by the government but rather provided to the government by third persons. Increasingly, the rights of these persons have become an important part of the debate regarding freedom of information laws. In 1987, President Reagan issued an Executive Order giving to those who submit information certain procedural rights, including the right to be informed that a request has been made for documents submitted by such a person, and the right to be heard prior to the release of the documents.[13]

Laws Protecting Whistleblowers

In the United States, open government laws or 'sunshine laws' are closely connected to the justifications for freedom of information provisions. (The term, 'sunshine laws' comes from an often repeated statement of Supreme Court Justice Louis Brandeis, 'Sunlight is said to be the best of disinfectants...'[14]) These laws, enacted in many of the states as well as by the federal government, include open-meeting laws,[15] laws providing public review of boards advising government agencies,[16] access to litigation materials,[17] and protection of whistleblowers. This essay will focus on one of these, whistleblower protection laws.

Whistleblower protection provisions illustrate how the rationale of the freedom of information statutes apply to these other laws. These whistleblower provisions protect employees who disclose certain types of wrongdoing by government officials. Most states in the United States have laws that protect public employees who disclose wrongdoing by government officials. The best known of the whistleblower laws is the Whistleblower Protection Act of 1989[18] applicable to federal employees. This Act was itself an expansion of the ground-breaking protection for federal employee whistleblowers in the Civil Service Reform Act of 1978.[19] As with freedom of information provisions, whistleblower protection can now be found in many countries.[20]

The remainder of this essay explores the unifying themes of freedom of information laws and the relationship of these themes to other open government laws, such as whistleblower protection. This exploration begins with an analysis of the relationship between the federal FOIA and administrative and constitutional theory in the United States and with the current discussions about the regulation of information generally. It moves to a discussion of the effects of the computer and internet revolutions on these laws. The analysis of these themes in the midst of the computer revolution provides a way of viewing the 'internationalization' of freedom of information and other open government laws. It also allows speculation regarding the future of these provisions.

The Federal Freedom of Information Act and Administrative and Constitutional Theory in the United States

Freedom of information provisions can appear to be insular bodies of specialized laws. They seem to form a body of technical, almost esoteric, rules and principles. Despite these appearances, freedom of information laws are deeply embedded in US administrative theory and partake of the general debate regarding administrative theory and practice. In turn, US administrative theory is closely linked to liberal thought. Recognition of these relationships offers several advantages. It provides a way of organizing and examining these laws; it exposes the inconsistencies and paradoxes besetting arguments supporting these provisions; and it allows prediction regarding the difficulties inherent in specific proposals.

Freedom of information laws in the United States cannot be fully understood without examining the relationship between these laws and the First Amendment which in the US guarantees, among other rights, the rights of free speech, free association and a free press. Freedom of information laws fill gaps in interpretations of the First Amendment. Similarly, the theories supporting First Amendment protection have been imported into discussions of freedom of information laws. Again, the federal FOIA provides a convenient example to explore these relationships.

Current discussions about the regulation of information are also helpful in understanding freedom of information laws. These discussions have focused on information more generally, but offer methods of analysis and insights which emphasize similarities between government information laws and more general attempts to regulate information. These similarities have been highlighted by the challenges which electronic technology have posed to the accepted principles of law applicable to information.

The reader not from the United States is asked to bear with what may at times seem like a parochial exercise, but I write about what I know best. This exploration should prove useful in the subsequent discussion of whistleblower protection laws and in speculation about the future of freedom of information provisions. It is no accident that the grounding of US administrative theory on liberal political thought exposes a constellation of ideas beneath freedom of information laws, many of which are of immediate currency outside the context of their creation. This currency and the ascendancy of liberal thought as exemplified in democracy and capitalism provide one explanation for the recent and rapid growth of open government provisions.

The Federal Freedom of Information Act and Administrative Theory

Freedom of information laws are logically part of administrative law. They share with administrative law the attempt to control administrative discretion. Like administrative law, they seek to regulate public bureaucracies. They also share with administrative law the differing and often conflicting justifications for such regulation. These differences and the conflicts inherent in them can be traced to different visions of the appropriate or 'ideal' administrative process.

To frame this discussion, I have chosen Thomas Sargentich's 'The Reform of the American Administrative Process: The Contemporary Debate' (Chapter 1) in part because his essay organizes and critiques proposals for administrative reform, including open government provisions. He does this through references to competing ideals of administrative law. To him, these ideals are not merely categories which facilitate description, but are competing visions based on conflicting and inconsistent answers to a fundamental question of administrative law – 'On what general normative principles may the use of often substantial public power by unelected agency officials in our political system be justified and, at least for the system as a whole, legitimated?' These ideals of administrative law, the Rule of Law Ideal, the Public Purposes Ideal and the Democratic Process Ideal, arise from different strains of liberal political thought. Each represents a vision that conflicts with competing visions of the administrative process. Each contains a core embodiment which represents a pure vision of the administrative process, but which confronts both the reality of the administrative process preventing its application, and an internal paradox that undermines its operative principles. The core embodiments are respectively: formalism, instrumentalism, and participation.

As a result, each ideal also contains an alternative expression that is less true to the ideal, but more likely of implementation. These alternative expressions of the three ideals are respectively: proceduralism, protection of the market, and political oversight. Although each alternative expression is consistent with the vision of administration underlying each ideal, it falls short of full implementation of that vision. As a result, it supports arguments that can be melded with those supporting some of the other ideals.

The history of the federal Freedom of Information Act demonstrates how that statute is related to these fundamental conceptions of administration contained in liberal political thought. The Rule of Law Ideal in its core embodiment requires that all exercises of public authority come from legal standards enacted by legislative bodies. Thus, it seeks to limit and confine administrative discretion. The alternative expression focuses instead on the importance of procedure in ensuring the proper exercise of that discretion although it fails to provide any substantive limitation on it.

If legal standards are to limit administrative discretion, those standards must be known. Without knowledge of these standards, it is difficult to believe that they will meaningfully limit administrative action. At the time of the enactment of the federal FOIA in 1966, a central concern of Congress was that public access to agency documents was necessary to protect against the application of secret law.[21] The FOIA's requirement that certain documents – rules and regulations, adjudicatory opinions, and relevant guides and manuals – be available without request seeks to ensure that the standards controlling the agency's exercise of public power are available to the public.

The concept of any-person access also implements that Rule of Law Ideal. Congress intended that this concept, by eliminating the need to explain the reasons why a requester sought information, would reduce agency discretion in evaluating individual requests. If the requested documents did not fall under an exemption claimed by an agency, any person, regardless of the reasons for which they sought the documents, was entitled to receive them.

The structure of the FOIA, however, is inconsistent with the Rule of Law Ideal for it grants considerable discretion to individual agencies in applying the exemptions to disclosure. Not only do agencies have discretion whether to claim an exemption or not, but these agencies also have discretion in initially interpreting the meaning of these broad exemptions. Because of the breadth of the exemptions and the discretion entailed in their application, the bulk of the litigation under the law has addressed their meaning. Despite extensive judicial interpretations of the exemptions, considerable discretion in their interpretation remains. Moreover, agencies also enjoy discretion in applying these standards to new categories of documents. Judicial interpretations, particularly regarding the exemption for properly classified documents, have conceded considerable agency discretion in the application of the exemptions.

Sargentich's articulation of the paradox or self-defeating characteristic of formalism, the core embodiment of the Rule of Law Ideal, resonates with the history of the federal FOIA.

Sargentich believes that the attempt to subject all administrative action to restraint by norms leads to norms of such indeterminancy that they fail to provide sufficient restraint.

Proceduralism is the response to the limitations of formalism. It seeks to channel administrative discretion by requiring that officials follow fair procedures in exercising their discretion. It seeks to regulate not the substance of decisions, but rather the process by which they are made.

Given the practical and theoretical restrictions on the core embodiment of formalism, reforms of the 1966 Freedom of Information Act have emphasized procedural rather than substantive reform. Although the 1974 amendments to the FOIA modified some of the exemptions, the thrust of the amendments was procedural. These amendments prescribed a number of procedures, including time limits for agency responses, provisions for administrative appeals, and criteria for charging fees for complying with requests. Similarly, a substantial portion of the Electronic Freedom of Information Act of 1996 addresses procedural issues. Michael Tankersley's essay, 'How the Electronic Freedom of Information Act Amendments of 1996 Update Public Access for the Information Age' (Chapter 2), examines these changes and places them in the context of previous procedural reforms.

The core embodiment of the Public Purposes Ideal, instrumentalism, stresses the role of administrative agencies in accomplishing important public tasks. In so doing, agencies rely on rational analysis in carrying out the affirmative obligations of government. Rather than fearing discretion, instrumentalism exalts it.

Unlike the Rule of Law Ideal, the Public Purposes Ideal conflicts with the concept of openness incorporated into the FOIA. An agency needs secrecy to examine alternative courses of action; frank discussions are necessary to apply rational criteria, and openness may create risks that such rational analysis will yield to political or social pressures.

The Public Purposes Ideal was not central to the enactment of the FOIA although at the time of its enactment, FOIA was seen as a way of improving agency decision-making. For example, information provisions encourage better articulation of the rationale for decisions, and, by making available the techniques of analysis, the law opens that analysis to challenge and refinement. The law, however, did consider the role of government in strengthening private decision-making, a goal that looks more to the alternative expression of this ideal of protecting the market.

From inception of the FOIA, Congress was aware that the FOIA would be used for purposes other than evaluating the performance of government officials. Government would hold great amounts of information useful to citizens, consumers, scientists, businesses and researchers. In this sense, the government would become a clearing house of information for commercial enterprises and for consumers. By the time of the 1974 amendments, the clearing-house function of the FOIA was seen by Congress as a central purpose of the law.[22] This clearing-house function, by providing information to commercial enterprises and to consumers, uses the market and private decision-making to accomplish the public good and principally views agencies as sources of the relevant information.

James O'Reilly's essay, 'Expanding the Purpose of Federal Records Access: New Private Entitlement or New Threat to Privacy?' (Chapter 3), describes the expansion of this clearing-house function under the Electronic Freedom of Information Act of 1996 and questions whether this expansion will significantly harm personal privacy and the commercial interests of those enterprises submitting information to the government. The expansion of the clearing-house function can in fact weaken rather than support private decision-making and the market. He contrasts the more limited function of ensuring government legality, basic to the Rule of Law Ideal, with the broader view that the government be a provider of information, a view more consistent with the alternative expression of the Public Purposes Ideal.

Two developments point, however, to instrumentalism and clear adoption of the basic premises of the Public Purposes Ideal. These developments, a concern with information management and the electronic dissemination of information, share much with instrumentalism. Information management focuses on the expertise of agencies and their ability through the application of rational criteria to manage information in the best interests of the public. Several information laws related to the FOIA emphasize information management. These include the Privacy Act of 1974,[23] the Paperwork Reduction Act,[24] the Computer Matching Act and Protection Privacy Act of 1988[25] and the Computer Security Act,[26] all of which address information management issues and mandate the development of management strategies. In so doing, they increasingly rely on agency expertise in accomplishing the management goals set out in these pieces of legislation. The future of the FOIA is likewise more closely linked to agency expertise in management and administration.

The electronic revolution has reinforced the importance of the management of information. The Electronic Freedom of Information Act shifts in many areas from an access model based on requests for information to a dissemination model based on affirmative obligations of government to provide a wide variety of information. This shift combines easily with the clearing-house function to make agency expertise increasingly important. This reorientation of federal information policy and of the FOIA shares much with instrumentalism.

This reorientation fails to consider the limitations of instrumentalism. Sargentich argues that instrumentalism's attempt to reach the optimal solution requires that virtually all factors be taken into account, thus depriving analysis of any content and leading to indeterminacy in outcome. Moreover, this reorientation fails to recognize the conflict between instrumentalism and the assumptions of openness supporting freedom of information provisions.

The Democratic Process Ideal rests on a participatory and representative decision-making process in which agency officials consider the views of those affected by administrative decisions. The administrative process is primarily political. The core embodiment of the Ideal, participation, seeks to transform the administrative process into a political one in which citizens directly participate.

Although the rhetoric of the federal FOIA has been strongly anti-bureaucratic, and thus shares with participation a disapproval of bureaucratic organization and function, the FOIA has not adopted the tenets of participation. The FOIA does not require participation in any administrative process or in any administrative decision. Rather, it only seeks to give persons access to government documents and records.

This role of the FOIA is more consistent with the alternative expression of the Democratic Process Ideal – political oversight. Citizens are given the information necessary to participate in the political process. By appealing to elected officials – Congress and the President, who oversee the bureaucracy – citizens are able to affect bureaucratic decisions and to protect their interests.

This relationship between the FOIA and the oversight function of politically responsible bodies connects the FOIA with the First Amendment. Access to information is necessary to effective participation in the political process which may be used to make agency officials democratically accountable for their decisions.

In this regard, the FOIA can also be seen to provide for a type of 'information equity' between interests groups who clash in these political arenas. Highly organized interests, subject to agency regulation, with close ties to the agency are likely to possess considerable information about bureaucratic action without freedom of information provisions. The FOIA gives less organized groups a way to obtain information necessary to contend with their more highly organized adversaries. Indeed, the history of the FOIA demonstrates how consumers and other groups have used the law to acquire important information about government policies and practices as the basis for political and public response.[27]

Provisions of the FOIA, such as those providing for fee waivers and for the payment of attorney fees to requesters who succeed in a judicial action to require agency compliance with the Act, incorporate this concept of 'information equity' underlying oversight. Portions of the fee waiver provisions of the 1974 amendments, the Electronic Freedom of Information Act of 1996, and other proposals which distinguish between groups of requesters seek, in part, to implement the goal of equality of access to government documents and records.

Although debate regarding creation of rights in persons who submit information to the government has often been viewed as a conflict between privacy and access, that debate can also be viewed as a part of the concern regarding 'information equity'. In particular, when the persons who submit information are large commercial enterprises who already enjoy close ties with administrative agencies, rules that make access to agency information more difficult can impede the ability of other groups to acquire sufficient information to address agency decisions that affect the interest of those commercial enterprises as well as those of less well organized groups.

Although perceived as an insular body of law, the FOIA is firmly embedded in administrative theory. Conflicts regarding information policy necessarily are part of the major debates about administrative legitimacy and decision-making.

Some conservative critics, however, see the FOIA as a misguided venture in regulation. Like many such ventures, its benefits are outweighed by its substantial costs to political and economic life. It is misguided because the unintended consequences of the law have over-whelmed any justifications supporting it. One of the best known (and bombastic) of these critiques is that by Antonin Scalia, now a Justice of the United States Supreme Court. His essay, 'The Freedom of Information Act Has No Clothes' (Chapter 4), captures the content and tone of some of these attacks.

The Freedom of Information Act and the First Amendment

The importance of the federal FOIA to the First Amendment follows from the emphasis of First Amendment precedent on the right to speak. Less developed is a First Amendment right of access to information. Although a combination of common law rights, the First Amendment, and other constitutional rights mandate open civil and criminal trials and, less clearly, access to court documents supporting dispositive orders, the First Amendment provides little ground for access to other types of government documents and records.

Indeed, one of the justifications for the enactment of freedom of information provisions rested on the need for such access as support for the First Amendment. This need is illustrated by a personal experience. When I lived in England, like many American tourists, I visited Hyde Park Corner to hear a variety of speakers rant and otherwise expostulate with the crowd regarding a range of government actions. Rather than an illustration of free speech, the visit was, for me, a demonstration that without access to information, the right of free speech is significantly diminished. The speakers could say what they wished but little attention was paid to their arguments not only because of the context of these speeches but also because of their content. Most of the speakers simply 'did not know what they were talking about'. In particular, in the case of political speech, the lack of information about the government conduct at issue reduced the credibility of the speaker and diminished the value of the right to speak. In the United States, this empowerment of the First Amendment right of free speech has been seen as an important justification of freedom of information.[28]

As the previous discussion of the Democratic Process Ideal suggested, the federal FOIA also supported the First Amendment right of free association. Without information about government decisions *and* the implications of these decisions for different groups, the need to associate and the impetus to do so is undermined. The right without the motivation or means of encouraging association can render that right empty and insignificant.

In the federal government and in the states, media interests were the earliest supporters of freedom of information provisions as well as the most politically potent group advocating such laws. The media, particularly the print media, played this role in the enactment and in subsequent amendments to the federal FOIA. The media remain ardent supporters of the law. Their support was particularly important in the passage of the 1974 amendments to the law over the veto of President Gerald Ford and in the successful defense of the law against significant restrictions on access sought by the Reagan administration.

Of course, the media's support correlates with their commercial interests. Their support also rests on the close connection between the First Amendment protections of a free press and access to information. Although the press are not among the groups most frequently using the law (delays in acquiring information may discourage such use when time is of the essence), the Act has provided the basis for a number of important exposés of government misconduct.[29]

Electronically Held Information and the Federal Freedom of Information Act

My colleague, James Boyle, in a yet unpublished work, has proposed the 'telephone test' for the seemingly ubiquitous discussions of the implications of the internet for almost any conceivable topic. The telephone test requires that you substitute the word telephone (or some analogous and relevant existing technology, such as television or radio) for the internet in any of these discussions. If the telephone fits as well as the internet, the author may be addressing an important topic, but it is unlikely to be intertwined with the internet or the computer revolution.

The link between electronically held information and the federal FOIA passes this telephone test. The shift from paper records to electronically held ones represented a change in technology and posed questions that were not addressed by the Act, which was drafted at a time when almost all government documents and records were in paper form. The technology of electronically held records raised issues that required interpretation of the law in light of this new technology. For example, the Act only applies to existing documents and records; the government is not required to create a document which did not previously exist. If the government uses a computer program to extract the requested document from a database, has it created a new document? Does it do so if it extracts information from a database in a way different from the way in which it does so for government purposes? How much programing is required before the government can legitimately argue that it is creating something new? These questions illustrate how electronically held documents challenge the concept of a document inherited from an age of paper records. The subtle shift in the second question above from document to information shows how the concept of document can be altered when *information* in a database can be retrieved in many different ways.

The change in technology also raised questions regarding other agency obligations under the law. Should a requester be able to obtain the document in the format that best serves the interest of the requester? Should the government be required to provide access to the software that it uses to manipulate the database?

Another issue requires slightly more explanation. Under the FOIA, an agency is required to segregate exempt portions of a document from non-exempt portions. When the requester receives a paper record with the segregated exempt portions removed, the requester is able to see word by word, or line by line, or page by page what has been removed and is able to judge the magnitude of deletions in light of the length of the document itself. With electronically held records, it is *much* easier than with a paper record to reformat the document so that the exempted portions simply disappear. The requester may find it difficult to determine how much has been deleted, and in some cases, where in the document the deletions have been made. Does this change in practice permitted by the change in technology significantly alter the rights provided by the FOIA?

These questions arise directly from the change in technology. The verification of this statement is that the arguments about these issues were based upon analogies to previous technology, with adversaries drawing on different aspects of that technology to form their analogies. The essay by Michael Tankersley in Chapter 2 describes how the Electronic Information Act of 1996 addresses these issues as well as long-standing ones in the administration of the Act.

The technological revolution regarding electronically held information has animated recent discussions of the regulation of information. These discussions are relevant to information held by the government and therefore to freedom of information provisions.

James Boyle in his essay, 'A Theory of Law and Information: Copyright, Spleens, Blackmail, and Insider Trading' (Chapter 5), approaches the regulation of information more generally. In my use of his essay as with Sargentich's, I do not pretend to capture in this essay the subtlety or nuance of the analysis. The conceptual richness of these works is another reason that I have included them so that a reader can appreciate the organization of this essay and has the material from which to draw conclusions different from the ones that I emphasize.

Like Sargentich, Boyle sees regulation of information as closely tied to the ways in which liberal theory envisions the role of the state. Liberal political thought limits the role of the state by separating the public and private spheres. This distinction plays an important role in the regulation of information; private activities are ones identified with property and with privacy and the ability to withhold information. In the public sphere, information should be freely available to all. To accomplish this division, law must regulate information differently in the public and private spheres.

In the private sphere, information is conceived of as property. This conception of information as property changes the legal entitlements of the holder of information. The conception of information as property poses significant obstacles to regulation of information and redistribution of the entitlements attached to its control.

Boyle's analysis suggests that *public information law* is likely to encounter difficulty in identifying the areas in which it is to operate. We should expect considerable uncertainty in determining where public information law ends and private rights in information begin.

Boyle also demonstrates that economic analysis cannot ease the difficulties in distinguishing public and private information. He identifies a paradoxical meaning of information that plagues attempts to use economic analysis to resolve conflicts in either public or private information law. Economic theory treats information as a condition of the economic model, that is, information is free and costless. At the same time, economists use that economic model, including its assumptions about information, to evaluate information as it would any other product. As Boyle says, '[P]erfect information is a defining conceptual element of the analytical structure used to analyze markets driven by the absence of information, in which imperfect information is actually a commodity.'[30]

For our purposes, and as a gross simplification of these ideas, we can view conceptions of information from a First Amendment or public political life perspective, from a privacy perspective or from a property one. These perspectives will prove useful in examining how freedom of information laws have responded to technological change.

The computer revolution and the internet have forced a reassessment of public information laws. This reassessment is part of a larger one which addresses more generally law and information. As applied to freedom of information laws, this reassessment allows us to see, as Boyle describes, what has been suppressed in the familiarity of legal and social relationships.

The combination of electronically held documents and the internet has suggested a much broader appraisal of the goals and purposes of the federal FOIA. In 1974, advocates of amendment to the law saw it as a way of providing access to a clearing house of government information. With the internet, government information could be easily available to anyone with a computer and a modem. By placing information on websites and providing links from websites to other collections of documents and records, the government could actively disseminate information. Reading rooms in which the FOIA requires some material to be placed could become virtual reading rooms, accessible anywhere. These reading rooms could contain commonly requested information or access to larger databases of information of value to specific groups of users.

Even when a specific request for information is required, electronic technology could allow that request to be made online at an agency website. On those sites, an agency's response to the request could also be electronic. Even within the access model, the internet and the computer revolution can transform practice and administration. Michael Tankersley's essay in Chapter 2 also explores how the EFOIA addresses these broader issues raised by these technological changes.

Electronic freedom of information laws have also directed attention to the character of information. The application of freedom of information principles to documents held electronically forces reassessment of those principles. In this context, James Boyle's essay suggests that a rich mixture of metaphor and contrasting concepts of information will be brought into this reassessment. Underlying these metaphors are some paradoxes of liberal political theory and thought: the distinction between the public and the private spheres; the contrasting conceptions of information as a good, subject to the restraints imposed by the economic theory, and, at the same time, as a free and costless commodity, which forms one of the principal assumptions of that theory; and the often inconsistent visions of information as property, as a public resource supporting both economic innovation and political rights, and as a unique and important aspect of personhood. It is with electronic freedom of information law that these conflicts, inconsistencies and paradoxes surface.

The dissemination of information can conflict with the privacy interests of persons in several ways. First, electronic dissemination of information changes the concept of public record. Before the advent of electronically held records, a paper record existed in a limited number of locations, if not a single place. Although it might be available, the difficulty of locating it limited access. In addition, public records regarding a specific person or group were likely to be scattered in many places. Compilation of these scattered records required efforts rarely justified. Dissemination through the internet removes the physical limitation on the concept of public document. The use of computer technology, either by the government or by requesters, permits the aggregation of information from these documents easily and quickly. That aggregation of information, all from public records, would be considerably less likely to exist without the internet and the dissemination of government documents.

The United States Supreme Court has never accepted the clearing-house function of the FOIA as a 'core purpose' of the law. Rather, according to the Court, the core purpose of the Act was to permit persons to understand the operations of government, particularly to examine suspected agency misconduct. When the FOIA requires a balancing of the interests in disclosure against the privacy interests affected by disclosure, the Court permitted only this 'core purpose' to be considered.[31] Thus, other important public values of disclosure, incorporated in the clearing-house concept, could not be considered. As a result, minimal violations of privacy, such as the disclosure of the address of a federal employee, would be sufficient to permit withhholding if the core purpose of the FOIA was not involved.

In his essay in Chapter 3, James O'Reilly argues that the Electronic Freedom of Information Act has repealed the core purposes doctrine and affirmed the importance of the government as a clearing house of information. He demonstrates why he believes that these aspects of the law combined with the technology of the internet create unacceptable risks to privacy. He also predicts dire consequences for organizations and businesses about which the government holds information.

Second, the dissemination of information electronically held by the government forces examination of the property rights or entitlements that will attach to such information. Although the question of property rights has lurked in the background of the debate regarding the rights of persons who submit information to the government, the role of property rights has come to the fore in the discussion of the dissemination of information held electronically by the government. Businesses and corporations submitting information to the government had often expressed concern that subsequent disclosure of that information interfered with, if not destroyed, important property rights in proprietary information, in trade secrets, and in research. These claims raised the conundrums of the definition of such rights. Academics tended to employ an economic or utilitarian analysis rather than other conceptions of property, such as those resting on natural rights or on property as a precondition to the preservation of political rights and freedoms. The essay, 'The Trade Secret Status of Health and Safety Testing Information: Reforming Agency Disclosure Policies' (Chapter 6), by Thomas McGarity and Sidney Shapiro illustrates this approach to the resolution of these claims. The debate, however, remained unfocused with few persons grappling with the implications of these contrasting conceptions of property.

The discussion of the role of government in the dissemination of electronically held information, on the other hand, highlighted the importance of the attachment of property rights. This emphasis was connected with the technology of such dissemination. Often the software programs permitting dissemination were created not by the government, but by independent contractors who retained proprietary interests in those programs. As already noted, attempts to acquire computer programs necessary to use government databases efficiently was a point of contention even when the government had created such software. The role of private property emerged, however, when those programs were created by third parties who retained property interests in them.

Government dissemination of electronically held information raised the issues of property more starkly. These issues gravitated to the center rather than the periphery of the discussion. The influential report of the Administrative Conference of the United States, the agency responsible for research regarding issues in the administration of government, addressed legal regulation of electronically held government information.[32] In discussing the dissemination of such information, the report emphasized the importance of property rights.

The report recognized that the government must decide when it would disseminate information from a database or when it should give the right to do so to private parties. The report, however, suggested that the decisions involved more than the licensing of government information. Dissemination could be nothing more than access to the raw data that formed the database. In this case, many, perhaps most requesters, would find the data difficult to use and interpret. Such use and interpretation required search programs, directories, menus and other such aids. If the government, however, provided these aids in each case, the government could retard private initiatives and innovation as these would not occur without the economic incentives that would be provided by ownership of the programs and procedures that would make the government data more valuable. The report identified the conflicts involved in such choices. Should the 'information' contained in the databases be seen as a public good to be developed and exploited by the government alone or, in the interests of the public, should private property rights be assigned to programs and guides necessary to make the 'information' useful? In fact, the term 'government information' has meaning only after this decision about the allocation of property rights has been made. The report relied upon cost-benefit analysis, to be applied in individual cases, as the way of resolving these conflicts. The dilemmas identified by the report, however, raise, as Boyle explains, other visions of information as well.

Freedom of information laws in the United States have been connected to liberal political theory regarding the role of state and the place of administrative agencies within it. These laws also draw upon varying conceptions of information and partake of the richness of metaphor and theory surrounding those conceptions. Rather than being isolated and esoteric bodies of law, freedom of information laws are intertwined with contemporary debates in modern American public law.

Before examining the 'internationalization' of these laws, a discussion which will close this essay, the next section examines a related body of law – protection of whistleblowers, that is, public employees who disclose various types of government misconduct. This body of law is often linked with freedom of information laws as an 'open government' provision and not surprisingly shares many of the same theoretical underpinnings. Like freedom of information laws, whistleblower protection provisions have gained acceptance outside of the United States.

Whistleblower Protection Laws

Thomas Devine's essay, 'The Whistleblower Protection Act of 1989: Foundation for the Modern Law of Employment Dissent' (Chapter 7), describes the development of federal laws designed to protect federal employees who disclose specific types of wrongdoing by government officials and employees. He discusses these federal laws in some detail, focusing on the 1989 Act, and examines the justifications for protection of federal employee whistleblowers. His article also identifies current issues in whistleblower protection and speculates regarding the future of such protections.

The federal law has provided an influential model for the states and many state provisions are patterned after or incorporate the federal protections.[33] Rather than repeat Devine's discussion, this section of the essay briefly summarizes the federal whistleblower provision before explaining how this provision and other similar laws relate to freedom of information laws.

The federal statute prohibits retaliation against federal employees who disclose information which they reasonably believe evidences certain types of government misconduct, including a violation of law, rule, or regulation, gross mismanagement, a gross waste of funds, an abuse of authority or a substantial and specific danger to public health and safety. The statute does not provide protection if the disclosure is prohibited by statute or by judicial interpretation of a statute or involves the disclosure of information classified in the interests of national defense or foreign affairs. Special avenues are provided for the examination of allegations regarding otherwise prohibited disclosures. The principal method of enforcement is administrative, with judicial review of the administrative action. Most agencies are covered, with a few exceptions such as the Central Intelligence Agency and National Security Agency. The law contains a provision, practically unique in federal law, which allows disciplinary action against agency officials charged with retaliation to be commenced by a specific official, the Special Counsel, outside of the agency.

The first federal provision was enacted in 1978. Prior to that date, few state or federal provisions protected whistleblowers. Most state and federal employees had to rely on the uncertain application of the First Amendment or a violation by an agency of its own procedures. Today, hundreds of federal and state laws protect both public and private sector whistleblowers. Whistleblower protection has become a pervasive and important part of employment law in the United States. The development of whistleblower protection over the last two decades can be described, without hyperbole, as a legal revolution.

Whistleblower protection laws are closely linked to freedom of information laws. Some of the earliest state provisions, such as that of Alaska, protected state employees who disclosed documents or records available under the state's freedom of information laws.[34] One of the first attempts to enact comprehensive protection for federal employees likewise connected that protection to the federal FOIA.[35]

The federal FOIA also provided an important justification for legal protection of whistleblowers. The FOIA established the principle that government documents and records were available to the public. Whistleblowing could thus be defended as vindicating the public's interest in access to government information. Protection of those federal whistleblowers was one way of implementing the policies underlying the freedom of information statute.

Whistleblower Protection and Administrative Theory

The whistleblower provision shares with the federal FOIA a reliance on one or another of the competing visions of administration described in Sargentich's essay and explored in the discussion regarding the federal FOIA. Thus, the presentation here is more attenuated and seeks principally to demonstrate how the same themes and issues run through the arguments regarding whistleblower protection.

The legislative deliberations surrounding the passage of the Civil Service Reform Act of 1978, which contained the first provision broadly protecting federal employee whistleblowers, relied heavily upon the Rule of Law Ideal. When introduced, the statute only protected disclosures reasonably believed to evidence a violation of law. This standard sought to preserve the rule of law by encouraging disclosures of violations of legal standards established by federal statutes. Sargentich's description of the Rule of Law Ideal notes the difficulty of limiting administrative discretion through statutory standards. Thus, it is not surprising that Congress amended the whistleblower provision to include violations of rules and regulations. This addition sought to incorporate internal agency standards developed in the exercise of its discretion under statutory authority, but which could be used as more specific standards against which to evaluate official conduct. The importance of the Rule of Law Ideal is not only illustrated by the history of the federal protection but also by the state statutes of general application.[36] Many of these statutes, unlike the federal law, limit protected disclosures only to those relating to violations of law, rule or regulation.

The protection of federal employee whistleblowers also draws on the Public Purposes Ideal. Disclosures regarding gross mismanagement, a gross waste of funds, or an abuse of authority lack specific standards against which the official conduct can be evaluated. These standards thus accept the exercise of considerable discretion on the part of government officials. In this sense, there is no 'rule' of law to be applied. Like the Public Purposes Ideal, these standards focus on whether agency discretion is exercised for the public interest. Moreover, the emphasis is on improving the internal management and administration of federal agencies. Like the federal provision, many state statutes do likewise.

Like the federal FOIA, the federal whistleblower provision rests on vindication of the Democratic Process Ideal. Citizens are given the information necessary to participate in the political process. Whistleblowing, however, challenges institutional authority in ways beyond other information provisions. Whistleblowing is a highly individual undertaking; it challenges institutional prerogative and undermines bureaucratic hierarchies. This aspect of whistleblower protection is illustrated by the relationship between it and the exemptions which an agency may claim under the federal FOIA. Most, but not all, of those exemptions are discretionary; an agency may claim the exemption, but it is not required to do so. Therefore, these discretionary exemptions are not legal prohibitions against the disclosure of documents or records or, indeed, of the information contained within them. An individual employee could thus be protected for the disclosure of documents regarding which the agency has claimed an exemption. This example demonstrates the importance attached to the decisions of individual employees by the whistleblower protection statute.

Whistleblower Protection and the First Amendment

As is the federal FOIA, whistleblower protection is closely connected to the First Amendment.

Like the FOIA, it vindicates the First Amendment by ensuring that persons have the information necessary to make meaningful the right of free expression. Congress intended whistleblower protection to strengthen the free speech rights of federal employees.[37] The First Amendment balancing test, uncertain in its application, was seen as an insufficient guarantee of these rights. In turn, one of the important justifications for protecting the First Amendment rights of public employees rests on the important contributions of these employees to debate regarding issues of public concern.

Protection of whistleblowers is particularly important to the vindication of the First Amendment rights of citizens. *When* information is available is as important as *whether* it is available. Persons need information about government misconduct at a time when some meaningful response is possible. The right to speak out or to seek political redress through association with others is not just a right of criticism, but a right to use democratic procedures in an attempt to change government action and policy before the effects of misconduct are fully felt. Otherwise, information can be hidden, even under a freedom of information provision. A person needs to know of government conduct before that person can request under the FOIA information regarding it. Whistleblowing can surface hidden information at a time which it is most useful.

The federal whistleblower protection statute requires, in some circumstances, a response to the allegations of a whistleblower. The government official responsible for receiving complaints from whistleblowers has authority to require the head of an agency to respond to allegations of wrongdoing which the official believes have merit. Such a response emphasizes rectification of the wrongdoing, but it also recognizes that allegations cannot be ignored but must be addressed by government officials. The federal whistleblower protection statute has recently been expanded to require an agency to respond to allegations of wrongdoing made by persons who are not federal employees.

Whistleblower Protection and the Regulation of Information

Like freedom of information provisions, whistleblower protection statutes participate in the more general discussion of the regulation of information. The discussion above examined the release of government information by whistleblowers from a First Amendment perspective. Whistleblower provisions also clearly have implications for both privacy and property based conceptions of information. Whistleblowers could disclose information that is protected by the whistleblower statute but which affects the privacy of individuals. On one level, the interrelationship between the Whistleblower Protection Act and the Federal Privacy Act demonstrates the conflict.

The Federal Privacy Act prohibits the disclosure of information contained within certain government records. The definition of these records, however, does not encompass all government documents and records. Thus, a whistleblower could make a disclosure that is protected by the whistleblower protection law for government records not covered by Privacy Act protections. Moreover, the whistleblower protection provision is not a document-and-records law in the same way as the federal FOIA and Privacy Act. The information protected in the whistleblower provision need not come from a government document or record. Indeed, it is an employee's access to information from a variety of sources that makes the employee's disclosures particularly important. For example, the employee may directly observe an egregious violation of law by agency officials, of which, not surprisingly, no document or record has been created. Thus, a whistleblower could disclose information affecting the privacy of third persons although that information is not contained in any government document or record.

The tensions between First Amendment and privacy conceptions, however, cannot be resolved simply by better drafting of the relevant statutory provisions. Statutory reconciliation would require a careful assessment of the scope of privacy protection and of the justifications for access under the First Amendment. This exercise, if conscientiously conducted, would involve the participants in the choices between incommensurate values described in James Boyle's essay.

Whistleblowing will implicate property conceptions of information in ways similar to that of the federal Freedom of Information Act. In a sense, whistleblowers can disclose information that private parties and the government may see as proprietary in the hands of private parties and convert it into public information widely available. In some instances, the government itself may be the party claiming such a proprietary interest. Again, the difficulties are deeply embedded more in our methods of thinking about information than in the content of particular statutes.

Whistleblower provisions share important attributes with freedom of information laws. Like those laws, whistleblower provisions are inextricably tied to debates in modern public law as well as to the unfolding discussion of the regulation of information.

The Increasing International Acceptance of Freedom of Information Provisions

As the introduction to this essay demonstrated, freedom of information laws, and to an extent whistleblower protection as well, have increasing international acceptance. Most advanced economic countries are subject to some form of freedom of information provision applicable to at least some types of government documents and records. Of particular note are the consideration of a freedom of information law in Great Britain and the enactment of one in Japan, both countries long known for their commitment to the secrecy of official information. These events mark a decided change in policy and illustrate the acceptance internationally of freedom of information principles. Debra Silverman in 'Freedom of Information: Will Blair Be Able to Break the Walls of Secrecy in Britain?' (Chapter 8) explores the development of the British proposal and shows the magnitude of the change that its consideration represents.

The Japanese freedom of information provision is also important because of the adoption of a freedom of information law in a country outside of Europe and the English speaking former colonies of Great Britain – Australia, Canada, and the United States. This dramatic change illustrates the potential for a world-wide application of these laws.

The changes occurring in Asia may be more extensive than the Japanese example alone suggests. For instance, the government of the Republic of Korea instituted in April of 1999 a program whose acronym is OPEN (Online Procedures Enhancement).[38] This program applies to a variety of requests for civil licenses, including those by contractors, and allows anyone to follow the permit process, from application through approval, by the use of a website in Korea.

One suspects that similar limited examples are occurring throughout the world, but do not receive the international attention paid to broadly applicable freedom of information provisions in major economic powers such as Japan and Britain. For example, Chile has recently adopted environmental legislation which gives citizens a right of access to environmental impact statements required under that law,[39] a form of public access previously unknown in that country.

Even before the computer revolution and the growth of the world wide web, freedom of information provisions in one country had direct impact on access to information about government and private activities in other countries. Because the United States Freedom of Information Act grants access to any person, citizens of other countries are able to access the huge number of documents and records held by federal agencies. The controversial book, *Spy Catcher*, describing Soviet infiltration of the British secret services, relied heavily upon documents obtained in the United States under the federal FOIA. Automobile safety is another example that applies to other US regulatory agencies as well. Documents submitted by foreign manufacturers to the National Highway Traffic Safety Administration in the United States provide information about the safety of automobiles sold in the manufacturer's domestic market as well. These documents also permit an assessment of the character of similar safety regulation in that country.

The provisions of the Electronic Freedom of Information Act make it increasingly likely that a person anywhere in the world with a computer and a modem could discover substantial amounts of information about private companies based in that country and about the activities of that person's government. The ease of the transferability of information and the value attached to access makes information held by the United States government internationally available.

The discussion of the freedom of information laws in the United States also enables speculation about the reasons for the increasing acceptance of freedom of information laws. Freedom of information laws are closely tied to liberal political thought; aspects of that thought may explain the international momentum for the adoption of these provisions.

Access to government information has long been connected with democratic participation in government. In his landmark book, *Privacy and Freedom*,[40] Alan Westin, in fact, defined democracy and authoritarianism in terms of information policy. Democratic governments were marked by significant restrictions on the ability of the government to acquire information about its citizens and ready access by citizens to information about the activities of government. Authoritarian governments were identified by the opposite set of policies: ready government access to information about the activities of citizens and significant limitations on the ability of citizens to acquire information about the government.

This informational definition of democracy easily fits with the Rule of Law Ideal which stresses the importance of restricting the role of government to the application of formal standards democratically arrived at. The ability to so limit the intrusion of government into private activities requires knowledge about the content and character of these rules as well as the compliance of government officials with them.

Citizen participation in democracy also benefits from access to government information. As noted above, the Democratic Process Ideal of political participation in the administration of government also supports the adoption of freedom of information provisions. This ideal can be seen as upholding citizen access apart from the American conception of the right of free speech contained in the First Amendment.

The attraction of a government bound by laws and rules that citizens participate in creating suggests a relationship between acceptance of democracy as form of government and the adoption of freedom of information provisions. Although this relationship may exist, the explanation of the increasing acceptance of freedom of information principles, however, must be more complicated. Many democratic governments, including Britain, the United States, Canada, Australia, and the nations of western Europe have lacked freedom of information provisions through much of their history as democratic governments.

In the United States, freedom of information provisions also play into a conception of administration which stresses the affirmative obligations of government, the requirement that government advance the public good. Government regulation and the extensive administrative structures of government in democracies with developed economies reflect similar circumstances. These realities draw on other strains of liberal political thought articulated in the Public Purposes Ideal.

The rhetoric of transparency draws heavily upon market justifications for access to government information. Only when rules and practices are known, can private economic actors have the information and confidence to invest. Access to information is one of the most fundamental ways in which governments can support the market. In the current international economic climate, these strains of thought are powerful arguments for freedom of information provisions.

It may also be fair to say that just as the computer revolution and the internet have influenced freedom of information laws in the United States, these technological changes have also offered an opportunity to examine anew the regulation of information. This reexamination need not necessarily lead to more freedom of information provisions. However, this examination is occurring at a time when the metaphors and theories provided by liberal thought have wide currency and acceptance. In these circumstances, the increasing adoption of freedom of information laws is not surprising.

Although the topic 'freedom of information laws' may first conjure images of noteworthy but peripheral statutory provisions, both narrow in scope and technical in content, these laws are closely connected to broad strains of liberal political thought. They are intertwined with an ongoing reassessment of the regulation of information; they are likely to become more important internationally.

Notes

1   *See generally* Stanley V. Anderson (1973), 'Access to Public Documents in Sweden', 21 Am. J Comp. L. 419, 421–24 (describing the history of public access in Sweden).
2   5 U.S.C. § 552 (1994 & Supp. IV 1998).
3   *See* Access to Information Act, R.S.C. ch. 111 (1980–1983).
4   *See* Freedom of Information Act, 1982 (Austl.).
5   The website of the British Home Office contains information about the proposed legislation which has been introduced in the House of Commons and provides links to other websites, including that of the House of Commons. *See* <www.homeoffice.gov.uk/foi/index.htm>
6   *See* 'Japan's Parliament Passes Freedom of Information Law', Dow Jones Int'l News Serv., May 7, 1999 (discussing the unanimous bill that Japan's parliament passed in order to increase public access). An English translation of this law can be found at <http://www.somucho.go.jp/gyoukan/kanri/translation2.htm>
7   *See* Amsterdam Treaty at Art. 255. *See generally* Inger O. Osterdahl (1998), 'Openness v Secrecy: Public Access to Documents in Sweden and the European Union', 23 E. L. Rev. 336. The treaty provisions are implemented through the codes of conduct applicable to the covered EU institutions.
8   *See* Council Directive 90/313, Art. 1, 1990 O.J. (L 158).
9   *See* H.R. 527, 106th Cong. (1999).

10   This portion of the Code of Conduct is described in 'Report on Openness within the European Union', Doc. No. A4–0476 (1998).

11   *See* Va. Code Ann. § 2.1–340 (Michie 1950 & Supp. 1999).

12   *See* 5 U.S.C. § 552(b)(1)–(9). The rather odd provision regarding oil wells is a historical record of the power of the oil industry in Congress at the time of the enactment of the federal FOIA.

13   *See* Executive Order No. 12,600, 52 Fed. Reg. 23,781 (1987).

14   *See* 'Other People's Money' 62 (National Home Library Foundation ed. 1933) (referring to publicity and corruption and the need for greater public access to our government).

15   5. U.S.C. § 552b (1994 & Supp. IV 1998).

16   *See* Federal Advisory Committee Act, § 10, 5 U.S.C. App. 2 (1994 & Supp. III 1997).

17   *See* Fla. Stat. Ann. § 69.08 (West Supp. 1995).

18   Pub. L. No. 101–12, 103 Stat. 16 (1989) (codified at 5 U.S.C. §§ 1201–1224 (1994 & Supp. IV 1998)).

19   Pub. L. No. 95–454, 92 Stat. 1111 (1978) (whistleblower provisions codified at 5 U.S.C. § 2302(b)(8) (1994 & Supp. IV 1998)).

20   These laws have been collected by the International Whistleblowing Campaign at the Government Accountability Project in Washington, D.C.

21   *See generally* 'American Bar Association Symposium on FOIA 25th Anniversary', 9 Govt. Inf. Q. 223 (1992) (describing history of FOIA); Jim Smith (1981), 'The Freedom of Information Act of 1966: A Legislative History Analysis', 74 Law Lib. J. 231 (explaining the FOIA's legislative history).

22   *See* Robert G. Vaughn (1991), 'Consumer Access to Product Safety Information and the Future of The Freedom of Information Act', 5 Admin. L. J. 673, 711 & n. 144 (Senator Ted Kennedy commenting on the clearing-house function and its benefits for citizens and their access to information).

23   5 U.S.C. § 552a (1994 & Supp. IV 1998).

24   44 U.S.C. §§ 3501–3520 (1994 and Supp. IV 1998).

25   5 U.S.C. § 552a(a)(8)–(13), (e)(12), (o)–(r), (u) (1994 & Supp. IV 1998).

26   40 U.S.C. § 759 (1994 & Supp. IV 1998).

27   *See generally* Evan Hendricks (1982), *Campaign for Political Rights, Former Secrets: Government Records Made Public Through the Freedom of Information Act.*

28   *See* 'Richmond Newspapers, Inc. v. Virginia', 448 U.S. 555, 575 (1979) (Chief Justice Burger suggested that the right to freedom of information is derived from the 'the common core purpose' of the explicit provisions of the First Amendment).

29   *See Former Secrets: Government Records Made Public Through the Freedom of Information Act*, *supra* note 27.

30   *See* James Boyle (1992), 'A Theory of Law and Information: Copyright, Spleens; Blackmail, and Insider Trading', 80 Cal. L. Rev. 1413, 1443.

31   *See* 'United States Dep't of Justice v. Reporters Comm. for Freedom of the Press', 489 U.S. 749 (1989); 'United States Dep't of Defense v. Federal Labor Relations Authority', 510 U.S. 487 (1994).

32   *See* Henry H. Perritt (1989), 'Electronic Acquisition and Release of Federal Agency Information: Analysis of Recommendations Adopted by the Administrative Conference of the United States', 41 Admin. L. Rev. 253.

33   *See generally* Robert G. Vaughn (1999), 'State Whistleblower Protection Statutes and the Future of Whistleblower Protection', 51 Admin. L. Rev. 581.

34   *See* Alaska Stat. § 39.51.020 (1980).

35   *See* The Federal Employee Act of 1975, S. 1210, 94th Cong. (1975).

36   *See* Vaughn, *supra* note 33.

37   *See generally* Robert G.Vaughn (1982), 'Statutory Protection of Whistleblowers in the Federal Executive Branch', Univ. of Ill. L. Rev. 615, 637–41 (describing the relationship of the whistleblower provision with the First Amendment).

38   *See* 'Seoul City's Anti-Corruption Efforts: A Systemic Approach' (visited Jan. 14, 2000) <http://www.metr.seoul.kr/eng/corrupt_fr.html>

39   *See* Environmental Law 19,300.

40   Alan Westin (1967), *Privacy and Freedom.*

[1]

ARTICLES

THE REFORM OF THE AMERICAN ADMINISTRATIVE PROCESS: THE CONTEMPORARY DEBATE

THOMAS O. SARGENTICH[*]

Numerous proposals to "reform" the American administrative process have been advanced in recent years. In this Article, Professor Sargentich discusses the contemporary debate about administrative reform in terms of deep normative controversies reflected in it. He argues that the contemporary debate may be understood in light of three competing ideals of the administrative process, which provide forceful but fundamentally different visions of the legitimacy and character of administration. The three ideals are the rule of law ideal, the public purposes ideal, and the democratic process ideal. Professor Sargentich examines these three ideals in terms of their core embodiments, the limitations of their cores, and the alternative expressions of the ideals that respond in part to the difficulties of realizing each core. In conclusion, this Article offers general perspectives on the contemporary reform debate in light of the basic normative structure constituted by the three competing ideals.

TABLE OF CONTENTS

*   Associate Professor of Law, American University. A.B., Harvard University, 1972; M.Phil., Oxford University, 1974; J.D., Harvard University, 1977.

386   WISCONSIN LAW REVIEW

I. INTRODUCTION

In recent years, the broad-scale reform of the American administrative process has attracted notable attention. Politicians, administrators, other participants in the administrative process, and scholars have generated a large literature recommending a diverse spectrum of proposals designed to improve the basic institutional relationships and methods of administrative decisionmaking.[1]

Debate has flourished, for instance, about recommendations for a more active role for the judiciary in reviewing and, where it deems

---

1. A useful summary of some of the main contemporary proposals for reforming the administrative process is found in G. ROBINSON, E. GELLHORN & H. BRUFF, THE ADMINISTRATIVE PROCESS 825-83 (2d ed. 1980). For other perspectives, see 1 SENATE COMM. ON GOVERNMENTAL AFFAIRS, STUDY ON FEDERAL REGULATION, S. DOC. No. 25, 95th Cong., 1st Sess. (1977); 2 SENATE COMM. ON GOVERNMENTAL AFFAIRS, STUDY ON FEDERAL REGULATION, S. DOC. No. 26, 95th Cong., 1st Sess. (1977); 3 SENATE COMM. ON GOVERNMENTAL AFFAIRS, STUDY ON FEDERAL REGULATION, S. DOC. No. 71, 95th Cong., 1st Sess. (1977); 4 SENATE COMM. ON GOVERNMENTAL AFFAIRS, STUDY ON FEDERAL REGULATION, S. DOC. No. 72, 95th Cong., 1st Sess. (1977); 5 SENATE COMM. ON GOVERNMENTAL AFFAIRS, STUDY ON FEDERAL REGULATION, S. DOC. No. 91, 95th Cong., 2d Sess. (1978); 6 SENATE COMM. ON GOVERNMENTAL AFFAIRS, STUDY ON FEDERAL REGULATION, S. DOC. No. 13, 96th Cong., 1st Sess. (1978); 6 Appendix SENATE COMM. ON GOVERNMENTAL AFFAIRS, STUDY ON FEDERAL REGULATION, S. DOC. No. 14, 96th Cong., 1st Sess. (1978); AMERICAN BAR ASSOCIATION COMM'N ON LAW AND THE ECONOMY, FEDERAL REGULATION: ROADS TO REFORM (1979); S. BREYER, REGULATION AND ITS REFORM (1982); R. LITAN & W. NORDHAUS, REFORMING FEDERAL REGULATION (1983); M. PERTSCHUK, REVOLT AGAINST REGULATION (1982); REFORMING REGULATION (T. Clark, M. Kosters, & J. Miller eds. 1980); S. TOLCHIN & M. TOLCHIN, DISMANTLING AMERICA: THE RUSH TO DEREGULATE (1983); L. W. WEISS & M. W. KLASS, CASE STUDIES IN REGULATION: REVOLUTION AND REFORM (1981); Gellhorn, *Reform as Totem—A Skeptical View*, REGULATION, May-June 1979, at 23; Kennedy, *Regulatory Reform: A Confused National Issue*, 28 AD. L. REV. 447 (1976); Strauss, *Regulatory Reform in a Time of Transition*, 15 SUFFOLK L. REV. 903 (1981).

it appropriate, redirecting agency behavior.[2] Others have proposed greater control over "single-mission" agencies by the assertedly broader-minded President and centralized Executive Office staff.[3]

Nor has Congress been overlooked. The recent debate has included calls for more aggressive legislative oversight of exercises of executive discretion.[4] Others, at least until recently, have supported inserting "legislative veto" provisions in statutes covering most agency rulemaking.[5] Such provisions purport to give Congress

---

2.   The most prominent of such recommendations has been a proposed amendment to the Administrative Procedure Act's standards of judicial review, codified at 5 U.S.C. § 706 (1982), which has been championed for years by Senator Dale Bumpers of Arkansas. *See* S. 2408, 94th Cong., 1st Sess. (1975). Although it has assumed a variety of forms during the recent debate, the so-called Bumpers Amendment would, in general, expand the role of courts in reviewing challenged agency action. *See* Kennedy, *The Bumpers Amendment: Regulating the Regulators*, 67 A.B.A. J. 1639 (1981); Levin, *Review of 'Jurisdictional' Issues Under the Bumpers Amendment*, 1983 DUKE L.J. 355; McGowan, *Congress, Court, and Control of Delegated Power*, 77 COLUM. L. REV. 1119, 1162-68 (1977); O'Reilly, *Deference Makes a Difference: A Study of Impacts of the Bumpers Judicial Review Amendment*, 49 U. CINN. L. REV. 739 (1980); Woodward & Levin, *In Defense of Deference: Judicial Review of Agency Action*, 31 AD. L. REV. 329 (1979); Wright, *Judicial Review and the Equal Protection Clause*, 15 HARV. C. R. - C. L. L. REV. 1, 4-8, 12-16 (1980).

3.   As with the other major reform proposals, the literature concerning an expanded Presidential role in overseeing the administrative process itself has expanded considerably in recent years. *See, e.g.*, AMERICAN BAR ASSOCIATION COMM'N ON LAW AND THE ECONOMY, *supra* note 1, at 73-84; Bernstein, *The Presidential Role in Administrative Rulemaking: Improving Policy Directives: One Vote for Not Tying the President's Hands*, 56 TUL. L. REV. 818 (1982); Bruff, *Presidential Power and Administrative Rulemaking*, 88 YALE L. J. 451 (1979); Byse, *Comments on a Structural Reform Proposal: Presidential Directives to Independent Agencies*, 29 AD. L. REV. 157 (1977); Cutler, *The Case for Presidential Intervention in Regulatory Rulemaking by the Executive Branch*, 56 TUL. L. REV. 830 (1982); Cutler & Johnson, *Regulation and the Political Process*, 84 YALE L. J. 1395 (1975); DeMuth, *The White House Review Programs*, REGULATION, Jan.-Feb. 1980, at 13; Eads, *Harnessing Regulation: The Evolving Role of White House Oversight*, REGULATION, May-June 1981, at 19; Verkuil, *Jawboning Administrative Agencies: Ex Parte Contacts by the White House*, 80 COLUM. L. REV. 943 (1980). *Cf.* Sierra Club v. Costle, 657 F. 2d 298, 400-08 (D.C. Cir. 1981) (discussing Presidential involvement in regulatory process and declining to overturn agency action on that basis).

4.   *See, e.g.*, 2 SENATE COMM. ON GOVERNMENTAL AFFAIRS, STUDY ON FEDERAL REGULATION, CONGRESSIONAL OVERSIGHT OF REGULATORY AGENCIES, S. DOC. NO. 26, 95th Cong., 1st Sess. (1977); Ribicoff, *Congressional Oversight and Regulatory Reform*, 28 AD. L. REV. 415 (1976). For a discussion of various efforts by Congress in the 1970's to reassert its power over the President and executive branch, see J. SUNDQUIST, THE DECLINE AND RESURGENCE OF CONGRESS (1981).

5.   *See, e.g.*, S. 1080, 97th Cong., 2d Sess. § 13, 128 CONG. REC. S2719-21 (daily ed. Mar. 24, 1982). The literature on the legislative veto is vast, although much of the constitutional discussion has been superseded by the Supreme Court's decision in Immigration and Naturalization Serv. v. Chadha, ___ U.S. ___, 103 S.Ct. 2764 (1983). *See infra* note 6. For examples of arguments on both sides of the debate concerning the legislative veto's efficacy, see Javits & Klein, *Congressional Oversight and the Legislative Veto: A Constitutional Analysis*, 52 N.Y.U. L. REV. 455 (1977); Martin, *The Legislative Veto and the Responsible Exercise of Congressional Power*, 68 VA. L. REV. 253 (1982). *See also* J. SUNDQUIST, *supra* note 4, at 344-66; Bruff & Gellhorn, *Congressional Control of Administrative Regulation: A Study of Legislative Vetoes*, 90 HARV. L. REV. 1369 (1977).

power to control agency decisions by passing binding legislative veto
resolutions, which themselves are not adopted by majorities of both
Houses of Congress and presented to the President for approval or
veto, as are bills or joint resolutions. Last summer, the Supreme
Court struck down on broad constitutional grounds a legislative
veto provision in an immigration statute, thereby indicating that a
resolution controlling the executive branch normally must be
adopted in a manner consistent with the bicameralism and presentation requirements.[6] Since then, much of the energy once devoted to
the legislative veto has been channelled into the task of framing constitutionally acceptable alternative methods for Congress to oversee
the use of administrative power.[7]

Other contemporary reform proposals have been equally far-
reaching, indeed government-wide, in their scope and implications.
The use of cost-benefit or similar analyses of regulations, such as
enshrined in President Reagan's 1981 Executive order dealing with
regulatory reform,[8] has generated wide attention.[9] So, too, have

---

6.   *Chadha,* ___ U.S. ___, 103 S.Ct. 2764 (1983). In his concurring opinion, Justice
Powell noted that the Court's decision, insofar as it was based on the presentment clause,
would "apparently . . . invalidate every use of the legislative veto." *Id.* at ___, 103 S.Ct. at
2788 (Powell, J., concurring). For a discussion of the case, see Strauss, *Was There a Baby in the
Bathwater? A Comment on the Supreme Court's Legislative Veto Decision,* 1983 DUKE L.J. 789.
7.   See Davidson, *After the Legislative Veto: Reflections from the Losing Side,* REGU-
LATION, July-Aug. 1983, at 23; Olson, *After the Legislative Veto: Restoring the Separation of
Powers,* REGULATION, July-Aug. 1983, at 19. However, since the Supreme Court's decision in
Chadha, see supra note 6, some statutes have been passed containing legislative veto provisions. *See* Tolchin, *In Spite of the Court, the Legislative Veto Lives On,* N.Y. Times, Dec. 21,
1983, at 14, col. 3 (national ed.).
8.   *See* Exec. Order No. 12,291, 3 C.F.R. 127 (1982). For discussion of this Execu-
tive order, see HOUSE COMM. ON ENERGY AND COMMERCE, 97TH CONG., 1ST SESS., REPORT ON
PRESIDENTIAL CONTROL OF AGENCY RULEMAKING (Comm. Print 1981); Raven-Hansen,
*Making Agencies Follow Orders: Judicial Review of Agency Violations of Executive Order
12,291,* 1983 DUKE L.J. 285; Rosenberg, *Beyond the Limits of Executive Power: Presidential
Control of Agency Rulemaking under Executive Order 12,291,* 80 MICH. L. REV. 193 (1981);
Shane, *Presidential Regulatory Oversight and the Separation of Powers: the Constitutionality of
Executive Order No. 12,291,* 23 ARIZ. L. REV. 1235 (1981).
9.   *See, e.g.,* HOUSE SUBCOMM. ON OVERSIGHT AND INVESTIGATIONS OF THE COMM.
ON INTERSTATE AND FOREIGN COMMERCE, 94TH CONG., 2D SESS., REPORT ON FEDERAL REGU-
LATION AND REGULATORY REFORM, 505-15 (Subcomm. Print 1976); Administrative Confer-
ence of the United States, Public Disclosure Concerning the Use of Cost-Benefit and Similar
Analyses in Regulation (Recommendation 79-4), 1 C.F.R. 305.79-4 (1983); De Long, *Defending Cost-Benefit Analysis: Replies to Steven Kelman,* REGULATION, Mar.-Apr. 1981, at 39; Kelman, *Cost-Benefit Analysis: An Ethical Critique,* REGULATION, Jan.-Feb. 1981, at 33; Kennedy, *Cost-Benefit Analysis of Entitlement Problems: A Critique,* 33 STAN. L. REV. 387 (1981);
Moss, *Cost-Benefit Analysis, Cost-Effectiveness Analysis and the Cotton Dust Standard: a Matter
of Life and Death,* 35 RUTGERS L. REV. 133 (1982); Rodgers, *Benefits, Costs and Risks: Oversight of Health and Environmental Decisionmaking,* 4 HARV. ENVTL. L. REV. 191 (1980);
Schwartz, *The Court and Cost-Benefit Analysis: An Administrative Law Idea Whose Time Has
Come—Or Gone?,* 1981 SUP. CT. REV. 291; Shaw & Wolfe, *A Legal and Ethical Critique of*

various "deregulatory" proposals that are designed to limit what their proponents consider the negative effects of federal regulation in certain industries and to permit a "freer" operation of the market.[10]

Alongside the economic critiques has evolved an emphasis on achieving broader public participation in agency decisionmaking. A range of proposals—calling, for instance, for intervenor funding, for enhanced efforts by agencies to inform the public about incipient policies, and for more specific procedural protections in traditionally less formal proceedings to allow affected groups to express their viewpoints on contemplated agency action—reflects the fundamental concern that the administrative process should be more responsive to the public, at least in its outward adherence to open, broad-based decisionmaking.[11] Other criticisms concentrate less on participation and responsiveness and more on different types of procedural restrictions that, it is said, are necessary to foster a more regularized, formalized, and procedurally fair process.[12]

Just as each of these types of reform proposals has been debated in its own terms, all have been implicated in recent congressional review of several omnibus "regulatory reform" bills.[13] If enacted,

---

Using Cost-Benefit Analysis in Public Law, 19 HOUS. L. REV. 899 (1982); Sunstein, *Cost-Benefit Analysis and the Separation of Powers*, 23 ARIZ. L. REV. 1267 (1981); Weaver, *Inhaber and the Limits of Cost-Benefit Analysis*, REGULATION, July-Aug. 1979, at 14; Weidenbaum, *On Estimating Regulatory Costs*, REGULATION, May-June 1978, at 14. *See generally* E.J. MISHAN, ECONOMICS FOR SOCIAL DECISIONS: ELEMENTS OF COST-BENEFIT ANALYSIS (1973); Coddington, *"Cost-Benefit" as the New Utilitarianism*, 42 POL. Q. 320 (1971).

10.   *See, e.g.*, S. BREYER, *supra* note 1; Breyer, *Analyzing Regulatory Failure: Mismatches, Less Restrictive Alternatives and Reform*, 92 HARV. L. REV. 547 (1979); Clark, *New Approaches to Regulatory Reform—Letting the Market Do the Job*, 11 NAT. J. 1316 (1979). *See generally* Baker, *Starting Points in Economic Analysis of Law*, 8 HOFSTRA L. REV. 939 (1980); Stewart, *Regulation, Innovation, and Administrative Law: A Conceptual Framework*, 69 CALIF. L. REV. 1256 (1981); Stewart, *The Reformation of American Administrative Law*, 88 HARV. L. REV. 1667, 1689-93, 1702-11 (1975).

11.   *See, e.g.*, 3 SENATE COMM. ON GOVERNMENTAL AFFAIRS, STUDY ON FEDERAL REGULATION, PUBLIC PARTICIPATION IN REGULATORY AGENCY PROCEEDINGS, S. DOC. No. 71, 95th Cong., 1st Sess. (1977).

12.   The effort to impose more formalized procedural constraints on agencies has been a mainstay of regulatory reform bills introduced in recent Congresses. For a discussion of the proceduralization of agency rulemaking during the 1970's, both as a result of legislation requiring more formalized rulemaking and of judicial innovation, see Pedersen, *Formal Records and Informal Rulemaking*, 85 YALE L.J. 38 (1975); Verkuil, *The Emerging Concept of Administrative Procedure*, 78 COLUM. L. REV. 258 (1978).

13.   Numerous such bills have been introduced and debated in Congress. For the 98th Congress, see H. R. 2327, 98th Cong., 1st Sess. (1983). For the 97th Congress, see H. R. 746, 97th Cong., 1st Sess. (1981), *reported in* H. R. REP. No. 435, 97th Cong., 2d Sess. (1982) (House Committee on the Judiciary); and S. 1080, 97th Cong., 1st Sess. (1981), *reported in* S. REP. No. 284, 97th Cong., 1st Sess. (1981) (Senate Committee on the Judiciary), and S. REP. No. 305, 97th Cong., 1st Sess. (1981) (Senate Committee on Governmental Affairs). For the

these bills would amend certain of the central procedural provisions of the Administrative Procedure Act (APA) for the first time since their enactment in 1946.[14] Although the bills differ in their particulars, in general they share the stated aim of achieving government-wide "reform" of the methods and institutions of administration in response to a wide range of perceived deficiencies. That an omnibus regulatory reform bill has not yet been, and may not be, enacted does not diminish the power of the basic criticisms of the administrative process that have shaped the emergence of this legislative debate. In fact, certain of the bills have proceeded relatively far along the path of legislative deliberation in recent Congresses.[15] Moreover, consideration of reform proposals has not failed to produce some statutory results, including the Regulatory Flexibility Act[16] and the Paperwork Reduction Act.[17]

Furthermore, the expressed desire on the part of many representatives for government-wide administrative reform has been matched by recent Presidents. President Reagan's 1981 Executive order on regulatory reform[18] is the latest in a succession of Executive orders on the general subject, each of which seems to indicate a Presidential determination of the need to assert greater control over the administrative process.[19] Without attempting here to assess such efforts, at least it has become clear, especially during the Reagan Administration, that numerous executive initiatives have been undertaken in response to pressures to curb proclaimed "excesses"

96th Congress, see H. R. 3263, 96th Cong., 1st Sess. (1979), *reported in* H. R. REP. No. 1393, 96th Cong., 2d Sess. (1980) (House Committee on the Judiciary); and S. 262, 96th Cong., 1st Sess. (1979), *reported in* S. REP. No. 1018, 96th Cong., 2d Sess., Pts. 1 & 2 (1980) (Joint Report of Senate Committees on Governmental Affairs and the Judiciary).

14. The APA is codified at 5 U.S.C. §§ 551-559 (1982). Its central procedural provisions have not been amended since its enactment except with respect to the public availability of agency documents and decisionmaking. *See* S. BREYER & R. STEWART, ADMINISTRATIVE LAW AND REGULATORY POLICY 29 n.49 (1979).

15. In 1982, the Senate passed, by a vote of 94-0, an omnibus regulatory reform bill, S. 1080. *See* 128 CONG. REC. S2693-722 (daily ed. Mar. 24, 1982). However, the House of Representatives did not adopt such a bill during the 97th Congress, leaving to later Congresses the task of reconsidering such proposals.

16. Regulatory Flexibility Act, Pub. L. No. 96-354, 94 Stat. 1164 (1980) (codified at 5 U.S.C. §§ 601-612 (1982)). *See generally* Stewart, *The New Regulatory Flexibility Act*, 67 A.B.A. J. 66 (1981); Verkuil, *A Critical Guide to the Regulatory Flexibility Act*, 1982 DUKE L.J. 213.

17. Paperwork Reduction Act, Pub. L. No. 96-511, 94 Stat. 2812 (1980) (codified at 44 U.S.C. §§ 3501-3520 (Supp. 1981)). A final regulation implementing the Paperwork Reduction Act was published in 1983 by the Office of Management and Budget. *See* 48 Fed. Reg. 13666 (proposed Mar. 31, 1983).

18. Exec. Order No. 12,291, *supra* note 8.

19. Exec. Order No. 12,044, 3 C.F.R. 152 (1979); Exec. Order No. 11,949, 3 C.F.R. 161 (1977); Exec. Order No. 11,821, 3 C.F.R. 926 (1976).

of regulation in such fields as consumer product safety, employee health and safety, and environmental protection.

The diverse themes in this contemporary debate, to be sure, are not entirely new or unprecedented. To an extent, they reflect the continuation of discussion over several decades about the nature and legitimacy of administrative decisionmaking in modern American government.[20] At the same time, the debate, as reflected in the various proposals noted above, is striking both for its intensity as well as for the sweep of its concerns and prescriptions.

One who would analyze the contemporary debate might proceed from a number of perspectives. It is not uncommon to discuss a specific effort or proposal in terms of its discrete rationale, application, and limitations.[21] One also could concentrate on an empirical study of the activities of certain agencies in particular areas of public policy.[22] Furthermore, one could undertake a historical survey of the debate, seeking for instance to compare the most recent proposals with earlier ones or to link the emergence of contemporary con-

---

20. For discussion of the recurrent "crisis" of the legitimacy of the American administrative process arising from its unstable place in our governmental system, see J. FREEDMAN, CRISIS AND LEGITIMACY: THE ADMINISTRATIVE PROCESS AND AMERICAN GOVERNMENT (1978). For some of the perennial calls for administrative reform, see PRESIDENT'S ADVISORY COUNCIL ON EXECUTIVE ORGANIZATION (THE ASH COUNCIL), A NEW REGULATORY FRAMEWORK: REPORT ON SELECTED INDEPENDENT REGULATORY AGENCIES (1971); J. LANDIS, REPORT ON REGULATORY AGENCIES TO THE PRESIDENT-ELECT, *reprinted in* SENATE COMM. ON THE JUDICIARY, 86TH CONG., 2D SESS., REPORT OF THE SUBCOMMITTEE ON ADMINISTRATIVE PRACTICE AND PROCEDURE (Comm. Print, 1960); COMM'N ON ORGANIZATION OF THE EXECUTIVE BRANCH OF THE GOVERNMENT (HOOVER COMM'N), LEGAL SERVICES AND PROCEDURES (1955); COMM'N ON ORGANIZATION OF THE EXECUTIVE BRANCH OF THE GOVERNMENT (HOOVER COMM'N), THE INDEPENDENT REGULATORY COMMISSIONS: A REPORT TO THE CONGRESS (1949); PRESIDENT'S COMM. ON ADMINISTRATIVE MANAGEMENT (BROWNLOW COMM.), REPORT OF THE COMMITTEE WITH STUDIES OF ADMINISTRATIVE MANAGEMENT IN THE FEDERAL GOVERNMENT (1937). *See also* Gellhorn, *Administrative Procedure Reform: Hardy Perennial*, 48 A.B.A. J. 243 (1962).

21. *See, e.g.,* Bruff & Gellhorn, *supra* note 5; O'Reilly, *supra* note 2.

22. *See, e.g.,* B. ACKERMAN & W. HASSLER, CLEAN COAL/DIRTY AIR (1981); R. KAGAN, REGULATORY JUSTICE: IMPLEMENTING A WAGE-PRICE FREEZE (1978). For a realist's reminder of the inevitability of complexity in the workings of the administrative process, see Guiseppi v. Walling, 144 F.2d 608, 619, 622 (2d Cir. 1944):

> While, then, the concept of 'administrative law' is invaluable, because it pulls together for comparative study and common use, techniques and ideas developed in scattered areas of administrative action, there is danger that that concept may yield inelastic uniformities. All administrators should not be treated identically. . . .
>
> . . . .
>
> Complexity is our lot, and we should not rail against its inevitable concomitants.

For the suggestion that administrative law should be studied in the context of particular agency functions, see Gellhorn & Robinson, *Perspectives on Administrative Law*, 75 COLUM. L. REV. 771 (1975). *See also* Gellhorn, *supra* note 1; Rabin, *Administrative Law in Transition: A Discipline in Search of an Organizing Principle*, 72 NW. U. L. REV. 120 (1977).

cerns with broader trends in American society.[23] The approach of
this Article differs from all of these, for it seeks primarily to understand the basic conceptual underpinnings of the major types of reformist argument reflected in key proposals for change, including
those noted at the outset. No claim is advanced here that all of the
strains and nuances in the debate may be reduced to a level of general conceptual controversy. It is suggested, however, that the central themes of the main reform proposals may be usefully illumi-
nated in terms of such controversy.[24]

It appears true that the daily practice of administration, both
by those in government and by others seeking to achieve a result
through government, seldom focuses for long on broad theory about
the nature and legitimacy of the administrative process. Although
administrative reformers employ arguments borrowing premises
from deeper normative positions, their concentration is likely to center on the concrete ends in view, not on basic concepts. Nonetheless,
it remains relevant to ask whether the contemporary debate about
administrative reform has any underlying intellectual structure, or
whether it simply reflects an accretion of disparate, largely ad hoc
proposals without broader organization or pattern. If the debate
may be seen to have such a structure, then one will be better able to
grasp the central constraints of key proposals, the chief relationships among different reformist positions, and the major terms and
limits of the debate itself.

II. A CONCEPTUAL FRAMEWORK FOR UNDERSTANDING ADMINISTRATIVE REFORM

This Article's thesis is that the contemporary debate does have
an underlying intellectual structure that revolves around the complex interrelationships among three mutually contradictory ideals
of the administrative process. The three ideals address the fundamental questions of the ultimate source of the legitimacy of the ad-

---

23.   *See generally* Keller, *The Pluralist State: American Economic Regulation in Com-
parative Perspective,* 1900-1930, in REGULATION IN PERSPECTIVE 56 (T. McCraw ed. 1981);
Vogel, *The 'New' Social Regulation in Historical and Comparative Perspective,* in REGULATION
IN PERSPECTIVE, *supra,* at 155.

24.   This Article concentrates on certain of the most visible proposals for government-wide administrative reform at the federal level during the past decade and, in particular, during the past four or five years. By emphasizing general conceptions of administrative
reform, I do not assume that any particular actor or reform proposal embraces (or rejects) all
of the elements of a given ideal of the administrative process. Furthermore, in discussing theories for the overt justification and criticism of the administrative process, I do not assume they
are necessarily the same as particular causes or motives for actions or positions in specific
situations.

ministrative process and the character of the decisionmaking engaged in by administrative actors. The ideals, for the sake of shorthand reference, will be called the rule of law ideal, the public purposes ideal, and the democratic process ideal.

By their very nature, these ideals embody their own governing pictures of how a well-regulated, legitimate, and rationally-functioning administrative process should operate. The pictures incorporate at their core a conception of administrative reality, or at least, administrative possibility within the limits of reality. If one were to infuse an ideal with personality, one might say that each one is steadily seeking its fuller realization in practice. The incessantly critical strain of each ideal is by no means accidental; each is a ready reservoir of premises and positions that may be used to support change of existing structures in order to lessen the always present distance between the actual process and the ideal itself. To this extent, the competing ideals are well-suited to reformist discourse: they stand, if you will, with one foot resting on the present administrative process, with certain understandings about its basic character and possibilities, and with another foot directed at the future.

Although their particular answers differ, the three ideals respond to the same fundamental questions. On what general normative principles may the use of often substantial public power by unelected agency officials in our political system be justified and, at least for the system as a whole, legitimated? Moreover, what is the characteristic mode of decisionmaking that principal actors in the administrative process, especially agency officials but also including judges or members of Congress, attempt to realize and ought to perfect? By resolving these fundamental issues in strikingly different ways, the rule of law, public purposes, and democratic process ideals stake out demonstrably distinct conceptual ground for subsequent defense and development. The distinctions among these three positions provide the basic pattern underlying the contemporary debate.

In addition, there is a central movement within the constellation of ideas giving body to the contemporary debate. This movement occurs within each ideal itself. Each ideal may be seen as having what will be referred to as a "core" embodiment as well as an "alternative" expression. The core embodiment represents the set of institutional commitments, predictions about the future, and normative premises that proponents of the ideal believe to be necessary for its full realization directly through the mechanisms of a reformed administrative process. For the rule of law ideal, for instance, the core embodiment is committed to realizing the demanding requisites of legal formalism within the actual, day-to-day operations of the administrative process. The theoretical underpinnings of this core, and of the other two, are developed in the succeeding sections.

But the main point to note here is that the very force that animates the core embodiment of each ideal—namely, single-minded devotion to a pristine, overarching vision of the legitimacy and character of administrative decisionmaking—risks the ideal's own undoing. In discussing reformist discourse, it is vital to recall that critical visions need to be rooted in some picture of reality that itself seems capable of being achieved, or approximately so, in the reasonably near future. If an ideal begins to appear wildly improbable in its assumptions about the actual process and its capacities for change, it gradually will cease to be a generative source of reformist criticism and will recede into the background as a construct of sheer imagination.

In the contemporary debate, the core embodiments of each of the three ideals seem caught in this basic difficulty. On the one hand, each core is committed to the most direct realization of the full promise of a powerful and central ideal within the context of a reformed administrative process. On the other hand, each core, if fully realized, would dramatically reorder the existing administrative process beyond the limits of mere reform. Ultimately, each core embodiment, taken in the fullness of its critical power, would require substantial and deep-seated alteration in that process in order to be fully realized. Since there is an abiding gap between the core embodiments and the existing administrative process, the direct realization of each core in the name of reform appears as deeply problematical as it does radically transformative of that process.

Furthermore, in some respects the core of each ideal, to be completely realized, requires reforms that undermine the fundamental ideal itself. To that degree, regardless of its normative power, each core is self-defeating.

Despite these difficulties, the three ideals are of central and continuing importance in understanding and restructuring the American administrative process within the terms of debate reflected in contemporary reformist criticism. Therefore, critics are driven to reformulate the basic ideals in order to preserve them. This reformulation is seen in the movement from a core embodiment to an alternative expression of each ideal.

Each alternative expression retains the underlying ideal's commitment to a particular conception of the legitimacy of the administrative process. At the same time, the alternative expression embraces an indirect method for realizing the values reflected in the ideal. Each alternative in effect trades a less direct means of realizing the fundamental ideal for a tighter fit between the expression itself and the existing administrative process. Thus, by its terms or implications, each ideal's alternative expression, as opposed to its core embodiment, is much less radically transformative of the administrative process. To that extent, the alternative expression is a more successful reformist vision because it provides a better account of the existing process and imposes on it less strenuous requirements for change. At the same time, the alternative expression is a less powerful normative vision precisely because it accepts an indirect method of vindicating its underlying legitimating principles.

This movement from a core embodiment to an alternative expression may be identified with respect to each of the three competing ideals in the contemporary debate. The following chart schematically identifies the three competing ideals, their core embodiments, and their alternative expressions:

Three Competing Ideals	Core Embodiments	Alternative Expressions
I. Rule of Law Ideal	A. Formalism	B. Proceduralism
II. Public Purposes Ideal	A. Instrumentalism	B. The Market
III. Democratic Process Ideal	A. Participation	B. Oversight

As will be discussed, each of the competing ideals, viewed in general terms and in relation to both core embodiment and alternative expression, has significant power in the contemporary debate. At the same time, each one has its own intrinsic weaknesses and limitations.

Given the wide array of arguments advanced to criticize the administrative process, it would be odd if different organizations of ideas in the contemporary debate could not exist. This Article does not contend that the foregoing conceptual framework is the only possible one.[25] The chief claims for this framework are threefold.

---

25.   Richard Stewart and Cass Sunstein employ a tripartite scheme to analyze certain background understandings said to inform judges in creating private remedies under public laws. Stewart & Sunstein, *Public Programs and Private Rights*, 95 HARV. L. REV. 1193, 1229-39 (1982). They call these background understandings the entitlement, production, and public values conceptions. Stewart and Sunstein's organization of ideas is quite different from that presented in this Article. Also, their conceptions are not designed to provide a framework within which to understand the contemporary debate about administrative reform. The three

First, this framework shows that the contemporary debate has a deep structure of basic oppositions among three distinct ideals of the administrative process. No one of these ideals may be abandoned within the terms of this debate, and each is at war with the others.

Second, this framework reveals an underlying dynamic within each ideal. This is the movement within each ideal from a core embodiment to an alternative expression, which occurs, it appears, in response to the central difficulties of realizing the core embodiment itself.

Third, despite the surface complexity and variety of the contemporary debate, this framework underscores that the reform debate is more self-contained and limited in scope than it may initially

---

ideals I discuss reflect fundamental normative commitments and conflicts about the legitimacy and character of administrative decisionmaking. Stewart and Sunstein's conceptions do not reflect such deep normative debates. Furthermore, I mean to explore not only a triad of general conceptions of administrative reform, but also the internal development within each dominant ideal from a core to a more indirect, alternative expression.

The protection of entitlements is a central part of the rule of law ideal, and a concern with economic production is shared by many who embrace elements of the public purposes ideal as developed in this Article. But those are only aspects of the more general ideals considered here. Moreover, the public purposes ideal discussed here differs considerably from Stewart and Sunstein's public values conception, which appears to be a rather open-ended position critical of the common law system, but focused on a medley of affirmative themes. *See id.* at 1238 (referring to the Progressive critique of the common law); *id.* at 1242 n.191 (speaking of the public values approach as "cultivat[ing] and weigh[ing] divergent conceptions of value" and aspiring "to the moral development of citizens and communities that reflectively and deliberately choose their own ends").

Patrick McAuslan discusses three competing ideologies in the context of English planning law: the "common law approach" that emphasizes the protection of private property; the "orthodox public administration and planning approach" that seeks to advance the public interest; and the "radical or populist approach" that advances the cause of public involvement in planning decisions. P. MCAUSLAN, THE IDEOLOGIES OF PLANNING LAW (1980). Although this triad has some affinities with the three ideals discussed here, McAuslan does not fully trace the three ideologies to their deep source in competing theories of the legitimacy of the administrative process in general. He is mainly concerned with analyzing different approaches to planning as such. In addition, McAuslan does not develop a distinctive sense of decisionmaking rationality associated with each of his different perspectives. In further contrast, he does not show internal development within each ideology, as is done here with respect to the core embodiments and alternative expressions of the three competing ideals. Finally, McAuslan does not underscore temporary alliances or overlaps that may be seen to exist among aspects of the competing ideas in his system.

Another conceptual treatment of topics in administrative law is Stewart, *The Reformation of American Administrative Law, supra* note 10. That article discusses the decline of a "traditional" model of administrative law that emphasized specifically legal constraints on agencies, and the emergence by the mid-1970's of an "interest representation" model of administration, that stressed the values of participation, responsiveness, and representation in administrative proceedings. Here, in contrast, there is no suggestion that any one of the general competing conceptions underlying the contemporary debate is in the ascendancy, or that any one is in decline or a state of disintegration. *See also infra* text accompanying note 136.

appear. Much of the debate's richness may be explained in terms of the efforts to work out the deep, competing normative commitments in the context of specific proposals.

The next three sections will discuss seriatim the three competing ideals. These sections will develop each ideal's basic premises and core embodiments. They also will discuss each core's limitations and the alternative expressions of each ideal. The concluding section will consider the question of overlaps and makeshift alliances among aspects of the three ideals in light of general perspectives on the contemporary debate.

III. The First Major Ideal of the Administrative Process Reflected in the Contemporary Debate: The Rule of Law Ideal

A. The Nature of the Rule of Law Ideal

The first central ideal reflected in the contemporary debate is the rule of law ideal. The ideal of the rule of law, as is often noted, commands the participants in the administrative process, notably including administrators but also including reviewing courts, to adhere to the dictates of public laws laid down in advance by the sovereign legislature. This ideal permeates administrative law in general, furnishing the foundational notion that agency action lacks legitimacy unless grounded in law, normally a statute. Not surprisingly, it also is central to the contemporary debate about administrative reform.[26]

The rule of law ideal is closely associated with a contractarian vision of the polity and a conception of legal rationality that may be referred to as legal formalism. In fundamental terms, the contractarian vision, as expressed, for instance, in Locke's political theory,[27] posits that there should be a realm of private autonomy within which individuals remain free to pursue their own ends in economic and social life relatively free from intrusions by officials of

---

26. The general concept of the rule of law is explicated in J. Rawls, A Theory of Justice 235-43 (1971). It is at the heart of what Richard Stewart has called the "traditional" model of administrative law. *See* Stewart, *The Reformation of American Administrative Law*, *supra* note 10. *See also* F. Hayek, The Road to Serfdom 72-87 (1944); P. Nonet & P. Selznick, Law and Society in Transition: Toward Responsive Law 53-72 (1978); Jones, *The Rule of Law and the Welfare State*, 58 Colum. L. Rev. 143 (1958).

27. *See* J. Locke, *The Second Treatise of Government*, in Two Treatises of Government (P. Laslett ed. 1960).

the state.[28] Public laws essentially mark the boundaries of the realm of private choice. Such laws are viewed as facilitative of private ordering in that they restrain official arbitrariness that otherwise might interfere with individual decisionmaking. In addition, the laws are seen as guarantors of public order that foster private liberty to act in a context relatively free from social disorder. Perhaps the core of the contractarian vision is the notion that public laws and the authorities established by them are legitimate to the extent that they rest on the consent of the governed.[29] The basis of such consent is the expectation that a law-governed system is necessary precisely in order to protect the sphere of private choice and, more particularly, to define entitlements. In this reasonably familiar sense, the premises of the contractarian vision presuppose the necessity of public laws, which provide the essential conditions of freedom.[30]

The jurisprudential conception most directly connected with the rule of law ideal is that of legal formalism. This much used term does not refer to a narrow view of legal rationality holding that every result in specific cases can and should be deduced as a matter of conceptual analysis from prior legal rules. Indeed, the usage here is not confined to any particular theory of the nature of rules or principles that furnish the basis of legal decisionmaking. Rather, legal formalism is used in a more generalized way to refer to a range of possible theories emphasizing the role of specifically legal constraints on public power, especially as it affects individuals' entitlements.[31] The dominant theme of a formalist perspective on the administrative process is that decisions about the use of public power are to be governed by legal norms—which for our purposes may include principles in Ronald Dworkin's sense or rules in H.L.A. Hart's sense[32]—that are presumed to be relatively autonomous from the

---

28.   *See* J. DICKINSON, ADMINISTRATIVE JUSTICE AND THE SUPREMACY OF LAW 32-36 (1927); F. HAYEK, *supra* note 26; J. LOCKE, *supra* note 27.

29.   Of course, there are various detailed expressions of contractarian theory embodying these notions. *See, e.g.,* J. RAWLS, *supra* note 26; P. RILEY, WILL AND POLITICAL LEGITIMACY: A CRITICAL EXPOSITION OF SOCIAL CONTRACT THEORY IN HOBBES, LOCKE, ROUSSEAU, KANT AND HEGEL (1982).

30.   *See* J. LOCKE, *supra* note 27, at § 222:

The Reason why Men enter into Society, is the preservation of their Property; and the end why they chuse and authorize a Legislative, is, that there may be Laws made, and Rules set as Guards and Fences to the Properties of all the Members of the Society, to limit the Power, and moderate the Dominion of every Part and Member of the Society.

See also Stewart, *The Reformation of American Administrative Law, supra* note 10, at 1672-73.

31.   *See generally* Kennedy, *Legal Formality,* 2 J. LEGAL STUD. 351 (1973).

32.   *See* R. DWORKIN, TAKING RIGHTS SERIOUSLY (1977); H.L.A. HART, THE CONCEPT OF LAW (1961).

sphere of frankly political decisions. On this persistently debated view, the sphere of politics is seen to generate value choices and to articulate them in legal norms. The legal realm is conceived to involve the use of such norms and the evolution of legal doctrine in concrete cases without any direct intrusion into politics.

The rule of law ideal's division of the world of public authority into presumptively distinct spheres of political and legal decisionmaking enables the ideal to provide within its own terms a ready explanation of and justification for legislative and judicial action. However, it is less able easily to account for administrative behavior. Under the ideal's premises, lawmaking by the sovereign legislature involves the enunciation of legal norms necessary for private freedom, and adjudication involves the application of legal norms in individual cases. Administration, by contrast, has no easily conceived central function in this bifurcated view of decisionmaking about law. On the one hand, to the extent that administrators themselves enunciate legal norms, as they assuredly do in rulemaking proceedings, their action partakes of the essential role of the legislature. But on the other hand, to the extent that administrators decide cases, as in adjudicatory proceedings, they share the fundamental task of courts.[33]

The rule of law ideal seeks to overcome this potential instability regarding the place of administrative decisionmaking by pragmatically acknowledging that administrative behavior may reflect either a rule-giving or a rule-applying mode. Whatever function is being performed, the key characteristic of any given administrative action on this view is that it must be authorized by and grounded in some prior public law. To the extent that this is achieved, the contractarian vision of the polity may be said to be upheld. Also, to this degree one may assert that law, rather than politics, ultimately has governed the administrative action; this is the essential residuum of the ideal's commitment to legal rationality as reflected in formalism. By embracing these basic ideas, the rule of law ideal recognizes that administrative decisionmaking functionally may correspond with either judicial or legislative decisionmaking. At the same time, the ideal requires that administrative action must be justified in essentially the same manner as the law-governed decisionmaking of courts, as distinct from the law-formulating decisionmaking of the legislature.

---

33. This dual character of administration has long been recognized. *See, e.g.,* Humphrey's Executor v. United States, 295 U.S. 602, 628 (1935) (noting that the FTC "acts in part quasi-legislatively and in part quasi-judicially").

400   WISCONSIN LAW REVIEW

This complex of notions furnishes the major premises of certain suggestions for reforming the existing administrative process. One example of a traditional notion put forward by some as a promising basis for significant reform, if it were more seriously applied, is the nondelegation doctrine. This doctrine bars Congress from abrogating its constitutional responsibility by delegating its legislative function to agencies.[34] The basic premises underlying the nondelegation doctrine may be seen as little more than somewhat narrowed restatements of those of the rule of law ideal itself. Like the ideal, the nondelegation doctrine holds, first, that legitimate agency action is necessarily governed by preexisting laws derived from the sovereign lawgiver and, second, that the process of legal decisionmaking engaged in by an agency must be traced specifically to the elaboration of legal norms, rather than to frankly political choice.[35]

Different approaches in judicial decisions applying the nondelegation doctrine may be explained in large measure in terms of the degree of specificity required of the authorizing statutes. Decisions rendered during the doctrine's heyday, notably *Schechter Poultry*[36] and *Panama Refining*,[37] emphasized the need for rather specific and determinate authorizations of actions undertaken by agencies. In later opinions, such as *Yakus*[38] and *Amalgamated Meat Cutters*,[39] which are considered to represent the doctrine's demise, courts have been much more willing to uphold extraordinarily broad authorizations by the legislature, so long as the tasks of administration have been marked out with some identifiable degree of definiteness, if not clarity, by intelligible principles in the authorizing statutes. Even though judicial decisions thus differ in their emphasis on the supposed rigors implicit in the nondelegation doctrine, in general their analysis proceeds on the basis of the rule of law ideal's main premises.

---

34.   A key issue in particular cases is how much in the way of legislative guidance, or standards, must be furnished by Congress when it empowers agencies to undertake administrative action in a given area. *See generally* S. BREYER & R. STEWART, *supra* note 14, at 59-85.

35.   See H. FRIENDLY, THE FEDERAL ADMINISTRATIVE AGENCIES 21-22 (1962):
We still live under a Constitution which provides that "all legislative Powers herein granted shall be vested in a Congress of the United States. . . ."; even if a statute telling an agency "Here is the problem: deal with it" be deemed to comply with the letter of that command, it hardly does with the spirit.

See generally Jaffe, *An Essay on Delegation of Legislative Power*, 47 COLUM. L. REV. 359 (1947); Wright, Book Review, 81 YALE L.J. 575 (1972).

36.   A.L.A. Schechter Poultry Corp. v. United States, 295 U.S. 495 (1935).

37.   Panama Ref. Co. v. Ryan, 293 U.S. 388 (1934).

38.   Yakus v. United States, 321 U.S. 414 (1944).

39.   Amalgamated Meat Cutters & Butcher Workers v. Connally, 337 F. Supp. 737 (D.D.C. 1971).

Just as the strengths of the nondelegation doctrine derive from its embrace of the powerful vision underlying the rule of law ideal, so, too, its ultimate instabilities as a doctrine by means of which to reform the administrative process can be traced to its embodiment of that ideal. As noted earlier, a key element of the ideal is the familiar contractarian vision of the polity, in which the legitimacy of government rests on the assumption that individual citizens have granted their consent to the legislature. Courts are in a sense restricted decisionmakers in this scheme, for their function is to employ legal norms in particular cases in accordance with the dictates of legal formalism. When courts invalidate administrative action as unauthorized because there has been an undue delegation of power to an agency, courts also are invalidating in a given case the statutory provision that purportedly governed the action in the first place. Such constitutionally-based nullification of legislative enactments in the administrative context presents the same conundra for courts that are raised so often in discussions of judicial review in general.[40] For present purposes, the chief difficulties are that when courts so invalidate statutes, they may appear to step beyond the role assigned to them under the rule of law ideal as mere expositors of legal norms, and in any event, in such circumstances they come into direct conflict with the premises of the vision of political legitimacy at the ideal's core. For these reasons, the rule of law ideal itself exerts a continuing pressure against the active application by courts of the nondelegation doctrine, even though the doctrine itself basically reflects that very ideal.

From this vantage point, one can grasp with greater sympathy the considerable challenge confronting those who, in the name of administrative reform, seek to "revive" the nondelegation doctrine. On the one hand, reformist proponents of the doctrine are able to borrow central aspects of a leading ideal of the administrative process in arguing, for instance in the manner of Justice Rehnquist, that Lockeian principles at the foundation of our polity support its wholehearted embrace.[41] On the other hand, these proponents inevi-

---

40. *See, e.g.,* A. BICKEL, THE LEAST DANGEROUS BRANCH (1962); J. ELY, DEMOCRACY AND DISTRUST: A THEORY OF JUDICIAL REVIEW (1980); Wechsler, *Toward Neutral Principles of Constitutional Law*, 73 HARV. L. REV. 1 (1959).

41. *See* American Textile Mfrs. Inst., Inc. v. Donovan, 452 U.S. 490, 543 (1981) (Rehnquist, J., and Burger, C.J., dissenting); Industrial Union Dep't v. American Petroleum Inst., 448 U.S. 607, 671 (1980) (Rehnquist, J., concurring in the judgment). *See also* Wright, *supra* note 35 (urging revival of nondelegation doctrine to limit agency discretion). *Cf.* Aranson, Gellhorn & Robinson, *A Theory of Legislative Delegation*, 68 CORNELL L. REV. 1, 63–67 (1982) (arguing for a revived nondelegation doctrine on the basis of the inefficiencies of the collective production of private benefits said to attend broad delegations).

tably confront the internal restraint embodied in the rule of law ideal itself regarding the proper role of courts as expositors of the law. Of course, constitutional norms take precedence over statutory ones, but in practice there remains persistent pressure against outright invalidation of a legislative judgment. Accordingly, to the extent that the rule of law ideal remains dominant, it seems likely that one may expect to observe continued bows in the direction of the nondelegation doctrine in criticisms of administrative action, as well as a prudent reliance on less drastic alternatives to the doctrine itself—such as a greater willingness simply to interpret statutes rather narrowly in order to avoid potential questions about undue delegations.[42]

B. *The Limitations of the Core Formalist Embodiment of the Rule of Law Ideal*

The core formalist embodiment of the rule of law ideal achieves its normative force by purporting to distinguish between blatantly political and more strictly legal decisionmaking, and by confining the administrative process to the latter. This fundamental aspiration depends upon the existence of relatively determinate and autonomous norms of public law, which ideally are to structure and guide specific agency decisionmaking.

In reality, however, the norms of public law often are remarkably indeterminate and sweeping in their scope. One sees this immediately by reviewing statutes that, for instance, authorize action in the "public interest, convenience and necessity."[43] Such a statutory standard plainly is designed to afford substantial room for the play of administrative discretion. In fact, one of the most familiar justifications for creating many administrative agencies and programs is that there must exist an institutional context for the exercise of executive discretion guided chiefly by specialized expertise about public problems.[44] The rule of law ideal's own premises simply do not pro-

---

42.   *See, e.g.*, National Cable Television Ass'n v. United States, 415 U.S. 336 (1974); Zemel v. Rusk, 381 U.S. 1 (1965); Kent v. Dulles, 357 U.S. 116 (1958). *See also* K. DAVIS, DISCRETIONARY JUSTICE: A PRELIMINARY INQUIRY 45-66 (1969). This is not to suggest that alternatives to the nondelegation doctrine are themselves necessarily freed of the conundra attaching to that doctrine. For instance, aggressive efforts by courts narrowly to construe broad delegations are subject to criticism precisely as an unduly activist approach to statutory construction, which may be said to be inappropriate in itself, or, from another perspective, a misleading posture to the extent that it is predicated on an asserted disavowal of judicial innovation.

43.   *See, e.g.*, Communications Act of 1934, 47 U.S.C. § 307(a) (1976).

44.   *See, e.g.*, J. LANDIS, THE ADMINISTRATIVE PROCESS (1938). *See also* Stewart, *The Reformation of Administrative Law, supra* note 10, at 1677-78.

vide an adequate account of the primary place of such discretion and expertise in the operation and development of the administrative process.

Given that highly open-ended legal norms are at the center, not the periphery, of administrative life, it often would be strained indeed to describe agency actions as truly grounded in law as distinguished from policy analysis, political choices, or bureaucratic patterns having at most an attenuated link with the law as such. The problem here is not that formalism can account for no open-ended legal norms, but rather that in administrative law such norms are dominant, not exceptional, and the premises of the formalist model do not acknowledge such a phenomenon. Examples of multifactored, open-ended agency decisionmaking that are difficult to account for under the formalist approach are not hard to identify. They range from adjudicative processes, such as licensing by the Federal Communications Commission, to complex rulemaking, such as that by the Environmental Protection Agency or the Occupational Safety and Health Administration. Because the rule of law ideal presupposes the existence of reasonably determinate and autonomous legal norms that constrain agency action, it cannot be realized so long as administrative decisionmaking is dominated by highly open-ended norms affording substantial room for the operation of discretion that may be guided as much by policy, political, or institutional factors as by specifically legal constraints.[45]

Several explanations, based largely on the asserted necessities or practical constraints of modern government, have been advanced to account for the predominance of such open-ended norms. In part, Congress may lack the time, staff, or other resources needed to delineate with precision the legal limits on agency action. Moreover, agency discretion often has been perceived as an independent value because it allows for experimentation, flexibility, and change without recourse to statutory amendment.[46] Also, as a political matter, it appears to be expedient for Congress to legislate in highly general terms. The less specific the proposed legislation, the more likely may be the achievement of the necessary consensus for enactment, which

---

45. Indeed, one may question as an initial matter whether any meaningful distinction in the administrative area may be drawn between "legal" and broadly "political" decisionmaking, especially so long as legal analysis is assumed to include consideration of the purposes of broad statutory delegations. For a general discussion of the breakdown of formalistic legal reasoning in the modern welfare state, see R. UNGER, LAW IN MODERN SOCIETY 192-223 (1976).

46. *See* J. LANDIS, *supra* note 44; Stewart, *The Reformation of American Administrative Law, supra* note 10, at 1695.

is difficult to accomplish even in the most propitious of circumstances. By such an approach, Congress may avoid the necessity of making certain controversial decisions about matters of public debate that may be expected to generate considerable clamor. At least, it assuredly is more convenient to assign such difficult tasks to agencies, from which Congress readily may seek to distance itself should the clamor become sufficiently widespread.

Even more fundamentally, the very character of statutory norms designed to criticize existing institutions—for instance, antidiscrimination norms, such as in legislation broadly prohibiting discrimination against the handicapped[47] —may require that they embody rather general and open-ended principles. If the critical norms were highly specific and thus strictly confined in their reference or implications, their force as catalysts of social change inevitably would be blunted. Thus, if the rule of law ideal is to allow for serious criticism of existing social institutions, it appears that it must be seen to permit open-ended principles in public law. To this extent, however, the ideal fosters the very condition that precipitates the frustration of its formalist aspirations.

These several factors, taken together, render highly problematical the full achievement of the formalist model of the rule of law ideal. They also may help to explain why, despite the ideal's continuing centrality in the theory of administrative law, its core embodiment has been the progenitor of relatively few contemporary proposals for reform.[48]

C. The Proceduralist Alternative to the Core Formalist Embodiment of the Rule of Law Ideal

A primary response by those embracing the basic vision underlying the rule of law ideal to the difficulties of realizing its formalist core is to place less concentration on substantive legal constraints on agency action and more emphasis on procedural limitations. Proceduralism continues to reflect the rule of law's commitment to

---

47.   *See* Rehabilitation, Comprehensive Services and Developmental Disabilities Amendments of 1978, Pub. L. No. 95-602, 92 Stat. 2955, 2982 (codified at 29 U.S.C. § 706 (1982)); Rehabilitation Act of 1973, Pub. L. No. 93-112, § 504, 87 Stat. 394 (codified as amended at 29 U.S.C. § 794 (1982)).

48.   The rule of law ideal's core is perhaps most consistent with efforts by Congress carefully to review and redraft as necessary the underlying substantive authorities of different agencies in order to be certain that statutory delegations are as clear and determinate as possible. Yet the center of gravity in the contemporary reform debate has been in the area of government-wide reform, not agency-by-agency statutory review. *But see* Federal Trade Commission Improvements Act of 1980, Pub. L. No. 96-252, 94 Stat. 374 (1980).

legal norms as necessary restraints on potentially overweening and arbitrary public power. However, proceduralism tends to deemphasize the place of determinate and autonomous legal norms as the guides of agency decisionmaking, while stressing in their place the need for broadly applicable procedural safeguards as the guarantors of a regularized and fair process.[49]

The animating image underlying the proceduralist critique of administration involves the application of the state's considerable powers in matters affecting discrete individuals. In such situations, the proceduralist's concern, not unexpectedly, is with fostering the autonomy and private rights of the person in a reasonably nonarbitrary process. The guiding idea is that of fairness toward the individual. Under this conception it is critical to afford each person a "day in court" when the state proposes to act against one's interests. It is essential from this perspective to provide a person the opportunity to understand and respond to any accusations or assertions that could lead to agency action against him or her. In particular cases, the full panoply of formalities associated with a judicial, trial-type process may be employed in the name of proceduralism.[50] Whatever the formalities employed, their rationale on these premises is to uphold a highly individualistic conception of fairness and regularity in administrative processes.

Of course, in an administrative context in which decisions affect large numbers of persons and groups in society, the image of a one-on-one encounter between the state and an individual often is somewhat amiss. Nonetheless, the basic project of assuring a nonarbitrary, fair, and regularized process with basic due process guarantees still is widely pursued, even if the means are modified to fit the realities of broad-scale policymaking, such as, for example, through agency rulemaking.[51]

Proceduralism has exerted a powerful influence on the development of administrative law, much of which consists, after all, of the procedural norms structuring adjudicatory and rulemaking proceedings.[52] To find other instances of proceduralism, one need look

---

49. *See generally* K. DAVIS, *supra* note 42.

50. *See generally* Friendly, *Some Kind of Hearing*, 123 U. PA. L. REV. 1267 (1975); Verkuil, *supra* note 12 (discussing, *inter alia*, various procedural safeguards brought to bear in different types of administrative proceedings).

51. *See* K. DAVIS, *supra* note 42, at 15-42, 98-120; Wright, *supra* note 35, at 577-80, 587-96. *See also* H.R. REP. No. 435, 97th Cong., 2d Sess. 22-23, 30-33 (1982) (discussing proposed changes in agency rulemaking procedures).

52. *See* 5 U.S.C. §§ 553, 556, 557 (1982) (setting forth requirements for rulemaking and adjudicatory procedures under the APA).

no farther than cases dealing with due process hearing rights[53] or
cases involving the review of agency action for possible arbitrariness
or capriciousness.[54] In the last context, some courts have adopted a
relatively assertive attitude toward administrative behavior that
has required agencies, if not to follow specific procedures as such, at
least to provide a reasonably full explanation of the basis for any
given decision. This, in turn, requires agencies to undertake a relatively careful decisional process in order to survive judicial review.
Such a tendency is reflected in the so-called "hard look" approach,
which requires that agencies take a hard look at the underpinnings
of their decision and provide a sufficient explanation of the reasons
for their ultimate choice in order to allow a reviewing court to determine whether in fact it was the product of reasoned decisionmaking.[55]

Although the proceduralist model has exerted considerable
practical influence in the development of administrative law, its
conceptual status is less secure. To a substantial degree, it represents an inherently unstable compromise. On the one hand,
proceduralism does not specifically advance the rule of law ideal's
commitment to substantive legal norms that govern legal decisionmaking and constrain agency action. On the other hand, proceduralism essentially maintains the rule of law ideal's vision of political
legitimacy, which is based on the contractarian notion of the polity
discussed above. In particular, proceduralism retains the ideas that
administrative action lacks legitimacy unless it is authorized by law
and that public laws promulgated by the legislature lack legitimacy
unless they may be said to rest on the consent of the governed.

This combination of commitments leads to an incompleteness
within proceduralism itself. By embracing the rule of law ideal's vision of political legitimacy, proceduralism embodies the ideal's conception of a demarcation between the spheres of public action and

---

53. *See, e.g.*, Vitek v. Jones, 445 U.S. 480 (1980); Greenholtz v. Inmates of Ne-
braska Penal and Correctional Complex, 442 U.S. 1 (1979); Meachum v. Fano, 427 U.S. 215
(1976); Bishop v. Wood, 426 U.S. 341 (1976); Mathews v. Eldridge, 424 U.S. 319 (1976);
Perry v. Sindermann, 408 U.S. 593 (1972); Board of Regents v. Roth, 408 U.S. 564 (1972);
Goldberg v. Kelly, 397 U.S. 254 (1970). *See generally* Monaghan, *Of 'Liberty' and 'Property'*,
62 CORNELL L. REV. 405 (1977); Saphire, *Specifying Due Process Values: Toward a More Responsive Approach to Procedural Protection*, 127 U. PA. L. REV. 111 (1978).

54. *See, e.g.*, Motor Vehicle Mfrs. Ass'n v. State Farm Mut. Auto. Ins. Co., ___ U.S.
___, 103 S.Ct. 2856 (1983); Ethyl Corp. v. EPA, 541 F.2d 1 (D.C. Cir.), *cert. denied*, 426 U.S.
941 (1976); Industrial Union Dep't v. Hodgson, 499 F.2d 467 (D.C. Cir. 1974).

55. *See, e.g.*, Greater Boston Television Corp. v. FCC, 444 F.2d 841 (D.C. Cir.
1970), *cert. denied*, 403 U.S. 923 (1971); Leventhal, *Environmental Decisionmaking and the Role
of Courts*, 122 U. PA. L. REV. 509 (1974). *See generally* S. BREYER & R. STEWART, *supra* note
14, at 291-305 (and cases cited therein).

private autonomy. In particular, proceduralism accepts—or at the very least never rejects—the rule of law ideal's vision of law as a constraint on public power that marks the boundaries of a realm of private rights. However, by abandoning the rule of law ideal's emphasis on substantive formalism and by stressing in its place the importance of proceduralism—or, if you will, procedural formalism—as a check on agency discretion, proceduralism fails to satisfy the conditions ultimately needed to realize its own political ideal. This is so because purely proceduralist restraints on agency action do not, and indeed they cannot, substantively delimit the sphere of public power, as distinct from the realm of private rights. If one wishes to accomplish such a task, one will need a substantive explanation of the basis for such a demarcation, which proceduralism lacks.

Such conceptual incompleteness plagues contemporary proceduralist proposals for administrative reform. Take, for instance, the so-called Bumpers Amendment, which for several years has been proposed by Senator Dale Bumpers.[56] Although not enacted, this amendment in 1982 was adopted in one version by the Senate by a vote of 94 to 0 and, in a somewhat different version, by the House Committee on the Judiciary.[57] The amendment essentially would broaden the scope of judicial review of agency action such as by requiring courts not to "presume" that challenged agency action is valid and by requiring courts to review issues of fact in informal rulemaking under a somewhat more stringent standard. Putting aside the amendment's details, which vary considerably from version to version, the proposal is grounded on a conviction that agencies tend to be too activist in their use of their broad delegations and, as a result, tend to trench excessively upon the private realm of social life.[58] This basic rationale represents a straightfor-

---

56.   *See supra* note 2.

57.   *See* 128 Cong. Rec. S2693-722 (daily ed. Mar. 24, 1982); H.R. Rep. No. 435, 97th Cong., 2d Sess. (1982).

58.   There are several versions of the Bumpers Amendment. A typical recent one is found in 128 Cong. Rec. S2713, 2718 (daily ed. Mar. 24, 1982) which provides that in "making determinations on questions of law, the court shall not accord any presumption in favor of or against agency action, but [using] its independent judgment . . . shall give the agency interpretation such weight as it warrants, taking into account the discretionary authority provided to the agency by law." *See also* S. Rep. No. 284, 97th Cong., 1st Sess. 164-73, 204-05 (1981) (noting that the reported version of the amendment was "premised on the basic constitutional principle that in a republic, legislative power must be exercised by elected representatives"). The Senate report also pointed out that "expertise, the strength of modern government, can become a monster which rules with no practical limits on its discretion." *Id.* at 164 (quoting New York v. United States, 324 U.S. 882, 884 (1951) (Douglas, J., dissenting)). *See* Ossola, *Two Versions of Bumpers Differ on Judicial Review*, Legal Times of Wash., Mar. 29, 1982, at 29, col. 1.

ward restatement of the rule of law ideal's commitments to establishing and enforcing a substantive demarcation between the public and private spheres.

However, the Bumpers Amendment does not even purport to accomplish such objectives. To the contrary, its major proponent has expressed serious doubt whether Congress ever could do much at all to narrow broad delegations that have contributed to a fundamental blurring of any substantive distinction between a truly public and a fundamentally private realm.[59] True to its proceduralist underpinnings, the amendment essentially would call upon the judiciary to "take a closer look" at challenged agency action.

The ultimate defense of the amendment is that agencies, by having to satisfy stricter standards of judicial review, may be expected in general to compile more complete records and, partly as a result, to engage in more cautious and self-restrictive deliberations under existing authorizations before reaching final positions. Whatever else may be observed about such an approach to administrative reform, in terms of the rule of law ideal itself, it is at best a partial solution to the problem it seeks to address. The underlying problem—assuring that agencies remain within the bounds of substantive law—can be addressed under the rule of law ideal by clarifying the limits of the law and by relying on courts to police them. To adopt the second step without even attempting the first one is to expand the judicial role without providing determinate guides that judges or administrators may follow. Such an approach borrows the rule of law rhetoric about the place of courts as the guardians of legal

---

The Bumpers Amendment in its various formulations has generated a critical literature discussing its prescriptions for asserted agency excess. *See generally* Levin, *supra* note 2; McGowan, *supra* note 2; O'Reilly, *supra* note 2; Woodward & Levin, *supra* note 2; Wright, *supra* note 2.

59. *See, e.g.,* 125 CONG. REC. S23,478-500 (daily ed., Sept. 7, 1979) (debate on the Bumpers Amendment, which was adopted by the Senate as an amendment to the Federal Courts Improvement Act of 1979). During this debate, Senator Bumpers stated that "Congress has demonstrated a remarkable ineptness in dealing with the bureaucracy. . . ." and that "[e]very law school freshman in the country knows that Congress cannot legally delegate the legislative power to anyone; yet we have been doing it." The Senator's explanation for the difficulty of directly redressing this perceived imbalance proceeded as follows:

The difficulty is that each of the broad legislative grants of power to agencies has already been particularized by the agencies themselves. These surrogates for Congress have spun out whole codes of regulations and interpretations. . . . Each of these specifications has acquired its own constituency of support, and it is not realistic to expect an elected Congress to tackle the massive task of reviewing the whole complex of administrative edicts now on the books.

Id. at 23,479-81.

constraints on administration[60] without providing the normative underpinnings necessary to give content to such an ideal.[61]

A similar dynamic may be seen in reform proposals calling for further formalization of the so-called informal rulemaking process.[62] Such proposals have been included in the major regulatory reform bills introduced in recent Congresses.[63] Formalizing informal rulemaking often is defended in the name of constraining the exercise of agency discretion and preventing excessive intrusions on the private sphere. Yet what would these proposals typically accomplish? Some of them would, for instance, provide for oral presentation or even cross-examination on material issues of fact in certain circumstances. Others would require agencies to compile with greater care a rulemaking file containing comments received during the rulemaking process. Commonly, the proposals also would impose a number of analytical burdens on agencies, such as the requirement of describing and evaluating reasonable alternatives to a proposed or a final rule. These and other provisions would tend to move informal rulemaking—originally conceived by the framers of the APA as a legislative-type process in which affected parties could voice their opinions, but in which agency decisionmakers would have rather broad latitude in reaching and justifying a final decision—well along the continuum of procedural detail in the direction of a fully formalized process. Such proposals, whatever their other attributes, share proceduralism's general inability to address the un-

---

60. See J. DICKINSON, supra note 28, at 37-38.

61. The Bumpers Amendment has been defended by some as likely to result in more aggressive judicial analysis of challenged agency action, and thus as a potential tonic for overzealous administration despite its lack of any clear substantive guidance to agencies on particular matters of public policy. Cf. McGowan, Regulatory Analysis and Judicial Review, 42 OHIO ST. L.J. 627, 631 (1981) ("And I see nothing in the [Bumpers] amendment, even as revised, that would stop me from going about the interpretative job in the way I like to think I always have.").

62. Under the APA, informal rulemaking is conceived as a relatively nonformal process calling for proposals, comments, and final decisions unencumbered by the procedural requirements associated with formal rulemaking or adjudications. In recent years, courts and Congress have contributed to the greater proceduralization of agency rulemaking. This has prompted some to describe the emergence of "hybrid" rulemaking, which represents a kind of midway position between the formal procedures associated with trial-type proceedings, 5 U.S.C. §§ 556, 557 (1982), and the nonformalized process associated with "informal" rulemaking under the APA, 5 U.S.C. § 553 (1982). For a discussion of administrative procedure as a continuum of decisionmaking modes running from a minimal "reasons" requirement to the maximum of trial-type procedures, with middle ranges consisting of various elements (notice, written comments, oral comments, selective cross-examination, a "record" requirement), see Verkuil, supra note 12.

63. See, e.g., H.R. 2327, 98th Cong., 1st Sess. (1983).

derlying substantive concern that animates the criticisms generating the reform efforts in the first place.[64]

Moreover, proposals to increase the procedural formality of administrative decisionmaking predictably would impose considerable costs in terms of sheer delay and institutional complication. They thus are likely to be viewed as counterproductive by those seeking primarily to make the process more timely and effective. They also are open to serious criticism for "overjudicializing" agency decisional processes, such as rulemaking, that many believe should not be burdened with formalities suited mainly to adversarial, adjudicative proceedings in court.[65] It may well be that some would welcome, or at least would not oppose, an even less efficient, more easily obstructed administrative process, but such a perspective hardly constitutes a satisfactory alternative basis on which affirmatively to reform the system.

IV. THE SECOND MAJOR IDEAL REFLECTED IN THE CONTEMPORARY DEBATE: THE PUBLIC PURPOSES IDEAL

A. The Nature of the Public Purposes Ideal

The second of the three competing ideals of the administrative process reflected in the contemporary debate may be called the public purposes ideal. Stated broadly, this ideal's central emphasis is to foster the realization of valued public ends. At bottom, the ideal necessarily starts with a conception—and there are various ones—of the

---

64.   This discussion emphasizes the "negative" strand of proceduralism as a set of constraints on agency action that reflect the commitments of the rule of law ideal. That model is to be contrasted with the commitment, discussed below in terms of the democratic process ideal, to employing agency processes as a means of representing the public's interests in administrative decisionmaking. *See infra* notes 102-34 and accompanying text.

One also may contrast proceduralism as a general expression of the rule of law ideal with the more particular notion of using agency processes to foster a conception of the inherent dignity and personality of each individual. On this latter view, the individual is seen as intrinsically worthy of respect and thus, for instance, deserving of a full explanation of decisions that will affect his or her interests. Such a view frequently is reflected in debate about procedural due process, which provides a suitable context because that doctrine typically is invoked in situations where the force of the state is brought to bear directly on the individual. *See* Mashaw, *Administrative Due Process: The Quest for a Dignitary Theory*, 61 B.U.L. REV. 885 (1981); Michelman, *Formal and Associational Aims in Procedural Due Process*, 18 NOMOS: DUE PROCESS 126 (1977); Saphire, *supra* note 53. *See generally* Summers, *Evaluating and Improving Legal Processes: A Plea for "Process" Values*, 60 CORNELL L. REV. 1 (1974).

65.   One response to the formalization of rulemaking procedures, with its attendant delays and expense, is reflected in various proposals for regulatory negotiation among affected interests with different sorts of checks imposed by agencies. For discussion, see, e.g., Harter, *Negotiating Regulations: A Cure for Malaise*, 71 GEO. L.J. 1 (1982); Stewart, *Regulation, Innovation, and Administrative Law: A Conceptual Framework, supra* note 10, at 1341-54.

nature of the ends or purposes to be advanced by administrative action. The ideal's chief premise is that the primary standard for criticizing the administrative process lies in its ability to promote, and at all costs not to impede, the achievement of such a conception. Unlike the rule of law ideal, the public purposes ideal does not place primary emphasis on legal norms as necessary constraints on public power. Rather, it mainly stresses the affirmative tasks of governmental policymaking in general and administrative action in particular.

The ideal's most direct embodiment may be referred to as instrumentalism, by which is meant the familiar notion that the significant worth of a policy inheres in its success as an instrument of the public good—that is, as a means whereby something valued may be achieved or furthered.[66] In the context of administrative reform, the instrumentalist critique holds that the legitimacy of the administrative process turns on its ability to realize valued public ends in an effective and efficient manner.

Plainly, the crucial variables that determine the nature of different instrumentalist conceptions of reform depend on the theories of the purposes to be rationally promoted and the allowable means of pursuing them. For present purposes, two main types of instrumentalist approaches that lie roughly toward opposite poles of a continuum of possible perspectives are of particular interest.

On one instrumentalist view, reflected in its essentials in the enduring New Deal conception of the expert agency put forward for instance by James Landis,[67] the public purposes to be achieved are those identified in an agency's authorizing legislation. The ultimate basis for this commitment is the notion that legislative enactments are the legitimate repositories of the sovereign will and, therefore, their guidance of and limitations on the expert agency must be taken quite seriously in identifying the goals to be promoted. Furthermore, on this view the allowable range of means for achieving given ends is presumed to be significantly contained, even if still capacious. This range includes the direct and necessary methods of promoting statutory ends so long as the methods may be fairly said to

---

66. The word "instrumental" is used here in its ordinary sense: "serving as a means or intermediary determining or leading to a particular result: being an instrument that functions in the promotion of some end or purpose. . . ." WEBSTER'S THIRD NEW INTERNATIONAL DICTIONARY 1172 (1976). Instrumentalism in this context conceives of the administrative process as an instrument of the public good. *Cf.* R. SUMMERS, INSTRUMENTALISM AND AMERICAN LEGAL THEORY 136-75 (1982) (contrasting instrumentalism with legal formalism and arguing that, whereas legal formalists conceive of law in terms of generally applicable norms, instrumentalists view law as a set of flexible tools designed to serve practical ends).

67. *See* J. LANDIS, *supra* note 44.

be consistent with an agency's central tasks under its authorizing legislation.

A second instrumentalist approach expands the range of desired ends along with the allowable means of reaching them, not by expressly countenancing the violation of statutes to be sure, but by assuming that broad delegations are consistent with a sweeping consideration of alternative goals and the widest possible variety of means for achieving them. This view is reflected, for instance, in various contemporary proposals for conducting agency rulemaking in accordance with the dictates of comprehensive cost-benefit analysis.[68] In general terms, the well-recognized principle underlying cost-benefit analysis is that the right, or rational, course of action is one which, within the general limits of law, maximizes social benefits while minimizing social costs, as conceived within the context of various possible theories of benefits and costs. Like classical utilitarianism, whose intellectual heritage cost-benefit analysis in part borrows, such an expanded instrumentalist conception exudes notable confidence about the power of human reason to predict and calculate the consequences of agency decisions and to select a course of conduct that will maximize desired ends and minimize undesired results.[69]

Whether approached from the perspective of Landis or of modern proponents of plenary cost-benefit analysis, the vision of bureaucratic instrumentalism in general furnishes valuable tools for justifying and criticizing administrative decisionmaking. In contrast with the rule of law ideal, instrumentalism does not emphasize an antinomy between law-making by the legislature and law-applying by the courts. Rather, instrumentalism seeks to establish a unified conception of rational administrative policymaking distinct from both the law-promulgating function of the legislature and the law-applying mode of the courts.[70] This attempt may be seen in the writings of the New Deal's defenders who emphasized the special role of agency expertise in realizing given policy ends[71] and in more recent discussions by those who embrace the perspective of "policy

68.   *See* sources cited *supra* note 9.

69.   *See* Diver, *Policymaking Paradigms in Administrative Law*, 95 HARV. L. REV. 393, 396-98 (1981); Weidenbaum, *supra* note 9. *See generally* R. LITAN & W. NORDHAUS, *supra* note 1.

70.   The instrumentalist model also incorporates a particularly activist image of administrators as realizers of an independently grounded public good. *See generally* J. LANDIS, *supra* note 44.

71.   *See, e.g.,* J. LANDIS, *supra* note 44.

science" as a foundation for understanding administrative behavior.[72]

In the contemporary debate, instrumentalism's core is reflected most prominently in legislative proposals to require agencies to conduct rulemaking in accordance with some version of a cost-benefit or similar analysis of alternative courses of action. The major claim for cost-benefit analysis itself is essentially the argument in favor of instrumentalism: it is designed to foster formally rational, instrumental decisionmaking by agencies. From this perspective, regulatory reform bills have been proposed that would, among other things, impose a cost-benefit analysis or similar requirement in order to make more "rational" the rulemaking process.[73] Such recommendations have been reflected in the policies of the Reagan Administration, which since 1981 has implemented an Executive Order on regulation that differs from its immediate predecessors primarily in terms of its wholehearted embrace of the basic premises of the cost-benefit technique.[74]

Other reflections of the instrumentalist perspective in the contemporary debate may be found in discussions of the appropriate degree of judicial deference to agencies concerning issues of fact and policy in contested cases. This continuing controversy is particularly vivid in recent commentary about the Bumpers Amendment, which as noted above would broaden the scope of judicial review of agency action.[75] A main counterargument to the amendment's proponents rests on the premises that agencies possess valued expertise in resolving issues of fact and policy, and courts must be allowed to

---

72. *See generally* L. LAVE, THE STRATEGY OF SOCIAL REGULATION: DECISION FRAMEWORKS FOR POLICY (1981); Diver, *supra* note 69, at 396-98 (and sources noted therein).

73. *See, e.g.,* H.R. 2327, 98th Cong., 1st Sess. (1983); S. 1080, 97th Cong., 1st Sess. (1981), *reported in* S. REP. No. 284, 97th Cong., 1st Sess. 65 (1981) (the committee report referred to the Senate bill's regulatory analysis provision as a type of cost-benefit analysis requirement in a "broad sense"). For discussion of cost-benefit and similar analyses, see sources cited *supra* note 9.

74. *See* Exec. Order No. 12,291, *supra* note 8. This order requires executive agencies to prepare a "Regulatory Impact Analysis" of all "major" rules, defined as ones likely to result in an "annual effect on the economy of $100 million or more," to cause a "major increase" in costs or prices, or to have "significant adverse effects" on competition or employment. *Id.* §§ 1(b), 3(a). A regulatory impact analysis is to include, *inter alia*, a description of all potential costs and benefits and "[a] determination of the potential net benefits of the rule." *Id.* § 3(d). The order provides that to the extent permitted by law, regulatory actions shall be consistent with the requirements that "the potential benefits to society . . . outweigh the potential costs to society" and the alternative chosen maximizes the total net benefit to society. *Id.* § 2.

Earlier Executive Orders calling for increasingly centralized executive branch oversight of the administrative process are cited *supra* note 19. *See also* sources cited *supra* note 8.

75. *See supra* notes 56-61 and accompanying text.

give some weight to their judgment. Agencies accumulate administrative expertise because they are called upon to address recurrent issues when making determinations about the effects of possible courses of action, as they are required to do under the model of instrumentalism. In contrast, courts do not tend continually to engage in decisionmaking about a relatively limited range of policy questions, and thus they cannot be presumed to have the same substantive and managerial experience.[76] From this vantage point, it is irrational to seek to rely primarily upon courts in policing agencies' exercise of their peculiar expertise.

Such an argument about the relative institutional incompetence of courts in areas of administrative policy and technical factual controversy has been acknowledged in various contexts by courts themselves. For instance, this position has figured centrally in some decisions applying the "arbitrary, capricious, an abuse of discretion" standard of review to complex issues of fact and policy in informal rulemaking.[77] In other contexts, however, courts have not embraced this perspective on the ground that it would displace them from their traditional role as active reviewers of the legality of agency action.[78]

To the extent that distinctions between issues of fact, policy, and law are blurred in particular cases, as they often are, it is difficult for the instrumentalist argument on behalf of a limited judicial role to prevail as a general matter. In such circumstances, the contention is more easily matched by a response rooted in the rule of law ideal's commitment to legal restrictions on public power and to the role of courts in policing such limits. Viewed in this light, the instrumentalist justification for judicial deference to expert administra-

---

76.   For a discussion of the relative lack of judicial expertise on matters of administration, see J. LANDIS, *supra* note 44, at 30-31, 125-55. *See also* Bazelon, *Coping with Technology Through the Legal Process*, 62 CORNELL L. REV. 817, 822-23 (1977); Freedman, *Crisis and Legitimacy in the Administrative Process*, 27 STAN. L. REV. 1041, 1056-60 (1975).

77.   The standard is stated in 5 U.S.C. § 706(2)(A) (1982). *See, e.g.*, Ethyl Corp. v. EPA, 541 F.2d 1, 34, 36 (D.C. Cir.), *cert. denied*, 426 U.S. 941 (1976) ("[t]his standard of review is a highly deferential one"; "[t]he immersion in the evidence is designed *solely* to enable the court to determine whether the agency decision was rational and based on consideration of the relevant factors") (emphasis in original).

78.   *See, e.g.*, Hi-Craft Clothing Co. v. NLRB, 660 F.2d 910, 914 (3d Cir. 1981) ("[a] reviewing court may not simply abdicate its responsibility by mumbling an indiscriminate litany of cases that extends 'great deference to administrative conclusions'"; "[i]n most instances, the matter is one of 'mixed law and fact'"). For a representative statement of the position that courts cannot stand entirely aside while agencies exercise discretion, see Volkswagenwerk Aktiengesellschaft v. Federal Maritime Comm'n, 390 U.S. 261, 272 (1968) ("'The deference owed to an expert tribunal cannot be allowed to slip into judicial inertia. . . .'") (quoting American Ship Bldg. Co. v. NLRB, 380 U.S. 300, 318 (1965)).

tive discretion stands in permanent tension with the rule of law's conception of the primacy of legal constraints on the public realm.

B. *The Limitations of the Core Instrumentalist Embodiment of the Public Purposes Ideal*

The core instrumentalist embodiment of the public purposes ideal, like the core of the rule of law ideal, provides a powerful and central normative perspective from which to criticize the contemporary administrative process. However, also like the core of the rule of law ideal, instrumentalism ultimately does not offer an adequate understanding or justification of the modern administrative process, which appears inevitably to operate in ways that lie beyond the purview of a fully instrumentalist vision.

In particular, instrumentalism focuses on the need for expert, rational analysis as the foundation of administrative decision-making. This image stands in sharp contrast to a system imbued with custom, habit, inertia, and "irrational" political intervention. Nevertheless, it would be difficult indeed to contend that such elements are not critical in various administrative contexts. The premises of the instrumentalist core of the public purposes ideal do not provide an adequate account of the undeniable importance of such forces in the administrative process. To that extent, instrumentalism's premises, taken on their own terms and despite their continuing importance, furnish a limited and ultimately problematical basis for a program of administrative reform.

Moreover, the instrumentalist core has an inherently self-defeating tendency to encourage broader and broader analytical undertakings in which the scope of contemplated ends and means is ever expanding. This tendency seems to be reflected historically in the shift in the center of gravity in instrumentalist critiques during recent decades from the "expertise" conception of Landis to the plenary cost-benefit balancing proposals prominent in the contemporary reform debate.[79] The apparent trend toward broadening the scope of instrumentalist analysis is consistent with the underlying goal of achieving a truly rational result. On instrumentalist terms, what would be more rational than the "most" optimal solution to a public policy problem that takes into account all reasonable ends and means? Although such a progression toward greater breadth of

---

79. *Cf.* Diver, *supra* note 69 (emphasizing the trend in agency rulemaking over the last several years toward concentration on a comprehensive analytical approach). *See generally* R. LITAN & W. NORDHAUS, *supra* note 1.

analysis seems inescapable, it leads ultimately to a perspective on the administrative process that lacks any firm normative moorings. To the extent that nearly everything is to be taken into account and virtually all factors must be balanced against all others, an expanded instrumentalist conception becomes increasingly empty, difficult to apply, and indeterminate in its results.

However much one may criticize the vagueness of the instrumentalist critique, such a view of administration can be especially useful in a regime in which political authorities seek a general cover for manipulating the process. Thus, the official justification of decisions may be cast, at least in part, in formally instrumentalist terms, but actual decisions in fact may be generated by essentially political factors—such as influence by dominant societal interests and *ad hoc* intervention in agency rulemaking by the Executive Office of the President. Such a possibility is more than a speculative concern, given the contemporary emphasis on Executive Office oversight of cost-benefit analysis conducted initially by agencies. At a minimum, the long-expressed alarm about the possible "capture" of the administrative process by dominant political forces cannot be assumed to have been obviated by the program of instrumentalism.

Furthermore, to the extent that expanded instrumentalism as an analytical approach becomes linked with Executive Office oversight of administration, the role of individual agencies as expert decisionmakers is likely to be substantially eroded. This is likely, at least, so long as actual power over the administrative process is wielded by Executive Office staff, whose perspectives frequently may differ from those of agency officials. On the one hand, such a result may be applauded by critics who decry the supposed narrowness of particular agencies and their asserted tendency to be dominated by regulated industries (and congressional committees and subcommittees), and who perceive a need for greater centralized direction by the President and those directly responsible to him. On the other hand, the basically instrumentalist view of agencies as valuable centers of managerial and substantive expertise is itself put at serious risk by such a program.[80]

Aside from sharing these general problems of instrumentalism, cost-benefit analysis generates a number of more specific doubts. As is often asked, is it really possible to determine in advance all of the

---

80. Thus arises one of the ironies of some instrumentalist reform proposals: by becoming allied with centralized executive oversight of agency action, they actually tend to undercut, rather than build upon, the underlying premise that agencies have a special expertise in addressing certain areas of public policy.

material consequences of all possible alternative means to all reasonable intermediate goals that would further some given ultimate end, and to assess these various consequences in terms of some common standards of "costs" and "benefits"? The theory of cost-benefit analysis, taken to its extreme, would require such a herculean undertaking in order to arrive at a truly rational result. However, it commonly is noted that, at least as a practical matter, cost-benefit analysis must take for granted some reasonably limited set of preconceived ends and means, and their selection will depend on choices that themselves are not founded on any cost-benefit analysis.[81]

Moreover, assuming a limited range of preconceived ends and means, will it actually be possible to measure with accuracy the benefits as well as the costs of the consequences of different possible agency actions? One must establish some common denominator in terms of which to assess or assign weights to various outcomes. However, the outcomes may have significantly differing characteristics and thus may not be readily susceptible to reduction to a common standard of measurement. Also, it frequently is observed that cost-benefit analysis may be systematically skewed by the particular difficulties of predicting and assigning values to the benefits, as opposed to the costs, of rules. Benefits, such as cleaner air or water, may be more difficult to predict and measure simply because of limits in our scientific understanding, for instance of the effects on human health and the environment of varying degrees of improvement in air or water quality. Also, benefits are especially difficult to state in quantifiable terms since they commonly are diffuse and long-term.[82]

More generally, cost-benefit analysis appears heedless of the view that there are certain values in society—moral, political, aesthetic, whatever—that many may consider worthy of pursuit even if they do not fully satisfy rigorous cost-benefit criteria. Clean air, clean water, and healthful working environments may be viewed as such fundamental values of nature and life itself that it would deny their basic worth to subject them to a cost-benefit standard of deci-

---

81. *See generally* Anderson, *The Place of Principles in Policy Analysis*, 73 AM. POL. SCI. REV. 711, 712 (1979); Coddington, *'Cost-Benefit' as the New Utilitarianism*, 42 POL. Q. 320 (1971). Indeed, the very concepts of what is to be included as a "cost" or "benefit" and how to measure them will depend on criteria antecedent to the performance of a cost-benefit analysis itself.

82. *See, e.g.,* SUBCOMM. ON OVERSIGHT AND INVESTIGATIONS OF THE HOUSE COMM. ON INTERSTATE AND FOREIGN COMMERCE, 94TH CONG., 2D SESS., REPORT ON FEDERAL REGULATION AND REGULATORY REFORM 505-15 (Subcomm. Print 1976). *See also* Rodgers, *supra* note 9.

sion. Whatever may be said in this regard about any particular value, cost-benefit analysis is subject to serious question because it denies that any values or combinations of values may be morally worthy of vindication on their own terms. This objection is a version of the broader point that a utilitarian ethics, by merging all particular goods into one general conception of the good, tends not to acknowledge the power of plural conceptions of values having distinct and independent claims of moral force.[83]

A frequent response to such various criticisms of cost-benefit analysis is that at least it forces regulators to become consciously aware of trade-offs that are inevitably made, and thus it requires regulators explicitly to weigh factors they might otherwise ignore or devalue. The technique is said to direct decisionmaking toward relatively objective matters and away from momentary, irrational, and often broadly political considerations.[84]

However, there appears no reason to suppose that trade-offs in specific cost-benefit terms are "inevitable" unless one has for other reasons adopted the central premises of cost-benefit methodology. Regulators may borrow from an abundant store of moral and political argument, apart from the particular line of analysis propounded by cost-benefit advocates. Also, there is a considerable difference between choosing an outcome because of its presumed cost-benefit ratio, on the one hand, and selecting an outcome on other grounds and then observing that it might be "translated" into cost-benefit terms if one were so inclined, on the other hand.

Moreover, even taking the above noted defense of cost-benefit methodology at face value, it represents a retreat from many of the central claims made for such analysis. As an expression of instrumentalist reasoning, cost-benefit analysis purports to provide a technique for determining the right result in an administrative context, or at least, the right range of results. It thus is put forward by its strongest proponents, to borrow a phrase, as a rule of decision. However, the foregoing response moves from this position to the defense of a multifactored balancing approach that essentially requires decisionmakers to focus on various conceivable alternatives, weigh

---

83.   *See* J. RAWLS, *supra* note 26, at 446-52; Kelman, *supra* note 9. *See generally* M. WALZER, SPHERES OF JUSTICE: A DEFENSE OF PLURALISM AND EQUALITY (1982).

84.   *Cf.* Coddington, *supra* note 81, at 323 ("The argument goes like this: Although the product of the study . . . may be of dubious value, . . . the process of arriving at [it] is worthwhile to the extent that it forces those involved to confront problems, define issues and generally think systematically about the project."); Rodgers, *supra* note 9, at 199 ("Formal decisionmaking techniques, including cost-benefit analysis, . . . invite modelling and a reasoned expression of future consequences. They sharpen analysis by uncovering assumptions and making explicit the factors pointing to the comparative advantages of options.").

their respective consequences, and otherwise hone analytical skills. This is a use of cost-benefit balancing as a tool—not a rule—of decision.[85]

When a shift has occurred to a defense of a multifactored balancing technique, proponents of cost-benefit analysis have moved to what may be considered a basically process-oriented perspective. Although balancing analysis is supposed to be conducted carefully, it leaves the substantive grounds for decision essentially open to administrative discretion. In this way, the perspective bears a certain resemblance to the method of courts that send back to agencies for further elaboration decisions reviewed and remanded under the so-called hard look approach. It would be error to confuse a process-oriented technique that basically requires more explanation of administrative action with cost-benefit analysis in its most fundamental form.[86]

C. The Market-Based Alternative to the Core Instrumentalist Embodiment of the Public Purposes Ideal

The primary alternative expression of the public purposes ideal takes seriously the manifest difficulties of realizing the instrumentalist core through direct action by administrative agencies. Instead, it seeks to achieve the public good through the indirect means of the market. The market, as is well known, is conceived as a set of economic institutions and relationships in which relevant actors are presumed to be capable of making, and to be routinely motivated to make, rational decisions in various situations of choice about the most efficient ways of achieving their own ends. Taken as a whole,

---

85.   *See Use of Cost-Benefit Analysis by Regulatory Agencies: Joint Hearings before the Subcomm. on Oversight and Investigations and the Subcomm. on Consumer Protection and Finance of the House Comm. on Interstate and Foreign Commerce*, 96th Cong., 1st Sess. 64-73 (1979) (testimony of Dr. Nicholas Ashford, Center for Policy Alternatives, M.I.T.). Dr. Ashford noted that "it is crucial to distinguish between using cost-benefit analysis as a decision tool—as an aid, as something which makes facts clear—and using it as a decision rule to guide agency action." *Id.* at 65. *See also* Identification, Classification and Regulation of Potential Occupational Carcinogens, 45 Fed. Reg. 5001, 5249 (1980) (quoting Dr. Ashford's testimony: "As a decisional tool, cost-benefit analysis can be useful in identifying the nature of the trade-offs; as a decisional rule it is useless.").

86.   It also may be the case that a particular statute does not permit cost-benefit or similar analysis in a given situation, or limits the consideration of costs in various ways. *See, e.g.*, American Textile Mfrs. Inst., Inc. v. Donovan, 452 U.S. 490 (1981); Union Elec. Co. v. EPA, 427 U.S. 246 (1976); Hercules, Inc. v. EPA, 598 F.2d 91 (D.C. Cir. 1978). *Cf.* EPA v. National Crushed Stone Ass'n, 449 U.S. 64 (1980); Industrial Union Dep't v. American Petroleum Inst., 448 U.S. 607 (1980); Portland Cement Ass'n v. Ruckelshaus, 486 F.2d 375 (D.C. Cir. 1973), *cert. denied*, 417 U.S. 921 (1974), *cert. denied*, 423 U.S. 1025 (1976); Environmental Defense Fund, Inc. v. Ruckelshaus, 439 F.2d 584 (D.C. Cir. 1971).

these decisions are assumed to embody the public interest, which thus is an aggregative conception defined in terms of the total of private wants and aversions expressed in the market.[87] On this view, the major function of the administrative process is to avoid interference with and, when necessary, to foster the conduct of largely nongovernmental decisionmaking.

To be sure, there are substantial differences between an instrumentalist commitment to bureaucratic action and a market-based critique of administration. The effort to view them here as aspects of a single, more encompassing ideal should not be allowed to obscure those differences. Basically, the former places direct faith in, while the latter tends to disavow, the administrative process as the primary arena in which public ends are to be pursued. At the same time, market theory retains the larger objective of the public good, while redefining it as the sum of private economic choices. Thus, both perspectives share the more general picture of a well-regulated administrative process as an effective and efficient promoter of valued public purposes. This broadly managerialist vision is retained by the market-based model even when, in some contexts, it claims that there should be no regulation or other type of administrative intervention in the market. In such contexts, the administrative process is essentially viewed as most effective when it is least active.

The market-based alternative is reflected, for example, in recent writings about the administrative process by now-Judge Stephen Breyer, who has undertaken a broad-ranging critique of regulation within the terms of this model.[88] One of its major premises is that the market alone has certain imperfections that do not permit it to operate, as pure theory would have it, as a fully efficient allocator of values. Accordingly, there is room for intervention by the administrative process in order to correct such imperfections to the greatest extent possible. For instance, the lack of adequate consumer information may be "corrected" by disclosure regulation in given cases, and the existence of certain externalities of productive processes, such as pollution, may be adjusted for by regulatory requirements. However, the central notion underlying such a critique re-

---

87.   While retaining this commitment, market-based theory also seeks to distinguish itself from a full-fledged utilitarian approach, which calls for plenary balancing of the whole range of predicted consequences of alternative courses of action. *See* Posner, *Utilitarianism, Economics, and Legal Theory*, 8 J. LEGAL STUD. 103 (1979). *See also* 1 A. KAHN, THE ECONOMICS OF REGULATION: PRINCIPLES AND INSTITUTIONS 1-17 (1970).

88.   *See* S. BREYER, *supra* note 1; Breyer, *supra* note 10. *Cf.* Breyer, *Two Models of Regulatory Reform*, 34 S.C.L. REV. 629 (1983) (contrasting a favored "case-by-case" approach to regulatory reform, illustrated by airline deregulation, with a disfavored "generic" approach seeking improvement through a single, government-wide statute).

mains: any administrative imposition should be geared primarily toward restoring the conditions required for a more perfect operation of market forces. At all costs, regulatory requirements should not be allowed to supplant or deeply to interfere with the market, for such results are viewed as leading inexorably to a fundamental misallocation of society's resources.

These ideas are reflected in the contemporary debate in various contexts, particularly including that of economic regulation. For example, it has been urged that power over matters of entry, pricing, and conditions of service in certain regulated industries should be returned generally to the market.[89] Such proposals have been buttressed by empirical studies that have been interpreted to support the view that prices would be lower, service would be improved, and competition would be more energetic if administrative interventions would be halted or at least relaxed.[90] Such an analysis proved to be persuasive enough, when combined with relevant political forces, to prompt federal legislation mandating substantial deregulation of the airline industry.[91] Other industries, such as trucking, remain on the agenda of deregulators who adhere to the underlying faith that the market knows best.[92]

Related proposals for administrative reform rest on the notion that if a regulated industry should not be deregulated, then the re-

---

89. See generally S. BREYER, *supra* note 1, which argues that the "clearest examples of a mismatch [between conditions of an industry and regulatory tools] arise when classical price and entry regulation is applied to a structurally competitive industry. In such cases, one should consider abolishing regulation and relying instead upon an unregulated market policed by antitrust." *Id.* at 197. For Breyer, the airline industry presents such a case, and thus he has strongly supported the deregulatory efforts in this area in recent years. *See id.*; Breyer, *supra* notes 10 and 88.

90. *See* S. BREYER, *supra* note 1; Breyer, *Two Models of Regulatory Reform*, *supra* note 88.

91. *See* Airline Deregulation Act of 1978, Pub. L. No. 95-504, 92 Stat. 1705 (codified starting at 49 U.S.C. § 1301 (1976)).

92. *See* Motor Carrier Act of 1980, Pub. L. No. 96-296, 94 Stat. 793 (codified starting at 18 U.S.C. § 1114 (1982)); G. ROBINSON, E. GELLHORN & H. BRUFF, *supra* note 1, at 834-37; S. TOLCHIN & M. TOLCHIN, *supra* note 1; Moore, *Deregulating Transportation*, REGULATION, Mar.-Apr. 1978, at 37, 41-44. Unlike the Airline Deregulation Act, the Motor Carrier Act did not provide for the phased transition to deregulation, and it preserved substantial ICC authority over entry and pricing in the trucking industry. *Cf.* American Trucking Ass'ns v. ICC, 659 F.2d 452, 465-74 (5th Cir. 1981) (holding that aspects of ICC's expression of deregulatory policies exceeded constraints on agency authority conferred by 1980 Act). *See also* Motor Vehicle Mfrs. Ass'n v. State Farm Mut. Auto. Ins. Co., ___ U.S. ___, 103 S.Ct. 2856 (1983) (holding National Highway Traffic Safety Administration acted arbitrarily and capriciously in rescinding requirement in Motor Vehicle Safety Standard 208 that motor vehicles produced after September 1982 be equipped with passive restraints); Claybrook & Drabble, *Good News: Deregulation Is Foundering*, Washington Post, Jan. 29, 1984, at D 7, col. 1 (asserting that in the Reagan Administration, "deregulation has been derailed because it deserves to be").

maining regulation itself should be rooted in the theory of the market. This conviction rests on the premise that regulation should exist when, but only when, it is necessary to correct market imperfections. Any regulation that satisfies this condition also must be tailored to be as consistent as possible with existing economic realities. Such a perspective provides the tools for criticizing standard regulatory controls, which often tend basically to compel or prohibit certain activities. For the economic critic, these regulatory edicts, or "command-and-control" regulatory requirements as they have been called,[93] frequently are seen as rather ham-fisted and ineffective because they restrict considerably the options of the industry being regulated. Greater flexibility, for instance in being able to choose among different pollution control technologies or devices,[94] is said to be necessary for an administrative regime to coexist with the market. Given the countervailing administrative pressures for determinacy, clarity, and ease of application of regulations, one can discern immediately the underlying tension in this attempt to make regulations consonant with the market.

In recent years, market-based arguments that manifest a basic hostility to regulatory activities have assumed striking prominence. In part, this may reflect the apparent vitality of an emphasis on economics in various fields of law. It also seems to reflect contemporary political pressures to shrink the scope of federal regulation.[95] In any event, an understanding of the current debate requires an awareness of not only the market-based theory's potential, but also its limits as a normative perspective from which to criticize the administrative process.

One of the chief constraints of the market-based conception is that it, like proceduralism, is ultimately an indirect and partial embodiment of its most general underlying ideal. The public purposes

---

93. *See* Clark, *supra* note 10, at 1317.

94. Another example is the "bubble" policy of the EPA, under which factories are treated as having a "bubble" over them and producers are required to limit total pollution from the plant rather than meet standards of pollution from individual sources. This allows increases in pollution from new or modified sources in a factory to escape full review under regulatory standards applying normally to such sources, so long as offsetting reductions in pollution emissions are made elsewhere within the plant. This approach is designed to permit producers to decide for themselves which pollutants to control, a decision that presumably will be guided by which pollutants are the cheapest to control, in order to satisfy the overall requirements. *See* Air Pollution Control, Recommendation for Alternative Reduction Options within State Implementation Plans, 44 Fed. Reg. 3740 (1979); Clark, *supra* note 10, at 1317. However, courts have overruled certain aspects of the policy under the Clean Air Act. *See, e.g.,* Alabama Power Co. v. Costle, 636 F.2d 323 (D.C. Cir. 1979); Asarco, Inc. v. EPA, 578 F.2d 319, 327-29 (D.C. Cir. 1978).

95. For discussion of these political pressures, see Vogel, *supra* note 23.

ideal holds that the role of administration is to advance valued ends in society. The market-based approach rejects the effort primarily to realize such an ideal directly through the operation of the administrative process. Instead, it relies mainly on the presumed efficiencies of the market, supplemented only to the extent necessary. This position requires fundamental faith in the market as an efficient mechanism for achieving the social good. However, the market-based theory itself, in many of its formulations, seems to call this faith into serious question.

For instance, many proponents of the market model themselves recognize a broad range of rationales for administrative intervention. These include the following: the existence of monopoly power that is capable of overcoming legitimate competition; the existence of natural monopolies in certain industries, such as utilities, where economies of scale are considerable; the lack of adequate consumer information; the existence of externalities, which involve costs imposed on society by productive processes that are not borne directly by the enterprises in question; the potential for unfair windfall profits resulting from the elimination of price ceilings when some suppliers have substantial inventories of a deregulated commodity; and the perceived need to eliminate "excessive" competition or to moderate distributional inequities that may result from a sudden or severe scarcity of a valued good.[96]

One is left with the unmistakable impression that the market surely requires a considerable degree of "perfection" even on the terms of some of its strongest supporters. At a minimum, one must question whether market-based theory does not recognize so many exceptions to its rule against governmental intervention that the rule itself should be considered the exception.

Furthermore, the market-based conception is persistently criticized for seeking to reduce all matters of public value to issues of individual, subjective preference. On its own terms, can the market be counted upon to realize important public values, given that presumably it is driven largely by the self-interested motivations of producers for profits and of consumers for lower prices and better goods and services?

Broadcast deregulation is one context in which such a question has been prominently debated. In particular, will the public values of the fairness doctrine,[97] with its emphasis on assuring the diversity of views aired in broadcasting, be upheld under a fully deregulated

---

96. *See* S. BREYER & R. STEWART, *supra* note 14, at 13-18; S. BREYER, *supra* note 1.
97. *See generally* Red Lion Broadcasting Co. v. FCC, 395 U.S. 367 (1969).

regime in which profit motivation will be the driving force behind corporate decisions about broadcasting? On the one hand, it has been argued that the public is likely to demand a diversity of views in broadcasting. On the other hand, it has been suggested that the economic realities of broadcasting, which depends for its survival on receipts from advertisers, may well prompt broadcasters to avoid controversial programming as much as possible. In the absence of administratively imposed requirements such as the fairness doctrine, these market incentives may result in even less variety in programming than prevails at present.[98] Whatever one's inclination regarding this debate, it certainly appears difficult to predict with any confidence whether public values of conceded importance will be upheld in a regime of totally private choice.

One possible response would be that the market's products by definition are expressive of the public good, and therefore one ought not to be overly concerned about, and ought not to argue on the basis of, premises concerning what is or is not a public value considered apart from decisions of the market. This response shares not only the appeal of simplicity, but also the limits of tautology. It is subject to serious question by those who hold to a vision of moral and social values that is in any basic respect independent of the subjective choices of hypothetical rational actors in the market.

In addition, the market-based model constricts considerably the terms of public debate by seeking to reduce issues of administrative choice to questions of economic rationality. This tendency is reflected, for instance, in the model's criticism of existing schemes of federal regulation on the ground that they embody "irrational" political compromises and predilections. Regulations also are condemned on the basis that they reflect "irrational" institutional tendencies to rely on precedent and to achieve enforceable, if not pristinely rational, standards.[99] These objections appear critical mainly from a particular economic point of view; they tend to reveal as much about the limited premises of the critique as about the matters being criticized.[100]

---

98. For general discussions of broadcast regulation, see Fowler & Brenner, *A Marketplace Approach to Broadcast Regulation*, 60 TEX. L. REV. 207 (1982); E. KRASNOW & L. LONGLEY, THE POLITICS OF BROADCAST REGULATION (2d ed. 1978).

99. *See* Breyer, *supra* note 10, at 552-84. For a discussion of general tensions between the economic and political perspectives on administration, see Reich, *Warring Critiques of Regulation*, REGULATION, Jan.-Feb. 1979, at 37.

100. From a different perspective, it could as easily be suggested that the life of the administrative process lies precisely in its adjustments to political pressures and institutional factors, however "irrational" some may view them to be. More generally, it has been argued that politics is inherently irrational and that this quality should not be scorned as deviance,

These and related concerns have been debated in an extensive and expanding literature that continues to produce new calls for deregulation and economic alternatives to regulation, on the one hand, and summonses to a wider conception of the administrative process, on the other hand.[101] Whatever one's attitude toward particular debates about the approach, it seems plain that it does not exhaust the possibilities for redirecting energies devoted to administrative reform.

V. The Third Major Ideal Reflected in the Contemporary Debate: The Democratic Process Ideal

A. The Nature of the Democratic Process Ideal

The third of the three competing ideals of the administrative process reflected in the contemporary debate is the democratic process ideal. The basic vision underlying this ideal is of a highly participatory, representative decisionmaking process in which relevant officials are held accountable for the extent to which they actively take into consideration the views of affected groups in formulating and implementing agency policy. This vision derives its intellectual force from democratic theory and its critique of nonrepresentative decisional processes.[102]

A number of contrasts may be drawn between this third ideal and the first two. Unlike the public purposes ideal, the democratic process ideal does not place primary emphasis on the purportedly expert status of administrative agencies or on the instrumentalist character of their decisionmaking. Rather, the third ideal conceives of administration primarily as a political process. Indeed, this ideal tends to assimilate the administrative process to the legislative process in the sense that it envisions the chief function of administration to be the representation of the views of interested members of

---

but rather should be seen as endemic to the human project of living in a society of one's fellows. *See* J. Plamenatz, Democracy and Illusion (1973).

101. For critiques of the economic approach, see Baker, *The Ideology of the Economic Analysis of Law*, 5 Phil. & Pub. Aff. 3 (1975); Horwitz, *Law and Economics: Science or Politics?*, 8 Hofstra L. Rev. 905 (1980); Kennedy, *Cost-Benefit Analysis of Entitlement Problems: A Critique*, 33 Stan. L. Rev. 387 (1981).

102. *See, e.g.,* J. Lively, Democracy (1977); C. Pateman, Participation and Democratic Theory (1970); E. Redford, Democracy in the Administrative State (1969). For present purposes, the distinction between a participatory democratic ideal and a conception of representative decisionmaking by elected political authorities is not central; both strands of analysis are embodied in what is referred to here as the democratic process ideal.

the public. In addition, there is no express resort on this ideal to an economic conception of the market as a central means of restraining and justifying agency action.[103]

The relationship between the democratic process ideal and the rule of law ideal is somewhat more complex. On the one hand, the democratic process ideal, unlike the rule of law ideal, does not attempt to separate the sphere of politics, as reflected in legislation, from the realm of legal decisionmaking, as reflected in administration (and judicial decisionmaking). Rather, the third ideal, in assuming that the administrative process is inherently political, basically borrows the guiding legitimating conception of democratic politics as the normative perspective from which to judge administration. In sharp contrast, the rule of law ideal confines the democratic ideal of interest representation to the legislature itself.

On the other hand, there is a certain affinity between aspects of the democratic process ideal and of proceduralism as a variant of the rule of law ideal. Both share the rhetoric of "fair" procedures and "open" decisional processes. Nevertheless, the highly individualistic conception of fair process underlying proceduralism is profoundly different from the picture of the collective pursuit of plural interests that informs the democratic process ideal. The former is directed at protecting the interests of discrete individuals on whom the force of government has been brought to bear. The latter, by viewing agencies essentially as surrogate legislatures, emphasizes the affirmative project by which agencies are to represent the interests of major groups in society. While acknowledging some relation between aspects of the democratic process ideal and proceduralism, then, one ought not to lose sight of fundamental distinctions between them.

The most direct expression of the democratic process ideal in the contemporary debate is the commitment generally to expand public participation in administration. "Participation" is viewed primarily as the opportunity to present opinions and recommendations to agency officials regarding pending matters that will directly affect the public's interests. Underlying this commitment to participation is a pluralist vision of political life as consisting of the competition among various groups or interests in society.[104] The task of successful administration, on this view, is to implement public law by selecting a compromise position that will be acceptable to the

---

103.   *See* Stewart, *The Reformation of American Administrative Law, supra* note 10.

104.   For a pluralist view of politics, see A. BENTLEY, THE PROCESS OF GOVERNMENT (1908); T. LOWI, THE END OF LIBERALISM (1969); D. TRUMAN, THE GOVERNMENTAL PROCESS (1951).

agency and a sufficient range of affected interests, such as consumers, producers, labor, and industry. Participation is seen as a way to foster necessary conditions for compromise and agreement, to inform officials about the relevant issues and views of affected interests, to allow concerned groups to become involved in decisional processes in which they have a stake, and to endow the administrative process with the appearance and as much as possible the reality of democratic responsiveness.

Various methods for promoting broader participation have been suggested. One is to foster a significant minimum degree of openness in the administrative process itself so that members of the public may become better informed about matters of importance to them, such as evolving enforcement policies. This approach basically assumes that when the public has access to such information, its members will be able to make their views known to the agency. Such a perspective is reflected in several laws enacted during the 1970's, including the Federal Advisory Committee Act (1972), amendments to the Freedom of Information Act (1974), and the Government in the Sunshine Act (1976).[105]

Related contemporary reforms call upon agencies to broaden efforts to inform the public of proposed actions that may affect their interests. For instance, President Carter's 1978 Executive order on regulations required agencies to take specific measures to notify the public about upcoming rulemaking proceedings in advance of the publication of a statutory notice of proposed rulemaking.[106] Another way to expand opportunities for public involvement is to fund intervention in agency proceedings by groups that otherwise would not be in a position to participate.[107] Richard Stewart has discerned further examples of the participatory ideal in judicial decisions involving the doctrines of intervention in agency proceedings and of standing to challenge an agency decision in court. As Stewart noted in 1975, such areas of the law saw considerable judicial innovation

---

105. *See* Federal Advisory Committee Act, 5 U.S.C. App. (1982); Freedom of Information Act, 5 U.S.C. § 552 (1982); Government in the Sunshine Act, 5 U.S.C. § 552b (1982).

106. *See* Exec. Order No. 12,044, *supra* note 19. Section 2(c) of that order required agencies to:

> give the public an early and meaningful opportunity to participate in the development of agency regulations. They shall consider a variety of ways to provide this opportunity, including (1) publishing an advance notice of proposed rulemaking; (2) holding open conferences or public hearings; (3) sending notices of proposed regulations to publications likely to be read by those affected; and (4) notifying interested parties directly.

107. *See* Boyer, *Funding Public Participation in Agency Proceedings: The FTC Experience*, 70 GEO. L.J. 51 (1981).

during the preceding decade. He argued that, at least in part, the innovation in that period reflected a judicial commitment to increase the opportunities for interest representation in administration.[108]

All of these examples have in common the effort to broaden public input into agency processes. Like the underlying notion of participation itself, they are largely process-oriented, for they do not purport to instruct agencies in substantive terms about the basis on which decisions should be reached. Rather, they seek to hold agencies to a relatively high standard of openness and responsiveness in their dealings with the public.

It might be suggested that, in the last few years, the core of the democratic process ideal has fallen on hard times, for the energies behind much of the contemporary debate have not been directed at opening up and making more participatory the administrative process. Nonetheless, this ideal exerts continuing influence, as it speaks to fundamental values in our administrative system. A discussion of administrative reform would be especially incomplete without recognition of its central role.

B. *The Limitations of the Core Embodiment of the Democratic Process Ideal*

A commitment to broader public participation in administration provides a forceful perspective for criticizing the existing system. However, despite its undeniable power, this core conception, like the cores underlying the first two ideals, ultimately furnishes an inadequate account and justification of the modern administrative process.

The participatory vision underlying the democratic process ideal requires for its full realization that the institutions in which it operates be governed by premises of responsiveness to the sentiments of the participants. Although imperfectly, Congress may be said to be so structured, for at least its membership finally depends on the continued favor of the electorate. However, as is well-recognized, the administrative process is not similarly structured either by law or custom.

Administrative decisionmaking occurs chiefly in hierarchical bureaucracies charged by law with making choices about public pol-

---

108.   Stewart, *The Reformation of American Administrative Law, supra* note 10.

icy.[109] Agency appointees normally are protected by civil service safeguards against the most obvious forms of political influence. To be sure, such appointees are subjected to a variety of political forces, including the views of significant groups of the public. But at bottom, agency decisions must be legally and bureaucratically justified, not grounded principally on the specific goal of representing the views of the affected public.[110] Indeed, when agencies arguably have come to act as mere representatives of certain groups in society, they frequently have been sharply criticized by members of Congress and the public itself as "captured" agencies failing to perform a neutral policymaking function as governmental institutions charged with general responsibilities under law.[111]

Given these realities, it is fundamentally difficult to achieve the goals of the participatory vision. Certainly, agencies may be made more aware on an *ad hoc* basis of the views of significant societal interests, such as by the importuning of members of Congress or of the President or his subordinates. Also, steps may be taken, as discussed in the previous section, to provide for a somewhat more open and participatory process. However, despite the continuing power of the democratic process ideal, the gap between its core embodiment and the existing process is so profound that the core, if fully realized, would radically transform rather than merely reform it. The core embodiment simply does not account for the practices of the hierarchical, specialized bureaucracies in which administrative action centrally resides.

In this light, the grand terms of the participatory vision inevitably seem only thinly realized in the proposals to reform the administrative process in its name. The creation of formal rights of participation, which basically are rights to express views to decisionmakers who remain as free as before in substantive terms to do as they will, seems hardly an adequate means of capturing in its fullness the

---

109. The hierarchical nature of public bureaucracies should not obscure that they, like other organizations, have complex informal patterns of interaction. For discussion of such patterns in the executive branch, see H. HECLO, A GOVERNMENT OF STRANGERS: EXECUTIVE POLITICS IN WASHINGTON 34-83 (1977). *See also* R. FRIED, PERFORMANCE IN AMERICAN BUREAUCRACY 32-33 (1976).

110. The point is not that the views of affected groups are not significant, as they clearly are, but rather that various political and bureaucratic pressures on agencies, combined with the frequently technical nature of the decisions, make it difficult to sustain the picture of agencies as representatives primarily of a broader public will—even assuming it were possible to identify such a will.

111. For discussion of the "capture" thesis, see M. BERNSTEIN, REGULATING BUSINESS BY INDEPENDENT COMMISSION 86-90, 155-63, 270 (1955); R. NOLL, REFORMING REGULATION 100 (1971); E. REDFORD, ADMINISTRATION OF NATIONAL ECONOMIC CONTROL 386 (1952).

430   WISCONSIN LAW REVIEW

power of the participatory model. Given the present institutional
realities of administration and the norms and rituals of the adversarial process that they foster, however, this may be all that can be
expected.

Furthermore, the program of the participatory ideal is undermined by the constraint of limited resources of both affected interest
groups and agencies. In practice, the interests that appear to have
the greatest access to the administrative process tend to be those
with reasonably significant standing in the broader community and
thus the political savvy, informational sources, and financial backing to organize when necessary to protect valued positions. Is it realistic to expect society to invest the resources that would be necessary to subsidize other groups in order to make the administrative
process truly as open and participatory as possible? Problems encountered by proposals for intervenor funding, as well as the difficult
future faced by many so-called pro bono legal organizations, suggest
a likely answer to this question.[112]

Moreover, strong institutional pressures almost certainly will
continue to be exerted by agencies themselves against opening up
and making more participatory the administrative process. In part,
such resistance is a perfectly understandable reaction to the likelihood that such reforms may prompt delays in an already cumbersome process. Criticism by agency officials of the Federal Advisory
Committee Act, for instance, reflects in significant measure a desire
for a more efficient administrative system.[113] At the same time,
agency opposition to a more participatory process is likely driven, at
least in part, by self-protective and self-serving commitments. In
any event, administrators are bound to continue their resistance and
thereby to contribute to the cumulative difficulties encountered by
the participatory vision of administrative reform.

---

112. For discussion of the problems of operating a system of agency funding of public
participation, see Boyer, *supra* note 107. For discussion of the uncertain future of pro bono
legal organizations, see COUNCIL FOR PUBLIC INTEREST LAW, BALANCING THE SCALES OF JUS-
TICE: FINANCING PUBLIC INTEREST LAW IN AMERICA (1976).

113. The inefficiencies of procedural requirements imposed on the operation of federal advisory committees have concerned commentators as well as federal officials. *See, e.g.*,
Cardozo, *The Federal Advisory Committee Act in Operation*, 33 AD. L. REV. 1 (1981). The Act's
definition of a covered advisory committee is broad and has been so interpreted by courts. *See,
e.g.*, National Nutritional Foods Ass'n v. Califano, 603 F.2d 327 (2d Cir. 1979); Consumers
Union v. HEW, 409 F. Supp. 473 (D.D.C. 1976), *aff'd mem.*, 551 F.2d 466 (D.C. Cir. 1977).
Various amendments to limit the Act's definition of a covered advisory committee have been
proposed in recent years. *See* H.R. 746, 97th Cong., 2d Sess. (1982), *reported by* H.R. REP. NO.
435, 97th Cong., 2d Sess. 92 (1982); S. 1080, 97th Cong., 1st Sess. (1981), *reported by* S. REP.
No. 305, 97th Cong., 1st Sess. 148 (1981). *See also* Recommendations of the Administrative
Conference of the United States, 1 C.F.R. § 305. 80-3 (1984).

Even more basically, the core of the democratic process ideal, by requiring that the administrative process represent a full range of interests and views on a particular matter, necessitates a bureaucratic decision about what interests and views are worth representing. Thus, in order for the ideal's core to be implemented, it is necessary, even if somewhat paradoxical, that an essentially nondemocratic decision be made about what democracy ultimately requires. To this extent, the attempt to realize the core of the ideal in the administrative context seems self-defeating.

C. The Alternative Expression of the Democratic Process Ideal: Political Oversight

The limitations of the core participatory conception are substantial enough to prompt many proponents of the democratic process ideal to reach for an alternative, if derivative, way to realize its values. In the contemporary debate, the major alternative expression of the democratic process ideal is the commitment to more active oversight of the administrative process by politically responsive officials.

What may be called the oversight model retains the ideal's underlying belief in the democratic process and its basic conception of administration as an essentially political process. At the same time, it abandons the emphasis on the ideal's direct realization through public participation in agency proceedings themselves. Instead, the oversight model relies on national political authorities—principally, the President and members of Congress—as the intermediaries whose job it is to impose the public's will on administrators. The basic project of administrative reform on this view is, put briefly, to promote greater control by the President and Congress over agency action.

In the contemporary context, this alternative expression of the democratic process ideal is particularly prominent in discussions about reforming rulemaking, as opposed to other decisionmaking processes. In significant measure, that emphasis may be explained by the tendency of many to single out federal regulation, rather than adjudicatory proceedings, as a central object of reform.[114]

---

114. The very title of the American Bar Association's influential 1979 report, FEDERAL REGULATION: ROADS TO REFORM, indicates the centrality of regulatory reform for critics of the administrative process. *See* AMERICAN BAR ASSOCIATION COMM'N ON LAW AND THE ECONOMY, *supra* note 1. In addition, explicitly political involvement in adjudicatory, as opposed to rulemaking, proceedings would raise due process concerns. *See generally* United Steelworkers of Am. v. Marshall, 647 F.2d 1189, 1215 n.28 (D.C. Cir. 1980); Action for Children's

The first major application of the oversight approach is the proposal to strengthen the role of the President and his immediate staff, located in the Executive Office of the President, in overseeing and, when necessary, checking the rulemaking decisions of agencies. To an extent, such a proposal calls mainly for more of what historically has tended to occur anyway, namely, a degree of Presidential supervision of executive agencies in the exercise of the President's constitutional duty to take care that the laws are faithfully executed. However, some critics would significantly expand the institutional powers of the Presidency and of officials in the Executive Office. The limits of Presidential involvement under existing law, and the respective merits and demerits of loosening the limits by statutory amendment, have been the subject of a lively controversy in recent years.[115]

Proponents of Presidential oversight of the regulatory process have argued that since the President is the single nationally-elected political official, he is uniquely qualified to impose on agencies the will of the public. Therefore, it is argued, the President should be given more power to do so. Opponents of the expansion of centralized executive oversight have urged that existing laws will not permit it, for it may undermine the intended role and powers of particular agencies under given authorizing statutes.[116] Moreover, opponents have asserted that such expansion is unwise because, in practice, it would encourage *ad hoc* political intervention in the administrative process that would impair a rational, coherent, and fair decisionmaking system. It also has been noted that, in reality, Presidential oversight largely means influence by subordinate, appointed officials in the Executive Office who are not themselves politically accountable to the extent the President is. Since the present Administration apparently is committed to increased Presidential oversight of the regulatory process,[117] the debate over these issues is likely to continue.

Television v. FCC, 564 F.2d 458, 477 (D.C. Cir. 1977); Sangamon Valley Television Corp. v. United States, 269 F.2d 221 (D.C. Cir. 1959), *cert. denied*, 376 U.S. 915 (1964).

115.   *See* AMERICAN BAR ASSOCIATION COMM'N ON LAW AND THE ECONOMY, *supra* note 1, at 73-84; Bruff, *supra* note 3; Byse, *supra* note 3; Eads, *supra* note 3; Verkuil, *supra* note 3. *See also* Sierra Club v. Costle, 657 F.2d 298 (D.C. Cir. 1981). *See also* other sources cited *supra* note 3.

116.   *See* STAFF OF THE HOUSE COMM. ON ENERGY AND COMMERCE, 97TH CONG., 1ST SESS., REPORT ON PRESIDENTIAL CONTROL OF AGENCY RULEMAKING (Comm. Print 1981). For a contrary view, see Memorandum of the Department of Justice, Proposed Executive Order entitled "Federal Regulation" (Feb. 13, 1981), *reprinted in* REPORT ON PRESIDENTIAL CONTROL OF AGENCY RULEMAKING, *supra*, at the appendix.

117.   *See* Exec. Order No. 12,291, *supra* note 8.

The second basic application of the political oversight model is found in proposals to expand congressional power over agencies. Traditionally, these proposals have stressed such mechanisms as more rigorous congressional oversight of agency behavior. Although such an approach has received some attention in the contemporary debate, particular concentration has been centered on the legislative veto mechanism.[118] At least until rather recently,[119] Congress displayed an increasing tendency to insert legislative veto provisions in an extraordinarily broad range of statutes.[120] The term "legislative veto" refers to a statutory provision that purports to authorize the legislative branch to disapprove or mandate an agency action by adopting a resolution—which may be passed by one or both Houses of Congress or even a committee of Congress—that is not presented to the President for approval or disapproval.[121] Scores of federal statutes contain such provisions.[122]

A longstanding dispute between Presidents and Congress over the constitutionality of such provisions intensified significantly in recent years, during which time numerous such provisions were enacted.[123] Last summer the Supreme Court dealt with three cases

---

118.   *See* J. SUNDQUIST, *supra* note 4, at 344 (referring to the legislative veto device as "a more timely and authoritative means of intervention in the administrative process" than the normal methods of congressional oversight).

119.   Congress' position has had to evolve in light of the Supreme Court's invalidation in June, 1983, of a one-House veto in an immigration statute. *See* Immigration and Naturalization Serv. v. Chadha, ___ U.S. ___, 103 S.Ct. 2764 (1983).

120.   *See* Schwartz, *The Legislative Veto and the Constitution—A Reexamination*, 46 GEO. WASH. L. REV. 351, 351-61 (1978). Indeed, there is some evidence that *Chadha* has not entirely halted this trend. *See supra* note 7.

121.   *See, e.g.,* J. BOLTON, THE LEGISLATIVE VETO: UNSEPARATING THE POWERS (1977); Dixon, *The Congressional Veto and Separation of Powers: The Executive on a Leash?*, 56 N.C.L. REV. 423 (1978); Ginnane, *The Control of Federal Administration by Congressional Resolutions and Committees*, 66 HARV. L. REV. 569 (1953); Jackson, *A Presidential Legal Opinion*, 66 HARV. L. REV. 1353 (1953); Olson, *The Unconstitutionality of Legislative Veto Provisions*, 10 SAN FERN. V.L. REV. 1 (1982); Watson, *Congress Steps Out: A Look at Congressional Control of the Executive*, 63 CALIF. L. REV. 983 (1975). *See also* J. SUNDQUIST, *supra* note 4, at 344-66.

122.   There are various estimates of the total number of federal statutes containing legislative veto provisions. *See Chadha*, ___ U.S. at ___, 103 S.Ct. at 2792 (White, J., dissenting) (stating that some 200 federal statutes contain such provisions); C.F. NORTON, STATISTICAL SUMMARY OF CONGRESSIONAL APPROVAL AND DISAPPROVAL LEGISLATION, 1932-1980 (Congressional Research Service, Sept. 14, 1981) (concluding that between 1932 and 1980, 193 statutes with legislative veto provisions were enacted); J. SUNDQUIST, *supra* note 4, at 345 & n.1 (1981) (concluding that, between 1932 and 1979, 113 laws were enacted with legislative veto provisions in them). In a study completed after the *Chadha* decision, the Office of Legal Counsel of the U.S. Department of Justice compiled a list of 126 public laws and 207 separate statutory sections containing legislative veto provisions. *See* Memorandum for the Attorney General from the Assistant Attorney General, Office of Legal Counsel (July 15, 1983).

123.   *See* Schwartz, *supra* note 120, at 351-61.

raising the constitutional issues.[124] In all of them, resolutions under legislative veto provisions had been adopted in order to nullify executive actions, and the courts of appeals had held that the veto provisions in question violated constitutional requirements.

The first case involved a one-House veto of the Attorney General's decision, following an administrative adjudication, to suspend the deportation of an alien under a provision of the Immigration and Naturalization Act.[125] The second case involved a one-House veto of a regulation adopted by the Federal Energy Regulatory Commission that implemented the "incremental pricing" provisions of the Natural Gas Policy Act; the thrust of the regulation had been to shift some costs of the deregulation of natural gas prices from residential to industrial consumers.[126] The third case involved a two-House veto of a Federal Trade Commission rule regulating warranty and disclosure requirements in connection with the sale of used cars.[127] In these three cases, opponents of the legislative veto argued that it violated both the general principles of the separation of powers and the particular procedures for legislative action set forth in article I, section 7, of the Constitution, calling for bicameral passage of bills and resolutions and their presentation to the President for approval or disapproval.[128] In turn, proponents urged that the legislative veto mechanisms, admittedly not contemplated specifically in the Constitution, nonetheless were authorized by the necessary and proper clause of article I, section 8, and that they were

---

124. *Chadha*, ___ U.S. ___, 103 S.Ct. 2764 (1983); Process Gas Consumers Group v. Consumer Energy Council of Am., Inc., ___ U.S. ___, 103 S.Ct. 3556 (1983), *aff'g* 673 F.2d 425 (D.C. Cir. 1982); Consumers Union of Am., Inc. v. FTC, 691 F.2d 575 (D.C. Cir. 1982), *aff'd mem.* ___ U.S. ___, 103 S.Ct. 3556 (1983).

125. Immigration and Naturalization Serv. v. Chadha, 634 F.2d 408 (9th Cir. 1980), *aff'd,* ___ U.S. ___, 103 S.Ct. 2764 (1983).

126. Consumer Energy Council of Am., Inc. v. Federal Energy Regulatory Comm'n, 673 F.2d 425 (D.C. Cir. 1982), *aff'd mem. sub nom.* Process Gas Consumers Group v. Consumer Energy Council of Am., Inc., ___ U.S. ___, 103 S.Ct. 3556 (1983).

127. Consumers Union of Am., Inc. v. FTC, 691 F.2d 575 (D.C. Cir. 1982), *aff'd mem.,* ___ U.S. ___, 103 S.Ct. 3556 (1983).

128. U.S. CONST. art. I, § 7, cl. 2 provides: "Every Bill which shall have passed the House of Representatives and the Senate, shall, before it becomes a Law, be presented to the President of the United States." If the President vetoes the bill, it will become law if repassed by two-thirds of each House of Congress. *Id.,* art. I, § 7, cl. 3 provides: "Every Order, Resolution, or Vote to which the Concurrence of the Senate and House of Representative may be necessary" also must be adopted by majorities of both Houses of Congress and then presented to the President for approval or veto; if vetoed, the item can take effect only if "repassed by two-thirds of the Senate and House of Representatives, according to the Rules and Limitations prescribed in the case of a Bill."

consistent with the flexible precepts underlying the separation of powers.[129]

In its decision in the immigration case, the Supreme Court ruled that the bicameralism and presentation requirements generally do apply to exercises of legislative power under article I and that the challenged nullification of the suspension decision itself was such an exercise of power. The Court's language was quite broad, indicating that it would be difficult indeed to distinguish between types of legislative veto provisions in applying the controlling constitutional requirements. In a vigorous dissent, Justice White decried the breadth of the Court's opinion, suggesting that it would have far-reaching consequences for the distribution of powers between the two branches in view of the large number of statutes containing analogous provisions.[130] Shortly after this decision was reached, the Supreme Court summarily affirmed the lower court rulings in the natural gas regulation and used car rule cases, lending further credence to the view that legislative veto provisions as a class run afoul of constitutional dictates.[131]

Although the long-running debate about legislative vetoes has now entered a new stage, one may anticipate continuing discussion of alternative mechanisms for increased congressional oversight of the administrative process. Indeed, as representatives of the executive branch themselves stressed during the recent years of heated exchange about the legislative veto, there is no shortage of such alternatives.[132] These include placing time limitations in statutory

---

129. In addition to raising constitutional issues, the cases before the Supreme Court presented various threshold and statutory questions. One of the major issues that arises in legislative veto cases is whether, assuming that the legislative veto provision is invalid, it is severable from the rest of the statute. If so, it may be struck down discretely without invalidating the remainder of the law. This issue requires a review of the statutory design in each situation to determine whether "'it is evident that the Legislature would not have enacted those provisions which are within its power, independently of that which is not.'" *Chadha*, ___ U.S. at ___, 103 S.Ct. at 2774 (quoting Buckley v. Valeo, 424 U.S. 1, 108 (1976); Champlin Ref. Co. v. Corporation Comm'n, 286 U.S. 210, 234 (1932)). *See also* Consumer Energy Council of Am., Inc. v. Federal Energy Regulatory Comm'n, 673 F.2d 425 (D.C. Cir. 1982), *aff'd mem. sub nom.* Process Gas Consumers Group v. Consumer Energy Council of Am., Inc., ___ U.S. ___, 103 S.Ct. 3556 (1983); EEOC v. Hernando Bank, Inc., 724 F.2d 1188 (5th Cir. 1984); Muller Optical Co. v. EEOC, 574 F. Supp. 946 (W.D. Tenn. 1983); EEOC v. Allstate Ins. Co., 570 F. Supp. 1224 (E.D. Miss. 1983).

130. *Chadha*, ___ U.S. at ___, 103 S.Ct. at 2792 (White, J., dissenting).

131. *See* Process Gas Consumers Group v. Consumer Energy Council of Am., Inc., ___ U.S. ___, 103 S.Ct. 3556 (1983), *aff'g* 673 F.2d 425 (D.C. Cir. 1982); Consumers Union of Am., Inc. v. FTC, 691 F.2d 575 (D.C. Cir. 1982).

132. *See, e.g., Congressional Review of Agency Rulemaking: Hearings before the Subcomm. on Rules of the House Comm. on Rules*, 97th Cong., 1st Sess. 4-70 (1981) (statement of Assistant Attorney General Theodore B. Olson). In the aftermath of *Chadha*, Congress has debated various alternative approaches to exercising oversight over the regulatory process in

authorizations and thus forcing periodic reauthorization of various administrative programs, confining the use of agency funds in a manner consistent with particular legislative objectives as expressed in appropriations legislation, and, of course, the familiar techniques of legislative oversight. Although such alternatives require Congress either to use the plenary legislative process in order to make its will legally effective or to rely mainly on advice or threats to agencies in the oversight context, they nonetheless constitute a formidable array of powers.

Even though the political oversight model, with its emphasis on Presidential and congressional supervision of agency action, has demonstrated considerable vitality in the contemporary debate, the model has significant shortcomings. In its essentials, it is an indirect and incomplete means of realizing its ultimate ideal. The guiding ideal is to achieve democratic responsiveness to public interests within the administrative process itself. The oversight approach does not seek to accomplish this directly, but instead attempts to rely on the President and Congress to make the public's views known to agencies. This reliance presupposes that the President and Congress are themselves responsive to a full range of public interests, but that presupposition is subject to serious question.

Relying on the President to oversee the administrative process is problematical on the premises of the democratic process ideal because the President has his own policies and programs that themselves are not necessarily designed to express the full range of the public's views and interests on particular administrative issues. Indeed, the President is an explicitly political actor with specific constituencies, preferences, and predilections. To rely on such an official to monitor the administrative process on behalf of all public interests is to risk ignoring that the President's political commitments reflect a subset of those of the polity. Moreover, even if it were possible to conceive of the President as a neutral ombudsman bringing to bear the full variety of public views and interests in the oversight of administration, one would be justified in asking why such a representative is necessary in the first place. If such were the case, why not simply rely on direct representation of the public's interests in the administrative process?

---

a manner consistent with the Supreme Court's decision. *See* 129 Cong. Rec. H4772-74 (daily ed. June 29, 1983) (discussing a proposal by Rep. Levitas, which would require a rule to be approved by both Houses of Congress and presented to the President, and one by Rep. Waxman, which would require a joint resolution to disapprove an agency rule); *Supreme Court's Ruling May Limit Hill's Power*, Washington Post, Sept. 11, 1983, at F 1, col. 1.

Similar concerns are raised by proposals to enhance the power of members of Congress over the administrative process. Such a method for achieving democratic responsiveness by agencies also is inherently an indirect one. It might be thought initially that Congress may be more capable than the President alone of representing the public's collective views and interests, if only because Congress itself is a collective body. However, in practice actual influence over the administrative process is wielded by specific members of congressional committees or their staffs. Like the President, members of Congress have particularistic political commitments that cannot be assumed to be equatable with the full range of the public's attitudes concerning matters of administration. Thus, as with the President, reliance on Congress as an indirect means of realizing the underlying democratic process ideal creates a definite potential for frustrating that very ideal.[133]

Moreover, absent undertakings to promote direct representation of the public's views in the administrative process, one may doubt whether many arcane issues that come to the fore in administrative decisionmaking are likely to generate broad-based political attention that will be channelled to the President or Congress and, through them, to agencies.[134] The problem is not merely one of mobilizing public interest. More generally, the problem is one of communicating to politically accountable officials the full range of the public's views in the absence of special efforts to broaden participation in the administrative process.

In the end, it is not unlikely that political officials acting under strengthened mandates of oversight will function significantly as conduits for particularly influential societal interests, such as important constituents of members of Congress or major supporters of and contributors to the President's party or allies. Even though this may not raise eyebrows from the perspective of realpolitik, it is inconsistent with the broad normative commitments of the democratic process ideal underlying the oversight model. That ideal, again, calls for channelling broad-based political views to adminis-

---

133. The influence of congressional staff underlies one of the arguments against the legislative veto as a method for enhancing legislative oversight of the executive branch. In essence, the argument is that congressional staff would have an inordinate amount of power if they could rely, expressly or implicitly, on the existence of legislative veto authority in conducting their ongoing negotiations with agency staff. *Cf.* Bruff & Gellhorn, *supra* note 5.

134. It is difficult to imagine, for instance, that there is a general public position concerning the percentage of peanuts that should be used as the benchmark for determining whether a substance is peanut butter—the issue that prompted one of the most infamous examples of delayed administrative action, which consumed more than ten years. *See* S. BREYER & R. STEWART, *supra* note 14, at 489.

trative officials in order to make the process more truly responsive to the democratic will—which is not the same as the heightened influence of a few of the most directly interested and powerful social groups.

VI. Conclusion: General Perspectives on Administrative Reform

As this Article has discussed, the contemporary debate about administrative reform does not consist merely of specific controversies about a plethora of discrete proposals or initiatives. Rather, there is a basic pattern in the debate that may be obscured if one considers it on a purely particularistic plane.

There are three major, competing ideals reflected in the debate that advance fundamentally different visions of a well-regulated, legitimate, and rationally-functioning administrative process. The rule of law ideal imagines a restrained and ordered process governed by norms of law; it seeks to achieve statutory aims in a manner consistent with the protection of private entitlements and adherence to legal limits. The public purposes ideal posits a more policy-oriented vision of administration; it prescribes the efficient and rational achievement of valued public purposes, or at least an effort to foster their realization by private economic actors. The democratic process ideal takes to heart the precept of democratic theory that choices among warring values in society should be made as the result of a basically participatory, representative process; it seeks to achieve this standard even in the context of hierarchical, bureaucratic institutions.

These three competing ideals reflect deep normative commitments that are central to the contemporary debate. At the same time, the ideals are in sharp conflict with one another. In particular, the core embodiments of each ideal, which reflect the most direct means of realizing the ideal within the operation of a reformed administrative process, are fundamentally critical of each other.

Thus, the core of the rule of law ideal rejects the open-ended character of the public purposes ideal and its tendency to emphasize policy-oriented, as opposed to strictly legal, decisionmaking by agencies. Conversely, the public purposes ideal refuses to accept the rule of law ideal's commitment to formalism as the basis of agency action.

At the same time, both the rule of law ideal and the public purposes ideal reject the democratic process ideal's notion of an open, participatory, and responsive administrative process that is seen as essentially political. The rule of law ideal rejects this conception by maintaining that administration is significantly apolitical in character and that duly-enacted laws are the bearers of values to be implemented, not created, by administrators. The public purposes ideal attacks the democratic process ideal by stressing the technical nature of expert administrative decisionmaking and by highlighting the irrationalities of a decisional process governed by political compromise.

In response, the democratic process ideal views both of the other ideals as misguided and illegitimate because they do not focus on the achievement of a democratic justification for the use of considerable public power by unelected agency officials. In particular, the democratic process ideal objects both to the bureaucratic and extremely rationalist propensities of the public purposes ideal and to the highly legalistic orientation of the rule of law ideal.

Despite these differences, each ideal, when viewed from an "internal" perspective, may be seen to encounter a common concern, albeit in different ways. Stripped to its essentials, each core embodiment appears to take for granted certain conditions of administrative life that seem substantially at odds with the possibilities of the existing administrative process. At the same time, each ideal is essential to understanding and justifying the administrative process in terms of the contemporary debate. Accordingly, a movement occurs in each ideal from a core embodiment to an alternative expression. The latter retains the ideal's basic theory of legitimacy, but it seeks to realize that legitimacy through some means other than one demanding the most direct transformation of the existing administrative process. In turn, however, each of the alternatives is subject to the charge of failing fully to achieve the ultimate ideal of which it is an expression, and each one has its own specific limitations.

The framework developed in this Article can account not only for deep clashes among the three ideals, but also for limited alliances among some of the ideas inhabiting more than one ideal. Certain aspects of the core embodiment of one ideal and the alternative expression of another ideal may be seen to "work" together in reformist discourse. It bears noting that the cores of different ideals do not combine with other cores; only alternative expressions combine in certain respects with the cores of other ideals. Moreover, these makeshift alliances are temporary and unstable because the alternative expressions ultimately are traceable to underlying ideals at odds with the competing cores. While not in any way denying the separateness of and competition among the three ideals, these *ad hoc* relationships highlight the complexity of the contemporary debate considered in terms of the framework put forward here. This complex interplay of ideas is ultimately derived from reformist visions that share the rich theoretical heritage of modern liberal thought, which itself has deep tensions and limited complementarities.

For instance, there is a degree of overlap in some of the ideas advanced on behalf of the formalist core of the rule of law ideal, on the one hand, and on behalf of the market-oriented model, on the other hand. Even though these two approaches ultimately posit very different justifications for administrative action, they both adhere to the notions that the public and private spheres must be kept separate, that legal norms help provide the necessary boundaries between the two realms, and more particularly that public laws should preserve private entitlements from undue impositions by the state. These themes often are linked together in reformist argument. For example, deregulation is defended chiefly in terms of a return to a "free" market, but also in terms of the need to eliminate legal intrusions on the "private" sphere that are said to be insufficiently confined by rules of law.

There also is a certain congruence between aspects of the core of the public purposes ideal, on the one hand, and of the political oversight model, on the other hand. Even though they represent distinct underlying visions of the legitimacy and character of administrative action, they both stress the multiplicity of goals and interests that must be balanced in the context of administrative decisionmaking. This shared theme frequently is found in arguments on behalf of an expanded role for the President and his staff in overseeing agency regulations. Such an expanded role is, of course, one means of pursuing the goal of political oversight of administrative decisions. But it also may be defended under the core of the competing public purposes ideal: the Executive Office of the President could be said to be the most competent institution for undertaking the government-wide balancing of costs and benefits of contemplated agency actions necessary to achieve the most instrumentally rational result.

In addition, there are certain connections among the ideas contained in the core of the democratic process ideal, on the one hand, and the proceduralist expression of the rule of law ideal, on the other hand. Although the ideals underlying these perspectives fundamentally differ, both approaches emphasize innovation in decisional processes, the language of fairness, and the interests of affected parties in becoming involved in administration. These notions commonly are relied upon in arguments on behalf of expanded public participation in administrative proceedings, which is claimed not only to enhance the openness and responsiveness of an essentially political process, but also to control agency discretion and to protect private entitlements by imposing procedural constraints on agencies in the name of the rule of law.

In view of the deep normative clashes and temporary alliances among aspects of the competing ideals, what can be said about the present state of the theory of administrative reform? In light of the limited overlaps among aspects of the cores of certain ideals and the alternative expressions of other ideals, is it possible to suggest that the conflicts reflected in the contemporary debate may be harmonized? Or given the fundamental tensions among the three ideals, is it more accurate to perceive irreducible normative tension underlying the contemporary administrative process?

It could be suggested that a degree of harmony might be achieved in terms of the alliances just noted among certain ideas inhabiting more than one ideal. The notion would be that such alliances may establish ways to bridge the gaps among the ideals and perhaps may point to a unified theory of administrative reform. This suggestion ultimately cannot succeed, however, because it fails to deal seriously with the fundamental clashes among the cores of the three competing ideals. The three ideals embody distinct visions of the legitimacy of administrative action and the character of administrative decisionmaking, and at these basic levels they are at war with one another. The ideals cannot be magically harmonized—even if aspects of them can be compared and combined on an *ad hoc* basis—without ignoring, or wishing not to notice, these deep conflicts.

For similar reasons, two well-established portraits of modern administrative theory cannot be accepted as fully adequate perspectives from which to understand the contemporary debate. The first portrait suggests that there is a continuing crisis in the American administrative process that should be resolved by developing an embracing theory of the legitimacy of administration in our political system.[135] This portrait aptly notes that the problem of administrative legitimacy is a longstanding one and that present concerns reflect recurrent dilemmas and doubts. However, the suggestion that the crisis of legitimacy should be resolved by a harmonizing theory or vision simply is inconsistent with the existence of deep normative conflicts at the root of the contemporary debate. In fact, the debate reveals major clashes among three competing ideals, which advance

---

135. *Cf.* J. FREEDMAN, *supra* note 20, at ix ("*I must confess my own hope that this book will persuade its readers of* the importance of understanding the recurrent sense of crisis attending the federal administrative agencies and of *the necessity of developing a theory of the legitimacy of the administrative process.*") (emphasis added).

their own forceful claims on the basis of distinct and to a large degree mutually incompatible premises.

The second portrait is one in which a traditional model of the administrative process, which might be assimilated here to the rule of law ideal, is seen to have disintegrated, leaving in its wake an array of alternative conceptions tending to lack overall structure or patterned relationships.[136] In analyzing the contemporary debate, however, it is not possible to say that any one "traditional" model is significantly more disintegrated or limited in its conceptual or programmatic promise than the other competing ideals. In some ways, the rule of law ideal and its expressions are among the most robust sources of reformist criticism. More generally, one cannot disregard any of the three competing ideals, for all of them are central to the contemporary debate. Furthermore, the different ideals, viewed as a group, do not lack structure or pattern in their relationships with each other.

In the end, the contemporary debate reflects major clashes among three competing ideals of the administrative process, as well as a parallel internal development within each ideal from a core embodiment to an alternative expression. No single conception at any level seems sufficiently moribund to permit the conclusion that any is necessarily much less vital than the others. Similarly, none appears particularly preeminent or in the ascendancy, either in theoretical or practical terms.

The contemporary debate about administrative reform may purport to represent a basic reevaluation of the existing process, but it does not. In fact, it is enmeshed in the complex dynamics surrounding the elaboration of and competition among deep, preexisting premises. A degree of self-consciousness about this predicament seems essential for a full awareness of the character and constraints of the main arguments advanced on behalf of administrative reform. Moreover, this understanding leads one to conclude that the contemporary debate is not likely to come to an end if and when, for instance, Congress enacts sweeping regulatory reform legislation or the President broadly rearranges patterns of executive behavior within legal limits. The debate about administrative reform exhibits fundamental tensions within reformist discourse that are likely to continue to fuel new proposals for change. In the midst of this ferment of ideas, however, one can discern an underlying intellectual structure that itself reflects the dominant but competing normative commitments of liberal political theory and legal thought.

---

136. *Cf.* Stewart, *The Reformation of American Administrative Law, supra* note 10.

[2]

HOW THE ELECTRONIC FREEDOM OF INFORMATION ACT AMENDMENTS OF 1996 UPDATE PUBLIC ACCESS FOR THE INFORMATION AGE

MICHAEL E. TANKERSLEY[*]

TABLE OF CONTENTS

---

   * Michael E. Tankersley is a Staff Attorney with Public Citizen Litigation Group, where his practice involves administrative law, constitutional law, civil rights, and consumer protection litigation. Mr. Tankersley is also Chair of the Committee on Government Information and Privacy of the Administrative Law Section of the Federal Bar Association, and teaches as an adjunct professor at Georgetown University Law Center.

INTRODUCTION

*[W]ithin the past decade, the public has grown accustomed to the
benefits of using information technology to reduce the burden and improve
the cost, quality, and timeliness of product and service delivery. Americans
now expect to solve a problem with one telephone call, obtain customer
service 24 hours a day, withdraw cash from automated teller machines
around the country, and get products delivered
almost anywhere overnight.*[1]

Thirty years after the passage of the Freedom of Information Act
(FOIA),[2] Congress tried to bring the statute, and the executive branch of
government, into the age of computers. The Electronic Freedom of Information Act Amendments of 1996 (1996 Amendments or Amendments)[3]
reflect Congress's recognition of the fact that, unlike thirty years ago, most
of the government's work-product is now generated electronically. More
importantly, the Amendments reflect the fact that computers have revolutionized the public's expectations of how quickly and efficiently information should be made available. For information requesters, the most critical
aspect of the 1996 Amendments is that Congress has sought to address
these expectations by fundamentally shifting the way that FOIA defines access to government records.

For the last three decades, public access to information under FOIA has
been defined by provisions of the statute that allow requesters to submit
broadly worded written requests for agency records. Requesters have
waited weeks, months, or even years for the government to respond. From
the time the statute was enacted, this "request-and-wait" paradigm has been
mired in paperwork and backlogs, and it has become increasingly unacceptable as the public has grown accustomed to being able to use digital
technologies to obtain instant access to information.

The 1996 Amendments shift the emphasis away from this "request-and-
wait" model. The new paradigm requires agencies to anticipate requests

---

　　1. S. REP. No. 104-8 at 15 (1995) (Senate Committee on Governmental Affairs).
　　2. Pub. L. No. 89-554, 80 Stat. 383 (1966) (codified as amended at 5 U.S.C. § 552
(1994 & Supp. II 1996)).
　　3. Electronic Freedom of Information Act Amendments of 1996, Pub. L. No. 104-
231, 110 Stat. 3048 (codified at 5 U.S.C. § 552 (Supp. II 1996)).

and make broad categories of records immediately available to the public at agency records depositories and, using telecommunications technology, at requesters' home computers. These provisions fundamentally alter the relationship between FOIA users and agencies, and the role of FOIA in federal information policy. The new model for public access requires that agencies be more forthcoming in making records immediately accessible to the public, and that requesters be more sophisticated in locating records and fashioning requests.

The changes imposed by this mandate for more affirmative disclosure and on-line access represent a revolutionary shift. In contrast, other parts of the 1996 Amendments reflect modest, evolutionary changes in the law. The Amendments contain provisions on electronic records that largely ratify the positions that agencies and the courts have gradually adopted over the past decade, and still leave some of the most difficult issues unresolved. Several other provisions in the 1996 Amendments seek to address the most pervasive problem with FOIA, namely the chronic delays in the processing of individual FOIA requests. These provisions, however, offer little that is new, and fail to provide any additional resources or enforcement mechanisms to cure the delays.

Section I of this Article describes the "request-and-wait" paradigm that has traditionally dominated public access under FOIA, frustrating users of FOIA. Section II describes how the 1996 Amendments shift the emphasis of FOIA by requiring agencies to make records of public interest available for immediate on-line access and in agency reading rooms. Section II then discusses how the provisions for electronic records interact with this new paradigm, and the problems and disputes likely to arise when implementing the new paradigm and interpreting the Amendments. Finally, Section III discusses how the 1996 Amendments attempt, once again, to address the delays that have crippled the "request-and-wait" process of providing access under FOIA for the past thirty years.

I. THE TRADITIONAL PARADIGM OF FOIA PROCESSING

FOIA's critical role in federal information policy is to provide access to records that federal agencies have little or no incentive to disseminate. If an agency wants to release information in its records, usually it can share the records with whomever it wishes. Corporations, journalists, researchers, and ordinary citizens routinely obtain information from the government without the formality or delay involved in a FOIA request because agencies, or at least agency employees, are willing to provide the information. FOIA provides a tool for prying loose information that the government is reluctant to disclose because it might be embarrassing, or because it is costly to release the information to the public.

For the last thirty years, FOIA has served this objective principally by providing that requesters may submit a written request to the agency and wait for the agency to respond. One of the handicaps of this "request-and-wait" ritual is that requesters usually have little, if any, information on what is in the agencies' files and how such files are arranged. Agencies often lack adequate indices of their records and, even if the files are indexed, rarely make any effort to publish this information to FOIA requesters. As a government task force recently observed, "[t]he public has no efficient and accurate way of learning what information the agency has [and no idea] how the files are arranged, how long they are kept, or where they are stored."[4]

Requesters are not required to formulate a precise request for specific documents or files. Instead, they need only submit a request that "reasonably describes" the records sought.[5] This intentionally liberal standard means that FOIA assists not only in obtaining government records, but also allows members of the public to require the government to search for and assemble records that, but for the request, the agencies may never have collected together. A requester with little or no information on the agencies' files can submit a request for all the agencies' records on a particular subject, person, or transaction. Even if the agency does not file its records according to the categories used in the request, the agency is required to have employees familiar with its records cull its files for the necessary information.[6] While the agency is required only to undertake a "reasonable" search and is not required to create "new" records, the task of searching for records can be substantial. "One of the greatest problems encountered in satisfying FOIA requests is that requests are often incompatible with the ways agency records are originally collected and organized."[7]

For requesters, however, the most significant problem with FOIA processing is delay. FOIA states that agencies shall "promptly" release records upon request,[8] but this directive has been mocked by lengthy delays in obtaining a response even to simple requests. In 1974, Congress amended the statute to require that agencies determine whether to release records within

---

4. DEPARTMENT OF THE INTERIOR, REPORT OF THE NAT'L PERFORMANCE REV. FREEDOM OF INFORMATION ACT REINVENTION TEAM, GATEWAY TO GOVERNMENT INFORMATION at 11 (1995) [hereinafter GATEWAY].

5. 5 U.S.C. § 552(a)(3)(A) (Supp. II 1996). *See* Truitt v. Department of State, 897 F.2d 540, 544-45 (D.C. Cir. 1990) (noting that requirement for reasonable description of records sought is consistent with congressional intent to create liberal standard for identification).

6. National Cable Television Ass'n, Inc. v. FCC, 479 F.2d 183, 192 (D.C. Cir. 1973).

7. Jamie A. Grodsky, *The Freedom of Information Act in the Electronic Age: The Statute Is Not User Friendly*, 31 JURIMETRICS J. 17, 41 (1990).

8. 5 U.S.C. § 552 (1994).

ten working days, but agencies routinely ignore this requirement and even simple requests are subject to protracted delays. Some of the most important agencies, such as the Federal Bureau of Investigation and the Department of State, take years to respond to FOIA requests.[9] Delays persist because "Congress has not funded the FOIA mission adequately at most of the agencies, and agency managers incur less trouble for FOIA failings than they would if they shifted resources and placed substantive agency programs at a disadvantage to better attend to their FOIA tasks."[10] Moreover, delays under the "request-and-wait" system can be useful to the government to dissuade requests or to postpone unwelcome disclosures when journalists or others seek records on a suspected or emerging scandal.[11]

The "request-and-wait" system, however, also creates problems for agencies because it generates enormous costs. Agencies have hired hundreds of information specialists, lawyers, and other staff to track requests, search for records, and review records for exempt materials.[12] One agency estimated that its average cost to process a FOIA request in 1994 was $349, and that the cost would increase to $544 per request by the year 2000.[13] Although computer technology has made finding, releasing and disseminating government information easier, agency records are largely organized in paper files, and processing requests for such records is labor intensive. The delays that harm requesters and the costs that burden agencies have persisted despite the use of new technologies.

A Department of Interior report summarized the operation of the "request-and-wait" system as follows:

> Despite the intention of the FOIA, the public's access to government information is inefficient, ineffective, and costly. Information is too difficult, expensive, and time consuming to find and obtain. The records management system is too paper and labor intensive, and its decentralization discourages public access. The public has little information about the FOIA process, and the information provided is not written in plain English. Some employees do not view FOIA requests

---

9. *See* Rabin v. United States Dep't of State, 980 F. Supp. 116, 122 (E.D.N.Y. 1997) (discussing that Department of State was inundated with 1,965 requests in 1995 alone); Aguilera v. Federal Bureau of Investigation, 941 F. Supp. 144, 148 (D.D.C. 1996) (describing that FBI estimates delay of 87 months before it can process request filed two years earlier); Electronic Privacy Information Center v. Federal Bureau of Investigation, 865 F. Supp. 1, 2 (D.D.C. 1994) (reporting FBI backlog of 11,651 requests).

10. JAMES T. O'REILLY, FEDERAL INFORMATION DISCLOSURE § 7.06, at 7-23 (1990).

11. *Id.* at 7-21.

12. *See* Andrew Blum, *Freedom to Battle for Data: FOIA Still Perplexes Some of Its Critics*, NAT'L L.J., Mar. 12, 1990, at 28-29 (discussing emergence of FOIA bureaucracy).

13. *See* GATEWAY, *supra* note 4, at 11, 14; Mark H. Grunewald, *Freedom of Information Act Dispute Resolution*, 40 ADMIN. L. REV. 1, 21 (1988) (estimating annual cost of administering FOIA as varying from $47 to $250 million).

as an essential part of their agency's mission.[14]

II. Shifting the Paradigm

A. *Making Records Available Without a Request*

The most important provisions of the 1996 Amendments to FOIA introduce a new paradigm in which agencies must affirmatively disclose more records and information about records, without waiting for a request. Agencies are now required to anticipate requests and make records available to the public without requiring FOIA users to submit a request and await a response. Moreover, the Amendments require that agencies provide requesters with indices and search aides to assist them in formulating their requests for records.[15] In theory, at least, these provisions significantly enhance the ability of requesters to obtain prompt disclosure under FOIA by giving requesters information on what agency files contain, and imposing an obligation on the agencies to make repeatedly requested records available without delay.

1. *Expanding the Categories of Records That Must Be Made Available for Immediate Access*

The Amendments require that many records that previously could be obtained only by filing a FOIA request be made available to the public for inspection and copying without a request.[16] FOIA, as adopted in 1966, divides agency records into three categories: (1) records that must be published in the Federal Register, such as substantive agency rules and descriptions of agency organizations; (2) records that must be either published and offered for sale, or deposited in agency "reading rooms" where the public may examine an index of the records and inspect and copy the records that interest them; and (3) all other agency records which, unless covered by one of FOIA's nine exemptions, must be made available to the public in response to a request.[17] Prior to the 1996 Amendments, the second category was of limited importance because the only records that agencies had to index and make available in their reading rooms were final opinions, statements of policy, staff manuals, and instructions affecting the public. For all other agency records, if the agency did not voluntarily make the record available on its own, the only way for the public to require dis-

---

14. *See* GATEWAY, *supra* note 4, at 2.

15. 5 U.S.C. § 552(a)(2)(D) (Supp. II 1996).

16. 5 U.S.C. § 552(a)(1)-(3) (1994 & Supp. II 1996).

17. 5 U.S.C. § 552(a)(2)(D) (Supp. II 1996).

closure under FOIA was to submit a request to the agency and endure delay.

The 1996 Amendments expand the types of records that agencies must make available under the second category to include those records identified in response to a FOIA request "which, because of the nature of their subject matter, the agency determines have become or are likely to become the subject of subsequent requests for substantially the same records."[18] Consequently, agency records that have been, or are likely to be, requested more than once must now be made available for public inspection and copying at agency reading rooms.

This provision was adopted with little fanfare considering the dramatic change it makes in agencies' affirmative obligations to make records available. The obligation to make records available without a request is no longer limited to formal agency pronouncements and manuals. Now, this obligation extends to all types of records in an agency's possession, whether written by the agency or obtained from a third party, and includes records that are informal or embarrassing to the government. Moreover, whether a record must be made available in the reading room is not determined by its function within the agency, but rather by requesters' interest in the record. Prior to the 1996 Amendments, many agencies adopted a practice of voluntarily making records that were frequently requested available in agency reading rooms in order to reduce the burden of responding to FOIA requests.[19] Requiring that *all* agencies adopt this practice for *any* record that is likely to be the subject of multiple requests significantly expands the volume of government records that agencies must make available in this manner.

2. *Requiring Agencies to Provide Access to Records On-line*

In addition to expanding their conventional reading rooms, agencies are required to make many records available on-line in electronic reading rooms. Previously, the only general law requiring that agency records be made available on-line was the Government Printing Office Electronic Information Access Enhancement Act of 1993.[20] This Act required that the Government Printing Office make available on-line the federal agency notices concerning rules, proposed rules, policy statements and similar materials that must be published in the Federal Register.[21] The 1996 FOIA Amendments provide that, by November 1, 1997, all federal agencies must

---

18. *Id.* § 552(a)(2).
19. *See* S. REP. NO. 104-272, at 13 (1996); H. REP. NO. 104-795, at 21 (1996).
20. Pub. L. No. 103-40, 107 Stat. 112 (codified at 44 U.S.C. § 4101 (1994)).
21. 44 U.S.C. § 4101(a)(1) (1994).

establish electronic reading rooms that make recent records in agency reading rooms available in electronic format. If an agency does not have the means to make these materials available on-line, then the information must be made available in some other electronic form, such as CD-ROM or disc.[22]

These electronic reading rooms must include traditional reading room records created after November 1, 1996, such as agency opinions, interpretations adopted by the agency, staff manuals and instructions to staff that affect the public. A wide variety of agency documents, ranging from formal manuals and policy statements to decisions in informal adjudications and position statements, must be made available on-line under this provision.[23] More significantly, the electronic reading rooms must also provide the public with access to any other type of record that the agency determines has been, or is likely to become, the subject of subsequent requests, if the record was created after November 1, 1996.[24]

The electronic reading room provisions of the Amendments represent an enormous expansion of agencies' obligations to create on-line depositories where the public can obtain immediate access to government records. Although agencies have increasingly been using the Internet and other electronic technologies to make government information accessible to the public, these activities have been confined to a few agencies and a few types of records.[25] None of the existing activities approach the large-scale elec-

---

22. Congress and the Clinton administration, however, have indicated a strong preference that agencies fulfill this requirement by making the records available over the Internet. *See* S. REP. NO. 104-272, at 11; OFFICE OF INFO. AND PRIVACY, DEP'T OF JUSTICE, Congress Enacts FOIA Amendments, FOIA UPDATE, XVII, No. 4, at 1 (Fall 1996).

23. *See* National Prison Project v. Sigler, 390 F. Supp. 789, 792-93 (D.D.C. 1975) (noting that parole board decisions denying inmate applications are reading room records); Public Citizen v. Office of the United States Trade Representative, 804 F. Supp. 385, 387-88 (D.D.C. 1992) (holding that Trade Representative's submissions to GATT panel containing agency's interpretation of United States' international legal obligations are § 552(a)(2) records); Stokes v. Brennan, 476 F.2d 699, 701-02 (5th Cir. 1973) (concluding that training course manual for health and safety officers falls within § 552(a)(2)).

24. Agencies are permitted to delete identifying details from these prior-released records in order to prevent a clearly unwarranted invasion of personal privacy, as with opinions, statements of policy, and other materials previously covered by § 552(a)(2). However, consistent with the computer redaction requirements described below, the agency must indicate the extent of any deletion from the prior-released records. Where technically feasible, the agency must also indicate the deletion at the place on the record where the deletion was made, unless doing so will harm an interest protected by the exemption in subsection (b) under which the deletion was made.

25. *See* General Accounting Office, Internet and Electronic Dial-Up Bulletin Boards: Information Reported by Federal Organizations, Report No. GAO/GGD-97-86, at 9 (June 1997); OFFICE OF TECHNOLOGY ASSESSMENT, ELECTRONIC DELIVERY OF FEDERAL SERVICES 138-39 (1993) [hereinafter ELECTRONIC DELIVERY]; HENRY H. PERRITT, JR., ELECTRONIC ACQUISITION

tronic posting of all types of agency records mandated by the 1996 Amendments, and most agencies appear to be totally unprepared to implement such electronic reading rooms. Indeed, it is remarkable that Congress adopted this provision without any comment on the breadth of its mandate, or any inquiry into the cost of implementation.

3. *Requiring Agencies to Provide Indices and Finding Aids*

The Amendments also require that agencies compile and publish information that will help requesters formulate requests. Agencies must make publicly available, upon request, "reference material" or a "guide" for requesting records or information from the agency.[26] These guides must include: (i) an index of all major information systems of the agency; (ii) a description of major information and record locator systems maintained by the agency; and (iii) a handbook for obtaining various types of public information from the agency under FOIA and other record laws.[27] Agencies are also required to make available an index of the previously released records that have been or are likely to be the subject of additional requests.[28] Congress hoped that this index would not only assist requesters in obtaining records that have been the subject of prior FOIA requests, but also would assist agencies in reducing FOIA backlogs, theorizing that agencies are able to process requests for prior-released records more quickly.[29] This index will initially be available through traditional agency reading rooms, but the Amendments also mandate that this index be made available through computer telecommunications by December 31, 1999.[30]

The information that should be provided in these indices has not been readily available in the past. Some sophisticated FOIA requesters have obtained and used agency logs of prior FOIA requests to identify useful records, or have studied the agencies' lists of record systems and files for guidance on drafting requests.[31] But agencies have rarely published these finding aids or encouraged FOIA users to consult them. Instead, the instructions published by agencies on how to use FOIA in the past have generally been limited to regulations or other formal, legalistic pronounce-

---

AND RELEASE OF FEDERAL AGENCY INFORMATION, REPORT PREPARED FOR THE ADMINISTRATIVE CONFERENCE OF THE UNITED STATES 26-72 (1988).

26. 5 U.S.C. § 552(g) (Supp. II 1996).

27. *Id.*

28. *See id.* § 552(a)(2)(E).

29. S. REP. No. 104-272, at 13 (1996).

30. 5 U.S.C. § 552(a)(2)(E) (Supp. II 1996).

31. Under the Federal Records Act, agencies must prepare schedules or lists describing their records and the retention periods for the records. 44 U.S.C. § 3303 (1994); 36 C.F.R. § 1228.22 (1997).

ments that are difficult to understand and provide no information on the records held by the agency. The difficulty in understanding agency instructions discourages public access to information.[32] Perhaps understandably, most agencies have not seen it as in their interest to encourage the use of FOIA. By imposing a legal duty on the agencies to provide indices and descriptions of major information systems, the 1996 Amendments are likely to promote greater use of FOIA and, hopefully, will also promote the submission of more precisely crafted requests.

The provisions in the 1996 Amendments requiring agencies to make records available without a request, and to disseminate information on agency records systems, are distinct from the Amendment's provisions for on-line reading rooms and could be implemented without using electronic technologies. These provisions, however, are all driven and inspired by the pervasive growth in the use of computers to archive and disseminate information. Businesses and agencies now use computer networks to archive and index virtually unlimited amounts of data, and to make the data available on demand in the time that it takes a modem to transmit the information. As a result, the traditional FOIA paradigm in which a requester submits a written request based on scant information about the government's holdings and waits indefinitely for a response, is now untenable. The Amendments reflect Congress's conviction that "[g]overnment agencies should use new technology to enhance public access to agency records and information."[33]

B. Resolving Electronic Records Issues in Favor of Access

For years, federal agencies resisted the application of FOIA to electronic data and urged courts to restrict public access to automated record systems. Arguments that FOIA should be interpreted to limit access to electronic records have, however, become increasingly untenable as the government's use of computer technology has become more pervasive and advanced. The 1996 Amendments resolve this issue in favor of requesters and reflect the prevailing consensus that the positions advanced by the government in

---

32. *See* GATEWAY, *supra* note 4, at 11 (discussing complexities in existing instructions as deterrent to public access).

33. Electronic Freedom of Information Act Amendments of 1996, Pub. L. No. 104-231, § 2(a)(6), 110 Stat. 3048 (codified at 5 U.S.C. § 552 (Supp. II 1996)). Representative Maloney captured the connection between technology and more direct public access in her floor remarks: "By using technology, government bureaucrats can avoid going through endless file cabinets hunting for information ... and ordinary American citizens can access that information without leaving their desks or driving to the post office, or in some cases having to contact any government workers at all." 142 CONG. REC. H10,451 (daily ed. Sept. 17, 1996) (statement of Rep. Maloney).

the past are inconsistent with meaningful public access.[34] These provisions, however, do not change the course of FOIA as much as they reflect its evolution; the pre-1996 FOIA can be, and has been, interpreted to reach the same result on these matters as the 1996 Amendments.

1. FOIA's Application to Electronic Records

Even before the 1996 Amendments, it was well established that FOIA applied to computer records.[35] The courts uniformly rejected the suggestion that records created by computers were not within FOIA, and held "that computer-stored records, whether stored in the central processing unit, on magnetic tape, or in some other form, are still 'records' for purposes of FOIA."[36] In 1988, the Administrative Conference recommended "that agencies should recognize that a 'record' includes information maintained in electronic form."[37] Two years later, the Department of Justice (DOJ) surveyed agencies on the application of FOIA to electronic databases and found that "no agency now treats its 'electronic record' file systems as beyond the FOIA's reach."[38] Nevertheless, the DOJ continued to contend, unsuccessfully, that some types of electronic records were not "records" for purposes of FOIA.[39]

The 1996 Amendments resolve this issue once and for all by, for the first time, adding a definition of the term "record," to the statute. The new defi-

---

34. *See infra* notes 35-38 and 50-57 and accompanying text (discussing rejection of argument that FOIA did not apply to electronic records and rejection of view that agency could elect to provide records in proper format).

35. *See infra* notes 36-38.

36. Yeager v. Drug Enforcement Admin., 678 F.2d 315, 321 (D.C. Cir. 1982) (citations omitted) (finding electronic records are covered under FOIA); *see* Long v. IRS, 596 F.2d 362, 364-65 (9th Cir. 1979), *cert. denied*, 446 U.S. 917 (1980) (concluding that widespread use of computers precluded any serious argument that "computer tapes are not generally within the FOIA").

37. ADMINISTRATIVE CONFERENCE OF THE UNITED STATES, RECOMMENDATIONS AND REPORTS, Recommendation No. 88-10 (1988) [hereinafter ACUS RECOMMENDATIONS); Henry H. Perritt, Jr. *Electronic Acquisition and Release of Federal Agency Information: Analysis of Recommendations Adopted by the Administrative Conference of the United States*, 41 ADMIN. L. REV. 253, 291 (1989) (noting prevailing view that computer-stored information is subject to FOIA and that Justice Department did not object to Administrative Conference recommendation on this point).

38. UNITED STATES DEP'T OF JUSTICE, REPORT ON "ELECTRONIC RECORD" ISSUES UNDER THE FREEDOM OF INFORMATION ACT 2 (Oct. 1990), *reprinted in The Electronic Freedom of Information Improvement Act: Hearing on S. 1098 Before Subcom. on Technology and the Law of the Comm. on the Judiciary*, 102d Cong. 33 (1992) [hereinafter DEP'T OF JUSTICE REPORT].

39. *See* Armstrong v. Bush, 721 F. Supp. 343 (D.D.C. 1989), *aff'd in part, rev'd in part*, 924 F.2d 282 (D.C. Cir. 1991) (noting agencies' contention that electronic mail records stored on backup tapes are not "records" under Federal Records Act and FOIA).

nition specifies that the term "record" and any other term used in FOIA in reference to information, "includes any information that would be an agency record subject to the requirements of this section when maintained by an agency in any format, including an electronic format."[40] The new definition thus makes explicit that FOIA covers information recorded in all types of media.

a. FOIA's Application to Computer Reference Materials

In defining "record" in this way, Congress also repudiated another potential limitation on access by rejecting the suggestion that library or reference materials compiled by agencies are not subject to FOIA. Because FOIA contained no definition of "record" prior to the 1996 Amendments, courts looked to the definition of "record" in the Records Disposal Act for guidance.[41] The Records Disposal Act definition, however, contains an exception for "library materials." Some courts cited this exception as a basis for concluding that certain agency databases containing reference materials, such as judicial decisions or medical abstracts, are not subject to FOIA.[42] The Senate proposed to incorporate a modified version of the Records Disposal Act definition into FOIA,[43] but the House Committee rejected this proposal. The House Committee Report cites *SDC Dev. Corp. v. Mathews*,[44] one of the decisions that relied on the "library materials" language in the Records Disposal Act to limit the definition of "record" under FOIA. The Report then states that the holding of *SDC Dev. Corp.* is inconsistent with FOIA because "information an agency has created and is directly or indirectly disseminating remains subject to the FOIA in any of its forms or formats."[45]

---

40. 5 U.S.C. § 552(f)(2) (Supp. II 1996).

41. 44 U.S.C. § 3301 (1994); *see* Forsham v. Harris, 445 U.S. 169, 183-84 (1980) (citing definition of "record" in Records Disposal Act as instructive, but not dispositive, under FOIA); Bureau of National Affairs v. United States Dep't of Justice, 742 F.2d 1484, 1493 (D.C. Cir. 1984) (stating Records Disposal Act treatment is relevant but is not dispositive under FOIA); Washington Post v. United States Dep't of State, 632 F. Supp. 607, 615 (D.D.C. 1986) (noting that material is considered "record" under Records Disposal Act supports conclusion that it is "record" under FOIA).

42. *See* SDC Dev. Corp. v. Mathews, 542 F.2d 1116, 1120 (9th Cir. 1976) (placing discrete reference materials outside reach of FOIA requests); Baizer v. United States Dep't of the Air Force, 887 F. Supp. 225, 227 (D.D.C. 1995) (holding that Dep't of Justice's computerized legal information database is not "record" under FOIA).

43. *See* S. REP. NO. 104-272, at 19 (1996).

44. 542 F.2d 1116 (9th Cir. 1976).

45. H. REP. NO. 104-795, at 20 (1996).

b. FOIA's Application to Computer Software

In the past, agencies have occasionally maintained that computer software is not a record under FOIA on the theory that software does not actually record agency information but, instead, consists of codes used to instruct computer hardware.[46] The claim that software is not a record was never considered to be persuasive, although it has long been recognized that some software, particularly proprietary software owned by private vendors, can give rise to difficult issues concerning agency control, and may be exempt under certain FOIA exemptions.[47] The 1996 Amendments do not directly address this issue, but the new definition of "agency record" makes clear that the medium in which software is recorded is irrelevant.[48] Software should be subject to release under FOIA unless it is not subject to agency control or is exempt under one of FOIA's exemptions.[49]

---

46. *See* DEP'T OF JUSTICE REPORT, *supra* note 38, at 40-46 (discussing claim that computer software is not record).

47. *See* PERRITT, *supra* note 25, at 295 ("Assuming the electronic form of the underlying data is a record, there is no apparent reason why software and indices are not records also."); American Bar Association Recommendation No. 102, § 1 (Feb. 12-13, 1990), *reprinted in* 15 ADMIN. L. NEWS 13 (1990) (stating that computer programs constitute "records" subject to FOIA).

48. The House Committee report on the 1996 Amendments observes that the form or format in which information is maintained is not relevant to the determination of whether the information is subject to FOIA:

This provision should restrain agencies from evading the clear intent of the FOIA by deeming some forms of data as not being agency records and not subject to the law. The primary focus should always be on whether information is subject to disclosure or is exempt, rather than the form or format it is stored in. This provision, however, does not broaden the concept of agency record. The information maintained on a computer is a record, but the computer is not.

H. REP. No. 104-795, at 20 (1996).

49. *See* Cleary, Gottlieb, Steen & Hamilton v. Department of Health and Human Services, 844 F. Supp. 770, 782-83 (D.D.C. 1993) (holding that computer program created by agency employee is agency "record" under FOIA but is exempt from disclosure under Exemption 5); Windels, Marx, Davies & Ives v. Deparment of Commerce, 576 F. Supp. 405 (D.D.C. 1983) (treating computer program, used to evaluate steel import prices, as record subject to FOIA, but exempt from release under Exemptions 2 and 7). The provision of the Senate Bill on the definition of record specifically excluded "computer software which is obtained by an agency under a licensing agreement prohibiting its replication and distribution." S. REP. No. 104-272, at 4 (1996). As noted above, the House rejected the Senate language and replaced it with a definition that did not include any specific exemptions. *See* S. REP. No. 104-272, at 31-32 (1996) (additional views of Senator Leahy) (discussing anticipated treatment of software under rejected Senate language).

2. FOIA's Application to Requests for Records in a Specific Form or Format

Although the government has generally conceded that electronic records are subject to FOIA, it sometimes contended that FOIA did not require agencies to make records available in electronic format and that making the information available on paper or microfiche satisfied agencies' obligations under the statute. In 1984, in *Dismukes v. Department of the Interior*,[50] a district court judge held that where there is no difference between the content of the electronic and paper formats, an agency "has no obligation under FOIA to accommodate plaintiff's preference [for a particular format, but] need only provide responsive, nonexempt information in a reasonably accessible form."[51]

This issue was never squarely addressed at the appellate level, but the result in *Dismukes* was widely condemned on both legal and policy grounds. The Administrative Conference's 1988 recommendation on the application of FOIA to electronic records concluded that "agencies should provide electronic information in the form in which it is maintained or, if so requested, in such other form as can be generated directly with reasonable effort from existing databases with existing software."[52] In 1990, the American Bar Association adopted a similar recommendation stating that, "[i]n responding to FOIA requests, agencies should release electronic information in the format in which it is requested, so long as the requested format already exists or may be generated by the agency with reasonable effort using available software and equipment."[53] Nevertheless, the DOJ continued to instruct agencies that they could rely on *Dismukes* by telling them it "has been held without contradiction by the courts that the agency, not the requester, has the right to choose the format of disclosure."[54]

---

50.   603 F. Supp. 760 (D.D.C. 1984).

51.   *Id.* at 763. In contrast, another court addressing a discovery request for access to an agency's computerized records concluded that providing 15,000 pages of paper print-outs of the records was inadequate, and ordered the agency to provide access to the computer tapes. Timken Co. v. United States, 659 F. Supp. 239, 242-43 (Ct. Int'l. Trade 1987).

52.   *See* ACUS RECOMMENDATIONS, *supra* note 37, at 50-51.

53.   American Bar Association Recommendation No. 102 (adopted Feb. 12-13, 1990), *reprinted in* 15 ADMIN. L. NEWS 13 (1990); *see* John M. Graham, *Fair Administration of the Freedom of Information Act After the Computer Revolution*, 5 COMP. L.J. 51, 69-70 (1984) (arguing that agencies should be required to release records in form specified by requester unless agency can show need to release information in other form).

54.   OFFICE OF INFO. AND PRIVACY, U.S. DEP'T OF JUSTICE, FREEDOM OF INFORMATION ACT GUIDE & PRIVACY ACT OVERVIEW 31 (1995) (citing *Dismukes*, unpublished opinions in *Coalition for Alternatives in Nutrition & Healthcare v. FDA*, No. 90-1025, slip op. at 3 (D.D.C. Jan. 4, 1991) and *National Sec. Archive v. CIA*, No. 88-119, slip op. at 1-2 (D.D.C. July 26, 1988), *aff'd on mootness grounds*, No. 88-5298 (D.C. Cir. Feb. 6, 1989)).

Despite *Dismukes*, FOIA requesters were often able to obtain records in electronic format. The DOJ encouraged agencies to "exercise sound discretion in complying with FOIA requests without 'unnecessary bureaucratic hurdles' in this regard"[55] and agencies often opted to make records available in electronic format rather than contest the issue.[56] As judicial familiarity with electronic records increased, *Dismukes* was increasingly viewed as unpersuasive. Courts recognized that providing access to hard copy versions of information stored in electronic format was not the same as providing access to the electronic records themselves, and "[n]othing in the FOIA excuses an agency from disclosing a particular record because it has disclosed the content elsewhere in a different format."[57]

The 1996 Amendments resolve this dispute in favor of requesters by explicitly rejecting *Dismukes*.[58] The Amendments require that agencies provide information in the format requested, including requests for records in electronic format, if the record "is readily reproducible by the agency in that form or format."[59] The Amendments also state that "[e]ach agency shall make reasonable efforts to maintain its records in forms or formats that are reproducible for purposes of this section."[60]

Thus, if an agency maintains records in electronic form, requesters are able to request a copy in electronic form, or any form "readily reproducible" from the agency's computers, such as paper or computer generated microfiche. Requesters can also specify formats. For example, if the agency maintains a database in a particular software format, requesters may request that the data be copied to an alternative format that is compatible with the

---

55. *See id.* (quoting President William J. Clinton, Memorandum for the Heads of Departments and Agencies on Freedom of Information Act, Oct. 4, 1993).

56. In response to the Department of Justice's 1989 questionnaire, a number of agencies reported that they were willing to provide a FOIA requester with the format the requester specified where it was not burdensome to do so. DEP'T OF JUSTICE REPORT, *supra* note 38, at 38-40. On the other hand, 59% of the agencies responding took the position that they had no obligation to provide requesters records in the particular electronic format specified by the requester, and 39% reported that they had no position on this issue. *Id.* at 6.

57. *See* Delorme Publ'g Co. v. National Oceanic and Atmospheric Admin., 907 F. Supp. 10, 12 (D. Me. 1995) (rejecting result in *Dismukes*); Petroleum Info. Corp. v. Department of the Interior, 976 F.2d 1429, 1437 n.11 (D.C. Cir. 1992) (rejecting contention that computer compilation of paper records did not have to be released because underlying paper records are public, particularly since paper records were not in "reasonably accessible form"); Armstrong v. Executive Office of the President, 1 F.3d 1274, 1282-87 (D.C. Cir. 1993) (rejecting contention that preserving paper print-outs of electronic mail fulfilled agency obligations to manage and safeguard electronic mail records under Federal Records Act).

58. *See supra* notes 50-57 and accompanying text (discussing holding and ramifications of *Dismukes*).

59. 5 U.S.C. § 552(a)(3)(B) (Supp. II 1996).

60. *Id.*

requester's database software, so long as the alternative format is readily reproducible from the agency's software. If the agency maintains records on mainframe computers, requesters may obtain the data in a format used by microcomputers unless the agency can demonstrate that its computers cannot produce that format.[61] Agencies may also be required to make an electronic copy of paper records to satisfy a request if the paper records are readily reproducible in electronic format by using imaging or scanning technology.[62]

3. FOIA's Application to Requests That Require Automated Searches

The 1996 Amendments also purport to address the disputes that have arisen between agencies and requesters over whether agencies are required to conduct automated searches of their electronic records in order to respond to FOIA requests. When Congress amended FOIA in 1974, it noted that, "[w]ith respect to agency records maintained in computerized form," the agencies' obligation to search for records includes "services functionally analogous to searches for records that are maintained in conventional form."[63] FOIA, however, does not require agencies to create new records that do not exist.[64] Agencies occasionally maintained that they were not required to search for and retrieve information in an electronic database, or write the programming necessary to find and retrieve database entries that were responsive to a FOIA request, on the theory that such activities would involve the creation of new records.[65]

Although the 1996 Amendments resolve this issue in favor of requesters, they still leave unclear how far agencies must go. The Amendments define "search" as a "review, manually or by automated means, [of] agency rec-

---

61. In general, agencies are required to be able to transfer their most valuable records to ASCII or EBCDIC formats for transfer to the National Archives, but other format conversions are also possible, depending on the nature of the data. *See* 36 C.F.R. § 1228.188 (1997).

62. OFFICE OF INFO. AND PRIVACY, DEP'T OF JUSTICE, Amendment Implementation Questions, FOIA UPDATE, at 5 (Winter 1997) [hereinafter, Winter 1997 FOIA UPDATE] .

63. S. REP. NO. 93-854, at 12 (1974).

64. *See* Kissinger v. Reporters Comm. for Freedom of the Press, 445 U.S. 136, 152 n. 7 (1980) (holding that if existing information is not contained within format covered by FOIA, agency has no obligation to reformat information); Forsham v. Harris, 445 U.S. 169, 186 (1980) (noting that FOIA only obligates an agency to provide access to those records which it in fact has created and retained); NLRB v. Sears, Roebuck & Co., 421 U.S. 132 (1975) (holding FOIA does not compel agencies to write opinions in cases where they would otherwise not be required to do so).

65. *See* Grodsky, *supra* note 7, at 23-29; DEP'T OF JUSTICE REPORT, *supra* note 38, at 21-26 (describing agencies' reasons for maintaining they had no obligation to create programs to perform FOIA searches).

ords for the purpose of locating those records responsive to a request."[66] Thus, the use of computer codes or programming to locate and retrieve computerized records constitutes a "search" and is not the creation of records.[67] The Amendments also state that agencies must make "reasonable efforts to search for the records in electronic form or format."[68] No electronic search is required if "such efforts would significantly interfere with the operation of the agency's automated information system."[69] The statute does not define "reasonable efforts," however, and the legislative history does little more than restate the position set forth in the 1974 legislative history: "[a]n unreasonable effort would significantly interfere with the operations of the agency or the agency's use of its computers. Electronic searches should not result in any greater expenditure of agency resources than would have occurred with a conventional paper-based search for documents."[70]

The new provisions may require agencies searching for electronic records to write or modify programs in order to respond to FOIA requests. In a separate statement, Senator Leahy, the principal Senate sponsor of the Amendments, observed that the "search" requirement, "in tandem with the 'record' status of agency software, holds some potential for compelled software creation" and "[a]gencies should be required to search and retrieve data according to new specifications where such retrieval activity does not disrupt agency functions."[71] The Amendments leave to the agencies and the courts the difficult issue of determining how much programming an agency may be required to do to meet its obligation to conduct a reasonable search.

4. *FOIA's Application to Requests That Require Computerized Removal of Exempt Information.*

In recent years, agencies such as the Department of Defense and the Department of State have begun using computer technologies to redact exempt information from records before release. If information is redacted in this manner, however, it may be difficult or impossible for the requester to determine whether the agency withheld a few words or many pages of information. The Amendments aid requesters by requiring agencies to indicate deletions from the released portion of a record. Where technically fea-

---

66. 5 U.S.C. § 552(a)(3)(D) (Supp. II 1996).
67. *See* H. REP. No. 104-795, at 22 (1996).
68. 5 U.S.C. § 552(a)(3)(C) (Supp. II 1996).
69. *See id.*
70. H. REP. No. 104-795, at 22 (1996).
71. S. REP. No. 104-272, at 28 (1996).

sible, agencies must also indicate the deletion at the place on the record where the deletion was made, unless including that indication would harm an interest protected by an exemption pursuant to which the deletion was made.[72]

When an agency mixes information from electronic records containing material that is exempt from disclosure under one of FOIA's nine exemptions,[73] with nonexempt material, it is often possible to use computer technology to segregate the exempt from the nonexempt and create a record that can be released. Courts and agencies have reached different conclusions on whether, when records would otherwise be exempt because they contain some exempt data, an agency may be required to write programs to separate and release the nonexempt data.[74] Remarkably, the 1996 Amendments do not directly address this issue. The Amendments contemplate some computer redaction as part of the government's obligation to release "any reasonably segregable portion" of a record containing exempt and nonexempt information. Moreover, the statute's requirement that each agency "make reasonable efforts to maintain its records in forms or formats that are reproducible for purposes of this section," indicates that agencies have an obligation to design their databases to release records under FOIA.[75] The Amendments do not, however, explicitly address whether agencies may be required to create programs in order to segregate computerized data for release, and the legislative history shows that the Congress that enacted the 1996 Amendments was divided on the issue.[76]

---

72. 5 U.S.C. § 552(b) (Supp. II 1996).

73. *Id.* (delineating nine categories of FOIA exemptions).

74. *See* Yeager v. DEA, 678 F.2d, 315, 319-23 (D.C. Cir. 1982) (finding computerized segregation not required); Long v. IRS, 596 F.2d 362, 364-65 (9th Cir. 1979) (requiring computerized segregation). In a subsequent case, a divided panel of the Ninth Circuit concluded that editing strategies suggested by the requester to permit disclosure of records containing exempt information were so extensive that they amounted to the creation of new records. Long v. IRS, 825 F.2d 225, 229-30 (9th Cir. 1987); *see also* Grodsky, *supra* note 7, at 29-31 (discussing *Long* and *Yeager*); Graham, *supra* note 53, at 59-68 (arguing that FOIA should be amended to require some agency use of "avoidance disclosure" techniques); DEP'T OF JUSTICE REPORT *supra* note 38, at 27-34 (discussing agency positions and practice concerning use of computer technologies to remove exempt information).

75. 5 U.S.C. § 552(a)(3)(B) (Supp. II 1996).

76. *Compare* S. REP. NO. 104-272, at 18 (1996) ("Agencies are not required to aggregate, compact, or modify electronic data in order to release it to FOIA requesters in nonexempt form. Agencies may do so as a matter of administrative discretion, just as FOIA requesters may modify their requests in order to encompass only nonexempt data.") *with id.* at 28 (including additional views of Senator Leahy) ("Agencies should make use of the capability to redact exempt information through electronic means, including through the acquisition of software packages for those purposes, whenever it is more efficient to do so.").

5. Deference to Agencies on Technical Issues

Not all of the Amendments are favorable to requesters because Congress also mandated that courts give deference to agency conclusions on technical issues concerning the electronic records. If an agency refuses to make records available in a particular format on the grounds that it is not "readily reproducible" by the agency in that format, the Amendments provide that a court reviewing the agency's decision must accord substantial weight to the agency's assessment of the reproducibility of the requested form or format of records.[77] Similarly, if an agency fails to indicate the extent of the material redacted on the grounds that this is not "technically feasible," the Amendments mandate that the court defer to the agency's determination on this issue.[78]

Courts are already inclined to give agencies deference on these issues, and these provisions of the 1996 Amendments will reinforce this tendency. Despite the FOIA's mandate that courts subject agency determinations to *de novo* review, the courts have repeatedly stated that agency statements concerning their ability to locate and segregate records should be accepted provided they are sufficiently detailed and there is no countervailing evidence or indication of bad faith.[79] Judicial review of agency decisions concerning the reasonableness and technical feasibility of producing electronic records should proceed on the same basis. The directive that courts give weight to agency determinations does not require courts to accept the agency's conclusion on these issues as dispositive. It does not preclude FOIA plaintiffs from offering evidence to show that the agency's claims are inaccurate, nor does it foreclose discovery into the basis for the agency's conclusions.

C. Problems with Implementing the New Paradigm

The level of public access mandated by the 1996 Amendments, and the access that the public will actually experience will be quite different, at least for the immediate future. Historically, many agencies have failed to comply fully with FOIA's affirmative disclosure provisions.[80] The 1996

---

77. 5 U.S.C. § 552(a)(4)(B) (Supp. II 1996).

78. *Id.*

79. *See* Pollack v. Bureau of Prisons, 879 F.2d 406, 409 (8th Cir. 1989) (noting agencies will win summary judgment if properly discharging obligations under FOIA); Weisberg v. United States Dep't of Justice, 705 F.2d 1344, 1350-51 (D.C. Cir. 1983) (determining adequacy of FOIA search under reasonableness standard); Perry v. Block, 684 F.2d 121, 127 (D.C. Cir. 1982) (discussing standard for evaluating adequacy of agency affidavits describing search).

80. GENERAL ACCOUNTING OFFICE, FREEDOM OF INFORMATION ACT: NONCOMPLIANCE WITH AFFIRMATIVE DISCLOSURE PROVISIONS, REPORT NO. GAO/GGD-86-68 (Apr. 1986).

440   *ADMINISTRATIVE LAW REVIEW*   [50:2

Amendments' mandate that agencies use new technologies to meet these obligations complicates the compliance issues. Individual agencies have successfully implemented a number of projects for making more information available to the public on-line. But government-wide initiatives, requiring all agencies to provide more public information, have repeatedly fallen short of the promises made in the government's rhetoric, and have even fallen short of the minimum standards required by law.[81]

For example, in December 1994, the Office of Management and Budget (OMB) announced the establishment of a "Government Information Locator Service" (GILS) that was designed to provide an on-line, government-wide directory of agency information systems that would allow the public to locate information resources held by various government agencies.[82] In 1995, Congress imposed a statutory requirement on the Director of OMB to establish such a service, and directed that GILS "shall identify the major information systems, holdings, and information products of each agency."[83] Three years later, however, this mandate is far from fulfilled. Several agencies, including the DOJ and the Department of Transportation, have failed to provide information on their major information systems for GILS.[84] Many agencies have made only nominal efforts to comply by providing GILS entries that are woefully incomplete. Only a few agencies have taken the requirement seriously and provided meaningful entries for GILS.[85] Thus, while GILS is useful as a source of information about some agencies, it generally does not provide a meaningful resource for locating government records. The failure to comply with the statutory mandate to establish GILS has, in large part, been due to lack of leadership by the OMB.[86]

The implementation of the 1996 Amendments has already been marred by similar problems. Agency resistance to implementing the Amendments, delays in meeting statutory deadlines, and disagreements over the interpretation of the Amendments will frustrate the promise of the Amendments for

---

81. *See Potholes on the Information Bridge to the 21st Century*, GOV. INF. INSIDER, Summer/Fall 1996, at A-8 [hereinafter *Potholes*] (listing agencies still not in compliance with GILS mandate); Jennifer J. Henderson & Patrice McDermott, *Arming the People " ... with the power knowledge gives"; An OMB Watch Report on the Implementation of the 1996 "EFOIA" Amendments to the Freedom of Information Act* (Apr. 1998) (describing agencies failure to implement the requirements of the 1996 Amendments).

82. OMB Bulletin 95-01, "Establishment of Government Information Locator Service" (Dec. 4, 1994) [hereinafter OMB Bulletin]; *see* MOEN & MCCLURE, AN EVALUATION OF U.S. GILS IMPLEMENTATION, 9-16 (1997).

83. 44 U.S.C. § 3511(a)(1) (Supp. I 1996).

84. *See* MOEN & MCCLURE, *supra* note 82, at 61; *Potholes, supra* note 81, at A-8.

85. *See* MOEN & MCCLURE, *supra* note 82, at 58-63.

86. *See id.* at 66-67; *Potholes, supra* note 81, at 12-14.

some time to come. Indeed, a year after the Amendments were enacted, it is already apparent that some of the provisions that are most important to achieving the new paradigm described above are not being implemented. A number of issues have emerged as areas of dispute.

First, the Amendments require that agencies, by March 31, 1997, provide the public with reference materials containing an index of all the agencies' major information systems. These provisions appear to be among the most straightforward to implement. Most agencies, however, have not implemented this mandate, and the scope of this requirement is already in dispute.

For example, Congress anticipated that the finding aides that agencies are required to provide under the 1996 Amendments would "supplement" GILS.[87] The OMB has frustrated this objective, however, by equating the FOIA requirement with OMB's own limited definition of what GILS should include. The FOIA requires that agencies provide to the public "an index of all major information systems of the agency," and "a description of major information and record locator systems maintained by the agency." In April 1997, the OMB issued a memorandum instructing agencies that they can satisfy this requirement by establishing a GILS "presence" as described in OMB's 1994 Bulletin on GILS.[88] The 1994 OMB Bulletin, however, limited GILS to (i) automated agency information systems (specifically excluding electronic mail and word processing systems); and (ii) agency "information dissemination" products, such as publications and databases made available to the public on-line.[89] Records systems organized manually in paper and microfiche files are not included. OMB has never updated the 1994 Bulletin to comply with Congress's 1995 statutory mandate that GILS cover the "major information systems" of each agency.[90]

Consequently, even if an agency follows the 1994 OMB Bulletin, its GILS records will be inadequate as a guide to agency records that are available under the FOIA because the bulk of agency records systems, which are still kept manually, are excluded. Moreover, since most agencies did not even compile the limited directory contemplated by the 1994 OMB

---

87. H. REP. No. 104-795, at 30 (1996).

88. OMB Memorandum M-97-10 (Apr. 7, 1997). The OMB rescinded Memorandum M-97-10 on April 23, 1998 and replaced it with a new guidance stating that agencies' reference materials should include its GILS presence "as well as any other major information and record locator systems the agency has identified.." Franklin D. Raines, *Updated Guidance on Developing a Handbook for Individuals Seeking Access to Public Information*, Apr. 23, 1998 [hereinafter *Updated OMB Guidance*].

89. OMB Bulletin, *supra* note 82, at Attachment A, 2.

90. 44 U.S.C. § 3511(a)(1) (Supp. I 1996).

Bulletin, they are not prepared to comply with their obligation to make publicly available the more comprehensive index and description of agency records required by FOIA.

In addition, Congress expected that OMB would take steps to ensure that agency guides for requesting records follow a common format and use common terminology to describe record systems and locator systems.[91] OMB has not undertaken to do so and, instead, has simply instructed agencies that each guides' description of the "'[t]ypes and categories of available information will vary from agency to agency, and agencies should describe their information resources in whatever manner seems appropriate."[92] Thus, the agency guides mandated by Section 552(g) provide little information on agency information systems and vary widely in format, detail, and content.

A second area of dispute over implementation has arisen because the DOJ has urged agencies to construe the Amendments to limit the agency records that must be made available on-line. The 1996 Amendments provide that, by November 1, 1997, each agency shall make available by electronic means final opinions, statements of policy, administrative staff manuals, and copies of records that are likely to become the subject of subsequent requests if the records were "created on or after November 1, 1996."[93] This mandate will be particularly difficult to implement for those agency records that are likely to become subject to subsequent requests, but are not in electronic form. Records may not be in electronic form because they were submitted to the agency on paper, created within the agency on paper, or, even if created by the agency electronically, were retained only in hard copy.

The DOJ has responded to agency concerns about this provision by asserting that the obligation is limited to records created by the agency. Thus, the DOJ construes the language "created on or after November 1, 1996," as not merely a temporal limitation, but an implied limitation on *who* created the records. According to the DOJ, records that were not generated by the agency, "but rather were generated elsewhere and were merely obtained by them for one purpose or another ... are not 'created' by the agency and should not be regarded as subject to the new electronic availability requirement."[94]

---

91. H. Rep. No. 104-795, at 30.

92. *See* OMB Memorandum, *supra* note 88, at 2; *Updated OMB Guidance*, *supra* note 88 at 2.

93. 552 U.S.C. § 552(a)(2) (Supp. II 1997).

94. *See* Winter 1997 FOIA Update, *supra* note 62, at 5; Dep't of Defense Freedom of Information Act Program, Final Rule, 62 Fed. Reg. 35,357 (1997) (to be codified at 32 C.F.R. § 286.7(b)(4)(iv)) (providing that Department of Defense "[c]omponents have no obligation to

This construction of the statute is, to put it mildly, strained. The statute does not limit this provision to records created by the agency, nor does the legislative history suggest that Congress contemplated such a limitation. The only authority the DOJ cites for this construction is the passage in *United States Dep't of Justice v. Tax Analysts* in which the Supreme Court states that an agency must either create or obtain a record for it to become subject to the FOIA.[95] This decision, however, undermines the DOJ's interpretation; Congress was aware that FOIA applies equally to records created or obtained by an agency,[96] but did not indicate any intention to limit this particular provision to those records created by the agency.[97]

In addition, the DOJ's construction cannot be justified on the ground that this is one of those rare situations where it is necessary to ignore the literal language and read limitations into the statute in order to avoid an absurd construction or avoid frustrating legislative intent.[98] There is nothing unreasonable in applying the statute as it is written and concluding that Congress believed that, if records are likely to become subject to multiple requests, agencies must take the necessary steps to make the records available on-line. These steps should include converting paper records to electronic form regardless of whether the records were generated inside or outside the agency. After all, Congress explicitly mandated that when an agency is presented with a single request for records in electronic format, the agency is required to convert the records to electronic form if the records are readily reproducible in that format, even if the records were generated outside the agency.[99] Moreover, even under the DOJ's interpretation,

provide electronic or hard copy reading room access to any (a)(2) record, including FOIA-processed (a)(2) records, originating outside their respective organizations"); Postal Service Records and Information Management Definitions, 63 Fed. Reg. 6480 (1998) (arguing that Congress only intended for records created by agency to be subject to this requirement).

95. *See* United States Dep't of Justice v. Tax Analysts, 492 U.S. 136, 144 (1989)).

96. SEN. REP. NO. 104-272, at 19 (1996) (citing *Tax Analysts*, 492 U.S. 136 (1989), and observing that "[a]ny item containing information that is in the possession and control of an agency is usually considered to be an agency record under FOIA").

97. *See* United States Dep't of Justice v. Landano, 508 U.S. 165, 178 (1993) (noting that if Congress intended to create rule allowing FBI to treat all sources as confidential under FOIA, it should have done so more clearly).

98. *See* United States v. Ron Pair Enter., Inc., 489 U.S. 235, 242 (1989) ("The plain meaning of legislation should be conclusive, except in the 'rare cases [in which] the literal application of a statute will produce a result demonstrably at odds with the intentions of its drafters.'") (quoting *Griffin v. Oceanic Contractors, Inc.*, 458 U.S. 564, 571 (1982)); Public Citizen v. Department of Justice, 491 U.S. 440, 454-55 (1989) (stating that literal reading of statute will not be followed where it would compel an odd or absurd result that is inconsistent with congressional intent).

99. 5 U.S.C. § 552(a)(3)(B) (Supp. II 1996); *see* Winter 1997 FOIA UPDATE, *supra* note 62, at 5. (suggesting that when records exist only on paper and requester seeks to have them converted to electronic form, agency is required to do so unless it determines that it cannot

if records generated by an agency after November 1, 1996 are likely to become subject to multiple requests, the agency is required to convert the records to an electronic form even if the records were never, or are no longer, available to the agency in electronic form.

Another issue that seems almost certain to give rise to disputes is how much discretion agencies have in deciding which records must be made available in traditional and electronic reading rooms because they are likely to become the subject of repeated requests. The statute provides that this requirement applies to "copies of all records, regardless of form or format" that "because of the nature of their subject matter, the agency determines have become or are likely to become the subject of subsequent requests for substantially the same records."[100] The "have become" language in this provision appears to establish an objective standard under which agencies must place any records that have become the subject of two or more requests in their reading rooms. The government, however, has focused on the phrase "agency determines" and has suggested that decisions about which frequently requested records are covered are to be committed to the agency's discretion.[101] This approach is likely to lead to disputes because permitting agencies to selectively exclude repeatedly requested records from the reading room would limit access and invite abuses. Moreover, courts typically have not found that this type of language leaves the decision to the unreviewable discretion of the agency.[102]

---

readily do so with a reasonable amount of effort).

   100.   5 U.S.C. § 552(a)(2)(D) (Supp. II 1996).

   101.   *See* Winter 1997 FOIA UPDATE, *supra* note 62, at 4. The Department of Defense's (DOD) regulations interpret this requirement to mean that the DOD shall decide on a case-by-case basis whether records fall into this category. The factors to be considered in making this determination are:

   (A) previous experience of the DOD with similar records;

   (B) particular circumstances of the records involved, including their nature and the type of information contained in them;

   (C) the identity and number of requesters and whether there is widespread press, historic, or commercial interest in the records;

   This provision is intended for situations where public access in a timely manner is important, and it is not intended to apply where there may be a limited number of requests over a short period of time from a few requesters. DOD Components may remove the records from this access medium when the appropriate officials determine that access is no longer necessary.

62 Fed. Reg. 35,357 (1997) (to be codified at 32 C.F.R. § 286.7(b)(4)); *see* 63 Fed. Reg. 7311, 7312 (1998) (to be codified at 49 C.F.R. 701.4(c)) (providing that AMTRAK shall make determination on which records are frequently requested records on a case-by-case basis using similar list of factors).

   102.   *See* Lincoln v. Vigil, 508 U.S. 182, 190-93 (1993) (holding decision by Director of Indian Health Services to discontinue program giving aid to handicapped Indian children was not subject to judicial review under Administrative Procedure Act); Arent v. Shalala, 70 F.3d

A subsidiary issue exists concerning how a FOIA user would challenge an agency's decision not to make records available in its reading room materials. Recent decisions have held that the judicial review provision of FOIA only permits a court to require an agency to produce a record that has been improperly withheld.[103] Therefore, this provision does not authorize a court to require an agency to publish materials in the Federal Register or place materials in reading rooms.[104] These decisions dodged the question of whether judicial review of these agency actions is nonetheless available under the Administrative Procedure Act (APA). Judicial review should be available under the APA to require agencies to publish or make records available without a request where the agency's decision not to do so was arbitrary and capricious or based on an erroneous construction of the statute.[105]

Perhaps the most pervasive problem in implementing the 1996 Amendments is that the electronic reading room requirement is an unfunded mandate. Congress generally assumed that implementing the electronic access provisions would reduce the overall cost of complying with FOIA.[106] Even before the 1996 Amendments, some agencies initiated plans to reengineer their FOIA procedures to offer a majority of their records through public reading rooms and the Internet on the theory that such procedures are more efficient.[107] But Congress did not give any specific attention to the cost of the technology or staff needed to establish on-line reading rooms, and many agencies are understandably hesitant to divert resources to acquiring better computer telecommunications facilities to respond to FOIA requests. Without specific funds devoted to implementing this mandate, many agencies will be slow to establish the computer systems necessary to provide on-line access to FOIA records as contemplated by the 1996 Amendments. On the other hand, some agencies that have, on their own initiative, made

---

610, 614-15 (D.C. Cir. 1995) (asserting court's jurisdiction to review FDA determination concerning standards for measuring retailer compliance with Nutrition Labeling and Education Act of 1990s voluntary food labeling guidelines).

103. See Tax Analysts v. IRS, 117 F.3d 607, 610 (D.C. Cir. 1997) (concluding that FOIA does not authorize court to require agency to make policy statements available in reading room); Kennecott Utah Copper Corp. v. United States Dep't of the Interior, 88 F.3d 1191, 1202-03 (D.C. Cir. 1996) (holding FOIA does not authorize courts to require Federal Register publication of materials covered by 5 U.S.C. § 552(a)(1)).

104. Tax Analysts, 117 F.3d at 610.

105. Cf. Chrysler v. Brown, 441 U.S. 281, 292, 317-18 (1978) (stating that FOIA does not provide submitter of records with cause of action to challenge agency decision to disclose its records; however, APA provides cause of action for judicial review of whether agency decision violates substantive restrictions on disclosure).

106. H.R. Rep. No. 104-795, at 21 (1996); see Electronic Delivery, supra note 25, at 149.

107. See Gateway, supra note 4, at 22.

agency records available on-line have found that the cost of complying with the new electronic reading room requirement is minimal.[108]

The Amendments also suffer from a significant omission; they do not require agencies to expedite processing where there are numerous requests for the same records pending in the agencies' backlog. If agencies with significant backlogs do not expedite processing such requests, the purpose of the reading room requirement will be frustrated. For example, if there is widespread interest in Department of State records on a particular current event, the 1996 Amendments require that the records be made available to the public once the first request for these records is processed. But the first request for the records may not be processed for years because the State Department has a significant backlog and processes requests in the order that they are received.[109] Because of this backlog, reading room access to the records may be delayed for years.

As discussed below,[110] the Amendments require agencies to expedite media requests where there is "urgency to inform the public concerning actual or alleged federal government activity."[111] The Amendments do not require, however, agencies to expedite the processing of records that are subject to multiple, backlogged requests. Agencies are permitted to adopt regulations identifying other categories of requests that shall receive expedited processing.[112] Hopefully, some agencies will adopt regulations that expedite processing where there are numerous requests in order to reduce backlogs and place records that are in demand in their reading rooms promptly.

Finally, the 1996 Amendments fail to address the problem of where records must be made available. Several courts have held that if an agency makes records available in its reading room, it has no obligation to provide a requester with copies of the records, even if it is prohibitively costly or impossible for the requester to travel to the reading room to examine the records.[113] This rule imposes a substantial obstacle for requesters of lim-

---

108. *See* 63 Fed. Reg. 2873 (1998) (stating that NRC concludes that cost of improving its Internet site to provide electronic reading room is minimal).

109. *See* Rabin v. United States Dep't of State, 980 F. Supp. 116, 122 (E.D.N.Y. 1997) (describing how State Department follows first-in, first-out processing and has backlog of over 1,200 FOIA requests).

110. *See infra* note 133 and accompanying text (discussing agency requirements to provide expedited requests).

111. *Id.*

112. 5 U.S.C. § 552(a)(6)(E)(i)(II) (Supp. II 1996).

113. *See* Oglesby v. Department of the Army, 920 F.2d 57, 70 (D.C. Cir. 1990) (concluding that records made available in agency reading rooms need not be provided in response to request); *see also* Tax Analysts v. United States Dep't of Justice, 845 F.2d 1060, 1065 & n.10 (D.C. Cir. 1988), *aff'd* 492 U.S. 136, 150-51 (1989) (noting that agency may not be required to

ited means who may effectively be denied access to records because the agency has made them available only in a reading room in Washington, D.C. The subsequent request provisions of the 1996 Amendments add to the problem by requiring agencies to place the most frequently requested records in reading rooms.

The legislative history of the 1996 Amendments states that Congress believed that agencies should provide copies of records in response to requests, even if the records have been deposited in agency reading rooms because "not all individuals have access to computer networks or are near agency public reading rooms."[114] No language, however, was added to the statute to implement this view or reject prior decisions that suggest the contrary result. For the time being, it appears that the issue will be resolved in favor of requesters. The DOJ has advised agencies to abide by the legislative history and respond to FOIA requests for materials that have been placed in agency reading rooms or computer systems under the new provision concerning records subject to repeated requests.[115]

III. STRUGGLING WITH THE OLD PARADIGM

The 1996 Amendments continue the struggle to overcome the delays that have crippled the "request-and-wait" system for processing traditional FOIA requests. The seeds of the 1996 Amendments were planted in the 1974 Amendments to the FOIA and, in many ways, the 1996 Amendments simply repeat the 1974 debate without providing substantially better answers.

Reducing delay was one of the principal objectives of the 1974 Amendments to the FOIA.[116] The 1974 House Report on those Amendments noted that "excessive delay by the agency in its response is often tanta-

---

release material that it has previously published or made available under 5 U.S.C. § 552(a)(2)); Nolen v. Rumsfeld, 535 F.2d 890 (5th Cir. 1976) (stating that FOIA only requires that agency make records available, not that agency deliver records to requester); Chamberlain v. United States Dep't of Justice, 957 F. Supp. 292, 296 (D.D.C. 1997) (holding that FBI fully complied with FOIA by making records requested by prisoner available for inspection at agency's reading room, particularly where agency claimed that records could not be copied without damaging them).

114. 142 CONG. REC. S10,716 (1996).

115. *See* Winter 1997 FOIA UPDATE, *supra* note 62, at 3; 56 Fed. Reg. 24,133 (1991) (to be codified at 32 C.F.R. § 286.7(b)(4)(ii)) (describing that Department of Defense may process request for reading room materials but has no obligation to do so).

116. *See* 120 CONG. REC. 17,016 (1974) (statement of Sen. Kennedy) (discussing loopholes in FOIA); *see also* Eric J. Sinrod, *Freedom of Information Act Response Deadlines: Bridging the Gap Between Legislative Intent and Economic Reality*, 43 AM. U. L. REV. 325, 330-33 (1994) (presenting examples of specific harms experienced by requesters resulting from agency delay).

mount to denial. It is the intent of this bill that the affected agencies be required to respond to inquiries and administrative appeals within specified time limits."[117] Congress set a strict statutory deadline of ten working days for agencies to respond to FOIA requests and provided that a requester may bring suit to compel a response if the agency fails to meet the statutory deadline.[118] When a requester brings suit, an agency may be given additional time to complete its review if the government can show that "exceptional circumstances exist and that the agency is exercising due diligence in responding to the request."[119] The legislative history shows that Congress expected courts would grant additional time to agencies only in truly extraordinary situations — not merely when agencies process large volumes of requests or are "unable to regularly meet standard deadlines."[120] President Ford vetoed the 1974 Amendments, saying that the strict deadlines set by Congress were unrealistic.[121] Congress overrode the President's veto.[122]

Congress, however, ensured that the new deadlines were unrealistic by failing to provide agencies with the funding necessary to process FOIA requests promptly.[123] Agencies inundated with FOIA requests, and short on resources, were able to win in the courts the flexibility that Congress refused to give them when it passed the 1974 Amendments. In the seminal case, *Open America v. Watergate Special Prosecution Force,*[124] the court held that the "exceptional circumstances" requirement was satisfied where the agency had experienced an unforeseen 3,000% increase in FOIA requests in one year, which created a massive backlog due to insufficient resources to process requests in a timely manner.[125] *Open America*, however, was generally interpreted as holding that if an agency could show that it had a backlog of FOIA requests, the agency could invoke the "exceptional circumstances" language.[126] Courts would routinely give agencies with a

---

117.   H.R. REP. NO. 93-876, at 6 (1974), *reprinted in* 1974 U.S.C.C.A.N. 6267, 6271.

118.   5 U.S.C. § 552 (a)(6)(A)(i) (Supp. II 1996).

119.   5 U.S.C. § 552(a)(6)(C)(i).

120.   S. REP. NO. 93-854, at 26 (1974).

121.   *See* MESSAGE VETOING H.R. 12,471, H.R. DOC. NO. 93-383, at 2 (1974), *reprinted in* HOUSE COMM. ON GOV'T OP., *Freedom of Information Act and Amendments of 1974; see also* SOURCE BOOK: LEGISLATIVE HISTORY, TEXTS, AND OTHER DOCUMENTS, 94th Cong., 1st Sess. 485 (Joint Comm. Print 1975); O'REILLY, *supra* note 10, § 11.04.

122.   *See* O'REILLY, *supra* note 10, § 11.04.

123.   *See* Sinrod, *supra* note 116, at 334 (describing congressional consideration and subsequent rejection of agencies' request for additional funding).

124.   547 F.2d 605 (D.C. Cir. 1976).

125.   *See id.* at 616.

126.   Summers v. United States Dep't of Justice, 729 F. Supp. 1379 (D.D.C. 1989) (holding that although author seeking information was from FBI and was working under publisher's deadline, author's request for expedited treatment of FOIA requests was not justified); The Nation Magazine v. Department of State, 805 F. Supp. 68, 73 (D.D.C. 1992) (citing *Open America,*

backlog a lengthy, if not open-ended, extension of their obligation to respond — even if the agency's backlog was longstanding and expected because of the limited resources devoted to FOIA processing.[127]

In addition, *Open America* held that an agency may fulfill its obligation to exercise "due diligence" in processing its backlog of requests by responding to requests on a first-come, first-serve basis.[128] First-in, first-out processing frustrates requesters with simple requests because lengthy delays result when agencies must process previous requests that are complex and/or involve voluminous records. Such processing may also frustrate journalists and others seeking a prompt disclosure of records related to current news stories.[129] "Too often agencies realize that a delay in responding to a press request for records can often moot the story being investigated and will ultimately blunt the reporter's desire to utilize the provisions of the Act."[130]

The 1996 Amendments seek to address the chronic delays that have continued under FOIA, despite the 1974 Amendments, by doubling the previous ten-day limit for initial responses, inviting agencies to employ better management systems to process requests, placing pressure on agencies to reduce backlogs and encouraging requesters to limit the scope of their requests in exchange for faster processing.

A. *Expansion of Agency Response Time*

Agencies claimed that the 1974 Amendments' mandate that agencies respond to FOIA requests within ten working days was unrealistic. As a concession, Congress doubled this time period for the initial response to twenty working days. For many agencies this change will have no effect. The ten day deadline has long been meaningless at most agencies (the FBI and the State Department being the most notorious examples) because the agencies are chronically backlogged with FOIA requests.[131] About one third of the federal agencies have little or no backlog, however, and the new deadline may frustrate requesters submitting requests to these agencies

---

547 F.2d 605, and refusing to order expedition of FOIA request on presidential candidate); Sinrod, *supra* note 116, at 347-50 nn.139-49 (citing cases). *But see* Ray v. United States Dep't of Justice, 770 F. Supp. 1544, 1549-50 (S.D. Fla. 1990) (denying agency's request for stay); Hunter v. Christopher, 923 F. Supp. 5, 8 (D.D.C. 1996) (denying request for stay).

127. *See Nation Magazine*, 805 F. Supp. at 73-74; *Rabin v. United States Dep't of State*, 980 F. Supp. at 123.

128. *Open America*, 547 F.2d at 616.

129. *See Nation Magazine*, 805 F. Supp. at 75 (rejecting magazine's request for expedited access to federal documents concerning presidential candidate Ross Perot).

130. S. Rep. No. 93-584, at 23 (1974).

131. *See* Sinrod, *supra* note 116, at 334-39 (describing backlogs and delays at State Department, INS and FBI).

if the agencies elect to take the full twenty working days to respond.

B. Expedited Processing

The Amendments require agencies to promulgate regulations that will allow two categories of requesters to break-out of the first-in, first-out system and obtain an expedited response: (1) requesters who can show that failure to obtain the records on an expedited basis will pose an imminent threat to the life or physical safety of an individual;[132] and (2) requesters who are primarily engaged in the dissemination of information to the public, if they can show that their request involves matters on which there is an urgent need to inform the public concerning "actual or alleged Federal Government activity."[133] Agencies may also adopt regulations providing for expedited processing for other categories of requests.[134]

The first provision largely codifies an exception for expedited processing that had been suggested by the courts. *Open America* recognized that an agency could not adhere to a first-in, first-out processing procedure

---

132.   5 U.S.C. § 552(a)(6)(E)(v)(I) (Supp. II 1996).

133.   *Id.* § 552(a)(6)(E)(v)(II). Other provisions of the 1996 Amendments challenge judicial decisions that have suggested that the FOIA's sole purpose is to disclose records of federal government activities. For example, recent Supreme Court cases have considered whether certain FOIA exemptions authorize agencies to withhold records. The cases have held that private purposes are not relevant, and the only "relevant 'public interest in disclosure' to be weighed" is whether disclosure will contribute "significantly to public understanding *of the operations or activities of the government.*" Department of Defense v. Federal Labor Relations Auth., 510 U.S. 487, 495 (1994) (quoting *United States Justice Dep't v. Reporters Comm. for Freedom of the Press,* 489 U.S. 749, 775 (1989)) (emphasis in original). Some lower courts have gone even further by making statements such as "FOIA does not require disclosure ... of all government documents but permits access 'only to information that sheds light upon the government's performance of its duties.'" Audubon Soc'y v. United States Forest Serv., 104 F.3d 1201, 1203 (10th Cir. 1997) (quoting *Sheet Metal Workers' Local No. 9 v. United States Air Force,* 63 F.3d 994, 996 (10th Cir. 1995) (citing *Hale v. United States Dep't of Justice,* 973 F.2d 894, 898 (10th Cir. 1992)).

The 1996 Amendments state that the purpose of FOIA is to require federal agencies to make records available to the public, subject to statutory exemptions, "for *any* public or *private* purpose." Pub. L. No. 104-231, § 2(a)(1), 110 Stat. 3048 (1996) (emphasis added). The chief architect of the 1996 Amendments described this finding as a signal to the Supreme Court that its conclusion, that only relevant public interest is disclosure of government operations, is inconsistent with congressional intent "and distorts the broader import of the Act effectuating government openness." S. REP. NO. 104-272, at 26-27 (1996) (additional views of Sen. Leahy). Whether this finding will be sufficient to convince courts to consider interests other than disclosure of government activities when determining if certain exemptions apply is unclear. *See* Bibles v. Oregon Natural Desert Ass'n, 117 S. Ct. 795 (1997) (reaffirming statements in *Department of Defense v. Federal Labor Relations Auth.* concerning public interest to be weighed).

134.   5 U.S.C. § 552(a)(6)(E)(i)(II) (Supp. II 1996).

when presented with a request that was exceptionally urgent.[135] The 1996 Amendments, however, do not address whether agencies can be required to expedite requests for reasons other than the two grounds set forth in the statute,[136] or those set forth in agency regulations. For example, past decisions have held that agencies may be required to expedite processing where delay poses a threat to the requesters' due process rights.[137] The Departments of Justice and Defense have decided to continue this exception by regulation, but some agency regulations do not recognize such an exception.[138]

The Amendments also clarify that an urgent need to inform the public can be sufficiently compelling to justify expedited processing.[139] Previously the only special treatment explicitly accorded to the press under the FOIA was found in the statute's provisions on fees.[140] The 1996 Amendments on expedited processing now accord a special status to the press in processing requests. As with the fee provisions, the requester bears the burden of showing that his or her request meets the requirements for expedition. Unlike the fee provisions, however, the information supporting the request for expedition must be presented in a statement certified to be true

---

135.   547 F.2d at 615-16. *See* Exner v. FBI, 542 F.2d 1121, 1123 (9th Cir. 1976) (approving first-in, first-out processing).

136.   *See supra* note 132-33 and accompanying text (discussing expedited processing).

137.   *See, e.g.*, Aguilera v. FBI, 941 F. Supp. 144, 149 (D.D.C. 1996) (ordering FBI to put plaintiff's FOIA request ahead of others to prevent loss of due process rights in upcoming trial for attempted murder); Cleaver v. Kelley, 427 F. Supp. 80, 81 (D.D.C. 1976) (holding that there is exceptional and urgent need that justifies putting request ahead of others where requester seeks exculpatory materials for upcoming criminal trial); Mayock v. INS, 714 F. Supp. 1558, 1567-68 (N.D. Cal. 1989), *rev'd and remanded*, 938 F.2d 1006 (9th Cir. 1991) (granting priority to requests by aliens who have urgent need for information for pending deportation or exclusion proceedings).

138.   *See* 62 Fed. Reg. 45,187 (1997) (to be codified at 28 U.S.C. § 6.5(d)(iii)) (stating that Department of Justice will expedite processing whenever it is determined that it involves "[t]he loss of substantial due process rights"); 62 Fed. Reg. 35,354 (1997) (to be codified at 32 U.S.C. § 286.4(d)(3)(iii)) (stating DOD will expedite in cases involving "an imminent loss of substantial due process rights and humanitarian need"). *But see* 62 Fed. Reg. 46,192, 46,194 (noting Consumer Product Safety Commission regulations include only exemptions set forth in Amendments).

139.   *See* The Nation Magazine v. Department of State, 805 F. Supp. 68, 73-74 (D.D.C. 1992) (concluding that magazine's interest in obtaining release of records, concerning presidential candidates, before election, was insufficient to justify requiring agency to make exception to first-in, first-out processing).

140.   5 U.S.C. § 552(a)(4)(A)(ii)(II) (1994) (limiting fees to charges for duplication where records are not sought for commercial use and request is made by representative of news media or by educational or noncommercial scientific institution whose purpose is scholarly or scientific research).

and correct to the best of the requester's knowledge and belief.[141] Any challenge to an agency's decision to deny expedition will be limited to the record before the agency at the time it denied the request.[142] The agency will have ten days to rule on the request for expedited processing and must provide an expedited appeal.[143]

These expedited processing provisions certainly have symbolic significance, but their practical effect is likely to be limited. The Amendments do not require that requests that qualify for expedited processing be processed within a specific time limit, but simply state that the agency must process the request "as soon as practicable."[144] If the request for expedited processing is denied, or if expedited processing is nominally granted but the agency does not process the request in a timely manner, the requester may file suit to compel the agency to disclose the material.[145] Such a suit, however, would certainly be handicapped by the difficulty of determining what constitutes an "urgency to inform the public"[146] under the statute, and by the lack of any specific statutory deadline for disclosure.

Moreover, the Amendments provide that if, after the requester files suit, the agency provides a complete response to the request for records, the courts shall not have jurisdiction to review whether the agency improperly delayed processing the request.[147] Thus, if an agency is opposed to prompt disclosure of the records sought under a request for expedited processing, it can easily frustrate expedited access and, at least, stall disclosure. The agency can deny an unwelcome request for expedition by saying that it does not perceive any special "urgency to inform the public of actual or alleged federal government activity,"[148] or on other grounds, and hope that the requester will not pursue the matter. If the requester happens to have the resources and tenacity to file suit, the agency can release the records before the court adjudicates the merits and moot the case without incurring any substantial penalty.[149] As a result, it is likely that few challenges to agency decisions on expedited processing will go to judgment and, consequently, the development of standards on how these provisions should be applied will occur predominantly within the agencies, with little independent oversight from the courts.

---

141. 5 U.S.C. § 552(a)(6)(E)(vi) (Supp. II 1996).

142. *Id.* § 552(a)(6)(E)(iii).

143. *Id.* § 552(a)(6)(E)(ii)(I).

144. *Id.* § 552(a)(6)(E)(iii).

145. *See id.*

146. *Id.* § 552(a)(6)(E)(v)(II).

147. *See* 5 U.S.C. § 552(a)(6)(E)(iv) (Supp II. 1996).

148. *Id.* § 552(a)(6)(E)(v)(II).

149. The agency could still be subject to a claim for the attorneys' fees and costs incurred by the requester in bringing suit. *See* H. REP. NO. 104-795, at 25 (1996).

C. Multi-track Processing

The Amendments encourage, but do not require, agencies to promulgate regulations implementing multi-track processing systems, in which small and large requests are processed separately.[150] The Amendments state that agencies may provide requesters with the opportunity to limit the scope of their requests in order to qualify for processing under a faster track.[151] Even before the Amendments, however, agencies recognized that the law permitted them to implement such multi-track processing systems.[152] Thus, these provisions do nothing more than confirm that agencies have this option if they choose to exercise it.

The Amendments also state that an agency that institutes multi-track processing must exercise due diligence within each track, but do not spell-out what this means in practice.[153] It is unclear whether an agency must devote equal staff and resources to each track, or whether it is permissible for the agency to devote most of its resources to processing simple requests. It is also unclear whether the obligation to exercise "due diligence" will prevent agencies from classifying requests based on the content of records requested and deferring processing of records that the agency is not anxious to disclose.

D. Delays in Processing Ordinary Requests

The Amendments continue to permit an agency in "unusual circumstances" to extend for a maximum of ten working days the statutory time limit for responding to a FOIA request by sending the requester a written notice setting forth the reason for such extension.[154] To invoke this provision, the delay in processing the request must arise from the need to search for and collect requested records from multiple offices, the volume of records requested or the need for consultation among components of an agency.[155] Thus, if the agency is unable to process the request within twenty working days for one of these reasons, it may extend the period for responding to up to thirty working days simply by sending a notice.

---

150. *See* 5 U.S.C. § 552(a)(6)(D) (Supp. II 1996).

151. *See id.* § 552(a)(6)(D)(ii). However, if a requester seeks to circumvent the procedures discouraging large requests by submitting several requests involving "clearly related matters," the agency is permitted to aggregate the requests and treat them as a single, large request. *Id.* § 552(a)(6)(B)(iv).

152. Aguilera v. FBI, 941 F. Supp. 144, 149 n.10 (D.D.C. 1996) (describing FBI's two-tiered system for processing requests).

153. *See* 5 U.S.C. § 552(a)(6)(D)(iii) (Supp. II 1996).

154. *See* 5 U.S.C. § 552(a)(6)(B)(I) (1994 & Supp. II 1996).

155. *See* 5 U.S.C. § 552(a)(6)(B)(iii) (Supp. II 1996).

In practice, however, when agencies take an extension for these or other reasons, more than an extra ten days is usually necessary to respond. As in the past, if the agency does not respond by the statutory deadline, the requester may file suit against the agency to compel it to respond. But if the agency can show that "exceptional circumstances" justify its delay in processing the request, and that the agency is exercising "due diligence" in responding to the request, the court may stay the action to give the agency additional time to complete its review.[156]

The Amendments still do not define "exceptional circumstances," but do purport to limit the ability of agencies to rely on ordinary backlogs to meet this requirement. FOIA now provides that "exceptional circumstances" do not include a delay that results "from a predictable agency workload of requests unless the agency demonstrates reasonable progress in reducing its backlog of pending requests."[157] The legislative history indicates that under these criteria, "agencies with backlogs must make efforts to reduce that backlog before exceptional circumstances will be found to exist."[158] The legislative history, however, does not define what "efforts" are sufficient and suggests that a host of other grounds can still be used by agencies to justify delays in processing.[159]

The 1996 Amendments also introduce new requirements to place pressure on requesters to limit their requests by providing that, when the agency can not meet the twenty working day deadline, the agency shall give the requester an opportunity to limit the scope of the request so that the request may be processed within statutory time limits, or the requester may arrange with the agency an agreed upon time frame for processing the original request or a modified request.[160] If the agency and the requester are unable to reach an agreement on a time limit or modification of the request, the agency is still obligated to process the request with "due diligence," but the statute does not define what this means.

It is unlikely that requiring agencies to negotiate with FOIA requesters on narrowing the request under these conditions will be very useful to requesters. An agreement to limit a request can be beneficial to a requester if

---

156.   *See id.* § 552(a)(6)(C)(i).

157.   *Id.* § 552(a)(6)(C)(ii).

158.   142 CONG. REC. S10717 (daily ed. Sept. 17, 1996).

159.   The House Report states:

   Agencies may also make a showing of exceptional circumstances based on the amount of material classified, based on the size and complexity of other requests processed by the agency, based on the resources being devoted to the declassification of classified material of public interest, or based on the number of requests for records by courts or administrative tribunals.

H. REP. NO. 104-795, at 24-25 (1996).

160.   5 U.S.C. § 552(a)(6)(B)(ii) (Supp. II 1996).

it secures quicker access or more certainty concerning when the agency will respond, but it may also result in the requester receiving incomplete information. FOIA requesters are at a significant disadvantage in negotiating these matters because the agency alone will have the information necessary to determine how long it will really take to process a request and to determine whether limiting the request will prevent the requester from uncovering the information it seeks. The requester generally will have to accept the agency's representations on these matters.[161] Thus, these provisions of the Amendments will be of little utility in the situations where FOIA is most critical — namely, where the agency has an incentive not to facilitate prompt release of information that the requester seeks.[162]

Moreover, FOIA does not give the requester anything that he or she can use as leverage against the agency in this "negotiation." The requesters' principal alternative is to initiate a costly lawsuit that may take considerable time to resolve.[163] Indeed, the 1996 Amendments are likely to protract such litigation because agencies are now allowed to insist on litigating a new issue, namely whether the requester's failure to agree to modify his or her request was unreasonable.

The Amendments state that if the requester refuses to "reasonably" modify the scope of the request or arrange an alternative time frame for processing a request in response to a request by the agency, this refusal "shall be considered as a factor" in determining whether "exceptional cir-

---

161. *See* Grunewald, *supra* note 13, at 31 (noting that one problem in resolving FOIA disputes is that "the inherent imbalance in knowledge between the agency and the requester of the facts relevant to the resolution of the dispute generates distrust that can often be overcome only by placing the matter in the hands of a neutral decisionmaker"). Prior to the 1996 FOIA Amendments, agencies were permitted to share information with requesters about where information they seek was likely to be located and negotiate modification of requests. Some agencies even adopted regulations encouraging agency personnel to assist requesters in revising overbroad requests rather than simply rejecting them. *See* 5 C.F.R. § 2502.6(d) (1997); 29 C.F.R. § 70.19(c) (1997). To the extent that the 1996 Amendments encourage this practice, they will be constructive.

162. The Amendments require agencies to provide information that will be useful to requesters in such negotiations, as FOIA now compels each agency to: (i) annually report the number of days it takes the agency to process particular types of requests, the number of backlogged FOIA requests and the staff and funds devoted to processing FOIA requests; 5 U.S.C. § 552(e) (Supp. II 1996); and (ii) provide the public with an index and description of its major information systems. 5 U.S.C. § 552(g). These annual reports and indices, however, will only partially cure the disparity in information.

163. Data compiled by the Administrative Office of the United States Courts show that in fiscal years 1994 and 1995, the median time from filing to final disposition in FOIA actions was approximately eight months (232.6 days in FY 1995, 239.6 days in FY 1994). The average disposition time was approximately one year (367.6 days in FY 1995, 384.6 days in FY 1994). *See* Grunewald, *supra* note 13, at 7-9 (stating that median disposition time for FOIA cases in district courts from 1979-85 ranged from seven to nine months).

cumstances" justify the delay in processing and require a stay of the lawsuit.[164] The statute, however, does not provide any standards for evaluating the reasonableness of the requester's refusal to modify a request or agree to an alternative date for processing a request. Nor does the statute give any guidance on how this factor, or other factors, should be weighed in determining whether exceptional circumstances exist.[165] This portion of the statute is also remarkably one-sided because it does not address the failure of agencies to act reasonably in negotiating over processing deadlines or modification of the scope of a request. The Amendments do not impose any penalty, burden or adverse consequences on an agency if it fails to agree to process a request in a reasonable period of time, or if the agency makes unreasonable demands that the requester modify his or her requests.

More generally, it is unlikely that the 1996 Amendments' provisions on processing requests will be effective in eliminating the hurdles that requesters face when confronted with agency delay. The critical problem for FOIA requesters is that the statute provides no meaningful sanctions to deter unreasonable delay in processing requests.[166] The 1996 Amendments continue to provide none. Moreover, the Amendments do not give real teeth to the "exceptional circumstances" and "due diligence" standards. *Open America* itself indicates that agencies should not be able to use ordinary, predictable backlogs to justify delays, but courts and agencies have, nevertheless, construed the decision as permitting agencies to obtain a stay based on ordinary backlogs. The legislative history of the 1996 Amendments strongly condemns this reading of *Open America* and clearly sets forth Congress's opposition to judicial tolerance for delays based on backlogs.[167] The statute, however, still contains the same highly subjective and malleable standards. It permits agencies to invoke many factors in addition to backlogs as a justification for delay. The statute also leaves courts that are reluctant to second-guess agency resource allocation decisions with little guidance on how to reconcile FOIA's mandate for prompt responses

---

164. 5 U.S.C. § 552(a)(6)(C)(iii) (Supp. II 1996).

165. *See id.* The legislative history, however, indicates that failure to agree to modify a request should not be dispositive. As reported by the House Committee, the bill contained language stating that the requester's unreasonable refusal to agree to limit a request, or refusal to agree to a time frame, "shall be exceptional circumstances." H. REP. NO. 104-795, at 3-4 (1996). By the time the bill reached the floor, however, this language had been changed to provide that the requester's refusal should only be considered "a factor" in determining whether exceptional circumstances exist. 142 CONG. REC. H10448 (daily ed. Sept. 17, 1996).

166. *See* O'REILLY, *supra* note 10, at 7-20 (finding that since "Act's Sanctions Provision Passage, no effective sanctions have been imposed on anyone"); Grunewald, *supra* note 13, at 33 ("Because the agency position of nondisclosure prevails unless and until it is reversed, the burden of delay falls exclusively on the requester.").

167. S. REP. NO. 104-272, at 28-29 (1996).

with the many reasons that agencies offer for delay.

In addition, the statute does not make clear what remedy a court may or should impose if an agency's failure to respond to a plaintiff's FOIA request is based solely on delays caused by backlog, and the agency is unable to demonstrate "reasonable progress" in reducing the backlog. If the remedy is for the court to order the agency to respond immediately to the plaintiff's request, the systemic backlog problem will not be relieved. Moreover, significant equity issues are raised by the fact that many FOIA requesters cannot afford to bring a court action to compel a response.[168] On the other hand, the decisions following *Open America* make clear that courts are not willing to compel an agency to respond to FOIA requests within the statutory deadlines when the agency claims that it lacks sufficient resources to eliminate its backlog, particularly when the agency's records contain sensitive law enforcement or national security information.

CONCLUSION

The Electronic Freedom of Information Act Amendments of 1996 mark an important transition between the statute's past and future. Congress struggled with FOIA's past by, once again, trying to cure the delays that have crippled FOIA from its inception. Congress also tried to update FOIA for the future in light of the growing use of electronic records by federal agencies, and the ability of telecommunications technologies to provide access more quickly and efficiently.

The Amendments also mix modest tinkering and major revision. The provisions of the Amendments concerning delays in processing requests provide little that is new and are unlikely to be any more successful than Congress's prior effort to attack backlogs without providing additional funding. The provisions on the application of FOIA to electronic records largely ratify the conclusions that agencies and courts have reached in adapting the statute to new technologies. In contrast, the new provisions requiring agencies to provide the public with descriptions of their record systems and affirmatively disclose records without waiting for a request promise to fundamentally change how access is provided under the FOIA. For the first time, all federal agencies are required to make broad categories of agency records immediately available to the public at agency records

---

168. *See* The Nation Magazine v. Department of State, 805 F. Supp. 68, 74 (D.D.C. 1992) (upholding first-in, first-out approach to FOIA requests and noting potential abuse if wealthy plaintiffs' requests were ultimately processed faster than less wealthy persons not parties to such suits); Rabin v. United States Dep't of State, 980 F. Supp. 116, 122 (E.D.N.Y. 1997) (stating that absent exceptional circumstances, it would be unfair to let plaintiff jump ahead of other requesters in backlog).

depositories and on-line.

The success of these Amendments will depend on whether agencies embrace or resist this new paradigm, and whether requesters act shrewdly in taking advantage of the new directives. In order for these Amendments to be implemented, the government must make a broader commitment to devoting resources to providing information to the public than it has in the past. To fully take advantage of FOIA's updated approach to providing access, requesters will need to be more aware of what information is made available under FOIA and where to find it. For both agencies and requesters, Congress's decision to emphasize the use of new technologies and shift FOIA away from the traditional "request-and-wait" procedures will change the meaning of public access under FOIA.

[3]

EXPANDING THE PURPOSE OF FEDERAL RECORDS ACCESS: NEW PRIVATE ENTITLEMENT OR NEW THREAT TO PRIVACY?

JAMES T. O'REILLY[*]

TABLE OF CONTENTS

INTRODUCTION

Government agencies have collected private information for centuries. The 1966 Freedom of Information Act (FOIA)[1] encouraged federal agen-

---

   * Visiting Professor of Law, University of Cincinnati; Section Chair, ABA Section of Administrative Law & Regulatory Practice; B.A. Boston College; J.D. University of Virginia.

cies to release information about their activities to private requesters within the general public. Some of this requested information included submissions about private persons which was held within government files. The FOIA's original intent limited the public's access right to only those inquiries having a "public" purpose. As the case law surrounding the FOIA developed, courts developed a balancing test to determine whether a requester's actual purpose met this express "public purpose" standard. This test allowed the courts to screen out those who sought government information for purposes other than the core purpose of studying the activities of the government itself. It thereby diminished the public's access to otherwise private government information.

In 1996, Congress effectively overruled three decades of established FOIA case law. The Electronic Freedom of Information Act Amendments of 1996 (1996 Amendments or Amendments)[2] allow any person to access government information for any reason, with little exception. The Amendments legitimize public use of the FOIA to access even private information, without regard to the purpose or motivation underlying the request.

This Article examines the background of the 1996 changes and predicts some of its consequences for agencies, requesters, and the general public. The change to the FOIA's actual language was very minor and no direct legislative history on the subject exists. Even so, the effect of this change may be to compel federal agencies to become libraries for private research about, or private espionage against, millions of persons or entities that interact with those agencies. This Article concludes that private person access to other persons' information may have become a new entitlement[3] for the Information Age.

FOIA AND ITS AMENDMENTS

Historically, the federal Freedom of Information Act[4] has permitted the general public to oversee the work of government agencies. The statute enabled "any person" to file a request for public access to a federal agency's

---

1. Pub. L. No. 89-554, 80 Stat. 383 (1966) (codified as amended at 5 U.S.C. § 552 (1994 & Supp. II 1996)).

2. Pub. L. No. 104-231, 110 Stat. 3048 (1996) (codified at 5 U.S.C. § 552 (Supp. II 1996)).

3. The administrative law term "entitlement" is best described as a judicially protectable right arising out of a statutory benefit or privilege. The landmark entitlement case, *Goldberg v. Kelly*, 397 U.S. 254 (1970), attributed specific judicial protections to the processes by which agencies handle determinations of entitled rights.

4. 5 U.S.C. § 552 (1994 & Supp. II 1996).

records.[5] The record-holding agency could then opt either to release them or to invoke one of nine exemptions from required disclosure.[6] The agency's decision was reviewable *de novo* in federal district court.[7] Agencies and courts traditionally judged these records requests with an eye towards the public's interest in knowing "what their government [was] up to."[8]

In 1996, an obscure portion of a complex amendment to the FOIA[9] declared, without legislative history explanation,[10] a set of findings that the purposes of the amended FOIA include improvement of public access to agency records concerning non-governmental private matters. This "findings" clause of the FOIA's 1996 Amendments[11] further stated that the FOIA's purpose "is to require agencies ... to make certain agency information available ... for *any public or private purpose*."[12] The law previously had been silent regarding purposes and courts consistently had construed the FOIA's purpose as focusing on government actions alone. As a result of the 1996 Amendments, an agency's evaluation of a private requester's purpose or motive can no longer pejoratively contrast this private purpose with what had been the core purpose of the FOIA: access for a public purpose. Additionally, courts can no longer bar governmental disclosure on the basis of requesters' motives when balancing disclosure and privacy interests.

Prior case law up to and including three recent Supreme Court deci-

---

5. *Id.* § 552(a)(3).

6. *See id.* § 552(b)(1) (providing exemption for national defense and foreign policy secrets); *id.* § 552(b)(2) (providing exemption for agency internal personnel rules and practices); *id.* § 552(b)(3) (providing for statutory exemptions); *id.* § 552(b)(4) (providing exemption for trade secrets); *id.* § 552(b)(5) (providing exemption for inter-agency or intra-agency memorandums or letters); *id.* § 552(b)(6) (providing exemption for personal files of agency personnel, disclosure of which would constitute unwarranted invasion of personal privacy); *id.* § 552(b)(7) (providing limited exemption for law enforcement investigatory material); *id.* § 552(b)(8) (providing exemption for reports connected with agencies regulating financial institutions); *id.* § 552(b)(9) (providing exemption for geological and geophysical information).

7. *See id.* § 552(a)(4)(B).

8. *See* United States Dep't of Justice v. Reporters Comm. for Freedom of the Press, 489 U.S. 749, 773 (1989) (holding that disclosure of FBI rap sheet is prohibited on basis of personal privacy exemption outlined in 5 U.S.C. § 552(b)(7)(C)).

9. Electronic Freedom of Information Act Amendments of 1996, Pub. L. No. 104-231, 110 Stat. 3048 (codified at 5 U.S.C. § 552 (Supp. II 1996)).

10. *See* H.R. REP. NO. 104-795, at 19 (1996); S. REP. NO. 104-272, at 10 (1996) (restating text of statute without explanation).

11. *See* § 2, 110 Stat. at 3048.

12. *Id.* (emphasis added).

sions[13] held that the FOIA[14] provided public access to the workings of federal agencies for the public purpose of monitoring how government performed its functions, but not for any private purpose. The 1996 Amendments "effectively overrule" that case law, as a district court has observed subsequent to passage of the Amendments.[15]

I. THE CHANGED STATUTE

A. *The Importance of the 1996 Change*

This Article regards the 1996 change not only as a reformulation of statutory intentions, but also as a reflection of the *de facto* evolution of the FOIA's use in recent years. Once this new statutory disclosure purpose is widely accepted by agencies and courts, the FOIA's new role will have many implications for Internet communications and other electronic information sources. This will create a very different landscape of FOIA utilization in the coming years.

Prior to the 1996 Amendments, agencies could, and often did, deny requests for copies of government agency files concerning private persons in situations where the requester sought the data for his or her own private purposes.[16] Consequently, agencies that chose not to employ a liberal prodisclosure approach to criminal and privacy-related records often successfully defended their denials on the basis that the disclosure request did not serve a public interest.

For example, agency A regulates person B; B's adversary, C, requests

---

13. *See* Bibles v. Oregon Natural Desert Ass'n, 117 S. Ct. 795 (1997) (finding that asserted public interest of knowing with whom government chose to communicate was insufficient under FOIA to warrant disclosure); United States Dep't of Defense v. Federal Labor Relations Auth., 510 U.S. 487 (1994) (holding that only public interest is weighed when assessing whether disclosure of employee addresses violates Privacy Act); *Reporters Comm.*, 489 U.S. at 771-72 (providing general sentiments of agencies and courts that although public has right to know "what their government is up to," such right ends when information pertains to private citizens and reveals little about agency conduct).

14. 5 U.S.C. § 552 (1994 & Supp. II 1996).

15. Voinche v. FBI, 940 F. Supp. 323, 330 n.4 (D.D.C. 1996), *aff'd*, No. 96-5304, 1997 WL 411685 (D.C. Cir. June 19, 1997), *cert. denied*, 66 U.S.L.W. 3178 (U.S. Nov. 3, 1997) (No. 97-383).

16. *See* Thomas v. Office of United States Attorney, 928 F. Supp. 245, 251 (E.D.N.Y. 1996) (denying FOIA request under law enforcement records exemption, 5 U.S.C. § 552(b)(7)(C), for file of criminal investigation where requester, a convicted criminal, only sought information to use in collateral challenge to his conviction); United Techs. Corp. v. FAA, 102 F.3d 688 (2d Cir. 1996) (denying aircraft manufacturer's FOIA request under FOIA trade secrets exemption, 5 U.S.C. § 552(b)(4), for third parties' design drawings of replacement parts for manufacturer's engine).

the documents filed by B. Before the 1996 Amendments, agency A could have denied C's request in order to protect B's privacy. The FOIA allowed C to study the actions of agency A, but did not allow C to use agency A as a library for the study of private parties like B. Since the passage of the Amendments, this evaluation is no longer available to agencies.

This change in the FOIA's purposes therefore eliminates the balancing factor of honoring only the more pure-minded public purposes.[17] As a result, it expands the private person's ability to probe for private records in agency files.

At this point, it is important to note two significant caveats. First, the motive and purpose analysis plays a role in those FOIA cases which involve a balancing of competing interests.[18] Second, agencies have continued to exercise their discretion to waive an exemption claim and disclose whatever they wish, provided that no express barrier to disclosure exists in law. The 1996 Amendments did not impact several of the FOIA exemptions, such as those for classified military records[19] and bank examiners' records.[20] Likewise, prior court decisions[21] had not affected these same exemptions since the likelihood that a balancing of interests would occur in these cases was remote.

B. *"Any Person" Access*

A conceptual flaw in the original FOIA generated some confusion. The FOIA granted information access rights to "any person."[22] It also replaced a section of the Administrative Procedure Act of 1946 (APA)[23] that had limited access rights to persons "properly and directly concerned."[24] "Any

---

17. *See Voinche*, 940 F. Supp. 323, 330 & n.4 (D.D.C. 1996) (noting that 1996 FOIA amendments "effectively overrule" *United States Dep't of Justice v. Reporters Comm. for Freedom of the Press*, 489 U.S. 749 (1989), which had "sharply limited the concept of 'public interest' under the FOIA to the core purpose for which it [had been] enacted: 'to shed [ ] light on an agency's performance of its statutory duties'").

18. *See* 5 U.S.C. §§ 552(b)(6), 552(b)(7)(C) (exemptions directly involving privacy of individuals).

19. *See id.* § 552(b)(1) (1994 & Supp. II 1996).

20. *See id.* § 552(b)(8).

21. *See* Bibles v. Oregon Natural Desert Ass'n, 117 S. Ct. 795 (1997); United States Dep't of Defense v. Federal Labor Relations Auth., 510 U.S. 487 (1994); *Reporters Comm.*, 489 U.S. 749, 771 (1989).

22. 5 U.S.C. § 552(a)(3)(A).

23. Pub. L. No. 79-404, 60 Stat. 237 (1946) (codified as amended at 5 U.S.C. § 551 (1994)).

24. *Id.* sec. 3(c), 60 Stat. at 238. This was the original 1946 APA's only concession to public access, codified prior to the FOIA as 5 U.S.C. § 1002. It was repealed by the 1966 FOIA. *See* 1 JAMES T. O'REILLY, FEDERAL INFORMATION DISCLOSURE §§ 2.02-.04 (2d ed.

person" access in the FOIA,[25] however, was further conditioned by exemptions which allowed withholding of some records.[26] In several situations, these exemptions required the agency and court to balance competing interests in privacy and disclosure.[27] Agencies and courts granted access to "proper" purpose requesters under these exemption balancing tests, while denying access to lesser requesters. Most frequently, this meant that agencies and courts could deny the commercially-motivated requester,[28] the prisoner seeking revenge,[29] or the curious bystander a federal record request under the exemptions to the FOIA. Access denial to those with merely venal, private motivations was based on the judicial interpretation that the purposes of the Act were to inform citizens about their government's workings, not to serve private purposes.[30] The 1996 Amendments altered this theory and invalidated those denial premises.[31]

C. *Changing the Focus*

The effect of the 1996 legislative "purposes" statement[32] is to turn the FOIA from a window for oversight of the actions of government into a library of resources about others. In this scenario, the government serves as data collector, assembler and intermediary. The previous version of the FOIA had instructed government agencies to disclose information about their own actions; now the FOIA instructs agencies to disseminate information about others.

Although the purpose is new, the conflict that inevitably results is not

---

1990 & Supp. 1997) [hereinafter O'REILLY] (discussing development of FOIA in 1950s and 60s).

25. 5 U.S.C. § 552(a)(3) (1994), *amended by* 5 U.S.C. § 552 (Supp. II 1996). *See* O'REILLY, *supra* note 24, § 4.06 (discussing "any person" access to information under FOIA).

26. *See* 5 U.S.C. § 552(b).

27. *See id.* §§ (b)(6), (b)(7)(C).

28. *See* United Techs. Corp. v. FAA, 102 F.3d 688 (2d Cir. 1996) (denying aircraft manufacturer's FOIA request under FOIA trade secrets exemption, 5 U.S.C. § 552(b)(4), for third parties' design drawings of replacement parts for manufacturer's engine).

29. *See Thomas*, 928 F. Supp. at 251 (denying FOIA request under law enforcement records exemption, 5 U.S.C. § 552(b)(7)(C), for file of criminal investigation where requester, a convicted criminal, only sought information to use in collateral challenge to his conviction).

30. *See* United States Dep't of Justice v. Reporters Comm. for Freedom of the Press, 489 U.S. 749, 773 (1989) (holding that purpose of FOIA is to disclose "information that sheds light on an agency's performance of its statutory duties").

31. The purpose of FOIA "is to require agencies ... to make certain agency information available ... for *any public or private purpose* ...." Pub. L. No. 104-231, sec. 2, 110 Stat. 3048 (1996) (codified at 5 U.S.C. § 552 (Supp. II 1996)) (emphasis added).

32. *See id.*

new. The FOIA's utility for private-versus-private conflicts has been observed for many years. For example, a dispute between a vehicle manufacturer and a local advocacy group concerning private labor hiring led to the Supreme Court's *Chrysler Corp. v. Brown*[33] decision in 1979. This decision legitimized the so-called "reverse-FOIA" litigation as a means to protect privacy interests of the data submitters.

D. Press Advocacy

The press rightly can claim credit both for the FOIA's passage and for its requirement that government agencies make access available to any private citizen, not merely a journalist or other person "properly and directly concerned" with the records.[34] The press was among the earliest users of the FOIA, but it soon grew tired of battling the bureaucracy over terms of exemptions from disclosure.[35] The majority of today's news stories about federal agency-related activities continue to arise from sources other than press requests for FOIA documents.[36] One could argue that the FOIA has led to the systematized "leaking" of agency documents to advocacy groups. These groups in turn have disseminated information to the press and the incremental benefit has aided the public. The more formal FOIA release of documents to the press operates this accountability mechanism, which is more rational than the traditional Washington "leak" of information to journalists by anonymous but "well-informed" sources.

E. Catching Up with Case Law

The change in the FOIA's purposes is perhaps a congressional reflection of what the FOIA had become — *de facto*. As mentioned briefly above, the FOIA's parentage aimed entirely at government activity. The FOIA's press sponsors were eager to attack secrecy in government operations. The political concessions of the Kennedy and Johnson administrations[37] inter-

---

33. 441 U.S. 281 (1979).

34. *See supra* notes 22-31 and accompanying text (discussing "any person" aspect of FOIA laws). The Administrative Procedure Act of 1946 contained the "properly and directly concerned" requirement. This selective dissemination barred the news media from access, so newspaper editors mounted a decade-long campaign. *See* O'REILLY, *supra* note 24, § 2.02 (discussing newspaper editors' campaign). The "any person access" language of the Freedom of Information Act of 1966 replaced the APA's language. The press considered but did not pursue a media-limited access provision in the FOIA's original draft. *See id.* §§ 2.02-04, 4.06 (discussing development of FOIA).

35. *See* O'Reilly, *supra* note 24 (noting that FOIA does not serve sufficiently press's need for timely information).

36. *See id.* § 3.02 (noting press's infrequent use of FOIA).

37. *See id.* §§ 2.06, 3.01.

sected with a common understanding that the FOIA would not reveal the actions of private persons in government, except as an adjunct to the mission of better agency accountability.[38]

By the mid-1970s, the FOIA had evolved from an accountability device for agency activity into a research tool for data about private persons. Early requesters typically included persons claiming that the agency had operated on secret policies,[39] had failed to adequately enforce a law against private persons, or had improperly preferred one contract offeror over another.[40] The agencies and the Justice Department had a vision that courts accepted: the "core purpose" of the FOIA was disclosure of government activities vis-a-vis the private regulated person. This purpose did not include the unrestricted public access to all of the government's information about private individuals.[41] The inclusion of the nine statutory exemptions[42] implicitly recognized this distinction. In particular, the sixth and a portion of the seventh exemptions required balancing of privacy interests.[43] The fourth exemption, regarding confidential business data, assumed that the FOIA disclosure process would have little effect on private persons' submissions of valuable data.[44]

II. THE "CORE PURPOSE" DEBATE

A. *Core Purpose and the* Reporters Committee *Case*

In 1989, the Supreme Court examined the balancing of public and private interests in a FOIA case involving the alleged criminal activities of Charles Medico.[45] Although Federal Bureau of Investigation (FBI) files contained Medico's arrest record, he retained some privacy interests. The Court balanced Medico's interests against the countervailing interests in

---

38. *See id.* §§ 2.01-.03.

39. *See* NLRB v. Sears Roebuck & Co., 421 U.S. 132, 137-38 (1975) (deciding whether disclosure was necessary to fulfill FOIA's purpose of avoiding the development of "secret law"). *See also* Vaughn v. Rosen, 523 F.2d 1136, 1140-43 (D.C. Cir. 1975) (reiterating view that FOIA exemption listed at 5 U.S.C. § 552(b)(2) protects from disclosure only routine "housekeeping matters" in which public presumably has no interest).

40. National Parks & Conservation Ass'n v. Morton, 498 F.2d 765 (D.C. Cir. 1974).

41. United States Dep't of Justice v. Reporters Comm. for Freedom of the Press, 489 U.S. 749, 774-75 (1989).

42. *See* 5 U.S.C. § 552(b)(1)-(9) (1994), *amended by* 5 U.S.C. § 552 (Supp. II 1996); *see also supra* note 6.

43. *See id.* §§ 552(b)(6), (b)(7)(C).

44. *See id.* § 552(b)(4).

45. *Reporters Comm.*, 489 U.S. at 762-63.

FEDERAL RECORDS ACCESS

FOIA disclosure.[46] The Court was persuaded by several provisions of the FOIA where Congress had expressed the "core purpose" of the statute as "contribut[ing] significantly to public understanding *of the operations or activities of the government.*"[47]

The Court held that the release of Medico's records would not serve this "core purpose" of public access for increased public understanding; "the public interest in the release of any rap sheet on Medico that may exist is not the type of interest protected by the FOIA."[48] Instead, the Court found that the FOIA served the people by "permitt[ing them] to know what their government is up to."[49]

While this finding is consistent with the Court's earlier examination of balancing interests,[50] *Reporters Committee* represents the first time the Court articulated the "core purposes" analysis. As a result, balancing became a judicial test of weighing the requester's motives, where the motives include such elements as identification of any agency misconduct, the requester's nonprofit status, the requester's relationships with news media, and the like. All of these factors contradict the FOIA's universal access principle of "mak[ing] the records promptly available to any person."[51]

B. Core Purpose and the FLRA Case

The Supreme Court subsequently examined the balancing of federal employee privacy rights against the public's disclosure right in *United States Department of Defense v. Federal Labor Relations Authority.*[52] In this case, the Court quoted from *Reporters Committee* and confirmed its "core purpose" analysis. At the same time, the *FLRA* Court balanced the purposes of the FOIA and ruled against the interest of the labor union requester.[53] Stating that the *Reporters Committee* precedent could be "easily" applied in this situation, the *FLRA* Court found that only a negligible public interest existed in the dissemination of federal employees' home addresses.[54] As disclosure would not open agency action to the light of public

---

46. *See id.* at 775.

47. *See id.* (quoting 5 U.S.C. § 552(a)(4) (1994) (emphasis in original)).

48. *Id.* at 775.

49. *Id.* at 773 (quoting Henry Steele Commager, *The New York Review of Books*, Oct. 5, 1972 at 7) (stating observation about government secrecy).

50. Department of Air Force v. Rose, 425 U.S. 352, 371-75 (1976) (noting that Congress's intention behind FOIA exemptions was to balance privacy of individuals against opening agency action to public scrutiny).

51. 5 U.S.C. §§ 552(a)(3) (1994 & Supp. II 1996).

52. 510 U.S. 487 (1994).

53. *See Federal Labor Relations Auth.*, 510 U.S. 487 at 495-502 (1994).

54. *See id.* at 497-98.

scrutiny in any meaningful way, the *FLRA* majority denied disclosure of the addresses,[55] despite criticism in Justice Ginsburg's concurrence that *Reporters Committee*'s core purpose approach had adversely "changed the FOIA calculus that underlies" the disclosure analysis.[56]

After the *FLRA* opinion, a 1997 short per curiam opinion again cited the public purpose of the FOIA in a reversal of a Ninth Circuit opinion.[57] The Ninth Circuit had held that disclosure of the Bureau of Land Management's mailing list was not forbidden under the FOIA's terms.[58] Instead, providing such information was in keeping with the public's interest in "knowing to whom the government [was] directing information."[59] In its opinion, the Supreme Court observed that the purpose for which a FOIA request is made has "no bearing on whether information must be disclosed under the FOIA."[60] Instead, the public's interest relates only to the degree to which disclosure would reveal an agency's direction of its statutory duties or inform the public of the government's activities.[61] Lower courts followed this direction, and therefore looked for a public purpose that would warrant disclosure.[62]

C. Adoption of the Core Purpose Test

Government interpretations of the core purpose test recognized the value of the "not for public purposes" defense available to agencies that opted to protect the secrecy of files. The Justice Department has liberally construed the Supreme Court's interpretation of the core purpose test[63] and, not surprisingly, has often asserted the absence of congruence between requesters' needs and numerous circuit[64] and district court[65] interpretations of the

---

55. *See id.* at 500-02.

56. *Id.* at 505-07 (Ginsburg, J., concurring) (stating *"Reporters Committee* 'core purpose' limitation is not found in FOIA's language").

57. Bibles v. Oregon Natural Desert Ass'n, 117 S. Ct. 795, 796 (1997) (per curiam).

58. Bibles v. Oregon Natural Desert Ass'n, 83 F.3d 1168 (9th Cir. 1996), *rev'd*, 117 S. Ct. 795 (1997).

59. *Id.* at 1171.

60. *Bibles*, 117 S. Ct. at 795-96.

61. *Id.* at 795 (citing *Reporters Comm.*, 489 U.S. 749, 773 (1989)).

62. *See, e.g.*, Bartholdi Cable Co. v. FCC, 114 F.3d 274, 282 (D.C. Cir. 1997); *In Re* Sealed Case, 1997 U.S. App. LEXIS 14521 (D.C. Cir. 1997); Wichlacz v. United States Dep't of Interior, 983 F. Supp. 325, 333 (E.D. Va. 1997), *aff'd*, 114 F.3d 1178 (4th Cir. 1997) (unpublished per curiam decision) (unpublished table decision).

63. *See* United States Dep't of Justice, Freedom of Information Act Guide & Privacy Act Overview 326 (1997) [hereinafter FOIA Guide].

64. *See* Massey v. FBI, 3 F.3d 620 (2d Cir. 1993).

65. *See* Thomas v. Office of U.S. Attorney, 928 F. Supp. 245, 250 (E.D.N.Y. 1996); Andrews v. United States Dep't of Justice, 769 F. Supp. 314, 316 (E.D. Mo. 1991).

FOIA's core purpose.[66] The official policy explications of the FOIA exemptions, issued annually by the Department of Justice's Office of Information and Privacy, emphasize to government agencies the value of asserting the "core purpose" defense against private requesters' desire for access to records about other private persons.[67]

D. Basis for Congressional Reversal

FOIA scholars have extensively criticized using the core purpose approach as a basis for denying FOIA requests.[68] The FOIA purposes are not debated in every FOIA case, but they become important in cases where an agency has and/or may exercise discretion for or against disclosure.[69]

The effect of the Supreme Court decisions[70] was to inhibit the degree of disclosure that advocates of FOIA reform preferred. Efforts to change the FOIA in this respect were not very visible. In 1996, the reform advocates successfully secured a change in a slightly-noticed FOIA amendment with no legislative history.[71] As a result of these efforts, agencies can no longer deny FOIA requests simply because such requests are based on private purposes. If this is the future trend of judicial interpretations, as is likely now that the purposes of the FOIA have been expressly broadened, the Amendments will have several major effects.

III. EFFECTS OF THE CHANGE

A. The Library Function

Disclosing requested information that promotes the government's accountability for its activities is not the equivalent of providing a library function for the general public, with research access to agency files concerning private submitters of information. The *Reporters Committee* standard[72] held steadfast to the FOIA's original purpose, the "core purpose" of

---

66. *See* FOIA Guide, *supra* note 63, at 326-27.

67. *See id.* at 326.

68. *See* Harry Hammitt, *FOIA: Limited by Core Principles?* 20 ACCESS REP. No. 5 at 3 (Mar. 2, 1994); O'REILLY, *supra* note 24, § 9.12.

69. *See* 5 U.S.C. §§ 552(b)(6), (b)(7)(C) (1994 & Supp. II 1996). *See also* United States Dep't of Defense v. FLRA, 510 U.S. 487 (1994) (discussing "unwarranted" invasion of personal privacy).

70. *See generally FLRA*, 510 U.S. 487; United States Dep't of Justice v. Reporters Comm. for Freedom of the Press, 489 U.S. 749 (1989); Department of Air Force v. Rose, 425 U.S. 352 (1976).

71. *See supra* note 10 and accompanying text.

72. *See Reporters Comm.*, 489 U.S. at 775 (1989) (finding that "Congress has once

promoting government accountability. The eventual effect of the new private-purpose entitlement may be to partially convert the agencies' statutory mission from one of enforcing action subject to accountability, into one of brokering information to requesters in the general public.[73]

Agencies screen incoming information, acting on the portions that suggest a problem and storing the remainder. Consider the taxpayer's view: a public that pays tax dollars for the regulation of widgets will readily allow a portion of those dollars to be spent on the oversight and accountability roles that the FOIA facilitates. Therefore, the taxpayers would ask: are widgets being adequately controlled? Are sufficient standards in place? Do inspectors catch the bad widget makers and prosecute them? Do the agency files reveal misconduct or malfeasance of the regulators? From this perspective, the FOIA is not a primary agency function, information is a raw material, and agency output is based on regulatory or benefit decisions. Apart from the National Archives and the Government Printing Office, the dissemination of vast amounts of privately-submitted data is not a normal function of traditional regulatory and benefit-awarding agencies.[74]

The 1996 Amendments approach the use and dissemination of information from a different perspective. Taxpayer funds now support a library function to and from which those taxpayers interested in the production of U.S. widgets can make requests for information about widgets, obtain widget data of all types, and compete more aggressively with the U.S. widgetmakers. Taxpayers interested in tort suits against the widget maker can identify witnesses or class plaintiffs' identities from submissions made by the regulated firms. As part of the next logical step, the widget maker would be compelled to record, collect and transmit to the controlling agency data that the agency does *not* intend to act upon. This information then becomes grist for the disclosure mill, with the agency acting as a conduit rather than as an accountable actor. As a result, such agency-released data will feed private actions with private motivations, such as civil litigation, contractor competition, nuisance claims, etc. Apart from the potential involvement of the Paperwork Reduction Act,[75] there is no barrier to an agency setting up a private data collection system which enables data to

---

again expressed the core purpose of the FOIA as 'contribu[ting] significantly to the public understanding *of the operations or activities of the government*'") (emphasis in original).

73. *See* O'REILLY, *supra* note 24, §§ 2.06A, 17.15A (noting how 1996 "private purpose" Amendments have adversely affected Supreme Court's prior "core values" approach and have allowed private actors access to agencies' private data solely for commercial use).

74. *See id.* § 2.06A (citing Durham v. United States Dep't of Justice, 829 F. Supp. 428, 433 (D.D.C. 1993)).

75. 44 U.S.C. § 3501, paras. 1-3, 5-6, 10 (1994 & Supp. I 1995) (requiring agencies to limit demands for information from private requesters, subject to exceptions and conditions).

flow directly into the agency's library of accessible information.

B. The Change and Law Enforcement

As the 1996 Amendments reversed the *Reporters Committee* decision,[76] the motive of the record requester is no longer determinative of its rights of access.[77] The majority of law enforcement cases, however, have been determined without regard to the requester's motives.[78] The great majority of FOIA cases for federal law enforcement agencies have involved confidential informants or disclosures that could potentially disrupt the prosecution of the enforcement case.[79] These cases are not affected by a balancing-of-interests analysis.[80]

The most visible effect of the 1996 Amendments in law enforcement cases will arise when agencies oppose the identification of a person named in an investigatory file that is no longer an active pre-prosecution document. In such a case, the agency may still invoke the privacy protection exemption to avoid diminishing the privacy interests of the named individual, but at a greater effort, since the previously available argument assailing a requester's purpose has been removed. Lists of antitrust investigators' potential witnesses, for example, would be very helpful to a commercial litigator attacking a merger. The agency cannot tilt the balancing test against a private requester on the basis that the requester's purpose is to examine the individual's acts, not purely the actions or misdeeds of the en-

---

76. *See* 2 O'REILLY, *supra* note 24, § 17.15 (describing how 1996 FOIA Amendment's have obliterated rule of *Reporters Comm.*, 489 U.S. 749 (1989) (requiring that plaintiff's request serve public interest before court would order agency disclosure)).

77. *See supra* notes 45-51 and accompanying text.

78. *See* NLRB v. Robbins Tire & Rubber Co., 437 U.S. 214 (1978) (holding that witness statements which NLRB intended to use at hearing on unfair labor practices were exempt from disclosure because such disclosure could have proven detrimental to NLRB enforcement actions); Davin v. FBI, 60 F.3d 1043 (3d Cir. 1995) (holding that government-submitted Vaughn index did not include specific factual recitation linking materials in question with claimed FOIA exceptions).

79. A statistical analysis of the exemption cases indicates that more cases involved interference with prosecution, *see* 5 U.S.C. § 552(b)(7)(A) (1994 & Supp. II 1996), and protection of confidential sources, *see id.* § (b)(7)(D), though the reported judicial decisions concerning law enforcement/personal privacy conflicts are also substantial. UNITED STATES DEP'T OF JUSTICE, FREEDOM OF INFORMATION CASE LIST 458-9 (Sept. 1996).

80. *See, e.g.*, Cleary v. FBI, 811 F.2d 421 (8th Cir. 1987) (finding FBI investigatory files exempt from disclosure despite fact that plaintiff already knew identities of FBI sources, since identities of FBI agents and interviewees were privileged under FOIA's unwarranted invasion of personal privacy exemption); Cucci v. DEA, 871 F. Supp. 508 (D.D.C. 1994) (holding that DEA and Customs Service were exempt under FOIA from disclosing requested documents since disclosure would constitute unwarranted invasion of personal privacy rights of law enforcement agents and support personnel).

forcement agency. A court would presumably view the disclosure request for a private purpose with merit equal to a "public" purpose request. Therefore, as a court would presumably order the same record to be released to another person claiming agency fraud or misfeasance, it likely would do the same for a private purpose request.

C. The Change and Personal Privacy Files

The FOIA exemption for identifiable individual privacy interests[81] requires a court to balance the individual privacy rights of the person named in the file against the public's interest in disclosure.[82] Prior to the 1996 Amendments, balancing had been a part of every litigated case involving this exemption. Therefore, agencies frequently included the "core purpose" test in their analyses.[83] The Amendments favor disclosure for a private purpose by removing the existing presumption that a FOIA requester must seek a record for a public purpose.[84]

Consider the following examples of private purpose requests. A competitor for a high federal appointment may submit a FOIA request for the resumes and financial statements of other successful applicants. If the controlling agency withholds the release of such information, claiming an exemption, and the withholding is litigated, the courts would force the agency to disclose the requested information under the 1996 Amendments. This would be true in spite of the fact that the requester is a very interested competitor for the same job as the subjects of the request. Likewise, that the requestor does not wish to investigate any agency misconduct makes no difference since the 1996 Amendments. Another example may be where a requester wants to sell services to persons on an agency information list. The 1996 Amendments have legitimized this as a basis for requesting access to an agency's records. The result is the same in either case: diminished protection for personal data within federal government agency files.

D. Commercial Research

The FOIA's slowly-recognized value as an intelligence-gathering device has spawned a variety of intermediaries, including law firms and FOIA-specific search bureaus created by law firms as a sideline business. The commercial customers of these firms have used the FOIA for their private purposes — to spy on competing vendors, manufacturers, importers, etc. So long as agencies did not apply the core values analysis to bar their pri-

---

81. 5 U.S.C. § 552(b)(6) (1994 & Supp. II 1996).
82. *See generally* 2 O'REILLY, *supra* note 24, § 16.
83. *See id.*
84. *See id.* § 17.15A.

vate fishing expeditions, the commercial FOIA enterprises were quite well off.

The change to the FOIA's purpose renders disclosure of this sort more likely. Ironically, these service organizations might become less necessary as the need to shield the requester's identity goes away. Since the 1996 Amendments, the competitive or adversarial requestor need not fear that an agency would use his or her true identity as a basis for denial of access. Some of the functional utility of these intermediary search sources remains, however, in that they shield the requestor's identity from public view. It is not newsworthy that a Washington, D.C., law firm requested Food and Drug Administration memoranda about the personal details of an employee who regulates cigarettes; however, it is banner headline material if its clients Philip Morris, Inc. or Liggett Group do so.

IV. NEXT STEPS

A. How Courts Should Apply the Change

The 1996 Amendments present courts with a different equation for FOIA balancing. The privacy-related balancing test that courts must perform when an agency exempts requested records will now more frequently favor the requester, regardless of that requester's motivations.[85] The curious busybody, creditor, or ex-spouse is now as much entitled to personal records as is the university professor with a history thesis to be verified from agency documents.

Courts can approach this change in different ways. One approach could be to deny exemption claims for documents affecting a privacy interest, without any regard for the individual expectations of the affected person. In the context of a criminal investigation, this means that the identities of any individual federal witnesses would be released upon anyone's request, including that of the target defendant.[86] Advocates may assert that if the

---

85. *See* United States Dep't of Justice v. Reporters Comm. for Freedom of the Press, 489 U.S. 749, 762 (1989) (enunciating balancing test).

86. This had been the principal use of the exemption at 5 U.S.C. § 552(b)(7)(C) (1994 & Supp. II 1996), and the courts had approached its use differently. *See, e.g.*, Rosenfeld v. United States Dep't of Justice, 57 F.3d 803, 811 (9th Cir. 1995) (stating government's interest in FOIA as opening agency action to public scrutiny dictates disclosure of identities); Providence Journal Co. v. United States Dep't of Army, 981 F.2d 552, 569 (1st Cir. 1992) (finding that unsubstantiated allegations do not maintain case against disclosure but emphasizing that courts must weigh public and private interests of each case); Safecard Servs., Inc. v. SEC, 926 F.2d 1197, 1206 (D.C. Cir. 1991) (holding that unless access to names and addresses of private individuals under FOIA 7(C) exemption is necessary to confirm or deny compelling evidence of agency misconduct, such information is exempt from disclosure).

FOIA's purpose is to advance private access for private purposes, then private submitters' rights should be secondary. Such a drastic outcome would diminish willingness to cooperate with agencies and could hinder data collection for those purposes that are truly "public" and have agency regulation in mind.[87]

Another approach could be to discard balancing altogether and demand that Congress establish a bright line rule through the adoption of statutes meeting the FOIA criteria for exemption via a specific statute.[88] This would qualify certain personal records as exempt, regardless of the interest of the person seeking access. The time and expense required for Congress to wrestle with dozens of statutes, however, would not justify the putative easier task of interpreting the FOIA.[89] The danger is that for many statutes, news that Congress was reopening and amending the reporting obligations of substantive laws would encourage demands for many unrelated changes to those laws' often-delicate balance of powers.[90]

The most likely approach will be a "yes, but" solution. In such an analysis, the court will weigh the ascertainable benefits to the public, from the specific requested disclosure as to any requester, against the individual harms to personal privacy.[91] Since the 1996 Amendments overruled decisions like *FLRA*, it is now legitimate for any person to access the federal employee address file to find a deadbeat debtor or a wandering ex-spouse — purposes which are wholly private. The courts may deal with this scenario by stating that, notwithstanding the legitimacy of the private inquiry for private purposes, the FOIA or the Privacy Act can still preserve the privacy of the record's submitter in these cases.[92]

---

87. *See* Douglas C. Michael, *Cooperative Implementation of Federal Regulations*, 13 YALE J. ON REG. 535, 553 (1996) (citing FOIA as impediment to industry disclosure).

88. *See* 5 U.S.C. § 552(b)(3) (1994 & Supp. II 1996) (exempting, under certain conditions, specific laws that provide for confidentiality of particular information). Data submitters are free to ask Congress to expressly determine confidential status of reports or submissions when Congress adopts the statute requiring the report. *See* 15 U.S.C. § 2055(a)(2) (1994) (protecting disclosure of industry trade secrets necessary in consumer protection investigations).

89. *See* Bernard W. Bells, *Using Statutory Interpretation to Improve the Legislative Process: Can It Be Done in the Post-Chevron Era?*, 13 J.L. & POL. 105, 148 n.226 (1997) (discussing role of Department of Justice in reconciling divergent agency interpretations of FOIA).

90. *See id.* at 154-55 (discussing tensions occurring among branches of government and small legislative groups during statutory interpretations).

91. *See* Voinche v. FBI, 940 F. Supp. 323, 330 (D.D.C. 1996), *aff'd*, 1997 WL 411685 (D.C. Cir.), *cert. denied*, 118 S. Ct. 370 (1997) (emphasizing that pubic interest under FOIA is to open agency action to public scrutiny; disclosure not furthering this end will be exempted for countervailing private interest).

92. 5 U.S.C. § 552(a) (1994 & Supp. II 1996).

The expectations of privacy under which a requested record was shared or file created are even more legitimate purposes for denying disclosure. These expectations were stronger when courts could limit disclosure via the core purpose balancing test.[93] As against the curiosity of creditors or competitors, the weight of post-1996 balancing should tip in favor of individual privacy rights in instances where there is more than a trivial expectation of nondisclosure.[94]

B. Predictions and Projections

The statutory authorization for using public agencies to research private records was a "sleeper," a statutory policy change that was not "heralded" by the sponsors of the 1996 Amendments.[95] This legislative change's quiet arrival was probably the result of the *de facto* use of the FOIA for that exact purpose over many years. Only the FOIA insiders, a relative few dozen agency professionals and a tiny clique of expert attorneys, recognized the potent barrier that core purpose analysis had become, and what benefits future requesters would gain from the FOIA's revised purposes.

C. FOIA and the Internet

The major effect of the 1996 Amendments will be in the area of Internet access, with secondary impacts in the commercial research and fundraising-dependent membership organizations. The Amendments were devoted to electronic access and computer-readable files, including a new command for the central preservation of one file containing the documents that the agency had previously released.[96] As an advocate for the Amendments has written, the Amendments shift the paradigm from a system where requesters experience delays in awaiting printed pages "to a model in which agencies anticipate requests and act to make records (and information on how to find additional records) available over online systems."[97]

---

93. *See supra* notes 45-51 and accompanying text.

94. Some records are categorically withheld because they are covered by the narrow reach of the Privacy Act, 5 U.S.C. § 552(a) (1994), but few FOIA requests become entangled in that statute's poorly-conceived morass.

95. *See* H.R. REP. NO. 104-795 at 19 (1996); S. REP. NO. 104-272 at 9-10 (1996) (stating that purpose of Amendments was to ensure and improve access to agency records and information and to maximize public's use of those records and information. In addition, goal was to promote agency compliance with statutory time limits).

96. *See* Pub. L. No. 104-231, sec. 4, 110 Stat. 3048, 3049 (1996) (codified at 5 U.S.C. § 552 (Supp. II 1996)). Before the Amendments, FOIA did not require agencies to retain copies of the records they had disclosed. *Id.*

97. Michael Tankersley, *Opening Drawers: A Requester's Guide to the Electronic Freedom of Information Act Amendments*, LEGAL TIMES, May 19, 1997, at 29.

If the new purpose of the FOIA is to endorse private researching to serve private purposes, it follows that Internet searchers will more readily examine privately-submitted information.[98] For example, if an environmental agency commands that a factory install a continuous emission monitor in its smokestack,[99] the agency conceivably could compel the factory to transmit electronically the monitoring data to the agency's office. The agency then could link — presumably for a fee — the factory's neighbors, anti-industry groups, or toxic tort plaintiffs into the flow of data. This is more likely to be true as more real-time monitoring devices become technologically feasible.

The three-way communication which results is not a conventional dialogue but a form of entitlement in which the sophisticated regulated company and the government regulator are accompanied into the enforcement decision process by those outsiders who access the same data via their computer links. Where government once engaged in dialogue (for better or worse) with regulated parties submitting information, now the agency engages in poly-logue with multiple "interested parties" who dial in for today's private data. The ideal of participative democracy may be achieved when the democratic institution takes on the role of arming all participants with private sector information.

The Internet is currently the international channel for information transfer.[100] Soon, all federal United States filings will be open to private searches by the world's curious and inquisitive requesters.[101] The polylogue that results will be open to multiple listeners around the world.

CONCLUSIONS

Government provides certain data services for public benefit, like weather reports; that is one of its duties. The transformation of access to *private* information into an entitlement, however, will challenge currently available services and the agencies that provide those services. The little-noticed Amendments of 1996 add a service function that was not part of the FOIA for its first three decades: data library for the world. Since the private person requesting FOIA access is more often than not asking about

---

98. *Cf. id.* at 29 (explaining FOIA's new provisions for making information available on Internet).

99. *See* JAMES O'REILLY ET AL., CLEAN AIR PERMITTING MANUAL § 21.09, at 12-13 (1995).

100. *See* Elizabeth Corcoran, *Scrambling for a Policy on Encryption Exports: As Technology Advances, US and Industry Seek Compromise That Balances Public, Private Fears,* WASH. POST, Feb. 25, 1996, at H1 (noting explosive growth of Internet use).

101. The FOIA allows "any person" access and does not require citizenship or U.S. residency. *See* 5 U.S.C. § 552(a)(3) (1994 & Supp. II 1996); O'REILLY, *supra* note 24, § 4.06.

other private persons' files, the FOIA has a *de facto* role as library, and the 1996 change in the FOIA's purpose validates that role.

Private access to agency files about private persons adds no value to the oversight role for which the FOIA was designed since the access is not being used to hold agencies accountable for their errors or misdeeds. The higher moral era of the journalistic "right to know" in the early 1960s idealized the public's accountability objectives. Today's FOIA request is more often than not a tool for corporate or private espionage.

In addition, public funds should not be appropriated to aid the efforts of privately-motivated FOIA requesters, as such requests do not protect the value of governmental efficiency. An agency's FOIA expenditures on private-versus-private inquiries will inevitably divert resources from the agency's other public duties and operations. This will require Congress to increase agency appropriations, which eventually are recouped by tax increases. For those agencies that already had been releasing private records for private motives, little will change. For those agencies like the FBI, however, which had previously invoked the FOIA's "core purpose" standard in denying access, the 1996 Amendments eliminate an easy exemption defense.

The new core value of the FOIA, stripped of any access-denying consideration of motives or purposes, is this: a poly-logue among the regulated, the regulator, and the new adversaries who are armed with information acquired from FOIA requests and from agency Internet sites. As these increase, the agencies' traditional role as surrogate for all the public will come to an end, and the agencies will become one among many well-informed critics of the affected persons or organizations. Those who once claimed "you can't fight city hall" now sense themselves empowered with an entitlement that is at least as strong in information terms as any agency has enjoyed.

THE FREEDOM OF INFORMATION ACT HAS NO CLOTHES

Antonin Scalia

THE FREEDOM of Information Act (FOIA) is part of the basic weaponry of modern regulatory war, deployable against regulators and regulated alike. It differs, however, from other weaponry in the conflict, in that it is largely immune from arms limitation debate. Public discussion of the act displays a range of opinion extending from constructively-critical-but-respectful through admiring to enthralled. The media, of course, praise it lavishly, since they understandably like the "free information" it promises and provides. The Congress tends to agree with the media. The executive branch generally limits its criticism to relatively narrow or technical aspects—lest it seem to be committing the governmental equivalent of "taking the Fifth." The regulated sector also wishes to demonstrate that it has nothing to hide, and is in any case torn between aversion to those features of the act that unreasonably compromise its interests and affection for those that unreasonably compromise the government's. Through the mutually reinforcing praise of many who should know better, the act is paraded about with the veneration normally reserved for the First Amendment itself.

Little should be expected, then, of efforts now under way in both houses of Congress to revise the act. But however dim the prospect for fundamental change, the FOIA is worth examining, if only as an academic exercise. It is the Taj Mahal of the Doctrine of Unanticipated Consequences, the Sistine Chapel of Cost-Benefit Analysis Ignored.

Antonin Scalia, the editor of Regulation, *is professor of law at the University of Chicago.*

Almost all of the Freedom of Information Act's current problems are attributable not to the original legislation enacted in 1966, but to the 1974 amendments. The 1966 version was a relatively toothless beast, sometimes kicked about shamelessly by the agencies. They delayed responses to requests for documents, replied with arbitrary denials, and overclassified documents to take advantage of the "national security" exemption. The '74 amendments were meant to remedy these defects—but they went much further. They can in fact only be understood as the product of the extraordinary era that produced them—when "public interest law," "consumerism," and "investigative journalism" were at their zenith, public trust in the government at its nadir, and the executive branch and Congress functioning more like two separate governments than two branches of the same. The amendments were drawn and debated in committee while Presi-

> The Freedom of Information Act is
> the Taj Mahal of the Doctrine
> of Unanticipated Consequences,
> the Sistine Chapel of Cost-Benefit
> Analysis Ignored.

dent Nixon was in the final agony of Watergate, and were passed when President Ford was in the precarious early days of his unelected term. The executive branch managed to make a bad situation worse, by adamantly resisting virtually all changes in the act, even those that Congress was obviously bent on achieving. By the time it realized the error of its obstinacy, it was too late: the changes had been drafted and negotiated among congressmen and committees without the degree of agency participation and advice that might have made the final product—while still unpalatable—at least more realistic. The extent of the disaster may be gauged by the fact that, barely two months after taking office as a result of the Watergate coverup, President Ford felt he had to veto a bill that proclaimed "Freedom of Information" in its title. It passed easily over his veto.

When one compares what the Freedom of Information Act was in contemplation with what it has turned out to be in reality, it is apparent that something went wrong. The act and its amendments were promoted as a means of finding out about the operations of government; they have been used largely as a means of obtaining data in the government's hands concerning private institutions. They were promoted as a boon to the press, the public interest group, the little guy; they have been used most frequently by corporate lawyers. They were promoted as a minimal imposition on the

---

The act and its amendments . . . were promoted as a boon to the press, the public interest group, the little guy; they have been used most frequently by corporate lawyers. . . . It is a far cry from John Q. Public finding out how his government works.

---

operations of government; they have greatly burdened investigative agencies and the courts. The House Committee Report estimated that the 1974 amendments would cost only $100,000 a year; a single request under them has cost more than $400,000. There has grown up, since 1974, an entire industry and profession based upon the Freedom of Information Act. An organization has been formed, the American Society of Access Professionals, composed of men and women (mostly government employees) who have made their careers in this field. A two-volume FOIA loose-leaf service, updated monthly, retails at $438 a year; another one, supple-

mented only semiannually, is somewhat cheaper. Every week the *Legal Times of Washington* runs a page or more of notable new FOIA filings —mostly to enable corporate lawyers to find out what it is that other corporate lawyers are trying to find out. The necessary training for any big-time litigating lawyer now includes not only the cross-examination of witnesses, but use of the Freedom of Information Act. In short, it is a far cry from John Q. Public finding out how his government works.

WHAT HAPPENED in the 1974 amendments to the Freedom of Information Act is similar to what happened in much of the regulatory legislation and rulemaking of that era: an entirely desirable objective was pursued singlemindedly to the exclusion of equally valid competing interests. In the currently favored terminology, a lack of cost-benefit analysis; in more commonsensical terms, a loss of all sense of proportion.

Take, for example, the matter of costs. As noted above, the 1974 amendments were estimated by Congress to cost $100,000 a year. They have in fact cost many millions of dollars —no one knows precisely how much. The main reason is that the amendments forbid the government from charging the requester for the so-called processing costs. Responding to a request generally requires three steps: (1) searching for the requested documents; (2) reviewing or "processing" them to determine whether any of the material they contain is exempt from disclosure, to decide whether the exemption should be asserted, and, if so, to make the line-by-line deletions; and (3) duplicating them. Before 1974, the cost for all of this work was chargeable to the requester; since 1974, step two has been at the government's expense. In many cases, it is the most costly part of the process, often requiring the personal attention of high-level personnel for long periods of time. If, for example, material in an investigative file is requested, someone familiar with the investigation must go through the material line by line to delete those portions, and only those portions, that would disclose a confidential source or come within one of the other specific exceptions to the requirement of disclosure. Moreover, even steps one and three are at the government's expense "where the agency determines that waiver or reduction of the fee is in the public interest because furnishing the information can be considered as primarily benefiting the general public." Even where the agency parsimoniously refuses to grant this waiver, the more generous judiciary sometimes mandates it—which happened, for example, in the case of the FOIA request by the Rosenberg children.

The question, of course, is whether this public expense is worth it, bearing in mind that the FOIA requester is not required to have any particular "need to know." The inquiry that creates this expense—perhaps for hundreds of thousands of documents—may be motivated by no more than idle curiosity. The "free lunch" aspect of the FOIA is significant not only because it takes money from the Treasury that could be better spent elsewhere, but also because it brings into the system requests that are not really important enough to be there, crowding the genuinely desirable ones to the end of the line. In the absence of any "need to know" requirement, price is the only device available for rationing these governmental services—and in many cases a price based on search and reproduction costs is simply not adequate.

Other features of the amendments reflect the same unthinking extravagance and disregard of competing priorities. Although federal agencies carry out a great many important activities, rarely does the law impose a specific deadline for agency action. Yet the FOIA requester is entitled by law to get an answer to his request within ten working days—and, if it is denied, to get a ruling on his appeal within another twenty. (There is a provision for an additional ten days "in unusual circumstances.") So the investigative agent who is needed to review a file must lay aside his other work and undertake that task as his top priority.

It is also rare that a federal official *must* be subjected to a disciplinary investigation— even for malicious baby-snatching under color of law, much less mere negligence. But if he should happen to trifle with an FOIA request, stand back! In a provision unique in the United States Code, the 1974 amendments specify that whenever a court considering an appeal from an FOIA denial

issues a written finding that the circumstances . . . raise questions whether agency personnel acted arbitrarily or capriciously

with respect to the withholding, the Civil Service Commission [now the Special Counsel of the Merit Systems Protection Board] shall promptly initiate a proceeding to determine whether disciplinary action is warranted against the officer or employee who was primarily responsible for the withholding.

In the courts, the statute provides that FOIA appeals shall "take precedence on the docket over all cases and shall be assigned for hearing and trial or for argument at the earliest practicable date and expedited in every way." (There is an exception to this preferential treatment for "cases the court considers of greater importance.") And if the requester taking the agency to court "has substantially prevailed," the court is authorized to make the government pay his attorney fees and litigation costs. One would have thought it infinitely more important to pay the attorney fees and litigation costs of persons who are erroneously or even frivolously prosecuted by the government — but of course the law makes no provision for such payment.

The preferred status of the FOIA requester in the courts is also evident in the standard of review. If a federal agency assesses a penalty against you or revokes a certificate that is necessary for your livelihood, it will do you no good to persuade a judge that the agency is probably wrong. The courts cannot reverse the agency merely because they disagree with its assessment of the facts. They can do so only when there is a lack of "substantial evidence" to support its finding. If, however, an agency denies a freedom of information request, shazam!—the full force of the Third Branch of government is summoned to the wronged party's assistance. The denial is subject to *de novo* review—which means that the court will examine the records on its own and come to its own independent decision. And whereas the general rule is that the citizen appealing to the courts must show that the agency acted improperly, in the case of an FOIA denial "the burden is on the agency to sustain its action."

THE FOREGOING DEFECTS (and others could be added) might not be defects in the best of all possible worlds. They are foolish extravagances only because we do not have an unlimited amount of federal money to spend, an unlimited number of agency employees to assign, an unlimited number of judges to hear and decide cases. We must, alas, set some priorities—and unless the world is mad the usual Freedom of Information Act request should not be high on the list.

Some other effects of the 1974 amendments, however, would be malignant even in a world without shortages. Prominent in this category is the provision which requires the courts to determine (again *de novo*) the propriety of classification of documents on the grounds of national security or foreign affairs. What is needful for our national defense and what will impair the conduct of our foreign affairs are questions of the sort that the courts will avoid—on the basis of the "political question" doctrine—even when they arise in the context of the most significant civil and criminal litigation. Imagine pushing the courts into such inquiries for the purpose of ruling on an FOIA request! This disposition appears even more incredible if one compares it with the provisions of the Foreign Intelligence Surveillance Act. There, for the much more compelling purpose of determining whether secret electronic surveillance will be allowed, the court must accept the certification of a high-level executive official that the information sought is necessary to the national defense or the conduct of foreign affairs unless, on the basis of the accompanying data, that certification is "clearly erroneous."

But the most ironic absolute defect of the '74 amendments was perhaps unintended at the time and seems to have gone virtually unnoticed since. The amendments have significantly reduced the privacy, and hence the autonomy, of all our nongovernmental institutions—corporations, labor unions, universities, churches, political and social clubs—all those private associations that form, as Tocqueville observed, diverse centers of power apart from what would otherwise be the all-powerful democratic state. Some of the activities of these associations should be open to public scrutiny, and prior to 1974 Congress made that judgment on a relatively specific basis, in enacting such disclosure statutes as the Securities Exchange Act, the Public Utility Holding Company Act, and the Labor-Management Reporting and Disclosure Act. Of course, in addition to those particular activities of private institutions that require *publication*, virtually all activities of private institutions may be subjected to *governmental investigation*—and increasingly are, to ensure compliance with the innumerable requirements of federal laws and regulations. By and large, it has been left to the agencies to determine when investigation is appropriate, and the courts have been most liberal in sustaining investigative authority.

The effect of the 1974 amendments to the Freedom of Information Act was to eliminate the distinction between investigation and publication. The "investigative files" exemption in the original act was narrowed so as to permit withholding of documents acquired or produced in a law enforcement investigation only if disclosure would cause specific damage to the investigative process or to particular private interests (for example, reveal the identity of a confidential source). The way things now work, the government may obtain almost anything in the course of an investigation; and once the investigation is completed the public (or, more specifically, the opponents or competitors of the investigated institution) may obtain all that the investigative file contains, unless one of a few narrow exemptions applies. There is an exemption (though the agency has discretion not to invoke it) for confidential commercial information. But there is none that protects an institution's consultative and deliberative processes—the minutes of a university's faculty meetings, for example. It is noteworthy that internal consultation and advice within the government itself is exempted from disclosure since, as the 1966 House Committee Report explained, "a full and frank exchange

> In other words, legislation that was supposed to lay bare the workings of government is in fact more protective of the privacy needs of government than of private institutions.

of opinions would be impossible if all internal communications were made public." But no such exemption exists for the internal communications of private organizations that come into the government's hands. In other words, legislation that was supposed to lay bare the workings of government is in fact more protective of the privacy needs of government than of private institutions.

THERE SEEMS LITTLE HOPE, however, that these absolute defects of the Freedom of Information Act, much less its mere extravagances, will be corrected. And once the fundamentally flawed

> ... once the fundamentally flawed premises of the '74 amendments are accepted, as they have been, all efforts at even minor reform take on an Alice-in-Wonderland air.

premises of the '74 amendments are accepted, as they have been, all efforts at even minor reform take on an Alice-in-Wonderland air. For example: The government is concerned about use of the Freedom of Information Act as a weapon in litigation. Requests by a litigant for judicially compelled production of documents from the opposing party's files (so-called discovery requests) can be kept within reasonable bounds by the court itself. But when the government is the adversary, there no longer is any need to use the judicial discovery mechanism. An FOIA request can be as wide as the great outdoors; and the government must produce the information within ten working days —or, as a practical matter, within such longer period as the requester is willing to negotiate. It is not only a good way to get scads of useful information; it is also a means of keeping the government's litigation team busy reviewing carloads of documents instead of tending to the trial of the case. The story is told of a criminal defense lawyer who negotiated a favorable plea for his client by filing an onerous FOIA request that would have taken weeks of the U.S. attorney's time. And why not? Anyone can file such a request, and surely the attorney is obliged to use all lawful means to serve the interest of his client.

Well, the government's proposed solution for this problem is to forbid FOIA requests by litigants once litigation has commenced. Apart from the practical difficulty of enforcing such

a ban, consider the Mad Hatter result it would produce: Absolutely anybody in the world (the FOIA requester does not, by the way, have to be a U.S. citizen) would be able to put the government through the inordinate trouble and expense of the FOIA process *except*—you guessed it—the person most legitimately interested in the requested information.

The defects of the Freedom of Information Act cannot be cured as long as we are dominated by the obsession that gave them birth— that the first line of defense against an arbitrary executive is do-it-yourself oversight by the public and its surrogate, the press. On that assumption, the FOIA's excesses are not defects at all, but merely the necessary price for our freedoms. It is a romantic notion, but the facts simply do not bear it out. The major exposés of recent times, from CIA mail openings to Watergate to the FBI COINTELPRO operations, owe virtually nothing to the FOIA but are primarily the product of the institutionalized checks and balances within our system of representative democracy. This is not to say that public access to government information has no useful role—only that it is not the ultimate guarantee of responsible government, justifying the sweeping aside of all other public and private interests at the mere invocation of the magical words "freedom of information."

> The act's defects cannot be cured as long as we are dominated by the obsession that gave them birth— that the first line of defense against an arbitrary executive is do-it-yourself oversight by the public and its surrogate, the press.

It is possible to save the desirable features of the FOIA—and even to give it teeth it did not have before 1974—without going to absurd extremes. But don't hold your breath. As the legislative debate is now shaping up, a few minor though worthwhile changes may be made, such as exemption of CIA case files. But the basically unsound judgments of the '74 amendments are probably part of the permanent legacy of Watergate. We need not, however, admire the emperor's clothes. ∎

[5]

California Law Review

VOL. 80   DECEMBER 1992   No. 6

A Theory of Law and Information: Copyright, Spleens, Blackmail, and Insider Trading

James Boyle

TABLE OF CONTENTS

1414   *CALIFORNIA LAW REVIEW*

A Theory of Law and Information: Copyright, Spleens, Blackmail, and Insider Trading

James Boyle†

In this Article, Professor Boyle undertakes an analysis of the law's treatment of information across four apparently disparate realms: copyright, genetic information, blackmail, and insider trading. He argues that questions of information regulation, commodification, and access are shaped by two neglected processes of interpretive construction. First, such issues are often decided by pigeonholing them into implicitly contradictory stereotypes of "public" or "private" information. These conflicting stereotypes have their roots in basic assumptions about politics, the market, and privacy in a liberal state. Second, Professor Boyle argues that tension between these stereotypes is often apparently resolved by the use of a seductive image: the romantic author whose original, transformative genius justifies private property and fuels public debate. Thus, conventional wisdom, courts, and even economic analysts are more likely to favor granting prop-

† Copyright 1992, James Boyle, Professor of Law, Washington College of Law, The American University. LL.B. 1980, Glasgow University; LL.M. 1981, S.J.D. 1986, Harvard University. This Article was written while I was a Visiting Professor at Boston University Law School and Harvard Law School. The research funds of those schools supplied valuable assistance.

As befits a piece that questions the notion of authorship and originality, this one is marked by fundamental intellectual debts. Four articles have been particularly influential: Peter Jaszi, *Toward a Theory of Copyright: The Metamorphoses of "Authorship"*; Duncan Kennedy, *The Structure of Blackstone's Commentaries*; Joseph W. Singer, *The Legal Rights Debate in Analytical Jurisprudence from Bentham to Hohfeld*; and Martha Woodmansee, *The Genius and the Copyright: Economic and Legal Conditions of the Emergence of the "Author."* I have also been influenced by the work of Rosemary Coombe, and by the prodigious and sophisticated oeuvre of Wendy Gordon. This Article draws on a theory of authorship and its relevance to property, romance, and interpretation that I first laid out in *The Search for an Author: Shakespeare and the Framers.* Earlier versions of this Article were presented at the 1991 Case-Western Conference on Intellectual Property and the Construction of Authorship, and at faculty colloquia at Harvard Law School and Boston University Law School. I would like to thank all of the participants for helping me to refine my ideas. Colleagues at Harvard Law School, American University, and Boston University were generous with their time. I have benefitted particularly from comments by Frank Michelman, Fred Schauer, Terry Fisher, Howell Jackson, Terry Martin, Mark Hager, Jack Beermann, Joe Singer, Rudy Peritz, Mark Rose, Margreta de Grazia, Steven Shavell, Louis Kaplow, Bob Bone, and David Seipp. William Alford's work on intellectual property in China was also extremely helpful. Anne Hollander, Gerry Moohr, and the rest of the participants in the Modern Legal Theory Seminar also helped me to refine my ideas. Jae Won Kim, Jennifer Ritter, David Dantzic, and Beth Silberman researched expertly. Above and beyond these other debts, however, this piece only exists because of a conversation carried on over the last eight years with my polymath colleague, Peter Jaszi. It is to him that I would like to dedicate it.

erty rights in information when the controller of this information can convincingly be ascribed the qualities of originality, creativity, and individuality, the defining attributes of romantic authorship. This is possible in the copyright domain and for manipulators, if not sources, of genetic information. Blackmailers and insider traders cannot so readily be fitted into the romantic author mold, and are classified instead as transgressors against, respectively, the "private" and "public" stereotypes of information. The Article concludes by assessing the impact of the implicit stereotypes on the politics of the "information age." Professor Boyle argues that an emphasis upon the ideology of authorship could be as important to an information society as the notions of freedom of contract and wage labor were to an earlier, industrialized society. This ideology of authorship, Professor Boyle contends, with its tendency to devalue the claims of sources and of audience, has the potential for strong detrimental effects on the political and economic structure of the "information age."

INTRODUCTION

It is hard, nowadays, to find a piece of futurology that *doesn't* say we are entering an information age. Yet there have been few systematic critical studies of the rhetorical, ideological, political, and, ultimately, legal structures through which we deal with information.[1] At the same

---

1. Among legal scholars, only the economic analysts of law have seemed interested in dealing holistically with information, rather than with the doctrinal categories into which law has traditionally divided it. The two most striking examples of the holistic approach are Frank H. Easterbrook, *Insider Trading, Secret Agents, Evidentiary Privileges, and the Production of Information,* 1981 SUP. CT. REV. 309, and Edmund W. Kitch, *The Law and Economics of Rights in Valuable Information,* 9 J. LEGAL STUD. 683 (1980). In a manner reminiscent of legal realist scholarship, these studies suggest that doctrinal divisions may obscure the need for enlightened policymaking. Easterbrook, for example, is concerned that, "[i]f the Court puts information cases in securities law or evidence law pigeonholes, it may overlook the need to consider the way in which the incentive to produce information and the demands of current use conflict." Easterbrook, *supra,* at 314. While I agree with the impulse to treat information holistically, my goals are rather different. Later in this Article, I argue that despite its holistic treatment of information, the law and economics literature is beset by a number of conceptual "baseline" and Hohfeldian errors, and that it presents an ideology of "authorial" incentive as if it were not ideology, but empirical fact. *See infra* Part IV.

Nonlawyers have come close to my concerns here. Kim L. Scheppelle's book *Legal Secrets* gives a thoughtful contractarian analysis of secrets in cases related mainly to fraud, privacy, and professional requirements of confidentiality. In the process she offers a critique of Chicago-style law and economics and an interesting defense of egalitarian informational ethics. KIM L. SCHEPPELLE, LEGAL SECRETS: EQUALITY AND EFFICIENCY IN THE COMMON LAW (1988). Literary critics have also contributed to the issue. In a recent book, Susan Stewart offers a fascinating analysis of the intersection of law and a range of "crimes of writing"—forgery, literary imposture, pornography, and graffiti—and the relevance of this intersection to notions of subjectivity and authenticity. SUSAN STEWART, CRIMES OF WRITING: PROBLEMS IN THE CONTAINMENT OF REPRESENTATION (1991). Bernard Edelman's *Le Droit Saisit par la Photographie* (published in English as BERNARD EDELMAN, OWNERSHIP OF THE IMAGE (1979)) goes in the other direction, giving an Althusserian analysis of law through an examination of intellectual property law relating to photographs. In the process he raises some of the problems of objectification, originality, and commodification that I deal with here. Finally, in a forthcoming work, Mark Rose offers an excellent analysis of the historical connections between "authorship" and copyright in England. MARK ROSE, AUTHORS AND

time, the area of legal doctrine that acknowledges that its main concern is information—conventionally defined intellectual property—is marked by severe disagreements over the most fundamental propositions. For example, within copyright there are continuing disputes over a wide range of basic issues—the classification of something as idea or expression, the definition of "fact works," and the dilemma of how to treat computer programs being some of the more obvious.[2] Areas outside intellectual property, although superficially commonsensical, are also beset by basic conceptual puzzles. Blackmail and insider trading both represent proscribed forms of trading in information that, when defined in abstract terms, seem to conform exactly to moral and legal norms accepted elsewhere in society. In the former case, why should private individuals be forbidden to make private agreements regarding the dissemination of privately held information? Insider trading is even more puzzling. Markets are built on structured inequality. Why should we not let people trade from a position of advantage in information, just as we let them trade from a position of advantage in wealth? Finally, if we look at the legal treatment of genetic information—which, with electronic information, may define the international economy of the immediate future[3]—we find a morass of formalism, circular arguments, and incoherent theories of property.

Taking these puzzles as its raw material, this Article attempts to develop a theory of law and information. Its aim is not to produce a formula for resolving all problems, but rather to show the themes repeated in, and the possibilities suppressed by, our current treatment of information issues. In particular, the Article argues that questions of information regulation, commodification, and access are shaped by the intersection of two neglected processes of interpretive construction. First, such questions are often decided by an uncritical process of pigeonholing into a number of stereotypes of "public" or "private" information. These stereotypes have their roots in relatively basic assump-

---

OWNERS: THE INVENTION OF COPYRIGHT (forthcoming 1993). Rose's work has both parallels to and differences from Woodmansee's pioneering article on the same issues in Germany, see Martha Woodmansee, *The Genius and the Copyright: Economic and Legal Conditions of the Emergence of the "Author,"* 17 EIGHTEENTH-CENTURY STUD. 425 (1984), and my discussion of the valences of an ideology of authorship for interpretation and entitlement, see James D.A. Boyle, *The Search for an Author: Shakespeare and the Framers,* 37 AM. U. L. REV. 625 (1988). For a critical comparison of our approaches, see David Saunders & Ian Hunter, *Lessons from the "Literatory": How to Historicise Authorship,* 17 CRITICAL INQUIRY 479, 491-500 (1991).

2. See Peter Jaszi, *Toward a Theory of Copyright: The Metamorphoses of "Authorship,"* 1991 DUKE L.J. 455, 464 ("At present, the surface patterning American copyright law is in apparent disarray. Judges and writers can not agree on the most basic propositions."); Jessica Litman, *The Public Domain,* 39 EMORY L.J. 965, 998 (1990) ("[T]here is ample precedent deciding almost every copyright issue in almost every conceivable direction.").

3. Those with a taste for ambiguous dystopias may care to look at *Neuromancer,* which offers a fictional vision of a world organized around the trade, control, and theft of genetic and electronic information. WILLIAM GIBSON, NEUROMANCER (1984).

tions about property, society, and privacy in a liberal state. Second, the tensions among and between these stereotypes are often lessened by an appeal to a particular (and particularly romantic) image of information production—the author who produces originality *ex nihilo* and thus should be rewarded with honor and property rights. The Article argues that the contradictions, assumptions, and lacunae of these two processes are an important part of any study of the current law of information, or the future social arrangements of the information society.

A note on method may be in order. The first half of this Article— with its concentration on the doctrinal and argumentative patterns generated by the apparent contradiction of "information property"—bears a certain resemblance to the structuralist legal theories of the early 1980s. Like the authors of those articles, I claim that understanding a particular set of tensions allows us to see patterns in otherwise diverse doctrinal developments, to relate legal issues to basic conflicts of political vision, to anticipate the structure of the rhetoric on both sides of any issue, and to see the moral and political inconsistencies in the way that we deal with information. This may sound suspiciously like overblown claims to have discovered the "fundamental contradiction" or even the driving wheel of history. My goal is rather different.

Structuralist and determinist accounts of social forces generally argue that one area of social life—the means and relations of production, the mediation of the fundamental tension between self and others, or the patterns of childrearing—is the *real* determinant of history. All else is chimera and superstructure. The claims I make here are much more modest. At most, I am trying to lay out the normative topography, the geography of assumptions within which issues are framed, possibilities foreclosed, and so on. This geography *matters* because it excludes some options from consideration (excludes them even from being seen, perhaps) or prompts a hasty leap to judgment, or because it is one of the many forces shaping the terrain of political struggle. But the ideas and ideologies I am describing are neither so deeply rooted in the culture that they can never be criticized, nor so determinate that they dictate only one solution: the process is neither a giant conspiracy nor a deterministic and inevitable deep structure of thought.

The second theme of this Article is its critique of romantic authorship. I claim that a series of concepts associated with the romantic notion of the "author" is offered as a device to mediate, defer, or apparently resolve the internal tensions of regulating information. Most of the time, courts accept the author gambit, even if the "author" is plainly recombining elements mined free of charge from the public sphere (or even the private body). My examples of this pattern come from copyright doctrine and the law of property in genetic information. Occasionally, however, for reasons apparently related to the pattern of tensions between public and private spheres, the author gambit is declined, and the putative "authors" are instead told they cannot profit from their use of information. Blackmail and insider trading are the two examples given here: both of these would seem like classic market transactions, were it not for the fact that they concern information and thus conjure up all the contradictions and tensions which beset the treatment of information in liberal social theory. The doctrine of blackmail defends the image of the private sphere by protecting an individual's subjectively defined "private" information from commodification in the marketplace. The prohibition of insider trading protects the image of the public sphere by imposing the ideas of formal equality on market transactions precisely because they concern *information*, rather than some other form of power or wealth. My thesis is strengthened by the fact that insider trading seems from scholarly reaction to lie particularly close to the line. Indeed, the acknowledged pioneer-critic of insider trading law relied heavily on the rhetoric of authorial, entrepreneurial genius to support decriminalization.[4] Perhaps insider traders can be authors after all.

This aspect of the Article, and particularly its discussion of the social construction of authorship, is reminiscent of poststructuralist criticism. My conclusion—with its reliance on both economic analysis and literary criticism, and with its attempt to imagine the effects of a transposition of the traditions of nineteenth century liberalism to the social relations of an information society—could fashionably be styled as postmodernist. Thus, for those who are interested, this Article presents a kind of layer cake of the intellectual methods of the last fifteen years. There was a reason behind this methodological eclecticism. My hope is that this piece will be seen as an example of constructive engagement between the main schools of legal scholarship, prompting economic analysts to consider the interpretive construction that grounds their theories, devotees of law and literature to look beyond the text to the structure of incentives through which the text was created, and critical legal scholars to take seriously their professed commitment to decoding the social construction of reality in a way that produces practical suggestions for change. Nevertheless, I have tried as far as possible to make sure that familiarity with these academic movements is not necessary to understand the central arguments presented here.

The structure of the Article replicates that of this introduction. In Part I, I set up the four subjects mentioned in the title of the Article. My aim is to treat them as academic conundrums worthy of solution in their own right and as case studies that help us to lay the groundwork for a theory of law and information.

In Parts II and III, I argue that the doctrinal disputes and confu-

---

4. *See infra* text accompanying notes 224-40.

sions in all of these areas can be usefully understood as reflections of a set of basic tensions—in particular the tensions between public and private, speech and property, formal equality and *restitutio in integrum.* These tensions are especially painful because speech, debate, and the exchange of information are so important to the liberal vision of politics and economics and to the construction of the public and private realms.

In Part IV, I turn to the area of information economics. The uncertainties and tensions in conventional legal and political discourse about information, combined with the obvious analytical importance of concepts such as incentives to production and barriers to exchange, make information issues seem particularly susceptible to economic analysis. Legal scholars now routinely turn to microeconomic concepts, whether of "the public goods problems of intellectual property" or the attributes of an "efficient capital market," to resolve problems in the production, generation, commodification, or use of information. Is this reliance on economic analysis warranted? Drawing on the recent theoretical literature and on the structure of tensions described in this Article, I argue that information economics is paradoxical or at least aporetic.[5] Consequently, it provides no real surcease from the difficulties of liberal state theory or from the indeterminate topography of "public" and "private."

Sometimes economists treat information as just another product, something that must be commodified if producers are to be given an incentive to produce it. At other times, they treat it as part of the structure of the market: infinite, perfect, and circulating without let or hindrance. I argue that contemporary microeconomics offers only the most intuitive basis for evaluating which "aspect" of information is fundamental to the analysis. Yet it also offers no convincing way of reconciling the competing "aspects" into a uniquely correct ordering of preferences or structure of tradeoffs. Any attempted reconciliation ends in paradox, a fact noted by at least one prominent pair of economists.[6] In fact, information presents almost the same kind of difficulties for neoclassical eco-

---

5. *Aporia*—and its adjectival form, aporetic—means literally, "in a state of doubt." Philosophers and political theorists have differed about the appropriateness of using the term "paradox" or "contradiction" to describe some of the situations I lay out in this Article. My claim is that information can (and must) be defined both as a commodity, the production and distribution of which can be analyzed within the model, and as a constituent part of the model itself. *Aporia* seemed the most appropriate word to use because whether one chooses to see this as a basic theoretical fault line, or a mere quibble that can be solved by changing the level and focus of the analysis, the nature of information is "in a state of doubt," and the outcome of any particular economic analysis will be profoundly different depending on which aspect is chosen. Because *aporia* might be an unfamiliar word to those who love neither classical rhetoric nor German idealist philosophy, I use the word "paradox" interchangeably. Unless specified otherwise, it is this double, and thus doubtful, quality of information to which I am referring. Other well-known paradoxes have similar structure—for example, the barber of Seville, who is both "a man" and "the barber," so if the barber shaves all the men who do not shave themselves . . . ? For an explanation of the paradox created by the idea of an informationally efficient market, see *infra* text accompanying notes 69-77.

6. *See infra* text accompanying note 83.

nomics that rent did for classical economics: it is the problem case in which the basic assumptions of the discipline come into conflict with each other.

Although some economic analyses acknowledge the indeterminacies involved in choosing which aspect of information to highlight, most are silent on the issue. In fact, such analyses are frequently "grounded" on a subtextual, and probably unconscious, appeal to a particular vision of information production—the stereotype of the romantic author which I referred to earlier. Consequently, I argue that although economics *frames* some of the issues of information regulation well, the perception that it is capable of routinely *settling* those issues is a false one, a false one with important consequences.

In Part V I argue that, within the legal system, the concept of property traditionally bears the burden of resolving the tensions between public and private, but that it does so in ways that merely restate those tensions. Thus, when we turn to a field that can best be described as *property in information,* we have a set of contradictions that is literally redoubled.

In Part VI, I test the above hypothesis by turning to the first of my puzzles or case studies, the structure of copyright doctrine. I trace the parallel evolution of the romantic idea of authorship—a notion that would have been alien to Shakespeare—and the development of the concept of intellectual property. My argument is that copyright offers a vitally important mediating strategy, a constellation of rhetorical, conceptual, and thematic ideas that seems to resolve the tensions I have described so far. That constellation is formed by the figure of the romantic author, the theme of "original creation," and the distinction between "idea" and "expression." It apparently provides a basis for partial and limited property rights without raising the specter of property as merely a utilitarian, revocable state grant, it justifies the giving of entitlements according to a labor theory of property without spreading those entitlements too widely, and it resolves the tension between public and private by giving the idea to the public world and the property right in expression to the writer.[7] By appealing to a particular notion of progress and of creation, the idea of "originality" downplays debts to language, culture, and genre and thus justifies the granting of limited monopolies, even monopolies centered around information.

The next two Parts explore the way in which the commodification of

---

7. This constellation of ideas appears to resolve so many of the paradoxes in the regulation of information that one finds it in other areas of information regulation—even ones far removed from literary creation. A particularly fascinating manifestation of this trend lies in the fact that many economists and economic analysts of law seem just as fascinated by the romantic vision of authorship as their econophobic precursors. One reason for this unlikely state of affairs could be that an unconscious reliance on the idea of romantic authorship conceals the *aporias* of information economics, even from the analysts themselves.

information raises different problems depending on whether the situation is typed as a "private" one or a "public" one. In the case of blackmail, discussed in Part VII, the ability to control information—alone out of all other social resources—seems to be central to our conception of personality. In the case of insider trading, discussed in Part VIII, we see information advantages, unlike other advantages in wealth or power, as subject to the norm of equality. In both cases, I argue that if we look at information holistically rather than within its narrower doctrinal boxes, these two longtime subjects of scholarly dispute can be explained if not actually resolved. In both, a refusal to commodify information is justified in part by an intuitive act of "typing" into realms of publicness or privateness, each with its own ideas about justice and its own theories of entitlement.

The mediating role of the author is also relevant to at least one of these two subjects. Blackmail offers us no convincing author figure on whom to pin a property right. But in insider trading, an area where decriminalization has been seriously suggested and defended, things are rather different. At the end of Part VIII I show that the germinal argument for the decriminalization of insider trading actually relies on an eerily perfect invocation of the rhetoric of the romantic author or, in this case, the romantic entrepreneur. This argument defines the entrepreneur in terms of originality, in terms of the creative destruction of settled arrangements. By this view, insider trading is a limited monopoly in information that rewards the entrepreneur for his or her efforts and thus ensures further entrepreneurial acts. Just as with copyright, society is purportedly compensated by the advances and contributions that the great genius throws off. In the face of such an essential contribution to human progress, what's a little monopoly here and there?

More generally, I claim that examination of insider trading scholarship and case law gives evidence of both of the processes this Article describes: the typing of information issues into "public" and "private" and the attractiveness of the author concept as a device to reconcile, or at least obscure, our conflicting notions about information.

The final puzzle, discussed in Part IX, comes from *Moore v. Regents of the University of California,*[8] a case that concerns ownership and control of genetic information. The *Moore* case presents, in miniature, each of the conflicts referred to in this Article: the clash between a vision of property rights as absolute or relative, between the public and private characterization of information, between the market and "privacy," and between natural rights and the rights of creative labor. My analysis attempts to show the consequences, for "sources" such as Mr. Moore, of an entitlement regime built around the notion of romantic authorship.

---

8. 793 P.2d 479 (Cal. 1990), *cert. denied,* 111 S. Ct. 1388 (1991).

In the Conclusion, I make three arguments. First, the Article demonstrates a particular method of "resolving" questions of information regulation by typing the issue into one of a series of contradictory visions of information. Second, despite Michel Foucault, postmodernism, and the death of the novel, the romantic vision of authorship is more important today than it was to Fichte and Krause, Pope and Macaulay. The facility with which the romantic vision appears to resolve the tensions I describe in this Article is one of the keys to its success or failure. Sometimes the romantic vision may be "right." Yet its ahistorical claims of universality and its overblown claims about the incentives necessary to production, to say nothing of its overweening romanticism, make it a dangerous template for the regulation of information. Using a string of examples, ranging from software development to the manufacture of pharmaceuticals, I argue that the romantic vision blinds us to the pragmatic, moral, and distributive claims of both "sources" and audience.

The final Section of the Conclusion is more speculative. Above and beyond my attempt to reorient long-running academic debates over copyright, blackmail, insider trading, and genetic information, this Article has a broader goal. It seems reasonable to assume that we are moving into a world that will increasingly be structured around the collection, manipulation, and use of information. At least at first, that world will be discussed, debated, and regulated using ideas about information that come from a society in which information had a rather different set of relationships to economic power and the rhetoric of entitlement. Consequently, the final Section of the Conclusion reflects on what the "information world" could, and should, look like.

One of our greatest cultural legacies is a collection of intellectual tools that help us to understand both the appeal and the limitations of the rhetoric of entitlement produced by a society like ours. Thus, we have a rich tradition of intellectual commentary on the production and distribution of tangible objects and on the consequences of the division between capital and labor, between ownership and control, between public and private. This commentary has produced conceptual tools such as the labor theory of value, the Pigouvian analysis of externalities, and the critique of the public/private split. Such tools have profound limitations and analytical shortcomings, but they do help us to uncover that which is suppressed or rendered invisible by the overwhelming familiarity of our social arrangements. The final Section of the Article attempts to imagine some of the equivalent tools for the *information* society.

One final note about method may be in order. My subject in this Article is "information." Elsewhere I have explained my rejection of the essentialist vision of language[9] and the disciplinary ideas associated with

---

9. James Boyle, *The Politics of Reason: Critical Legal Theory and Local Social Thought,* 133 U. PA. L. REV. 685 (1985).

it.[10] I see this Article as a continuation of that work, rather than as a renunciation of it. If I am not claiming that there is some preexisting, essential component that ties together every "information" issue "properly so-called,"[11] then what holds the examples used in this study together? My attitude towards definition in this Article has been pragmatic, in the looser sense of that term. With Felix Cohen, I believe that a "definition . . . is *useful* or *useless*. . . . [It] is useful if it insures against risks of confusion more serious than any that the definition itself contains."[12]

In this Article, I have focused on the communication and manipulation and trade of knowledge—whether found in RNA, typeface, programmer's code, or blackmailer's photographs—and on the parties who are seen as the rightful owners, controllers, or audiences of that knowledge. This has led me into cognate issues presented by copyright law, even though *Pierre Menard: True Author of Don Quixote* and *The Name of the Rose* are not normally seen as "information."[13] Bringing these disparate areas together does have its advantages. Each of these areas involves situations in which tangible control of a single *res* is not enough. The same compromising photograph in a blackmailer's hands, piece of software, best-selling novel, or genetic program plugged into a vat of gene-spliced *E. coli* can be used to produce an infinite number of copies. In each, it is the message rather than the medium that is central to the analysis. In each, one is forced to confront the division and disaggregation of the property concept, and so on.

To some, this approach may seem doubtful. Professional economists have concentrated on "innovation" rather than "information"—particularly in coverage of intellectual property, but occasionally even in their coverage of such issues as insider trading. I chose quite deliberately to move away from this literature and to use a broad and open definition

---

10. James Boyle, *Ideals and Things: International Legal Scholarship and the Prison-House of Language*, 26 HARV. INT'L L.J. 327 (1985) [hereinafter Boyle, *Ideals and Things*]; James Boyle, *Thomas Hobbes and the Invented Tradition of Positivism: Reflections on Language, Power, and Essentialism*, 135 U. PA. L. REV. 383 (1987) [hereinafter Boyle, *Thomas Hobbes*].

11. *See* 1 JOHN AUSTIN, LECTURES ON JURISPRUDENCE 167 (Robert Campbell ed., 5th ed., London, John Murray 1885).

12. Felix S. Cohen, *Transcendental Nonsense and the Functional Approach*, 35 COLUM. L. REV. 809, 835-36 (1935).

13. Patent law offers just as rich a field for analysis. I excluded it partly because of exhaustion and lack of space, but also because of a tentative judgment that it depends on a similar conceptual structure to that of copyright law. Both areas apply a notion of "originality" that suppresses the importance of culture, language, and scientific community. Both exhibit the same structural pattern of internal binary division, although the content of the divisions is not identical. (Consider the copyright protection of expression, not idea, and the patentability of function, not form.) In each case, it is the *manifestation* of the appropriate kind of genius that receives protection, while the remainder is given to the public realm. My own background leads me to use the idea of romantic authorship as the organizing concept. I leave open the question of whether a similar analysis could be performed using the idea of the "inventor."

of information as my organizing concept. In part, this choice stems from the belief that there are interesting things to be said about both levels of generality, and that information was the conceptual box into which my particular theoretical interests fit most neatly. My choice also stems from the fact that the studies that concentrate on "innovation" are destined to repeat the paradigm of the original transformative genius, rather than subjecting it to critical assessment in each of the new contexts in which it is deployed.[14] By themselves, of course, these explanatory remarks could not *justify* my choices. In the end, it will be the work created from the materials thus assembled that either justifies or discredits the criteria of inclusion. For epistemological reasons, if for no others, the proof of this pudding *is* in the eating.

---

14. Some writers seem to assume that production, whether industrial or literary, is marked by two distinct forms—one representing imitative, organic, normal science, the other transformative, original innovation. This is as true of Schumpeter as it is of Wordsworth. *See* JOSEPH A. SCHUMPETER, THE THEORY OF ECONOMIC DEVELOPMENT (Redvers Opie trans., Oxford University Press 1961) (1934). I am heartened to find that one of the most empirically detailed and historically sensitive *economic* studies of technology and innovation echoes my dissatisfaction with this conclusion. Paul David explains that he has found it much more useful to conceive of innovation in terms of modification of particular existing processes rather than in terms of sweeping industry-wide transformation.

> [T]he economist's now conventional conceptualization of technological innovation as a change of a neoclassical production function—an alteration of relationships between inputs and output across the entire array of known techniques—has turned out to be less helpful than one might wish. On more than one occasion, regrettably, it has led historical discussions of invention and diffusion into paradox and confusion.

PAUL A. DAVID, TECHNICAL CHOICE, INNOVATION AND ECONOMIC GROWTH: ESSAYS ON AMERICAN AND BRITISH EXPERIENCE IN THE NINETEENTH CENTURY 2 (1975). David's conclusion is that

> a deeper understanding of the conditions affecting the speed and ultimate extent of an innovation's diffusion is to be obtained only by explicitly analyzing the specific choice of technique problem [sic] which its advent would have presented to objectively dissimilar members of the relevant (historical) population of potential adopters.
>   . . . Doing so, however, calls sharply into question the penchant historians of technology have displayed for separating their task into two distinct undertakings: writing the 'history of common practices' and the 'history of inventions,' and supposing that it will prove useful to continue to pursue each enterprise rather independently of the other.

Id. at 5. In this Article, I stress that the fixation on authors, inventors, and entrepreneurs tends to obscure the importance of continuity, indebtedness, and evolution and to overemphasize that of transformation, originality, and revolution. Having claimed that this vision of creation undervalues genre, tradition, and source, I point out that it also ignores the contradictory roles that information is expected to play—even within the world of microeconomics. Consequently, I argue that one cannot draw the kind of general conclusions that most economists and historians have drawn about the relationship of any particular kind of information, *or* innovation, to some abstract legal form. For obvious reasons, my use of the larger conceptual category of information facilitates this argument considerably. David's account, with its stress on dissimilar circumstances, particular empirical evidence, and the intimate relationship between the "innovation" and the practices it modifies, seems to me to support at least part of this effort.

I
Four Puzzles

A. *Copyright*

Nothing is more familiar to the student of intellectual property than the claim that it is an area of unusual conceptual difficulties. We even have judicial authority for the proposition that copyright approaches "nearer than any other class of cases belonging to forensic discussions, to what may be called the metaphysics of the law, where the distinctions are, or at least may be, very subtle and refined, and, sometimes, almost evanescent."[15] At first sight the current state of copyright doctrine would appear to justify that conclusion. The newcomer to the field is quickly dazzled by the apparently basic questions that surface even in relatively mundane cases. What is the distinction between idea and expression?[16] Are the page numbers in the West Law Reports or the alphabetical compilations of names in a telephone directory actually copyrightable?[17] What are the criteria for deciding such cases: The originality of the work? The amount of labor that has gone into it?[18] The potential loss to the original compiler, or potential profit to the copying

---

15. Folsom v. Marsh, 9 F. Cas. 342, 344 (C.C.D. Mass. 1841) (No. 4,901).

16. "Nobody has ever been able to fix that boundary, and nobody ever can." Nichols v. Universal Pictures Corp., 45 F.2d 119, 121 (2d Cir. 1930) (Hand, J.); *see also* Peter Pan Fabrics, Inc. v. Martin Weiner Corp., 274 F.2d 487, 489 (2d Cir. 1960) (Hand, J.) ("Obviously, no principle can be stated as to when an imitator has gone beyond copying the 'idea,' and has borrowed its 'expression.' "). The more fundamental question, however, is not *how* to draw the distinction between idea and expression, but *why* to draw it.

> Why is it that copyright does not protect ideas? Some writers have echoed the justification for failing to protect facts by suggesting that ideas have their origin in the public domain. Others have implied that "mere ideas" may not be worthy of the status of private property. Some authors have suggested that ideas are not protected because of the strictures imposed on copyright by the first amendment. The task of distinguishing ideas from expression in order to explain why private ownership is inappropriate for one but desirable for the other, however, remains elusive.

Litman, *supra* note 2, at 999 (footnotes omitted). At a later point, I will argue that the contradictory ideological structure described in these pages is the most plausible explanation for the copyright's reliance on the idea-expression dichotomy. *See infra* Part VI.

17. *See* L. Ray Patterson & Craig Joyce, *Monopolizing the Law: The Scope of Copyright Protection for Law Reports and Statutory Compilations*, 36 UCLA L. Rev. 719, 720-28 (1989) (recounting a district court's willingness to grant, and a circuit court's willingness to affirm, a preliminary injunction against the use of West page numbers by Mead Data Central's LEXIS service). *But see* Feist Publications v. Rural Tel. Serv. Co., 111 S. Ct. 1282, 1297 (1991) (holding that telephone white pages are not entitled to copyright protection and that use of them does not constitute infringement).

18. *See* Justin Hughes, *The Philosophy of Intellectual Property*, 77 Geo. L.J. 287 (1988) (investigating the two "grand" theories for intellectual property—labor and personality); Alfred C. Yen, *Restoring the Natural Law: Copyright as Labor and Possession*, 51 Ohio St. L.J. 517 (1990) (advocating the restoration of copyright law's natural law heritage, in part through an investigation of the rights an author should be granted for her labor).

party, or to society?[19] Can anyone own "facts"?[20] Does a computer program such as "Windows" infringe the copyright of the Apple operating system if it has a similar "look" or "feel," regardless of whether that look or feel is produced by lines of computer code that in no way resemble the original work?[21] What is the extent of the "fair use" exception to copyright?[22] How far does the "public domain" extend and how are we to conceive of it?[23] The list of questions could be extended almost infinitely. Indeed, in a comment on the state of "fact works" doctrine that could well be applied to the whole field of copyright, one scholar put the point succinctly: "[T]here is ample precedent deciding almost every copyright issue in almost every conceivable direction."[24] Is there something particular about intellectual property that explains this apparent doctrinal chaos?

---

19. Wendy J. Gordon, *Towards a Jurisprudence of Benefits: The Norms of Copyright and the Problem of Private Censorship,* 57 U. CHI. L. REV. 1009, 1037-49 (1990) (book review).

20. "The most notable features of present-day copyright doctrine relating to 'fact works' are its incoherence and instability." Peter Jaszi, *Fact Works and All That—A (Slightly) Structuralist Overview, in* FUNDAMENTALS OF INTELLECTUAL PROPERTY LAW PRACTICE BEFORE AGENCIES, COURTS AND IN CORPORATIONS 348, 348 (1987).

21. A federal district judge granted a preliminary ruling in favor of Apple. *Apple Suit Advances,* L.A. TIMES, Mar. 7, 1991, at D2.

22. For example, the Supreme Court refused to allow *The Nation* to copy excerpts of President Ford's autobiography despite the fact that news reporting is mentioned as one of the statutory exemplars of the fair use exception. "The promise of copyright would be an empty one if it could be avoided by merely dubbing the infringement a fair use 'news report' of the book." Harper and Row, Publishers v. Nation Enters., 471 U.S. 539, 557 (1985). If the reporting of excerpts of an ex-president's memoirs by a news magazine is seen merely as an *assertion* of "news reporting," then what counts as actual news reporting, sufficient to meet the fair use test? For a magisterial study of fair use law, which actually discusses both the utilitarian and the utopian goals that copyright law ought to promote, see William W. Fisher III, *Reconstructing the Fair Use Doctrine,* 101 HARV. L. REV. 1659, 1661-95 (1988). Fisher is more sanguine about the *Nation* case.

Later in this Article, I argue that even the defenders of an expansive fair use doctrine have paid insufficient attention to the role of this doctrine in constructing the public domain—that is, in providing or disseminating the raw material out of which future intellectual creations may be built. *See, e.g.,* Litman, *supra* note 2. Landes and Posner are, by contrast, very careful to mention this aspect of copyright doctrine and seem to agree that its importance is underrated—a phenomenon for which they offer no particular explanation. William M. Landes & Richard A. Posner, *An Economic Analysis of Copyright Law,* 18 J. LEGAL STUD. 325, 357-61 (1989).

23. *See* Litman, *supra* note 2, at 968, 999 (arguing that "justifications for the public domain become least satisfactory at the most fundamental level" and proposing that public domain should be understood "not as the realm of material that is undeserving of protection, but as a device that permits the rest of the system to work by leaving the raw material of authorship available for authors to use"). Occasionally, judges seem willing to recognize this side of the public domain although they generally "balance" their commentary by a tip of the hat to the idea of original genius.

> In truth, in literature, in science and in art, there are, and can be, few, if any, things, which, in an abstract sense, are strictly new and original throughout. Every book in literature, science and art, borrows, and must necessarily borrow, and use[s] much which was well known and used before. . . . No man writes exclusively from his own thoughts, unaided and uninstructed by the thoughts of others. The thoughts of every man are, more or less, a combination of what other men have thought and expressed, although they may be modified, exalted, or improved by his own genius or reflection.

Emerson v. Davies, 8 F. Cas. 615, 619 (C.C.D. Mass. 1845) (No. 4,436).

24. Litman, *supra* note 2, at 998.

B. Blackmail

Why is blackmail illegal? The crime is defined as an "[u]nlawful demand of money or property under threat to do bodily harm, to injure property, to accuse of crime, or to expose disgraceful defects."[25] It is easy to understand that the demand of money is unlawful when the accompanying threats are of bodily harm or property damage. After all, these threats themselves are illegal on other grounds. It is also possible to explain why you cannot demand money as the price of refraining from accusing someone of a crime. But what about the case where a private individual asks another private individual for money as the price of not revealing legally obtained information about activities perfectly legal in themselves: "If you do not pay me $100, I will reveal to your boyfriend the fact that I saw you coming out of another man's house at two o'clock in the morning." After all, in this case it would be perfectly legal to carry through with the threat. Clearly the person being blackmailed does not wish to pay, but then many of us do not wish to pay when others ask money from us, telling us that if we do not comply with their demands they will carry out some legal and unpleasant course of action. How is blackmail different from a baseball team "demanding" concessions from a city and local residents (in the form of tax reductions and parking spaces, for example) under threat of moving the team to another city? It begs the question to say that the baseball team has a right to do so, whereas the blackmailer does not. That, after all, is exactly the point we are supposed to be explaining.

Scholars have been drawn to blackmail like wasps to a picnic. Landes and Posner, Goodhart, Nozick, Coase, and Epstein have all suggested explanations[26]—none terribly convincing. The commodification of this kind of information is generally reviled and legally prohibited, yet no one has explained why.[27] *Is* there a reason?

---

25. BLACK'S LAW DICTIONARY 170 (6th ed. 1990).

26. *See* ARTHUR L. GOODHART, ESSAYS IN JURISPRUDENCE AND THE COMMON LAW 175-89 (1931); ROBERT NOZICK, ANARCHY, STATE, AND UTOPIA 84-86 (1974); Ronald H. Coase, *The 1987 McCorkle Lecture: Blackmail,* 74 VA. L. REV. 655 (1988) (examining blackmail from an economic perspective and focusing in particular on the British response to blackmail); Richard A. Epstein, *Blackmail, Inc.,* 50 U. CHI. L. REV. 553 (1983) (arguing that blackmail should be illegal not so much because it is inherently coercive but rather because it necessarily leads to, and is inseparable in reality from, fraud, peculations, and other forms of illegality); William M. Landes & Richard A. Posner, *The Private Enforcement of Law,* 4 J. LEGAL STUD. 1, 42-44 (1975) (articulating and defending an economic model in which law is enforced by private entities and applying this model to blackmail).

27. James Lindgren, *Unraveling the Paradox of Blackmail,* 84 COLUM. L. REV. 670, 671 (1984). Lindgren's own explanation concerns third party rights, and I will discuss it later. *See infra* text accompanying notes 164-67.

C. Insider Trading

Securities law sometimes prohibits certain individuals from trading in securities on the basis of material nonpublic information. All scholars seem to agree that, despite widespread popular support for sanctions against insider trading, the reasons for such sanctions are hard to identify. In fact, a recent article *supporting* the prohibition of insider trading started with the following startling admission: "American jurisprudence abhors insider trading with a fervor reserved for those who scoff at motherhood, apple pie, and baseball. *The commonly stated reasons for this reaction to insider trading are many and unpersuasive. The case law barely suggests why insider trading is harmful.*"[28] Needless to say, those arguing *against* the criminalization of insider trading are even less charitable towards the reasons offered. In the ubiquitously cited work on the subject, Henry Manne argued that prior to 1910 no one had ever publicly questioned the morality of insider trading.[29] Further, he claimed that since that time no one has explained why insider trading is morally or economically wrong.[30]

At first blush, it seems that Professor Manne has a point. Our society distributes wealth through a market system built on inequality of economic power and normally exalts an individual who is able to convert some temporary advantage in knowledge or economic power into a position of market advantage. Why not here? And why is it that, just as with blackmail, so many people share the sense that insider trading is wrong but find it hard to explain the reason?

D. Spleens

So far, I have given three brief and general descriptions of areas of doctrine. My last example is longer and comes from a single case,[31] the rhetoric and reasoning of which is so extraordinarily revealing that it

---

28. James D. Cox, *Insider Trading and Contracting: A Critical Response to the "Chicago School,"* 1986 DUKE L.J. 628, 628 (emphasis added) (footnote omitted). For assessments even more critical, see Harold Demsetz, *Perfect Competition, Regulation, and the Stock Market, in* ECONOMIC POLICY AND THE REGULATION OF CORPORATE SECURITIES 1, 11-16 (Henry G. Manne ed., 1969); J.A.C. Hetherington, *Insider Trading and the Logic of the Law,* 1967 WIS. L. REV. 720; Michael Moran, Insider Trading in the Stock Market: An Empirical Test of Damages to Outsiders (Center for the Study of American Business, Washington University Working Paper No. 89, July 1984).

29. HENRY G. MANNE, INSIDER TRADING AND THE STOCK MARKET 1 (1966) ("Prior to the year 1910 no one had ever publicly questioned the morality of corporate officers, directors, and employees trading in the shares of corporations.").

30. Most of the commonly cited scholarly critiques of insider trading, Manne claimed, were "largely statements of conclusions." *Id.* at 5. The congressional hearings of 1933 and 1934 were no better: "[T]o say that the practice was vicious or unscrupulous was . . . not a reasoned answer. Worse than that, the emotional tone of the arguments probably intimidated anyone who tried to defend the practice or even make cogent inquiries." *Id.* at 10.

31. Moore v. Regents of the Univ. of Cal., 793 P.2d 479 (Cal. 1990), *cert. denied*, 111 S. Ct. 1388 (1991).

deserves extended consideration.[32] In 1976 John Moore started treatment for hairy-cell leukemia at the UCLA Medical Center. His doctors quickly became aware that some of his blood products and components were potentially of great commercial value. They performed many tests without ever telling him of their commercial interest, and took samples of every conceivable bodily fluid, including sperm, blood, and bone marrow aspirate. Eventually, they also removed Mr. Moore's spleen, a procedure for which there was an independent medical reason, but only after having first made arrangements to have sections of the spleen taken to a research unit. In 1981 a cell line established from Mr. Moore's T-lymphocytes was patented by the University of California, with Mr. Moore's doctors listed as the inventors. At no time during this process was Mr. Moore told anything about the commercial exploitation of his genetic material. The likely commercial value of the cell line is impossible to predict exactly, but there were "reports in biotechnology industry periodicals predicting a potential market of approximately $3.01 Billion Dollars by the year 1990 for a whole range of [such lymphokines] . . . ."[33] There were no estimates in the case for the markets *after* 1990.

This case hinges on issues of information—on at least two levels. On the most obvious level, Mr. Moore was not told about his doctors' financial interest in exploiting his genetic material, an interest that might well have conflicted with the demands of responsible medical care. Dealing with this issue, the Supreme Court of California had no difficulty in ruling that Mr. Moore had stated a cause of action for breach of fiduciary duty or lack of informed consent. After all, he had been denied information in which he had a legitimate interest and which the doctors had a corresponding duty to provide.

On a slightly more abstract level, this case concerned the ownership and control of another kind of information, genetic information. T-lymphocytes are white blood cells that have, coded into their genetic material, "blueprints" or "programs" for the production of lymphokines, proteins that regulate the immune system. If these genetic "programs"

---

32. And I am not the only one to think so. *See, e.g.,* Bernard Edelman, *L'Homme Aux Cellules D'Or,* 34 RECUEIL DALLOZ SIREY 225 (1989); Bernard Edelman, *Le Recherche Biomedicale Dans L'Economie De Marche,* 30 RECUEIL DALLOZ SIREY 203 (1991); John J. Howard, *Biotechnology, Patients' Rights, and the* Moore *Case,* 44 FOOD DRUG COSM. L.J. 331 (1989); Patricia A. Martin & Martin L. Lagod, *Biotechnology and the Commercial Use of Human Cells: Toward an Organic View of Life and Technology,* 5 SANTA CLARA COMPUTER & HIGH TECH. L.J. 211 (1989); Thomas P. Dillon, Note, *Source Compensation for Tissues and Cells Used in Biotechnical Research: Why a Source Shouldn't Share in the Profits,* 64 NOTRE DAME L. REV. 628 (1989); Stephen A. Mortinger, Comment, *Spleen for Sale:* Moore v. Regents of the University of California *and the Right to Sell Parts of Your Body,* 51 OHIO ST. L.J. 499 (1990). For the most brilliantly macabre title in the related literature, see Erik S. Jaffe, Note, *"She's Got Bette Davis['s] Eyes": Assessing the Nonconsensual Removal of Cadaver Organs Under the Takings and Due Process Clauses,* 90 COLUM. L. REV. 528 (1990).

33. *Moore,* 793 P.2d at 482 (quoting plaintiff's complaint).

from the T-lymphocytes can be isolated, they can then be used to manufacture large amounts of the valuable lymphokine through a variety of recombinant DNA processes. For example, whole vats full of bacteria can be "told" to manufacture the particular lymphokine just as a computer word processing file can issue the same commands to any compatible printer. The key issue in the case was whether Mr. Moore owned the genetic information coded into his cells, or indeed, whether he owned the cells from which that information had been extracted. The court held that he had no property rights in either.

A fascinating array of reasons is offered for this decision. First, the court appears to believe that Mr. Moore had "abandoned" his cells when he consented to their removal. This argument is hard to square with the rest of the decision, however, where—while ruling on the issue of whether he had stated a cause of action in tort—the court did everything but hold as a matter of law that Mr. Moore had *not* been given sufficient information to consent to the removal.[34] Second, the court argued that the cells were not property anyway because California's genetic material statute "[b]y restricting how excised cells may be used and requiring their eventual destruction . . . eliminates so many of the rights ordinarily attached to property that one cannot simply assume that what is left amounts to 'property' or 'ownership' for purposes of conversion law."[35] By implication, one cannot assume that property rights exist in exotic and highly regulated substances, such as plutonium, which are subject to exactly the same types of regulation. In fact, since almost every kind of property is regulated, what can the court mean?

The court also said that Mr. Moore could not sue under conversion for violation of rights to his cells based on the rights of publicity or privacy. These, the court suggests, are not *really* matters of property law, so Mr. Moore has no remedy in conversion. Thus, though Johnny Carson has an enforceable interest in the phrase "Here's Johnny"[36] (a phrase uttered by someone else), Mr. Moore does not have one in his own DNA.

---

34. It also ignores the possibility that one can give up one stick from the bundle of property rights, but still retain the rest. This is an idea fundamental to all modern concepts of property, but particularly to intellectual property.

35. *Moore*, 793 P.2d at 492.

36. Carson v. Here's Johnny Portable Toilets, Inc., 698 F.2d 831, 836 (6th Cir. 1983). A disagreeable picture of Mr. Carson emerges from the suit, and one is left wishing that the defendant, who described himself as "The World's Foremost Commodian," *id.* at 833, could have taken his place on television. Judge Kennedy, in dissent, attacked the decision because (among other reasons) the phrase "Here's Johnny" "can hardly be said to be a symbol or synthesis, *i.e.,* a tangible 'expression' of the 'idea,' of Johnny Carson the comedian and talk show host." *Id.* at 844 (Kennedy, J., dissenting). This formulation—one that might have made even Hegel blanch—shows the power of the idea/expression distinction, even outside its normal ambit. Kennedy also mused that Ed McMahon might have a better claim to the phrase, as he was the one who actually used it. *Id.* at 839 n.5. Nevertheless, Judge Kennedy was willing to admit that a distinctive racing car could be an "expression" of the "idea" of the driver normally associated with it. *Id.* at 844 (citing Motschenbacher v. R.J. Reynolds Tobacco Co., 498 F.2d 821 (9th Cir. 1974)).

In any event, the court argues that since everyone's genetic material contains information for the manufacture of lymphokines, the particular genetic material is "no more unique to Moore than the number of vertebrae in the spine or the chemical formula of hemoglobin."[37]

Finally, in perhaps its most interesting twist, the opinion concluded that Mr. Moore could not be given a property right in his genetic material because to do so might hinder research. To back up this argument the court painted a vivid picture of a vigorous, thriving public realm. Communally organized, altruistically motivated, and unhampered by nasty property claims, the world of research is moving dynamically towards new discoveries: "At present, human cell lines are routinely copied and distributed to other researchers for experimental purposes, usually free of charge. This exchange of scientific materials, which still is relatively free and efficient, will surely be compromised if each cell sample becomes the potential subject matter of a lawsuit."[38] This argument is a convincing one: property rights in the world of research would only slow down discovery. Convincing, that is, until one reads in the very next column that "the theory of liability that Moore urges us to endorse threatens to destroy the economic incentive to conduct important medical research."[39] Property rights given to those whose bodies can be mined for valuable genetic information will hamstring research because property is inimical to the free exchange of information. On the other hand, property rights *must* be given to those who do the mining, because property is an essential incentive to research. Do these assertions contradict one another? Do they tell us anything about the doctrinal chaos of copyright or the anomalies of blackmail and insider trading? Is there a reason that the court is willing to give Mr. Moore an entitlement to "decisional," but not to *genetic,* information? Finally, does the decision give us any logical or ideological hints about the future legal regime covering biotechnology? I would say that the answer to each question is yes.

I have presented four puzzles. My claim is that each one is best understood as a conflict over the use of information and that the conflict is structured by a recurring pattern of contradictions. It is to that pattern I now turn.

---

37. *Moore,* 793 P.2d at 490. The court claims that "[b]y definition, a gene responsible for producing a protein found in more than one individual will be the same in each." *Id.* at 490 n.30. One's first reaction is to wonder whether the reasoning here is disingenuous or merely accidentally fallacious. Later in this Article, the court's concern with "originality" and "uniqueness" will be compared to the concerns stressed by the romantic notion of authorship. My claim is that such a comparison helps us to understand the court's almost obsessional desire to prove that Mr. Moore's spleen was not unique, whereas the doctor's research products were. *See infra* Section IX.C.

38. *Moore,* 793 P.2d at 495 (footnotes omitted).

39. *Id.*

II
PUBLIC AND PRIVATE IN THE LIBERAL STATE

[T]he state as a state abolishes *private property* (i.e. man decrees by *political* means the *abolition* of private property) when it abolishes the *property qualification* for electors and representatives, as has been done in many of the North American States. . . . The *property qualification* is the last *political* form in which private property is recognized.

But the political suppression of private property not only does not abolish private property; it actually presupposes its existence. The state abolishes, after its fashion, the distinctions established by *birth, social rank, education, occupation,* when it decrees that birth, social rank, education, occupation are *non-political* distinctions; when it proclaims, without regard to these distinctions, that every member of society is an *equal* partner in popular sovereignty . . . . But the state, none the less, allows private property, education, occupation . . . to manifest their *particular* nature. Far from abolishing these *effective* differences, it only exists so far as they are presupposed; it is conscious of being a *political state* and it manifests its *universality* only in opposition to these elements.[40]

There are many reasons to doubt Karl Marx's prescience as a theorist of the modern liberal state. But any American lawyer would have to acknowledge that he was right about one thing: the centrality of the public-private distinction to any understanding of the legal system. The liberal state depends on the idea of equality. That, after all, is one of the key differences between the liberal and the feudal idea of politics. Liberalism mandates an end to status distinctions in politics. There can be no restriction of the franchise to a particular social class, no weighting of the votes of the nobility. Thus we have equality, but only inside the public sphere. Citizens are equal, but only in their capacities as citizens, not as private individuals. Each is guaranteed an equal vote, but not equal influence. We draw a line around certain activities—voting, appearing in court, and so on—and guarantee equality within this realm. Outside that line is the private sphere, the world of civil society. It is the private sphere that contains all the real differences between people—differences of wealth, power, education, birth, and social rank. This line-drawing allows us to use the language of egalitarianism to defend a society marked precisely by a highly stratified distribution of wealth or power.[41]

The real dilemma of liberal theory is that it must exalt the virtues of

---

40. Karl Marx, *On the Jewish Question, in* THE MARX-ENGELS READER 24, 31 (Robert C. Tucker ed., 1972).

41. One of Marx's more intriguing suggestions is that the public sphere of the liberal state is attractive because it is a diminished and distorted form of a truly just, egalitarian society. While the Eastern European state socialist societies never provided anything except a dystopian model of

egalitarianism, of each person's voice counting equally and, at the same time, confine that egalitarianism to the public sphere. Our vision of society must be a vision of two separate spheres, with two different governing principles, two different theories of justice, and even two different *personae* to go with them.

> Where the political state has attained to its full development, man leads, not only in thought, in consciousness, but in *reality,* in *life,* a double existence—celestial and terrestrial. He lives in the *political community,* where he regards himself as a *communal being,* and in *civil society* where he acts simply as a *private individual,* treats other men as means . . . and becomes the plaything of alien powers.[42]

The law is implicated in every stage of this process.[43] First of all, the law draws, and in a more complex way depends on, the line between public and private. The central fear of the liberal political vision is that unrestrained state power will invade the private sphere. And yet the only force available to police the state *is* the state. The rule of law appears to be the answer to this dilemma. By policing the lines between public and private and between citizens and other citizens, the law offers us the hope of a world that is neither the totalitarian state nor the state of nature. In this sense, both the *role* of law and the *rule* of law depend on the public/ private division.

On a more mundane level, both lawyers and citizens perceive issues through the lens of the public/private distinction. Controversial political and moral issues often resolve themselves as being questions of *placement* in either the public or private realms.[44] Access to medical professionals,

---

drearily brutal oppression, the concern with the limits of egalitarian justice is an issue that bids fair to obsess liberal societies for the foreseeable future.

    42. Marx, *supra* note 40, at 32.

    43. This discussion can offer no more than a summary of the basic ideas. It would take an entire article to discuss the full ramifications of the law's role in the public/private distinction. In fact, particularly good ones have already been written on the influence of legal thought on classical economic thought, *see* Duncan Kennedy, *The Role of Law in Economic Thought: Essays on the Fetishism of Commodities,* 34 AM. U. L. REV. 939 (1985), on the decline in credibility of the public/ private dichotomy, *see* Duncan Kennedy, *The Stages of the Decline of the Public/Private Distinction,* 130 U. PA. L. REV. 1349 (1982), on the history and reasons for the continued survival of the distinction, *see* Morton J. Horwitz, *The History of the Public/Private Distinction,* 130 U. PA. L. REV. 1423 (1982), and on the paradoxes produced by the fact that the market can seem public from the perspective of the family, but private from the perspective of the state, *see* Frances E. Olsen, *The Family and the Market: A Study of Ideology and Legal Reform,* 96 HARV. L. REV. 1497 (1983). For a discussion of the prominence of the public/private distinction in tort law, see James Boyle, *The Anatomy of a Torts Class,* 34 AM. U. L. REV. 1003, 1023-34 (1985).

    44. Marx also thought that law played a vital role in this process, at least with respect to religion.

> Man emancipates himself *politically* from religion by expelling it from the sphere of public law to that of private law. Religion is no longer the spirit of the *state,* in which man behaves, albeit in a specific and limited way and in a particular sphere, as a species-being, in community with other men. . . . It is no longer the essence of *community,* but the essence

for example, is in the private sphere. My access depends on my resources; there is no constitutional guarantee to equal health care, or even to minimal health care. Access to legal professionals, however, is at least partly in the public sphere. When I am tried for a crime that may carry a substantial jail term, I have the right to an attorney whether or not my private resources will let me pay for one.[45]

This example suggests one last important point about the public/ private distinction in law: our conception of justice differs depending on whether we are dealing with public law or private law. A driver negligently knocks over a pedestrian. If the victim is poor, homeless, and out of work, the law is likely to put him back in exactly that position. Tort damages, after all, are compensatory. If the victim is a $200,000 a year investment banker, the injurer is likely to find himself paying out a lot more in lost wages, among other things. Yet when we turn from private law to public law, the picture changes completely. Should the law punish an assault against an investment banker more seriously than an offense against a homeless person? Our sensibilities are outraged at the thought (even if we suspect this frequently may be the reality). In the private sphere our ideal of justice is, broadly speaking, *restitutio in integrum.* In public law we aim for equality.[46]

One of the claims of this Article is that every dispute about property rights in information resolves itself into a dispute about whether the issue "is" in the public or the private realm. This rhetoric of geographic placement suggests that we are engaged in a factual inquiry about the location of a preexisting entity within a well-charted and settled terrain. Nothing could be further from the truth. In fact, the process is one of contentious moral and political decisionmaking about the distribution of wealth,

---

of *differentiation.* . . . It is now only the abstract avowal of an individual folly, a private whim or caprice.

Marx, *supra* note 40, at 33. In this sense, the defining feature of the liberal theory of politics is that it moves religion, wealth, and social class from the realm of public law to that of private law. We can no longer condition public office on a particular religion or social class, nor can we allow citizens to buy shorter jail time or purchase exemptions from military service. We can, however, allow private associations to exclude on the basis of religion or private individuals to purchase better health care or education.

45. Gideon v. Wainwright, 372 U.S. 335, 345 (1963) (establishing, under the Sixth Amendment, a right to counsel for all defendants accused of serious crimes). *See generally* ANTHONY LEWIS, GIDEON'S TRUMPET (1964) (describing details of *Gideon*).

46. The question is even more complicated than this, because the tension is reproduced at each level of the inquiry. *Gideon* is a perfect example of the playing out of this issue in constitutional law. *See* 372 U.S. 335. First, we have to decide whether the norm of equality applies. Our notion of equal justice fairly obviously does include access to legal services and does not include access to medical services. But even if we say that the norm of equality should apply, we have to decide what equality *means*, with the choice normally being between formal equality and substantive equality. In *Gideon v. Wainwright,* equality means substantive equality—the accused has a right to an actual lawyer, not merely to a hypothetical lawyer if he can pay for one. In First Amendment issues, however, we all have merely a formally equal right to speak—the state is not understood to be constitutionally bound to pay the cost of getting my advertisement into the newspaper.

power, and information. The supposedly settled landscape is in fact an ever-changing scene that folds back onto itself like a Möbius strip. The market, for example, is on the public side of the map when we are talking about commercial exploitation of private information about families. As citizens we feel the need to keep the impersonal, public world of commerce out of our private realm of home and hearth. Yet the market is simultaneously on the private side of the line as against the state. When the FDA requires a drug company to reveal details of its internal testing practices, the company lobbyists will probably stress the importance of defending private enterprise against public meddling. If a geography metaphor is appropriate at all, the most likely cartographers would be Dali, Magritte, and Escher.

My own views on information issues are strongly influenced by two goals. The first is egalitarian—having to do with the relative powerlessness of the group seeking access to or protection of information. The second is the familiar radical republican goal of creating and reinforcing a vigorous public sphere of democracy and debate.[47] Yet, for all of the usual postmodern, pragmatist reasons, I would not suggest that we erect these two criteria into a new grand theory. All of the problems of value-choice, contradiction, and indeterminacy of meaning would reappear in the new theory. Thus, I have no criteria that would "replace" the language of public and private, at least no criteria that would algorithmically resolve the questions I put forward here. Why, then, do I spend so much time taking apart that language? My point is that because there is in fact no intelligible geography of public and private, the attempt to resolve issues through a process of line-drawing gives us only an empty exchange of stereotypes, "illusions about which one has forgotten that this is what they are; metaphors which are worn out and without sensuous power; coins which have lost their pictures and now matter only as metal, no longer as coins."[48] Those illusions, however, have considerable motive power and this Article aims to show where they take us. Even without a grand theory, it may be somewhere we do not want to go.[49]

---

47. For an excellent discussion of the tensions between these ideas, see Frank Michelman, *Law's Republic,* 97 YALE L.J. 1493 (1988).

48. FRIEDRICH W. NIETZSCHE, THE PORTABLE NIETZSCHE 47 (Walter Kaufman ed. & trans., 1982).

49. For the methodological and epistemological argument behind this position, see Boyle, *supra* note 9. For an elegant critique of (*inter alia*) my approach, see Pierre Schlag, *The Problem of the Subject,* 69 TEX. L. REV. 1627 (1991). To me it seems that Professor Schlag develops an epistemological and ontological argument that epistemological and ontological reasoning can provide no basis for normative arguments, and then uses that same kind of reasoning to conclude, in a strikingly normative manner, that we *should not* argue normatively. *See generally* James Boyle, *Is Subjectivity Possible? The Post-Modern Subject in Legal Theory,* 62 U. COLO. L. REV. 489 (1991). This seems like a fourfold contradiction. Understandably enough, Professor Schlag disagrees with this assessment. Pierre Schlag, *Foreword: Postmodernism and Law,* 62 U. COLO. L. REV. 439, 449-51 (1991) (pointing out the apparent contradiction in placing postmodernism in the service of a traditional ethical program and claiming that a romanticized ethical subject reappears in the wake of

Now, having introduced the public/private split, let us turn to the second part of this conceptual background, the particular role of information.

III
INFORMATION IN THE LIBERAL STATE

Information plays a central, if not defining, role in both the public and the private worlds of the liberal political vision. When we talk about the private world of the family and the home, we define these institutions partly by the idea of an entitlement to withhold information—privacy.[50] The right to withhold information is also one of the main forms of protection given to private citizens facing an accusing state. Fourth and Fifth Amendment protections are the classic cases, but the attorney-client privilege is also a good example.

In the private world of the market, information is again a defining feature. The analytical structure of microeconomics includes "perfect information"—meaning free, complete, instantaneous, and universally available—as one of the defining features of the perfect market. At the same time, the *actual* market structure of contemporary society depends on information *itself* being a commodity—costly, partial, and deliberately restricted in its availability. When I discuss information economics,[51] this paradox will be of central importance.

Finally, in the public world of politics—which is defined in the liberal vision by the information-centered ideas of debate, exchange, and decision—the free flow of information is a prerequisite for atomistic citizens to form and then communicate their preferences in the great marketplace of ideas. At the same time, a citizen's access to information is thought to be as important a check on governmental activity as that provided by the rule of law. This point was made most famously by James Madison: "A popular Government, without popular information, or the means of acquiring it, is but a Prologue to a Farce or a Tragedy; or, perhaps both. Knowledge will forever govern ignorance; And a people who mean to be their own Governors, must arm themselves with the power which knowledge gives."[52]

---

the deconstructive project); Pierre Schlag, *Normative and Nowhere to Go,* 43 STAN. L. REV. 167 (1990).

50. Admittedly, conventional privacy doctrine covers a great deal more than the right to withhold information. Nevertheless, it seems fair to say that other areas of privacy doctrine are explained partly in informational terms, *cf.* Rust v. Sullivan, 111 S. Ct. 1759 (1991) (upholding federal regulations banning use of Title X funds by medical clinics that advise clients about the availability of and means of obtaining abortions), and that control over private *information* is a vital part of the contemporary conception—whether legal or lay—of privacy.

51. *See infra* Part IV.

52. Letter from James Madison to W.T. Barry (Aug. 4, 1822), *in* THE COMPLETE MADISON 337, 337 (Saul K. Padover ed., 1953).

So far I have argued that information, loosely defined, is central to our conception of the family, the market, and the democracy. I claimed that there are tensions "between spheres" in the roles we expect information to play. For example, the public interest in a sphere of vigorous debate and discussion often clashes with the demands of personal privacy. In contrast, claims to own certain information in the market mix uneasily with the values of the First Amendment.[53] I also have claimed that, within spheres, information is often conceived of in apparently conflicting ways. Looking at the market through the lens of microeconomics, we find that information is both an analytical prerequisite for the model and a commodity to be traded under the model. In First Amendment theory, analysts sometimes talk as if information exchange had its own inevitable tilt towards democratic values and the good life ("the cure for bad speech is more speech"). At other times they present the First Amendment as the jewel in the crown of liberalism, drawing its nobility precisely from the fact that it is value neutral as to content ("I loathe what you say but would die for your right to say it").[54]

Some might ask for explanations: Why do we think such different things about information? This is a vital question, and I am not sure that I can answer it satisfactorily. Part of the answer seems to be that the matrix of conflicts between the theories of justice that we apply to the family, the market, and democracy is overlaid by another set of conflicts caused by the fact that information is conceived of as both *finite* and *infinite*, as both product and process. As an infinite good, information seems to be that magical thing—a gift that can be given without making the giver any poorer. I explain Pythagoras' theorem to you, or teach you how to work out the area of a circle. Afterwards, I seem no poorer in the sense that we both have the knowledge. This is the positive side of the public goods dilemma. The same unit of the good apparently satisfies the needs of an infinite number of consumers. Perhaps this is one of the reasons that in moments of high moral or ideological conflict, we often

---

53. *See, e.g.,* Harper & Row, Publishers v. Nation Enters., 471 U.S. 539 (1985) (holding that the Copyright Act bars unauthorized use of quotations from a public figure's manuscript); *see also* Rosemary J. Coombe, *Objects of Property and Subjects of Politics: Intellectual Property Laws and Democratic Dialogue*, 69 TEX. L. REV. 1853 (1991); Alfred C. Yen, *A First Amendment Perspective on the Idea/Expression Dichotomy and Copyright in a Work's "Total Concept and Feel,"* 38 EMORY L.J. 393 (1989).

54. Some might believe that these contradictions result from the broad definition of information that I have adopted in this piece: nothing forces us to adopt the broad definition, and it is only with the broad definition that commodification seems to conflict with the perfect market, copyright with the First Amendment. With the use of sensible subdivisions—into copyright issues, First Amendment issues, privacy issues, insider trading issues, commodification issues, efficient capital market issues, and so on—these problems would disappear, or at least lose their salience. I am unconvinced by this argument, and I find support for my disbelief in the recurring problems that I pointed out within the law and rhetoric of copyright, blackmail, and insider trading. Given my vision of language and definition, however, I can imagine no "proof" of my method, save its usefulness to the reader.

reach for a solution that involves giving the parties more information. If we are thinking of information as a resource that is infinite in this sense, then the distribution of wealth does not seem to have been changed. Yet there are occasions when courts and scholars switch perspectives. Far from being an infinite resource, a good that may be given infinitely without impoverishing the giver, information is reconceived as a finite good, whose production and distribution are subject to the same economic laws as any other. Suddenly it becomes necessary to give producers an incentive to produce more information. Mandatory information transfer is suddenly viewed as an inefficient, forced exchange that undermines the incentives necessary to produce more information.[55]

So far, I have described information's various roles separately and in a rather static and synchronic way. But the historical importance of the connection between information, the market, and liberal democracy should not be underestimated. Perhaps the most familiar version of the relationship comes originally from the philosophers of the Scottish Enlightenment: commerce was desirable largely because it would force people from widely separated areas to talk to each other, to obtain information about the beliefs and practices of others, and inexorably to question the basis for their own. Thus, the invisible hand would subject social practices and traditions to the test of reason. *Doux commerce* would be the crucible in which superstition and myth were burnt away and the rationalism of the Enlightenment brought to the provinces. This message was extraordinarily influential on the political theorists of the early American republic.[56] In later years, both in Scotland and in the United States, the message changed. Increasingly, both the Scots and the American republicans began to worry that commerce would produce enormous disparities in wealth and power (including power over information) and that these disparities would be subversive of the republican form of government.[57] Sadly, this change of emphasis never received the same attention as the original optimistic message.[58]

---

55. Anthony T. Kronman, *Mistake, Disclosure, Information, and the Law of Contracts,* 7 J. LEGAL STUD. 1, 9-32 (1978) (arguing that forced disclosure of deliberately acquired information is undesirable because it impedes production of information at socially desirable levels); Saul Levmore, *Securities and Secrets: Insider Trading and the Law of Contracts,* 68 VA. L. REV. 117 (1982) (arguing against a disclose-or-abstain rule in insider trading on grounds of both fairness and efficiency).

56. *See, e.g.,* GARRY WILLS, INVENTING AMERICA: JEFFERSON'S DECLARATION OF INDEPENDENCE (1978).

57. *See* Robert W. Gordon, *"The Ideal and the Actual in the Law": Fantasies and Practices of New York City Lawyers, 1870-1910, in* THE NEW HIGH PRIESTS: LAWYERS IN POST-CIVIL WAR AMERICA 51 (Gerard W. Gawalt ed., 1984).

58. Two hundred years later, Horkheimer and Adorno amazed American college students by suggesting—in considerably less graceful language—that, even in capitalism, there was still mythology and iconography. More surprising still, they argued that these new "mythologies" might be all the more secure precisely because of the effect of disparities of power on the type of abundant but nonrandom "information" provided to the public. MAX HORKHEIMER & THEODOR W. ADORNO, DIALECTIC OF ENGLIGHTENMENT 28 (John Cumming trans., 1990).

If the concept of information has potentially conflicting roles to play in family, market, and state, and if information itself is sometimes conceived of as infinite and sometimes as finite, how are social problems involving information decided? Much of the time the answer is, "by drawing lines." We "type" certain situations or conflicts as "public" or "private" and then act as if we have solved the problem. Unfortunately, we have merely restated it. As I pointed out earlier, the notion of "private" is defined in one common understanding largely by the idea of the justified ability to withhold information. Yet the same word, with its connotations of "that-with-which-we-cannot-interfere," conjures up the freedom of the market from state intervention. The fact that we think of the private sphere as encompassing both the market (*vis-à-vis* the state) and the family (*vis-à-vis* the market *and* the state) produces a Laocoön of ideological and rhetorical contradictions.[59]

For example, many consumers do not wish biographical details, provided to a retailer for another purpose, to be traded in the flourishing direct marketing industry. They might argue that this information is "private" and that the state should step in to prevent the companies involved from passing it on, compiling it into larger databases, or whatever. Others might want the state to protect the private sphere of home and family from information coming in from the outside. The telemarketing phone call interrupting the family dinner is the most frequently used example. In both cases, the classification as "private" is supposed to trigger, or at least justify, state protection. Yet the owners of the databases would protest the unfairness of the public world of the state interfering in a *private* disposition of *private* property—in this case involving mailing lists or databases of consumer information. The telemarketers might say the same thing, but they would probably also claim that—since information, rather than some other form of property is involved—the issue is one which should be settled by appeal to the constitutional norms that govern the public realm.[60] In other words, they might argue both that the government should not interfere because this is a private activity in the market and that the government should

---

59. *See* Olsen, *supra* note 43.

60. When I first wrote this passage, I had intended these as purely hypothetical examples. Since that time, Congress enacted the Telephone Consumer Protection Act, originally introduced by Senator Hollings, which outlaws most autodialers. Pub. L. No. 101-243, 105 Stat. 2394 (1991) (to be codified at 47 U.S.C. § 227). Much debate preceded the law's passage. "Calling autodialers an 'outrageous invasion' of people's homes, Sen. Hollings said privacy rights outweigh concerns about the free speech of marketing companies." Edmund L. Andrews, *Curtailing the Telephone Robots,* N.Y. TIMES, Oct. 30, 1991, at D1, D24. The Portland, Oregon, ACLU disagreed. One of their lawyers, Mr. Charles Hinkle, is "representing a small business against an Oregon law banning the commercial use of autodialers." *Id.* at D24. His arguments? The ban would interfere with free speech and would violate the constitutional commitment to equality in public life—in this case the Equal Protection Clause—since it distinguishes between commercial and non-commercial speech. *Id.*

not interfere because this is a public issue of free speech—and equal protection, for that matter.[61]

If there really were an intelligible geography of public and private, and a unitary concept of information, then we might hold up the hope that one set of claims could be proved to be "true" and the other "false." But since the era of the legal realists, that hope has seemed chimerical.

The story cannot end here, however. One of the themes of this Article is that the implicit frameworks within which the regulation of information is discussed are contradictory—or at least aporetic—and indeterminate in application. As far as the rhetoric of public and private goes, that seems an unexceptionable conclusion.[62] Since that rhetoric dominates popular discussion of information, I explored at some length the multiple ways in which liberalism portrays information as central to both public and private realms. It is hard to read public debates on any issue involving information without coming to the conclusion that a great deal of it is an exercise in line-drawing or typing, increasingly isolated from the moral and political ideals the lines are supposed to represent. Perhaps this is the best we can do. But then again, perhaps not.

So much for public debate. Is scholarship any different? Increasingly, scholarly discussions of information are turning away from liberal constitutionalism and rights theory and towards the language of

---

61. The same, familiar tensions play themselves out in the public sphere of debate. Do private citizens have a right of access to privately held communications media in order to participate in public debate? The citizens would portray the television station as a means of public communication tinged with a public interest, *cf.* Munn v. Illinois, 94 U.S. 113 (1876) (upholding a state statute that regulated grain storage charges on public interest grounds), and would demand state intervention to prevent public debate from being ceded to a satrapy of private interests. The television station would portray such intervention as an illegitimate public interference with private property. Similarly, does a person who participates in the public world of politics lose her property right in reputation, a property right normally protected by the imposition of a universal tort duty to refrain from defamation? The list of similar questions goes on. On top of these issues lie the conflicts between the vision of information as both finite and infinite. Is someone really "taking" anything from you when they learn of your address or your consumption patterns and sell those facts to a thousand databases? You still have all the "goods" that you had before—except, of course, that peculiar good that exists in the *negation* or restriction of information.

62. Although the academic literature is relatively silent regarding the conflicting requirements that liberal state theory puts on information, most academics would admit, I think, that the language of public-ness and private-ness is relatively useless for resolving *any* important issue. I do not mean to say that it is meaningless to talk of "public" and "private" issues. On the contrary, those terms are central to public discourse. They are also the accepted way in which competing political beliefs are expressed. Hence the old saw that conservatives think the market is private and the bedroom is public and liberals think the exact opposite. Robert H. Mnookin, *The Public/Private Dichotomy: Political Disagreement and Academic Repudiation,* 130 U. PA. L. REV. 1429, 1430-31 (1982) (discussing the malleability of terms like public and private but noting their prominence in the discourse of political disagreement). But although they are vital terms with which to express normative conclusions, they are poor guides to analysis or decisionmaking. When lawyers or state theorists attempt to use them as *operative terms,* the "all-things-to-all-people" quality that makes them so useful in political debate simply produces an endless array of mirror-image arguments of the kind described above.

microeconomics.[63] Whether the issue is copyright,[64] patent,[65] insider trading,[66] blackmail,[67] or simply "valuable information,"[68] some of the most ambitious recent scholarship employs some kind of economic approach. Yet, microeconomics provides no surcease from the paradoxes of information. As I will try to show in the next Part, those paradoxes are just as central to the discipline of economics as they are to liberal political theory.

---

63. SCHEPPELLE, *supra* note 1, provides an excellent contractarian critique of this tendency. *See also* ECONOMIC IMPERIALISM: THE ECONOMIC APPROACH APPLIED OUTSIDE THE FIELD OF ECONOMICS (Gerard Radnitzky & Peter Bernholz eds., 1987).

64. *See, e.g.,* Landes & Posner, *supra* note 22, at 325 (applying economic models to determine the extent to which "copyright law can be explained as a means for promoting efficient allocation of resources"); John S. Wiley, Jr., *Copyright at the School of Patent,* 58 U. CHI. L. REV. 119 (1991) (arguing that although copyright and patent law serve essentially the same goals—justice for creators and efficiency for consumers—patent law is logically coherent while copyright law is not); *see also* Fisher, *supra* note 22 (proposing reformation of the fair use doctrine in particular and using economic analysis to support his proposal).

65. *See, e.g.,* George Bittlingmayer, *Property Rights, Progress, and the Aircraft Patent Agreement,* 31 J.L. & ECON. 227 (1988) (discussing difficulties of allowing property rights in ideas and using the Aircraft Patent Agreement as an illustration); Frank H. Easterbrook, *Intellectual Property Is Still Property,* 13 HARV. J.L. & PUB. POL'Y 108, 118 (1990) (arguing that patent law should treat physical and intellectual property identically, because "[r]ights to exclude are not monopolies just because the property involved is an intangible rather than something you can walk across or hold in your hand"); Louis Kaplow, *The Patent-Antitrust Intersection: A Reappraisal,* 97 HARV. L. REV. 1813 (1984) (discussing conflicts between patent and antitrust law and the resulting paradoxes); Edmund W. Kitch, *The Nature and Function of the Patent System,* 20 J.L. & ECON. 265 (1977) (arguing that the patent system is desirable because it increases output of resources used for technological innovation).

66. In insider trading scholarship, it would be briefer to cite those articles that do not rely on economic analysis. However, the following list may give some indication of the breadth of approaches subsumed under the heading. *See, e.g.,* MANNE, *supra* note 29 (examining generally the parameters of the insider trading problem, traditional legal solutions, and arguments for and against prohibiting the activity); Dennis W. Carlton & Daniel R. Fischel, *The Regulation of Insider Trading,* 35 STAN. L. REV. 857 (1983) (arguing that insider trading might be allowed in some cases as an efficient way to compensate corporate managers); William J. Carney, *Signalling and Causation in Insider Trading,* 36 CATH. U. L. REV. 863 (1987) (arguing that the opposition to insider trading may be unfounded because such activity causes very little harm); Cox, *supra* note 28 (arguing for continued regulation of insider trading and criticizing arguments that such trading is justified because it increases allocative efficiency); Christopher P. Saari, Note, *The Efficient Capital Market Hypothesis, Economic Theory and the Regulation of the Securities Industry,* 29 STAN. L. REV. 1031 (1977) (arguing that empirical findings underlying efficient capital market theory cast doubt on the SEC's assumption that stricter prohibitions on insider trading are the best means of protecting investors).

67. *See, e.g.,* Coase, *supra* note 26; Epstein, *supra* note 26; Landes & Posner, *supra* note 26, at 42-43.

68. *See, e.g.,* Easterbrook, *supra* note 1 (discussing the Supreme Court's treatment of discrete doctrinal areas of information law and attempting to unify them within a broader theory of property rights in information); Kitch, *supra* note 1 (using price and finance theory to analyze welfare consequences of law on ownership of information by firms and employees).

IV
THE ECONOMICS OF INFORMATION

As usual, information has not one role, but many. The analytical structure of microeconomics includes the concept of "perfect" information—meaning free, complete, instantaneous, and universally available— as one of the defining features of the perfect market.[69] At the same time, the *actual* market structure of contemporary society depends on information being a commodity—costly, partial, and deliberately restricted in its availability. To put it briefly, *perfect information is a defining conceptual element of the analytical structure used to analyze markets driven by the absence of information, in which imperfect information is actually a commodity.*[70] If an analogy is needed, imagine a theology that postulates ubiquitous God-given manna—food from heaven—in its vision of the heavenly city, but otherwise assumes that virtue and hard work are both maximized under conditions of scarcity. Now use that theology as the basis for a practical discussion of the ethics of food shortages.[71]

This basic theoretical *aporia*[72] explains the weakness of much economic analysis of information regimes. My point is not that the reality is more complicated than the abstraction. That would be a critique of all abstractions, and abstractions are necessary to life. My claim is that information is a problem case for that specific set of abstractions we call economic theory, that it can and must be represented within the theory in two conflicting ways, and that certain concrete problems follow as a result. Some economists believe that these problems can be solved by

---

69. For reasons related to the *aporia* described here, economists have tried to refine the concept of perfect information so as to limit the breadth of the concept. The accepted formulation seems to be that "[i]ndividuals are unsure only about the size of their *own* commodity endowments and/or about the returns attainable from their *own* productive investments. They are subject to technological uncertainty rather than market uncertainty." Jack Hirshleifer, *The Private and Social Value of Information and the Reward to Inventive Activity,* 61 AM. ECON. REV. 561, 561 (1971) (assessing private and social value in a perfect market of technological information and discussing implications of these values for the patent system); *see also* Peter A. Diamond, *The Role of a Stock Market in a General Equilibrium Model with Technological Uncertainty,* 57 AM. ECON. REV. 759 (1967) (explaining how the stock market deals with technological uncertainty). *But see* Sanford J. Grossman & Joseph E. Stiglitz, *On the Impossibility of Informationally Efficient Markets,* 70 AM. ECON. REV. 393 (1980) (arguing that informationally efficient markets are impossible because either prices would perfectly reflect the available information about the market, denying compensation to those who spend resources to obtain such information, and thus undermining the incentive to produce, or would introduce an extra cost into the price so that it no longer reflected perfectly the available information).

70. Having always wanted to imitate my ancestor and attach my name to a Law, I would like to call this Boyle's Paradox. Somehow, I doubt that the name will catch on.

71. Actually, the analogy underestimates the point, as the discussion will show in a moment. In any event, like microeconomics, religions are replete with mediating devices between the ideal and the actual. Consider, for example, how the conflict between an ideal vision of a perfectly merciful God and the actual reality of starving children, is mediated through a variety of conceptual devices including "original sin" and "God moves in mysterious ways." The economic ideas discussed in this section have more esoteric names, but the basic function is similar.

72. *See supra* note 5.

changing the level of analysis—from perfect to imperfect markets, from imperfect information as commodity to imperfect information as transaction cost to perfect information as component of the analytical structure—just as Russell and Whitehead believed that they could banish paradoxes from mathematics by segregating the component parts of the paradox on different levels of analysis. Gödel's Theorem convinced mathematicians of the impossibility of getting rid of this pattern of circularity, recursive definition, and self-swallowing analysis. Sadly, with some notable exceptions that I shall discuss in a moment, economists seem to have avoided any comparable moment of professional modesty.[73]

The first manifestation of this paradox in information economics is the fact that the requirements of "motivation" and those of "efficiency" seem contradictory.[74] For example, if markets are to be efficient, the

---

73. For some qualified exceptions to this statement, see JACQUES H. DRÉZE, *A Paradox in Information Theory, in* ESSAYS ON ECONOMIC DECISIONS UNDER UNCERTAINTY 105 (1987) (arguing that the value of information can be negative as well as positive); Torben M. Andersen, *Some Implications of the Efficient Capital Market Hypothesis,* 6 J. POST KEYNESIAN ECON. 281 (1983-1984) (arguing that the concept of information does not have any well-defined meaning in efficient capital market); Grossman & Stiglitz, *supra* note 69. The classic article calling for a more rigorous treatment of information was George J. Stigler, *The Economics of Information,* 69 J. POL. ECON. 213 (1961). According to Stigler, "One should hardly have to tell academicians that information is a valuable resource: knowledge *is* power. And yet it occupies a slum dwelling in the town of economics. Mostly it is ignored . . . ." *Id.* at 213. Reading the economic literature on information, one is tempted to believe that there was a reason for the marginalization of information noted by Stigler: information plays the same role for neoclassical economics that rent did for classical economics. It is the problem case in which the internal tensions of the discipline come to the surface.

74. Many economists do not see a paradox here because microeconomics is, after all, the study of trade-offs. As I will show in a moment, economic analysts of law tend to start by thinking of information as a commodity and then to introduce the free circulation of information as a countervailing factor that needs to be "balanced" against the need to commodify. *See* Landes & Posner, *supra* note 22, at 326 ("Copyright protection . . . trades off the costs of limiting access to a work against the benefits of providing incentives to create the work in the first place.").

Actually, except for the fact that it ignores the distributional side of things, this is not a bad formulation in that it tends to recast every issue as an ad hoc balancing act, depending on highly contextual and specific local factors. Yet by downplaying the extent to which this "balancing act" diminishes the scientific pretensions of the pure version of the theory, economic analysis attempts to keep its credibility while maintaining the illusion of rigor. Professional economists employ this tone of certainty less often than practitioners of "law and economics." *Compare id.* at 333 ("*In principle,* there is a level of copyright protection that balances these two competing interests optimally . . . . We shall see . . . that various doctrines of copyright law, such as the distinction between idea and expression and the fair use doctrine, can be understood as *attempts* to promote economic efficiency . . . .") (emphasis added) *with* Hirshleifer, *supra* note 69, at 572 (because of the possibility of speculation on prior knowledge of invention and the uncertainties of "irrelevant" risks, patent protection may or may not be necessary in order to produce an appropriate incentive to invention).

It also makes one a little skeptical to note that, when done by economic analysts of law, this ad hoc balancing of empirically unspecified and unquantified factors tends to track the distinctions made by the existing case law with surprising fidelity—surprising, that is, unless one had already assumed that the common law was working its way towards the economically efficient solution. *See* George L. Priest, *The Common Law Process and the Selection of Efficient Rules,* 6 J. LEGAL STUD. 65 (1977). In recent years, however, it seems that economists have begun to acknowledge that the problems in reconciling efficiency and incentives in information issues go deeper than this. *See*

prices must perfectly reflect available information. Yet information is costly to obtain. If prices perfectly reflect available information, with no part of the price going to the producer of the information, then there is no incentive to produce more information. To postulate efficiency in the production of information we must assume away the incentive necessary to produce. To postulate the incentive is to make efficiency impossible. It looks like a classic paradox. This is not an observation confined to those skeptical of information economics, some of the most sophisticated economists writing in the area have acknowledged this problem: "There is a fundamental conflict between the efficiency with which markets spread information and the incentives to acquire information."[75] Are property rights in information a transaction cost that impedes the full and efficient circulation of information? It might seem obvious that they are. After all, perfect information is one of the elements of the perfect market. If information can be commodified, then a host of transaction costs are introduced into information flow and a limited monopoly is granted in the midst of a system supposedly based on competition.[76]

Yet the picture changes when information is viewed not as an element within the theoretical structure of the economic system, but rather

---

Grossman & Stiglitz, *supra* note 69, at 405. Lawyers, too, have had their moments of skepticism, the most famous being Stephen Breyer, *The Uneasy Case for Copyright: A Study of Copyright in Books, Photocopies, and Computer Programs,* 84 HARV. L. REV. 281 (1970). The most sophisticated recent analyses have been those of Wendy Gordon. *See* Wendy J. Gordon, *Fair Use as Market Failure: A Structural and Economic Analysis of the* Betamax *Case and Its Predecessors,* 82 COLUM. L. REV. 1600 (1982); Wendy J. Gordon, *An Inquiry into the Merits of Copyright: The Challenges of Consistency, Consent, and Encouragement Theory,* 41 STAN. L. REV. 1343 (1989) [hereinafter Gordon, *Merits of Copyright*]; Gordon, *supra* note 19.

75. Grossman & Stiglitz, *supra* note 69, at 405.

76. This clash is a general one, not limited to information questions. Judge Easterbrook has recently argued that both judges and economists overstate the extent to which intellectual property rights (and in particular, patent rights) confer a monopoly. Intellectual property rights, he argues, are no different from rights to tangible property.

> Problem: Patents are not monopolies, and the tradeoff is not protection for disclosure. Patents give a right to exclude, just as the law of trespass does with real property. . . . A patent *may* create a monopoly—just as an auto manufacturer *may* own all of the auto production facilities—but property and monopoly usually differ.

Easterbrook, *supra* note 65, at 109. If Easterbrook is merely pointing out that the economic consequences of granting different patents will be different given the varying possibilities of substitute goods and so forth, the point is a good one. Indeed, it is precisely such empirical difficulties that undermine economists' more sweeping statements about the efficiency of the patent system as a whole. *See* Hirshleifer, *supra* note 69. As to his other point, Easterbrook may be right that judges overestimate the monopolistic qualities of *intellectual* property.

Nevertheless, his article, like many pieces of economic analysis, seems to commit the opposite error—to underestimate the extent to which *all* property rights can have monopolistic or quasimonopolistic effects. Property rights are frequently trumps *against* market forces; this point causes considerable problems for economic analysis. Thus, an economist would ask: "If I value your house more than you do (measured by our relative ability and willingness to pay), why should I not be able to compel you to sell it to me whether you like it or not?" Indeed, the general tendency in Chicago-school economic analysis is to use offering price rather than asking price as a measure. *See* Duncan Kennedy, *Cost-Benefit Analysis of Entitlement Problems: A Critique,* 33 STAN. L. REV. 387 (1981); *cf.* C. Edwin Baker, *The Ideology of the Economic Analysis of Law,* 5 J. PHIL. & PUB.

as a commodity produced and distributed according to the rules of that system. In fact, most economic analysis of information takes this "commodity perspective."[77] From that perspective, the goal of the analysis is to discover the level of property rights that will produce the optimal level of production. Take the classic case of *International News Service v. Associated Press.*[78] Associated Press (AP) operated a news-gathering service. An international network of correspondents and wire services provided news which was printed in the AP papers. Unfortunately for AP, International News Service (INS), which operated a far less expansive news-gathering apparatus, made a practice of free riding on AP's efforts. INS employees would gather news from AP's noticeboards and from early editions of its East Coast newspapers and would then reprint the news, often taking advantage of the time differential between the east and west coasts.

The *INS* case raises a difficult question for economic analysis. One line of rhetoric and analysis indicates that we should secure to producers the fruits of their labors, and thus induce them to produce more. Without some legally protected interest in the news it gathers, AP will presumably be under a competitive disadvantage. News will become a "public goods problem." Unable to exclude its competitors from the fruits of its efforts, AP will be driven to cut back its news-gathering activities—as will all the other newspapers. Thus, though consumers might be willing to pay for a higher level of news gathering, it will be impractical for any individual newspaper to provide such a service. Put this way, the majority's creation of a legally protected interest in freedom from

---

AFF. 3 (1975). Under that measure, a forced sale would be moving resources to their highest use value.

But because we make a pretheoretical classification of the issue as being about "settled property rights," we use asking price rather than offering price as the measure of value. You get to keep the house unless your asking price is equal to or lower than my offering price—in other words, unless you are willing to sell it to me. Yet, if there is a "public interest" involved, or an existing clash of land uses, we shift doctrinal boxes into eminent domain or nuisance and change our measure of valuation back to offering price. We need a general principle or algorithm that would identify those issues that should be analyzed in terms of the free-flowing calculus of utility (and offering price) and those issues that should be analyzed in terms of settled property rights (and asking price). Absent such a principle, economic analysts seem to be guilty of exactly that kind of mushy ad hoc balancing for which they reproach other legal scholars. *See* Duncan Kennedy & Frank Michelman, *Are Property and Contract Efficient?*, 8 HOFSTRA L. REV. 711 (1980).

It is, of course, true that there may be no problem as to any given property right. You may loathe my house, and the patent may be for a device that no one wants to use. This hardly resolves the more general theoretical problem, however, and it also tends to reduce all property (and intellectual property) questions into endlessly particular, empirical inquiries—negating the possibility of exactly the kind of grand statements about the efficiency or inefficiency of entire doctrinal areas for which economic analysis is renowned.

77. Obviously, there are a number of reasons for this—many of them good ones. Later in this Article, I will suggest that one of the not-so-good reasons is an unacknowledged and largely unconscious reliance on a particular model of authorship as the norm against which to measure all information issues. *See infra* Section X.B.

78. 248 U.S. 215 (1918).

unfair competition in news gathering is the perfect solution to the public goods problem. By allowing commodification, it ensures continued production and avoids the prisoner's dilemmas set up by the alternative regime.

Yet one cannot solve the problems of economic analysis merely by adopting the commodity perspective—leaving perfect competition and information efficiency concerns aside. The problem of the free flow of information reappears within the new model. For example, should we approach the question of "fair use" in copyright through the lens of the commodity perspective? If we do so, will we only tolerate limitations on intellectual property rights when those limitations are necessary to minimize transaction costs or accomplish well-defined public goals? The most sophisticated scholarly analysis takes this approach.[79] Consequently, it tries to preserve incentives for creators, even establishing a typology of "fair uses"—assigning or denying property rights in part according to whether those uses would tend to reduce the reward available to the author.[80] Yet the analysis largely ignores the opposite perspective, that of the efficient flow of information. If we switch the perspective, we see that one important purpose of "fair use" law is to make sure that future creators have available to them an adequate supply of raw materials. From this perspective, too many "incentives" could convert the public domain into a fallow landscape of private plots.

To their credit, some economic analysts have attempted to reconcile the two perspectives. Thus, for example, Landes and Posner describe copyright as constructed by the tension between the need to grant legally protected interests to authors in order to motivate them and the need to limit the rights of authors so as to allow future creators legal access to the raw materials they need.[81] This seems reasonable enough, but it also leaves them dangerously close to the mushy "balancing" analysis from which economics was supposed to provide surcease. At the same time, the *aporia* reappears in the question of classification *within* the theory. For instance, how are we to classify a telephone directory of agents and

---

79. *See* Fisher, *supra* note 22.

80. *Id.* at 1766-79.

81. Landes & Posner, *supra* note 22, at 326. In another context, one might expect that Landes and Posner would engage in one of those charming "assume a can opener" flights of fancy, in which we merely assume that authors will contract for the right to use exactly the inspirational sources needed, no less and no more. After all, Judge Posner can imagine that contingency fee lawyers will come flocking to prisons in order to pursue meritorious claims for damages: "Encouraging the use of retained counsel thus provides a market test of the merits of the prisoner's claim. If it is a meritorious claim there will be money in it for a lawyer; if it is not it ought not to be forced on some hapless unpaid lawyer." McKeever v. Israel, 689 F.2d 1315, 1325 (7th Cir. 1982) (Posner, J., dissenting). Why should he not imagine T.S. Eliot paying small royalties to everyone from Dante to the inventors of the tarot pack? Interestingly, Landes and Posner seem to assume from the beginning that such a solution is completely impractical. Instead, the best way to encourage production is to limit the creator's legally protected interests *ab initio.* Perhaps authors are allowed to exist in a world less stringently constricted by the devices of economic fantasy.

publishing houses or an index price measure in a futures market in books? Is the former—the information necessary to make the market run—something that should be freely available? Is the latter a commodity in which the creators must be able to claim a legitimate intellectual property right if we are to encourage continued production of information? Or is it exactly the other way around?[82]

My argument is not merely that analysts are concentrating too much on motivating creators and not enough on the free flow of information. I am claiming that a change in the focus of the analysis does not dispose of these difficulties; it merely reverses their "polarity." There are issues that economists tend to analyze by thinking of information *as information* rather than as a commodity—for example, the discussion of the efficient capital market hypothesis. Yet, as some economists have pointed out, unless the questions of commodification and incentive are worked into the analysis, the theory ends in paradox as soon as the slightest costs or imperfections are introduced into it. The best example comes from Grossman and Stiglitz's description of the self-destructing futures market.

> [W]henever there are differences in beliefs that are not completely arbitraged, there is an incentive to create a market. (Grossman, 1977, analyzed a model of a storable commodity whose spot price did not reveal all information because of the presence of noise. Thus traders were left with differences in beliefs about the future price of the commodity. This led to the opening of a futures market. But then uninformed traders had two prices revealing information to them, implying the elimination of noise.) But, because differences in beliefs are themselves endogenous, arising out of expenditure on information and the informativeness of the price system, *the creation of markets eliminates the differences of beliefs which gave rise to them, and thus causes those markets to disappear.* . . .

> Thus we could argue as soon as the assumptions of the conventional perfect capital markets model are modified to allow even a slight amount of information imperfection and a slight cost of information, the traditional theory becomes untenable. . . .

> . . . [B]ecause information is costly, prices cannot perfectly reflect the information which is available, since if it did, those who spent resources to obtain it would receive no compensation.[83]

---

82. Recourse to the traditional categories of copyright law—expression may be owned but not ideas or facts—merely begs the question. We *could* choose to analyze expression in our "commodity" mode and facts and ideas in our "free circulation of information" mode. Having thus assumed away the very *aporia* we need to resolve, we could study the production of texts under the current regime—to find our methodology triumphantly confirmed as we rediscovered the very pattern of choices that we ourselves had made moments before.

83. Grossman & Stiglitz, *supra* note 69, at 404-05 (emphasis added). The time lags, or other

Switching perspectives again, we might think that commodification is the answer. A futures market produces information—in the form of the price of futures contracts. We do not normally think of price as a public good, but it seems to fit all of the criteria. In this case, it is a valuable commodity that takes considerable effort to create and is available thereafter at a marginal cost near zero.[84] If we wish to eliminate the

---

imperfections in the transmission of information through price, that are necessary for those who create information to trade on it, are crucial to the discussion of insider trading. *See infra* Part VIII. In an article that studies the informational mechanisms of market efficiency, Ronald Gilson and Reinier Kraakman have argued that the "efficiency paradox" occurs only when the market is fully efficient: "While we do argue that an evolutionary bias pushes the market *toward* efficiency, the Efficiency Paradox arises only when *full* efficiency is achieved. Our very emphasis on information costs recognizes that prices need *not* be perfectly efficient with respect to any particular information." Ronald J. Gilson & Reinier H. Kraakman, *The Mechanisms of Market Efficiency*, 70 VA. L. REV. 549, 623 (1984). Nevertheless, they acknowledge that this notion of limits does not explain the apparent inconsistency between Grossman and Stiglitz's conclusions and their own analysis of two particular market mechanisms—universally informed and professionally informed trading—an analysis which does "explicitly point[] to reaching just such an efficient equilibrium." *Id.* To their eyes, however, "the conflict between these perspectives is more apparent than real." *Id.* Their solution is an interesting variation of an analysis that should be familiar by now. Briefly put, their idea is that the first trader who gains access to or develops some useful information will be able to profit from it—thus receiving an adequate incentive—and that the equilibrium can thereafter be maintained at a very low cost.

> The empirical literature does not demonstrate that the originators of [a useful] insight failed to earn a return on their efforts. Rather, it is reasonable to suppose that they did earn an acceptable return on the information, but that the secret was subsequently dissipated through discovery by competitors (or even academics). So understood, the question posed by the Efficiency Paradox is *not* whether incentives exist to induce the *original* innovation. Rather, the puzzle is to explain how an efficient equilibrium is *maintained* once the innovation becomes so widely known that profit is no longer possible for those who exploit it.
>
> . . . Because of joint cost characteristics, maintenance of the equilibrium is effectively costless, and the Efficiency Paradox disappears.

Id. at 625 (footnote omitted). The first part of the argument, which locates the incentive in the originator's temporally limited monopoly in trading on the value of the information, is very similar to Hirshleifer's musings about the patent system, *see* Hirshleifer, *supra* note 69, as well as to Manne's description of insider trading as the necessary compensation for entrepreneurial acts, *see infra* text accompanying notes 224-40. Given a privilege to trade, the originator does not need a legally protected interest (on the model of copyright or patent, say) in order to encourage future information creation. The second part of the analysis employs a traditional philosophical method for getting around state/process paradoxes—paradoxes such as Zeno's tale of the arrow that can never reach its target since it must pass though an infinite series of smaller and smaller distances. With the initial process simply postulated, we have no trouble thinking about the arrow quivering in the target, the equilibrium being maintained. Yet, as I think Kraakman and Gilson would agree, if we move from the abstract modeling of *possible* market mechanisms to the actual analysis of a particular market, we have moved too quickly, because to postulate this is to assert that which must be proved. In the abstract there is no way of knowing whether the temporal advantage of being first in possession of information and having a privilege to trade is an *inadequate* compensation, requiring greater intellectual property rights, or an *over*compensation that will encourage too many traders to invest too much in the acquisition of information so as to gain an advantage over other traders. *See* Eugene F. Fama & Arthur B. Laffer, *Information and Capital Markets*, 44 J. BUS. 289 (1971).

84. *Cf.* Harold Demsetz, *The Private Production of Public Goods*, 13 J.L. & ECON. 293 (1970). As Demsetz points out, the key feature of the public good is that "it is possible at no cost for additional persons to enjoy the same unit of a public good." *Id.* at 295. Why, then, is price not a public good?

public goods problem, the answer might be to commodify the price measure—to assert an intellectual property right in the price output of the market—in order to prevent others from gaining free access to the information. Yet if there is one thing that microeconomics cannot justify treating as a public good, surely it is price.

If all of this seems like an Alice-in-Wonderland conclusion, it is worth considering the case of *Board of Trade v. Dow Jones & Co.*,[85] in which the court recognized that Dow Jones had a "proprietary interest in its indexes and averages which vests it with the exclusive right to license their use for trading in stock index futures contracts."[86] The court pointed out, however, that "[t]he extent of defendant's monopoly would be limited, for as defendant points out, there are an infinite number of stock market indexes which could be devised."[87] The *Dow* case does not go as far as the "secret stock market" I proposed half-jokingly, but it does exemplify the ineradicable tension between the notion of perfect information and frictionless markets and the notion of commodification and property rights.

This internal tension in the analysis always leaves open the question whether a particular issue is to be classed as a public goods problem for which the remedy is commodification,[88] or a monopoly of information problem for which the remedy is unfettered competition.[89] The problem

---

85. 456 N.E.2d 84 (Ill. 1983). For the connection between this case and the *INS* case, see Douglas G. Baird, *Common Law Intellectual Property and the Legacy of* International News Service v. Associated Press, 50 U. CHI. L. REV. 411 (1983).

86. *Dow Jones*, 456 N.E.2d at 90.

87. *Id.*

88. Alternatively, the solution could be some form of state tax and transfer scheme to accomplish the same ends. This "commodification" solution may seem to run against the conventional wisdom that public or collective goods are those from which others cannot be excluded. If the good can be commodified, one might ask, surely that means that it was never a public good in the first place? From my perspective, this difficulty hinges on a certain confusion over baseline assumptions about legally protected interests, a confusion that is relatively common in the writing of nonlegally trained economists. Economists tend to think that an undifferentiated property concept has resolved many of the questions of internalization/externality, tend to lay no clear distinction between the physical and the legal exclusion of users of public goods, tend to underestimate the extent to which property rights can be fragmented, and tend to insist on a somewhat naive separation between public and private law. The real problem with public goods is that a failure by their users to internalize their full costs will lead to underproduction. (Although some economists believe that in some cases, it may actually lead to *over*production. Hirshleifer, *supra* note 69, at 569.) Demsetz makes a similar point.

> Frequently there is confusion between the public good concept, as I understand it, which states that it is possible at no cost for additional persons to enjoy the same unit of a public good, and a different concept, that might be identified as a collective good, which imposes the stronger condition that it is *impossible* to exclude nonpurchasers from consuming the good.

Demsetz, *supra* note 84, at 295. A central idea behind much of the law and economics literature since Coase is that many of the problems traditionally solved by recourse to the state taxation system can be just as well served by a system of limited property rights such as those found in copyright or patent.

89. For example, consider the following:

of classification is not merely an empirical one. Even the existence of precise empirical evidence (of a kind currently unavailable for any area of information regulation except, arguably, stock market prices) would not, alone, reveal the right answer unless we had also decided on what level of generality the analysis was to be undertaken. In *Feist Publications v. Rural Telephone Service Co.*,[90] for example, the Supreme Court denied copyright protection to the compilers of a white pages phone directory. The logic of the analysis I just applied to the *INS* case might seem to indicate that it was necessary to give the compilers of the directory some protection. After all, directories raise classic public goods problems. The cost of creation is high, yet it is possible at minimal extra cost for additional users to enjoy the same unit of the good thus created. In other words, it is expensive to make and cheap to copy. The Court was not disposed to agree. Partly by means of doctrinal line-drawing (copyright rather than unfair competition) and partly by means of definitional fiat (telephone directories are not original, so in that sense nothing truly new is being created), the Court moved away from the "sweat of the brow" theory and denied the compilers copyright protection.

At first, it appears that the *Feist* opinion has nothing to tell us about economic analysis. On closer inspection, it becomes apparent that the Court was not so much rejecting the commodity perspective as it was changing the level of generality of the analysis. From Justice O'Connor's perspective, it was the structure of copyright law as a whole that strikes the right balance between the need to reward producers and the need to maintain competition and the free flow of information. Since copyright law as a whole allows the commodification of expression but not the ideas or facts which that expression contains, and since the Court finds this particular arrangement of facts to be "unoriginal," no legally protected interest can be recognized. It is only once this prior decision about

---

It is true that under a patent system there will, in general, be some shortfall in the return to the inventor, due to costs and risks in acquiring and enforcing his rights, their limited duration in time, and the infeasibility of a perfectly discriminatory fee policy. On the other side are the recognized disadvantages of patents: the social costs of the administrative-judicial process, the possible anti-competitive impact, and restriction of output due to the marginal burden of patent fees. As a second best kind of judgment, some degree of patent protection has seemed a reasonable compromise among the objectives sought.

But recognition of the unique position of the innovator for forecasting and consequently capturing portions of the *pecuniary* effects—the wealth transfers due to price revaluations—may put matters in a different light. The "ideal" case of the perfectly discriminating patent holder earning the entire technological benefit is no longer so ideal. For, the same inventor is in a position to reap speculative profits, too; counting these as well, he would clearly be over-compensated.

. . . Do we have reason to believe that the potential speculative profits to the inventor, from the pecuniary effects that will follow release of the information at his unique disposal, will be so great that society need take no care to reserve for him any portion of the technological benefit of his information? The answer here is indeterminate.

Hirshleifer, *supra* note 69, at 571-72 (footnote omitted).

90. 111 S. Ct. 1282 (1991).

the level of generality has been made that the questions of efficiency and incentive can intelligibly be posed.

For all of these reasons, economic analysis of information regimes is extraordinarily indeterminate. A person reading the confident statements of legal scholars about the superior efficiency of the patent regime over the copyright regime,[91] or the economic inefficiency of insider trading regulation[92] and of the law of fraud,[93] would be surprised to find that economists cannot agree over the basic question of whether, in the absence of commodification, there will be under- or over-investment in the production of information. Kenneth Arrow takes a position that seems to support the Court's result in *INS*. He argues that without property rights, too little information will be produced, because producers of information will not be able to capture its true value.[94] Fama and Laffer, on the other hand, argue that too *much* information will be generated, because some information will be produced only in order to gain a temporary advantage in trading, thus redistributing wealth but not achieving greater allocative efficiency.[95] In other words, in the absence of information property rights, there may be inefficient investment of social resources in activities that merely slice the pie up differently, rather than making it bigger. Hirshleifer gives a similar analysis of patent law, ending with the conclusion that patent law may be *either* a necessary incentive for the production of inventions *or* an unnecessary legal monopoly in information that overcompensates an inventor who has already had the opportunity to trade on the information implied by his or her discovery.[96] It is hard to think of a more fundamental uncertainty.[97]

---

91. *See* Wiley, *supra* note 64.

92. *See infra* text accompanying notes 224-40.

93. *See* Easterbrook, *supra* note 1; Kronman, *supra* note 55; Levmore, *supra* note 55.

94. Kenneth Arrow, *Economic Welfare and the Allocation of Resources for Invention, in* THE RATE AND DIRECTION OF INVENTIVE ACTIVITY: ECONOMIC AND SOCIAL FACTORS 609, 617 (National Bureau of Economic Research ed., 1962). The Arrow article itself offers some lovely examples of the tensions between efficiency and anticompetitive provision of incentives. It is interesting to note that Arrow, writing for The RAND Corporation, believes that even with intellectual property rights it is unlikely that sufficient knowledge will be produced. He therefore suggests that "for optimal allocation to invention it would be necessary for the government or some other agency not governed by profit-and-loss criteria to finance research and invention." *Id.* at 623. Arrow uses this idea to offer a partial defense of the "cost-plus" method of developing weaponry for the military. "This arrangement seems to fly in the face of principles for encouraging efficiency, and doubtless it does lead to abuses, but closer examination shows both mitigating factors and some explanation of its inevitability." *Id.* at 624. Michael Perelman, most emphatically *not* writing for The RAND Corporation, uses a similar logic to reach a conclusion sufficiently indicated by his title. *See* Michael Perelman, *High Technology, Intellectual Property, and Public Goods: The Rationality of Socialism,* 20 REV. RADICAL POL. ECON. 277 (1988).

95. Fama & Laffer, *supra* note 83, at 298.

96. Hirshleifer, *supra* note 69, at 572-73.

97. The problem is further compounded by the fact that many professional economists seem to have a naive, prerealist understanding of law. In particular, I found the following recurrent mistakes. Professional economists often talk as though there was a natural suite of property rights that automatically accompanied a free market. They make strong and unexplained assumptions that

It is my argument in this Article that much contemporary economic analysis conceals these tensions, *aporias,* and empirically unverifiable assumptions by relying unconsciously on the notion of the romantic author. I have tried to show that most issues in information economics could be portrayed (in the absence of more detailed empirical information) as *either* public goods problems for which the state has wisely chosen the remedy of commodification in order to avoid underproduction *or* as potential monopolies in which intolerable transaction costs are introduced into the free flow of information. In later Parts, I will argue that this choice is often concealed by an implicit reliance on the author notion, a reliance that tends to push the analysis towards the incentives/commodity vision of information. This could have serious negative consequences since it will lead analysts (and governments) to support a greater commodification of information than is actually warranted. Such a discourse could also be used cynically to protect existing information monopolies. Economists would be mainly concerned by the possible efficiency losses implicit in such a result. In the Conclusion, I argue that there are also profound distributional issues which should concern us—particularly if we believe that information is becoming one of the primary resources in the international economy.

So much for the theory. What about the facts? The empirical evidence, of which there is surprisingly little, seems to justify these conclusions, or at least to cast doubt on current assumptions about the level of international intellectual property protection necessary to promote research and innovation. A historical, statistical study of the effect of patent protection on the development of drugs in both developed and developing countries from 1950 to 1989 found:

> [T]he existence of a patenting system is not a prerequisite for inventions.
>
>   . . . .
>
> The relationship between patent systems and their influence on the inventive capacity of developed countries was also tested. Two different tests using Yule's coefficient showed conclusively

---

certain types of activities (for example, trading on superior information) will "naturally" be allowed, but that certain others (for example, trading on superior physical strength) will not be. This kind of error also creeps into the work of some lawyer-economists such as Easterbrook and Levmore. *See generally infra* Part VIII (discussing insider trading). To the extent that they do use the concept of property, economists tend to assume that "absolute" property rights are the default position. The debates between Laffer and Arrow show the results of these shortcomings. For example, both Arrow and Laffer seem to assume that the "natural" unregulated position is that one would have "privileges" but not "rights" to trade in information. But if there is no such thing as a natural, unregulated market, we would have to compare the efficiency of *all* of the possible legal positions—particularly since the legal system actually uses the full suite of Hohfeld's jural correlates in its regulation of different kinds of information. For an excellent description of the many different legal relationships around valuable information, see Easterbrook, *supra* note 1, at 313-14.

that, for those countries in which nearly all inventions are made, the relationship is not significant.

. . . The hypothesis that the number of inventions would increase along with the world-wide increase in patent systems was also considered, but it was concluded that there is no significant relationship between these two variables, either in the United States or in the world at large.[98]

The certainty of these conclusions warrants some skepticism. A small correlation (Yule's association coefficient = 0.15) between patent protection and invention was observed in developed countries.[99] As the authors observe, there is a much more significant correlation between economic development and invention (Yule's association coefficient = 0.94).[100] Yet when the question is what level of intellectual property rights to maintain domestically, the latter correlation is of dubious relevance—at least for developed countries. On the other hand, the absence of a strong correlation between patent and invention is significant, and the study certainly tends to undermine the claims made by the developed world that a stronger international regime of intellectual property is necessary to encourage innovation.

Finally, while all such studies warrant methodological skepticism, the studies that support intellectual property protection seem even more problematic. One study estimated that without patent protection sixty-five percent of new drugs produced by the U.S. pharmaceutical industry would not have reached the market.[101] The analysis was based, however, on data supplied by the pharmaceutical industry in response to a questionnaire on the impact of patent protection on research and development. The problems with such a method are fairly obvious.

In another context, the paradoxes and empirical uncertainties of economic analysis might be of mainly theoretical interest. In discussions of information, they are of immediate practical relevance to almost every issue. In part this is because economists—to their great credit—have been in the forefront of attempts to treat information holistically.[102] Another reason may lie in the perception that information issues are somehow more "intangible." Escaping more easily from the absolutist, formalist, and physicalist notions of tangible property, information has historically seemed more amenable to a utilitarian calculus.[103] Conse-

---

98. Pablo Challú et al., *The Consequences of Pharmaceutical Product Patenting,* 15 WORLD COMPETITION 65, 115 (1991).

99. *Id.* at 68.

100. *Id.* at 70.

101. Edwin Mansfield, *Patents and Innovation: An Empirical Study,* 32 MGMT. SCI. 173, 174-75 (1986).

102. *See supra* note 1.

103. To my knowledge, copyrights and patents are the only types of property that have an explicitly utilitarian constitutional basis. Congress is empowered "[t]o promote the Progress of

quently, these issues are often debated in economic terms—both inside and outside the academy. When the U.S. Trade Representative argued that the General Agreement on Trade and Tariffs (GATT) should be used to pressure other countries to increase their levels of intellectual property protection, she turned to the language of necessary economic incentives, rather than to the labor theory of property or the language of natural rights.[104] Once again, the simplistic claim arises that more protection of intellectual property means more innovation and invention.

There is another reason that economics shapes the debate of information issues. Neoclassical price theory is not only the most sophisticated utilitarian language available, but also the one whose disciplinary assumptions—consumer sovereignty, exogenous preferences, and so on—best reflect a liberal vision of the production, distribution, and exchange of information.[105] The "marketplace of ideas" is more than just a ran-

---

Science and useful Arts, by securing for limited Times to Authors and Inventors the exclusive Right to their respective Writings and Discoveries." U.S. CONST. art. I, § 1, cl. 8. The Clause demonstrates two important characteristics of intellectual property. First, intellectual property seems more *chosen*—more of a social artifact—than other types of property, though in fact it is not. Second, partly because of this, intellectual property is almost always discussed in terms of the social benefits it will bring. The person who is asked why he should have the right to pile his flax by the tracks regardless of the inconvenience to the railroad company is likely to say "because it's *my* land." The author who is asked why he should have some legally protected interest in a work after it has been conveyed through the marketplace cannot appeal so easily to any naturalistic or physicalist notion of property. This phenomenon is evidenced also in respect for different types of property rights; "nice" people, who would not steal a record from a record store even if they were sure they were unobserved, nonetheless tape albums they did not buy. For all of these reasons, intellectual property intuitively seems a fit subject for a utilitarian calculus of social interests. What better language than economics in which to discuss "the way in which the incentive to produce information and the demands of current use conflict"? Easterbrook, *supra* note 1, at 314. As a result, intellectual property in particular was subject to economic analysis long before other doctrinal areas. *See, e.g.,* Arnold Plant, *The Economic Aspects of Copyright in Books,* 1 ECONOMICA 167 (1934). Interestingly, this 1934 article argues for *diminished* copyright protection. *Id.* at 194-95.

104. My preferences, as I earlier said, would be for complete protection of intellectual property. And so the higher the protection, the more I think it benefits the developing countries, who thereby then attract the transfer technology, investment, and creative endeavor. And of course, the more you protect intellectual property, those established firms are willing to pour more into research and development to try to address mankind's problems, whether they be disease or constructive building of agricultural crops or what have you, all for the benefit of peoples wherever they may be located.

News Briefing by U.S. Trade Representative, FED. NEWS SERVICE, Jan. 17, 1992, *available in* LEXIS, Nexis Library, FEDNEW File (Carla Hills, Remarks on the Signing of a Bilateral Memorandum of Understanding with the People's Republic of China).

105. There may also be a more indirect relationship between the exaltation of individuality, creative innovation, and utilitarianism. Schumpeter thought there was:

[T]he typical entrepreneur is more self-centered than other types, because he relies less than they do on tradition and connection and because his characteristic task—theoretically as well as historically—consists precisely in breaking up old, and creating new, tradition. Although this applies primarily to his economic action, it also extends to the moral, cultural, and social consequences of it. It is, of course, no mere coincidence that the period of the rise of the entrepreneur type also gave birth to Utilitarianism.

SCHUMPETER, *supra* note 14, at 91-92. The reader may notice the similarity between Schumpeter's vision of the entrepreneur and the idea of authorship described here. This connection will be explored in the discussion on insider trading. *See infra* Part VIII.

1456   *CALIFORNIA LAW REVIEW*   [Vol. 80:1413

dom metaphor: it is an accurate summation of many of the assumptions that our society brings to the discussion of information issues. In a moment, I will argue that this metaphor brings still more problems in its wake.

If microeconomics has become one of the most attractive languages in which to discuss questions of information, then it is almost inevitable that the specific blindnesses[106] of economic analysis will be replicated in information policy. Thus, to the particular difficulties of the economic analysis of information are added the more general difficulties of the economic analysis of law—baseline problems, wealth effects, and so on. These have been analyzed elsewhere, so I will not dwell on them here.

To sum up, there are at least two types of theoretical problems in microeconomic analysis of information. The first stems from the contradictory roles that information plays in the market and in microeconomic theory—information as both perfect and imperfect, property rights in information as both necessary incentives and dubious transaction costs, and so on. The second type of problem stems from the conflict between the assumptions of microeconomic analysis and actual social behavior. For example, when poor schoolchildren are convinced by relentless advertising and peer pressure that they "need" hugely expensive basketball shoes, even a staunch advocate of liberal economics may begin to doubt both the descriptive accuracy and prescriptive fairness of an unswerving application of the norms of "consumer sovereignty" and "exogenous preferences."[107]

What conclusions do we draw from the combination of these two theoretical problems? The pessimistic conclusion would be that one of the most influential ways we have to discuss issues of information is a theory so indeterminate that it frequently functions as a Rorschach blot for dominant social beliefs and the prejudices of the analyst. At the same time, this theory tends structurally to undervalue issues of power and inequality.

Call that the pessimistic conclusion. Is there an optimistic one? My answer would be a guarded "maybe." It is a good idea to focus on incentives to production, on transaction costs, and on the problems created by the presence or absence of legally protected interests. It is certainly a good idea to try to discover actual effects of a particular regime of infor-

---

106. I do not necessarily mean this as an insult. *All* theoretical schemes function like blinders, focusing attention on certain phenomena while ignoring others. In its current incarnation, the economic analysis of law tends to ignore wealth effects, structural ("irrational") oppression, the possibility of manufacturing needs as well as products, and so on. To the extent that a more or less sophisticated version of economic analysis becomes the discourse of power in the regulation of information, such issues would *tend* to be ignored or at least marginalized. From my perspective, these seem to be exactly the issues that deserve our attention.

107. Bob Gordon offers the following definition of "economist": "An economist is a person who believes that advertising is a means of conveying information."

mation regulation. By and large, economists have not actually done this, but at least they have talked about it. The tendency of economic analysis to go at least one layer below reified doctrinal concepts is also to be welcomed. One could imagine a type of information economics that was sensitive to baseline errors, offer-asking problems, and wealth effects, that questioned the reality of exogenous preferences, and that openly acknowledged the tension between perfect information and "information as commodity." If this economics also paid more attention than is currently fashionable to the diminishing marginal utility of wealth, I, for one, would be pleased.

If all of these things were done, what epistemological *status* and practical *effect* would information economics have? It would be a little less imperial, a lot more modest, and much more empirical. Its conclusions would be more carefully hedged than they are now, and it would openly declare its partiality—the inherent prejudices of any utilitarian, efficiency, or welfare-maximizing calculus and the political consequences of the distinction between allocation and distribution.

To some, this judgment may seem strange in light of my claims that information economics is beset by a basic paradox or *aporia*. If the discipline is truly paradoxical, surely it is useless?—no matter how chastened its conclusions. The answer, I think, is that economics is only useless if one makes a particular positivist and scientist set of assumptions about the kind of knowledge a theory has to provide in order to qualify as a theory. Admittedly, both professional economists and economic analysts of law—and not merely those from the Chicago school—sound in their more expansive moments as if they subscribe to those assumptions. But that is no reason for the rest of us to do so. Neoclassical price theory is a valuable tool which enriches our understanding of the world. Like all theoretical systems it has blind spots and moments of formal "undecidability." Used with an awareness of its paradoxes and its blind spots, an awareness of the unconscious process of interpretive construction that conceals its indeterminacy, it would nevertheless be a valuable theoretical tool. Seen this way, economics would be a spur to concentrate on incentives and information flow, to worry about perverse motivations and unintended consequences. It would, in short, be more a rough-and-ready set of analytical techniques and reminders than a Newtonian science.

Whether or not this is the economics we should have, it is not the economics we have at the moment. With a few significant exceptions, we have an economics more like my pessimistic picture—an aporetic discipline which, as I hope to show in the rest of this Article, often conceals its indeterminacy through romance. To understand the origins of that romance, we must first look at the liberal conception of property.

V

Property in the Liberal State

Like information, property has a vital role in liberal state theory. That role imposes certain conflicting requirements on the concept of property itself.[108] Legal realism, Lockean political theory, critical legal thought, and law and economics have all stressed—each in its own vocabulary—the idea that property is perhaps the most important way in which we attempt to reconcile our desire for freedom and our desire for security.[109] How can we be free and yet secure from the freedom of others, secure and yet free to do that which we want to do?[110] The most obvious way to deal with this apparent contradiction is to conceive rights of security

> in a manner that both makes them appear to be absolute and negates the proposition that they restrict the legitimate freedom of action of others. Thus if we define liberty as free actions that do not affect others at all, and rights as absolute protection from harm, the contradiction vanishes.[111]

The traditional Blackstonian definition of property does just that. But there are irresoluble conceptual tensions in any such formulation, a point which has considerable relevance to intellectual property law, as we will see later. Vandevelde states the problem in the following way:

> [A]t the beginning of the nineteenth century, property was ideally defined as absolute dominion over things. Exceptions to this definition suffused property law: instances in which the law declared property to exist even though no "thing" was involved or the owner's dominion over the thing was not absolute. Each of these

---

108. *See generally* Francis S. Philbrick, *Changing Conceptions of Property in Law,* 86 U. PA. L. REV. 691 (1938); Joseph W. Singer, *The Legal Rights Debate in Analytical Jurisprudence from Bentham to Hohfeld,* 1982 WIS. L. REV. 975; Kenneth J. Vandevelde, *The New Property of the Nineteenth Century: The Development of the Modern Concept of Property,* 29 BUFF. L. REV. 325 (1980).

109. To put it in the simplest terms possible, property is a strong barrier against potentially dangerous other people but, at least since the decline of classical legal thought, a weaker barrier against the state. *See, e.g.,* Hawaii Hous. Auth. v. Midkiff, 467 U.S. 229 (1984) (holding that the condemnation of property for the purpose of limiting the concentration of property ownership constitutes a public use within the meaning of the Fifth Amendment); Poletown Neighborhood Council v. City of Detroit, 304 N.W.2d 455 (Mich. 1981) (allowing a municipality to condemn and transfer private property to a development corporation for the public purpose of expanding its economic base). Constitutional rights, on the other hand, are generally a strong barrier against the state, but a weak barrier against "private" parties. Or, as one of my colleagues puts it, the full panoply of constitutional restraints applies to the actions of the dogcatcher in Gary, Indiana, but not to Exxon or General Motors. The best explanation of property as a mediator between freedom and security comes from Singer, *supra* note 108, and I am indebted to his analysis.

110. *See* THOMAS HOBBES, LEVIATHAN 139-43 (Bobbs-Merrill 1958) (1651); JOHN S. MILL, ON LIBERTY 70-86 (David Spitz ed., Norton 1975) (1859); Boyle, *Thomas Hobbes, supra* note 10; Duncan Kennedy, *The Structure of Blackstone's Commentaries,* 28 BUFF. L. REV. 205, 209-21 (1979).

111. Singer, *supra* note 108, at 980.

exceptions, however, was explained away. Where no "thing" existed, one was fictionalized. Where dominion was not absolute, limitations could be camouflaged by resorting to fictions, or rationalized as inherent in the nature of the thing or the owner. . . .

As the nineteenth century progressed, increased exceptions to both the physicalist and the absolutist elements of Blackstone's conception of property were incorporated into the law. . . . This dephysicalization was a development that threatened to place the entire corpus of American law in the category of property. Such conceptual imperialism created severe problems for the courts. First, if every valuable interest constituted property, then practically any act would result in either a trespass on, or a taking of, someone's property, especially if property still was regarded as absolute. Second, once property had swallowed the rest of American law, its meaningfulness as a separate category would disappear. On the other hand, if certain valuable interests were not to be considered property, finding and justifying the criteria for separating property from nonproperty would be difficult.[112]

To the extent that there was a replacement for this Blackstonian conception it was the familiar "bundle of rights" notion of modern property law, a vulgarization of Hohfeld's analytic scheme of jural correlates and opposites, loosely justified by a rough-and-ready utilitarianism and applied in widely varying ways to legal interests of every kind. The euphonious case of *LeRoy Fibre Co. v. Chicago, Milwaukee & St. Paul Railway*[113] is used in many a first-year class to illustrate the conceptual shift. Could a flax maker be found guilty of contributory negligence for piling its stacks of flax too close to the tracks? The majority bridled at the very thought. The flax maker was piling its flax on its own property, after all. "[T]he rights of one man in the use of his property cannot be limited by the wrongs of another. . . . The legal conception of property is of rights. When you attempt to limit them by wrongs, you venture a solecism."[114] Though the majority's circular reasoning[115] carried the day, it is Holmes' partial concurrence that pointed to the future. Rather than imagining an absolute sphere of rights surrounding the property lines like a glass bubble, Holmes would be happy to remove the flax-piling entitlement from the bundle of property rights for whatever swathe of the property "was so near to the track as to be in danger from even a

---

112. Vandevelde, *supra* note 108, at 328-29.

113. 232 U.S. 340 (1914).

114. *Id.* at 350.

115. If the railroad had a duty not to cause the destruction only of that property kept at a reasonably safe distance from the track, where was the wrong? To put it another way, why isn't the majority venturing a solecism by allowing the "wrong" of the flax-stacker (in stacking the flax by the tracks) to limit the "rights" of the railroad company to operate their property?

prudently managed engine."[116] He also directed a few sanguine, if vaguely crocodilian, comments towards the majority on the subject of their concern about the apparent relativism of his concept of property.

> I do not think we need trouble ourselves with the thought that my view depends on differences of degree. The whole law does so as soon as it is civilized. Negligence is all degree—that of the defendant here degree of the nicest sort; and between the variations according to distance that I suppose to exist and the simple universality of the rules in the Twelve Tables or the Leges Barbarorum, there lies the culture of two thousand years.[117]

Presumably, the majority consoled itself with the fact that its concern with absolutism and universality was 2000 years out of date. In any event, the writing was on the wall. Property was no longer conceived of as absolute, as a guaranteed trump against the interests of the majority or the state, or as related to any physical thing. Indeed, so thoroughly had the conception been relativized that courts were willing to admit that there could be property rights restricted to particular interests, to be asserted against one person rather than another, and only in some situations and moments. But if this is the case, where is our shield against other people or the state? If the flax-piling entitlement can be stripped from seventy yards of the LeRoy Fibre Company's land merely because there would be utilitarian benefits to letting the railroad run unmolested, then why not from 100 yards, or from the whole parcel? Instead of an absolute, unchanging, and universal shield against the world, property is now merely a bundle of assorted entitlements that changes from moment to moment as the balance of utilities changes. It seems that the modern concept of property has given us a system that works on the day-to-day level, but only at the price of giving up the very role that property was supposed to play in the liberal vision.

Thus, when we turn to intellectual property, an area which throughout its history has been less able to rely on the physicalist and absolutist fictions which girded the traditional conception of property, we will see not only an attempt to clothe a newly invented romantic author in robes of juridical protection, but also to struggle with, mediate, or repress one of the central contradictions in the liberal world view. This, then, is the redoubled contradiction of which I spoke earlier. If it is to protect the legitimacy and intellectual suasion of the liberal world view, intellectual property law (and indeed, all law that deals with information) must accomplish a number of tasks simultaneously. It must provide a conceptual apparatus that appears to mediate the various tensions associated with the role of information in liberal society. Thus, for example, it must

---

116. *LeRoy Fibre,* 232 U.S. at 353 (Holmes, J., concurring in part).
117. *Id.* at 354 (citation omitted).

explain why a person who recombines information from the public sphere is not merely engaging in the private appropriation of public wealth. It must explain how we can motivate individuals, who are sometimes postulated to be essentially self-serving and sometimes to be noble, idealistic souls, to produce information. If the answer is "by giving them property rights," it must also explain why this will not diminish the common pool or public domain so greatly that a net decrease in the production of information will result. (Think of overfishing.) It must carve out a sphere of privacy and at the same time ensure a vigorous sphere of public debate and ample information about a potentially oppressive state. It must do all of this within a vision of justice that expects formal equality within the public sphere, but respects existing disparities in wealth, status, and power in the private. And all of these things must be accomplished while using a conception of property that avoids the theoretical impossibilities of the physicalist, absolutist conception, but that at the same time is not too obviously relativistic, partial, and utilitarian.

VI
COPYRIGHT

So far, I have argued that because of the contradictions and tensions I have been describing, there are certain structural pressures on the way that a liberal society deals with information. When we turn to the area of law conventionally recognized as dealing with information—intellectual property, and in this case copyright—we will find a pattern, a strategy that attempts to resolve these tensions in the liberal view of information. On one level, understanding this pattern helps to make sense (if not coherence) of the otherwise apparently chaotic world of copyright. On another level, understanding the conceptual strategy developed in copyright illuminates most of the other areas that concern information—even if those areas are not conventionally understood as relating to copyright.

Although intellectual property has long been said to present insuperable conceptual difficulties, it actually presents exactly the same problems as the liberal conception of property generally. It merely does so in a more obvious way and in a way which is given particular spin by our fascination with information. All systems of property are both rights-oriented and utilitarian, rely on antinomial conceptions of public and private, and present insuperable conceptual difficulties when reduced to mere physicalist relations. But when they are conceived of in a more abstract and technically sophisticated way, systems of property immediately begin to dissolve back into the conflicting policies to which they give a temporary and unstable form. In personal or real property, however, one can at least point to a pair of sneakers or a house, say "I own that," and have some sense of confidence that the statement means something. As *LeRoy Fibre* shows, of course, it is not at all clear that such confidence is justified, but at least physical property presents itself as an apparently coherent feature of social reality. This is a fact of considerable ideological and political significance. In intellectual property, the response might be "What do you mean?"

As Martha Woodmansee discovered, this point was made with startling clarity in the debates over copyright in Germany in the eighteenth century. Encouraged by an enormous reading public, by several apocryphal tales of writers who were household names yet still lived in poverty, and by a new, more romantic vision of authorship, writers began to demand greater economic returns from their labors. One obvious strategy was to lobby for some kind of legal right in the text—the right that we would call copyright. To many participants in the debate the idea was ludicrous. Christian Sigmund Krause, writing in 1783, expressed the point pungently.

> "But the ideas, the content! that which actually constitutes a book! which only the author can sell or communicate!"—Once expressed, it is impossible for it to remain the author's property. . . . It is precisely for the purpose of using the ideas that most people buy books—pepper dealers, fishwives, and the like, and literary pirates excepted. . . . Over and over again it comes back to the same question: I can read the contents of a book, learn, abridge, expand, teach, and translate it, write about it, laugh over it, find fault with it, deride it, use it poorly or well—in short, do with it whatever I will. But the one thing I should be prohibited from doing is copying or reprinting it? . . . A published book is a secret divulged. With what justification would a preacher forbid the printing of his homilies, since he cannot prevent any of his listeners from transcribing his sermons? Would it not be just as ludicrous for a professor to demand that his students refrain from using some new proposition he had taught them as for him to demand the same of book dealers with regard to a new book? *No, no, it is too obvious that the concept of intellectual property is useless. My property must be exclusively mine; I must be able to dispose of it and retrieve it unconditionally.* Let someone explain to me how that is possible in the present case. Just let someone try taking back the ideas he has originated once they have been communicated so that they are, as before, nowhere to be found. All the money in the world could not make that possible.[118]

Along with this problem go two more fundamental ones. The first is the recurrent question of how we can give property rights in intellectual products and yet still preserve the inventiveness and free flow of informa-

---

118. Christian S. Krause, *Über den Büchernachdruck,* 1 Deutsches Museum 415-17 (1783) (emphasis added), *quoted in* Woodmansee, *supra* note 1, at 443-44.

tion that liberal social theory demands. I shall return to this question in a moment. The second problem is the more fundamental one. On what grounds can we justify giving the author this kind of unprecedented property right at all, even if the conceptual problems could be overcome? We do not think it is necessary to give car workers residual property rights in the cars that they produce—wage labor is thought to work perfectly well. Surely an author is merely taking public goods—language, ideas, culture, humour, genre—and converting them to his or her own use. Where is the moral or utilitarian justification for the existence of this property right in the first place?

The most obvious answer is that authors are special, but why? And since when? Even the most cursory historical study reveals that our notion of "authorship" is an invented concept of relatively recent provenance. Medieval church writers actively disapproved of the elements of originality and creativity that we now think of as essential components of authorship.

They valued extant old books more highly than any recent elucubrations *and they put the work of the scribe and the copyist above that of the authors.* The real task of the scholars in their view was not the vain excogitation of novelties but a discovery of great old books, their multiplication and the placing of copies where they would be accessible to future generations of readers.[119]

Woodmansee quotes a wonderful definition of "book" from a mid-eighteenth-century dictionary that merely lists the writer as one mouth among many—"[t]he scholar and the writer, the papermaker, the type founder, the typesetter and the printer, the proofreader, the publisher, the book binder, sometimes even the gilder and brass-worker, etc."—all of whom are "fed by this branch of manufacture."[120] Other studies show that authors were seen as merely another type of craftsman—an appellation which Shakespeare might not have rejected—or at their most exalted, as the crossroads where learned tradition met external, divine inspiration.[121] But since the tradition was mere craft, and the glory of the divine inspiration was to be offered to God rather than to the vessel he had chosen,[122] where was the justification for preferential treatment in

---

119. ERNST P. GOLDSCHMIDT, MEDIEVAL TEXTS AND THEIR FIRST APPEARANCE IN PRINT 112 (1943) (emphasis added), *quoted in* JOHN W. SAUNDERS, THE PROFESSION OF ENGLISH LETTERS 20 (1964).

120. GEORG H. ZINCK, ALLGEMEINES OECONOMISCHES LEXICON col. 442 (3d ed. n.p. 1753), *quoted in* Woodmansee, *supra* note 1, at 425.

121. *See* Boyle, *supra* note 1, at 628-33.

122. This view persisted for some time:

Nevertheless, I had to be told about authors. My grandfather told me, tactfully, calmly. He taught me the names of those illustrious men. I would recite the list to myself, from Hesiod to Hugo, without a mistake. They were the Saints and Prophets. Charles Schweitzer said he worshipped them. Yet they bothered him. Their obtrusive presence prevented him from attributing the works of Man directly to the Holy Ghost. He therefore

the creation of property rights? As authors ceased to think of themselves as either craftsmen, gentlemen,[123] or stenographers for the Divine Spirit, a recognizably different, more romantic vision of authorship began to emerge. At first, it was found mainly in self-serving tracts. But little by little it spread through the culture so that, by the middle of the eighteenth century, it had come to be seen as a universal truth about art.[124]

---

felt a secret preference for the anonymous, for the builders who had had the modesty to keep in the background of their cathedrals, for the countless authors of popular songs. He did not mind Shakespeare, whose identity was not established. Nor Homer, for the same reason. Nor a few others, about whom there was no certainty that they had existed. As for those who had not wished or who had been unable to efface the traces of their life, he found excuses, provided they were dead.

JEAN-PAUL SARTRE, THE WORDS 61-62 (Bernard Frechtman trans., 1964).

123. I use the male form deliberately. It is true that despite the obstacles placed in their way, a number of women authors established themselves on the literary scene. To say, however, that they participated in the "invention" of romantic authorship, or to claim that such a notion accurately reflected the parts of their own creative practices that they thought most valuable, seems to me to be going too far. In this historical analysis, gender-neutral language might actually obscure understanding. See SANDRA M. GILBERT & SUSAN GUBAR, THE MADWOMAN IN THE ATTIC: THE WOMAN WRITER & THE NINETEENTH CENTURY LITERARY IMAGINATION (1988); see also ANN RUGGLES GERE, COMMON PROPERTIES OF PLEASURE: TEXTS IN NINETEENTH CENTURY WOMEN'S CLUBS 647 (1992); MARLON B. ROSS, THE CONTOURS OF MASCULINE DESIRE: ROMANTICISM AND THE RISE OF WOMEN'S POETRY (1989); Martha Woodmansee, On the Author Effect: Recovering Collectivity, 10 CARDOZO ARTS & ENT. L.J. 279 (1992).

A significant exception to this line of thought is provided by Professor Linda Lacey who, in a fascinating and thought-provoking article, provides a feminist-influenced view of authorship that I would argue is just as romanticized as the vision I discuss here. Linda J. Lacey, Of Bread and Roses and Copyrights, 1989 DUKE L.J. 1532. Professor Lacey argues that authors have been stigmatized as female and therefore, unlike all other rights-holders, have had their property rights limited. I would disagree with the tendency to romanticize the individual creator for the reasons given in this Article. Moreover, I simply cannot agree that other forms of property are not limited for reasons of social policy, commonweal, convenience of administration, or what-have-you. For a criticism of this kind of "absolutist" picture of property rights, see supra note 108, infra text accompanying notes 243-49.

124. For comprehensive development of these ideas, see Boyle, supra note 1; Jaszi, supra note 2. This line of thought can be traced back to Foucault. Michel Foucault, What Is an Author?, in TEXTUAL STRATEGIES: PERSPECTIVES IN POST-STRUCTURALIST CRITICISM 141 (Josueé V. Harari ed., 1979). Woodmansee provided the paradigm for actual research, and her article gives a marvellous account of the "rise" of intellectual property in Germany. Woodmansee, supra note 1. For the linkage between romantic authorship and intellectual property in England, see Mark Rose, The Author as Proprietor: Donaldson v. Becket and the Genealogy of Modern Authorship, 23 REPRESENTATIONS 51 (1988). See also N.N. FELTES, MODES OF PRODUCTION OF VICTORIAN NOVELS (1986). But see John Feather, Publishers and Politicians: The Remaking of the Law of Copyright in Britain 1775-1842 Part II: The Rights of Authors, 25 PUBLISHING HIST. 45 (1989). For the same linkage in France, see Carla Hesse, Enlightenment Epistemology and the Laws of Authorship in Revolutionary France, 1777-1793, 30 REPRESENTATIONS 109 (1990). And for the United States, see CATHY N. DAVIDSON, THE REVOLUTION AND THE WORD: THE RISE OF THE NOVEL IN AMERICA (1986). My ideas on this issue were strongly influenced by participation in the 1991 Conference on Intellectual Property and the Construction of Authorship at Case Western University. Some of the papers from that Conference have been collected in the Cardozo Arts and Entertainment Law Journal. Symposium, Intellectual Property and the Construction of Authorship, 10 CARDOZO ARTS & ENT. L.J. 277 (1992). I should note here that I am concentrating on the romantic vision of the author, because that is the image with which I am most familiar, and the rhetoric of which seems most persuasive. I do not mean to imply that a similar project could not be undertaken using some different version of the romantic creator—the great inventor, say. In either case, originality provides the hook with which one can both justify and limit monopoly.

Woodmansee explains how the decline of the craft/inspiration model of writing and the elevation of the romantic author both presented and seemed to solve the question of property rights in intellectual products.

Eighteenth-century theorists departed from this compound model of writing in two significant ways. They minimized the element of craftsmanship (in some instances they simply discarded it) in favor of the element of inspiration, and they internalized the source of that inspiration. That is, inspiration came to be regarded as emanating not from outside or above, but from within the writer himself. "Inspiration" came to be explicated in terms of *original genius,* with the consequence that the inspired work was made peculiarly and distinctively the product—and the property—of the writer.[125]

In this vision, the author was not the journeyman who learned a craft and then hoped to be well paid for it. The romantic author was defined not by mastery of a prior set of rules, but instead by the transformation of genre, the revision of form. Originality became the watchword of artistry.[126] To see how complete a revision this is, one need only examine Shakespeare's wholesale lifting of plot, scene, and language from other writers, both ancient and contemporary. To an Elizabethan playwright, the phrase "imitation is the sincerest form of flattery" might have

---

125. Woodmansee, *supra* note 1, at 427.

126. The notion of originality brought its own burdens, particularly during the mid-19th-century zenith of the cult of the romantic author. The pitiable account of the obsessive author in George Borrow's *Lavengro* is a fine example.

[The misfortune which befell me] was neither more nor less than a doubt of the legality of my claim to the thoughts, expressions, and situations contained in the book; that is, to all that constituted the book. How did I get them? How did they come into my mind? Did I invent them? Did they originate with myself? Are they my own, or are they some other body's? . . . I at length flung my book, I mean the copy of it which I possessed, into the fire, and began another.

But it was all in vain; I laboured at this other, finished it, and gave it to the world; and no sooner had I done so than the same thought was busy in my brain, poisoning all the pleasure which I should otherwise have derived from my work. How did I get all the matter which composed it? Out of my own mind, unquestionably; but how did it come there—was it the indigenous growth of the mind? And then I would sit down and ponder over the various scenes and adventures in my book, endeavouring to ascertain how I came originally to devise them, and by dint of reflecting I remembered that to a single word in a conversation, or some simple accident in a street, or on a road, I was indebted for some of the happiest portions of my work; they were but tiny seeds, it is true, which in the soil of my imagination had subsequently become stately trees, but I reflected that without them no stately trees would have been produced, and that, consequently, only a part in the merit of these compositions which charmed the world—for they did charm the world—was due to myself. Thus, a dead fly was in my phial, poisoning all the pleasures which I could otherwise have derived from the result of my brain sweat.

GEORGE BORROW, LAVENGRO 332-33 (Ernest Rhys ed., Everyman's Library 1909) (1851). (In keeping with the theme of this footnote, I should say that I am indebted to Peter Jaszi for pointing out this passage to me.) To understand the contemporary attitude towards sources, it is worth comparing this notion of originality, and its profound "anxiety of influence," with the classical one described *infra* note 128.

seemed entirely without irony. "Not only were Englishmen from 1500 to 1625 without any feeling analogous to the modern attitude toward plagiarism; they even lacked the word until the very end of that period."[127] To the theorists and polemicists of romantic authorship, the reproduction of orthodoxy would have been proof that they were not the unique and transcendent spirits they hoped themselves to be.[128]

It is the originality of the author, the novel creation the author fashions out of the raw materials provided by culture and the common pool, that "justifies" the property right. At the same time, the postulate of originality offers a strategy for resolving the basic conceptual problem pointed out by Krause: what concept of property would allow the author to retain some property rights in the work but not others? In the German debates, the best answer was provided by the great idealist, Fichte. In a manner that is now familiar to lawyers trained in legal realism and Hohfeldian analysis, but which must have seemed remarkable at the time, Fichte disaggregated the concept of property in books. The buyer gets the physical thing and the ideas contained in it. *Precisely because the originality of his spirit was converted into an originality of form* the author retains the right to the form in which those ideas were expressed.

> [E]ach writer must give his thoughts a certain form, and he can give them no other form than his own because he has no other. But neither can he be willing to hand over this form in making his thoughts public, for no one can *appropriate* his thoughts without thereby *altering their form*. This latter thus remains forever his

---

127. HAROLD O. WHITE, PLAGIARISM AND IMITATION DURING THE ENGLISH RENAISSANCE 202 (1935). During the mid-16th century "imitative composition enjoyed general and unquestioned acceptance." *Id.* at 42. It was not until the very end of the century that any writer made use of Martial's figurative expression "plagiarius" (man-stealer) with the connotation literary thief. *Id.* at 120.

128. Contrast the views of the mid-16th century: "As for the theoretical treatises which discussed literature, they were unanimous in asserting the necessity of imitation, varying only in the emphasis they placed upon the classical safeguards for originality." *Id.* at 59. Even in the 1580s, as writers began to object to imitation,

> [o]f all the objections to imitation which were raised, only those of Churchyard and of one anonymous author were directed against imitation *as such.* All the rest opposed only what classical critics had pointed out as incorrect: piracy, secrecy, perversity, servility, superficiality. And of all those who demanded originality of invention, not one used the term in its modern sense of individual fabrication. All sought originality just as classical critics declared that it should be sought: through individual adaptation, reinterpretation, and, if possible, improvement of the best which each writer could find in the literature of his own and earlier days.

Id. at 118-19. The difference between the classical sense of originality (which defined itself around the adaptive reproduction of past knowledge) and the romantic conception of originality (which demanded radical innovation) could hardly be more marked. The former vision celebrates, while the latter vision minimizes and even denigrates, the influence of "sources"—genre, tradition, past learning, and shared language. This tendency to underemphasize and devalue sources is of profound importance to the law of information in general and intellectual property in particular.

exclusive property.[129]

American copyright law strikes exactly the same theme. In the famous case of *Bleistein v. Donaldson Lithographing Co.,*[130] which concerned the copyrightability of a circus poster, Oliver Wendell Holmes was still determined to claim that the work could become the subject of an intellectual property right because it was the original creation of a unique individual spirit. Holmes' opinion shows us both the advantages and the disadvantages of a rhetoric that bases property rights on "originality."[131] As a hook on which to hang a property right, "originality" seems to have at least a promise of formal realizability. It connects nicely to the romantic vision of authorship. It also seems to limit a potentially expansive principle, the principle that those who create may be entitled to retain some legally protected interest in the objects they make—even after those objects have been conveyed through the marketplace. But while the idea that an original spirit conveys its uniqueness to worked matter seems intuitively plausible when applied to Shakespeare[132] or Dante, it has less obvious relevance to a more humdrum act of creation by a less credibly romantic creator—a commercial artist in a shopping mall, say. The tension between the rhetoric of Wordsworth and the reality of suburban corporate capitalism is one we will explore further later in the Article. In *Bleistein,* this particular original spirit had only managed to rough out a picture of energetic-looking individuals performing unlikely acts on bicycles, but to Holmes, the principle was the same. "The copy is the personal reaction of an individual upon nature. Personality always contains something unique. It expresses its singularity even in handwriting, and a very modest grade of art has in it something irreducible, which is one man's alone. That something he may copyright . . . ."[133] This quality of "uniqueness," recognized first in great spirits, then in creative spirits, and finally in advertising executives, expresses itself in originality of form, of expression.

In the language of romantic authorship, uniqueness is by no means the only characteristic of the author. Originality may imply iconoclasm. The romantic author is going beyond the last accepted style, breaking out

---

129. Johann G. Fichte, *Proof of the Illegality of Reprinting: A Rationale and a Parable* (n.p. 1793), *quoted in* Woodmansee, *supra* note 1, at 445 (emphasis added by Woodmansee).

130. 188 U.S. 239 (1902).

131. *See id.* at 248-52.

132. In fact, of course, Shakespeare engaged regularly in activity that we would call plagiarism but which Elizabethan playwrights saw as perfectly harmless, perhaps even complimentary. This not only shows the historical contingency of the romantic idea of authorship, it may even help to explain some of the "heretical" claims that Shakespeare did not write Shakespeare. Most of the heretics use the fact of this supposed plagiarism and their knowledge of the timeless truth of the romantic vision of authorship to prove that someone else, preferably the author of the borrowed lines, must have written the plays. After all, the Immortal Bard would never stoop to copy the works of another. Once again, originality becomes the key. *See* Boyle, *supra* note 1.

133. *Bleistein,* 188 U.S. at 250.

of the old forms. This introduces an almost Faustian element into the discussion. The author is the maker and destroyer of worlds, the irrepressible spirit of inventiveness whose restless creativity throws off invention after invention. Intellectual property is merely the token awarded to the author by a grateful society.

A passage from Professor Litman bears repeating at this point:

> Why is it that copyright does not protect ideas? Some writers have echoed the justification for failing to protect facts by suggesting that ideas have their origin in the public domain. Others have implied that "mere ideas" may not be worthy of the status of private property. Some authors have suggested that ideas are not protected because of the strictures imposed on copyright by the first amendment. The task of distinguishing ideas from expression in order to explain why private ownership is inappropriate for one but desirable for the other, however, remains elusive.[134]

I would say that we find the answer to Professor Litman's question in the romantic vision of authorship, of the genius whose style forever expresses a single unique persona. The rise of this powerful (and historically contingent) stereotype provided the necessary raw material to fashion some convincing mediation of the tension between the imagery of public and private in information production.

To sum up, then, the idea/expression division which has so fascinated and puzzled copyright scholars apparently manages, in one stroke:

1. To provide a *conceptual basis* for partial, limited property rights, without completely collapsing the notion of property into the idea of a temporary, limited, utilitarian grant by the state, revocable at will. The property right still *seems* to be based on something real—on a distinction that sounds formally realizable, even if, on closer analysis, it turns out to be impossible to maintain.

2. To provide a *moral and philosophical justification* for giving the author such a property right. After all, through his originality of spirit, the author has created something entirely new out of the raw material of the public domain. The argument is almost like Locke's labor theory: one gains property by mixing one's labor with an object. But where Locke's theory, if applied to a modern economy, might have a disturbingly socialist ring to it, Fichte's theory bases the property right on the originality of every spirit as expressed through words. Every author gets the right—the writer of the *roman á clef* as well as Goethe—but because of the concentration on originality of expression, the residual property right is only for the workers of the word, not the workers of the world. Even after it is analogized to sculptures and paintings, software and music, it will still have an attractively circumscribed ambit.

---

134.   Litman, *supra* note 2, at 999 (footnotes omitted).

3. To resolve (or at least conceal) the *tension between public and private*. In the double life that Marx described, information is both the lifeblood of the noble, disinterested citizens of the public world and, at the same time, a commodity in the private sphere to which we must attach property rights if we wish our self-interested producers to continue to produce.[135] By disaggregating the book into "idea" and "expression," we can give the idea (and the facts on which it is based) to the public world and the expression to the writer, thus apparently mediating the contradiction between public good and private greed.

Thus, the combination of the romantic vision of authorship and the distinction between idea and expression appears to provide a conceptual basis and a moral justification for intellectual property, does not threaten to spread dangerous notions of entitlement to other kinds of workers, and mediates the tension between the schizophrenic halves of the liberal world view. Small wonder that it has been a success. Small wonder that, as I hope to show in this Article, the language of romantic, original authorship tends to reappear in discussion of subjects far removed from the ones Fichte had in mind. Like insider trading. Or spleens.

A final question remains before I can proceed. Has the structure I have just described been rendered superfluous by economic analysis and public goods theory? An economist might say that the difference between the author and the laborer is that the author is producing a public good and the laborer is (generally) producing a good that can be satisfactorily commodified and alienated using only the traditional lexicon of property. The distinctions drawn from the idea of romantic authorship might appear to be surplus—unnecessary remnants of a conceptualist age.

It is certainly true that some articles decry the language of "idea" and "expression" and offer the prediction that those terms will be used as mere summations of the underlying economic analysis[136]—in the same way that "proximate cause" is used as a way of expressing a conclusion about the desirable reach of liability. But this kind of response mistakes both the popular and the esoteric power of the language of romantic authorship. As the rest of this Article will show, the romantic vision of authorship continues to influence public debate on issues of information—far beyond the traditional ambit of intellectual property. I tried to show earlier[137] that the language of economic analysis provides no neat solutions to the problems of information regulation—precisely because economic analysis is marked by the same *aporiàs* as the rest of public discourse. In this situation of indeterminacy and contradiction, it is the romantic vision of authorship that frequently structures technical or

---

135. *See supra* text accompanying note 40.
136. *See, e.g.,* Wiley, *supra* note 64, at 123-24.
137. *See supra* Part IV.

scholarly economic analysis—providing the vital initial choices that give the analysis its subsequent appearance of determinacy and "common sense" plausibility. Scholars may criticize the distinctions that flow from the romantic vision, but they should not imagine themselves to be free from its influence. This point will be particularly obvious when we get to the unlikely—and distinctly unromantic—subject of insider trading.

In the next Part I turn to the question of blackmail. One of my aims in this Article is to pick examples that illustrate different aspects of the structure of information regulation I describe here. Copyright offers the idea of romantic authorship as a way of reconciling the demands of private property and the public realm. By contrast, blackmail is a situation in which the state *forbids* the commodification of information, precisely because it concerns the private sphere of home, hearth, and personal self-definition.

VII
BLACKMAIL

Blackmail is of academic interest primarily as a proving ground. Each new generation of scholars comes to it, as to some muddy and treacherous test track, to try out their new theories.[138] The test is an apparently simple one: to find out whether their approach will answer the question, "Why is blackmail illegal?"

Before we plunge headlong into that morass, however, it is worth focusing on the qualities that make blackmail problematic in the first place. When scholars talk about the difficulties of explaining blackmail, they are generally referring to a restricted subsection of the doctrine. It is easy to explain attempts to extort money by threats that would be illegal to carry out and to explain why a blackmailer cannot ask money as the price of keeping silent about some violation of the law. The hard case to explain is the situation in which one person asks another person for money as the price of not revealing legally obtained information about activities perfectly legal in themselves. The example I gave earlier was, "If you do not pay me $100, I will reveal to your boyfriend the fact that I saw you coming out of another man's house at two o'clock in the morning."[139] The information was legal to acquire and would be legal to reveal, the conduct was legal to engage in, yet it is illegal to demand money for keeping quiet.[140] In Hohfeldian terms, the sale of a privilege

---

138. By far the best survey comes from Professor James Lindgren. *See* Lindgren, *supra* note 27. Though I disagree with Lindgren's own explanation of blackmail, his article is an excellent introduction to the field, and one to which I am indebted.

139. *See supra* text accompanying note 25.

140. Lindgren formulates the problem in this way: "I have a legal right to expose or threaten to expose [a] crime or affair, and I have a legal right to seek a job or money, but if I combine these rights it is blackmail." Lindgren, *supra* note 27, at 670-71 (footnotes omitted). While this is clearly an advance on other formulations, it tends to gloss over the variety of the legally protected interests

has been criminalized but the privilege itself has been retained. How is this different from any other situation in which one economic actor makes a bargain with another to forego a legal course of action that the second party wishes to avoid? To put it another way, what is the qualitative difference between a blackmailer's demands for money and a baseball team's demands for tax breaks, rezoning, and direct grants as the price of not moving to another a city?[141]

The attempts to explain the criminalization of blackmail point in very different directions, and I could not begin to cover the full range of explanations here. Instead, I will use this Part to illustrate three kinds of attempted explanations: economic theories, libertarian theories, and third party theories. I will argue that all three fail to explain blackmail, and that we need a theory that focuses on the various roles that information is expected to play within our society. Admittedly, such a theory gives an answer of a different type than the ones sought by the theorists I cite here. To me, however, that answer seems both more credible and more useful.

A. Economic Theories

Landes and Posner believe that the prohibition of blackmail springs from the state's attempt to prevent (inefficient) private enforcement of the law. In other words, the prohibition of blackmail is supposed to help the state keep its monopoly in law enforcement.

> Were blackmail, a form of private enforcement, lawful, the public monopoly of enforcement would be undermined. Overenforcement of the law would result if the blackmailer were able to extract the full fine from the offenders . . . . Alternatively, the blackmailer might sell his incriminating information to the offender for a price lower than the statutory cost of punishment to the criminal, which would reduce the effective cost of punishment

---

involved. The legal relationships involved are not all actually "rights," but a mixture of privileges, powers, and immunities. This tendency to reduce all legal relationships to a single "right" concept appears to play a role in undermining Lindgren's own theory. Later in this Article, I will argue that there are other cases in which the legal system makes it illegal to commodify various privileges and powers—for example, parents may arrange private adoptions, but they may not sell babies to adoptive parents. It is in this context that blackmail should be understood.

141. There is something else in the blackmail question that makes it an irresistible puzzle for legal scholars, but a matter of little concern for courts, practicing lawyers, or citizens. Blackmail just *seems* undeniably bad. It is the combination of the rule's intuitive moral sense and the lack of an obvious theoretical justification that leads scholars to believe that there is an answer out there if only they think hard enough about it. In that sense, blackmail is like other jurisprudential puzzles, such as the definition of law, which intrigue the novice and tantalize the professional by their apparent simplicity, only to confound and confuse anyone who proposes a theory.

This idea of the tasks of jurisprudence is rendered problematic by the essentialist vision of language on which it rests. *See* Boyle, *Ideals and Things, supra* note 10; Boyle, *Thomas Hobbes, supra* note 10. I will argue here that a related problem besets the analysis of blackmail.

to the criminal below the level set by the legislature.[142]

The first problem with this argument is its assumption that legislators will identify the optimal level of activity and set fines accordingly. What mechanism would operate to make self-interested legislators, concerned mainly with reelection, choose the correct level of an activity?[143] This argument appears to presume too easily the existence of a perfect market for legislation.

The second problem with the argument is that it does not explain the hard case I mentioned earlier—the case when both revelation and silence on the part of the blackmailer and the act on the part of the victim would be entirely legal. Thus, for instance, if George Bernard Shaw is secretly eating rack of lamb despite his publicly announced vegetarianism, his butcher may not make him pay for the privilege of silence.[144] At the beginning of their section on blackmail, Landes and Posner note that blackmail appears at first sight to be an efficient way of enforcing the law, "the moral as well as the positive law."[145] Yet (rightly or wrongly) Shaw is not assumed by most people in this society to be violating a moral law—thus the threat of over- or underenforcement does not seem to arise.

Perhaps realizing these difficulties, Landes and Posner then offer a slightly different explanation for the criminalizing of the sale of humiliating as well as incriminating information.

> The social decision not to regulate a particular activity is a judgment that the expenditure of resources on trying to discover it and punish it would be socially wasted. That judgment is undermined if blackmailers are encouraged to expend substantial resources on attempting to apprehend and punish people engaged in the activity.[146]

This is an ingenious suggestion, but there are a number of problems with it. First of all, the implications Landes and Posner draw from "the decision not to regulate" seem problematic in the extreme. All over the United States there are parents trying to find out if their children—whether infant or adult—are eating their greens, doing their homework, smoking cigarettes or dating the "wrong people." The idea that the legal system ought to step in to prevent them from investing time in checking up on any legal activity does not survive prolonged scrutiny, no matter

---

142. Landes & Posner, *supra* note 26, at 42.
143. *Cf.* DENNIS C. MUELLER, PUBLIC CHOICE (1979) (surveying legislator and voter behavior from an economic point of view); Jack M. Beermann, *Interest Group Politics and Judicial Behavior: Macey's Public Choice,* 67 NOTRE DAME L. REV. 183 (1991); Jonathan R. Macey, *Special Interst Groups Legislation and the Judicial Function: The Dilemma of Glass-Steagall,* 33 EMORY L.J. 1 (1984).
144. Nor for the silence of the lambs.
145. Landes & Posner, *supra* note 26, at 42.
146. *Id.* at 43.

how attractive it might be to the children involved. To put it another way, it is already stretching a point to claim that criminal statutes are accurate judgments of the efficient level of an activity. It is going altogether too far to claim also that the *absence* of criminal statutes represents a measured judgment by the legislature that "research" on such behavior would be inefficient.

The second problem with the argument is its leap to the deduction from negative evidence. It is strange to imagine that by failing to criminalize behavior we are making a reasoned judgment that information about that behavior should never be gathered. One can imagine all sorts of reasons we might have for failing to criminalize behavior that would not prevent us from wanting to have news gathered and spread. A politician makes repeated sexist or racist jokes, an air force officer in charge of nuclear weapons is a moody alcoholic, a candidate for a teaching position has awful teaching evaluations at a prior school—in each case, we can acknowledge some social value to the information despite the fact that the behavior concerned is perfectly legal. Posner and Landes would need to show *both* that: (1) noncriminalization was a conclusive judgment that the information was not worth the investment of social resources and (2) forbidding citizens to trade in it would have a meaningful effect on its acquisition. Yet (2) seems empirically doubtful in the extreme, while (1) seems just plain wrong.

One response to these problems might be that Landes and Posner object only to monetary incentives to engage in this kind of research. Where affection and sentiment or public or private interest supply the motive, we might hope that all is for the best—my examples notwithstanding. Of course, if there are enough nonmonetary incentives to investigate legal behavior, then the prohibition of monetary incentives would be irrational, a use of the state's cumbersome and expensive machinery in the service of a goal that is already unreachable. But even if the empirical question were dealt with adequately (and Posner and Landes do not deal with it at all), such a response brings a new school of problems in its wake. If we concentrate only on occasions involving monetary incentives to gather information, the theory as stated seems unable to distinguish rationally between paid concealment and paid revelation. If adultery is legal in this particular state, does that represent a judgment that we do not want resources devoted to the discovery of adultery? Thinking of the blackmailer, Landes and Posner would presumably say, "Yes." Does this logically require that we prohibit newspaper reporters from following Gary Hart, or one spouse from hiring private detectives to check on the other?

Just at this point in their article, Landes and Posner reverse tack, apparently without realizing it: "We therefore predict that in areas where there is a public monopoly of enforcement, bribery, like blackmail, will be prohibited, while in areas where there is no public monopoly it will be permitted. And so we observe."[147] This may seem to deal with the spouse example. But it completely undercuts their idea that the decision not to regulate implies a judgment that resources should not be spent trying to acquire the information. There is no public monopoly of enforcement of George Bernard Shaw's vegetarianism, yet "private enforcement"—through blackmail—is illegal. In many states there is no public monopoly of enforcement of prohibitions against adultery, certain types of plagiarism, or violation of the individual's professed creed—yet blackmail is not permitted.

Perhaps Landes and Posner are saying that we should minimize the gathering of information about activities that are not illegal and which private parties have no right to restrain. If that is the idea, then they seem again to be ignoring the possibility that blackmail may well be one of the least important motives for gathering information. Prurience, moral disapproval, or simple curiosity can lead citizens to pry, as can the desire to help another human being, to gain status as a gossip, or to achieve political power. Surely if we wished to avoid this kind of wasteful "research," the solution would be to criminalize it, or at least to allow the injured party to bring suit under an enormously expanded tort of intrusion on seclusion. Under their plan, the only person deterred will be the person who wants to sell directly to the individual concerned. Sales to other parties—the tabloids, for example—are untouched, as are all the other nonmarket incentives for engaging in investigation. If this is an attempt to prevent the socially wasteful investment of resources, then it is a signally ineffective one.[148] Though thought-provoking, Landes and Posner's theory focuses on probably the least important market and on only one motive for gathering information. It also neglects empirical considerations that might rob it of any significance, deploys the concept of monopoly enforcement in apparently contradictory ways, and ignores the case in which the information-gathering is paid for *ex ante* rather than *ex post*.

---

147. *Id.*
148. Lindgren also makes some of these points in his critique of Posner. At the same time, however, he makes what I consider to be an error, at least tactically, in his criticisms of Posner and other economic theorists such as Ginsburg. In both cases, he criticizes theories that focus on the inefficiency of investing resources in acquiring "blackmailable" information, because they cannot explain the prohibition of blackmail using accidentally acquired information. To this, I think Posner would simply respond that problems of formal realizability and difficulties of proof would more than justify drawing the rule so as to include the person who accidentally learns of some scandalous behavior as well as the person who waits, night after night, with camera in hand. In my discussion of Coase and Ginsburg, I reformulate this criticism in a way that does not appear to be countered by the formal realizability argument. *See infra* text accompanying notes 149-52.

Ginsburg[149] and Coase[150] take a more promising economic approach. Both focus on the fact that, if blackmail is allowed, there will be incentives for potential blackmailers to invest in discovering information that could be used to blackmail others. "Blackmail involves the expenditure of resources in the collection of information which, on payment of blackmail, will be suppressed. It would be better if this information were not collected and the resources were used to produce something of value."[151] This is, in fact, an ingenious explanation of blackmail. But again there are a number of problems.

The first problem, as Lindgren points out, is that it does not explain the prohibition of "accidental blackmail" (such as the clergyman seen *in flagrante delicto* through a wind-fluttered curtain). Let us assume the response to this critique is, as I suggested earlier, that of formal realizability. Drawing the boundaries this way will make it easier to enforce. The second problem is that the argument appears to rest on an unacknowledged empirical assumption about the prevalence of accidental blackmail as opposed to "deliberate blackmail" (the individual who sets out to "get the dirt on someone"). If the information necessary for deliberate blackmail is costly relative to the likely benefits to be gained, then rational actors would be deterred anyway. Thus, even when the practice is legalized, most blackmailers would be of the accidental type. Yet the accidental blackmailer's discovery of the information is unaffected by the rule change. Thus we might be forbidding a potentially productive exchange, leaving the accidental blackmailer who would rather have been paid off than gossip, but would rather gossip than keep quiet, to spill the beans. To make the argument with any confidence we would need to figure out the proportion of accidental blackmail to deliberate blackmail under both rule systems, and the relative utility functions of gossip for both types of blackmailers. It could be the case that our attempt to prevent the socially wasteful investment of resources will block mutually beneficial transactions—those between eager victims and accidental blackmailers who place a low value on gossip.

The third problem is the quick move to judgment that "nothing of value" has been produced. The measure being used here is not the subjective willingness of the parties to pay. Because of its moral repulsiveness, it seems intuitively believable that blackmail produces nothing of value. But is this really the case? What measure of social value is being used? On the part of a victim, the blackmail payment represents "the avoidance of a loss," rather than a "gain," but we are surely not saying that all situations where parties pay to avoid losses are criminal. Con-

---

149. Douglas Ginsburg, Blackmail: An Economic Analysis of the Law (n.d.) (unpublished manuscript, on file at the Harvard University Law Library).
150. Coase, *supra* note 26.
151. *Id.* at 674.

sider the behavior of the baseball team, negotiating with its host city for a better deal. As Coase himself admits at the end of his article,

> The problem is that all trade involves threatening not to do something unless certain demands are met. Furthermore, negotiations about the terms of trade are likely to involve the making of threats which it would be better if they were not made (and in this Pigou is right). But it is only certain threats in certain situations which cause harm on balance and in which the harm is sufficiently great as to make it desirable that those making them should be prosecuted and punished.[152]

Having implicitly accepted that all of the theories would criminalize transactions now understood to be perfectly legal, Coase concludes by wondering whether the British system, with its broad grant of discretion to judge and jury, represents the best answer. This seems a perfectly sensible response on the level of policy. Yet it also represents an abandonment of the rationalist project in this case, with no consideration of the more general questions that such a rejection seems to raise.

These are not the only possible criticisms of economic theories of blackmail. We could turn Landes and Posner on their heads and argue that blackmail would function, by and large, as an effective way to police social norms, coupled with a relatively efficient buyout provision. If the victim was willing to pay more for the information than the public would (whether through tabloid bounty or Gennifer Flowers celebrity), then the blackmailer would sell silence. On its face, a resource has been moved to its highest use-value. Only Landes and Posner's rather dubious assumption about the efficiency of both positive and negative judgments by legislatures allow them to avoid this interpretation. Viewing blackmail as a secondary method of social control, it is not entirely clear how one can both stay within the strange world of economic assumptions and yet declare that the information "has no value." For all of the reasons listed, the economic theories of blackmail seem to fail according to their own standards.[153] This is a point that Coase seems almost to acknowledge at

---

152. *Id.* at 675-76.

153. When I presented this paper at Harvard Law School, Professor Henry Hansmann suggested that blackmail theorists could come up with a new variant of the economic explanations—arguing that by denying the possibility of direct sale, blackmail operates as an incentive to encourage the revelation of information in which society has an interest. Although this was a spontaneous creation (to the best of my knowledge) it seems to be the least problematic of the economic hypotheses. Nevertheless, it still runs into some of the same problems as the other economic theories; in particular, it asserts—without evidence—that the gain from the total value of the information revealed by the existence of blackmail doctrine would be greater than the loss caused by the blocking of many potentially efficient transactions between blackmailers and victims eager to pay for silence. If disclosure of items in the public interest is the goal, why do we not rely on the economists' default assumption that the market will provide? There *is* a market for tidbits of disgraceful news about the mighty, whether that market is *The New York Times* or *The National Enquirer*. In other situations, economists are prone to say that—if the public interest is truly great enough—then the market will

the end of his article.

Perhaps the central problem with all such theories from my perspective, however, is that they seem so far from the social understanding of blackmail. Would social judgments about the normative status of blackmail turn on empirical issues about the relative frequency and costliness of its accidental versus its deliberate varieties? Of course, explanations of the law do not have to assume that social actors understand their own institutions. Yet in the case of blackmail, the goad to answer the puzzle comes partly from the juxtaposition of the almost universal sense that the practice is wrong and the difficulty of distinguishing it from "lawful" transactions. To discard the importance of social perceptions is also to challenge a large part of the motive for undertaking the theoretical inquiry in the first place. Finally, as I will point out later, there seems to be a particular problem here for economic analysts. How do we move from a picture of relentlessly rational actors, consumer sovereignty, and exogenous preferences to a world in which we assert that citizens think blackmail has nothing to do with information costs, but are deluded? For me at least, that is a puzzle. It looks like a theory of false consciousness. But that is exactly the kind of theory most economic analysts of law claim to be avoiding.

B. *Libertarian Theories*

Blackmail is also a very troublesome topic for libertarians. If contract is the central metaphor for mutually beneficial social relationships and government intervention in free exchanges is a paradigmatic evil, how can blackmail be wrong? Driven by this logic, some libertarians are willing to argue that blackmail is permissible,[154] but two of the most prominent libertarians, Robert Nozick and Richard Epstein, think it should be criminalized, though each gives a different explanation for this apparent exception to their principles.

Epstein, in his article *Blackmail, Inc.,* argues that if blackmail were legal, it might lead to further crimes as the victim sought money to pay off his blackmailer.[155] This idea seems extremely implausible, being both logically unrequired and subject to some obvious practical difficulties. Why should we suddenly start assuming that this particular monetary pressure would drive the victim to crime? Consider the entirely legal forms of "pressure" that can be put on individuals in our society—ranging from the advertising that encourages us to define our self-worth in

---

price the resource appropriately. In other words, the victim would lose the bidding war. Why assume, in this particular instance, that transaction costs are high enough that we must rely on a paternalistic clause which forbids parties to contract?

154. *See* WALTER BLOCK, DEFENDING THE UNDEFENDABLE 53-54 (1976); MURRAY N. ROTHBARD, THE ETHICS OF LIBERTY 124-27 (1982).

155. Epstein, *supra* note 26, at 564-65.

terms of consumer goods that not all of us can afford to the action of a company in laying off workers, many of whom have mortgages or medical bills that place an intolerable financial burden on them. Each of these might conceivably lead to crime. Yet somehow it seems doubtful that Epstein would criminalize the advertising of Air Jordans, or the practice of plant closings. Besides, as Lindgren points out, it would be in Blackmail, Inc.'s interests to set the payments at a level not likely to provoke rash criminal activity.[156] An incarcerated victim is an unpromising target for blackmail.

Epstein also speculates that the blackmail victim, unlike other persons needing money, would probably not be able to get a loan because of the difficulty of specifying the reason she needed the money. Again, this seems implausible. In my (admittedly limited) experience, providers of consumer credit, credit cards, and home equity loans care only about one's ability to pay. The liberal state may or may not be indifferent as to "ends," but lenders certainly seem to be.

There also seems to be a familiar baseline error here: imagining a hypothetical change of rule, but failing to adjust behavior to conform to the new rule. If blackmail were *legal,* surely lenders would find it an acceptable investment. Imagine a lender contemplating a further loan to a borrower who already owes the lender money. If paying off Blackmail, Inc., will allow the borrower to keep a lucrative job or social position, then a blackmail loan would seem like a better investment than a loan for a new car. If lenders are supposed to be irrational, presumably Blackmail, Inc., would be smart enough to develop a good credit division. Rather than exploring either of these possibilities, Epstein imagines that Blackmail, Inc., will stupidly encourage the victim's slide into crime. Thus, not only will they open themselves to suit and to criminal charges for conspiracy, but they will also forfeit the advantages Epstein has just conferred on them by legalization. Admittedly, a firm this stupid doesn't deserve a break, but why assume such irrationality on the part of all concerned?

Finally, as Epstein himself notes, it would seem intuitively plausible that a rational blackmail industry would pick rich victims—victims who might not *need* credit. Blackmailers would prefer rich victims because of the diminishing marginal utility of wealth[157] and because there would probably be a statistically significant correlation between those who have something to lose in terms of reputation and association and those who

---

156. James Lindgren, *More Blackmail Ink: A Critique of* Blackmail, Inc., *Epstein's Theory of Blackmail,* 16 CONN. L. REV. 909, 921 (1984).

157. This is an economic concept about which Chicago-school economists (and econo-libertarians such as Epstein) generally maintain an intriguing silence. Of course, one *can* differentiate between wealth-maximizing and more strictly utilitarian versions of economic analysis. But what is the advantage of doing so?

have money. The street person is an unlikely victim of blackmail, the minimum wage worker scarcely more likely, and, if there are any costs of investigation at all, we would need some empirical evidence of the break-even point before we could say whether those who are most likely to be blackmailed would not also be likely to have substantial resources or credit on demand. Epstein's conclusion that, unlike kindred transactions, "only blackmail breeds fraud" seems, like religious encyclicals about the depraving effects of rock music, to have little in the way of logic to recommend it.

Epstein has another string to his bow. Working from libertarian assumptions, he sees most nonphysical crimes to be grounded in fraud or deceit. Thus, for him, "[t]he puzzle . . . is somewhat transformed, as the question might be better asked, why is it that [the victim] escapes criminal punishment for deception, not why is [the defendant] punished for blackmail."[158] In the end, he cannot entirely solve this problem so he pushes it to one side, confident that the blackmail problem, at least, has been resolved: "Blackmail should be a criminal offense even under the narrow theory of criminal activities because it is the handmaiden to corruption and deceit."[159] We have already dealt with the corruption argument. What about deceit? The trouble here is that this answer seems to avoid the question. The blackmail puzzle asks why the law allows citizens to keep secrets, and to reveal secrets, but not to make others pay for the keeping of secrets. To say that secret-keeping in some wider sense should be illegal, and to use this as an explanation of blackmail's illegality, is hardly likely to satisfy those who have been seeking a solution to the problem. For someone like Lindgren, this is similar to "solving" Epinimides' paradox (that all Cretans are liars, Epinimides himself being from Crete) by suggesting that Epinimides was actually from Ios.

In another interesting libertarian analysis, Robert Nozick has argued that blackmail should be illegal because it is "not a productive activity."[160] The proof of its "unproductivity" comes, for Nozick, from his belief that one party to the exchange would be no worse off if it were prohibited.

> Though people value a blackmailer's silence, and pay for it, his being silent is not a productive activity. His victims would be as well off if the blackmailer did not exist at all, and so wasn't threatening them. And they would be no worse off if the exchange were known to be absolutely impossible.[161]

This idea is an interesting one, but it collapses as soon as it is exposed to the world of legal powers, privileges, and immunities. There are many

---

158. Epstein, *supra* note 26, at 565.
159. *Id.* at 566.
160. NOZICK, *supra* note 26, at 85.
161. *Id.* (footnote omitted).

cases in which I would be better off (in some sense) if the other party did not exist at all. The neighboring landowner wishes to build a structure that will deprive my courtyard of sunlight, but is willing to forego building for payment. Perhaps Nozick would respond that even if this landowner did not exist, some landowner must exist and thus—at least potentially—I would face the same problem. But even this kind of confession and avoidance does not solve the problem.

Nozick seems to be relying on an implicit but indefensible baseline. The alternative to blackmail is silence, and thus the victim may seem better off if blackmail is illegal. But the alternative to blackmail may be, not silence, but revelation. This is a point that those libertarians who believe blackmail should not be criminalized have made loudly and often.[162] To put it another way, Nozick is making a category error, confusing the *person* with the legally protected interest. The victim might be better off if the blackmailer did not exist, but Nozick instead is arguing for the disappearance of one of the blackmailer's legally protected interests, leaving intact exactly the ones that can do the victim harm. It is true that all those with secrets to hide would be better off if no one ever discovered them. But the law of blackmail cannot get rid of the person who discovers a secret; it merely makes it impossible for him to sell that secret. Nozick has not stripped the blackmailer of the privilege of disclosure, but merely the ability to commodify silence. He is therefore wrong to say that victims "would be no worse off if the exchange were known to be absolutely impossible."[163] In such a situation, blackmailers who put a low value on the celebrity of being a gossip, but who would instead have accepted a small payment for silence, will now disclose. In such a situation, victims might justifiably conclude that they would have been better off if *Nozick* had never existed!

Nozick might choose to reformulate his position by combining the incentives point discussed by Coase with his own definition of unproductive exchanges. The idea here would be that prohibiting blackmail would discourage rational actors from investing resources in trying to "get the dirt on someone" and thus minimize the number of "unproductive exchanges." Such a response, however, has two major problems. First and most fundamentally, there is the difficulty in crafting a noncircular definition of unproductive exchanges, and one that does not also criminalize a host of other transactions. So far, this is something that Nozick has been unable to do. Second, this argument appears to rest on the same unacknowledged empirical assumption about the prevalence of accidental blackmail as opposed to deliberate blackmail. Thus Nozick might be forbidding a potentially productive exchange, leaving the accidental blackmailer who would rather have been paid off than gossip, but

---

162. ROTHBARD, *supra* note 154, at 243.
163. NOZICK, *supra* note 26, at 85.

would rather gossip than keep quiet, to spill the beans. To make the argument with any confidence we would need to figure out the proportion of accidental blackmail to deliberate blackmail under both rule systems, and the relative utility functions of gossip for both types of blackmailers. Of course, neither Nozick nor Epstein can do this.

C.   Third Party Theories

James Lindgren's analysis offers to resolve the paradox of blackmail by reference to third party interests.

> [M]y own view is that the key to the wrongfulness of the blackmail transaction is in its triangular structure. As Epstein notes, the transaction implicitly involves not only the blackmailer and his victim but always a third party as well. This third party may be, for example, the victim's spouse or employer, the authorities, or even the public at large. When a blackmailer tries to use his right to release damaging information, he is threatening to tell others. To get what he wants, the blackmailer uses leverage that is less his than someone else's. Selling the right to go to the police involves suppressing the state's interests. And selling the right to inform others of embarrassing (but legal) behavior involves suppressing the interests of those other people. Why should this threatener be able to gain personal advantages by coercing others, using leverage that is not really his?[164]

In one sense, Lindgren is on the right track here. Certainly his article contains an impressive survey and critique of other theories, and his theory at least asks us to look at the reaction of other individuals in the society. But the analysis is flawed by a series of errors based on conceptual slippage in the definition of key terms. In what sense, exactly, is the leverage that the blackmailer uses "less his than someone else's"? First of all, one should note the vagueness of the terms. Is a legally protected interest being asserted here, or merely an "interest" in the same sense that many people have an interest in seeing Madonna's new video? At times, Lindgren seems to be moving from the latter to the former, thus presuming the point he is obliged to prove. Second, if Lindgren is asserting that the blackmailer has "no right" to capitalize on the latter kind of interest, he seems to be restating the very problem he has set himself to solve. For the realist scholars of the 1920s, the slippage from "no right to control" to "no saleable privilege to reveal" represents a prototypical Hohfeldian error. The ability to analyze such issues clearly is exactly the thing that distinguishes post- from pre-Hohfeldian analysis.[165]

---

164. Lindgren, *supra* note 156, at 922-23. Lindgren's full explanation of his theory is given in Lindgren, *supra* note 27.

165. *See* WESLEY N. HOHFELD, FUNDAMENTAL LEGAL CONCEPTIONS AS APPLIED IN JUDICIAL REASONING AND OTHER LEGAL ESSAYS (Walter W. Cook ed., 1923); *see also* Hitchman

Third, whatever kind of "interest" this is, Lindgren is mistaken if he believes that one may not sell access to something one does not own. Many bargains involve one party using access to a resource or market he or she does not own as leverage to persuade another party to contract. If I sell a popcorn concession in my baseball stadium to you, you will be interested only because you know this will give you access to a group of potential consumers. You would never pay me merely for refraining from exercising my right to deny you access to the physical space that I own. Without the crowd, my sale of this right would be worthless to you, just as the blackmailer's promise to forebear from exercising the privilege of revelation would be worthless without third parties who will not otherwise be told of the secret. I own neither those consumers nor their appetites, but I do control access to them while they are at the game. Is this transaction somehow despicable because the economic leverage I use is access to someone else's appetite, whether for popcorn or for gossip? I will probably lease the stand to the person who pays the most, perhaps increasing the cost of popcorn to those who attend the game. In some sense, therefore, I sell my right of exclusion, using the "interests" of others as my economic leverage, and yet I am not forced to incorporate their interests fully into my calculation.[166]

When we renegotiate, I may threaten to lease to someone else unless you pay me more. As far as one could tell, Lindgren's analysis is unable to distinguish this case from blackmail. "Why should this threatener be able to gain personal advantages by coercing others, using leverage that is not really his?"[167] But as this analogy should make clear, the phrase "not really his" contains a fatal ambiguity. The leverage is not really mine, in the sense that I do not own the baseball fans and their appetites, or the audience for gossip, but it is "really mine" in the sense that I have legally protected interests that allow me to grant or withhold physical *or informational* access. If we ignore the judgmental possessive, "mine," with its associated connotation of the absolute concept of property, then the legal relationships become much clearer. Lindgren's theory—at least in any strong form—fails to distinguish blackmail from innumerable legal transactions.

Coal & Coke Co. v. Mitchell, 245 U.S. 229 (1917); Morton Horwitz, The Transformation of American Law 1870-1960, at 152-56, 193-202 (forthcoming Oxford University Press) (unproofed ed.); Walter W. Cook, *Privileges of Labor Unions in the Struggle for Life,* 27 Yale L.J. 779 (1918).

166. The baseball example, like many cases of blackmail, involves a situation close to a bilateral monopoly. Obviously, there are limits—for example, substitute goods (other baseball teams, other activities, other foods)—but the ability to sell the legally protected interest still gives considerable power to the party possessing it.

167. Lindgren, *supra* note 156, at 923.

D. Shared Problems

Before I finish the critical part of my coverage of blackmail, I would like to point out three characteristics of the articles I have discussed so far. The first is best exemplified by Nozick, Posner, and Epstein. Their arguments show an interesting willingness to relinquish, or at least modify, a principle they normally hold dear. The principle is consumer sovereignty, or the personal definition of self-interest. Why is blackmail such a difficult case for them? Seeing that the law prohibits a transaction, seeing that the transaction is apparently dependent only on the coercion involved in the relinquishment of a legal privilege, and yet finding the transaction indefensible, they are placed in an agonizing position. To suggest, as the legal realists did, that coercion is inherent in the legal system, that the core of a consensual *laissez faire* system is completely dependent on institutionalized coercion, is not a solution that appeals to them.[168] Besides, it is not clear that even that admission would solve the puzzle of blackmail. (In formal terms, it would merely put other transactions on the same level as blackmail—hardly an attractive solution in either theoretical or practical terms.) At the same time, all three wish to put the law of blackmail within the class of "rational social institutions," and thus they must find some logical explanation of its wrongfulness. The explanation must contain some principle to distinguish between this state interference in a "consensual transaction" and all the other state interferences in "consensual transactions." Otherwise, they might be seen to have accepted the premise of liberals and radicals that paternalistic intervention is frequently necessary in the economic system in order to mitigate the effects of unequal power.[169]

Second, it is also noticeable that even in combination, all the theories—but particularly the economic and libertarian ones—fail to grasp the social meaning of blackmail. Put another way, I doubt that anyone—even on the streets of Cambridge—would respond to the question, "Why is blackmail illegal?" by appealing to notions of inefficient incentives for information production or of unproductive exchanges. Of course, there is nothing wrong with giving an explanation for a body of law that conflicts with the explanations of those in the society governed by such laws. But Nozick, Epstein, Posner, and Coase are increasingly forced towards theories that diverge so widely from popular ideas that the only explanation for the discrepancy seems to be the false consciousness of those concerned. For theorists in other traditions this would be unexceptionable. Yet for libertarians and economic analysts to accept

---

168. *See* Robert L. Hale, *Bargaining, Duress, and Economic Liberty,* 43 COLUM. L. REV. 603 (1943).

169. *See* Duncan Kennedy, *Distributive and Paternalist Motives in Contract and Tort Law, with Special Reference to Compulsory Terms and Unequal Bargaining Power,* 41 MD. L. REV. 563 (1982).

the idea of false consciousness is to throw their theories—strongly dependent on a particular version of rational choice—into doubt.

The third observation could be made about all of the articles, but it is most clearly at work in Lindgren's. We could call it "Kantian anthropology." At times, Lindgren seems to assume that because there is a rule prohibiting blackmail and the practice seems intuitively bad, there must be a single general principle underlying both prohibition and revulsion. The task that he sets himself, and that he (rightly) sees as the basic goal of the other studies of blackmail, is to find this missing principle. This is certainly one way to understand legal institutions. Its premise is that social institutions should have a rational basis, expressible in terms of general principles, and those that do not should disappear from the earth. Its descriptive, rationalist anthropology dovetails nicely with its prescriptive, principled critique. As a method of legal studies, its premises are so widely shared that they are not often subject to question. Its weapons also have undeniable critical bite, particularly when deployed against someone who is working within the same genre of scholarship. Indeed, the persuasiveness of my critique of the other blackmail theorists depends on both author and reader presupposing these background conventions. But just as information questions make more apparent the weaknesses in the liberal vision of property and in the conceptual structure of efficiency and incentive discourse in economics, so too they highlight the contentious quality of this vision of legal scholarship.

I would claim that we cannot understand blackmail unless we look at it in the context of the ideology and institutions of a liberal society, a society that often presupposes different theories of justice and methods of treating people in the realms of the family, the market, and the state. We get a different picture if we look at legal institutions and moral beliefs in light of the history, social arrangements, and ideology of this actual society, rather than in an unspecified and featureless world of legal hypotheticals and pure rationality.

Let us use a nonblackmail hypothetical for a moment. Consider the contract rules about penalty clauses and liquidated damages. We could come up with a rationalistic explanation of the difference, based perhaps on allocative efficiency or the Rawlsian original position. But although such an explanation would be useful, it would also ignore the absolute terror that liberal social theory in general and classical legal thought in particular have of private law assuming a redistributive function. This concern is built on moral ideals and ideas of political theory, but it is also built on concerns of legitimacy and of the apparent soundness of an entire ideological view of the world.

Any study of legal ideology would note two problematic conclusions deduced from the supposedly nonredistributive nature of contract law: (1) the court should merely interpret the will of the parties, because to go further would be to move from being an instrument of the parties' bargain to being an independent redistributive actor; and (2) punitive damages are inappropriate in contract law, which functions only to achieve the results the contract would have reached. The obvious conflict comes when the parties apparently *specify* punitive damages. If it shares that ideological background, the court is faced with a contradiction. That contradiction helps explain the confused and confusing distinction between illegitimate "punitive damages" and legitimate and mutually agreed upon "liquidated damages." The perspective of rational managers of the legal system, dealing with one technical problem of doctrine at a time, underestimates the extent to which these answers fit into a world already structured by history, ideology, and political vision.[170]

How does this insight help us to understand blackmail? To answer that question I must return to my discussion of public and private. My thesis here is that one of the main reasons that blackmail is illegal (and strongly perceived to be wrong) is that there is a strong social belief, sometimes consciously articulated and sometimes unconsciously held, that not everything should be reduced to the universalizing logic of the money relation. In particular, the private realm of home and hearth should be protected against the relentless instrumentalism of market transactions. This belief is given a particular "spin" by our practice, within that sphere, of defining the norm of justified protection largely by reference to the right to withhold and control information. Intuitively, blackmail seems like the intrusion of market logic into the realm that should be most "private." To put it another way, we do not think that we should commodify relationships in the private realm. To commodify is itself to violate the private realm.[171] To commodify a violation of privacy, then, is doubly reprehensible.

Two features of blackmail doctrine seem to me to support this inter-

---

170. This is not to say that, since societal institutions have nonrational elements, we must give up the tools of reason (although my claim is that those tools are less powerful than is often assumed). But it does offer an interesting insight into the kind of theorizing that assumes the correctness of a strongly held social belief and works to fashion a principled justification for it—rather like putting a slipcover onto an existing chair.

Looking at issues in the way I suggest here also helps us to understand the connections between apparently diverse questions. The will theory of contracts, the doctrine of no duty to act, and the continued constitutional challenges to punitive damages, for example, all share certain premises about the role of private law *vis-à-vis* the distribution of wealth. Thus, an attack on one principle is often perceived as an attack on them all.

171. In this, as in much of the discussion of commodification in this Article, I have found Peggy Radin's work to be invaluable. Margaret J. Radin, *Market-Inalienability,* 100 HARV. L. REV. 1849 (1987). Professor Radin does not discuss blackmail, or information issues as such, nor does she use the public/private split to explain social reluctance to commodify certain types of information. Nevertheless, she does discuss many of the issues analyzed here, including the commodification of body parts, and I found those discussions to be extremely helpful. She also touches on the commodification of celebrity personae, *id.* at 1857 n.33, and on the issue of market inalienability in tort law, *id.* at 1876-78.

pretation. First, by and large we allow the victim (and the blackmailer's assessment of the victim's subjective beliefs) to determine whether or not particular information involves a "disgraceful defect." A vision of blackmail that did not focus on privacy, but instead wanted to prohibit the commodification of information about a particular menu of behavior and practices, would either list topics about which individuals could not be blackmailed or appeal to an objective or community standard. In fact, we choose to protect George Bernard Shaw's secret carnivorousness to exactly the same extent that we protect secret marital infidelity, despite the different tolerance for such practices in society as a whole. The comparison to the law of libel is instructive.

Second, we only prohibit the *commodification* of private information. This reinforces my earlier arguments about the multiple contradictory stereotypes about information. Unless I have gone so far as to commit an additional tort such as intrusion upon seclusion, I am allowed to reveal all of the information I discover—without penalty. The privilege is retained, but the sale of the privilege is criminalized. When freely revealed, information—even relatively private information—fits readily into the public, First Amendment stereotype: information is the lifeblood of the public realm, that which we must not regulate if we are to maintain the free flow of ideas. The attempt to commodify, however, undermines the First Amendment stereotype, allowing the privacy vision to take over. In the Part on insider trading, I will argue that the reverse mechanism explains the prohibition of trading on material, nonpublic information.[172] There, the "public" view of information, the idea of presumptive equality in this resource alone, operates to give insider trading law a powerful rationale.

Seen this way, blackmail is analogous to a different set of crimes. To understand blackmail we would not compare it to the robber's demand for a wallet. Instead, we would compare it to other situations where commodification of something "private" is made illegal, despite the fact that, at a slightly greater level of abstraction, the transaction looks like an ordinary market exchange. Thus the analogies would be to the voidability of contracts for sexual services or the prohibition of babyselling. I can give sexual favors, but not enforce a contract for them. I have the power to arrange a private adoption of my child, yet I cannot sell that power, nor the child.[173]

---

172. *See infra* Part VIII.

173. There are many other examples. In the wrongful birth cases, the refusal of many courts to include the costs of raising a child as part of the "damage" attributable to a neligently performed sterilization operation stems partly from the desire to keep the market out of the realm of home and hearth. Courts produce a whole set of arguments ranging from the ineffable benefit of extra children to the difficulty of quantification, the duty to mitigate damages, and the impossibility of tracing the chain of causation. Yet a moment's analysis of each of these reasons reveals that other tort issues pose far greater difficulties. In the end, one is hard put not to conclude that the court is really

Many scholars find this kind of response unsatisfying. Even if there are "irrational" or "sentimental" or "romantic" reasons behind a legal institution, should we not work to complete the Enlightenment project— to bring institutions to account in the court of reason? I have both a fancy philosophical response and a mundane practical response to this suggestion. The fancy philosophical point is that there *is* no pretheoretical, preclassified reality from which we can begin to analyze our institutions. *This* context or *that* context may not be inevitable, but there will be some context, some prior social construction of reality. Wittgenstein's analysis of language games,[174] Feyerabend's and Kuhn's (very different) work on the scientific method,[175] Rorty's neopragmatism[176]—all seem to cast doubt on the idea of a world not already socially constructed, while leaving open the question of consequences that flow from exploring the limits of the particular, overlapping contexts in which we find ourselves.

My more mundane response is that it is important to understand the limitations of a system that "decides" issues by typing them as public or private. To say that, however, is not to hold up the possibility of a pure analysis that would treat the issue of blackmail in a "neutral" framework. No such framework is available. On a local basis, I still believe in arguments about the desirability of a prohibition of blackmail—arguments based on judgments about consequences, on analogies to other kinds of behavior, even on the idea of incentives to engage in particular kinds of information-gathering. Those arguments, however, will not discover some universalizable principle that underpins both the proscription of blackmail and its social support. Instead, they will be both over- and underinclusive. They will point towards the prohibition of acts that we allow, while not explaining our prohibition of other transactions. The goal of the blackmail theorists, to provide the single rational explanation is not only unmet but—I would argue—unreachable.

What then is the benefit of the analysis I offer here? What does it profit us to understand that information issues are resolved partly by the typing of issues into "public" or "private" categories? How does it help us to understand that blackmail prevents the commodification of subjectively defined private information partly because of a romantic notion of privacy, home, and hearth, and an associated belief that we must keep the market away from that realm if we hope to maintain it? First, I think

---

imposing a particular belief about those areas that should not be subject to market quantification— no matter how real the loss.

174. LUDWIG WITTGENSTEIN, PHILOSOPHICAL INVESTIGATIONS (G.E.M. Anscombe trans., 3d ed. 1953).

175. PAUL K. FEYERABEND, AGAINST METHOD: OUTLINE OF AN ANARCHIST THEORY OF KNOWLEDGE (1975); PAUL K. FEYERABEND, PROBLEMS OF EMPIRICISM (1981); THOMAS S. KUHN, THE STRUCTURE OF SCIENTIFIC REVOLUTIONS (1962).

176. RICHARD RORTY, CONSEQUENCES OF PRAGMATISM (1982); RICHARD RORTY, PHILOSOPHY AND THE MIRROR OF NATURE (1979).

it is descriptively useful. To understand how information issues should be resolved, we need first to understand how they *are* resolved.

Second, the analysis gives us an ability (albeit very limited) to prognosticate. In the Conclusion, I point out that any analysis of an "information society" has to deal with the conflicting valences of our various visions of information as public and as private, as commodity and as "that which must never be commodified." Blackmail doctrine points out the lengths to which we are prepared to go to give individuals sovereignty over information pertaining to them. This surely is an important idea in any society in which the collection, manipulation, distribution, and use of information plays a significant role.

Third, dealing specifically with the blackmail puzzle, the analysis sets out a reason for the problems with the existing blackmail literature. The very notion of "reason," "theory," and "principle" adopted by the blackmail theorists makes it almost impossible for them to find such a reason, theory, or principle underlying blackmail. There is an old joke about a drunk looking for his car keys under a street light, even though he had dropped them several hundred feet away. When asked to explain his behavior, he points out that while the keys might not be there, it was the only place he could see anything. To a certain extent, the Kantian anthropology of the blackmail theorists has the same problem. They wish both to engage and to ignore the socially constructed nature of markets, coercion, and privacy. To put it another way, the society in which the kind of principle for which they are looking could be found would be the society in which social forms were already transparent to rational analysis; that is to say, the society for which it was not necessary.

Finally, the persistent mistakes made by the most sophisticated analysts of blackmail—the category and baseline errors, the failure to take into account changes in behavior if a new rule is presumed, the conflation of different legally protected interests into an undifferentiated "right" concept—all of these turn out to be mistakes that are instructive for the remainder of the literature on law and information. In the next Part, the analysis of insider trading doctrine will reveal the persistence of such errors in a case in which the commodification of information is apparently prohibited because of the public rather than the private stereotype of information. At the same time, examination of the germinal critique of insider trading doctrine will show that the language of romantic authorship can appear where least expected.

VIII
INSIDER TRADING

Our era aptly has been styled, and may well be remembered as, the "age of information." Francis Bacon recognized nearly 400 years ago that "knowledge is power," but only in the last generation has it risen to the equivalent of the coin of the realm. Nowhere is this commodity more valuable or volatile than in the world of high finance, where facts worth fortunes while secret may be rendered worthless once revealed.[177]

The above quotation comes from an insider trading case. Anthony Materia worked as a copyholder for a financial printer. One of his duties involved reading documents aloud to a proofreader who checked their accuracy. In this case, the documents concerned a forthcoming tender offer. Although the names of the companies had been erased, Mr. Materia—whom the Court of Appeals described as "an avid market watcher"[178]—was able to work out the identity of the intended target. He did this by checking the details revealed in the tender offer documents against a variety of publicly available types of information. In another context, one could imagine Mr. Materia's wit, hard work, and eye for an opportunity being held up as exemplary American entrepreneurial virtues. In the context of this case however, with its persistent overtones of fraud and deceit, the Second Circuit found little to admire in Mr. Materia's conduct and disapproved of the enthusiasm with which he pursued his extracurricular interests. At one point Judge Kaufman noted drily, "If copyholding was Materia's vocation, the stock market appears to have been equally consuming."[179] Having determined the identity of the target company, Mr. Materia invested heavily. "Within hours of each discovery, he purchased stock, and within days—after the offer had been made public—he sold his holdings at substantial gains."[180]

In the broadest possible terms, we could say that the question presented by *Materia* is, "When may an individual profit from access to material, nonpublic information?" In an earlier case, *United States v. Chiarella,*[181] which had strikingly similar facts, the same court had held that *"[a]nyone—corporate insider or not—who regularly receives material nonpublic information may not use that information to trade in securities without incurring an affirmative duty to disclose."[182] The Supreme Court did not agree. To Justice Powell, writing for the majority, the court of appeal's decision was too concerned with one particular goal of the Securities Exchange Act.

> Its decision . . . rested solely upon its belief that the federal securities laws have "created a system providing equal access to information necessary for reasoned and intelligent investment decisions." The use by anyone of material information not gener-

---

177. SEC v. Materia, 745 F.2d 197, 198 (2d Cir. 1984), *cert. denied,* 471 U.S. 1053 (1985).
178. *Id.* at 199 n.2.
179. *Id.* at 199.
180. *Id.*
181. 588 F.2d 1358 (2d Cir. 1978), *rev'd,* 445 U.S. 222 (1980).
182. *Id.* at 1365.

ally available is fraudulent, this theory suggests, because such information gives certain buyers or sellers an unfair advantage over less informed buyers and sellers.[183]

Justice Powell was not inclined to see the Securities Exchange Act as a document with such relentlessly egalitarian aims or such a broad reach to effect them. "Formulation of such a broad duty, which departs radically from the established doctrine that duty arises from a specific relationship between two parties, should not be undertaken absent some explicit evidence of congressional intent."[184]

In *Materia,* the Second Circuit tried again. Having seen their general duty to "disclose regularly received material nonpublic information" rejected by the Supreme Court, they recast the issue in terms of misappropriation.[185] Seen this way, Mr. Materia's offense was that he had "misappropriate[d] nonpublic information in breach of a fiduciary duty and trade[d] on that information to his own advantage."[186] It was this action that violated Section 10(b) of the Securities Exchange Act and Rule 10b-5. This time, with the issue framed not as the existence of formally equal public access to information, but instead as the protection of private information from something the court called "misappropriation,"[187] the Supreme Court was not inclined to disagree.[188] Given our earlier discussion of tensions in the regulation of information, this choice between an equal access view and a quasiproperty rights view should not be surprising.[189]

---

183. Chiarella v. United States, 445 U.S. 222, 232 (1980) (quoting *Chiarella,* 588 F.2d at 1362).

184. *Id.* at 233 (citation omitted). The majority seemed to feel that some degree of inequality inheres in the very idea of a market. Thus, "not every instance of financial unfairness constitutes fraudulent activity under § 10(b)." *Id.* at 232. In the later case of Dirks v. SEC, 463 U.S. 646 (1983), the Court amplified its acceptance of the idea that certain participants in the marketplace could be allowed to exploit their position of informational advantage as a form of compensation for some real or imagined public function.

> Congress has expressly exempted many market professionals from the general statutory prohibition set forth in § 11(a)(1) of the Securities Exchange Act. . . . We observed in *Chiarella* that "[t]he exception is based upon Congress' recognition that [market professionals] contribute to a fair and orderly marketplace at the same time they exploit the informational advantage that comes from their possession of [nonpublic information]."

Id. at 657 n.16 (quoting *Chiarella,* 445 U.S. at 233 n.16). Market professionals are private actors who perform a public function and are given license to exploit the information that comes their way, as a payoff. The private right secures the public role. Again, the parallel to copyright is striking.

185. This theory had been suggested in the *Chiarella* case, but since it was never submitted to the jury, Chiarella's conviction had been overturned and the resolution of the issue left "for another day." *Chiarella,* 445 U.S. at 238 (Stevens, J., concurring).

186. SEC v. Materia, 745 F.2d 197, 203 (2d Cir. 1984), *cert. denied,* 471 U.S. 1053 (1985).

187. *Id.* at 202-03. The court was understandably vague in explaining the idea of misappropriation. Was the information property, and if so, whose? If it was not property, could it be misappropriated? Would a third party, overhearing the same information in an elevator, have been "misappropriating" it? Or was the court merely saying that Mr. Materia's contractual fiduciary duties authoritatively allocated opportunities for information gathering, thus conditioning the offense on the breach of a private agreement?

188. Materia v. SEC, 471 U.S. 1053 (1985), *denying cert. to* 745 F.2d 197 (2d Cir. 1984).

189. This choice also split the Supreme Court. Whereas the majority in *Chiarella* saw

The conflicts between the court of appeals and the Supreme Court in *Materia* and *Chiarella* are variations on a deeper thematic conflict. Why should insider trading be illegal at all? Earlier in this Article, I pointed out that we live in a society that distributes wealth through a market system built on the inequality of economic power and that normally exalts an individual who is able to convert some temporary advantage into a position of market gain. Even those who think insider trading should be criminalized agree that "[t]he case law barely suggests why insider trading is harmful."[190] Critics of the current law argue that insider trading is consistent with norms found elsewhere in society,[191] that it injures no one,[192] that insider trading would be impossible in an efficient capital market,[193] that insider trading operates as a method of compensation for entrepreneurial excellence,[194] and that corporations would regulate it themselves if they believed it to be harmful.[195]

My attitude toward these criticisms is somewhat unusual. Critics of insider trading regulation could rightly claim that it is inconsistent with many of the norms that we apply to market behavior. There is something strange in the discovery of a statutory island of egalitarianism at the very heart of capitalism. But this island is not the only manifestation of egalitarian ideals in the rules defining market transactions. The law of fraud and mistake, the rule against perpetuities, the doctrine of unconscionability, and (the populist understanding of) antitrust all have

---

disparities of information as an inevitable part of a market, the dissent believed that the mere fact of disparate access is crucial to a 10b-5 case. Thus, in the view of Justices Blackmun and Marshall, an earlier Supreme Court case "len[t] strong support to the principle that a structural disparity in access to material information is a critical factor under Rule 10b-5 in establishing a duty either to disclose the information or to abstain from trading." *Chiarella*, 445 U.S. at 251 (Blackmun, J., dissenting) (citing Affiliated Ute Citizens v. United States, 406 U.S. 128 (1972)); *see also* United States v. Chestman, 947 F.2d 551, 564-67 (2d Cir. 1991) (en banc) (plurality opinion), *cert. denied*, 112 S. Ct. 1759 (1992). On the multiple confusions of the case law, see 6 ALAN R. BROMBERG & LEWIS D. LOWENFELS, SECURITIES FRAUD & COMMODITIES FRAUD § 7.5(510)-(513) (1991). For scholarly reactions to the misappropriation theory, see Manning G. Warren III, *Who's Suing Who? A Commentary on Investment Bankers and the Misappropriation Theory*, 46 MD. L. REV. 1222 (1987); Elliot Brecher, Note, *The Misappropriation Theory: Rule 10b-5 Insider Liability for Nonfiduciary Breach*, 15 FORDHAM URB. L.J. 1049 (1987); Karen A. Fischer, Comment, *The Misappropriation Theory: The Wrong Answer to the* Chiarella *Question*, 32 N.Y.L. SCH. L. REV. 701 (1987). Of course, as I tried to show earlier, the conflict goes far beyond insider trading. For an application to intellectual property of cognate principles derived from the *INS* case, see *supra* text accompanying notes 77-82, as revised by a countervailing desire to promote competition, see Leo J. Raskind, *The Misappropriation Doctrine as a Competitive Norm of Intellectual Property Law*, 75 MINN. L. REV. 875 (1991).

190. Cox, *supra* note 28, at 628.

191. Hetherington, *supra* note 28.

192. "[I]nsiders' profits are not outsiders' losses but evidence of more efficient resource allocation." Moran, *supra* note 28, at 1.

193. "The SEC first should recognize that in an efficient market, where prices are by definition 'fair,' it is impossible for investors to be cheated by paying more for securities than their true worth." Saari, *supra* note 66, at 1069 (footnote omitted).

194. *See* MANNE, *supra* note 29, at 138-41.

195. *See* Carlton & Fischel, *supra* note 66, at 862-63.

egalitarian components.[196] These rules are not all concerned with informational egalitarianism. Nevertheless, there is something undeniably counterintuitive about the prohibition against insider trading. One might expect that those who are normally skeptical of egalitarian regulation of market transactions would make much of this apparent anomaly, while those more hospitable to egalitarian notions would be keen to explore the dynamics of this egalitarian theme in the treatment of information. The former group might be expected to defend inequality in this particular context in straightforward normative terms—much as Rand or Hayek do,[197] for example. The latter group might be expected to investigate this apparent "information exception" to our tolerance for market inequality. Does the structure of public and private which I described earlier mean that it is easier to argue for egalitarian results with issues that are presented in terms of inequalities of information, rather than straightforward inequalities of wealth or power? The popular support for insider trading regulation offers some support for that hypothesis, as does the marked absence of articulate explanations of what is wrong with insider trading in the first place. Consequently, one might expect to find the informational-equality hypothesis explored at some length.

In fact, the actual scholarship on insider trading is often very different. In particular, the area is dominated by economic analysis that, with some significant exceptions, exemplifies in a rather unreflective way the *aporia* in information economics that I described earlier.[198] The analyses

---

196. Kim Scheppele's work is particularly good at showing how economic analysis fails to explain the concern of the courts hearing fraud cases with issues of power and inequality—exactly the types of issues that a more egalitarian (or in her case, Rawls-influenced contractarian) vision of the law of "legal secrecy" would concentrate on. *See* SCHEPPELE, *supra* note 1; *see also* Kronman, *supra* note 55.

197. *See* FRIEDRICH A. HAYEK, THE CONSTITUTION OF LIBERTY 81-102 (1960); FRIEDRICH A. HAYEK, LAW, LEGISLATION AND LIBERTY (1979); FRIEDRICH A. HAYEK, THE ROAD TO SERFDOM (1944); AYN RAND, THE VIRTUE OF SELFISHNESS (1964).

198. *See supra* text accompanying notes 69-98. With the exception of Gilson and Kraakman, very few scholars have attempted to integrate the literature dealing with the efficient capital markets hypothesis with the actual mechanisms of market efficiency and the associated problems of incentive and transaction cost. *See* Gilson & Kraakman, *supra* note 83. Gilson and Kraakman argue that (in at least two market mechanisms) the limited temporal monopoly on information will allow the first party to develop it to reap a reward, while subsequent imitation or learning by other traders will move the market towards an efficient equilibrium, thus harmonizing the "incentive" and the "efficiency" sides of the information debate. I am skeptical about this idea—or at least about its more general implications—for the reasons given in the discussion of information economics. *See supra* text accompanying notes 82-93. Gilson and Kraakman propose the legalization of (certain kinds of) insider trading together with a requirement that insiders identify themselves and the size of their trade at the time of the trade. Gilson & Kraakman, *supra* note 83, at 629-34. I believe that such a proposal must be based on a firm empirical analysis of the costs and benefits of allowing insider trading (including the incentives that result from existing disparities in information, *see* Hirshleifer, *supra* note 69) versus the costs and benefits of prohibiting insider trading (including lessened incentives to produce the information that would otherwise be traded, *see* Fama & Laffer, *supra* note 83, at 297-98). Kraakman and Gilson explicitly acknowledge this problem, but do not consider it to be a fatal flaw.

of insider trading regulation tend to be divided into two broad camps: those scholars who see insider trading as primarily an issue of the incentives necessary to produce information, and those scholars who focus on the efficient capital markets hypothesis. Both analyses face a fundamental problem. Just as physicists must think of light as both a particle and a wave, so economists must see information as both a prerequisite for market efficiency and a good whose producers must be motivated. If incentives are to be offered for the gathering of information, then the market cannot be informationally efficient. On the other hand, if no incentives are offered, the theory cannot explain how the information is

---

To be sure, any increase in informational efficiency from insider trading may alter the incentives to create the information because it reduces the opportunity to exploit informational disparities through trading. Because the derivatively informed trading mechanism does not disclose the information itself, however, it will not reduce the returns to information creators who exploit their information through production rather than trading, and concern over an impact on allocation is thereby minimized.

Gilson & Kraakman, *supra* note 83, at 632 n.218.

This claim would depend, presumably, on two things: first, that there is the opportunity to exploit the information through production rather than trading, and second, that the trading mechanism informs traders sufficiently to make the market move towards an efficient equilibrium but insufficiently to permit others to guess the information, thereby nullifying the information creator's trading advantage. Imagine an insider under the old rules who invests time and money to deduce that one of Polaroid's rivals has developed a newer and better instant camera. Such a person could trade on the knowledge through production, or by selling Polaroid shares short. Because some insider trading rules allow delay in reporting the trade or disclosing the information, the trader could benefit from the time lag—again, either in production or through trading. Now imagine the same trader under the new rules. Kraakman and Gilson seem to argue that while the incentives offered by trading have been changed, the returns offered by production have not. I am not sure why this is the case. Under a regime of instant disclosure of identity and size of sale, many traders might draw negative conclusions about Polaroid from short sales by industry insiders. There would certainly be less incentive to invest in information creation for trading. Why would investment in production be any different? What difference would it make if the trader buys the Polaroid license cheaply and floods the market with cut-price Polaroids before the new camera arrived on the scene, rather than, say, selling Polaroid short? It seems dubious to assume that because this is classed as "production" the returns would not be diminished—"production," too, is a datum, and other traders and consumers might draw similarly negative inferences. There seems to be no reason to assume that, as a general matter, production decisions can benefit more from *precise* knowledge (in other words, that a new camera is coming out, rather than just that the stock price is going down). The important distinction is not so much between production and trading as between the creation of information that is and that is not socially valuable. Actually, we might benefit from prohibiting traders from investing in this kind of information creation, although to say so for sure we would need to know more about the frequency of serendipitous, socially valuable discoveries occurring in searches originally designed to yield a trading advantage.

Perhaps when Kraakman and Gilson talk about "production" they have in mind something like the production of the Polaroid camera in the first place, and thus the incentives they are talking about are incentives to engage in fundamental research and development, not distributionally advantageous market research. In that case, the conclusion seems more intuitively convincing. Part of the reason that it is convincing, however, might be that the creator of the information would have some kind of intellectual property right to exploit through production, rather than having a mere privilege to trade. Yet, as I argued in the discussion of information economics, to identify those "creators" who should be the beneficiaries of property rights, we must first resolve exactly the tension that Kraakman and Gilson are dealing with—the tension between incentive and efficiency. *See supra* Part IV.

supposed to get to the market in the first place. By itself, this kind of theoretical conflict might not seem to be cause for alarm. After all, physicists can tell us a lot about refraction, reflection, and light-sails even if they must use the contradictory metaphors of particle and wave to do so. Yet as I tried to show earlier,[199] when it comes to some practical questions of information regulation—such as fair use or insider trading—the choice between which aspect of information is to be stressed seems to create a corresponding uncertainty in the results of the analysis.

In the next Sections, I attempt to extend this analysis by focusing on some of the most influential economic scholarship on the disclosure of information and then on the first real scholarly challenge to insider trading. My claim is that a concentrated study of the economic literature on disclosure shows the extent to which the indeterminacy of the underlying analysis is concealed only by a number of conceptual baseline errors and ad hoc assumptions. When I turn to Henry Manne's challenge to the regulation of insider trading, I argue that it is reliance on a notion remarkably similar to romantic authorship that gives his analysis its apparent determinacy. In the conclusion I argue that this ensemble of baseline error, non sequitur, and romance is worthy of study because it is used to justify expansive intellectual property rights far beyond insider trading.

A. Economic Analysis of Information Disparities

The more expansive law-and-economics literature treats insider trading as a case study in regulating the disclosure of valuable information. To the skeptical outsider, the outstanding features of this analysis—whether supporting or opposing the prohibition of insider trading—seem to be: (1) persistent baseline errors, (2) the use of ad hoc claims about behavior in order to give the analysis a spurious determinacy, and (3) the tendency to ignore contradictions or *aporias* in the theory at the moment policymaking conclusions are to be drawn.

1. Baseline Errors

The best examples of baseline errors in discussions of insider trading probably come from the cases,[200] but the law-and-economics literature

---

199. *See supra* text accompanying notes 74-97.

200. For example, Chief Justice Burger in *Chiarella* said,

   As a general rule, neither party to an arm's-length business transaction has an obligation to disclose information to the other unless the parties stand in some confidential or fiduciary relation. This rule permits a businessman to capitalize on his experience and skill in securing and evaluating relevant information; it provides an incentive for hard work, careful analysis, and astute forecasting. But the policies that underlie the rule also should limit its scope. *In particular, the rule should give way when an informational advantage is obtained, not by superior experience, foresight, or industry, but by some unlawful means.*

Chiarella v. United States, 445 U.S. 222, 239-40 (1980) (Burger, C.J., dissenting) (emphasis added)

runs a close second. Consider the following analysis of the economics of disclosure requirements, drawn from Professor Levmore's *Securities and Secrets: Insider Trading and the Law of Contracts,*[201] the article that introduced the happy phrase "optimal dishonesty."[202] Professor Levmore's argument rests on an exploration of the intersections and analogies between insider trading and the more general rules of disclosure in contract law. According to Professor Levmore, legal rules forcing a mining corporation to disclose discovery of a large ore deposit on a farmer's land would "hurt both present and future shareholders and, in some instances, society as a whole."[203] But the shareholders are "hurt" only if we assume that they are entitled to the amount of profit to be made in nondisclosing situations. And that is the very thing we are trying to decide. Are the Chicago Bears' shareholders "hurt" by the criminal law rules which prohibit the employment of their linebackers as muggers after the game is over? The assumptions about the regime of rules dictate which advantages (in strength, knowledge, information) may be exploited and which may not. Levmore's comment is either redundant (any change of entitlements will hurt those who lose protection and help those who gain it) or circular. He assumes the current rule is right, uses that as the baseline to measure losses—but not gains—and then finds the choice of rule mysteriously confirmed.[204]

Judge Easterbrook uses exactly the same example, and makes a similar baseline error, although in his case it leads him to overgeneralization and non sequitur. "Is it unfair for a geologist, after studying the attributes of farmland, to buy the land without revealing that the land likely covers rich mineral deposits? If the answer is yes, then fairness means that no one may appropriate the value of the information he has created."[205] But this simply is not true. Imagine an argument that if we prohibit an athlete from using his strength to take my money by force, fairness means that we must also prohibit him from using his strength to get a job on a football team. Again, the assumptions about the regime of rules dictate which advantages may be exploited and which may not. To

---

(citation omitted). Since the definition of insider trading identifies exactly what *are* "unlawful means," the use of "unlawful means" to define insider trading is an underwhelming analytic technique.

201. Levmore, *supra* note 55, at 133-44.

202. *Id.* at 140.

203. *Id.* at 133.

204. The same problem bedevils many other articles. For example, Carlton and Fischel argue that if insider trading were harmful, companies would prohibit it themselves. *See* Carlton & Fischel, *supra* note 66, at 862-66. This seems dramatically to underestimate the importance of the fact that under the current rules insider trading *is already illegal*. Manne's argument that entrepreneurs will seek employment inside firms so as to engage in insider trading is subject to the same difficulties. MANNE, *supra* note 29, at 138-41.

205. Easterbrook, *supra* note 1, at 324.

say that a particular advantage may not be exploited in one area does not commit us to the view that it may not be exploited in another.

We find a similar mistake in Easterbrook's argument that an attack on insider trading is an attack on the division of labor itself.

> People do not have or lack "access" in some absolute sense. There are, instead, different costs of obtaining information. An outsider's costs are high; he might have to purchase the information from the firm. Managers have lower costs (the amount of salary foregone); brokers have relatively low costs (the value of the time they spent investigating); Sherlock Holmes also may be able to infer extraordinary facts from ordinary occurrences at low cost. The different costs of access are simply a function of the division of labor. A manager (or a physician) always knows more than a shareholder (or patient) in some respects, but unless there is something unethical about the division of labor, the difference is not unfair.[206]

Again, the conclusion simply does not follow. Easterbrook seems to be operating on two assumptions. The first is that anyone in a position of power has some kind of natural right to the advantages they would be able to wring from that position if unrestrained by rules. The football player example sufficiently demonstrates the flaws in this argument. Alternatively, perhaps the assumption is that a market comes with an automatic set of default positions and one of them is "allow trading on superior information." It would be hard to find any lawyer since the legal realists who would defend this position. His second assumption seems to be that if we prohibit any person from profiting from any position of inequality, we are logically committed to a root and branch attack on all inequalities everywhere. But this would be obviously incoherent. If the assumption is the narrower one—that forbidding citizens to profit from a single one of the advantages conveyed by the division of labor implies that we must forbid anyone to profit from any advantage from the division of labor—then Judge Easterbrook is making a category mistake. Dogs have four legs and cats have four legs, but that does not imply that cats are dogs or that rules affecting cats must be applied to dogs—unless, of course, we have previously committed ourselves to treating all four-legged animals alike.

The second typical baseline problem in discussion of trading on superior information occurs at the moment when the analyst imagines a change in the rules, but fails to modify the rest of the analysis. For example, when Levmore does think of shifting the baseline to a different pattern of entitlements, he assumes either irrational behavior or a failure to adjust behavior to the new regime. In his argument about mineral

---

206. *Id.* at 330.

exploration, for example, he claims that under a full disclosure regime farmers would ask prices so high that they would hold up the sale or even stop exploration altogether—his assumption being that no company would prospect if it had to disclose the fruits of its efforts to sellers.[207] He offers no reasons why rational parties would suddenly begin to engage in holdout behavior after the change in rules. He also seems to ignore the fact that changes in rules produce changes in behavior. Under the new regime, we would expect extensive use of pre-exploration option contracts on promising pieces of land, for example. Such contracts would allow companies to factor in estimates of exploration costs, potential profits discounted by the likelihood of a find, and so on. Farmers would simply do the same type of calculation in reverse. By ignoring this kind of possibility, Levmore can premise his examination of a new rule on the continuation of the pattern of dealing that would have been produced by the old rule. Needless to say, the new rule looks irrational.

None of this should be taken to imply that it is wrong to worry about the level of reward necessary to produce information. One could imagine a situation, *not* constructed with baseline fallacies, circular definitions of "damage," and inconsistent assumptions of irrational behavior, in which a society would be hurt by contracts made on the basis of fuller disclosure.[208] But to have any impact on policy, the analysis would have

---

207. Levmore, *supra* note 55, at 133.

208. An unpublished essay by Steven Shavell from Harvard Law School's "Discussion Paper Series" avoids most of these pitfalls. Steven Shavell, Acquisition and Disclosure of Information Prior to Economic Exchange, Discussion Paper No. 91 (Apr. 1991) (unpublished manuscript, available from Harvard Law School). Limiting his conclusions to the world of his model, Professor Shavell argues that sellers should be required to disclose so that they do not have unduly high incentives to acquire information, but that buyers should sometimes be allowed to conceal their information. Briefly stated, the argument is that we must distinguish between information that has social value and that which has no social value. We only want to encourage production of the former. Professor Shavell takes as a definition of "socially valuable information" "that which allows an action to be taken that raises the value of the good to the party who possesses it." *Id.* at 4 n.6. Professor Shavell wishes to avoid rules that would simply achieve a different distributive effect with no impact on allocative efficiency. We do not wish to give incentives to acquire information that will merely make one party or the other richer, but we do wish to give incentives to produce information if it will help in moving resources to their use-value. Under a rule of compulsory disclosure for sellers, sellers will only invest in information-gathering when the chances of the information revealing something positive, multiplied by the amount of the increase in value the information would allow the seller to recoup, would be greater than the chance of the information revealing something that would *decrease* the value of the property multiplied by the amount of the decrease in value.

Shavell is careful not to generalize his approach to other issues of information inequality. Interested by the method, I have tried to imagine how one might do so. One difficulty would be that once we go beyond the model, we can contemplate situations in which the seller can profit by "selling short" (such as in insider trading)—offsetting the losses involved in the sale of his current portfolio by trading on the knowledge that the price of similar goods is likely to fall. This raises some problems for the baseline measurement of socially valuable information. In certain kinds of markets, the seller will be able to "raise the value" of his property whether the information is positive or negative. But the increased value depends at least partly on the possibility of silence. A basic problem appears to arise here. The decision whether or not we want individuals to invest in

to show that the hypothetical situation was actually likely to be *our* situation. This is exactly what Levmore does not do.

2. Ad Hoc Claims About Behavior

The same article offers a fine example of ad hoc claims about behavior by different parties under different sets of rules. Professor Levmore sets himself the task of deciding whether disclosure rules are necessary for (1) termite-infested-house sellers and (2) farmers and mineral companies. "Homeowners . . . need not be offered an incentive [by a rule which allows sellers to withhold information] to inspect for termites. As soon as there is a fleeting rumor of a termite infestation in the neighborhood, every sensible owner calls in the experts and prepares to take corrective measures."[209] Thus Levmore argues that when society does not compel disclosure, both buyers and sellers will inspect, leading to a waste of resources.

> This efficiency-based distinction is most compelling in the case of the ore discovery. Unlike the owner of an infested house, the farmer is not likely to drill in his fields for minerals. There will be a net societal loss if we do not encourage exploration, and there is no reason to think that the farmer will be inclined to explore unless he is privy to the buyer's information. *The buyer, of course, will not explore if he must disclose the fruits of his efforts.*[210]

Levmore fails to offer proof for any of these generalizations. The first two seem to rest on stereotyped assumptions about the relative foresight and sophistication of home buyers and farmers. Similarly, they assume an absence of a well-functioning secondary market in geology experts or mining options. The last statement, that no mineral explora-

---

information depends on the effect of the research on the asset's price, but the asset "price" depends on the postulated rules of disclosure. In the concrete example given, the rule of compulsory disclosure would tend to undermine the possibility of selling short. Therefore, sellers would not invest in acquiring information when they knew it was likely to be of this kind. (Since the "seller" is also a "buyer" with respect to other units of the fungible good, the possibility of trading advantageously would appear to depend on the relative *in*efficiency of informational market mechanisms similar to those discussed in Gilson & Kraakman, *supra* note 83.)

Factoring in the empirical uncertainties of information costs, we might find that a compulsory disclosure rule would produce underinvestment by sellers in information likely to be negative, or that the absence of a compulsory disclosure rule would lead to inefficient investment in information gathering merely to gain an advantage over other traders, thus causing distributional changes but no increase in allocative efficiency. *See* Fama & Laffer, *supra* note 83, at 292. Once again, the efficiency claims seem to be in tension with the incentive claims, *see* Grossman & Stiglitz, *supra* note 69, while the baseline price measure appears both to decide and to depend on the regime of information disclosure. I am unsure whether a similar point could be made about the capital asset pricing model used to determine the existence of efficient markets. *See* Gilson & Kraakman, *supra* note 83, at 561 n.41.

209.   Levmore, *supra* note 55, at 135.
210.   *Id.* (emphasis added).

tion will ever take place if the explorer has to pay (postdisclosure) market price for mineral-bearing land, is simply false. Gathering information does have costs, but one cannot stipulate *a priori* that they must always be so high that concealment is necessary to protect the information.[211] The claim is also analytically incoherent for the reasons discussed in the subsection concerning baseline errors.[212]

3. *Ignoring Contradictions in the Theory*

The influential Note, *The Efficient Capital Market Hypothesis, Economic Theory and Regulation of the Securities Industry,*[213] provides an example of the ingenious use of contradictory economic analysis, and baseline errors at the same time. The Note's author, Christopher Saari, admits that unregulated markets "may or may not" lead to optimal production of information and cites economists to prove it. The Note points out that Kenneth Arrow argues that production of information will be "*less* than optimal because producers of information will not be able to capture its true value due to inability to acquire necessary property rights" in the information they produce.[214] The same footnote proceeds to cite Jack Hirshleifer and Eugene Fama and Arthur Laffer, who argue that "production of information will be *greater* than optimal because some information will be produced solely for trading advantages that produce wealth distribution rather than for allocational purposes."[215] These two charmingly contradictory arguments do not lead the author to question the determinacy of the analysis, but instead to cite yet another economist for the proposition that "production of information in unregulated markets may not be strictly optimal, but will lead to better resource

---

211. *Cf.* Hirshleifer, *supra* note 69.

212. *Supra* Section VIII.A.1. And these failings are made even more disturbing by the fact that many of these articles use a persistent rhetoric of scientific certainty to cover up their extreme judgmental moralism. Here is Professor Levmore excoriating a farmer who is nasty enough to ask the mineral company *questions* about what they are doing. He begins by comparing the farmer to a house owner who holds out on (and holds up) a development.

> The owner of the 3001st tract of land who demands a high price is really the despicable character. Similarly, the seller who, to preserve a fraud claim, asks specific questions *about activities he would otherwise never engage in* is really the contemptible party. Like eminent domain, optimal dishonesty operates to deny a windfall to a passive party when to do otherwise might lead to a net societal loss.

Levmore, *supra* note 55, at 142 (emphasis added). Of course, the question of whether the farmer would engage in the activities *himself* is irrelevant. (Wasn't that Adam Smith's basic point?) And to call the farmer "passive" strikes one as judgmental labeling rather than economic science. It also seems to go against everything Coase ever taught us about joint activities. If, on the other hand, these statements reflect the ideology of the romantic author, then we might expect that the parties who get the rights are those who can most readily be portrayed as active romantic innovators, rather than passive, unoriginal sources. *That* picture seems to fit fairly well.

213. Saari, *supra* note 66.

214. *Id.* at 1068 n.197 (emphasis added) (citing Arrow, *supra* note 94, at 617 n.190).

215. *Id.* (emphasis added) (citing Fama & Laffer, *supra* note 83; Hirshleifer, *supra* note 69).

allocation than any other alternative."[216] That is, we cannot agree what happens in "unregulated" markets—but "regulated" ones are bound to be worse.

This assessment is political dogma masquerading as analysis. In fact, given economists' acknowledgement that "public goods" may require regulation in order to avoid free rider problems and their frequent claim that information is a public good, this is the worst place to make such a claim. It does not help to find that Arrow and Laffer agree that "unregulated" markets will not produce the right amount of information, but can't agree whether they will over- or underproduce. Worse still, later in his analysis of markets for the production of information, Arrow states that—even allowing for commodification of information—"unregulated" markets will underproduce and that some major form of state intervention is probably necessary.[217] This position is hardly consistent with the earlier proposition that "production of information in unregulated markets . . . will lead to better resource allocation than any other alternative."

The claim is not only analytically unsupported, it is also conceptually incoherent, depending as it does on a completely untenable set of assumptions about the ground rules in a "natural" market. Would those rules require disclosure, or not? The question has no answer, in part because there is no "natural," unregulated state of affairs. Without the rules of contract, tort, and property there would not be a market. Barring a belief in classical legal thought, how could we claim that the particular set of (common law?) rules found in this country at this time is any more natural, neutral, or nonregulatory than the rules imposed by the SEC? As I pointed out before, reading much of the economic literature, one might imagine that the legal system came with preset, default positions that sounded something like this: "Protect owners against physical invasion of land, allow formation of contracts when information is concealed, nullify contracts where lies are told."[218] But this is silly. The choice is not between "regulated" and "unregulated" but between different kinds of regulation.[219] Judge Posner has claimed that economic analysis is the true heir of legal realism. On the evidence of these arguments one is tempted to call this "the case of the murdering heir."

B. Insider Trading Law as a Puzzle

For my purposes, the interesting thing about insider trading law is that it represents a commitment to a far-reaching, publicly popular, egal-

---

216. *Id.* (citing Harold Demsetz, *Information and Efficiency: Another Viewpoint,* 12 J.L. & ECON. 1 (1969)).

217. Arrow, *supra* note 94, at 623.

218. *See, e.g.,* Easterbrook's arguments discussed *supra* text accompanying notes 205-06.

219. *See* Hale, *supra* note 168, at 626-28.

itarian program of regulation—a commitment that is valued despite the fact that the program is expensive to administer and difficult to police. What is more, the prohibition of insider trading is merely the capstone of a larger structure that places affirmative obligations to reveal information on companies involved in the securities market. This structure is defended by far-reaching appeals to egalitarian norms.

The SEC puts relatively onerous reporting requirements on both companies and individuals and even attempts to police the information revealed to make sure that it is not misleading. Thus, for example, income projections that might gull an unsuspecting investor are forbidden, and the form of disclosure required is designed explicitly to put the novice, so far as is possible, on par with the experienced investor.[220] Courts, administrators, and scholars say things about the evils of disparate access to information that they would never say about disparate access to wealth or to other forms of power or property. They even worry about the evils of structural disparities in access, not merely about cases where one individual has mistreated another. This concern is hardly popular nowadays, even in a presumably hospitable field such as civil rights.[221] Yet all this takes place in the securities market, in the very heart of capitalism, and in the face of practical difficulties of administration and sustained academic criticism. Surely this is a puzzle.

In this Section, I examine the internal structure of this puzzle, tracing its competing, circular arguments and its self-swallowing definitions. My claim is that the internal structure of the debate over insider trading reproduces once again the matrix of ideological tensions in the liberal theory of justice that I identified earlier—public versus private, free flow of information versus property, the norm of equality versus the norm of return to the *status quo ante,* and so on.

Using this framework I would argue that it is precisely the fact that insider trading is trading on information that helps us to understand why it is ideologically feasible to subject it to egalitarian regulation. After all, this trading is a market transaction. In the repetitive and contradictory division of the world into public and private, the market is supposed to be exactly the place that stands outside the norm of equality. Rich and poor both get one vote. Leaving the voting booth as formally equal citizens, they turn instantaneously into members of civil society. One returns to the stock exchange, the other to the unemployment line. The writ of equality does not run to the marketplace. Yet the nonrational

---

220. Professor Epstein would probably argue that it was an uncompensated taking of the latter's hard-won expertise. *See* RICHARD A. EPSTEIN, TAKINGS: PRIVATE PROPERTY AND THE POWER OF EMINENT DOMAIN (1985).

221. *See* Wards Cove Packing Co. v. Atonio, 490 U.S. 642 (1989) (evidence that skilled, high-paying jobs are filled predominantly by whites and unskilled, low-paying jobs are filled predominantly by minorities is insufficient to establish a prima facie case of discrimination).

1502 *CALIFORNIA LAW REVIEW* [Vol. 80:1413

association of information with the public sphere, with the world of debate and discussion, makes it easier to talk about insider trading using the language of equality and fairness.

What is more, we are dealing with something commonly thought of as "market information." As I pointed out earlier, the basic model of the perfect market in microeconomics depends on the idea that all parties are "informationally equal," in that they all possess perfect information. It does not, needless to say, depend on all parties being equal in wealth or possession of legally protected interests. Thus, at first blush it might seem that one would be "arguing downhill" in claiming that a party should not be able to trade on the basis of undisclosed nonpublic material information.[222] At the very least, it would seem that microeconomic discourse would be more hospitable to this precise form of egalitarian regulation. As we will see, things are actually much more complicated. Yet the unreflective first plotting of information as a "public" matter and (to a lesser extent) the apparent congeniality of economic theory to ideas of informational egalitarianism remain vitally important to the political acceptability of the insider trading laws.[223] One thesis of this Article is that our intuitive ideological mapping matters, whatever the outcome of more prolonged reflection.

If the analysis presented so far is correct, some idea akin to "authorship" ought to be offered as a device to mediate these tensions between public and private, between the norm of equality and the norm of return to the status quo, between imperfect information as property *in* a market and perfect information as a property *of* a market. What would an

---

222. Although, of course, the transaction costs involved make this simplistic assumption extremely problematic, and the section on law and economics shows some of the other possible conclusions one could draw. In one sense, I see this issue as a playing out of the "paradox" proposed earlier. *See supra* text accompanying note 70.

223. If this hypothesis were right, one would expect to see a diverging pattern of treatment of informational inequalities and (other kinds of) wealth inequalities—particularly after the abandonment of the most Lochneresque visions of *laissez faire*. In the late nineteenth century, courts would seldom allow plaintiffs to get out of bargains by showing evidence of *either* wealth inequalities or information inequalities. (Though there is certainly a convincing story in American legal history that claims that classical legal thinkers had to work quite hard to ignore older doctrines such as "just price." These were the doctrines that allowed juries to inquire into the relative wealth and power of the parties—whether this particular merchant was "grinding the faces of the poor." As such, these doctrines were anathema to a legal consciousness built on the beliefs that Marx described—the idea that the inequalities of civil society were taboo as far as the state was concerned.) In any event, under the influence of a will theory of contract and a *caveat emptor* theory of bargaining, it was hard even to explain why there should be contractual redress for disparities in information or power.

But note the relative changes in these doctrines since the early part of the twentieth century. Courts are still uneasy about striking down bargains merely because of disparities in wealth or power between the parties. Yet they seem much more comfortable imposing disclosure requirements, extensive and non-derogable "duties to warn," and even requirements that the particular class and educational requirements of potential purchasers be taken into account in constructing warnings. Informational egalitarianism is clearly not as threatening as economic egalitarianism—hardly an unimportant fact to understand as we enter the "information age."

author figure look like in insider trading, and what would be its most important characteristic? From my perspective, the key feature of authorship as a mediating device lies in its romance—by which I mean both the homage to imagination, originality, and the unique spirit that is typical of the Romantic movement in literature and the actual romanticization of the character of this original creator and destroyer—this Faustian figure.

In the stereotyped story line that goes with this construct, the romantic author spurns convention and loathes routine. He may even violate social mores. Nevertheless, society gains so much from the original creations he throws off that these matters can be overlooked or perhaps even cherished. If the theme of originality supplies the conceptual basis on which to rest the claim to property, the romanticization of the author supplies both the emotional justification for the normative claim and the device by which it can be limited where necessary. Who can resist the argument, "Senator, you're no Van Gogh"? (Although, as *Bleistein* shows, the same rhetoric allows even the humblest contributions to be conclusively presumed "unique.")

Insider trading scholarship is the last place one would expect to find odes to romantic authorship. And yet my claim has been that the author device is almost irresistible because of the conceptual neatness and emotional appeal of the way in which it mediates the contradictions in the regulation of information. If we find the language of romantic authorship incongruously used to defend insider trading, I would claim that my argument is strengthened.

The germinal defense of insider trading comes from Henry Manne.[224] His supporters claim that all subsequent discussions of the criminalization of insider trading "raise, without acknowledging it, the questions first raised by Henry Manne."[225] Manne's book begins with a lengthy economic analysis of insider trading and with a consideration of the effects of various insider trading rules. But after 110 pages of such analysis, he has this to say:

> This somewhat laborious discussion of what happens in the stock market does not constitute a strong argument *against* a proposal to bar all insider trading. Indeed it is not intended for that purpose at all, but merely to point out that no strong arguments along these lines are available in *defense* of such a proposal. . . .

> But the debate is far from over. . . . [T]he argument developed in the following three chapters is that a rule allowing insiders to trade freely may be fundamental to the survival of our corporate system. People pressing for the rule barring insider

---

224. MANNE, *supra* note 29.
225. Carney, *supra* note 66, at 868.

trading may inadvertently be tampering with one of the well-springs of American prosperity.[226]

The wellspring to which he is referring is entrepreneurship. Manne begins his normative argument with a reprise of Schumpeter's argument on the role of entrepreneurship and its likely demise under the rigid and routinized conditions of modern organizational life—conditions which might seem inimical to the entrepreneurial spirit.[227]

Schumpeter's basic argument was that without dynamic innovation from inventors and entrepreneurs, competition would lead to diminishing returns on capital—as more capital goods were added to a market in which the supply of labor was (at least relatively) fixed.[228] Eventually such a process could lead to the point where no further capital accumulation took place. Inventions and recombinations of productive factors make capital more productive, shifting the factor-price frontier to the right. Yet as soon as a great innovator arises, competitors will imitate the innovation, returns on capital will be driven down once again, and the process will repeat itself. Thus, for both Manne and Schumpeter, originality, iconoclasm, and innovation are simultaneously the keys to economic development and the identifying characteristics of the entrepreneur.[229] Manne takes pains to point out that this innovation is crucial

---

226. MANNE, *supra* note 29, at 110.

227. *Id.* at 124-27. Manne has to tread carefully here. As Schumpeter describes him, the entrepreneur is the enemy of tradition whose "conduct and . . . motive are 'rational' in no other sense. And in *no* sense is his characteristic motivation of the hedonist kind." SCHUMPETER, *supra* note 14, at 92. This tends to fit the idea that routinization and bureaucracy will undermine the opportunities for entrepreneurship. But when Manne goes on to argue that entrepreneurs need more profits if they are to be motivated, the entrepreneur suddenly switches hats from the nonrational creator and destroyer to the economically rational actor who, presumably, would find a modern corporation entirely congenial.

228. SCHUMPETER, *supra* note 14; *see* PAUL A. SAMUELSON & WILLIAM D. NORDHAUS, ECONOMICS 113, 188-89 (14th ed. 1992).

229. Schumpeter lists the entreprenuer's principal motivations as
the dream and the will to found a private kingdom . . . the will to conquer: the impulse to fight, to prove oneself superior to others, to succeed for the sake . . . of success itself. . . . Finally there is the joy of creating, of getting things done, or simply of exercising one's energy and ingenuity.
SCHUMPETER, *supra* note 14, at 93. Dream, will, success for the sake of success, nonrational imperatives, and above all, the joy of creating and transforming—these descriptions paint a picture of the genius romantic author, particularly when he claims that the entrepreneur comes from that portion of society distinguished by "super-normal qualities of intellect and will." *Id.* at 82 n.2. His analysis is certainly an interesting answer to a wider question: to whom do we attribute the growth of civilization, of culture, of capital—to the individual who makes the change, or to the society, culture, public domain, and workforce that make that change possible? Schumpeter's book is a premier (and unusually convincing) example of the argument that attributes growth to the iconoclastic individual. The argument takes the form of "but for" causation—"but for the entrepreneur . . ." Manne goes one step further, concluding from the "but for" argument an entitlement to some share of the proceeds—both on grounds of just dessert and on utilitarian grounds to encourage further production. This style of argument is of course exactly the style of argument that justifies property rights for the (great) author and then, by analogy for all authors—provided only they make something original. Originality and individuality become the central

even though the entrepreneur seems (like the author) merely to be recombining elements that already exist. Those elements are information and productive factors in the former case, language, genre, and perhaps even plot in the latter.

For Schumpeter the entrepreneur's function is to make new combinations of productive factors, that is, to bring them together in a new way. Routine business management is a critical function in the successful operation of a corporation, but it will characterize the work of corporate executives *only after* productive factors have been successfully combined for the first time.[230]

Entrepreneurs have been identified as the agents of development, and creative originality has been identified as the mark of the entrepreneur.[231] Manne now turns to the question of incentives. Following Berle and Means, he believes that ownership and control are separated in the modern corporation. Diverging from them, he argues that entrepreneurs will probably seek positions within firms and make their money from stock trading rather than stock ownership. In making that argument he also diverges from Schumpeter, who did not believe that large returns were necessary to motivate the entrepreneur. Rather, Schumpeter believed that the satisfaction of innovation or creation sufficed.[232]

At first, Schumpeter's point that large returns are not a necessary incentive for entrepreneurial effort seems correct. The supply would appear to be determined solely by personal, psychological forces. Entrepreneurs do appear in government and in salaried

---

qualities we look for in conferring property rights. It should be noted, however, that Schumpeter thinks that economic reward to the entrepreneur is not central to entrepreneurship—precisely because the motivations of the iconoclast are not "rational" money-grubbing ones. This tension between romaticizing the author and making utilitarian arguments about the need to encourage authorship reappears throughout this study. In the English edition of the book, Schumpeter also denied the charge that he was glorifying the entrepreneur.

> [O]ur analysis of the the rôle of the entrepreneur does not involve any "glorification" of the type, as some readers of the first edition of this book seemed to think. We do hold that entrepreneurs have an economic function, as distinguished from, say, robbers. But we neither style every entrepreneur a genius or a benefactor to humanity, nor do we wish to express any opinion about the comparative merits of the social organisation in which he plays his rôle, or about the question whether what he does could not be effected more cheaply or efficiently in other ways.

Id. at 90 n.1.

230. MANNE, *supra* note 29, at 116. At another point Manne describes the entrepreneur in decidedly Faustian terms, as "this upsetter of stable societies, this creator of disruptive forces." *Id.* at 119.

231. "[T]he typical entrepreneur is more self-centred than other types, because he relies less than they do on tradition and connection and because his characteristic task—theoretically as well as historically—consists precisely in breaking up old, and creating new, tradition." SCHUMPETER, *supra* note 14, at 91-92.

232. Schumpeter makes explicit the point that, although he views the entrepreneur as the engine of capitalist development, economic gain is not a vital motivation for the entrepreneur. In his view, two out of three of the goals of the entrepreneur "may in principle be taken care of by . . . social arrangements" other than the profit motive. *Id.* at 94.

positions, and the temperament for innovation may turn up in such nonentrepreneurial professions as the clergy or teaching. But surely these are the exceptions, and, though data would be difficult to obtain, the indications are that entrepreneurial talent tends to concentrate in those industries, professions, and positions providing the greatest potential for very substantial profits.[233]

Thus, where Schumpeter saw the rigidity of modern bureaucratized capitalism and the swings of the business cycle as the major enemy of entrepreneurship, Manne sees an absence of reward to the entrepreneur as the biggest problem. In one of his more lyrical and romantic moments, he uses exactly the Faustian imagery we saw earlier to introduce his claim that we need to secure to entrepreneurs the fruits of their labors: "What then is the nature of the return to this upsetter of stable societies, this creator of disruptive forces?"[234] His answer? Profits from insider trading. The argument here gets a little incoherent.

Certain events or developments lend themselves peculiarly to exploitation by insiders. Not surprisingly, many of these are items that corporate employees or others close to the corporation will have produced. Higher earnings or the concommitant [sic] dividend increase are clear examples. New products or inventions, new ore discoveries, oil finds, or successful marketing or management techniques also will generally be known first to those in the company responsible for the development.[235]

The clear implication is that insider trading will be the result of *beneficial changes* produced by innovative "upsetters of societies and creators of disruptive forces." Society benefits by the improved allocation of productive resources and thus should not begrudge the entrepreneur/insider his or her cut.[236] This is nice rhetoric but bad analysis. The insider makes money off information that will cause the future stock price to diverge widely from the current price in either direction. Thus, being a lousy manager and selling short before the impending bankruptcy becomes public knowledge will net the same return as being a good manager and recouping part of the increase in stock price. Manne has based his argument on originality and uniqueness, but something can be uniquely bad as well as uniquely good.

The idea is confusing in other ways. The unsupported claims about the placement of entrepreneurs and their stock trading habits, the cate-

---

233. MANNE, *supra* note 29, at 122-23. Given Manne's own thesis, this would imply that, at present, either few entrepreneurs are in large companies or that they are there and are trading illegally.

234. *Id.* at 119.

235. *Id.* at 55.

236. Indeed, for the reasons given above, it is only through innovation that capital accumulation will continue.

gory errors inherent in certain of his generalizations, the difficulty in delineating those insider trading opportunities that were the result of entrepreneurial activity, all of these lead us to wonder if something else is going on under the text. At one point, Manne asks himself who should be allowed to trade. Suddenly, from the heady language of the creator and destroyer of societies, the relentless romantic innovator, Manne swoops down to the realities of corporate personnel. The conceptual whiplash is rather like that produced in *Bleistein* when the rhetoric of a Van Gogh or a Monet is used to justify intellectual property in an advertising poster.

> The last form of the "person-is-not-entitled" objection to insider trading is that individuals making insider profits are frequently far removed from a time or place or job in which they could perform any entrepreneurial service for the company. It is, however, extremely difficult to identify individuals performing the entrepreneurial function or to know the precise moment at which an individual performs an entrepreneurial act. . . .
>
> Directors, large shareholders, executives, lawyers, investment bankers, or many other individuals may, at one time or another, perform an entrepreneurial function. Most of the time, however, they will not be innovating. And for any particular development, many individuals may have made contributions. Who, among the lawyers, bankers, and executives involved, can be given full credit or the correct portions of credit for conceiving the desirability of a merger, searching out the most likely firm, and effectuating the desired plan? An entrepreneurial function has been performed, and the individuals involved will have some claim against the subsequent flow of inside information. But any attempt by an outsider to correlate the contribution and the reward on a one-for-one basis will probably fail. The contribution of an individual may be so subtle—so much a result simply of his being there—and yet so critical that we must be very cautious in concluding that no reward is deserved.[237]

This magnanimity does not extend to mere menial workers whose jobs are deemed incapable of giving rise to original contributions and who thus deserve no share of the reward. Once again, "sources" get a rough break if they do not come close enough to fit the image of the great author. What is more, the dividing line seems a little arbitrary. Lawyers are author/entrepreneurs, but secretaries are not. Then again, Manne's intended audience is a legal one so we might understand a certain rose-tinted view of the lawyer's role.

To review: after spending half of his book on economic analysis of

---

237. MANNE, *supra* note 29, at 156-57.

the market in information, Manne concludes that his "somewhat laborious discussion . . . does not constitute a strong argument *against* a proposal to bar all insider trading."[238] Harking back to my discussion of information economics, I would agree—at least so far as the skeptical judgment about the determinacy of economic analysis is concerned.[239] Some moral or theoretical *a priori* is required in order to ground the analysis. Ultimately, Manne pins his hopes on a Faustian vision of entrepreneurship, a vision which puts innovation (and not mere labor) at the heart of the issue and which seeks to reconcile society to the granting of a monopoly rent by promising the entrepreneur the spin-off profits from her innovative actions. In all significant respects, this is the romantic theory of authorship all over again.

Manne's theory fails because it cannot separate "bad" originality from "good" originality. It fails because it can neither justify nor limit the class of people entitled to cash in on insider information. It fails because he has only the most tenuous argument to connect insiders and entrepreneurs in the first place. For these reasons and others, Manne's book has proved more influential in raising the topic of insider trading regulation than in actually solving that problem. But though the opponents of insider trading regulation may claim that they have gone far beyond his approach, they fail to grasp the crucial moment in Manne's analysis—the moment when an indefinite body of economic ideas about information is given normative content by *romance*.[240] In this case, the romance is attached to the dynamic innovator, the person who is put at the center of all economic development. Though Manne's theory fails to convince, it nevertheless offers a revealing picture of the role of romantic authorship in discussions of information regulation. In the next Part, that same romance is used to endow the manipulators, rather than the sources, of genetic information with the right to profit from its development.

IX
SPLEENS

So far, I have argued that issues of information will tend to revolve around a set of tensions—between public and private, between the norm of equality and the norm of the return to the status quo, between the public domain and the private right, between the idea of property as an absolute shield against potentially oppressive others and the idea of prop-

---

238. *Id.* at 110.

239. *See supra* text accompanying notes 69-97.

240. Drawing on the ideas advanced in the discussion of information economics, *see supra* Part IV, one might ask the other critics of insider trading regulation the extent to which their ideas achieve apparent determinacy without recourse to such romantic notions only by underplaying the kinds of paradoxes discussed in Grossman & Stiglitz, *supra* note 69.

erty as a bundle of rights, utilitarian in both derivation and application. Public discourse in general and legal discourse in particular must appear to mediate these tensions. Otherwise, particular regimes of information regulation will seem "ungrounded," "contrary to institutional logic," "dangerous in their precedential implications," or simply "wrong."

For example, we might have a normative theory that argued that any individual who mixes her labor with information should thereby acquire a legally protected interest in it.[241] Yet if we accept the labor theory of property for information, why not for all property? Unless we have some articulated limiting principle, our information property regime will "subvert" our general property regime.

At the same time, any information property regime requires a moral justification of the fact that the individual is being granted a private monopoly rent for recombining language, genre, and ideas that were harvested free of charge from the public domain. Coupled to this moral argument we would need a prudential argument that this particular *level* of property rights would not lead to the privatization of the fertile fields of the public domain—converting it into a patchwork of inaccessible, and increasingly barren, private estates.[242] To give an extreme example, think of granting Shakespeare's heirs a property right in perpetuity over Romeo and Juliet's plot, or Turing's estate a property right in all computer technology. How likely would future Turings or Shakespeares be under such a regime?

Finally, since information property is more obviously de-physicalized than other property rights, we would need some hook on which to

---

241. This is certainly a theory which reappears time and again in the regulation of information. *See* International News Serv. v. Associated Press, 248 U.S. 215, 234-42 (1918) (recognizing a quasiproperty right in news); *see also* Feist Publications v. Rural Tel. Serv. Co., 111 S. Ct. 1282, 1294-95 (1991) (rejecting the "sweat of the brow" theory, but holding that choices of selection and arrangement may imbue a compilation with sufficient originality for copyright).

242. Wendy Gordon and William Fisher provide the two most impressive examples of such a combined moral-utilitarian analysis in the field of copyright. *See* Fisher, *supra* note 22; Gordon, *Merits of Copyright, supra* note 74. Yet in their prudential analyses of the optimal level of property rights, both articles concentrate more on the level of property rights necessary to encourage authors to produce than on the countervailing need to keep a large amount of information free from property rights so that authors and creators will have the necessary raw materials with which to work. Using the language of this Article, the private property component of the prerequisites of information production gets more attention than the public domain component. *See* Litman, *supra* note 2. This problem occurs even in the best and most sophisticated copyright literature. One explanation of this emphasis might be the power of the vision of authorship I have described in this Article. The romantic vision of authorship emphasizes creativity and originality and de-emphasizes the importance of sources, genre, and conventions of language and plot. Thus, when economists and legal scholars come to do their analyses, most see the issue as determining the extent of property necessary to motivate and reward the creative spirit, rather than the extent of the public domain necessary to give the magpie genius the raw material she needs. (Emerson on Shakespeare.) Landes and Posner's work on copyright offers a significant exception; however, they themselves point out that this is a "neglected consideration." Landes & Posner, *supra* note 22, at 332. In this Part, the tendency of author-discourse to devalue "sources" will be an important element of my analysis of the *Moore* case.

hang the legally protected interest. In other words, we would need some convincing and apparently firm set of attributes that we could identify as the property that the author, inventor, or artist could own, even after the particular book, machine, or print has been sold. If property is to fulfill its ideological function of apparently securing the individual from the dubious affections of the state and other parties, this set of attributes would have to be something more reified than some general injunction to protect whatever today's utilitarian calculation indicates we should.

In the Part on copyright law, I argued that the figure used to "solve" these problems is the romantic author. The conceptual device of the romantic author makes credible the division between idea and expression. The romantic author stands with one foot in civil society and the other in the public domain of political, artistic, and scientific interchange. The author takes facts, genre, and language from the public domain, works on them, adds the originality of spirit presumptively conferred on him by the themes of romanticism, and produces a finished work. The ideas (and the facts on which they are based) return to the public domain, thus enriching it for the future. But because his originality has marked the form of the work as "unique," the form or expression becomes his alone. Together, the *figure* of the romantic author, the *theme* of originality, and the *conceptual distinction* between idea and expression seem to offer one of the most convincing mediations of the tensions described earlier. This assemblage of mediating devices is so convincing, in fact, that I argued we should expect to find it well beyond the familiar realm of copyright. *Moore v. Regents of the University of California*[243] seems to support that thesis.

Earlier in this Article, I described some of the bizarre features of the *Moore* opinion.[244] At first sight, the case looks as though it has been deliberately constructed to provide a foil for law professors' lectures on bad legal reasoning. The court bumbles and pontificates, apparently at random. The reader is left to make the transitions as best she can. What connects this confused discussion of the difference between the right of publicity and the right of property to the claim that limited property rights are not really property rights at all? What, if any, relevance does the question-begging discussion of whether or not Mr. Moore's cells were unique have to the idyllic picture the court paints of research carried on free from the dead hand of property rights? How is the idyllic picture reconciled with the court's later claim that the researchers themselves must be given property rights in order to provide the vital incentives necessary for their work? My claim is that these otherwise inexplicable features of the case support the theory developed in this Article. The apparently random shifts of topics, inconsistent jurisprudences of prop-

---

243. 793 P.2d 479 (Cal. 1990), *cert. denied,* 111 S. Ct. 1388 (1991).
244. *See supra* text accompanying notes 31-39.

erty, and ostensibly conflicting claims about originality and incentives are best explained as a manifestation of the structure I described when I discussed copyright.[245]

A. Worrying About Property

The court in *Moore* worries about the classification, limitation, and relativization *of* property. It also worries about the utilitarian justification *for* property. One theme of this Article is to suggest that these strands of the opinion express the same concerns in different words.

1. Limitations on Property

The best place to begin the argument is at the moment that the court confronts these issues head on, in its discussion of regulatory limitations on property. In this case, the limitations that concern the court do not come from the law of copyright, but instead from a statute that regulates the use and disposal of human tissue. "By restricting how excised cells may be used and requiring their eventual destruction, the statute eliminates so many of the rights ordinarily attached to property that one cannot simply assume that what is left amounts to 'property' or 'ownership' for purposes of conversion law."[246]

This limitation is not as extreme as the claim presented earlier by Krause in his eighteenth-century attack on the very notion of intellectual property: "No, no, it is too obvious that the concept of intellectual property is useless. My property must be exclusively mine; I must be able to dispose of it and retrieve it unconditionally."[247] Nevertheless, there is something peculiar in seeing a late-twentieth-century California court talk about the implications we can draw from elimination of the rights ordinarily attached to property. From a practical point of view, such comments invite counterexamples. Most countries put extensive restrictions on the use, reproduction, transfer, and disposal of banknotes with-

---

245. My analysis here focuses on the reasons that the court gives for its decision, the assumptions on which that decision is based, and the structure of the rhetoric in which the decision is justified. I am *not* implying that the court's decision is indefensible on other grounds. One obvious concern in giving patients property rights over their own bodies is that it holds out the possibility of a market in organs in which the poor and the needy sell everything from kidneys to corneas. A court or legislature convinced of the evils of such a system might reject the commodification of organs for entirely different reasons than the court in *Moore*—although the case for prohibiting sale would be less compelling in situations where the organ must be removed for other reasons. Concerns like these seem to have been at the root of the National Organ Transplant Act, 42 U.S.C. §§ 273-274f (1988). One of the interesting things about the *Moore* case is that it says so little about these kinds of concerns and so much about the concerns that would dominate if one was viewing the issue through the author paradigm. Since my concern is with the general effect of author-thinking on the interests of sources and audience, it is that aspect of the case on which I concentrate here.

246. *Moore,* 793 P.2d at 492.

247. Krause, *supra* note 118, at 415-17, *quoted in* Woodmansee, *supra* note 1, at 444.

out prompting any soul-searching about property rights in money.[248] To a greater or lesser extent, similar types of restrictions could be found for cars, plutonium, motor oil, beachfront houses, and air conditioners.

From a slightly more theoretical perspective, the court's comment is even more puzzling. After all, in contemporary legal discourse the most common conception of property is the bundle of legally protected interests, held together by competing and conflicting policy goals. The removal of one or more sticks from the bundle should have no particular implications for the legally protected interests that remain. This point should be more rather than less obvious in questions of intellectual property. The author claims a right in the work that is severable from the material object bought by the reader. An author cannot prohibit the reader from burning the book, nor from telling acquaintances about it, nor from stealing the ideas. Even the jokes may be fair game, if retold under the right circumstances. The one prohibited act is the copying of expression—and even in that case there are exceptions. Thus, to reason from the "normal incidents of ownership" in a case like this is to adopt a formalistic and absolutist vision of property like that of Krause, and to do so in the area least suited to it.

2. *Utilitarian Justification* of *Property*

The court does not see itself as formalist, of course. The majority says explicitly that "when the proposed application of a very general theory of liability in a new context raises important policy concerns, it is especially important to face those concerns and address them openly."[249] Yet, when the court does address them, it does something very curious. The majority opinion describes the existing state of affairs—a world in which "sources" have no property rights over the products developed from their body fluids, tissue, or genetic information. "At present, human cell lines are routinely copied and distributed to other researchers for experimental purposes, usually free of charge. This exchange of scientific materials, which still is relatively free and efficient, will surely be compromised if each cell sample becomes the potential subject matter of a lawsuit."[250] This assessment is a fine example of the rhetoric of the public domain. Property rights of "sources" are portrayed as impediments to innovation, an unnecessary drag on research. This principle is potentially an imperialistic one. One could imagine the same argument being made against copyright, or in favor of the legalization of insider

---

248. Thanks to David Seipp for this example.

249. *Moore*, 793 P.2d at 488. It is interesting to contrast this view with their equally strong opinion that the "important policy concerns" worrying the dissent should be handled elsewhere. "Shedding no light on the Legislature's intent, philosophical issues about 'scientists bec[oming] entrepreneurs' are best debated in another forum." *Id.* at 492 n.34 (quoting *id.* at 514 (Mosk, J., dissenting)) (citation omitted).

250. *Id.* at 495 (footnote omitted).

trading. As I pointed out at the beginning of this Article, commodification of information can always be portrayed as *either* a time-consuming and unjust impediment to, *or* a necessary prerequisite for, the free circulation of information.[251]

Indeed, this is exactly what happens. A moment later, information property rights of scientists are portrayed as necessary incentives to innovation. This assertion is not supported by data or analysis. It simply flows from the assumptions of romantic authorship. As my discussion of information economics makes clear,[252] it is *possible* that if we do not give property rights to sources of genetic information, not enough will be brought to researchers in the first place. It is also *possible* that researchers would be given adequate incentives by the quest for scientific preeminence and by the joy of research, and that the competitive advantage of those who are first to bring a product to market would be a sufficient incentive for research and development. The court does not consider these alternative possibilities, not because they are weighed and rejected or because the existence of the patent system precludes them altogether, but because the ideology of romantic authorship makes them disappear.

3. *Characterization* as *Property*

The court also worries about the characterization of certain legally protected interests as "property" rights. The plaintiff and the court of appeal had relied strongly on analogies from privacy right cases dealing with the antinomially named "right of publicity." When the California Supreme Court addressed the cases cited by the plaintiff,[253] its main concern was whether or not the right of publicity is "really" a property right.

> These opinions hold that every person has a proprietary interest in his own likeness and that unauthorized, business use of a likeness is redressible as a tort. But in neither opinion did the authoring court expressly base its holding on property law. Each court stated, following Prosser, that it was "pointless" to debate the proper characterization of the proprietary interest in a likeness.[254]

From a legal realist perspective of legally protected interests, the question is indeed pointless: classification of the legally protected interest is dependent on the *purpose* the interest has to serve. Thus, rather than staring at the legally protected interest in an attempt to divine

---

251. *Compare* International News Serv. v. Associated Press, 248 U.S. 215 (1918) *with* Feist Publications v. Rural Tel. Serv. Co., 111 S. Ct. 1282 (1991).

252. *See supra* Part IV.

253. *Moore,* 793 P.2d at 490 (citing Motschenbacher v. R.J. Reynolds Tobacco Co., 498 F.2d 821 (9th Cir. 1974); Lugosi v. Universal Pictures, 603 P.2d 425 (Cal. 1979)).

254. *Id.* (citations omitted).

whether it was "really" property,[255] one would decide the goals of this particular interest and would then discuss whether the remedies attached to a "property" right would be sufficient to achieve them. The court, however, having tipped its hat to Dean Prosser, is not willing to follow him. "For purposes of determining whether the tort of conversion lies, however, the characterization of the right in question is far from pointless. Only property can be converted."[256] Nevertheless, having raised the question of classification, the court declines to settle it. Instead, the majority simply assumes that the "right of publicity" is not a property right, in part because of its classification as a right that protects privacy. This is a shame because, if seen a little less formalistically, the publicity rights cases themselves present a fascinating example of the tensions discussed in this Article.

B. *Public and Private; Publicity and Privacy*

The famous Warren and Brandeis article that formed the basis of much of the law of privacy[257] attempted to ground the right to exclude others in a person's privacy interest—the legitimate desire to keep certain information from the eyes of the public. Their article implies that the interest is more than just a property right in information about oneself. The vision they invoke is the cozy private sphere of the home, not the bustling private sphere of the market. Indeed, to allow the market to commodify one's privacy might be to accelerate exactly the trends that Warren and Brandeis found so disturbing. If one understands the concern that animates this area of the law to be the protection of privacy, rather than the protection of private property, Mr. Moore's analogy might seem to be correspondingly weaker. To a judge, taking someone's genetic information is unlikely to seem intuitively as much of a violation of "privacy" as publishing facts from a diary without the consent of the author.

Yet despite their classification under the law of privacy, the publicity rights cases on which the plaintiff relied pay great attention to the importance of commodification, alienation, and transfer of the protected

---

255. *See generally* WITTGENSTEIN, *supra* note 174.
   This is connected with the conception of naming as, so to speak, an occult process. Naming appears as a *queer* connexion of a word with an object.—And you really get such a queer connexion when the philosopher tries to bring out *the* relation between name and thing by staring at an object in front of him and repeating a name or even the word "this" innumerable times. For philosophical problems arise when language *goes on holiday*. And *here* we may indeed fancy naming to be some remarkable act of mind, as it were a baptism of an object. And we can also say the word "this" *to* the object, as it were *address* the object as "this"—a queer use of this word, which doubtless only occurs in doing philosophy.
Id. at 19e.
256. *Moore,* 793 P.2d at 490.
257. Louis D. Brandeis & Samuel D. Warren, *The Right to Privacy,* 4 HARV. L. REV. 193 (1890).

interest, and little or no attention to the concerns that so worried Warren and Brandeis. The *Motschenbacher* case[258] turns on a racing driver's ability to commodify the distinctive image of his car and use it to advertise cigarettes. The *Carson* case[259] explains at length that Mr. Carson already licenses the phrase "Here's Johnny" to a chain of clothing stores in which he holds a twenty percent interest. The *Hirsch* case[260] holds that "Crazylegs" Hirsch should be able to sell the right to use his nickname, and thus that it cannot be used without his consent to promote the sale of products that remove hair from women's legs. The *Lugosi* case[261] allows Mr. Lugosi a partial monopoly over the commercial exploitation of a particular image of Dracula.

It is also worth noting that in each case the plaintiffs did not expend great labor, emotion, or even originality in creating the protectible "mark." It was Ed McMahon's distinctive voice and phrasing that made Mr. Carson's introduction more than a pleasantry. Mr. Motschenbacher did not design the car that formed the tangible basis of the image he was allowed to exploit. "Crazylegs" Hirsch was given his nickname by someone else. Mr. Lugosi's right of publicity protected a figure drawn from a book Mr. Lugosi did not write, portrayed in films he did not write, direct, or produce, and based on an historical figure[262] who actually did very different (though equally unpleasant) things.

To a greater or lesser extent, therefore, each case treats fame as a partial public good—something unique and personal that can be gainfully exploited only if it can be commodified and others excluded from its use except on pain of payment. This, of course, was exactly what Mr. Moore wanted the court to say about his genetic information. Why did they refuse? Neither formalism, nor the functional requisites of the biotechnology industry, nor the dictates of economic efficiency seems sufficient to explain the decision.

Perhaps the court is applying an authorship theory after all. Perhaps the deep assumption here is that a celebrity is the author of his or her *fame,* and that the phrases, nicknames, and images that are associated with the fame are, as Judge Kennedy put it in his dissent in the Carson case, actually expressions of the essential celebrity.[263] To be famous, after all, is to stand out from the crowd, to be thought unique. There is also a strong popular belief that having labored to create this unique mark, the celebrity is entitled to have it protected. Mr. Moore's

---

258. Motschenbacher v. R.J. Reynolds Tobacco Co., 498 F.2d 821 (9th Cir. 1974).

259. Carson v. Here's Johnny Portable Toilets, Inc., 698 F.2d 831 (6th Cir. 1983).

260. Hirsch v. S.C. Johnson & Son, Inc., 280 N.W.2d 129 (Wis. 1979).

261. Lugosi v. Universal Pictures, 603 P.2d 425 (Cal. 1979).

262. a/k/a Vlad the Impaler.

263. By far the most sophisticated development of this idea is in Rosemary J. Coombe, *Author/izing the Celebrity: Publicity Rights, Postmodern Politics and Unauthorized Genders,* 10 CARDOZO ARTS & ENT. L.J. 365 (1992).

genetic endowment could certainly be seen as something he got without expending labor.[264]

But what about uniqueness and originality, the other fundamental prerequisites for an author to have exclusionary property rights in his creation? In one of its most surprising passages, the court says that not only was Mr. Moore's genetic information produced without the relevant labor, it was insufficiently original to justify property rights.

> Lymphokines, unlike a name or a face, have the same molecular structure in every human being and the same, important functions in every human being's immune system. Moreover, the particular genetic material which is responsible for the natural production of lymphokines, and which defendants use to manufacture lymphokines in the laboratory, is also the same in every person; it is no more unique to Moore than the number of vertebrae in the spine or the chemical formula of hemoglobin.[265]

This passage is remarkable partly because it is nonsensical. It was precisely the unique properties of Mr. Moore's genetic "programs," the fact that his virus-infected cells overproduced lymphokines, that made his tissue and bodily fluids such an important part of Dr. Golde's research. If the issue was one of unique value, or unusual ease of extraction, clearly Mr. Moore's cells are not like everyone else's. Both seawater and gold ore contain gold molecules. That does not stop a cubic foot of gold ore from being more valuable than seawater containing the equivalent amount of gold. If the issue is statistical uniqueness, again it is exactly the unusual degree to which Mr. Moore's cells overproduced lymphokines that made them worth fighting about. The court offers the weak argument in support of its position that "[b]y definition, a gene responsible for producing a protein found in more than one individual will be the same in each."[266] Both Steve Timmons and I can jump and hit a volleyball. Only one of us, however, will be asked to endorse shoes, or to play on the U.S. Olympic team. But by the court's logic, since both Steve and I are "playing volleyball" we are both "volleyball players" and are therefore "the same."

But the argument about uniqueness is not merely nonsensical. It is also irrelevant to the question of whether or not Mr. Moore should be able to sue in conversion—irrelevant that is, unless the issue is once again being restated, whether consciously or unconsciously, in terms of the ideology of authorship.

---

264. Although most labor theories of property have as their most basic postulate the ownership of one's own body. It is from this *a priori* naturalistic property right that labor theorists deduce the case for one's ownership of the fruits of that body's work.

265. Moore v. Regents of the Univ. of Cal., 793 P.2d 479, 490 (Cal. 1990), *cert. denied,* 111 S. Ct. 1388 (1991).

266. *Id.* at 490 n.30.

Thus there are two distinct reasons why Mr. Moore is arguing against the grain of the implicit structure I have described. First, the market has taken from him the most "private" information of all, information about his own genetic structure. Yet our intuitive notions of privacy are constructed around the notion of preventing disclosure of intimate, embarrassing, or simply "personal" socially constructed facts about ourselves to others like ourselves. I could stare at my own genetic code all day and not even know it was mine. Even if I could "read" DNA, it is hard to imagine that I would be upset by revelation of my genetic code, or at least, that I would experience the particular complex of anger, shame, and righteous indignation that we associate with "a violation of privacy." For example, I would be less upset if someone chose to reveal that I carry the recessive gene for blue eyes than if they disclosed my preference in underwear—though neither is unusual or (to the best of my knowledge) aesthetically or socially reprehensible. There is something in the way that our culture has constructed the notion of privacy that makes it more hospitable to the protection of *"social"* facts than *"natural"* facts.[267] Even with the obvious borderline cases—hereditary diseases, for example—revelations are only thought to be violative of a person's privacy when some particular social significance has been given to the genetic coding.

The difficulty with Mr. Moore's case is that (1) no one would think worse of him for having a genetic makeup that could be mined for a socially valuable drug and (2) specialized knowledge would be necessary to make the connection between the "facts revealed" by his genetic makeup and his "inner life." One could draw the mild and reformist conclusion that our notion of privacy, based as it is on the revelation of intimate social facts comprehensible to a lay audience, does not adequately protect the interests of individuals in genetic information.

Second, if the thesis of this Article is correct, decisionmakers will tend—consciously or unconsciously—to look at questions of information through the lens of the romantic vision of authorship. The publicity rights cases seem to view protected nicknames, catchphrases, fangs, and cars as the expression of some underlying celebrity persona—the marks of a fame that is definitionally original and presumptively the result of

---

267. Of course, this distinction breaks down fairly quickly. For one thing, there is no such thing as a "theory free" description of facts, so that all "natural" facts can be seen as "social" facts if only one picks the right definition of "society." Thus, more precisely, we could say that the ordinary language notion of privacy protects an individual's subjectively defined "personal information" from the gaze of the peer group that the individual has chosen to recognize.

The more the revealing party seems to profit by the information, the more we allow the "victim" of the unwanted disclosure to define the sphere of privacy. Thus a butcher would probably not be found to have violated George Bernard Shaw's privacy rights if he revealed in a letter to *The Times* that Mr. Shaw secretly broke his vegetarian principles by eating pork pies. If, on the other hand, the butcher demanded £100 on pain of disclosure, we call it "blackmail" and *prohibit* the commodification of the information.

1518   *CALIFORNIA LAW REVIEW*   [Vol. 80:1413

hard work. These qualities sound suspiciously like the analytical structure of romantic authorship in copyright law. If Mr. Moore's claim is not to the protection of his "privacy" *tout court,* but rather the protection of his ability to commodify the genetic information derived from his cells, then the inquiry shifts from privacy to the "right of publicity," from the home and the secret to the market and the commodity. Once that shift is made, we are led to ask, "Who is the *real* author of the genetic information at issue here?" Reading this case, however, one gets the sense that the court thinks that Mr. Moore has not exhibited that mixture of arcane labor and dazzling originality that we associate with the romantic author. This sense is deepened when the court moves on to talk about the comparative rights of Mr. Moore and the doctors and researchers.

C. The Author and the Source

Having decided that Mr. Moore does not own the actual cells taken from his own body, the court uses the University of California's patent to trump his claim to the cell line developed by Dr. Golde and the other researchers.

> Finally, the subject matter of the Regent's patent—the patented cell line and the products derived from it—cannot be Moore's property. This is because the patented cell line is both factually and legally distinct from the cells taken from Moore's body. Federal law permits the patenting of organisms that represent the product of "human ingenuity," but not naturally occurring organisms. Human cell lines are patentable because "[l]ong-term adaptation and growth of human tissues and cells in culture is difficult—*often considered an art . . . ,*" and the probability of success is low. It is this *inventive effort* that patent law rewards, not the discovery of naturally occurring raw materials.[268]

The conceptual structure of patent law contains many of the same oppositions as that of copyright, and in this excerpt the court deploys them to great effect. There is something wonderful in the way that Mr. Moore becomes a "naturally occurring raw material," whose "unoriginal" genetic material is rendered unique and valuable by the "inventive effort," "ingenuity," and "artistry" of his doctors. If we look at this case through the lens of the romantic author, then Mr. Moore's claim is as ridiculous as if Huey Long had laid claim to ownership rights over *All the King's Men* or the baker of madeleines to *Remembrance of Things*

---

268. *Moore,* 793 P.2d at 492-93 (first emphasis added) (citations and footnotes omitted). It should be noted that although the court can justifiably say that the themes of originality, inventive effort, and functional use are appropriate to a discussion of patent law, these are in fact the themes that organize the entire opinion, and not merely the section on patent law. The mention of artistry—largely irrelevant in the patent law context—further supports my thesis.

Past. Authorship devalues sources. In its implicit application of authorship analysis to this case, the court similarly devalues sources. The fact that this can be accomplished in the face of the strong naturalistic presumption that one owns one's own body, and in the face of the ethically unattractive behavior of Mr. Moore's doctors, is a testament to the rhetorical power of the ideas involved.

Thus, to a greater extent than the other issues this Article discusses, the *Moore* case may indicate both the contentious value judgments loaded into the conceptual apparatus of authorship and the way that discussions of entitlement to control information are carried out through the metaphor of "authorship," even in fields far from copyright. Seen this way, Mr. Moore's case seems to have been designed to fail the authorship test. The court thinks that his rights are already too limited to be property, that his genetic information is too natural to be a creation, that it is neither private enough to be protected by the law of privacy nor original or creative enough to be protected by the rights of publicity. Viewed through the lens of authorship, Mr. Moore's claim appears to be a dangerous attempt to privatize the public domain and to inhibit research.[269] The scientists, however, with their transformative, Faustian artistry, fit the model of original, creative labor. For them, property rights are necessary to encourage research. What should we think about this desire to cast around in every situation until we find the people who most resemble authors, and then to confer property rights on them?

There is one last irony in the *Moore* case. The California Supreme Court does not leave Mr. Moore entirely without recourse. As I mentioned in the introduction to this Article, the court acknowledges that doctors have a duty to disclose any financial interests they have in the treatment of a patient. Thus, while discussing genetic information, the court views Mr. Moore as a "naturally occurring raw material," a public domain to be mined by inventive geniuses. Conversely, when discussing his role as a consumer of medical services, Mr. Moore is transformed into a sovereign individual with an unchallengeable entitlement to the facts necessary to make informed decisions.[270] As far as the majority is

---

269. There is a parallel here to Levmore's discussion of farmers who own land that, unbeknownst to them, contains valuable mineral deposits. If a mineral company seeks to buy the land, should it be able to respond dishonestly to the farmer's inquiry about possible mineral deposits? Levmore is convinced the answer is yes: in fact he calls it "optimal dishonesty" and says that the farmer's behavior in attempting to find out the full value of his land is "despicable" because he has no intention of mining the land himself. Levmore, *supra* note 55, at 137-42.

270. This part of the decision spawns a whole new set of puzzles. What will be the measure of damages for the violation of this legally protected interest? Are damages to be decided with no reference to the value of the drugs or cell lines produced from the patient who has failed to give consent? What if the doctor believes that the patient will not give his or her consent to such research, but also believes that the patient's cells are likely to be invaluable in developing a hugely profitable drug? In that situation, a rational doctor in a position like that of Doctor Golde will

concerned, Mr. Moore is the author of his own destiny, but not of his spleen.

X
CONCLUSION

A. *"Typing" Information Issues*

There are a number of reasons that one might classify the kinds of issues I have discussed here under the heading "information." One might believe that one had a master theory—a single set of principles capable of resolving all significant conflicts, or simply a single set of functional goals to be rescued from messy doctrinal particularity. For example, as discussed earlier, Judge Easterbrook was concerned that putting information cases in traditional legal pigeonholes would cause the Court to "overlook the need to consider the way in which the incentive to produce information and the demands of current use conflict."[271] My aim here was rather different.

First of all, I had a descriptive and analytic goal. I wished to attack from a different angle a series of problems that have puzzled scholars and frustrated courts. The conventional way of addressing these issues is a particularistic one. The legal system commodifies, refuses to commodify, or makes illegal the commodification of certain kinds of information. Scholars then take each issue on its own merits. They ask, "Why is blackmail illegal?" or, "Why does the state forbid insider trading?" or even, "Why does copyright doctrine extend protection to expression but deny it to ideas?" Instead, I asked a series of questions about the roles that information is expected to play in the institutions of a liberal state— in the family, in the market, and in the world of politics and public debate. My aim was to remain faithful to the subtlety and complexity of the material by dealing with each issue in some detail. If I had to abandon that goal temporarily in order to summarize my conclusions here, I would say that the ideology of a liberal society presents different reified visions of information—as the lifeblood of the disinterested debate in the public world, as the instantaneous omniscience of the actors in the perfect market, as that which must be commodified if we are to encourage more information to be produced, as that potential public manifestation of themselves that individuals must be able to control if we are to protect the cozy world of the home, the family, and the persona. And so on, and so on.

Most analysts start by assuming a certain level of deductive rational-

---

decide not to inform, will pay the damages for breach of the duty to disclose or for battery and will still come out ahead. The obvious way to avoid undermining the patient's sovereign power of decision would be to base the damages in part on the patient's proportional contribution to the profitable drug. But how different is that from a "property" right?

271. Easterbrook, *supra* note 1, at 314.

ity in the construction of our social institutions.[272] They assume that there really is some logical reason that blackmail should be prohibited. After all, most of us feel so strongly that blackmail is "wrong" that it is easy to imagine that a little further reflection and a better set of analytical tools will uncover the principle that distinguishes the blackmail demand from the rent bill, or from the baseball stadium's negotiation with its host city. Alternatively, analysts critique the current position—but again, they assume the deductive rationality of the institutions they analyze. Thus, the critics of insider trading regulation seem puzzled by the fact that legislative history, scholarly analysis, and judicial exposition offer no rationale for prohibiting a practice that, when described in abstract terms, seems to them entirely compatible with the norms of a free market society. In the place of this fuzzy thinking, they offer economic analyses of secrecy, justifications of "optimal dishonesty," and models of the efficient capital market, confident that their prescriptions are not marred by the flaws of the ideas they criticize.

In my view, blackmail is illegal because we have a vision of "privateness" that is constructed in part around the control of *information*[273]— as opposed to, say, wealth, health care, or housing.[274] We "romanti-

---

272. For a discussion of the relevance of the assumption that social institutions are subject to critique by reason, and an analysis of the *conservative* objections to such an idea, see James Boyle, *A Process of Denial: Bork and Post-Modern Conservatism*, 3 YALE J.L. & HUMAN. 263, 299-314 (1991).

273. *See, e.g.*, Whalen v. Roe, 429 U.S. 589, 599-600 (1977) (defining privacy in terms of "the individual interest in avoiding disclosure of personal matters, and . . . the interest in independence in making certain kinds of important decisions") (footnotes omitted). This definition of privacy focuses on retention and control of information to protect the person and the life plan. One interpretation of this idea is that information is the only *resource* or form of wealth the need for which can be convincingly derived from the liberal theory of personhood. This may be one reason that state laws regulating abortion that incorporate theories of when life begins can be disturbing. *See, e.g.*, Webster v. Reproductive Health Servs., 492 U.S. 490, 504-07 (1989) (refusing to consider the constitutionality of the preamble to Missouri's abortion law where the theory of life contained therein was not used to justify regulation of abortion). For an interesting analysis of information rights in light of current Supreme Court doctrine, see Francis S. Chlapowski, Note, *The Constitutional Protection of Informational Privacy*, 71 B.U. L. REV. 133 (1991).

274. An inexact analogy may help to demonstrate the profoundly contingent, socially constructed nature of our notion of "public sphere" and "privacy." Imagine a society in which everyone lived in communal dormitories with socialized childrearing, limited taboos about public displays of sexual behavior, and so on. Imagine also that universal access to excellent health care was seen as a defining, essential quality of the society. Then imagine a person in that society who offered permanently to give up her right to health care, in return for some release from communal obligations. Such a transaction might well be seen as no more legitimate than an attempt by a citizen in this society permanently to renounce her vote or her right to counsel, perhaps even to sell herself into slavery. Such a transaction might seem to violate the "logic" of the public sphere. Conversely, imagine the way that "privacy" would be seen in such a society. Certainly, an individual whose neighbor in the dormitory threatened to reveal some unpleasant fact would be unhappy, but would that society necessarily have thought "control of information about oneself" to be an important principle of social organization, as opposed to, say, "policing those who shirk their social duties"? My point is not that certain forms of social organization *necessarily* produce certain principled normative concerns. Rather, a process by which we imagine changes in fundamental aspects of our

cize"[275] a notion of subjective control of private information, refusing to allow the information to be commodified. The best analogy to blackmail, then, is not monopoly or monopsony, but something like the "wrongful birth" cases in which many courts refuse to recognize the costs of raising a child as "damage" flowing from a negligently conducted sterilization operation. In both cases, we make a pretheoretical judgment that an activity is "private," and only then do we "deduce" that it must be kept from the ruthless, instrumental logic of the market.

Insider trading is another situation in which someone trades from a superior position in nonpublic information. This is not just any information, but information of great value. In blackmail, we pigeonholed the issue into the "private" world of information about home and family. In insider trading, on the other hand, we label the issue as "public," subject to the norms of equality rather than the norms of the market, precisely because it is material *information* and not some other form of wealth or power. Hence, there is a strand in the cases and in the scholarly writings that applies the norm of equality to *all* regular dealings in material nonpublic information. But there is also a strong vision that information should be traded just like every other commodity—a vision that would deny the special public status of information. Thus, there is an equally strong—perhaps now, a stronger—tendency to see insider trading in terms not of formal public equality, but rather in terms of private misappropriation and theft.

The disagreements in courtrooms and scholarly journals about the proper characterization of insider trading help to point out the limits of my argument. The typing I am describing is neither so deeply rooted in the culture that it can never be criticized nor so determinate that it dictates only one solution. At most, I am trying to lay out the structure within which issues are now framed, possibilities foreclosed, and so on. The structure matters, because it excludes some options from consideration (excludes them even from being seen, perhaps), or prompts a hasty leap to judgment, or because it is one of the many forces shaping the terrain of political struggle. But the process of typing is neither a giant conspiracy nor a deterministic and inevitable deep structure of thought.

Finally, let me say that this process of typing information issues as public or private[276] is not "irrational," in the derogatory sense of that

---

social life reveals the *contingency* of our own beliefs. In fact, the relationship of social form to normative structure is highly contingent—perhaps a dormitory-based social system would be *more* concerned with privacy than we are—but this contingency is concealed precisely by the fact that members of any given society share a basic normative structure.

275. I use the word to mean that as a society we project onto an institution or set of actions an emotional and intellectual charge—in this case a positive one—and that we then perceive that charge as already being contained *within* the romanticized object. *See* PETER L. BERGER & THOMAS LUCKMANN, THE SOCIAL CONSTRUCTION OF REALITY (1980); Boyle, *supra* note 9.

276. And typing them into the conflicting ideas about what public and private *mean*.

term. There are, to be sure, reasons why we think the control of information about ourselves is fundamental to the preservation of the self. There are reasons why a right to control private information will command more support in this society than a right to control some other critical resource—food, for example. There are reasons why the claim that "everyone should trade from a position of roughly equal information" seems merely "fair," whereas "everyone should trade from a position of roughly equal wealth" seems like socialism. Those reasons are a complex of ideology, anthropology, history, New Deal institutions, class interest, noble ideal, Enlightenment epistemology, and so on. It would take a better philosopher than I to lay them out fully, and one with more hubris to believe that exactly the correct mix could be identified. But it is in the process these "reasons" explain—the process of "typing" information issues that I have described in this Article—more than in the language of microeconomics or Rawlsian rights theory that we find answers to the question, "Why are insider trading and blackmail illegal?"

I would also draw another, modestly realist, conclusion from this process and the conflicting stereotypes about information on which it relies. During the process of typing issues as public or private, analogies and metaphors play a vital role. In some cases, however, we become the prisoners of our metaphors. While this observation has a long and distinguished history in other areas of legal doctrine,[277] the information field has been curiously immune to it.

In the area of electronic information services, the *Prodigy* case is a particularly good illustration.[278] Prodigy has been defending itself from charges that its electronic bulletin boards censored notices critical of Prodigy and did not censor anti-Semitic speech. The ACLU wanted neither form of restriction; B'nai Brith wanted only the latter. An article from *Network World* offers a series of classic "public and private" characterizations, shored up by metaphors that refer back to the information technology of yesteryear.

> Prodigy's bulletin board editing policies are, in essence, electronic publications, the spokesman added. He said Prodigy has the right to edit or delete material, just as newspapers have a right not to print letters to the editor.
>
> Jerry Berman, director of the American Civil Liberties Union's Information Technology Project in Washington, D.C., said the ACLU agrees with Prodigy's assertion that it has the

---

277. Cohen, *supra* note 12.

278. *See* Barnaby J. Feder, *Computer Concern Assailed on Anti-Semitic Notes*, N.Y. TIMES, Oct. 24, 1991, at A21; Barnaby J. Feder, *Computer Speech—Also Free*, N.Y. TIMES, Oct. 30, 1991, at A24; Barnaby J. Feder, *Toward Defining Free Speech in the Computer Age*, N.Y. TIMES, Nov. 3, 1991, § 4, at 5; Michael W. Miller, *Prodigy Computer Network Bans Bias Notes from Bulletin Board*, WALL ST. J., Oct. 24, 1991, at B1, B6.

right to edit public bulletin board systems. But he said a Prodigy policy limiting the types of private electronic messages users can send is a gray area.

Some new Prodigy rules prohibit users from sending unsolicited messages protesting pricing policies to the Prodigy advertisers. . . .

Berman said these restrictions may be justified because Prodigy is a private service, but they could also be seen as an unjustifiable restraint of free speech.[279]

The metaphors are contested, of course. Organizations such as Electronic Frontier compare electronic bulletin boards to public parks.[280] In another article, Berman drew on the shopping mall cases to suggest that "[t]he courts may some day hold that electronic shopping networks like Prodigy are the public forums of the 21st century."[281] The process by which bulletin boards are analogized to shopping malls, which in the past had been analogized to the Roman forum, is a fascinating one. Berman then suggests that Congress should regulate electronic mail under "common carrier principles."[282]

The tropes change as the context changes. In libel cases, for example, courts have analogized electronic information services to bookshops or for-profit libraries,[283] rather than to newspapers that publish libelous information. The difficulty comes when the analogy alone seems to decide the issue.

"There is some debate in legal circles on the extent to which videotext service providers must screen publicly posted messages," said Benjamin Wright, a lawyer in Dallas who specializes in electronic communications law. "If the law sees the provider as more like a newspaper, then the duty to screen is higher. But if the law sees the provider as more like a telephone company, a communications common carrier, then the duty is lower."[284]

Parks? The U.S. Mails? Federal Express? A telephone company? Community newspaper? Regulated television station? Common carrier? Who is to say? There are advantages—in familiarity, evocativeness and tradition—to this particular kind of analogical reasoning. Nevertheless,

---

279. Barton Crockett, *DA Probes BBS Practices at Prodigy,* NETWORK WORLD, Apr. 15, 1991, at 4.

280. *See infra* note 305.

281. Jerry Berman & Marc Rotenberg, *Forum: Free Speech in an Electronic Age,* N.Y. TIMES, Jan. 6, 1991, § 3, at 13.

282. *Id.*

283. "CompuServe's CIS product is in essence an electronic, for-profit library that carries a vast number of publications and collects usage and membership fees from its subscribers in return for access to the publications." Cubby, Inc. v. Compuserve Inc., 776 F. Supp. 135, 140 (S.D.N.Y. 1991).

284. Peter H. Lewis, *The Executive Computer: On Electronic Bulletin Boards, What Rights Are at Stake?,* N.Y. TIMES, Dec. 23, 1990, § 3, at 8.

it is hard to repress an occasional wish to frame the issue as whether a specific type of regulation will help or hinder the kind of society that we wish to create,[285] rather than filtering it through an additional layer of simile and metaphor. The difference in the two methods is not the difference between rational analysis and figurative speech[286]—our vision of the good society is, of necessity, an analogical one too. Still, it would be unfortunate if we decided how to regulate the most important technologies of the next century based mainly on their formal resemblances to the physical environs or commercial settings in which the public information of the nineteenth century found its home.

B. The Search for an Author

The second goal of this Article was more complicated. Recognizing the existence of contradictory pictures of information and the role of the public/private distinction in information issues is only the beginning of the project. At the end of my description of the conceptual elements of information issues—property, the public/private distinction, and information economics—I outlined the ideological and practical prerequisites for the law of intellectual property. Our assumptions about state, market, family, and information present a task for the law of information. Given these assumptions, intellectual property law, and the law of information in general, must appear to reconcile a series of apparently incompatible demands if it is to appear credible.

It must provide a conceptual apparatus that appears to mediate the various tensions associated with the role of information in liberal society. Thus, for example, it must explain why a person who recombines information from the public sphere is not merely engaging in the private appropriation of public wealth. It must explain how we can motivate individuals, who are sometimes postulated to be essentially self-serving and sometimes to be noble, idealistic souls, to produce information. If the answer is "by giving them property rights," it must also explain why this will not

---

285. The best summation of the Prodigy debate itself may have come at the end of a *Boston Globe* article:

> Industry analyst Gary Arlen has a different view. What may have happened, he says, is that Prodigy unwittingly attracted people looking for a real communications network instead of consumers eager to spend money in an electronic shopping mall.
>
> Citing a computer magazine editorial, he says, "Prodigy's message to its subscribers seems to be 'Shut up and shop.'"

Chris Reidy, *Computer Flap: Is Speech Free on Prodigy?*, BOSTON GLOBE, Jan. 30, 1991, at 35.

286. This is one of my disagreements with the economic analysts of information issues. Easterbrook, for example, believes that the problem with intellectual property issues is that abstract (and I would say, metaphoric) terms conceal from the court the real functional requisites of the information market. Yet to engage in economic analysis is (at least as Judge Easterbrook does it) to abstract certain aspects of a complex social situation, whether of blackmailing, baby-selling, book-writing or boat-covering—and to declare that this is *really* a market. And that, of course, is a metaphoric, analogical process.

CALIFORNIA LAW REVIEW [Vol. 80:1413

diminish the common pool or public domain so greatly that a net decrease in the production of information will result. (Think of overfishing.) It must carve out a sphere of privacy and at the same time ensure a vigorous sphere of public debate and ample information about a potentially oppressive state. It must do all of this within a vision of justice that expects formal equality within the public sphere, but respects existing disparities in wealth, status, and power in the private. And all of these things must be accomplished while using a conception of property that avoids the theoretical impossibilities of the physicalist, absolutist conception, but that at the same time is not too obviously relativistic, partial, and utilitarian.[287]

The constellation of ideas that seems most successfully to reduce the salience of these tensions in copyright law is the *figure* of the romantic author, the associated *theme* of originality, and the *conceptual distinction* between idea and expression. This triad manages to make it seem that intellectual property rights are more than just a utilitarian grant by the state; to limit the ambit of something that sounds very much like a labor theory of property rights; and to divide the author's creation so that the idea goes into the world of public exchange, while the expression remains the author's. In explaining the history of this constellation of ideas, I tried to show that the idea of authorship is socially constructed and historically contingent. In particular, the romantic vision of authorship plays down the importance of external sources by emphasizing the unique genius of the author and the originality of the work. This "author gambit" is so attractive that it is found far beyond conventional intellectual property law, a fact of no small importance.

The current trend seems to be to assume that economics is the most appropriate theoretical language in which to discuss questions about the regulation of information. But the turn to microeconomics does not rob the idea of romantic authorship of all significance. In my discussion of information economics, I tried to show that economic analysis of information questions is paradoxical or at least aporetic. I suggested that these problems could be traced to the fact that perfect information is a defining conceptual element of the analytical structure used to analyze markets driven by the absence of information, in which imperfect information itself is a commodity. The implication was that informationally efficient markets are not merely difficult to achieve, but impossible.

The paradoxes of information in liberal state theory reappear in microeconomics. Economists analyze some information from the "commodity" side and other information from the "perfect information" side, but they can neither produce a theoretical metaprinciple that justifies

---

287. *Supra* pp. 1460-61.

their shifts nor completely purge the disfavored aspect from their analysis. It seems perfectly possible to invert the hierarchies, so that one could analyze the free availability of futures market prices as a public goods problem, or copyright as an intolerable transaction cost.

The most obvious manifestation of this basic indeterminacy is the difficulty that economists have in theorizing about the amount of information that will be produced in an "unregulated" market. Will it be too much or too little? Many economists say that information is a classic public good, apparently taking as a theoretical *a priori* about public goods problems the assumption that too *little* of the good will be produced. Yet some economists think that the absence of property rights will lead to the production of too *much* information. Thus, the use of some general body of "public goods theory" to analyze information issues seems impossible.[288] Each information issue needs to be examined on its own, in a particularistic, highly empirical way—a style not often found in the current literature. In the absence of such particular, empirical data, and some convincing theoretical grounding, economics offers little more than a partial checklist of issues and tradeoffs. And that is where the author comes in again. In a strange mixture of Wordsworth and Coase, Byron and Stigler, the values of romantic authorship seem to seep—consciously or unconsciously—into economic analysis. And because in most conflicts the paradigm of authorship tends to fit one side better than the other, this romantic grounding provides economic analysis with at least the illusion of certainty. Authors tend to win.

In Parts VIII and IX, I claimed that both scholars and courts have

---

288. Professor Steven Shavell suggests to me that when professional economists talk about "public goods" they do *not* mean that there is a general category of goods that share the same economic characteristics, manifest the same dysfunctions, and thus benefit from similar corrective solutions. Most economists, he argues, would agree that there is no such thing as "public goods"— merely an infinite series of particular problems (some of overproduction, some of underproduction, and so on), each with a particular solution that cannot be deduced from the theory but that instead would depend on local empirical factors. If this is what economists think, I would be happy to agree. Certainly, lawyer-economists often seem to have more expansive ideas. *See* Landes & Posner, *supra* note 22, at 326 ("A distinguishing characteristic of intellectual property is its 'public good' aspect."); *see also* Demsetz, *supra* note 28; Easterbrook, *supra* note 1; Kitch, *supra* note 1. Mainstream economics texts and articles also make more general claims. JAMES M. BUCHANAN, THE DEMAND AND SUPPLY OF PUBLIC GOODS (1968); Paul A. Samuelson, *Contrast Between Welfare Conditions for Joint Supply and for Public Goods,* 51 REV. ECON. & STAT. 26 (1969); Earl A. Thompson, *The Perfectly Competitive Production of Collective Goods,* 50 REV. ECON. & STAT. 1 (1968). This seems to be true of economists of all political opinions and theoretical types. DAVID HEMENWAY, PRICES AND CHOICES: MICROECONOMIC VIGNETTES (1977); Perelman, *supra* note 94. Finally, detailed articles *by* economists often make the same mistakes that one would expect of someone working with a reified and overly general "public good" vision of information. Arrow, *supra* note 94. Nevertheless, there are articles putting forward ideas consistent with Shavell's point of view, *e.g.,* Hirshleifer, *supra* note 69, although it is noticeable that these articles generally adopt the tone of a protestant dissenter, rather than that of normal science. In the end, my conclusion has to be that Professor Shavell is committing the entirely laudable error of being too kind to his colleagues.

wide recourse to the author gambit. In the *Moore* case, the court found, like Krause,[289] that Mr. Moore's claims raise concerns about the limitation and justification of property and the nature of privacy. Eventually, it is the celebration of original, creative, artistic modification of naturally existing raw material and the need to motivate society's creators that justify giving property rights to the doctors but not to Mr. Moore.[290] Even the right-of-publicity cases seem to reflect this body of ideas, allowing the commodification of the "expressions" of a unique celebrity persona. In both areas, those who do not look like authors find that their property claims are rejected. Mr. Moore presents us with a powerful picture of the unfortunate consequences that can ensue if the court decides you are part of the public domain. Ed McMahon, the World's Foremost Commodian, and the manufacturers of Crazylegs depilatory cream may present less compelling claims to our sympathy, but they all suffer some significant consequence in part because they do not fit the author paradigm.

In Part VIII, the relevance of the romantic author to economic and utilitarian analysis becomes clearer still. As an example I used the original defense of insider trading by Henry Manne. Manne admits that his economic analysis of insider trading provides no strong reasons to legalize the practice. Again, it is a figure akin to the romantic author who provides the outcome-determinacy the analysis otherwise lacks. Drawing on Schumpeter's theory of economic development, Manne conjures up a romanticized vision of the entrepreneur/innovator as the creator and destroyer of settled arrangements. Manne, with the aid of a few category errors, declares that profits from insider trading will function as the entrepreneur's reward—temporary monopoly rents that lie at the heart of capitalism. The parallel to copyright and patent is striking.

In the other writing on insider trading and on the right to withhold valuable information, echoes of the author appear again and again. Professor Levmore's article on insider trading and contract law styles as "contemptible" the farmer who "to preserve a fraud claim, asks specific questions about activities he would otherwise never engage in" and advocates his own proposed doctrine as a way "to deny a windfall to a passive party when to do otherwise might lead to a net societal loss."[291]

---

289. *See* Krause, *supra* note 118.

290. In other words, the argument on behalf of the doctors that we must secure for producers the fruits of their labors in order to encourage research has an equal and opposite counterpart. The opposing argument identifies Mr. Moore as a co-producer in terms of dessert and argues that unless individuals are rewarded for allowing their genetic material to be used for research, too little genetic material will be made available to researchers. The California Supreme Court avoids, suppresses, or counters this argument by appealing to its audience's reverence for the original, creative laborer who transforms the environment, and whose property rights are appropriately limited by their very function. The ideal of authorship first *identifies* the researchers as the relevant parties and then *justifies* their property rights.

291. Levmore, *supra* note 55, at 142.

The judgmental moralism and the preference for the active, dynamic, exploring mineral company rather than for the "contemptible," "passive" farmer are not required by the economic analysis. Indeed, one could paint a perfectly respectable series of economic vignettes in which the absence of a right to expect disclosure held up transactions and encouraged strategic behavior on the part of farmers who could never rely on the representations of buyers of their land. Instead, the choice to start the analysis from a preference for the "active," inventive party seems to represent the same romanticization of the innovating, transforming author figure. If one starts from this perspective, then the farmer, like the baker of Proust's madeleines or Mr. Moore, has no *moral* right to the profits the innovator makes from the new object—even though that object was created from raw material supplied by the hapless source. Whatever coating of economics is subsequently put over this pretheoretical orientation, the outcome derives from the initially hidden, and probably unconscious, moment of romance. Judge Easterbrook's arguments about the division of labor seem to be marked by a similar pretheoretical preference for Faust and the individual creator, rather than for Job and the public domain.

I am certainly not saying that authors are bad, or claiming that we never need to give property rights to the creators of information in order to encourage further production. The protection and exaltation of authorship is a compelling and attractive idea. The need to reward producers in order to encourage continued production is a real concern, although, of course, the question of just who is a "producer" continues to be a problem. Just as the typing of information issues into public and private may produce felicitous and attractive results, the concern with the motivation of authors may, in any individual case, be exactly what is needed. But I stress the "may." Of the examples I gave above, Proust's baker may have no claim to our heartstrings or our utilitarian goals, while the farmer and Mr. Moore may have considerably more. Yet to the extent that we decide information issues by forcing them into a Procrustean concept of authorship, we risk a tendency to ignore the countervailing moral and utilitarian concerns. This risk arises not because we reject these concerns, but because the veil of authorship obscures them. Consider the following.

Centuries of cultivation by third world farmers produce wheat and rice strains with valuable qualities—in the resistance to disease, or in the ability to give good yields at high altitudes. The biologists, agronomists, and genetic engineers of a western chemical company take samples of these strains, engineer them a little to add a greater resistance to fungus or a thinner husk. The chemical company's scientists fit the paradigm of authorship. The farmers are everything that authors should not be: their contribution comes from a community rather than an individual, tradition rather than an innovation, evolution rather than transformation. Guess who gets the intellectual property right? Next year, the farmers may need a license to resow the grain from their crops. Calling this practice "the great seed ripoff," Representative John Porter actually introduced a resolution into Congress that would have called for the United States not to proceed with intellectual property negotiations under the GATT until there has been a study on "protecting the rights of those in the Third World."[292] A news article on the resolution immediately follows this observation by offering a view of this issue from the other side, that is to say, from within the author-centered view of intellectual property: "The 'industrial world' view on the issue is that poor countries pirate drug recipes or high-yield seeds, violating the patent laws of industrial countries to avoid paying royalties on the order of $3 billion a year to U.S., Japanese and European firms."[293]

Other examples abound. Shamans from the Amazon basin often have generations of lore about the properties of herbs and flowers. Some of the these plants are placebos; others are extremely valuable.[294] Drug companies have found that if they test the plants from the shamans' "black bag," they yield a high percentage of valuable drugs.

> While skeptics may argue that the lore of native healers is mere superstition, the ethnobotanists see shamanic knowledge as the result of a trial-and-error process refined over thousands of years. Ethnobotanists hope to take a scientific short cut to discovering new uses for the tens of thousands of plants with which native peoples are intimately familiar.[295]

One of the most fascinating experiments reported by the *New York Times* involved the AIDS virus. In test tube trials, "[o]f the 20 plants collected on the shaman's advice, five killed the AIDS virus but spared the T cells. But of 18 plant species gathered randomly, just one did so."[296] There is, of course, no guarantee that any of these plants would be suitable for human consumption, but they are now being tested.

A more widely publicized example concerns vinca alkaloids from the rosy periwinkle—a plant that is native to Madagascar. The plant was used indigenously to treat diabetes. It was investigated by the Lilly company and forms the basis of a compound now used in chemotherapy treatment.[297] According to the British newspaper *The Independent*, the

---

292. David Judson, *Lawmaker Urges U.S. to Come Clean on "Seed Ripoffs,"* GANNETT NEWS SERVICE, July 19, 1990, *available in* LEXIS, Nexis Library, GNS File.

293. *Id.*

294. Daniel Goleman, *Shamans and Their Lore May Vanish with Forests,* N.Y. TIMES, June 11, 1991, at C1.

295. *Id.*

296. *Id.*

297. The example is actually a more complex one. When tested as a drug to ameliorate the symptoms of diabetes, the alkaloids derived from the periwinkle did not perform well. Subsequent

plant "has yielded a drug to cure Hodgkin's disease and a trade in the drug worth $100m a year."[298] The article goes on to quote the World Wide Fund for Nature to the effect that "[i]f Madagascar had received a significant part of this income, it would have been one of the country's largest (if not the largest) single sources of income."[299] In the days of recombinant DNA techniques, genetic information may be one of the largest resources of the developing countries. "Madagascar is the unique home of perhaps 5 per cent of the world's species. It is the biological equivalent of an Arab oil sheikhdom. Yet, without an income from its huge biological wealth, it has chopped down most of its forests to feed its people."[300] Now *there's* a place to deploy our economic analyses of public goods, free riders, and the tragedy of the commons. Precisely because they can find no place in a legal regime constructed around a vision of individual, transformative, original genius, the indigenous peoples are driven to deforestation, or slash-and-burn farming. Who knows what other unique and potentially valuable plants disappear with the forest, what generations of pharmacological experience disappear as the indigenous culture is destroyed. In both cases, a large part of the problem is that indigenous peoples share in none of the profits of development. While it is always possible that huge profits could destroy the culture just as effectively as penury, the decision to impose the author vision without acknowledging, or even understanding, its implications is also the decision to ignore these problems.

These facts have not gone completely unnoticed. Environmental groups and groups devoted to the preservation of indigenous peoples have criticized the way that tribal lore and biological largesse find no place in the language of intellectual property. Dr. Jason Gray, Director of Cultural Survival, put the position simply:

> "It's a question of intellectual property rights. People whose medical lore leads to a useful product should have a stake in the profits. Unless we return some profits to them, it's a kind of theft. We have to figure out ways to make the rain forests pay for themselves, so these peoples can continue to exist."[301]

This "colonial" form of intellectual property has been around for hundreds of years. In 1800 the Makushi Indians showed explorers the plant from which they extracted curare for their arrowheads. Western chemists found that curare was an excellent muscle relaxant. It is still

---

testing showed that the drug had other, equally valuable uses. How, then, should we value the contribution of Madagascar's flora and indigenous medical lore? At zero? If we do, how are we to avoid the public goods problems, or tragedy of the commons problems that I discuss below?

298. Fred Pearce, *Science and Technology: Bargaining for the Life of the Forest,* INDEPENDENT, Mar. 17, 1991, at 37.

299. *Id.*

300. *Id.*

301. Goleman, *supra* note 294, at C6.

being used to this day. According to Dr. Mark Plotkin of Conservation International, "The Makushis never received any compensation for the discovery of a product worth millions."[302]

In the future, plans to set up data banks on the genetic resources of tropical rain forests raise concerns that companies will no longer have any incentive either to preserve the forest or to reward its inhabitants for the use of their lore. Precisely because of our increasing ability to record genetic information *as information,* the connection of that information to its natural habitat will become less necessary. Conrad Gorinsky, a Guyanan biologist working in Britain,

> calls the current plans "bunker biology," because they ignore the traditional tribal knowledge that is the fount of our wisdom. He fears that the [proposed treaty on genetic sovereignty] could act as an incentive for companies to loot the biological riches of the rain forests over a few years, secreting the results in their laboratories and gene banks. A gene in the lab, they will argue, is worth two in the bush. But once the riches are taken, who will save the rain forest then?[303]

A patent lawyer or an economist could argue that we cannot criticize intellectual property regimes for failing to maintain the genetic diversity of the biomass (or whatever). Perhaps that is true, although it seems highly problematic to me. But even if we close our eyes to the distributional, environmental, and other "subsidiary" effects of our intellectual property regimes, even if we analyze those regimes solely on their ability to maintain and increase the production of information, we find that, for the reasons developed in this Article, they are unlikely to achieve that very restricted goal. An author-focused regime that makes the contributions of sources "invisible" is unlikely to reward those contributions—even when an economic analysis might show this to be desirable. Sources may become a "commons" whose exploitation is justified or obscured by an author theory, leading to predictably tragic results— cutting down the genetic miracle of a rain forest to grow subsistence crops, for example. The result *may* be a reduced flow of genetic material to laboratories and a consequent reduction in research and innovation. The same general analysis can be applied to restrictive decisions about the fair use exception in copyright,[304] to the application of patent law to computer programming tricks worked out long ago by hackers,[305] and

---

302. *Id.*

303. Pearce, *supra* note 298.

304. The *Kinko's* decision, for example. Basic Books, Inc. v. Kinko's Graphics Corp., 758 F. Supp. 1522 (S.D.N.Y. 1991). The restriction of the doctrine of fair use may seem initially to go the other way. In one sense, a restricted fair use exception will guarantee a higher level of payment to "sources." The difference, of course, is that you only benefit from the restriction of fair use if the legal system already classifies you as an author.

305. Some computer scientists and software developers have been resolutely opposed to the

even to the willing participation of subjects in genetic research programs.

It is not only "sources" that tend to suffer from the blindnesses of the authorial vision. Audiences suffer too—even as they sometimes benefit from the incentive mandated by the authorial vision. As I pointed out in the discussion of the conflicting roles of information, copyright scholars have recently begun to comment critically about the tensions between their discipline and the ideals of the First Amendment. They are right to do so. Whether the issue is access to electronic information, the photocopying of materials for classroom use, the quoting and paraphrasing of passages from an ex-president's biography, or the general issue of the privatization of the public domain, author-talk often *presumes* the very relationship between the incentives of property rights and the availability of information that it must *prove*. The opposing positions of the United States and the Third World on the intellectual property provisions debated during the Uruguay Round of negotiation on the GATT show the implications that these presumptions have for international development as well as for domestic debate.[306] Less obvious, but no less important, are the effects that the regime of intellectual property will have on the international audience for literary work, political debate, or scientific exchange.

My point here is a simple one. Much of the current case law and scholarly literature gives the impression that if we wished to consider issues of distributive justice, international development, or citizen interest in a thriving public domain, we would have to give up a rigorous analytical system that carefully balances incentives for production against the needs of current use. From my perspective, nothing could be further from the truth. The current analysis is massively indeterminate at every stage. It is based on claims for which there is inadequate empirical evidence. It relies on an aporetic set of economic ideas in which most issues could convincingly be portrayed *either* as a public goods problem requiring commodification *or* as a monopoly/transaction cost problem requiring competition and the free flow of ideas. As a system, it is held

---

application of intellectual property to information technology. One of the developers of the Lotus program, Mitch Kapor, has been a powerful critic of the effects of intellectual property on the "electronic frontier," founding a group by that name to counter the orthodox wisdom about the necessity of property rights to encourage development. Richard Stallman, an MIT computer scientist, has founded a group called the "League for Programming Freedom" specifically to challenge what he sees as the inhibiting effects of commodification on both the development of new technology and the *dispersal* of market power over information technology. Finally, an underground group called "Nu Prometheus" has dedicated itself to stealing and revealing the "source codes" for single supplier CPU's such as the MacIntosh as a way to encourage other suppliers to compete with Apple. The idea of theft in the service of competition is a perfect example of the conflicts I describe in this Article.

306. *See, e.g.,* Clyde H. Farnsworth, *U.S. Warns on Global Trade Talks,* N.Y. TIMES, Nov. 30, 1988, at D1 ("Brazil opposes stronger protection for intellectual property and freer trade in services—two major American objectives."). *See generally* Eric Wolfhard, *International Trade in Intellectual Property: The Emerging GATT Regime,* 49 U. TORONTO FAC. L. REV. 106 (1991).

together by definitional fiat, despite the fact that the definitions of "idea," "expression," "parody," "originality," "fact work," "fair use," "nonobviousness," and "natural law" merely reproduce the very tensions they were designed to resolve. Finally, the system is both grounded on and imbued with an ahistorical and romanticized vision of authorial creation: it takes as universal premise that which should be its occasional conclusion.

Admittedly, there are a number of things the authorship vision does well. It conceals the indeterminacy of much of the utilitarian analysis. More positively, the concerns it stresses are real ones. Authors and inventors often *do* need to be encouraged, protected, lauded, and rewarded. The romantic vision of authorship offers an attractive idea of creative labor—transcending market norms, incorporating both work and play, and entailing a world in which workers have a real connection to and control over the fruits of their labors. This is a vision that we might want to expand far beyond the limited realm of property in information. As currently constructed however, intellectual property in particular and information issues in general seem to be in the thrall of an idea that is taken as truth where it should be questioned as dogma.

C. The Future

In this Article, I have assumed that we are moving towards a society more centrally concerned with the production, manipulation, and use of information. As assumptions go, this seems to be a reasonable one. Obviously, any judgment about the best way to analyze information issues will depend in part on the fears (and hopes) we have about this process. Classical liberalism lays great stress on the dangers posed by a runaway state, and so liberalism as a political doctrine has much to say about the best means for the restraint of state power. What fears do we have about information and the much heralded information age? From here it is hard to tell what the future holds, or what kind of ideas and cultural traditions will be of use. Inevitably we rely on historical analogies to grasp the situation, and just as inevitably, the analogies mislead as well as enlighten. In an information world, what would be the equivalent of Hegel's and Weber's analyses of the public/private split, Marx's labor theory of value, or Pigou's analysis of externalities? Here are three possibilities that draw on the ideas developed in this Article.

1. Information Class

My concern in this Article has been with ideas and lines of thought that tend to be suppressed by the current way of thinking about information and society. This is a familiar intellectual exercise. Writing about the industrial revolution and the transformation of capitalism, Marx turned the rhetoric of private property and entrepreneurialism on its head, arguing that wealth was socially produced but privately appropriated. According to Marx, law, ideology, religion, and philosophy all operated to obscure this "skimming off" of surplus value. In place of a market theory of value and the confused positivist/natural right theory of property of his time, he offered a labor theory of value, transforming workers from "another factor of production" into "the *real* producers of value."[307]

One danger that might be dimly prefigured in this Article is that we are moving towards a new, highly stratified class system—a world broadly divided between manipulators of information and "sources." In a society where one group compiles, modifies, redesigns, and commodifies information gleaned in part from the genes, consumption patterns, and culture of the rest of the population, the rhetoric of justification and entitlement bids fair to be based on author-talk. Just as the market/natural right vision of property could be used to claim that workers were receiving exactly the proportion of social wealth to which they were entitled, so the authorship vision can be used—both rhetorically and theoretically—to obscure, undervalue, or simply ignore the contributions of "sources." Precisely because author-talk is genuinely attractive, because it does express desirable moral and utilitarian ideas, its power is likely to be all the greater. How does one break the grip of a rhetoric of entitlement that systematically obscures and undervalues the contributions of one part of the population and magnifies those of another part of the population? One method is to propose an alternative rhetoric of entitlement. For Marx, the labor theory of value was the *true* theory, rather than a way of thinking that helped to expose the partiality and contentious quality of the settled arrangements of his society. By contrast, the argument in this Article merely aspires to show the suppressed side of information and intellectual property, not to dethrone the author and crown the source instead.

The examples here ranged from the *Moore* case to insider trading, from copyright doctrine to indigenous medical lore in the Amazon and the tragedy of the commons in the forests of Madagascar. Using them, I argued that for complex reasons relating to the ideology of public and private spheres in a liberal society, the regime of intellectual property is built around a particular romanticized conception of authorship. I argued that this regime often has the effect of devaluing sources and that, even within the conventional language of policy analysis, such a devaluation seems sometimes to have very bad consequences. (Sometimes it has very good ones—but more by accident than by design.) This, surely, is

---

307. This is not to say that I am arguing in favor of the labor theory of value. One of the achievements of marginalism in economics and legal realism in property law was to point out the flaws of both the Marxist labor theory of value and the conventional vision of property which it opposed.

something we want to know. Apart from this pragmatic concern, I have a more intangible one—*Ideologiekritik* rather than policy analysis. Marx's errors notwithstanding, it *is* important to see the lacunae and contentious assumptions involved in a particular society's discourse of entitlement—the language in which entitlement to that particular society's primary resources is both described and justified.[308] To have a critical understanding of the rhetoric of entitlement in an information society, one would need an analysis of conventional discourse about information as well as of the more complicated, more sophisticated, and more highly formalized version of that discourse provided by the language of microeconomics. I have tried to provide both here.

2. Information Overload

My second alternative future is strongly counterintuitive, for it discards not only the basic assumption of post-Enlightenment thought that more information is always a good,[309] but also the assumption that the rate of progress of science and society will vary directly with the rate of accumulation of information. I offer the idea anyway, not because I believe it will necessarily happen, but because the very possibility of this set of events tends to be suppressed by the uncritical acceptance of an Enlightenment view of information.[310]

It could be that we are headed for an information overload—a brownout caused by overproduction and consumption of information. This is an idea that ought to be familiar to the legal profession. During the '80s, bright young lawyers worked hundreds of thousands of hours on contested tender offers and leveraged buyouts. They pored through corporate documents, built up electronic databases to keep track of their research, searched for any case, treatise, or law review article that could

---

308. I think that Foucault would have agreed with this point, even as he would have insisted (again rightly in my view) that grand theory offers exactly the wrong method to *find* and criticize this "discourse."

309. *See* DRÉZE, *supra* note 73.

310. I say this in part because what little writing there is on the impact of "the information society" on law has been profoundly meliorist and optimistic. *See, e.g.,* M. ETHAN KATSCH, THE ELECTRONIC MEDIA AND THE TRANSFORMATION OF LAW (1989). Professor Katsch believes that greater access to information may undermine "abstractions of the law," "such as rights." *Id.* at 262-65. He seems to believe that this process will make the law more "humane," a word that appears here—as it does in some early critical legal theory, *see* Boyle, *supra* note 272—to be an antonym of "abstract." Yet his other positions seem marked by a mainstream liberalism that prods me into wondering whether he wants "abstractions" like "the right of free speech" to be undermined. When he says that the information age will make law more like a conversation, I find myself wondering who will get to talk and who will have to listen. Finally, when he says that privacy will "change," *id.* at 168-97, I find myself beset by dystopian images entirely unlike the ones that appear, from his tone, to be intended by that phrase. All of Professor Katsch's assessments may be right—a transformation devoutly to be wished, no doubt—but it is hard to escape the conclusion that he is able to be so vague and yet so optimistic precisely because he is talking about information—the lifeblood of the Enlightenment. It is from that feeling of unexamined possibilities, contrariness, and general "humbuggery" that this dystopia arises.

give their side an edge, and checked every possible line of authority on computerized legal research services. They even rechecked the final product an hour before filing just to make sure that no more recent decision had been added. On the other side, opposing attorneys did exactly the same thing. Even if one believes that all those takeovers actually led to a more efficient allocation of resources, it is hard to believe that the legal process would not have been just as efficient and just as equitable if both sides had commanded a slightly lower level of effort.

We could describe this legal equivalent of the nuclear arms race in terms of market failure, inefficient discovery rules, prisoners' dilemmas, or hyperlexis. But any thorough analysis would have to concede that one of the problems was not just hyperlexis, but Hyper-LEXIS—an explosion of the availability of information that, under a particular set of societal assumptions and background rules, sometimes leads to a socially irrational investment of resources. There is no *a priori* reason that the idea must be confined to the adversary system. We might imagine a world in which inventors were overwhelmed by the difficulty of searching patent banks, where specialists found it impossible to keep up in their fields, where researchers worked in increasing isolation—an isolation produced by the sheer quantity of available information. Increasing specialization, balkanization of the disciplines, an irrational fixation on "authority" and cross reference, and a scholarly habit of conspicuous citation,[311] even an erosion of public debate by information overload—these signs are not so very alien to the world we live in that we can afford to dismiss them completely. Nor are they so different from the results one would expect in a world that romanticizes authorship and focuses overwhelmingly on incentives to the immediate producer. That might be food for thought.

In the 1930s, welfare economists used the example of the factory that pours pollution into the air but pays nothing for its use. In that case, they declared, a failure to internalize all externalities causes overproduction. If the full social costs of production were taken into account, the current high levels of production might prove uneconomical. Maybe a future Pigou will write an analysis of the blindness of information economics at the close of the twentieth century[312] and will point

---

311. I have to say that I like the irony of saying this at the end of a huge Article whose myriad footnotes are the fruit of every electronic research service the world has to offer.

312. *Cf.* D.M. Lamberton, *The Emergence of Information Economics, in* COMMUNICATION AND INFORMATION ECONOMICS: NEW PERSPECTIVES 7, 7-22 (Meheroo Jussawalla & Helene Ebenfield eds., 1984).

The emergence of information economics can be seen as a response to the deficiencies of economic theory based on perfect knowledge, the failures of policy, or the spectacular advent of intelligent electronics with greatly enhanced capacity for communication, computation, and control. Whichever is the preferred interpretation, it remains a personal judgment whether the battle for recognition and respectability has only just been joined, is well advanced, has been won or perhaps been lost.

Id. at 7.

out that we were oblivious to the "information pollution" we were creating, that our economics did not force us to internalize the consequences of our overproduction, leaving us free to continue to "pollute."[313] Like the welfare economics of the thirties, the economics of information might well lay part of the blame on an ideological insistence on the image of the isolated economic actor. For us, that actor is the author. Our romance is almost as great as the romance with which the classical economists endowed the self-reliant economic atoms of the *Lochner* era.

3. Information Politics

What of the realms in which the author-figure apparently does not play so great a role? What of public debate, privacy, or requirements for disclosure of information advantage in market transactions?[314] Here I am most optimistic. My own views are loosely egalitarian and I favor an expanded and decentralized view of democracy.[315] But egalitarianism and democracy are norms that liberalism confines to a comparatively narrow sphere—as evidenced by everything from the state action requirement to the notion of formal equality in the public sphere. One way to express my conclusions is that, on information issues, liberal political theory is less restrictive. Consequently, from my perspective many of the criticisms aimed at liberalism are less powerful. Precisely because information is conceived of as being different from other forms of wealth and power, precisely because it seems like an "infinite" resource, it does not get exiled to the world of civil society. Information disparities are not simply taken as "given," as a postulate that must be accepted before we begin. Thus, to me it seems that judges are more willing to strike down bargains on the basis of information disparities than other forms of (nonphysical) power disparities, that legislatures are willing to criminalize

---

313. Because of the "infinite" vision of information I discussed earlier, we do not view information as a good, the maximization of which is sometimes harmful. But a moment's reflection should reveal occasions when the unbridled growth of information may actually be hurtful. Some decisions become *harder* with more information. *See* DRÉZE, *supra* note 73. When we think of information not as a good, but as the lifeblood of the public sphere of debate, or the perfect information of a market model, we ignore the *constraints* produced by overproduction. For example, given a retrieval system of a limited capacity, I will prefer to have a smaller database that will give me answers 50% of the time than to add the information necessary to give answers 100% of the time but which so overwhelms my abilities to retrieve and process data that I can only find the answer 40% of the time. In neoclassical price theory, these kinds of trade-offs are exactly the ones that market decisions make so well. Yet the point of this paper has been to show that the double quality of information—both part of the model and a good to be traded under the model—may prevent the operation of economic feedback mechanisms on the level of market behavior, and may make questions of microeconomic analysis undecidable on the level of scholarship. As the case of the polluting factory shows, the parallel to welfare economics operates at both levels, the practical and the theoretical.

314. Of course, as I tried to show earlier, the author ideal often does appear in that particular issue, especially when analyzed by Professor Manne.

315. While admitting that these are abstractions that do not resolve concrete cases, that they frequently contradict each other, and so on, and so on.

insider trading but not other forms of market advantage, that people who see nothing wrong in the state refusing to fund abortion clinics find *Rust v. Sullivan* troubling. When we are analyzing disclosure requirements or the extent of a duty to warn, we are more willing to look at outcomes and results, rather than uniformly equal access—to take into account the actual educational level, social class, and native language of those who are the targets of the warnings, rather than conclusively assuming a formal equality.

Whatever the practical limits of these "exceptions"—and at the moment I would accept them to be enormous—it seems that we apply egalitarian norms more broadly when we are dealing with information rather than with some other form of wealth or power. If we are indeed moving towards an "information-based society"—whatever that means—then we are doing so with a reservoir of egalitarian cultural understandings and political ideals. This fact, in and of itself, guarantees nothing at all. But it is not unimportant, and from my perspective, it is a very good thing.

What about privacy? Egalitarian and redistributive political solutions can be supported by arguments keyed to the requirements of the individual ("to flourish, every human being needs . . .") or supposedly deduced from abstract distributional principles. The interesting thing about privacy is that it follows the former strategy and thus offers up a view of human personality that has normative implications about the control of resources. To be fully a person, one must have control over (fill in the blank). The resource named is information. Again, a society that often has a hard time imagining that persons need control over food, shelter, medical care, and so on, can find room for the idea that the most intimate sphere of personhood must be defined in part by a right to control information—the right of privacy.

When Warren and Brandeis wrote their article, this may not have seemed like much of a challenge to the distribution of power in society. In a society based on the transmission, accumulation, and manipulation of information, it might seem rather more of one. Of course, it could turn out that the ideal of privacy was precisely the basis needed for a discourse of entitlement in an information society. It could be manipulated to allow an electronic society to justify the appropriation of intimate details, just as the labor theory of property was used by Locke to "boot himself up" into market society. Again, one must resist the temptation to reason from rhetoric to reality. Nevertheless, it seems to me that the gradient of argument runs the other way. Using the concept of privacy, one is arguing downhill when challenging the imperial tendencies of a data-based society and arguing uphill when supporting them.

The question that remains to be answered is whether the social harm we should be most concerned about is underproduction, overproduction, the tragedy of the commons, the commercialization of an electronic public sphere, the corrosive effect of information technology on privacy, or merely straightforward distributional inequity. This Article cannot answer that question. Indeed, I have tried to show that there are conceptual reasons why the question is unanswerable in the abstract. But my argument does show that the way that we currently think about information may actually blind us to important aspects of each one of those problems, making us that little bit more helpless in the face of them. On the other hand, some of our current ideas about information offer reservoirs of strategy, tactics, and social belief that—when viewed in the abstract—seem egalitarian in the extreme. To someone like me, who believes a lot of our social ills come from the restriction of egalitarian norms, that fact has an optimistic ring.

We should be careful in drawing too strong a conclusion from this analysis. I have tried to offer a theory of information, but the theory is more like a road map or a tool kit than a blueprint or an algorithm. One cannot *deduce* social consequences from the existence of an authorship theory of intellectual property or an information-centered vision of privacy. This Article can point out tendencies and gradients of argument. It can describe the process of typing information as public or private, finite or infinite. It can work out some of the reasons that the romantic vision of authorship spreads far beyond copyright. It can show the *aporias* at the heart of information economics. It can prognosticate about the way that the rhetoric and ideology of the past will interact with the social arrangements of the future. It can suggest that the information age may be constructed in part around the conflicting valences of a romantic, individualistic notion of information production, an egalitarian notion of public information, and a theory of privacy based on a notion of positive liberty. Ultimately, however, it must end on a note of uncertainty. And that, it strikes me, is entirely appropriate to both its subject and its theme.

[6]

VOLUME 93   MARCH 1980   NUMBER 5

HARVARD LAW REVIEW

THE TRADE SECRET STATUS OF HEALTH AND SAFETY TESTING INFORMATION: REFORMING AGENCY DISCLOSURE POLICIES

Thomas O. McGarity* and Sidney A. Shapiro**

Manufacturers of new drugs, pesticides, and other substances are often required by law to provide federal regulatory agencies with costly test results as a prerequisite to obtaining clearance to go to market. In this Article, Professors McGarity and Shapiro analyze the circumstances under which this information should be made available to the public. Balancing the interests for and against disclosure, they conclude that virtually all test results should be disclosed, although competitors should generally be forbidden for some period of time from making use of the disclosed information in their own test programs.

RECOGNIZING that market mechanisms, even as enhanced by a tort compensation system, do not adequately protect man and the environment from the risks posed by new products, chemicals, and technologies, Congress has empowered several federal regulatory agencies to proscribe the sale of certain products which endanger the public. In making the risk-benefit assessment prerequisite to such a determination, an agency relies upon the results of experimental testing submitted by the proponents of the product. The controversial question whether, and to what extent, such data should be publicly disclosed has recently arisen in several contexts, including approval of new drugs, antibiotics, and food and color additives by the Food and Drug Administration (FDA); and approval of pesticides and chemicals by the Environmental Protection Agency (EPA).

In almost all of these instances, the private regulatees who submit the studies have successfully forestalled most efforts by

* Associate Professor of Law, University of Kansas. B.A., Rice University, 1971; J.D., University of Texas, 1974.

** Associate Professor of Law, University of Kansas. B.S., University of Pennsylvania, 1970; J.D., 1973.

The assistance of the University of Kansas Research Fund is gratefully acknowledged. The authors would like to express their appreciation to Malcolm Burns, Edward Gray, Thomas Krattenmaker, Jeffrey Miller, and Richard Pierce for their comments on earlier drafts of this Article. The authors would also like to acknowledge the assistance of Janice Jacobs, Class of 1981, University of Kansas Law School.

agencies and interested citizens to disclose their contents by claiming that health and safety data are statutorily protected "trade secrets." Moreover, the recent Supreme Court decision in *Chrysler Corp. v. Brown*,[1] by effectively allowing parties to assert trade secrecy claims against agencies, threatens to continue to restrict disclosure.

In Part I, this Article will examine the disclosure question, exploring the social costs and benefits of requiring publication of health and safety testing data. Powerful interests are at stake in balancing the desirability of disclosure against the need for confidentiality. Disclosure may, for example, reduce the incentives for new product research and development by preventing companies from fully recouping the high costs of generating the required test data, and by making it easier for competitors to duplicate and license breakthroughs. Nondisclosure, on the other hand, may hamper scientific progress, deny consumers the opportunity to make fully informed product use decisions, increase the risks that agency decisions based on faulty data or analysis will remain undiscovered, and encourage potentially hazardous duplicative human testing.

Following an explication of the competing policy considerations behind disclosure and nondisclosure, current law is examined in Part II. Present agency disclosure policies are governed by a patchwork of often inconsistent statutes, which generally prohibit agencies from releasing "proprietary information." This raises two important issues. First, where there is conflict between statutes or their underlying policies, agencies and courts must determine the scope of particular enactments and decide which policies shall prevail. *Chrysler* provides some guidance, but fails to cast light on the crucial question of what kinds of information should receive "trade secret" protection and is likely to chill salutary agency attempts to permit disclosure. Second, it is crucial to establish whether health and safety data fall within the scope of "proprietary information" or should be exempted from "trade secret" status. Absent specific statutory language to the contrary, agency regulations generally have uncritically labeled health and safety data as proprietary and thus exempted such information from disclosure under the Freedom of Information Act (FOIA).[2]

An examination of various regulatory schemes in Part II reveals great disparities in the manner in which health and safety testing data are treated across product areas: drug test-

---

[1] 441 U.S. 281 (1979).

[2] 5 U.S.C. § 552 (1976).

ing data remain secret, antibiotic and additive testing data are fully disclosed, while chemical and pesticide data are disclosed subject to compensation for later use by competitors. No underlying principle justifies these differences in approach. This Article concludes that the competing interests for and against disclosure are best accommodated in *each* of the product categories by a system of full disclosure, with innovation incentives protected by means other than nondisclosure. While the pesticide and chemical approaches offer one such alternative, the costs of administering a compensation scheme are substantial. A better solution, elaborated in Part III, would be to couple disclosure with generic "exclusive use periods" which guarantee a data submitter that no one else can use its data to register a product for a specific number of years. Congress should act decisively to mandate such a system. If Congress does not act, specific agency action is recommended to improve the present systems and encourage congressional action.

Before proceeding, it is essential to clarify what sorts of information fall within the category "health and safety testing data." Under the approach recommended below, the breadth of this definition will determine the fate of large amounts of important, sensitive information. For our purposes, the definition of "health and safety study" adopted by the Toxic Substances Control Act (TSCA)[3] will suffice: "any study of any effect of a chemical substance or mixture on health or the environment or on both, including underlying data and epidemiological studies, studies of occupational exposure to a chemical substance or mixture, toxicological, clinical, and ecological studies of a chemical substance or mixture."[4] For drugs, efficacy data are also included. Therefore, the results of any product testing that involves laboratory animals or human subjects fall within the scope of health and safety testing data. The question whether background data, notably chemical identities, proportions, or manufacturing processes should be included is a difficult and sensitive issue discussed below.[5] There are good reasons why the latter sorts of information may warrant protection even if study data are to be released.

I. WEIGHING THE POLICIES FOR AND AGAINST DISCLOSURE

Few would quarrel with the desirability of open government, with the inputs and outputs of governmental decision-

---

[3] 15 U.S.C.A. §§ 2601–2629 (West Supp. 1979).

[4] *Id.* § 2602(6).

[5] *See* pp. 876–78 *infra*.

making subject to public scrutiny. This presumption in favor of disclosure was codified in the FOIA, which guarantees citizens access to certain information possessed by federal agencies. Public access to health and safety data is especially desirable since disclosure enables individuals to decide whether their use of a product poses an unacceptable risk to their own health despite generic agency approval. Nondisclosure may also hamper scientific progress and needlessly endanger human participants in product testing. Yet certain current federal regulatory schemes involving the submission of health and safety testing data effectively reverse the FOIA's salutary presumption in the name of "trade secret" protection.[6] Nondisclosure is chiefly supported by the fear that disclosure will diminish research incentives by reducing the profitability of discovery.

As this Part will demonstrate, an analysis of the competing policy considerations demands that health and safety data be disclosed except where research incentives would be substantially and demonstrably hindered, and could not be protected by methods other than nondisclosure. The case for disclosure is clear; the case for nondisclosure is weakened by conflicting economic studies as well as the existence of alternative means for protecting research incentives.

A. Reasons for Disclosure

Strong policy considerations support disclosing fully the health and safety data submitted to administrative agencies. As this Section will develop, disclosure should improve agency effectiveness, permit better informed consumer choice, avoid wastefully duplicative testing, and promote scientific innovation.

1. Agency Effectiveness. — An agency faces a difficult task in predicting the likely social consequences of a product's use solely on the basis of experimental testing data submitted by the product's proponent. Data are often scientifically inconclusive, permitting reasonable scientists to arrive at different interpretations. Proper regulatory decisionmaking therefore requires the exercise of "scientific judgment."[7] In addition, test sponsors, because of their financial interest in agency approval, often will design and report studies in the light most

---

[6] *See, e.g.*, pp. 868–69 *infra*.

[7] McGarity, *Substantive and Procedural Discretion in Administrative Resolution of Science Policy Questions: Regulating Carcinogens in EPA and OSHA*, 67 GEO. L. J. 729, 741–43 (1979).

favorable to their products.[8] After a product is approved, agencies rarely have the time and resources to reevaluate the original test data in light of changing scientific evaluational criteria. Thus, questionable industry interpretations can remain undetected for years. In one case, fifteen years elapsed between the original regulatory decision to accept the manufacturer's interpretation that the pesticide "heptachlor" did not cause cancer in rats and later evaluation of the same data, buttressed by independent experimentation, finding strong evidence which indicated that "heptachlor" was very likely carcinogenic.[9]

Traditionally, the scientific community minimizes these problems and biases by subjecting one scientist's research results and methods to formal and informal review by other scientists.[10] If, however, the data submitted to agencies may not be disclosed, the data and test methodology never enter the normal peer review channels and are therefore not subject

---

[8] *See* Shapiro, *Divorcing Profit Motivation from New Drug Research: A Consideration of Proposals to Provide the FDA with Reliable Test Data*, 1978 DUKE L.J. 154, 162–63. This problem was graphically illustrated by a situation in which the FDA discovered that G.D. Searle & Co., a drug company, had "made a number of deliberate decisions which seemingly were calculated to minimize the chances of discovering toxicity and/or to allay FDA concern." *Preclinical and Clinical Testing By the Pharmaceutical Industry, 1976: Joint Hearings Before the Subcomm. on Health of the Senate Comm. on Labor and Public Welfare and the Subcomm. on Administrative Practice and Procedure of the Senate Comm. on the Judiciary*, 94th Cong., 2d Sess., pt. 3, at 25 (1976) (statement of Alexander M. Schmidt, M.D., Comm'r, FDA). The discrepancies associated with Searle's presentation were so serious that FDA recommended to the Department of Justice that grand jury proceedings be instituted against Searle. *Id*. at 30. Over the FDA's objections, the U.S. attorney in Chicago dropped the case without presenting it to a grand jury. Washington Post, June 1, 1979, at A9, col. 1.

[9] *See* Testimony of Samuel S. Epstein, M.D., at 59A, 65A–68A, *In re* Velsicol Chem Corp., FIFRA Docket No. 384 (E.P.A. Dec. 24, 1975) (expedited hearing before EPA Administrator); Velsicol Chem. Corp., Consolidated Heptachlor/ Chlordane Hearing, 41 Fed. Reg. 7552, 7566–67 (E.P.A.), *aff'd sub nom.* Environmental Defense Fund, Inc. v. EPA, 548 F.2d 998 (D.C. Cir. 1976), *cert. denied*, 431 U.S. 925 (1977).

[10] H. Anderson & J. Goldsmith, Peer Review and Openness of Information in the Process of Making Environmental and Other Technical Decisions 20–21 (June 11, 1976) (paper prepared for Comm. on Environmental Decision Making, Nat'l Academy of Sciences) [hereinafter cited as Peer Review]; Letter from FDA Commissioner Donald Kennedy to Senator Edward M. Kennedy (May 5, 1978), *reprinted in Drug Regulation Reform Act of 1978: Hearings on S. 2755 Before the Subcomm. on Health and Scientific Research of the Senate Comm. on Human Resources*, 95th Cong., 2d Sess. 841–42 (1978) [hereinafter cited as Kennedy Letter]; *Drug Regulation Reform Act of 1978: Hearings on H.R. 11611 Before the Subcomm. on Health and the Environment of the House Comm. on Regulatory Reform*, 95th Cong., 2d Sess. 1989–90 (1978) (statement of David Rall, M.D.) [hereinafter cited as *House Hearings on Drug Regulation Reform*].

to scrutiny by independent scientists.[11] Cast adrift in such scientific isolation, agency scientists may be more prone to misjudge the accuracy or usefulness of the data submitted. Although agency scrutiny is intended to prevent drug testers from making extravagant claims on account of their data, or even from falsifying the data,[12] the FDA itself admits that its review "has not been entirely sufficient to ensure the integrity or usefulness of [submitted] data."[13] Similarly, a recent independent review of EPA pesticide decisionmaking concluded that the data relied upon were woefully inadequate to support the agency's approval of certain pesticides.[14]

Without traditional peer review, agencies also become prisoners of the expertise of their own scientists. A long series of both independent and FDA reports have documented serious deficiencies in the quality of scientists that can be attracted and retained by the agency.[15] Ironically, this deficiency can be tied to the confidentiality problem. Where professional staff are prohibited from using any materials with which they work in normal peer activities[16] such as publishing, the scientific atmosphere in the agency is stifled and the professional growth of its staff is seriously hampered.[17]

---

[11] *Extending and Amending FIFRA: Hearings Before the Subcomm. on Department Investigations, Oversight, and Research of the House Comm. on Agriculture,* 95th Cong., 1st Sess. 58–59 (1977) (statement of Environmental Defense Fund and Nat'l Audubon Soc'y) [hereinafter cited as *1977 FIFRA Hearings*]; AMERICAN ASSOCIATION FOR THE ADVANCEMENT OF SCIENCE, SCIENTIFIC FREEDOM AND RESPONSIBILITY 20–22 (1975); Peer Review, *supra* note 10, at 18–19; Kennedy Letter, *supra* note 10, at 842.

[12] There have been several prominent instances of such fraud. *See* Shapiro, *supra* note 8, at 166–68. Two former executives of Biometric Testing, Inc., a testing laboratory, recently pleaded guilty to charges of conspiring to falsify data for drug manufacturers. Washington Post, Oct. 6, 1979, at A3, col. 5.

[13] Kennedy Letter, *supra* note 10, at 843.

[14] *See* STAFF OF SUBCOMM. ON ADMINISTRATIVE PRACTICE AND PROCEDURE OF THE SENATE COMM. ON THE JUDICIARY, 94TH CONG., 2D SESS., THE ENVIRONMENTAL PROTECTION AGENCY AND THE REGULATION OF PESTICIDES 34 (Comm. Print 1976) [hereinafter cited as KENNEDY REPORT].

[15] *See* REVIEW PANEL ON NEW DRUG REGULATION, U.S. DEP'T OF HEALTH, EDUCATION & WELFARE, FINAL REPORT app. E, at 12–17, 21–24, 31–34, 36–37, 40 (1977) [hereinafter cited as DRUG REGULATION REPORT].

[16] Many FDA scientists refuse to discuss their work with outsiders for fear of inadvertently disclosing trade secrets, thereby foreclosing practically all contact for these scientists with others in their respective fields. Letter from Anita Johnson, Health Research Group, *et al.*, to HEW Hearing Clerk at 6 (n.d.).

[17] *Drug Regulation Reform Act of 1978: Hearings on S. 2755 Before the Subcomm. on Health and Scientific Research of the Senate Comm. on Human Resources,* 95th Cong., 2d Sess. 645–46 (1978) (testimony of Anita Johnson, Environmental Defense Fund) [hereinafter cited as *Senate Hearings on Drug Regulation Reform*]; *id.* at 668 (testimony of Sidney Wolfe, Health Research Group); *House Hearings on Drug Reg-*

Nondisclosure also may foster a pro-industry bias in agency decisionmaking. Where health and safety data are withheld from the public, industry representatives confront overworked agency personnel under conditions where there is no opportunity for independent observers to scrutinize the existing data and advocate their own inferences based upon their independent policy judgments.[18] As a result, the agency is more likely to accommodate the objectives of its regulatees and perhaps expose the public to serious health risks.[19]

In an open system, by comparison, the agency would not be deprived of the pluralism that is vital to the exercise of informed scientific judgment. Instead, the agency would receive helpful assistance in assessing data from independent scientific and public interest groups[20] and from other pharmaceutical and pesticide companies who may wish to comment.[21] Although the pharmaceutical industry belittles these benefits, contending that few consumers or independent scientists would actually read the disclosed data,[22] public interest groups,[23] the EPA,[24] and the FDA[25] contend that even limited added participation can improve the quality of agency decisions.[26] The fact that consumer representatives and independ-

---

ulation Reform, supra note 10, at 1992 (statement of David Rall, M.D.); DRUG REGULATION REPORT, *supra* note 15, at 35; Kennedy Letter, *supra* note 10.

[18] Whether agencies are systematically biased toward the agencies they regulate has been addressed elsewhere. *See, e.g.*, DRUG REGULATION REPORT, *supra* note 15, at 1 ("FDA is neither pro- nor anti-industry in its review and approval of new drugs"); Stewart, *The Reformation of American Administrative Law*, 88 HARV. L. REV. 1669, 1686 (1975) ("[The] various theses of systematic bias in agency policy are not universally valid."). The EPA is presently regarded by some as retaining the pro-industry attitude of the Office of Pesticides Programs of the Department of Agriculture when that office was transferred to EPA. *See* KENNEDY REPORT, *supra* note 14.

[19] The FDA has been criticized for approving certain drugs and devices later determined to be potentially dangerous to their users. *See, e.g.*, Goldstein, *DES — Still a Threat*, TRIAL, June 1976, at 66, 69, 74–75; Note, *The Intrauterine Device: A Criticism of Governmental Complaisance and An Analysis of Manufacturer and Physician Liability*, 24 CLEV. ST. L. REV. 247, 259–60 (1975); Note, *Liability of Birth Control Pill Manufacturers*, 23 HASTINGS, L.J. 1526, 1533–34 (1972).

[20] *Senate Hearings on Drug Regulation Reform, supra* note 17, at 668 (testimony of Sidney Wolfe, Health Research Group).

[21] *Id.* at 646 (testimony of Anita Johnson, Environmental Defense Fund).

[22] *Id.* at 293 (testimony of C. Joseph Stetler, President, Pharmaceutical Mfrs. Ass'n).

[23] *See* Memorandum of Amicus Curiae Environmental Defense Fund in Opposition to Plaintiffs' Motion for Preliminary Injunction at 2, 4, 16–17, Amchem Prods., Inc. v. EPA, No. 76-2913 (S.D.N.Y., filed Nov. 20, 1978).

[24] *See 1977 FIFRA Hearings, supra* note 11, at 148 (statement of Douglas M. Costle, Adm'r, EPA).

[25] Kennedy Letter, *supra* note 10, at 845.

[26] *See* Bazelon, *Risk and Responsibility*, 205 SCIENCE 277, 278 (1979); Jacks, *The*

ent scientists lack the time or resources to scrutinize all health
and safety data is an insufficient reason to deprive them of the
opportunity to analyze that which they deem important.
Moreover, an open system could have an important prophy-
lactic effect. The threat of scrutiny by critical outsiders may
motivate industry[27] and agency scientific personnel[28] to analyze health and safety data more carefully.

Agency isolation also has a deleterious impact on public
confidence and agency morale. For example, the FDA asserts
that present secrecy policies prevent it from satisfactorily answering its critics, limiting public confidence in its judgments[29]
and causing deep resentment among FDA staff, who cannot
reveal data that would help rebut public attacks against their
decisions.[30] These attitudes, in turn, can result in a more
inefficient process, slowing the approval of beneficial drugs or
pesticides.[31]

2. Independent Consumer Judgment. — The public's interest in the full disclosure of health and safety data extends
beyond the scientific accuracy of agency decisionmaking.
Members of the public have a legitimate interest in knowing
the full health effects of products which receive agency approval so that they can decide for themselves whether to use
them. Indeed, information of this sort is essential to a true
market economy.[32] Agencies, of course, do strive to protect
consumer safety, but do so via very broad risk-benefit determinations for classes of consumers.[33] Since a licensed chemical

---

Public and the Peaceful Atom: Participation in AEC Regulatory Proceedings, 52 TEX.
L. REV. 466, 500–06 (1974).

[27] *Senate Hearings on Drug Regulation Reform, supra* note 17, at 626 (statement
of Marcia D. Greenberger, Center for Law and Social Policy); *id.* at 670 (testimony
of Anita Johnson, Environmental Defense Fund); Kennedy Letter, *supra* note 10, at
843.

[28] *Senate Hearings on Drug Regulation Reform, supra* note 17, at 646 (testimony
of Anita Johnson, Environmental Defense Fund).

[29] *See Regulatory Reform — Federal Power Commission, Food and Drug Administration: Hearings Before the Subcomm. on Oversight and Investigations of the House
Comm. on Interstate and Foreign Commerce*, 94th Cong., 1st & 2d Sess., pt. 2, at
572 (1975–1976) (statement of Alexander Schmidt, Comm'r, EPA).

[30] Crout, *New Drug Regulation and Its Impact on Innovation*, in IMPACT OF
PUBLIC POLICY ON DRUG INNOVATION AND PRICING 249 (S. Mitchell & E. Link eds.
1976).

[31] *See FDA's Review of Initial IND Submissions: A Study of the Process for
Resolving Internal Differences and an Evaluation of Scientific Judgments*, in 2 RE-
VIEW PANEL ON NEW DRUG REGULATION, U.S. DEP'T OF HEALTH, EDUCATION &
WELFARE, INTERIM REPORTS C-43 (1977).

[32] *See* 2 P. AREEDA & D. TURNER, ANTITRUST LAW ¶ 402 (1978).

[33] *See generally* Gelpe & Tarlock, *The Uses of Scientific Information in Environmental Decisionmaking*, 48 S. CAL. L. REV. 371 (1974); McGarity, *supra* note 7;

may harm certain individuals more than it helps them, individual consumers should have available to them information to make decisions, balancing personal risks and benefits.[34] Even if most consumers would never take the time to read health and safety data before making purchasing decisions, consumer oriented media in consultation with scientific experts could use some of this information to inform the public of potential risks.[35]

   3. Unnecessary Duplicative Testing. — Where nondisclosure of health and safety data by one firm forces a second company to replicate the first company's tests in order to obtain approval for a substantially identical product, the second company's duplicative testing may pose unjustifiable risks to human test subjects and inflict unnecessary suffering on numerous additional laboratory animals. Such duplication also wastes scarce scientific resources. A system of full public disclosure of health and safety testing data, although not the only way to prevent these costs of duplicative testing,[36] would be one way to minimize such costs.

   In drug testing, and to a limited extent, pesticide testing, human experimentation is necessary since the human body may interact with a chemical in a manner different from that indicated by preliminary testing in animals.[37] The possibility that human test subjects may suffer unpredictably adverse reactions to a drug in the initial experiment is thought justified by the assumption that such testing will lead to the wisest risk-benefit decision for society as a whole.[38] By contrast, patients

---

Comment, *Implementing the National Environmental Policy Act Through Rulemaking: The Implications of* Natural Resources Defense Council, Inc. v. Nuclear Regulatory Commission, 126 U. Pa. L. Rev. 148 (1977).

[34] Knowledge of the data is particularly important for workers who tend to be "involuntary consumers" of toxic substances. Workers in pesticide plants have in the past been informed that the substances they were working with were harmless, when in fact health and safety data in the files of their employers and of the EPA led to the opposite conclusion. Kennedy Report, *supra* note 14, at 37–41.

[35] Probably the most widely read periodical of consumer-oriented media is *Consumer Reports*, which is published by Consumers Union, a frequent FOIA litigator. Interestingly, that magazine's recent report on the household insecticide diazinon (sometimes called spectracide) was impeded because the extent to which it was contaminated by a toxic impurity was considered by the EPA to be confidential as proprietary data. *Poisons That Don't Belong at Home*, 44 Consumer Rep. 364, 364 (1979).

[36] Such systems include compensated use of disclosed information, *see* pp. 874–76 *infra*, and abbreviated application procedures for previously licensed products, *see, e.g.*, 21 C.F.R. § 314.1(f) (1979).

[37] Wescoe, *A Producer's Viewpoint*, in National Academy of Sciences, How Safe is Safe? 30 (1974) [hereinafter cited as How Safe is Safe?].

[38] *See* Dyck & Richardson, *The Moral Justification for Research Using Human*

in the duplicative test face risks which cannot be similarly defended.[39]

In drug testing, duplication can needlessly deprive ill patients of proven treatments. In the typical drug testing experiment the medical performance of a group of ill patients given the test drug is compared to that of a control group of other ill patients who are usually given a placebo. Of necessity, the latter group of patients is temporarily denied effective treatment and put at risk for no other purpose than to replicate what is already known. Indeed, two German legal scholars have suggested that when such unnecessary inferior treatment predictably leads to a fatality rate higher for the control group than the group receiving the experimental drug, the treating physicians, under German law, would be guilty of manslaughter.[40] Duplicative drug testing can therefore pose risks to human subjects with very little corresponding social gain.

In addition to the special problem of human testing, duplicative testing can be socially wasteful since the safety of the product in question has already been demonstrated.[41] Duplication is particularly unaffordable because of the present shortages of scientific manpower in the fields of pharmacology and toxicology,[42] of clinical physicians available to conduct human drug trials,[43] and of adequate laboratory, animal, and clinical

---

Subjects, in BIOMEDICAL ETHICS AND THE LAW 243–44 (J. Humber & R. Almeder eds. 1976); Lowry, *A Scientist's Viewpoint*, in HOW SAFE IS SAFE?, *supra* note 37, at 113.

[39] Defenders of one system that requires such duplicative tests claim that they can eliminate this problem by cautioning duplicative testers against any unwarranted risks suggested by the original data. *See, e.g.*, Letter from Pfizer, Inc., to FDA Hearing Clerk at 22–23 (Aug. 15, 1977) (comments on DRUG REGULATION REPORT, *supra* note 15); Letter from SmithKline Corp. to FDA Hearing Clerk at 6 (Aug. 11, 1977) (same).

[40] *Experiment Gelungen, Patienten Tot*, DER SPIEGEL, Sept. 11, 1978, at 54. *See generally* Burkhardt & Kienle, *Controlled Clinical Trials and Medical Ethics*, THE LANCET, Dec. 23, 1978, at 1356–59.

It should also be noted that it is unlikely that the subjects in a duplicated test are fully apprised of the fact that the data the test will yield are almost exclusively for commercial purposes and have little to do with advancing medical knowledge. Hence, such researchers may well violate the legal and ethical requirements of obtaining the informed consent of the subjects. Crout, *supra* note 30, at 249.

[41] DRUG REGULATION REPORT, *supra* note 15, at 35; *Senate Hearings on Drug Regulation Reform*, *supra* note 17, at 1597 (testimony of Roger Noll); Kitch, *The Patent System and the New Drug Application: An Evaluation of the Incentives for Private Investment in New Drug Research and Marketing*, in REGULATING NEW DRUGS 102 (R. Landau ed. 1973).

[42] *See House Hearings on Drug Regulation Reform*, *supra* note 10, at 1990 (testimony of David Rall, M.D.). *See also* COMMISSION ON HUMAN RESOURCES, NATIONAL RESEARCH COUNCIL, PERSONNEL NEEDS FOR BIOMEDICAL AND BEHAVIORAL RESEARCH 48–49 (1978) [hereinafter cited as PERSONNEL NEEDS].

[43] *See* PERSONNEL NEEDS, *supra* note 42, at 89–91; Mirkin, *Drug Therapy and*

testing facilities.[44] Moreover, committing scarce scientific resources to duplicative testing may act as a drag on scientific innovation by diverting research and development expertise to unproductive uses.

Duplication has been defended on the grounds that science normally verifies experimental results through replication.[45] The duplication that occurs, however, is not intended as scientific verification; rather, it is performed only to obtain a drug license. It will occur only when business prospects make it attractive and then only to the extent necessary to pass agency approval. Moreover, if the original testing information were not treated as proprietary, it would be subject to an open process of peer scrutiny, which, like replication, could ensure some verification.[46] Finally, regulatory processes that provide agencies with safety data based on actual consumer experiences to augment experimental data could lessen the need for additional verification.[47]

4. Hampering Innovation. — Suppressing scientific data can also hamper innovation by preventing researchers from becoming fully apprised of scientific findings relevant to their work.[48] A panel of the President's Science Advisory Committee asserted that "[n]ot allowing the academic research community access to the detailed results of safety testing can do

---

the Developing Human: Who Cares?, 23 CLINICAL RESEARCH 106, 112 (1975); Trout, *Problems in Drug Research and Development*, in INTERSECTIONS OF LAW AND MEDICINE 57–66 (G. Morris & M. Norton eds. 1972).

[44] *House Hearings on Drug Regulation Reform, supra* note 10, at 1990 (testimony of David Rall, M.D.); S. REP. No. 334, 95th Cong., 1st Sess. 104 (1977).

[45] *See, e.g., Federal Insecticide, Fungicide, and Rodenticide Act: Hearings Before the House Comm. on Agriculture*, 95th Cong., 1st Sess. 321–22 (1977) (statement of John E. Donalds, Dow Chemical U.S.A.) [hereinafter cited as *1977 Agriculture Hearings*].

[46] *See* pp. 841, 843–44 *supra*.

[47] The Senate has approved the FDA's request for the authority to approve certain drugs provisionally, conditional on the requirement that market experience be monitored by the manufacturer and reported back to the agency. S. 1075, 96th Cong., 1st Sess., §§ 128–129, 125 CONG. REC. 13,471 (1979). *See generally*, REVIEW PANEL ON NEW DRUG REGULATION, U.S. DEP'T OF HEALTH, EDUCATION & WELFARE, INTERIM REPORT: EXPANSION OF FDA'S STATUTORY AUTHORITY IN THE PAST — MARKETING PERIOD FOR NEW DRUGS 13–19 (1977). In addition, the FDA is seeking to improve physician and hospital reports systems concerning adverse drug reactions. REVIEW PANEL ON NEW DRUG REGULATIONS, U.S. DEP'T OF HEALTH, EDUCATION & WELFARE, INTERIM REPORT: ADVERSE DRUG REACTION REPORTING SYSTEMS 9–21 (1977).

[48] DRUG BIOEQUIVALENCE PANEL, OFFICE OF TECHNOLOGY ASSESSMENT, DRUG BIOEQUIVALENCE 48 (1974); PANEL ON CHEMICALS & HEALTH, PRESIDENT'S SCIENCE ADVISORY COMMITTEE, CHEMICALS AND HEALTH 126 (1973) [hereinafter cited as CHEMICALS AND HEALTH]; PRESIDENT'S SCIENCE ADVISORY COMMITTEE, HANDLING OF TOXICOLOGICAL INFORMATION 5 (1966).

much to slow our progress in the understanding of the presence or absence of unfortunate effects of chemicals on people."[49] It might be argued that scientists will be alerted to new developments through information obtained informally from colleagues and published articles or directly from the sponsoring company or its investigators.[50] But in fact, firms are not always willing to disclose health and safety data, since, if released, the data would no longer be proprietary.[51] For example, some companies condition disclosure on the availability of patent protection.[52] Also, if a company were to publish only some of its data, its selection of which data to reveal might not correspond to the needs of the scientific community. In the final analysis, while companies may occasionally publish data as a contribution to scientific knowledge, much data will be kept secret out of economic self-interest.[53]

B. *The Argument Against Disclosure*

The case for nondisclosure reflects legitimate concerns, but is undermined by conflicting and uncertain evidence. The key question is whether confidentiality is necessary to foster research and innovation. This Section examines that dilemma and concludes that industry has not yet come forth with convincing evidence that research incentives would be appreciably harmed by disclosure of health and safety data. Moreover,

---

[49] CHEMICALS AND HEALTH, *supra* note 48, at 126. *See also* Kennedy Letter, *supra* note 10 at 843:

> FDA is one of the largest repositories of drug information in the world. On matters such as pharmacokinetics, estimation of human risks from animal studies, potential new uses for older drugs, and techniques to reduce human risk and increase the scientific validity of drug testing, information of immense value to humanity may be locked away in the agency's files. We lack the resources to explore that storehouse of data for information of general scientific interest. But if we are permitted to make those data available to scientists, I believe that some will take an interest, and that large benefits may well result.

[50] Letter from R. Keith Cannan, Chairman, Division of Medical Sciences, National Research Council, to Senator Hubert Humphrey (n.d.), *reprinted in Hearings on Interagency Coordination in Drug Research and Regulation Before the Subcomm. on Reorganization and International Organizations of the Senate Comm. on Government Operations*, 88th Cong., 1st Sess. 1896 (1963).

[51] *See* p. 862 *infra*.

[52] Letter from Eli Lilly & Co. to FDA Hearing Clerk at 2 (Aug. 12, 1977) (comments on DRUG REGULATION REPORT, *supra* note 15) ("At Eli Lilly and Company our commitment to the free and full exchange of scientific information, in keeping with scientific tradition, is of long standing. *After patent protection is established*, our company and its scientists have a policy of submitting for publication all pertinent data . . ." (emphasis added).).

[53] *See* Whyte, *Drug Company Concerns and Opportunities — How We Will Cope*, 30 FOOD DRUG COSM. L.J. 338, 340 (1975).

there are methods other than nondisclosure to protect research incentives.[54]

   1. Legitimate Concerns About Research Incentives. — The slow current pace of discovery and innovation in industries subject to agency health and safety approval requirements warrants serious concern. For example, from October, 1975 to June, 1978, the FDA approved only six drugs that the agency regarded as "important" therapeutic gains,[55] despite the fact that drug testing data was not disclosed.[56] Present regulatory systems force a product down a tortuous path from discovery to marketability: the average drug requires between 4.5 and 8.5 years of testing at an average cost of 2.7 to 4.7 million dollars,[57] while the average pesticide requires 5 to 7 million dollars.[58] The fear is that the disclosure of health and safety testing data will further erode the ability of a company to reap the benefits of innovation, reducing the incentives to engage in research.

   Potential detriments to an innovator from disclosure of health and safety testing data can be easily identified. Where a product is not protected by a patent, the data could be submitted by a competitor in support of an application to a regulatory agency for approval of an equivalent product.[59] In light of the time and expense of testing, this would deprive an innovator of substantial lead time and impose on it a significant cost disadvantage. Pharmaceutical and pesticide manufacturers also allege that testing data could be used by competitors to obtain foreign licenses to market competing products.[60] Such "piracy" may be aided by the fact that patent

---

[54] *See* p. 857 *infra.*

[55] *See How the FDA Rates Prescription Drugs,* 43 CONSUMER REP. 578 (1978). The FDA also classified 20 drugs as "modest therapeutic gains." *Id.* at 579–81.

[56] *See* pp. 868–69 *infra.*

[57] Clymer, *The Economics of Drug Innovation,* in THE DEVELOPMENT AND CONTROL OF NEW DRUG PRODUCTS 112 (M. Pernarowski & M. Darrach eds. 1971). *See generally* Schnee & Caglarcan, *The Changing Pharmaceutical Research and Development Environment,* in THE PHARMACEUTICAL INDUSTRY 96–97 (C. Lindsay ed. 1978).

[58] *See* S. REP. NO. 334, 95th Cong., 1st Sess. 30 (1977).

[59] *See* F. Dworkin, Impact of Disclosure of Safety and Efficacy Data on Expenditures for Pharmaceutical Research and Development 12 (Apr. 1978) (Staff Paper, Economic Analysis Group, FDA Office of Planning and Evaluation). Apart from nondisclosure, this problem may be avoided by not permitting one company to submit another company's testing data, or by forcing the latter to pay the former. *See* p. 875 *infra.*

[60] *See, e.g., 1977 FIFRA Hearings, supra* note 11, at 465 (statement of Jack E. Early, President, Nat'l Agricultural Chems. Ass'n); *1977 Agriculture Hearings, supra* note 45, at 324 (statement of John E. Donald, Dow Chem. U.S.A.); *Senate Hearings on Drug Regulation Reform, supra* note 17, at 296–97 (testimony of C. Joseph Stetler,

protection may be unavailable in certain significant foreign markets.[61] Disclosure of health and safety testing data may also provide competitors with insights concerning their own research in similar areas for related products.[62] Such insights could lead to a breakthrough that would undermine the ability of the original innovator to reap the benefits of its innovation.

It might be argued that the nondisclosure of health and safety data is not necessary to protect innovating firms from competition since the seventeen-year monopoly granted by the patent system affords the needed shield. The drug and chemical industries, however, have identified three reasons why the patent system may be inadequate to protect their incentives for innovation.

First, some discoveries are unpatentable because they do not meet the statutory requirement of being new, novel and nonobvious.[63] For example, innovations that are easily synthesized from other known chemicals or which constitute the discovery that a known drug can be used for a previously unknown purpose may be unpatentable because they will be considered "obvious."[64] For pesticides, innovations lack patent protection if they are composed of active ingredients that were known to kill pests before the attempt to patent them[65] or, possibly, if they are biological pesticides such as pest diseases.[66]

The extent of protection that the patent laws provide is also affected by the fact that actual protection can be shorter than the prescribed seventeen-year period. Although in some

---

President, Pharmaceutical Mfrs. Ass'n); *id.* at 678 (testimony of Robert B. Clark, President, Hoffmann-LaRoche, Inc.).

[61] *Senate Hearings on Drug Regulation Reform, supra* note 17, at 303 (Memorandum of Pharmaceutical Mfrs. Ass'n) (Argentina, Brazil, Canada, India, Italy, Mexico, and Spain do not give meaningful patent protection for drugs). In addition, in major markets such as France, Germany, and Great Britain, some new drugs are not patentable and others, while patentable, may turn out to be difficult to protect against infringement. *Id.* at 305.

[62] Dworkin, *supra* note 59, at 12; *see Senate Hearings on Drug Regulation Reform, supra* note 17, at 293 (statement of C. Joseph Stetler, President, Pharmaceutical Mfrs. Ass'n); *id.* at 674–75 (testimony of Robert B. Clark, President, Hoffmann-LaRoche, Inc.); Whyte, *supra* note 53, at 340; Letter from Pfizer, Inc., to FDA Hearing Clerk at 25 (Aug. 15, 1977).

[63] Kitch, *supra* note 41, at 86–87; *see* 35 U.S.C. §§ 101–103 (1976).

[64] Kitch, *supra* note 41, at 96–98; *see* 35 U.S.C. § 103 (1976).

[65] *See 1977 Agriculture Hearings, supra* note 45, at 360 (testimony of J. Conner, General Counsel, Nat'l Agricultural Chems. Ass'n). Carbon tetrachloride and lead arsenate are two such ingredients. *Id.*

[66] The Supreme Court has recently agreed to decide whether novel biolgical organisms are patentable. Application of Bergy, 596 F.2d 952 (C.C.P.A.), *cert. granted*, 100 S. Ct. 261 (1979).

cases, a pending patent application will deter competitors from marketing a substitute even before the patent is granted so that there is "effective" protection for more than seventeen years,[67] in other cases, companies may shorten the "effective life" of a patent by filing an application as early as possible in the research and development process, often long before that process and agency approval are complete.[68] The latter possibility occurs often enough so that the average effective life of a drug patent is estimated at only about twelve to thirteen years[69] and that of a pesticide patent at only about seven to ten years.[70]

Finally, a patent may offer effective protection from competition only for the time it takes competitors to invent a noninfringing substitute product. For drugs, a later substitute, known as a "follow-on" drug, may be a distinct innovation or merely a molecular modification of the innovation itself. These follow-on drugs are possible because the original innovator may not anticipate and patent all the chemical variants of its drug, thereby allowing the development of a competing product based on the concept embodied in the original patent.[71] Follow-on drugs can rapidly follow an original drug innovation onto the market. For example, a survey of the markets for seven therapeutic drugs found that the mean time period between the marketing of the innovation and the appearance of the first follow-on drug was only three years.[72]

2. *Evaluation of the Nondisclosure Argument.* — On the basis of current information, it is uncertain that disclosure of

[67] Kitch, *supra* note 41, at 84–85.

[68] *Id.* at 85; Pracon, Inc., Study to Assess Impacts of Releasing Safety and Effectiveness Data on the Pharmaceutical Industry's Incentives to Invest in and Conduct Research and Development Program, FDA Contract 223-77-8052, at 81–82 (n.d.).

[69] D. SCHWARTZMAN, INNOVATION IN THE PHARMACEUTICAL INDUSTRY 180 (1976) (average effective patent life for period 1966–1973 was 13.1 years; for 1970–1973, 12.4 years); Forman, *Drug Patents, Compulsory Licenses, Prices and Innovation*, in THE ECONOMICS OF DRUG INNOVATION 185 (J. Cooper ed. 1969) (12.0 years); Lasagna, *The Development and Regulation of New Medications*, 200 SCIENCE 871, 871–72 (1978) (about 11 years).

The range of protection, however, is considerable. About one-sixth of new drug innovations receive either greater than 17 years of effective protection and about another one-sixth receive effective protection for less than 10 years. D. SCHWARTZMAN, *supra*, at 170.

[70] *See 1977 Agriculture Hearings, supra* note 45, at 236 (supplementary statement of Nat'l Agricultural Chems. Ass'n).

[71] *See* D. SCHWARTZMAN, *supra* note 69, at 306.

[72] Pracon, Inc., *supra* note 68, at 58. *See also* Kemp, *The Follow-on Development Process and the Market for Diuretics*, in DRUG DEVELOPMENT AND MARKETING 255, 260–61, 265–67 (R. Helms ed. 1975) (follow-on competition within one to four years in diuretics market) [hereinafter cited as DRUG DEVELOPMENT].

health and safety data would actually have a serious adverse impact on innovation. First, disclosure of such data may not give competitors significant licensing and intelligence advantages. Second, empirical evidence is in conflict over whether profitability in the relevant industries is so precarious or sensitive that disclosure of health and safety data, where not currently permitted, would substantially destroy research incentives. Unless industry comes forward with better evidence in these two areas, uncertain fears about the incentives for innovation should not stand in the way of disclosure.

Strong evidence contradicts several of the arguments for nondisclosure. For example, HEW estimates that seventy-five percent of all drugs sold in 1976 were manufactured by only one source.[73] Innovating companies may protect their patent positions by attempting to patent a broad spectrum of chemicals similar to the one under active investigation[74] or may enforce their patent rights against related follow-on products under the "doctrine of equivalents."[75] Under the latter concept, when two chemicals work in substantially the same manner and accomplish the same result, they may be considered the same for purposes of patent infringement even though they differ in name, shape or form.[76] Even without patent protection, market imperfections can protect the ability of an innovator to reap monopoly benefits. In the drug area, for example, a recent Federal Trade Commission (FTC) study concluded that physicians display a strong and continued preference for the first brand of a product to appear and for follow-on brands marketed by the same firm.[77] The study found that these preferences existed even where the innovative drug was not patented and thus subject to almost immediate competition.[78] A useful example is Eli Lilly's patent on the analgesic

---

[73] *Pricing of Drugs: Hearings Before the Subcomm. on Health and Scientific Research of the Senate Comm. on Human Resources and Subcomm. on Antitrust and Monopolies of the Senate Comm. on the Judiciary*, 95th Cong., 1st Sess. 29–30 (1977) (testimony of Robert Derzon, Adm'r, Health Care Financing Adm'n) [hereinafter cited as *Pricing of Drugs Hearings*].

[74] Dworkin, *supra* note 59, at 12.

[75] *See* 7 A. DELLER, WALKER ON PATENTS §§ 546, 571–572 (2d ed. 1972).

[76] *See* Graver Tank & Mfg. Co. v. Linde Air Prods. Co., 339 U.S. 605, 608–09 (1950).

[77] *See* FEDERAL TRADE COMMISSION, SALES PROMOTION AND PRODUCT DIFFERENTIATION IN TWO PRESCRIPTION DRUG MARKETS 76 (1977) (Staff Report) [hereinafter cited as FTC STAFF REPORT]; *accord, Pricing of Drugs Hearings, supra* note 73, at 31 (1977) (testimony of Robert Derzon, Adm'r, Health Care Financing Adm'n). However, the FTC did recognize that innovative competition may persuade physicians to alter their preferences. FTC STAFF REPORT, *supra*, at 76.

[78] FTC STAFF REPORT, *supra* note 77, at 77. *But see* Pracon, Inc., *supra* note 68, at 53–55.

Darvon. Although its patent expired in 1971, Darvon still retained a ninety percent market share in 1979.[79] While recent public interest in lower cost generic drugs[80] could lessen the effect of physician brand loyalty, to date, acceptance of generic drugs has been slow.[81]

The ability of competitors to use disclosed health and testing data to gain an advantage in obtaining foreign licenses must be seriously questioned in light of the findings of a FDA report. In a study of the nine foreign markets accounting for two-thirds of all foreign drug sales by American multinational firms,[82] the FDA found that the effect of releasing data would be minimal in all but one of those countries.[83] In some cases, data required by federal agencies would be either unacceptable[84] or unnecessary[85] to achieve foreign regulatory approval. The FDA also suggested that market imperfections would provide significant protection beyond that granted by foreign patent laws.[86] An eminent economist has noted that American companies do not show substantially lower sales in countries where they are unable to obtain patent protection and where regulatory standards are low, enabling competitors to obtain a drug license by only submitting published medical journal articles.[87] He therefore labeled estimates of the sales at risk from releasing data a "gross overstatement."[88]

Underlying the uncertainty about the effect on research

---

[79] Smith, *Federal Government Faces Painful Decision on Darvon*, 203 SCIENCE 857, 857 (1979).

[80] *See generally Substitute Prescription Drug Act: Hearings on H.R. 1963 Before the Subcomm. on Consumer Protection and Finance of the House Comm. on Interstate and Foreign Commerce*, 95th Cong., 2d Sess. (1978); *FDA Drug List: Key to Generic Substitution*, FDA CONSUMER, Feb. 1979, at 15.

[81] Lublin & Laroslovsky, *Generic Drugs Provide No Big Savings So Far in Nation's Health Bill*, Wall St. J., Dec. 7, 1978, at 1, col. 6.

[82] U.S. FOOD & DRUG ADMINISTRATION, SUPPLEMENTARY ANALYSES OF THE IMPACT OF PROVISION IN S. 2755 REGARDING DISCLOSURE OF SAFETY AND EFFECTIVENESS DATA ON FOREIGN MARKETS OF U.S. MULTINATIONAL FIRMS 1 (n.d.) [hereinafter cited as FDA SUPPLEMENTARY ANALYSES].

[83] *Id.* at 3. Based on data supplied by the Bureau of Drugs, the FDA analysis led to a prediction of minimal impact in all but one of the countries. When different data from the International Federation of Pharmaceutical Manufacturers and from FDA assessments were substituted, predictions were for a minimal impact in five and six countries, respectively, with somewhat more serious consequences predicted in the remaining countries. *Id.* at 2–3, 5.

[84] *Id.* at 1, 7–9.

[85] *See Senate Hearings on Drug Regulation Reform, supra* note 17, at 250 (testimony of Donald Kennedy, Comm'r, FDA).

[86] FDA SUPPLEMENTARY ANALYSES, *supra* note 82, at 5.

[87] *House Hearings on Drug Regulation Reform, supra* note 10, at 2162 (testimony of Prof. Roger Noll).

[88] *Id.*

incentives of government disclosure policies is a conflict in empirical evidence about the profitability of the industries that must routinely obtain agency approval on health and safety grounds. In the case of the drug industry, which perhaps has received the greatest scrutiny from economists, there is support both for those who would argue that profitability is so low that any decrease in the benefits to be reaped from research could be catastrophic and for those who would argue that profitability is so high that substantially reduced protection of testing results would still not make investment in drug research worse than alternative investment opportunities.

One set of economists has suggested that ethical drug firms may be shifting resources away from drug research and development (R&D) and into activities offering more promising rates of return.[89] Some empirical results support this conclusion and show that the rate of return on R&D for drugs is less than for comparable alternative investments.[90] One such study found an expected average rate of return of three percent for drugs, as compared to an expected average rate of ten percent in other industries.[91]

These results seem implausible. If the rate of return for drugs was in fact seven percentage points below other comparable investments, drug industry R&D investment would drastically decline. Instead, in constant dollars, it has been at a steady level or, at worst, has declined by some small amount.[92] In absolute terms, most major pharmaceutical firms have consistently increased their research spending, while only a small number of firms have either eliminated or sharply reduced R&D expenditures.[93] One explanation for this appar-

---

[89] Grabowski, Vernon & Thomas, *The Effects of Regulatory Policy on the Incentives to Innovate: An International Comparative Analysis*, in IMPACT OF PUBLIC POLICY ON DRUG INNOVATION AND PRICING 47, 53 (S. Mitchell & E. Link eds. 1976).

[90] *See* D. SCHWARTZMAN, *supra* note 69, at 146; Clymer, *The Economic and Regulatory Climate: U.S. and Overseas Trends*, in DRUG DEVELOPMENT, *supra* note 72, at 137, 141–42.

[91] D. SCHWARTZMAN, *supra* note 69, at 146, 160.

[92] *See* Grabowski, Vernon & Thomas, *supra* note 89, at 53–54.

[93] Schnee & Caglarcan, *supra* note 57, at 97. *See also* Temin, *Technology, Regulation, and Market Structure in the Modern Pharmaceutical Industry*, 10 BELL J. ECON. 429, 431 (1979). Professor Schwartzman believes that the increase in investment can be explained by the fact that some firms expect to do better than the average return based on their previous performance, that firms must maintain some research if they are to compete successfully, and that firms may simply be gambling that they can produce a drug which is immensely successful. D. SCHWARTZMAN, *supra* note 69, at 147–48. *See also* Clymer, *The Economics of Drug Innovation*, in THE DEVELOPMENT AND CONTROL OF NEW DRUG PRODUCTS 109, 126 (M. Pernarowski & M. Darrach eds. 1971). Another group of economists has suggested that the adjustment of R&D spending to lower rates of return might not have occurred yet because of a

ently irrational behavior may be that the foregoing return calculations are in error. The unavailability of accurate profit information from drug manufacturers on which to base estimates may have caused a substantial understatement of present research profit expectations.[94]

Some economists have argued that the conventionally calculated rate of return, which is historical in perspective, merely reflects the research success of companies in the 1960's and does not yet measure the less successful research results of the present period.[95] They also contend that those accounting methods overstate profits by failing to match income generated, which occurs some years after the R&D, with the costs attributable to that income.[96] Finally, these economists suggest that the resulting overstatement of income may be greater for the pharmaceutical industry than other domestic industries because it spends a disproportionately greater amount on R&D.[97]

In an attempt to avoid some of these accounting infirmities, economists have recalculated firm profit rates by capitalizing R&D expenditures instead of treating them as expenses — a mechanism which more fully reflects the relationship between later-arriving income and the expenses that created it.[98] When R&D costs are capitalized, pharmaceutical profits decline, sometimes by a considerable amount.[99] But when these studies compare the resulting rates to those of other industries, using various methodologies, the pharmaceutical industry still

---

lag in industry reaction. Grabowski, Vernon & Thomas, *Estimating the Effects of Regulation on Innovation: An International Comparative Analysis of the Pharmaceutical Industry*, 21 J.L. & ECON. 133, 158 (1978).

These theories lack plausibility, however, since according to Professor Schwartzman's study, drug industry research is far less profitable than alternative investments. In such circumstances, a more immediate change in the pattern of investment would be expected.

[94] *See* Scherer, *Commentary*, in DRUG DEVELOPMENT, *supra* note 72, at 121, 121–22.

[95] D. SCHWARTZMAN, *supra* note 69, at 63, 138.

[96] *Id.* at 137–38; Ayanian, *The Profit Rates and Economic Performance of Drug Firms*, in DRUG DEVELOPMENT, *supra* note 72, at 81, 82–83; Brozen, *Foreword* to K. CLARKSON, INTANGIBLE CAPITAL AND RATES OF RETURN 7–8 (1977); Bloch, *True Profitability Measures for Pharmaceutical Firms*, in REGULATION, ECONOMICS, AND PHARMACEUTICAL INNOVATION 147, 148 (J. Cooper ed. 1976); Stauffer, *Profitability Measures in the Pharmaceutical Industry*, in DRUG DEVELOPMENT, *supra* note 72, at 97, 99–101.

[97] Ayanian, *supra* note 96, at 82; Stauffer, *supra* note 96, at 97, 112–13.

[98] K. CLARKSON, *supra* note 96, at 36–40; Ayanian, *supra* note 96, at 82–83, 88–91; Bloch, *supra* note 96, at 154–55.

[99] K. CLARKSON, *supra* note 96, at 64 (30% decrease); Ayanian, *supra* note 96, at 88 (25% decrease); Bloch, *supra* note 96, at 155.

remains significantly more profitable than average.[100] In one such comparison, it still exceeded the mean average for other industries by thirty-three percent.[101]

This conflict concerning pharmaceutical profitability cannot be resolved on the basis of available public evidence. The economic studies seem to understate the present rate of return and accounting data appear to overstate it. This absence of relevant information confounds any attempt to determine how sensitive drug industry research incentives would be to switching from nondisclosure to disclosure of health and safety testing data.[102] Information from the drug industry itself further contributes to the confusion. While belittling its profitability to stave off data disclosure, the industry has presented a more favorable profit picture to the readers of business publications who might purchase drug company stocks.[103]

---

[100] K. CLARKSON, *supra* note 96, at 64 (12.89% versus median of 9.6% for selected industries); Ayanian, *supra* note 96, at 89 (13.69% versus median of 12.4% for firms in Fortune 500); Temin, *supra* note 93, at 432. *See also* Brozen, *supra* note 96, at 2.

Some economists have attributed some portion of this higher return to the fact that the drug industry is more risky than other industries. *See* Schnee & Caglarcan, *The Economic Structure and Performance of the Ethical Pharmaceutical Industry*, in THE PHARMACEUTICAL INDUSTRY 23, 38–39 (C. Lindsey ed. 1978). Other economists have disputed that any difference in risk exists since examples of unstable or occasionally below average company profits are difficult to find. Schifrin, *The Ethical Drug Industry: The Case for Compulsory Patent Licensing*, 12 ANTITRUST BULL. 893, 910 (1967). The capital asset pricing model predicts that ethical drug stocks are in fact riskier than the market, but not to the extent reflected in the higher returns seen above. A composite beta for the industry, computed by a weighted sales average of major corporations in the industry, is 1.10, suggesting that the ethical drug industry is only some 10% riskier than the risk level of the average market portfolio (which carries a beta of 1). *See* 4 Value Line Investment Survey 592–607 (Oct. 26, 1979). *See generally* Modigliani & Pogue, *An Introduction to Risk and Return: Concepts and Evidence*, in V. BRUDNEY & M. CHIRELSTEIN, CASES AND MATERIALS ON CORPORATE FINANCE 1156–63 (1979); Pogue & Lall, *Corporate Finance: An Overview*, in MODERN DEVELOPMENTS IN FINANCIAL MANAGEMENT 26, 28–31 (S. Myers ed. 1976).

[101] K. CLARKSON, *supra* note 96, at 64.

[102] A second confounding factor is the fact that a decision as to future investment decisions will be made by pharmaceutical industry managers whose individual management perspectives will affect their investment decisions. As a consequence, an FDA-sponsored study concluded:

> [W]e think a negative impact *will* occur if safety and effectiveness data are disclosed, but the net reaction of the industry will be largely determined by the managements of individual firms, each differing in terms of financial resources, risk-taking propensity, product mix, non-pharmaceutical diversification and general views — optimistic vs. pessimistic — about firm and industry futures.

Pracon, Inc., *supra* note 68, at 87.

[103] *See, e.g.*, *Eli Lilly: New Life in the Drug Industry*, BUS. WEEK, Oct. 29, 1979, at 134 ("Like the premature reports of Mark Twain's death, . . . the bleak assessments of the drug industry's future have proven to be highly exaggerated."); Baris, *SmithKline's Revival*, N.Y. Times, Sept. 16, 1979, § 3, at 1, col. 4.

C. *Weighing the Interests For and Against Disclosure*

Even were the choice merely between the polar extremes of pure disclosure and pure nondisclosure of health and safety testing data, current information would compel disclosure. Nondisclosure frustrates agency effectiveness and consumer free choice while imposing significant duplicative testing costs. Proof that secrecy is necessary to promote research investment is at best equivocal. Patents and market imperfections provide some protection for research incentives, even if data are disclosed. It is conceivable that industry may one day establish that profit rates are so dangerously low that nondisclosure of health and safety testing data is essential to facilitate product innovation. Since such information is uniquely within the control of industry and since the case for disclosure is substantial, the burden of establishing the need for secrecy properly belongs with the individual regulated industries.

The case for disclosure is stronger when one departs from examining only pure disclosure and nondisclosure systems. Along with a basic disclosure scheme one may build in protections for the intelligence and licensing advantages relinquished by data producers. Alternatively, a basic nondisclosure scheme may be supplemented with protections against duplicative testing or mechanisms to promote agency effectiveness. Some of these "mixed" systems will be evaluated in the next Part of this Article by examining several of the systems currently in operation.

II. AN EXAMINATION OF CURRENT LAW

This Part explores the manner in which present law accommodates the competing interests for and against disclosure of health and safety testing data by examining the general structure of the law, the specific regulatory frameworks, and the effect of recent court decisions. An agency, in deciding whether to disclose health and safety data, is faced with two separate questions. First, the agency must decide the extent to which "proprietary information" — a general term used here to encompass the terms "trade secrets," "confidential business information," or "privileged information" — may be disclosed to the public. This determination is complicated by the fact that a patchwork of statutes, including the FOIA, the Trade Secrets Act, and the agency's own substantive regulatory scheme, addresses the issue of disclosure of proprietary information.[104] Second, the agency must determine whether

---

[104] A number of separate statutes in the United States Code, many of which are safety statutes, contain some provision for protecting proprietary information in gov-

the health and safety data it has received qualify as proprietary information. Where it is ultimately found that the health and safety data should be disclosed, the agency must be prepared to answer the possible charge that forced disclosure constitutes a taking of property without just compensation. This Part will address these questions before examining specific agency practices.

A. Resolving the Statutory Tangle

The question whether an agency can release proprietary information is complicated by the existence of laws which both encourage and discourage disclosure. The FOIA requires agencies to release all governmental information except that which may fall into nine categorical exceptions.[105] The pertinent exception here is "exemption four," which exempts "trade secrets and commercial or financial information obtained from a person and privileged or confidential."[106] The Trade Secrets Act establishes criminal penalties for the disclosure of "proprietary information" unless such disclosure has been "authorized by law."[107] Recently, in *Chrysler Corp. v. Brown*,[108] the Supreme Court delineated the interaction among these two statutes and the provisions regarding disclosure in specific regulatory statutes.

---

ernment files. Many of the statutes concerning the disclosure of such information simply reference the protection supplied by 18 U.S.C. § 1905 (1976). *See, e.g.*, Energy Supply and Environmental Coordination Act of 1974, § 11(d), 15 U.S.C. § 796(d) (1976); Flammable Fabrics Act § 4(c), 15 U.S.C. § 1193(c) (1976). Some also reference exemption four of the Freedom of Information Act, 5 U.S.C. § 552(b)(4) (1976), which protects trade secrets. *See, e.g.*, Consumer Product Safety Act § 6(a)(1), 15 U.S.C. § 2055(a)(1) (1976); Federal Fire Prevention and Control Act of 1974, § 20, 15 U.S.C. § 2217 (1976). Finally, still other statutes have their own unique "trade secret" provisions. *See, e.g.*, 7 U.S.C. § 12-1 (1976) (Dep't of Agriculture); 15 *id.* § 46(f) (FTC).

[105] 5 U.S.C. § 552(b)-(c) (1976).

[106] *Id.* § 552(b)(4).

[107] 18 *id.* § 1905. The section provides:

Whoever, being an officer or employee of the United States or of any department or agency thereof, publishes, divulges, discloses, or makes known in any manner or to any extent *not authorized by law* any information coming to him in the course of his employment or official duties . . . *which information concerns or relates to the trade secrets, processes, operations, style of work, or apparatus, or to the identity, confidential statistical data, amount or source of any income, profits, losses, or expenditures* of any person, firm, partnership, corporation, or association; or permits any income return or copy thereof or any book containing any abstract or particulars thereof to be seen or examined by any person except as provided by law; shall be fined not more than $1,000, or imprisoned not more than one year, or both; and shall be removed from office or employment.

(Emphasis added).

[108] 441 U.S. 281 (1979).

In *Chrysler*, the Chrysler Motor Corporation sued to enjoin the Defense Department from releasing information about Chrysler's employment of women and minorities pursuant to a private request for disclosure of the information under the FOIA. Chrysler claimed that the information was proprietary and that the FOIA and the Trade Secrets Act prohibited its release. The United States Supreme Court held that Chrysler enjoyed no direct private right of action to enjoin a violation of the Trade Secrets Act, but that a violation of the Act could be enjoined under section ten of the Administrative Procedure Act (APA),[109] which provides that a reviewing court shall "hold unlawful and set aside agency action . . . not in accordance with law."[110] The Court reasoned that "any disclosure that violates [the Trade Secrets Act] is 'not in accordance with law' within the meaning of the [APA]."[111]

The Court opened the door to greater governmental disclosure by holding that the FOIA exemptions are not absolute and that an agency has discretion to release information within an FOIA exemption.[112] The Court also held, however, that information that falls within the Trade Secrets Act may not be released.[113] The Court rejected the government's argument that since the FOIA exemptions are discretionary, the FOIA itself authorizes regulations which permit the release of the information within the "authorized by law" proviso of the Trade Secrets Act.[114] In rejecting this interpretation, the Court reasoned that since materials exempt from disclosure under the FOIA are outside that Act's mandate that information *must* be disclosed, the government could not rely on the FOIA as congressional authorization for the release of such information.[115]

The government also argued that the provision commonly referred to as the "housekeeping statute,"[116] which provides

---

[109] *Id.* at 318. Jurisdiction to review agency action under the APA is governed by 28 U.S.C. § 1331 (1976). *See* Califano v. Sanders, 430 U.S. 99 (1977).

[110] 5 U.S.C. § 706(2)(b) (1976).

[111] 441 U.S. at 318.

[112] *Id.* at 294. The Court found that the language of the FOIA itself, the nature of the judicial review provisions which concern only the person requesting the information, and the legislative history all clearly indicate the nonmandatory nature of the exemptions. *Id.* at 290–94. The Court also noted that in other statutes, where Congress wanted to make an exemption mandatory, it clearly stated that purpose in the statute. *Id.* at 293 n.14.

[113] *Id.* at 317–18.

[114] *Id.* at 303–04.

[115] *Id.*

[116] 5 U.S.C. § 301 (1976). The section provides:

The head of an Executive department or military department may prescribe regulations for the government of his department, the conduct of its employees,

that an executive department may prescribe such regulations as are necessary to carry out its business, provided the authorization to release the information.[117] Again, the Court disagreed with the contention and found instead that Congress intended that provision to authorize only "procedural" rules concerning the organization of an agency and not "substantive" rules permitting the release of proprietary information.[118]

The *Chrysler* Court served notice that for an agency's disclosure regulation to satisfy the Trade Secrets Act there must be some identifiable "nexus" between the disclosure regulation and the delegation of legislative authority for its promulgation.[119] Two kinds of statutory authorizations conceivably can satisfy the Court's criteria. First, Congress occasionally has given an agency explicit authority to release particular kinds of information that otherwise might be subject to a trade secrecy claim.[120] As will later be developed, both the Toxic

---

the distribution and performance of its business, and the custody, use, and preservation of its records, papers, and property. This section does not authorize withholding information from the public or limiting the availability of records to the public.

[117] 441 U.S. at 308–09.

[118] *Id.* at 310–11. The Court in *Chrysler* suggested one final way around the Trade Secrets Act. The Court cautioned that it had not attempted "to determine the relative ambits of Exemption 4 and § 1905." *Id.* at 319 n.49. The Court further postulated that if the material fell within § 1905, but not within exemption four, as nonexempted information it would have to be released pursuant to the FOIA, satisfying the requirement of § 1905 that disclosure be "authorized by law." *Id.* But the Court warned that it was unlikely that the coverage of the two statutes differed in light of the similarity of language of the two provisions. *Id.* Both statutes use the term "trade secrets," so at least for that type of information, the statutes are probably coextensive. *Compare* 18 U.S.C. § 1905 (1976) *with* 5 *id.* § 552(b)(4). The language of exemption four concerning "confidential . . . commercial or financial information" is also similar to the coverage in § 1905 of "the identity, confidential statistical data, amount or source of any income, profits, losses, or expenditures of any [entity]."

Apparently all of the lower courts that have considered the issue have concluded that the scope of the two provisions is coextensive. *See, e.g.*, National Parks & Conservation Ass'n v. Kleppe, 547 F.2d 673, 686 (D.C. Cir. 1976); Westinghouse Elec. Corp. v. Schlesinger, 542 F.2d 1190, 1204 n.38 (4th Cir. 1976), *cert. denied*, 431 U.S. 924 (1977); Charles River Park "A", Inc. v. HUD, 519 F.2d 935, 941 n.7 (D.C. Cir. 1975); Ditlow v. Volpe, 362 F. Supp. 1321, 1323–24 (D.D.C. 1973), *rev'd on other grounds sub nom.* Ditlow v. Brineger, 494 F.2d 1073 (D.C. Cir.), *cert. denied*, 419 U.S. 974 (1974); *cf.* Pharmaceutical Mfrs. Ass'n v. Weinberger, 401 F. Supp. 444, 446 (D.D.C. 1975) (parties stipulated that coverage was coextensive). Nevertheless, some commentators have argued that § 1905 is narrower than its language and hence not coextensive with the FOIA. *See* Clement, *The Rights of Submitters to Prevent Agency Disclosure of Confidential Business Information: The Reverse Freedom of Information Act Lawsuit,* 55 TEX. L. REV. 587, 613–17 (1977); Comment, *FDA Disclosure of Safety and Effectiveness Data: A Legal and Policy Analysis,* 1979 DUKE L.J. 286, 303–09.

[119] 441 U.S. at 304.

[120] *See* pp. 874–75 *infra. See also* Brookwood Medical Center, Inc. v. Califano, 470 F. Supp. 1247 (N.D. Ga. 1979).

Substances Control Act and the Federal Insecticide, Fungicide and Rodenticide Act explicitly authorize the release of health and safety data and thus meet the *Chrysler* criteria. Second, Congress often gives an agency general rulemaking authority beyond that which the housekeeping statute confers. Arguably, such individual grants of authority would meet the Court's criteria, but this is a much closer question under the "nexus" test than cases in which explicit disclosure authority is given.[121]

The *Chrysler* Court was correct in holding the APA available to plaintiffs aggrieved by threatened agency disclosure. In enacting the FOIA, Congress did not affirmatively remove the constraint of the Trade Secrets Act upon agencies. But to make that constraint anything more than academic, it must be enforceable. Given the draconian nature of the criminal penalties provided by the Trade Secrets Act for its violation, it was appropriate for the Court to effectuate another means of enforcement. By recognizing the applicability of the APA's "in accordance with law" provision, the Court held that one who submits the information to the government may act to enforce administrative compliance with the Trade Secrets Act.

The consequence of *Chrysler* is that agencies will be unable to disclose proprietary information without fairly explicit statutory authority. Therefore, if health and safety data are proprietary information, agencies may not disclose the data without such a mandate. But the scope of "proprietary information" is an entirely separate question.

B. Defining "Proprietary Information"

The Trade Secrets Act, the FOIA, the Food, Drug, and Cosmetic Act, and most other federal statutes dealing with proprietary information, make no attempt to define that term.[122] Therefore, it is open to question whether health and

---

[121] The continued vitality of one pre-*Chrysler* case which dealt with such a situation is uncertain. In Westinghouse Elec. Corp. v. Nuclear Regulatory Comm'n, 555 F.2d 82 (3d Cir. 1977), Westinghouse sought to enjoin the Agency from enforcing regulations that provided for disclosure of proprietary information when the public interest in disclosure exceeded the submitter's interest in secrecy. *See* 10 C.F.R. § 2.790 (1979). The Court of Appeals for the Third Circuit held that the Agency had validly issued the regulations under its authority to make such rules and regulations as may be necessary to carry out the purposes of the Atomic Energy Act, 42 U.S.C. §§ 2011–2281 (1976). 555 F.2d at 89. Therefore, information made public pursuant to the regulations came within the Trade Secrets Act's exemption for disclosure authorized by law. *Id*. at 94. However, agency attempts to use general rulemaking authority to support disclosure regulations may find *Westinghouse* weak authority after *Chrysler*.

[122] Congress has attempted to define "protected information" only in the context of health and safety information. *See* Toxic Substances Control Act § 14(b), 15 U.S.C.

HARVARD LAW REVIEW [Vol. 93:837

safety testing data should receive the protections mandated for proprietary information. Traditionally, agencies and courts have employed the broad common law definition of trade secrets to set the boundaries of proprietary information, including health and safety testing results within its scope. But the applicability of such a definition to the public law context of information submitted to government agencies is undermined by the very different considerations which led to a broad definition of "trade secrets" in the private law area. In some limited circumstances, courts have defined proprietary information by balancing the need for privacy against the need for disclosure. While such a method is more responsive to the underlying policy considerations, its implementation may be troublesome. Recently, Congress has attempted to override the "trade secrets" problem in two pieces of legislation, the Toxic Substances Control Act (TSCA)[123] and the amendments to the Federal Insecticide, Fungicide, and Rodenticide Act (FIFRA),[124] by explicitly excluding health and safety testing data from the ambit of proprietary information protection.[125] While this is a tidy, and, as will be argued later, a desirable solution, it is not completely free of problems.

1. The Common Law Definition. — The *Restatement of Torts*, embodying the common law definition, defines a trade secret as "any formula, pattern, device or compilation of information which is used in one's business and which gives him an opportunity to obtain *an advantage over* competitors who do not know or use it."[126] Strict application of this definition would classify virtually all undisclosed health and safety testing data as trade secrets since such data invariably give the owner a competitive advantage where competitors cannot market the same product without reproducing the data.[127]

---

§ 2613(b) (1976); Federal Insecticide, Fungicide, and Rodenticide Act § 10(d)(1), 7 U.S.C.A. § 136h(d)(1) (West Supp. 1979).

[123] 15 U.S.C. §§ 2601–2629 (1976).

[124] 7 U.S.C.A. § 136 (West Supp. 1979).

[125] *See* note 122 *supra*.

[126] RESTATEMENT OF TORTS § 757, Comment b at 5 (1939) (emphasis added). The oft-quoted factors for determining trade secrecy ensure very broad protection for plaintiffs:

Some factors to be considered in determining whether given information is one's trade secret are: (1) the extent to which the information is known outside of his business; (2) the extent to which it is known by employees and others involved in his business; (3) the extent of measures taken by him to guard the secrecy of the information; (4) the value of the information to him and to his competitors; (5) the amount of effort or money expended by him in developing the information; (6) the ease or difficulty with which the information could be properly acquired or duplicated by others.

Id. § 757, Comment b at 6.

[127] Courts have been unwilling to go so far as to conclude that *all* health and safety testing data is proprietary under the *Restatement* definition, but neither have

But the common law definition was tailored to private contexts where public policy almost exclusively focuses on the unjust enrichment and competitive harm resulting when someone acquires a business intangible through the breach of a contract or a confidential relationship.[128] The essence of the common law concept of trade secret is thus wrongdoing on the part of the defendant.[129] Although on rare occasions a court will suggest that the common law of trade secrets encourages research and development,[130] the *Restatement* eschews any policy of encouraging innovation.[131]

When the question of defining proprietary information appears in the public context of whether health and safety data submitted to an agency should be publicly disclosed, the interests of the public in disclosure and the protection of innovation incentives pose important considerations which the common law definition was not designed to handle. The *Restatement* approach, with its emphasis on culpability and misappropriation, is ill-equipped to strike an appropriate balance between the competing interests of regulated industries and the general public. Therefore, lumping health and safety testing data with all other types of proprietary information is inherently suspect.

2. *Balancing Approaches*. — In other contexts, courts have employed a test which balances the need for privacy against the need for disclosure in order to define proprietary information. For example, such a method has been recognized in determining whether information would be protected as proprietary during the discovery process under the Federal Rules

---

they identified any health and safety testing data that does not fall within the definition. *See* Dow Chem. Co. v. Costle, 464 F. Supp. 395 (E.D. Mich. 1978); Chevron Chem. Co. v. Costle, 443 F. Supp. 1024 (N.D. Cal. 1978).

[128] Many different kinds of confidential relationships can give rise to trade secret liability such as employment relationships, contractual relationships, negotiations for the purchase of a business, stockholder-company relationships, and licensee-licensor relationships. *See* 12 BUSINESS ORGANIZATIONS, MILGRIM, TRADE SECRETS 5-1 to -124 (1978). Trade secret liability can also arise from industrial espionage. *See, e.g.,* E.I. duPont deNemours & Co. v. Christopher, 431 F.2d 1012 (5th Cir. 1970), *cert. denied*, 400 U.S. 1024 (1971).

[129] "It is the employment of improper means to procure the trade secret, rather than the mere copying or use, which is the basis of the liability . . . ." RESTATEMENT OF TORTS § 757, Comment a at 3–4 (1939). A blatant breach of confidence may result in liability even though the plaintiff has not kept the information completely secret. *See, e.g.,* Ultra-Life Laboratories, Inc. v. Eames, 240 Mo. App. 851, 867, 221 S.W. 2d 224, 233 (1949); Vulcan Detinning Co. v. American Can Co., 72 N.J. Eq. 387, 67 A. 339 (N.J. 1907).

[130] *See* Kewanee Oil Co. v. Bicron Corp., 416 U.S. 470, 482 (1974); Water Servs., Inc. v. Tesco Chems., Inc., 410 F.2d 163, 171 (5th Cir. 1969).

[131] RESTATEMENT OF TORTS § 757, Comment b at 7 (1939). *See also* von Kalinowski, *Key Employees and Trade Secrets*, 47 VA. L. REV. 583, 589 (1961).

of Civil Procedure[132] and whether documents subpenaed in certain agency rulemaking proceedings could be publicly disclosed by the agency or must be held confidential.[133]

While a balancing approach to determining whether health and safety data are proprietary information would enable courts and agencies directly to consider the competing interests in the public's need to know versus the need to protect incentives for innovation, there are several problems. If the balancing approach is performed case-by-case, vast amounts of agency staff and lawyer time could be consumed in holding hearings, making determinations, and preparing for judicial review of decisions. Also, the fact that particular health and safety data would not qualify as proprietary information under the balancing approach does not mean that such data, although not eligible for *full* protection as proprietary information, should not receive some form of protection.

3. Wholesale Redefinition. — Completely excluding health and safety testing data from the protections afforded to proprietary information clears the way for a comprehensive scheme of disclosure and protections specifically geared to such data. Congress recently adopted such an approach in both the TSCA and the FIFRA, as amended.[134] The desirability of this approach will be explored as specific regulatory schemes are examined in a later section. Its chief drawback lies in the problems created by making the definition of health and safety so crucial. Costly fights over the definition have already begun.[135]

C. Constitutional Issues Regarding Forced Disclosure

While strong policy arguments favor disclosure of health and safety data, plaintiffs in several pending cases have argued that forced disclosure constitutes an unconstitutional taking of property without just compensation.[136] While this argument

---

[132] 48 F.R.D. 487, 505 (1970); *see, e.g.,* Covey Oil Co. v. Continental Oil Co., 340 F.2d 993 (10th Cir.), *cert. denied,* 380 U.S. 964 (1965). *See also* 8 C. WRIGHT & A. MILLER, FEDERAL PRACTICE AND PROCEDURE § 2043 (1970).

[133] FCC v. Schreiber, 381 U.S. 279 (1965). *See generally* Cohn & Zuckman, FCC v. Schreiber: In Camera *and the Administrative Agency,* 56 GEO. L.J. 451 (1968).

[134] *See* note 122 *supra.*

[135] *See* pp. 876-79 *infra.*

[136] The following undecided cases involve challenges to the constitutionality of the 1978 FIFRA amendments. Chevron Chem. Co. v. Costle, No. 79-532 (D. Del., filed Nov. 13, 1979); Union Carbide Agricultural Prods. Co. v. Costle, No. 76 Civ. 2913 (S.D.N.Y., filed July 5, 1979) (order granting preliminary injunction); Mobay Chem. Co. v. Costle, No. 79-591D (W.D. Pa., filed May 1, 1979); Monsanto Chem. Co. v. Costle, No. 79-00366C(2) (E.D. Mo., filed Mar. 30, 1979); American Cyanimid Co. v. Costle, C.A. No. 77-226 (D.N.J., filed Nov. 30, 1978).

seems devoid of merit, at least one court has issued a preliminary injunction barring implementation of the 1978 amendments to the FIFRA pending resolution of the question.[137] The current litigation raises two issues: (1) whether health and safety data submitted to the government pursuant to a licensing requirement is "property" within the meaning of the takings clause; and (2) whether government publication of such data constitutes a "taking" of the property.

1. Property. — While the issue is a fruitful subject for academic debate, it seems reasonable to conclude that proprietary information comes within the concept of property protected by the fifth amendment takings clause.[138] In *Zotos International, Inc. v. Kennedy*,[139] a federal district court held that the identity of the ingredients in Zotos' cosmetics was property for purposes of due process protection.[140] The FDA itself has apparently conceded that health and safety data are property.[141]

2. Taking. — Assuming that health and safety data are property within the meaning of the takings clause, disclosure as a condition to receiving a license or registration nevertheless need not constitute an unconstitutional "taking." In *Westinghouse Electric Corp. v. NRC*,[142] Westinghouse challenged the Nuclear Regulatory Commission's (NRC) rules governing the disclosure of proprietary information submitted during licensing and rulemaking proceedings. Under those rules,[143] all information submitted in hearings was to be placed in a public file.[144] The Third Circuit dismissed as "fanciful" Westinghouse's claim that this scheme ran afoul of the takings clause.[145] Stressing that license applicants are under no compulsion whatsoever to submit data to the agency, the court ruled that "[a] voluntary submission of information by an applicant seeking the economic advantages of a license can hardly be called a taking."[146] Like the petitioner in *Westing-*

---

[137] Amchem Prods. Inc. v. Costle, No. 76-2913 (S.D.N.Y. July 10, 1979).

[138] Trade secrets, like other business intangibles, fit well within the traditional Benthamite bundle of property rights with only one important exception: the right of the owner of a trade secret is never exclusive. The secret may always be discovered independently and used.

[139] 460 F. Supp. 268 (D.D.C. 1978).

[140] The court focused mainly upon the inadequacy of the notice that the FDA gave to Zotos of the basis for its conclusions prior to making a final decision. *Id.* at 278.

[141] *See* 39 Fed. Reg. 44,602, 44,612 (1974).

[142] 555 F.2d 82 (3d Cir. 1977).

[143] 10 C.F.R. § 2.790 (1979).

[144] *Id.* § 2.790(a).

[145] 555 F.2d at 95.

[146] *Id.*

house, one who submits health and safety studies to the EPA or the FDA has a choice between maintaining the confidentiality of the information and obtaining a license or registration. Forcing the submitter to make that choice can hardly be called a taking.[147]

Forced disclosure should survive a takings claim as a reasonable regulation of interstate commerce, analogous to a state's exercise of the "police power."[148] The widely used balancing test which weighs the public benefit against the private harm,[149] suggests that government publication of health and safety studies is constitutional. Even when disclosed, health and safety data still have a substantial residuum of value to the data producer.[150] Most important, they allow access to the market, which is something the innovator did not have prior to producing the data and which is the reason for developing the data in the first place. The fact that the data are also available to competitors for the same purposes does not eliminate their value to the data producer. A statute requiring disclosure of health and safety data results in only a partial diminution in their legitimate value.

On the other side of the balance are the public interests in greater competition, in avoiding duplicative research, in monitoring and participating in regulatory decisions, and in making informed decisions in the marketplace.[151] These are powerful

---

[147] An analogy to the well-established eminent domain law principle that government action can constitutionally take away value that it has created in the first instance, *see, e.g.*, United States v. Fuller, 409 U.S. 488, 492 (1973); United States v. Cors, 337 U.S. 325, 334 (1949); Reichelderfer v. Quinn, 287 U.S. 315, 319 (1932), may be helpful. The property interest for which pesticide and drug companies claim compensation exists only because of a government-imposed barrier to entry into the market. Their claim that disclosure would deprive them of a commercial advantage depends entirely upon the fact that the government requires the data as a precondition to issuing a license. Thus, to the extent that a data submitter has any "property" interest as a result of this barrier to entry, it is "property" given by the government and hence no compensation need be paid upon disclosure.

[148] United States v. Carolene Prods. Co., 304 U.S. 144, 147 (1938); Consumer Mail Order Ass'n v. McGrath, 94 F. Supp. 705, 711 (D.D.C. 1950), *aff'd per curiam*, 340 U.S. 925 (1951); 1 J. SACKMAN, NICHOLS' LAW OF EMINENT DOMAIN § 1.42[6], at 1-150 to -151 (3d rev. ed. 1979); *see* 1 R. ANDERSON, AMERICAN LAW OF ZONING § 7.03 (1976) (definition and scope of police power).

[149] *See, e.g.*, Plater, *The Taking Issue in a Natural Setting: Floodlines and the Police Power*, 52 TEX. L. REV. 201 (1974) (collecting tests of other scholarly commentators).

[150] The Supreme Court relied partly on the substantial residuum of value left to the claimant in Penn Cent. Transp. Co. v. New York City, 438 U.S. 104, 136 (1978), holding that no "taking" occurred where the Penn Central was denied application to erect an office tower above Grand Central Station, a designated "landmark site." *See also* Andrus v. Allard, 100 S. Ct. 318, 326–28 (1979) (regulations prohibiting the sale of eagle feathers upheld since economic benefit of their possession not destroyed).

[151] *See* pp. 840–48 *supra*.

public interests, going directly to the health, safety, and welfare interests underlying police power regulations. When weighed against the limited diminution in value, these interests tip the balance decisively in favor of constitutional legitimacy. The courts, not surprisingly, have agreed with this analysis in other contexts.[152] A disclosure model reflecting a governmental determination that the public interest in disclosure outweighs any resulting competitive harm should be afforded considerable judicial deference under traditional commerce clause and police power analysis.[153]

D. Specific Regulatory Policies

Despite the fact that the question of disclosure versus non-disclosure of health and safety testing data implicates similar public policy considerations across several areas of regulation, very different regulatory responses have emerged in the several product areas. With respect to drug licensing, the harsh effects of a general "no disclosure" rule are mitigated only by the release of summaries and the use of outside advisory committees.[154] In sharp contrast, information pertaining to the safety of antibiotics and food and color additives is routinely disclosed.[155] Testing data for pesticides and toxic substances are also disclosed, but special compensatory devices have been fashioned for the original developer of such information.[156] No principled reason is evident for such disparate treatment of essentially the same problem. This Section analyzes each of these systems, revealing that the use of the common law definition of trade secret creates several problems, and that administrative difficulties threaten the viability of any comprehensive solution to the present confusion.

152

[I]t is too plain for argument that a manufacturer or vendor has no constitutional right to sell goods without giving to the purchaser fair information of what it is that is being sold. The right of a manufacturer to maintain secrecy as to his compounds and processes must be held subject to the right of the State, in the exercise of its police power and in promotion of fair dealing, to require that the nature of the product be fairly set forth.

Corn Prods. Refining Co. v. Eddy, 249 U.S. 427, 431–32 (1919); *see, e.g.*, National Fertilizer Ass'n v. Bradley, 301 U.S. 178 (1937); Savage v. Jones, 225 U.S. 501, 524–25 (1912); Speert v. Morgenthau, 116 F.2d 301, 305 (D.C. Cir. 1940).

[153] *See generally* L. TRIBE, AMERICAN CONSTITUTIONAL LAW § 5–6, at 238 (1978) (broad protective scope of commerce power regulation; judicial review "largely a formality"); *cf.* 4 R. ANDERSON, *supra* note 148, § 25.26 (presumption of regularity of zoning decision pursuant to police power); G. GUNTHER, CASES AND MATERIALS ON CONSTITUTIONAL LAW 191–94 (9th ed. 1975) (broad federal commerce power authority to regulate economic problems).

[154] *See* pp. 868–72 *infra*.

[155] *See* pp. 872–73 *infra*.

[156] *See* pp. 873–76 *infra*.

1. Drugs. — Before a drug may be shipped in interstate commerce, its safety and effectiveness must be established by scientific experimentation.[157] The FDA has taken the position that health and safety testing data supporting the approval of a new drug cannot generally be released to the public.[158] The FDA applies the *Restatement* definition of trade secret to conclude that such health and safety testing data fall within the Food, Drug and Cosmetic Act's prohibition against "revealing . . . any information acquired under [this chapter] . . . concerning any method or process which as a trade secret is entitled to protection."[159]

FDA reasoning on the application of the *Restatement* definition is straightforward. A New Drug Application (NDA) "is personal to the manufacturer who files it."[160] Therefore, a follow-on applicant may not rely on undisclosed information in an approved NDA in support of licensing even the identical drug.[161] But, the FDA finds nothing in the regulatory scheme which would prevent it from accepting publicly disclosed health and safety data of a prior applicant in the NDA of a follow-on applicant.[162] The FDA concludes that such information, if undisclosed, provides the developing company with significant cost and lead-time advantages over competitors and hence is a trade secret under the *Restatement* definition.[163] The FDA's failure to consider any public policy interests in

---

[157] 21 U.S.C. § 355 (1976). The applicant submits the animal testing information, as well as other information, to the FDA in the form of a Claimed Investigational Exemption for a New Drug (IND) and may then ship the drug interstate for human testing if the FDA does not object within 30 days. 21 C.F.R. § 312.1(a) (1979). The human data is submitted to the FDA in the form of a New Drug Application (NDA). *Id.* § 314.1. For a description of the nature and organization of the human testing, see J. GIBSON, MEDICATION, LAW AND BEHAVIOR 124–45 (1976); Pines, *A Primer on New Drug Development*, FDA CONSUMER, Feb. 1974, at 12.

[158] 21 C.F.R. § 314.14(e)-(g) (1979); *see* 39 Fed. Reg. 44,633–35 (1974).

[159] 21 U.S.C. § 331(j) (1976); *see* 21 C.F.R. § 20.61 (1979); 39 Fed. Reg. 44,612 (1974).

[160] USV Pharmaceutical Corp. v. Weinberger, 412 U.S. 655, 664 (1973).

[161] *See* 39 Fed. Reg. 44,634 (1974).

[162] *Id.*

[163] *Id.* at 44,612, 44,634; *see* p. 862 *supra*. The FDA was influenced in its choice of definitions by the fact that the Supreme Court, in holding that state statutes making it a crime to steal trade secrets were not preempted by federal patent laws, noted that the *Restatement* definition was widely relied upon. Kewanee Oil Co. v. Bicron Corp., 416 U.S. 470, 474 (1974); *cf.* Aronson v. Quick Point Pencil Co., 440 U.S. 257 (1979) (federal patent law held not to preempt state contract law). Although the Court used the *Restatement* definition solely for the purpose of defining the scope of the common law tort in the state of Ohio, the FDA could "find no reason why it should be utilized for determining commercial damages but not for purposes of the Freedom of Information Act." 39 Fed. Reg. 44,612 (1974).

favor of disclosure exemplifies the fallacy of applying the *Restatement* definition in the regulatory context.[164]

This restrictive approach has led to pressure for greater disclosure. For example, the plaintiffs in *Johnson v. HEW*[165] are seeking to compel the agency to disclose the animal testing data filed by Smith, Kline & French in behalf of their drug Tagamet. The fact that the drug is patented, the plaintiffs argue, makes it impossible to prove a "likelihood of substantial competitive injury" should the testing data be released.[166] The intervening drug company contends that even when a drug is patented, it would still suffer competitive harm if the information were released, since competitors could use the information to license substitutes after the patent expired and to license the product immediately in foreign markets where United States patents are not recognized.[167] The court has not yet resolved this issue.[168]

Although drug safety and health testing data are not generally disclosed in full, the drug regulatory scheme does attempt to accommodate the policies underlying the pro- and antidisclosure arguments. The fact that follow-on manufacturers cannot rely on undisclosed testing data of competitors helps maintain research incentives by protecting an innovator's headstart and investment in testing. On the other side of the balance, the FDA does release summaries of data in order to inform the public of the basis for approving a new drug[169] and employs outside consultants to improve agency effectiveness.

The FDA believes that it may make summaries public even

---

[164] *See* p. 863 *supra.*

[165] 462 F. Supp. 336 (D.D.C. 1978).

[166] *Id.* at 337. Such a showing must be made if the information is to be covered by the trade secret exemption in the FOIA, 5 U.S.C. § 552(b)(4) (1976). National Parks & Conservation Ass'n v. Morton, 498 F.2d 765, 770 (D.C. Cir. 1974).

[167] 462 F. Supp. at 337.

[168] The court held that the existence of a patent did not, as a matter of law, make the trade secret exemption unavailable, and ordered further proceedings. *Id.* at 338.

[169] *See* 21 C.F.R. § 314.14(d), (e)(2)(ii) (1979); 39 Fed. Reg. 44,615, 44,635–36 (1974).

The FDA also decided not to protect testing information in two other limited circumstances. If the information had previously been lawfully disclosed to persons not within certain categories, the FDA will consider it available for public disclosure. 21 C.F.R. § 314.14(e)(1) (1979). The FDA reasons that secrecy is the essence of the definition of "trade secret." *See* Carson Prods. Co. v. Califano, 594 F.2d 453, 461–62 (5th Cir. 1979). Additionally, except in extraordinary circumstances, where the new drug application has been abandoned, disapproved, or declared unnecessary, the FDA will no longer protect the information. 21 C.F.R. § 314.14(f)(1)–(5); *see* 39 Fed. Reg. 44,637 (1974). FDA reasons that if the information will not support an NDA, it is of no commercial value to competitors.

where they contain some reference to testing information since an innovator can suffer no real competitive harm from the release of fragmented and limited data.[170] This view has, however, been challenged in *Syntex Corp. v. Califano*.[171] The plaintiffs in that case are seeking to prevent the release of a report by FDA investigators which contains excerpts of the testing data submitted by the firm. The report examined the possibility that the FDA had approved a Syntex drug on the basis of fraudulent animal testing information.[172] The company argued that although the information is in summary form, the report would reveal much of its testing data and thus have some intelligence value to competitors.[173] The court refused to grant summary judgment for the FDA on the question of trade secrecy and ordered the matter to trial to determine if even the summary portions of the testing data could be released.[174]

Even if their use survives legal challenge, "summaries" are hardly a replacement for the complete disclosure of testing information.[175] The necessary selectivity of such conclusory summaries precludes normal peer review since the reviewer is unable to examine all of the data used.[176] The FDA apparently agrees that summaries are insufficient substitutes for actual data, since it has asked Congress to authorize the release of all testing information.[177] It also encourages its own advisory committees to evaluate the raw experimental data instead of relying on summaries[178] and requires for its own approval process the use of "full reports" which include the raw experimentation data.[179] If the FDA needs "full reports" to determine the sufficiency of the experiments undertaken, any mean-

---

[170] 39 Fed. Reg. 44,636 (1974); Syntex Corp. v. Califano, [1978–1979 Transfer Binder] FOOD DRUG COS. L. REP. (CCH) ¶ 38,221, at 38,896–98 (D.D.C. 1979).

[171] [1978–1979 Transfer Binder] FOOD DRUG COS. L. REP. (CCH) ¶ 38,221 (D.D.C. 1979).

[172] *Id.* at 38,897.

[173] *Id.* at 38,898.

[174] *Id.* at 38,899.

[175] However, some officials in the pharmaceutical industry and some independent scientists believe that the summaries largely obviate the need to disclose testing information. *See Senate Hearings on Drug Regulation Reform, supra* note 17, at 293 (statement of C. Joseph Stetler, President, Pharmaceutical Mfrs. Ass'n); *id.* at 674 (statement of Robert B. Clark, President, Hoffmann-La Roche, Inc.); *id.* at 767 (statement of Louis Lasagna, M.D.).

[176] *See* Peer Review, *supra* note 10, at 18–19; Kennedy Letter, *supra* note 10, at 845.

[177] *See, e.g.*, Kennedy Letter, *supra* note 10, at 841–47.

[178] *See* FOOD & DRUG ADMINISTRATION, COMMISSIONER'S REPORT OF INVESTIGATION OF CHARGES 750 (1975).

[179] 21 C.F.R. § 314.1(c)(2) (1979).

ingful independent scientific review would need to be based on information of the same scope.

To augment further its expertise and ease agency isolation, the FDA heavily relies on outside medical consultants organized into standing advisory committees.[180] The pharmaceutical industry believes that the success of this system obviates the need to disclose testing data.[181] While undoubtedly their use has served the FDA well, advisory committees are imperfect substitutes for open peer review. Although the Advisory Committee Act specifically provides that committees should represent balanced viewpoints,[182] a recent study has found that most consultants are appointed at the suggestion of present members, resulting in an "old boy" network.[183] Additionally, committees usually review only limited aspects of the research submitted;[184] hence, they can only affect a limited portion of the FDA's responsibilities.

Finally, advisory committees are constrained by trade secret law in the same manner as the FDA. If the advisory committee deliberations involve proprietary information, the meeting must be closed[185] and committee members may not discuss the data with outsiders. This impedes effective peer review of the committees,[186] reduces the intellectual attrac-

---

[180] *See* REVIEW PANEL ON NEW DRUG REGULATION, U.S. DEP'T OF HEALTH, EDUCATION & WELFARE, INTERIM REPORT: THE USE OF STANDING ADVISORY COMMITTEES BY THE BUREAU OF FDA 18–22 (1977) [hereinafter cited as USE OF STANDING ADVISORY COMMITTEES]. The committees, at the FDA's discretion, may also have nonvoting public interest representatives. 21 C.F.R. § 14.80(b)(2) (1979).

[181] *Senate Hearings on Drug Regulation Reform, supra* note 17, at 674 (statement of Robert B. Clark, President, Hoffmann-La Roche, Inc.); *id.* at 682 (statement of Richard M. Furlaud, Chairman & Chief Executive Officer, Squibb Corp.); *House Hearings on Drug Regulation Reform, supra* note 10, at 1984 (statement of C. Joseph Stetler, President, Pharmaceutical Mfrs. Ass'n).

[182] Federal Advisory Committee Act § 5(b)(2), *reprinted at* 5 U.S.C. app. (1976).

[183] USE OF STANDING ADVISORY COMMITTEES, *supra* note 180, at 41–42, 44–45; *see* Peer Review, *supra* note 10, at 19. One government committee warns:

> The "old boy network" is not without its advantages . . . . On the other hand . . . [i]ts chief danger is that it tends to become a self-perpetuating system for insiders, from which important segments of the scientific (or other) community may be excluded, and may result in decisions that are one sided and parochial.

USE OF STANDING ADVISORY COMMITTEES, *supra* note 180, at 45.

[184] USE OF STANDING ADVISORY COMMITTEES, *supra* note 180, at 20–25, 27–28. The FDA has established a system of priorities to determine which parts of its activities will be reviewed by its advisory committees. 21 C.F.R. § 14.171(a)–(c) (1979). Past experience has indicated that the committees spend almost all of their time reviewing selected NDA's and human (clinical) drug testing guidelines with little or no review of animal test results (investigational new drug notice files). USE OF STANDING ADVISORY COMMITTEES, *supra* note 180, at 22–25.

[185] 5 U.S.C. § 552b(c)(4) (1976); 21 C.F.R. §§ 14.27(b)(3), 171(f) (1979).

[186] Without such peer review, some scientists believe that the advisory committee structure may not produce acceptable advice. *See* Peer Review, *supra* note 10, at 19.

tiveness of the job,[187] and prevents advisory committee members from publicly defending their conclusions.[188]

  2. Antibiotics and Additives. — An antibiotic[189] or a food[190] or color[191] additive is subject to seizure by the FDA unless it is marketed pursuant to an agency regulation stating the conditions of its manufacture and use.[192] Such regulations are issued upon proof that an additive is safe[193] or that an antibiotic is safe and effective[194] for the uses for which it is intended. Normally, the applicant submits animal tests for both types of products[195] and human tests for antibiotics.[196] Once the regulation is approved for antibiotics or a regulation is proposed for additives, in the absence of extraordinary circumstances, the FDA releases almost all of this test data.[197]

  The FDA's disclosure of the test data may be subject to

---

[187] *See* p. 842 *supra.*

[188] *See* p. 844 *supra.*

[189] An "antibiotic drug" is "any drug intended for use by man, containing . . . a substance which is produced by a microorganism and which has the capacity to inhibit or destroy microorganisms in dilute solution (including the chemically synthesized equivalent of any such substance)." 21 U.S.C. § 357(a) (1976).

[190] A "food additive" is "any substance the intended use of which results or may reasonably be expected to result, directly or indirectly, in its becoming a component or otherwise affecting the characteristics of any food." *Id.* § 321(s). *See generally* Lehmann, *More Than You Ever Thought You Would Know About Food Additives* (pt. 1), FDA CONSUMER, Apr. 1974, at 10; Sunshine, *Regulatory Aspects of Food Additives — Yesterday, Today and Tomorrow*, 31 FOOD DRUG COSM. L.J. 264 (1976).

[191] A "color additive" is any material which when added to a food, drug, or cosmetic, or to the human body, is capable of imparting color thereto. 21 U.S.C. § 321(t)(1) (1976).

[192] *See id.* § 334(a) (general seizure authority); *id.* § 357(b) and 21 C.F.R. § 431.1–.20 (1979) (for antibiotics); 21 U.S.C. § 348(c)(1) (1976) and 21 C.F.R. § 170.10 (1979) (for food additives); 21 U.S.C. § 376(b) (1976) and 21 C.F.R. § 71.20 (1979) (for color additives).

[193] 21 U.S.C. § 348(c)(3)(A) (1976) (for food additives); *id.* § 376(b)(1) (1976) (for color additives). *See generally* Harkins, *Food Additive Safety Evaluation*, 32 FOOD DRUG COSM. L.J. 182 (1977). It must also be established that the additive does not induce cancer when ingested by man or animal. 21 U.S.C. § 348(c)(3)(A) (1976) (for food additives); *id.* § 376(b)(5)(B) (for color additives). *But see* Pub. L. No. 95-203, § 3, 91 Stat. 1451 (1977) (18-month moratorium on applicability of 21 U.S.C. § 348 (1976) as applied to saccharin carcinogenicity). This provision, the so-called Delaney Anticancer Clause, has been the subject of great controversy, because it allows for no balancing of the risks posed with the benefits gained. *See* Allera, *An Overview of How the FDA Regulated Carcinogens Under the Federal Food, Drug, and Cosmetic Act*, 33 FOOD DRUG COSM. L.J. 59 (1978); Henteleff, *The Delaney Myths*, 33 FOOD DRUG COSM. L.J. 396 (1978).

[194] 21 U.S.C. § 357(a) (1976) (antibiotics).

[195] 21 C.F.R. § 430.20(b)(6) (1979) (antibiotics); *id.* § 171.1(c) (food additives); *id.* § 71.1(c) (color additives).

[196] *Id.* § 430.20(b)(6)(iii).

[197] *Id.* § 431.71(e)–(f) (antibiotics); *id.* § 171.1(h) (food additives); *id.* § 71.15(a)–(b) (color additives). *See also* 39 Fed. Reg. 44,602, 44,631–32 (1974).

challenge. Since the issuance of a regulation allows a competitor to market an identical product without duplicating the original testing data, the FDA believes that the data have no value to others and therefore lack any proprietary value.[198] But this conclusion ignores the fact that test data may be valuable to competitors seeking regulatory permission to sell the product for additional uses.[199] The FDA's position may thus be legally vulnerable because under the *Restatement* definition of trade secrets, to which the agency generally adheres, information only need be of "some" commercial value to be considered proprietary.[200]

While the FDA's interest in promoting disclosure is commendable, its position may be reversed by the courts. Even if permitted to stand, the regulatory schema for antibiotics and additives may provide no real protection for research incentives apart from that offered by patents and market imperfections. To the extent that these provide incomplete protection, the pace of innovation may be undesirably slowed.[201]

3. *Pesticides and Toxic Substances.* — The FIFRA, as amended, and TSCA share a common approach to the health and safety data confidentiality problem that distinguishes them from the statutes that the FDA administers. Rather than leave the confidentiality question to the relevant agency, the EPA, Congress attempted in both statutes to make health and safety data available to the public and to protect the original innovator by either forcing those who rely upon a registrant's data to compensate the data producer for its use or preventing such use for a fixed period of years. After briefly describing the applicable statutes, this subsection will focus on the compensated disclosure idea.

Under the FIFRA, as amended,[202] any manufacturer of a chemical that may be used to control any pest must obtain a registration for that product from the EPA.[203] Applicants for

---

[198] 39 Fed. Reg. 44,602, 44,632 (1974).

[199] Since an additive will often be approved for a limited purpose, such as use in a particular food, the testing data may be valuable to others who seek approval of the additive for other uses. *See* Sunshine, *Food Company Concerns and Opportunities — How We Will Cope*, 30 FOOD DRUG COSM. L.J. 345, 347 (1975). However, the industry has not attacked the disclosure scheme, in part because it has been the normal practice of the relevant industries to disclose the information in scientific journals, or to customers or other scientists. 39 Fed. Reg. 44,602, 44,632 (1974).

[200] *See* p. 862 *supra*.

[201] *See* pp. 850–51 *supra*.

[202] 7 U.S.C.A. § 136 (West Supp. 1979).

[203] In order to register a pesticide product, a manufacturer or formulator must demonstrate that:

(A) its composition is such as to warrant the proposed claims for it; (B) its labeling and other material required to be submitted comply with [FIFRA];

a new registration must provide, *inter alia*, comprehensive animal studies designed to ascertain the probable effects of the pesticide upon humans.[204] Moreover, if at any time after registration, the EPA has reason to believe that the studies available to it do not adequately support the prior regulatory approval, it may require the registrant to produce additional "defensive" data.[205] The TSCA grants the Administrator of the EPA power to order testing of any chemical substance or mixture of substances if he or she finds that the chemical may present an unreasonable risk of injury to health or the environment, that insufficient data exist to predict the health effects of the chemical, and that testing is necessary to develop such data.[206]

   (a) Overview: Compensated Disclosure. — Both the TSCA and the FIFRA as amended specifically exempt health and safety studies from the protections otherwise afforded to proprietary information.[207] This type of provision falls squarely

---

(C) it will perform its intended function without unreasonable adverse effects on the environment; and (D) when used in accordance with widespread and commonly recognized practice it will not generally cause unreasonable adverse effects on the environment.

Id. § 136a(c)(5).

[204] *See* 43 Fed. Reg. 37,336 (1978) (to be codified at 40 C.F.R. § 163.80–.86). In addition to these requirements, the Federal Food, Drug, and Cosmetic Act (FFDCA), 21 U.S.C. §§ 301–392 (1976), provides that raw agricultural commodities that are contaminated with pesticide residues shall be deemed adulterated (and therefore subject to seizure) unless the EPA has prescribed a tolerance for that pesticide and the residue is within the limits of that tolerance. *Id.* § 346a(a). Registrants of pesticides that will be applied to farm crops must therefore submit a petition for a tolerance to the EPA with accompanying health and safety studies. Interestingly, the pesticide tolerance section of the FFDCA is not included in that statute's prohibition against the release of trade secrets. *Id.* § 331(j). Thus, while data to support pesticide registrations is subject to the FIFRA's explicit trade secret prohibition, the same data, when used to support a tolerance is only subject to the general prohibition of the Trade Secrets Act, 18 U.S.C. § 1905 (1976).

[205] 7 U.S.C.A. § 136a(c)(2)(B) (West Supp. 1979).

[206] 15 U.S.C. § 2603(a) (1976). The Administrator must promulgate the testing requirement by rule. The rule must include the identification of the substance to be tested and standards for the development of test data. Interested persons must be given an opportunity to comment upon the rule, including an opportunity to present testimony orally. *Id.* § 2603(b)(1), (5).

Reporting requirements are another source of information on the health effects of chemicals subject to the Act. The Administrator must promulgate rules requiring manufacturers to submit lists of health and safety studies conducted by them, known to them, or reasonably ascertainable by them. *Id.* § 2607(d).

[207] *Id.* § 2613(b); 7 U.S.C.A. § 136h(d)(1) (West Supp. 1979) (FIFRA).

The term health and safety study means any study of any effect of a chemical substance or mixture on health or the environment or on both, including underlying data and epidemiological studies, studies of occupational exposure to a chemical substance or mixture, toxicological, clinical and ecological studies

within the "except as otherwise provided by law" proviso of the Trade Secrets Act[208] and therefore satisfies *Chrysler*.[209] Both statutes obviate the need for duplicative testing; the TSCA excuses a company from testing a chemical if such would be duplicative of other tests already performed or in the process of being performed[210] and the FIFRA generally permits competing registrants to rely upon data already in EPA's files.[211] However, both statutes do provide significant protections for innovators. Under the TSCA, a manufacturer may seek reimbursement from other companies that use its test results to gain an exemption from testing within five years of submission of those results.[212] If the parties cannot agree upon adequate compensation, the EPA Administrator must determine a "fair and equitable" reimbursement.[213] Under the 1978 FIFRA amendments, a complex scheme permits later registrants and the public to use the data of initial registrants: (1) Later registrants may use data submitted prior to 1970, without compensation to or permission from the originating party. (2) Data submitted after January 1, 1970 in support of pesticides containing active ingredients registered prior to the effective date of the 1978 FIFRA amendments may be used without compensation only after fifteen years from the date that the data are submitted. For use before that time, the later registrant must pay compensation as agreed between the parties or, if no such agreement can be reached, as determined by an arbitrator appointed by the Federal Mediation and Conciliation Service, whose decision will be subject to appeal only for fraud, misrepresentation or other misconduct. (3) Data submitted in support of pesticides containing active ingredients that are initially registered after 1978 may be used only after the original registration has been in existence for ten years, regardless of whether the later registrant is willing to compensate. After the ten years of exclusive use, the later registrant must compensate the data producer for fifteen years from the submission of the data in accordance with sentence (2) above.[214] In cases where the EPA orders data to be produced

---

of a chemical substance or mixture, and any test performed pursuant to this chapter.

15 U.S.C. § 2602(6) (1976).

[208] *See* p. 858 & note 107 *supra*.

[209] *See* p. 860 *supra*.

[210] 15 U.S.C. § 2603(a) (1976).

[211] 7 U.S.C.A. § 136a(c)(1)(D) (West Supp. 1979).

[212] 15 U.S.C. § 2603(c)(3) (1976).

[213] *Id*. § 2603(c)(4)(A).

[214] 7 U.S.C.A. § 136a(c)(1)(D) (West Supp. 1979). Significantly, the follow-on

to maintain an existing registration, existing registrants must share in the costs of producing the data or face cancellation of their registration.[215] Disputes over the proportion of costs attributable to each registration are to be resolved by arbitration.[216]

In enacting both the TSCA and the 1978 FIFRA amendments, Congress balanced the public interest in disclosing health and safety data against the public interest in the innovation that would result from keeping them secret and defined "proprietary information" to exclude all health and safety data. These Acts, however, have raised major administrative problems which threaten their viability.

(b) Problems with Compensated Disclosure. — The TSCA and the FIFRA, as amended, mandate disclosure while requiring reimbursement for the costs of health and safety studies. However, exactly what falls within the rubric "health and safety study" is unclear. The TSCA, for example, prevents disclosure to the extent that manufacturing processes would be revealed,[217] but the scope of the exception may be the subject of future litigation. Substantive and administrative problems also plague the computation of compensation awards. The following subsections will address these difficulties and search for solutions.

(i) Scope of "Health and Safety Study." — The principle problem in determining the scope of "health and safety study" has arisen with respect to the question whether the identity of a tested chemical must be disclosed as part of a health and safety study. This question is unique to the TSCA, because the identities of marketed products such as pesticides, food additives, drugs, and most chemicals are generally easily ascertainable through chemical analysis. The TSCA, however, can require health and safety studies to be performed for chemicals such as catalysts that may never enter the stream of commerce.[218]

Environmental groups argue that the TSCA's legislative history strongly supports an interpretation of "health and safety study" that would include chemical identity.[219] More-

---

applicant can secure its registration before the data compensation determination is made. Thus, the competing product can be on the market during the time that the parties argue about the appropriate amount of compensation. *Id.*

[215] *Id.* § 136a(c)(2)(B).

[216] *Id.* § 136a(c)(2)(B)(iii).

[217] 15 U.S.C. § 2613(b)(1)(A) (1976).

[218] *See* Eastman Kodak Co., Comments on Proposed Premanufacture Notification Requirements and Review Procedures 16–17 (Mar. 23, 1979).

[219] *See* Premanufacture Notification Requirements and Review Procedures, 44

over, they argue that the nondisclosure of chemical identity prevents independent scientists from conducting additional tests comparing the tested chemical to others whose toxicological effects are better known, and searching the scientific literature for assistance.[220]

Industry representatives deny these allegations, noting that it is standard practice to test a substance "blind" (without any knowledge of its chemical identity).[221] They also doubt that environmental groups or independent scientists will perform additional tests on very many products.[222] Confidential manufacturing processes frequently can be deduced from knowledge of the chemical structure of a substance[223] and the knowledge of the mere existence of a chemical can be an important commercial advantage to competitors.[224] For example, a company might manufacture a chemical and then stockpile it for several years to preserve its option to market it at an economically propitious time. Revealing even the fact that a particular company is manufacturing a particular chemical could destroy this marketing advantage.[225]

A proposed EPA solution that would mask the chemical identity until production begins[226] provides an appropriate resolution for the vast majority of chemicals. This would protect a company's headstart while providing interested parties with the chemical identity at the time that full-scale manufacturing begins so that they may evaluate the studies and begin environmental and workplace monitoring. Once production begins, the public interest in knowing the identity of chemicals to which it is being exposed probably outweighs whatever

Fed. Reg. 2242, 2255–56 (1979); Letter from Natural Resources Defense Council, Inc., to Blake A. Biles at 2–3 (Aug. 14, 1978).

[220] Environmental Defense Fund, Comments on Proposed Premanufacture Notification Requirements and Review Procedures 5 (Mar. 26, 1979); EPA Support Document, Premanufacture Notification Requirements and Review Procedures 178 (1979) [hereinafter cited as Support Document].

[221] *See* Lubrizol Corp., Comments on Proposed Premanufacture Notification Requirements and Review Procedures 13 (Mar. 26, 1979).

[222] *See* Letter from James T. O'Reilly, Proctor and Gamble Co., to Blake A. Biles at 4 (July 15, 1978). One company has even offered to make samples available to bona fide public interest groups for testing. *See* Lubrizol Corp., *supra* note 221, at 94–95.

[223] *See* U.S. Dep't of Commerce, Comments on Proposed Premanufacture Notification Requirements and Review Products 11 (Mar. 26, 1979) [hereinafter cited as Commerce Department Comments].

[224] *See* Lubrizol Corp., *supra* note 221.

[225] *See* Eastman Kodak Co., *supra* note 218, at 18; Polaroid Co., Comments on Proposed Premanufacture Notification Requirements and Review Procedures 27 (Mar. 23, 1979).

[226] EPA Premanufacture Notification Requirements and Review Procedures, 44 Fed. Reg. 2242, 2256–57 (1979).

marketing advantages are lost through revealing chemical identities with health and safety studies, especially since competitors can in most cases analyze a product to determine the unrevealed identities of chemicals contained therein.[227]

For a small minority of chemicals, however, the EPA's proposed rules could cause hardship. Some companies use chemicals in undetectable forms or quantities in certain products. While the amount of chemical used is small, it can perform an exceedingly important role in the marketability of the final product.[228] Other companies use some chemicals only as intermediates or catalysts within the confines of the company; these chemicals never become available to competitors for analysis.[229] Disclosure of such chemical identities could cause great economic harm to an innovating company without providing appreciable benefits to the public at large. One solution might be to reveal chemical identity for these substances only to bona fide market and public interest groups subject to enforceable protective orders. This, however, would require the agency to draw difficult distinctions between bona fide and non-bona fide groups. Alternatively, the EPA could specify some minimum amount of product below which generic chemical identification would be possible. Small amounts of a chemical should result in very little exposure to nonworkers, and workers' safety can be protected by informing them of the properties of the generically named chemical and labelling that chemical generically in the workplace. A "small quantities" exception would require labor and public interest groups to trust the EPA to make adequate evaluations of the studies for those chemicals subject to the exception. It would also require the EPA to spend time addressing claims that particular chemicals fell within the exception. On the whole, however, these disadvantages seem small in comparison to the potential loss of incentives to invest in the development of such chemicals that might otherwise result. Unfortunately, because the TSCA relies on a broad definition of "health and safety study,"[230] the agency is probably precluded from administratively promulgating a "small quantities" exception. Ultimately, Congress may have to resolve this question.

Apart from the question of chemical identities, there is

---

[227] *See* Commerce Department Comments, *supra* note 223, at 11.

[228] Examples of this problem include perfumes in consumer products and trace chemicals in photographic supplies. *See* Proctor and Gamble Co., Comments on Proposed Premanufacture Notification Requirements and Review Procedures (Mar. 26, 1979); Eastman Kodak Co., *supra* note 218, at 16–17.

[229] *See* Eastman Kodak Co., *supra* note 218, at 17.

[230] *See* p. 839 *supra*.

another problem associated with the scope of "health and safety study." Neither the TSCA, nor the FIFRA, as amended, specifies who has the burden of "sanitizing" new and existing health and safety reports that may include information that does not come within the definition of "health and safety study" and is legitimately considered proprietary. Agency employees will understandably be reluctant to send full copies of health and safety reports to data requesters if doing so might run afoul of the Trade Secrets Act[231] or a similar proscription in the agency's own statute.[232] But the agency is equally reluctant to scour each of the hundreds of pages in the reports for possible proprietary information. The EPA has attempted to solve this dilemma by requiring the original data submitter to mark clearly all portions of health and safety studies that it considers proprietary.[233] While this approach may place some outer bounds on the data that the agency will not disclose, unless data producers modify their recently adopted practice of stamping every page of health and safety data "trade secret," the EPA will still have to monitor industry claims. Under the TSCA, the EPA intends to require the data submitter to substantiate any trade secrecy claims at the time it submits the data.[234] The difference between the two monitoring approaches is reflected in the fact that the EPA currently has hundreds of thousands of unsanitized health and safety studies for pesticides while its TSCA files are presently empty.

The fact that all confidentiality determinations are subject to judicial review makes the TSCA approach the preferred one. Under that approach, confidentiality litigation will begin before humans and the environment are exposed to the chemical. Under the FIFRA approach, persons are likely to request data only after the product has been on the market for some time. At this point, the delay of litigation will operate in favor of the manufacturer who asserted the secrecy claim. The longer it can litigate about whether data should be released to environmental groups, the longer it will be before those groups have the opportunity to petition the agency to take the product off the market. The TSCA approach will initially be more burdensome to the agency, because it will require agency employees to resolve some confidentiality claims that might not otherwise be questioned and may encourage unnecessary litigation. However, once the agency and the courts have decided

---

[231] 18 U.S.C. § 1905 (1976).

[232] *See, e.g.*, 7 U.S.C.A. § 136h(f) (West Supp. 1979) (FIFRA).

[233] 44 Fed. Reg. 59,764, 59,773–77 (1979); 43 Fed. Reg. 59,060, 59,061–62 (1978).

[234] 44 Fed. Reg. 59,764, 59,773–77 (1979).

a few early cases, the TSCA approach should have the salutary effect of encouraging data submitters to make realistic claims at the outset. In addition, harsh penalties for bad faith assertion of trade secrecy protection could help prevent abuses.

(ii) Measuring and Apportioning Compensation. — While the idea of requiring follow-on manufacturers to compensate the original innovator for its testing costs is an appealing solution to the disclosure problem, fashioning a workable compensation scheme presents severe practical difficulties. Since the TSCA[235] and the FIFRA[236] seek to allocate a portion of the *actual* costs of producing the data, they fail to compensate the original submitter for its lost monopoly profits.[237] Hence, the protection for research incentives is incomplete in comparison to that provided by forcing later applicants to reproduce health and safety tests.[238] But a cost system is more practical than other candidates. A "fair market value" approach to measuring compensation is a highly abstract test in the data compensation context where there are no relevant markets that the decisionmaker may use for comparison. The "cost of production" test at least has the advantage of being reasonably ascertainable; the fair market value test has no moorings. A "reasonable royalty" test is also fraught with problems. This approach, commonly used for setting damages in patent infringement cases,[239] sets compensation at the level "which a licensee would be willing to pay and still make a reasonable profit out of use of the patented article."[240] Like the market value approach, the reasonable royalty test could lead to long

---

[235] The TSCA requires a follow-on applicant to make a "fair and equitable reimbursement . . . for a portion of the costs incurred by" the data producer. 15 U.S.C. § 2604(h)(2)(B)(i) (1976).

[236] The FIFRA is somewhat unclear. It requires the follow-on applicant to make an offer "to compensate the original data submitter." 7 U.S.C.A. § 136a(c)(1)(D) (West Supp. 1979). Conceivably, this language would authorize an award not limited to cost. However, another provision states that "defensive data" produced at the request of the Administrator after a pesticide is registered may be used by any current registrant, but only on the condition that it agree to pay a portion of the cost of producing the data. *Id.* § 1361(c)(2)(B). This suggests that Congress meant for data compensation in general to include only the cost of producing the data.

[237] Note that the discussion here concerns only those chemicals that are unpatentable or that have expired patents.

[238] If incentives suffer, a "cost plus a fixed percentage" system could be used. Such a system would not hurt the practicality of a cost-based system.

[239] *See, e.g.*, 35 U.S.C. § 284 (1976); 4 A. DELLER, *supra* note 75, § 413, at 669–82 (2d ed. 1965); *id.* § 413, at 221–24 (1979 Supp.); Wilson & Lewis, *Elements of Recovery in a Patent Infringement Suit*, 42 J. PAT. OFF. SOC'Y 742, 743–52 (1960).

[240] Beatty Safway Scaffold Co. v. Up-Right, Inc., 306 F.2d 626, 632 (9th Cir. 1962), *cert. denied*, 372 U.S. 934 (1963).

and difficult compensation proceedings that would necessarily have to be carried out on a case-by-case basis.[241]

Even the cost of production test will involve some difficulties in determining and allocating costs. The FIFRA suggests no method for apportioning the costs of data production among users. The TSCA, however, directs the Administrator to consider, among other factors, "the effect on the competitive position of the person required to provide reimbursement in relation to the person to be reimbursed and the share of the market for such substance or mixture of the person required to provide reimbursement in relation to the share of such market of the persons to be reimbursed."[242] While apportionment according to market share may seem simple, the problems of determining the relevant market and assessing market shares can be formidable.[243] The suggestion is also meaningless in the typical situation where the follow-on producer has not yet begun to manufacture the product and therefore has a market share of zero.[244] In any event, in light of the wide discretion afforded the EPA under the TSCA, and the Federal Mediation and Conciliation Service under the FIFRA, few advance compensation agreements and much litigation and arbitration can be expected.

Another problem lies in determining what portion of an innovator's costs should be eligible for reimbursement. A follow-on applicant might legitimately argue that all of the data generated by the original applicant were not necessary to obtain the license. The EPA avoids having to resolve these sorts of disagreements under the FIFRA by requiring every follow-on applicant for a technical grade registration to cite all data in the EPA's files and to offer to compensate all of the producers of those data.[245] In addition to the administrative

---

[241] *See, e.g.*, Georgia-Pacific Corp. v. U.S. Plywood Corp., 318 F. Supp. 1116, 1120 (S.D.N.Y. 1970) (listing the many factors relevant to determining a reasonable royalty rate), *modified sub nom.* Georgia-Pacific Corp. v. U.S. Plywood-Champion Papers, Inc., 446 F.2d 295 (2d Cir.), *cert. denied*, 404 U.S. 870 (1971).

[242] 15 U.S.C. § 2603(c)(3)(A) (1976). *See also id.* § 2604(h)(2)(B). The House Report indicates that the purpose for including these guidelines was to protect small businesses. H.R. REP. No. 94-1341, 94th Cong., 2d Sess. 21 (1976). Beyond this, Congress was willing to give the agency very little guidance. *See id.*

[243] *See* Advance Notice of Proposed Rulemaking, Data Reimbursement Under Sections 4 and 5 of The Toxic Substances Control Act, 44 Fed. Reg. 54,284, 54,286–87 (1979).

[244] The EPA has recognized the possibility of assessing market share at the end of some predetermined period following testing and marketing. *Id.* at 54,287. This, of course, would delay the compensation of the data producer.

[245] Regulations for the Enforcement of the Federal Insecticide, Fungicide, and Rodenticide Act: Compensation for Use of Data, 44 Fed. Reg. 27,945, 27,946–48

burden that would otherwise result, the EPA stresses that sound scientific decisions must be made on the basis of all of the information available to the decisionmaker.[246] Compensated disclosure therefore imposes substantial transaction costs upon the parties and the agency. In implementing this approach, the agency should attempt to make the process function as smoothly as possible. The EPA could eliminate a great deal of future friction by promulgating guidelines for measuring and allocating compensation.[247] It is interesting to note that many of the implementation problems are absent during the ten year exclusive use periods which the FIFRA applies to data submitted in support of pesticides containing active ingredients that are initially registered after 1978.[248] This thought will be pursued in the next Part.

III. RECOMMENDATIONS FOR REFORM

In the context of the policy considerations presented in Part I, the specific schemes presented in Part II may be succinctly critiqued. Application of the common law definition of trade secrets has been unsatisfactory since it has resulted in nondisclosure of drug health and safety data without regard to the public policy interests in favor of disclosure, and because it has led to full disclosure of antibiotic and additive safety data where no other special protections for research incentives exist. Neither of these outcomes strikes any real balance between the reasons for disclosure and the need to retain incentives for innovation. The TSCA and the FIFRA, by excluding health and safety data from the ambit of proprietary information, permit development of a scheme specifically geared to health and safety testing data. The resulting pattern of compensated disclosure protects innovation incentives while at the same time permitting disclosure, but the costs of arriving at proper reimbursement awards may be substantial. These conclusions suggest the desirability of finding new methods of striking the balance.

(1979) (to be codified at 40 C.F.R. § 162) [hereinafter cited as 1979 FIFRA Compensation Regulations]. These regulations have recently been challenged in the District Court for the District of Columbia by the National Agricultural Chemicals Association and CIBA-Geigy Corporation. *See* 3 CHEM. REG. REP. (BNA) 885 (1979). The agency has not yet grappled with this problem under the TSCA.

[246] *See* 1979 FIFRA Compensation Regulations, *supra* note 245, at 27,946.

[247] The EPA has made public its intention to establish precisely such guidelines for the TSCA. *See* 44 Fed. Reg. 54,284 (1979) (to be codified at 40 C.F.R. § 774).

[248] *See* p. 875 *supra*.

A. Recommended Congressional Action:
Exclusive Use Periods and Full Disclosure

In enacting the TSCA and amending the FIFRA, Congress has implicitly recognized that disclosure is desirable and that the interests that would be protected by nondisclosure can be safeguarded by other means. This conclusion is supported by the FDA's failure to find any satisfactory substitute for the full disclosure of drug safety testing data.[249] And even if the conclusion is wrong, the affected industries are better able to come forward with information supporting any request for increased protection than is the public to negate industry's claim.[250]

Congress could require the disclosure of all health and safety testing data and protect innovation by increasing patent protection or directly subsidizing research.[251] But extending patent protection poses special problems[252] and additional direct funding may be of doubtful political feasibility. The exclusive use period mechanism suggested in the FIFRA[253] points to the most attractive solution to the problem across all of the relevant fields.[254] Under this approach, the health and

---

[249] *See* pp. 869–72 *supra*.

[250] *See* pp. 851–52 *supra*.

[251] In the patent area, chemical and drug patents could be made easier to obtain and/or longer lasting. Federal encouragement could come by way of direct payment or tax incentives. Government subsidization of drug and pesticide research is already sizeable. For example, the National Cancer Institute's 1978 budget included $52.7 million for detection and diagnostic research. U.S. OFFICE OF MANAGEMENT & BUDGET, THE BUDGET OF THE UNITED STATES GOVERNMENT, FISCAL YEAR 1980, app., at 406 (1979). Also, the Division of Research Resources of the National Institute of Environmental Health Sciences in 1978 planned to spend $49.0 million for research at university-affiliated hospitals, $21.7 million for laboratory animal and primate related research, and $38.3 million for biomedical research. *Id*. app., at 416.

[252] Congress may be reluctant to provide individual exceptions to the patent laws' general provisions, especially because it might affect treaty obligations. *See* Paris Convention for the Protection of Industrial Property, July 14, 1967, 21 U.S.T. 1583, T.I.A.S. No. 6923.

[253] In the 1978 FIFRA Amendments, Congress gave the originator of an active pesticide ingredient a 10-year lead time during which its data could not be used by another company. However, Congress superimposed upon this a scheme that requires compensation for data used during the 15-year period following submission. *See* p. 875 *supra*. Since this combined approach is subject to all of the undesirable elements of the data compensation approach, it is less desirable than the pure lead time approach.

[254] Such a "head start" is also finding increasing favor in common law trade secret cases. *See, e.g.*, Analogic Corp. v. Data Translation, Inc., 371 Mass. 643, 647–49, 358 N.E.2d 804, 807–08 (1976); Carboline Co. v. Jarboe, 454 S.W.2d 540, 552–53 (Mo. 1970). *See also* Northern Petrochem. Co. v. Tomlinson, 484 F.2d 1057, 1061 n.5 (7th Cir. 1973).

safety data would be immediately available to the public, but competitors could not use the data to register competing products for a fixed period of time. While informing the public to the same extent as the FDA's full disclosure approach to food additives,[255] the exclusive use period would place the data producer in almost the same position for a pre-determined period that it would occupy under the FDA's nondisclosure approach for drugs.[256] The only detriment to the data producer stems from the "intelligence value" that the data may provide for competitors.[257] Nevertheless, the producer's "headstart" will be very valuable and should provide protection for research incentives.

The exclusive use period approach has several advantages. First, it recognizes that the public interest in disclosure of health and safety data can only be served by actual disclosure. Second, the duration of the exclusive use period can be adjusted to ensure adequate research incentives. Third, it balances the relevant competing interests generically, thereby avoiding the transaction costs that inevitably accompany case-by-case determinations. Yet, it provides the flexibility to permit different exclusive use periods for different product categories (for example, drugs), if warranted by differential concerns for innovation.

The exclusive use period approach is not without its disadvantages, however. Since it relies on monopoly profits as an indirect stimulus to innovation, consumers will have to pay monopoly prices during the exclusive use period. However, prices will be tempered by the fact that competitors may duplicate the testing data in order to enter especially attractive markets. Second, because the use period is established generically, it is probable that some data submitters will receive too much of an advantage, while others not enough, than if a balance were struck on a case-by-case basis. Given the modest ability of economists to predict the incentive stimulating and competition enhancing effects of any particular regulatory action, this criticism of a generic approach, however, may well presume an accuracy for the case-by-case method that does not in fact exist. While the exclusive use period approach may not be the ideal solution to the balancing problem, it is probably the best solution that is not hopelessly quixotic.[258]

---

[255] *See* pp. 872–73 *supra.*

[256] *See* pp. 868–69 *supra.*

[257] *See* p. 850 *supra.*

[258] Another potential problem with the exclusive use period involves data required by the agency after the product has been on the market for some time, commonly called "defensive data." Strict application of the exclusive use period approach would

A more telling criticism of the exclusive use period approach is that it would permit duplicative testing of drugs, posing potential health hazards to those involved.[259] This period could be minimized by giving the FDA authority to ban any duplicative testing that would endanger patients during the exclusive use period. After such a determination, the FDA should also be permitted to shorten the exclusive use period to reflect the increased barrier to entry.

It is certainly possible that the drug and chemical industries need long exclusive use periods. Yet since the information needed to support this conclusion is peculiarly within their control,[260] the burden should be upon them to justify the necessity of any particular exclusive use period. To date, the wide ranging and unfocused congressional hearings on this subject, especially concerning pesticide and drug reform, have not yet actually called upon the companies to justify their contentions that the monopoly profits attributable to exclusive use of data are socially desirable. This is not to suggest that a congressional committee is incapable of conducting this sort of inquiry. However, it is likely that the industries will continue to avoid answering the crucial questions that make or break their case for monopoly profits if the only forum continues to be the congressional hearing. An independent commission, the General Accounting Office, or the Office of Technology Assessment might be more effective forums for gathering the necessary information. Alternatively, the FDA or the EPA might, pursuant to general grants of rulemaking authority, conduct such investigations. Whatever the locus of the investigation, it is important that the investigator have subpena

---

give the first competitor to produce the required data a fresh exclusive use period. While this is an inefficient solution to the problem, it would be unfair to allow the remaining competitors to take a "free ride" on the data producer's work effort. The best solution to the defensive data problem is to force all licensees to agree before the research is started to share the costs of producing the data requested by the agency. If the licensees cannot agree how to proportion the costs among themselves, a pro-rata apportionment could be statutorily imposed.

[259] *See* pp. 845–47 *supra*.

[260] *See* pp. 851–52 *supra*. Whoever sets the exclusive use periods should consider (1) the extent of protection already afforded by the patent system; (2) how much extra consumers will pay because of the added anticompetitive effects of a given period of exclusive use for unpatented products; (3) how much of this additional profit will be channelled into research and development of new products; and (4) how many new products would likely result. Data bearing on these points would include current profit margins in competitive versus noncompetitive markets, current production levels in those markets, the percentage of current profits invested in R&D in the relevant industries, and historical comparisons between new products produced and dollars invested. It should be noted that these are the sorts of data that have been noticeably absent from congressional consideration of recent pesticide and drug reform packages.

power to verify for itself industry claims.[261] Once the information is available, the duration of the exclusive use period necessary to strike the balance between innovation and competition could be determined by Congress, or, perhaps more efficiently, by the relevant agency pursuant to a congressional grant of authority. But until the crucial information becomes available, it is not likely that Congress or any other decision-maker will strike an adequate balance.

B. Recommendations for Agency Action: The FDA Should Abandon the Restatement Definition

The FDA is on record as having asked Congress to authorize the release of all drug testing information.[262] If Congress does not act as recommended by the preceding section, the FDA may not be helpless. In light of the inappropriateness of the *Restatement* definition of trade secrets in the regulatory context,[263] the willingness of courts and Congress to adopt more restrictive definitions of "proprietary information,"[264] and the lack of any definition of that phrase in the applicable drug regulation statutes,[265] the FDA should abandon the *Restatement* definition. In its place, the FDA should substitute a balancing test[266] and proceed to weigh the interests for and against disclosure. The FDA's authority to promulgate such a regulation lies in its power to make regulations for the efficient enforcement of its statutory duties.[267] As Part I demonstrated, unless the drug industry comes forward with very persuasive evidence of the need for protection, the rulemaking should conclude that all health and safety test data are *not* proprietary information and hence should be disclosed. Such action by the FDA would probably force the drug industry to

---

[261] Recently, the FDA's Office of the Assistant Secretary for Planning and Evaluation was forced to abandon a study of the economic impact of various alternative trade secret policies on industry research incentives, partly because drug sponsors said they were unable to identify R&D expenditures in a manner that would have satisfied the study design. REVIEW PANEL ON NEW DRUG REGULATION, U.S. DEP'T OF HEALTH, EDUCATION & WELFARE, INTERIM REPORT: AN EVALUATION OF FDA'S TRADE SECRETS AND FREEDOM OF INFORMATION POLICIES 72 (1977).

[262] *See* Kennedy Letter, *supra* note 10, at 841–42.

[263] *See* p. 863 *supra*.

[264] *See* pp. 863–64 *supra*.

[265] *See* p. 868 *supra*.

[266] This would require the FDA to abandon its position that action would more appropriately be left to Congress. *See* 39 Fed. Reg. 44,634 (1974).

[267] 21 U.S.C. § 371(a) (1976); *see* 21 C.F.R. § 10.40 (1979). An agency may reverse a prior interpretation of a regulatory statute with an adequately documented conclusion that the former construction was inappropriate, erroneous, or contrary to the public welfare. *See* K. DAVIS, ADMINISTRATIVE LAW TEXT § 17.07 (1972).

seek redress from Congress, if not the courts. This in turn might spur Congress to give drug health and safety testing data the scrutiny that it deserves. If the actions taken under the TSCA and the FIFRA are any indication of Congress' pulse, Congress will take health and safety testing data out of the realm of proprietary information and establish special protections for innovation incentives. As noted in the previous Section, this would be desirable.

IV. Conclusion

The public has for too long been deprived of the information necessary to judge the performance of agencies involved with health and safety protection and to make informed individual health and safety decisions concerning drugs and pesticides. The industries that produce products posing possible health and safety threats to the public have been surprisingly successful in convincing or forcing regulatory agencies to protect health and safety data under an inappropriate definition of "proprietary information" that focuses exclusively upon competitive harm. Fortunately, Congress has intervened in the pesticide and toxic substance regulatory arenas to provide that health and safety data are not proprietary. To protect the incentives allegedly jeopardized by making health and safety data public, Congress provided a data compensation scheme that operates at great administrative cost. Especially in light of these costs, an exclusive use period approach would be preferable to the compensation approach.

Unfortunately, Congress has failed entirely to address the parallel, but much more serious problem of drug health and safety data. It would be desirable if the pharmaceutical industry, to eliminate the social waste and possible human injury associated with duplicative testing, would join the FDA in devising an acceptable solution — possibly along the lines of the exclusive use period approach advocated here. But if the industry continues its opposition to the FDA's reform efforts, the FDA could possibly precipitate the needed congressional action by abandoning its nondisclosure approach and, by redefining "proprietary information," adopt instead a full disclosure approach. This would force drug manufacturers to take their "lost innovation" claims directly to Congress, a result that is entirely appropriate, because manufacturers ought to bear the burden of demonstrating that the need for further innovation justifies monopoly profits.

Congress could react to drug company pressure in one of three ways. First, it could simply reverse the agency and make it clear that health and safety data should receive absolute proprietary protection. The FIFRA experience, however, indicates that Congress is not likely to disregard the substantial policies favoring data release to secure the benefits of the possible innovation that may flow from further research. Second, Congress might do nothing and allow the public to suffer whatever deleterious effects might result from lost innovation. Congress, however, is not likely to adopt a posture of benign neglect in the face of drug industry protests that the "drug lag" is endangering the health of American patients, despite the present lack of substantial evidence that monopoly profits will reduce this lag.

The fairest and most practical option is the exclusive use period approach. Congress could ratify the FDA's redefinition of "proprietary data" or, if the FDA proves unwilling to take the initial step, redefine the term itself so as to exclude health and safety data as it has recently done in the chemical and pesticide areas. Then, after an appropriate body has made a thorough investigation of the facts and has made reasonable predictions about the efficacy of barriers to entry in stimulating drug research, Congress or the agency pursuant to congressional authority could provide for a generic period of exclusive use that represents a balance between the need for innovation and the policies of encouraging competitive pricing and discouraging duplicative testing. In addition, Congress should give the FDA the authority to ban duplicative tests that endanger their human participants.

Congress has in the past studiously avoided resolving this continuing paradox in the American free enterprise system. No free enterprise economy can function properly unless consumers are informed. Yet consumers cannot become informed if industry-generated data on important aspects of products they consume remain secret; nor can competition produce an efficient marketplace when secrecy erects barriers to entry. On the other hand, competition and consumer sovereignty do not breed innovation. An innovator must be secure in the knowledge that he will reap the benefits of his efforts. Congress has moved to resolve these inherent contradictions in the toxic substance and pesticide areas. Congress should take parallel action with respect to drug regulation. FDA pressure, in the form of changing its antiquated approach toward proprietary information, could prove to be the necessary catalyst.

[7]

THE WHISTLEBLOWER PROTECTION ACT OF 1989: FOUNDATION FOR THE MODERN LAW OF EMPLOYMENT DISSENT

THOMAS M. DEVINE*

TABLE OF CONTENTS

* Legal Director, Government Accountability Project. J.D., 1980, Antioch School of Law; B.A. 1974, Georgetown University. The author wishes to acknowledge and thank the too often tireless legal research and initial drafting assistance from countless students at the University of the District of Columbia Law School; Donald Aplin, former clinical director of the Government Accountability Project (GAP); and Jasmin Keshet, Esq., Legal Director of the Movement for Quality Government in Israel, who assisted with final research while working with GAP as part of a grant from the New Israel Fund. Mr. Devine may be contacted via e-mail at whistle47@aol.com.

INTRODUCTION

Good faith whistleblowers[1] represent the highest ideals of public service and the American tradition for individuals to challenge abuses of power. They live by the Code of Ethics for Government Service by "put[ting] loyalty to the highest moral principles and to country above loyalty to persons, party or Government department."[2] They act as the human factor that is the Achilles heel of bureaucratic corruption. Even dissenters with the basest of

---

1. In the federal civil service system, whistleblowers are those employees or applicants for employment who are protected under 5 U.S.C. § 2302(b)(8) (1994) for lawfully disclosing information that they reasonably believe evidences illegality, gross waste, gross mismanagement, abuse of authority, or a substantial and specific danger to public health or safety. If disclosure is specifically prohibited by statute, or by Executive Order as classified on national security grounds, an employee is only protected if the disclosure is made to the agency chief or delegee, an agency Inspector General, or the U.S. Office of Special Counsel. *See infra* note 14.

Relevant regulations have defined "whistleblower" consistently with the statutory boundaries. *See* 5 C.F.R. § 1250.3(c) (1987). Case law has provided definitions and guidance for the boundaries of protected whistleblowing speech categories beyond disclosures of illegality, which under § 2302(b)(8) cover violations of "any law, rule or regulation." "Gross waste" is "a more than debatable expenditure that is significantly out of proportion to the benefit reasonably expected to accrue to the government." Smith v. Department of Army, 80 M.S.P.R. 311, 315 (1998) (citing Embree v. Department of Treasury, 70 M.S.P.R. 79, 85 (1996)). The amount of money involved can be as low as $15,000, indicating a negligible de minimis standard. *Id.* "Abuse of authority" also is a qualitative, rather than a quantitative category for protected speech. "An 'abuse of authority' occurs when there is an 'arbitrary or capricious exercise of power by a federal official or employee that adversely affects the rights of any person or that results in personal gain or advantage to himself or other preferred persons.'" Ramos v. Department of the Treasury, 72 M.S.P.R. 235, 241 (1996) (citing D'Elia v. Department of the Treasury, 60 M.S.P.R. 226, 232-33 (1993)). The definition does not incorporate a de minimus threshold.

By contrast, quantified impact is necessary to establish "gross mismanagement," which is "a decision that creates a 'substantial risk of adverse impact upon the agency's ability to accomplish its mission.'" Sazinski v. Department of Hous. and Urban Dev., 73 M.S.P.R. 682, 686 (1997) (citing Coons v. Department of the Navy, 63 M.S.P.R. 485, 488 (1994)). Perhaps the most significant category in terms of tangible impact is "substantial and specific danger to public health or safety," defined in an illustrative fashion by Congress and administrative precedent as follows: "[o]nly disclosures of public health or safety dangers which are both substantial and specific are to be protected. Thus, for example, general criticism by an employee of the Environmental Protection Agency that the agency is not doing enough to protect the environment would not be protected under [§ 2302(b)(8)]. However, an allegation by a Nuclear Regulatory Commission engineer that the cooling system of a nuclear reactor is inadequate would fall within the whistleblower protections." *Id.* (citing S. REP. No. 95-969, at 21 (1978)). The perceived danger does not have to affect the public at large. Threats to even a limited number of government personnel are sufficient for Whistleblower Protection Act coverage. *See* Wojcicki v. Department of the Air Force, 72 M.S.P.R. 628, 634-35 (1996).

2.   5 U.S.C. § 7301 note (1994) (Code of Ethics for Government Service).

motives can make positive contributions if their disclosures are accurate and significant. They provide the pluralism of views and competitive diversity of information necessary for the checks and balances in a democracy.[3]

In this context, it is not surprising that the civil service system long has had a love-hate relationship with dissenters. Whistleblower protection is a policy that all government leaders support in public[4] but few in power will tolerate in private.[5] Laws protecting freedom of dissent have been long on rhetoric and short on genuine substance. As a result, until passage of the Whistleblower Protection Act of 1989 (WPA or the Act),[6] most statutory free speech protections tended to be counterproductive — scandal containment laws that created an increased chilling effect.

An attempt to transcend this phenomenon has been the evolving system of federal statutory law that began with the whistleblower protection provision in the Civil Service Reform Act of 1978 (Reform Act or CSRA).[7] In addition to overhauling the structure of civil service law, the Reform Act outlawed eleven prohibited personnel practices[8] as affirmative defenses against merit system violations.[9] Within five years of the Reform Act's passage, fear of reprisal doubled — from nineteen to thirty-seven percent — and was the reason cited by would-be whistleblowers who remained silent observers instead of challenging significant government misconduct that they personally witnessed.[10]

---

3. *See* TOM DEVINE, THE WHISTLEBLOWER'S SURVIVAL GUIDE: COURAGE WITHOUT MARTYRDOM 1-2, 5-7 (1997).

4. As Representative Derwinski remarked during congressional deliberations, "[t]he term 'whistleblower' is like 'motherhood,' and we are all for whistleblowing evidently." *Markup Meetings on H.R. 11,280 of the House Comm. on Post Office and Civil Service*, 95th Cong. 19 (1978).

5. One commentator explained: "Don't be an oddball; don't be a radical; don't be a whistleblower. If you fit into any of those categories, your position . . . will range narrowly from uncomfortable to untenable. . . . Being a Democrat or a Republican is just a party affiliation. Don't make waves is a religion." Florence Isabell, *Dissidents in the Federal Government*, 4 CIV. LIB. REV., Sept./Oct. 1977, at 72, 75.

6. Pub. L. No. 101-12, 103 Stat. 16 (1989) (codified at 5 U.S.C. §§ 1201–1222 (1994 & Supp. III 1997)).

7. Pub. L. No. 95-454, 92 Stat. 1111 (1978). As referenced in note 1, *supra*, the relevant prohibited personnel practice protecting freedom of dissent is codified at 5 U.S.C. § 2302(b)(8) (1994).

8. *See* 5 U.S.C. § 2302(b)(1)-(11) (1994 & Supp. III 1997).

9. *See* 5 U.S.C. § 2301 (1994). For an exhaustive review of the statutory birth of whistleblower protection, see generally Robert G. Vaughn, *Statutory Protection of Whistleblowers in the Federal Executive Branch*, 1982 U. ILL. L. REV. 615 (1982).

10. MSPB: Office of Merit Systems Review and Studies, *Blowing the Whistle in the Federal Government: A Comparative Analysis of 1980 and 1983 Survey Findings*, 31, 34 (1984).

In light of the Reform Act's track record, the resulting silence was not surprising. The law only created a direct cause of action and conventional administrative hearing for whistleblowers to challenge demotions or disciplinary actions greater than a two week suspension — leaving unaddressed common forms of harassment such as reassignment to bureaucratic Siberia, elimination of duties, career paralysis, and paper trails like reprimands and other preliminary discipline that could make termination inevitable.[11] For most forms of retaliation, federal workers could only receive relief through being championed by the federal Office of the Special Counsel (OSC or Special Counsel).[12] Unfortunately, for extended periods this agency's approach ranged from neglect to overt hostility. After its 1978 creation until passage of the Whistleblower Protection Act of 1989, the Special Counsel conducted only one hearing to restore a whistleblower's job — in 1979.[13] Meanwhile, the OSC taught courses to agency leaders on how to fire whistleblowers with impunity, even tutoring federal managers when necessary. Most objectionable, the OSC regularly served as a source of free "discovery" by sharing with agencies the evidence from aggrieved whistleblowers seeking help, and by conducting and sharing with agencies the results from investigations of the complainants who sought OSC assistance.[14]

Results were only marginally better for those who had the right to a due process administrative hearing before the newly created civil service appeals forum, the Merit Systems Protection Board (MSPB or Board).[15] In reported decisions of the Board between 1979 and passage of the Whistleblower Protection Act of 1989, dissenters exercising their appeal rights only prevailed on the merits four times out of more than two thousand appeals where the whistleblower defense was raised — none prevailed after 1984.[16]

---

11. *See* DEVINE, *supra* note 3, at 27-39. Jurisdiction conferring eligibility for an administrative hearing was limited under 5 U.S.C. § 7701 (1994) to disciplinary actions greater than 14 day suspensions and actions based on unacceptable performance. For a general introduction on employee access to Board hearings, *see* Robert A. Maroldo, Jr., *An Overview of MSPB Appellate Jurisdiction*, 81 F.M.S.R. 9 (1981).

12. *See* 5 U.S.C. §§ 1213 (1994 & Supp. III 1997).

13. *See* In Matter of Frazier, 1 M.S.P.B. 163 (1979), *aff'd*, Frazier v. MSPB, 672 F.2d 150 (D.C. Cir. 1982).

14. For an in-depth discussion of abuses by the Office of the Special Counsel and the counterproductive nature of whistleblower protection under the Civil Service Reform Act, see generally Thomas M. Devine & Donald G. Aplin, *Abuse of Authority: The Office of the Special Counsel and Whistleblower Protection*, 4 ANTIOCH L.J. 5 (1986).

15. *See* 5 U.S.C. §§ 1201-1206 (1994).

16. *See* Anderson v. Department of Agric., 82 F.M.S.R. 5043 (1982); Plaskett v. Department of Health & Human Servs., 82 F.M.S.R. 5095 (1982); Spadaro v. Department of Interior, Office of Surface Mining, 18 M.S.P.R. 462 (1983); Sowers v. Department of Agric., 24 M.S.P.R. 492 (1984).

The circumstances surrounding passage of the Whistleblower Protection Act highlight the contrast between rhetorical support and functional intolerance. Superficially, there was an overwhelming mandate encouraging government employees to publicly voice dissent challenging improper practices within their organizations. Congress seldom takes any significant action unanimously. It unanimously passed the Whistleblower Protection Act twice.[17]

Similarly, no President in recent memory has admitted to opposing whistleblower protection.[18] Yet, in an election year and despite unanimous passage of the Whistleblower Protection Act of 1988, President Reagan pocket-vetoed it.[19] Even after Congress unanimously overrode his veto, the law continued to be ineffective due to resistance from the agencies charged with its implementation.

Since passage of the 1994 amendments,[20] encouraging patterns are beginning to emerge. New trends suggest that respect for the WPA's good government free speech mandate[21] may be taking hold. Based on traditions to date, however, the price of progress will be eternal persistence. The legal system's schizophrenic perspective on dissent reveals the inherent consequences of secrecy — sharp contradictions between policies set in the public eye and those implemented outside it. This Article will summarize how Congress's 1978 attempt at executive branch whistleblower protection failed, and analyze the significant changes adopted in 1989 and 1994 to strengthen the law of dissent. Finally, the Article surveys results since the

---

17. On October 3, 1988, the House passed Senate Bill 508, the Whistleblower Protection Act of 1988, by a 418-0 vote. *See* 134 CONG. REC. 28,128 (1988). On October 7 the Senate concurred without dissent. *See id.* at 29,544. The Senate already had passed a slightly-modified version of the bill on August 2. *See id.* at 19,961. On March 16, 1989, the Senate approved Senate Bill 20, the Whistleblower Protection Act of 1989, by a 97-0 vote. *See* 135 CONG. REC. 4535 (1989). On March 21 the House suspended the rules and passed the Act without dissent. *See id.* at 5026.

18. Typical of the unlimited rhetorical support whistleblowers have received in the abstract were the 1981 remarks of President Reagan, who expressed his wish to make it clear that his Administration assured protection and proper investigation of allegations "to every whistleblower in the Federal Government." *MSPB Recommends Agency "Outreach" Efforts to Encourage Whistleblowing*, Gov't Empl. Rel. Rep. (BNA) No. 936, at 8 (Nov. 2, 1981).

19. *See* Memorandum of Disapproval of S. 508, PUB. PAPERS 1391, 1392 (Oct. 26, 1988). Reagan took a sharp turn from his earlier unqualified support for whistleblowers: "Enactment of S. 508 would have redesigned the whistleblower protection process so that employees who are not genuine whistleblowers could manipulate the process to their advantage simply to delay or avoid appropriate adverse personnel actions." *Id.*

20. Act of Oct. 29, 1994, Pub. L. No. 103-424, 108 Stat. 4361 (1994).

21. 5 U.S.C. § 1201 (note) (Whistleblower Protection: Congressional Statement of Findings and Purpose) (1994).

latest legislative revision, with recommendations for loopholes that must be filled in order for the rhetoric of whistleblower protection to be credible.

I.   PROVISIONS OF THE WHISTLEBLOWER PROTECTION ACT OF 1989

Congress recognized the immensity of the 1978 law's failure[22] and attempted an ambitious balancing act through the Whistleblower Protection Act.[23] Rejecting the proposals of employee advocates to scrap the Civil Service Reform Act's administrative law system,[24] Congress reasoned that a structural overhaul was premature. Although the agencies charged with carrying out the 1978 law's legislative intent had undercut Congress's mandate rather than pursuing it, the model would not be scrapped yet. Instead, Congress opted to give its 1978 structure a second chance by reducing the agencies' discretionary authority, imposing detailed rules to achieve the original legislative intent and increasing employee due process rights.

There are four cornerstones to the modified structure — (1) giving whistleblowers control of their cases through an Individual Right of Action (IRA), providing expanded subject matter and personal jurisdiction for MSPB hearings; (2) making the Office of Special Counsel a risk-free option by eliminating previous discretionary authority that the Special Coun-

---

22. The Senate Report on the Act operated from the premise that "Congress'[s] well-intentioned efforts to protect whistleblowers have thus far had little effect." S. REP. NO. 100-413, at 5 (1988). Referencing the MSPB survey conclusion that fear of reprisal had doubled, Senator Levin set the context for the first Senate vote on the Act: "These statistics are a clear sign that the system has not worked as intended and needs to be improved." 134 CONG. REC. 19,981 (1988). Before the October floor vote, Senator Grassley summarized the net impact of the 1978 reforms: "The Government still hands out the same prizes to whistleblowers — harassment, demotion, transfer and discharge." *Id.* at 15,117. Senator Cohen echoed those sentiments before final Senate passage of the 1989 Act: "In short, the existing process has not protected legitimate whistleblowers at all." 135 CONG. REC. 2787 (1989). The prime target for the condemnations was the Office of the Special Counsel. Senator Grassley pointed out that "the agency set up to investigate whistleblower claims, the Office of Special Counsel, has become a rubberstamp for reprisals against the whistleblower." 134 CONG. REC. 15,117 (remarks of Sen. Grassley). Before the final floor vote Representative Sikorski succinctly summarized the congressional consensus about the OSC: "Set up as the employee's watchdog, it's been used as a pit bull for those hiding waste and fraud." 135 CONG. REC. 5032 (1989).

23. Pub. L. No. 101-12, 103 Stat. 16 (1989) (codified at 5 U.S.C. §§ 1201-1222 (1994 & Supp. III 1997)).

24. *See Whistleblower Protection Act of 1987: Hearing on S. 508 Before the Subcomm. on Federal Services, Post Office and Civil Service of the Senate Comm. on Governmental Affairs,* 100th Cong. 234-35, 260-64 (1987) (testimony of Edward Wright, counsel for the Whistleblower Coalition, and testimony of Thomas Devine, Legal Director, Government Accountability Project) [hereinafter *1987 Senate Hearings*]; *Hearings on Whistleblower Protection Act of 1986 Before the House Subcomm. on Civil Service of the House Comm. on Post Office and Civil Service,* 99th Cong. 151 (1986) (testimony of Julie Loeb, Chairman of the Coalition Against Government Waste) [hereinafter *1986 House Hearings*].

sel had abused to undermine whistleblowers' legal interests; (3) expanding the scope of protection by eliminating prior loopholes, broadening the shield for protected conduct, and expanding the scope of illegal employer conduct; and (4) creating more realistic legal burdens-of-proof in order to enable whistleblowers to prevail.

A. Findings and Statement of Purpose[25]

These provisions definitively resolve fundamental, bitter disputes over interpretation of the 1978 statute. The findings reaffirm that Congress views whistleblowing as a public service, the protection of which increases the effectiveness of the civil service system, and also reaffirms that the Office of the Special Counsel was created to achieve that objective.[26]

The "Purpose" section[27] focuses on the Office of Special Counsel, clarifying its mandate and summarizing the principle that limits the OSC's discretionary authority. Congress left no doubt that the OSC is a remedial agency whose mission is to defend individual victims of merit system violations. The OSC had insisted it was a civil service prosecutor responsible for serving the merit system generally.[28] The OSC's "primary" purpose is protecting employees generally, and whistleblowers in particular, from

---

25. *See* Whistleblower Protection Act § 2, 103 Stat. at 16 (1989), (codified at 5 U.S.C. § 1201 note (1994)).

26. *See id.* § 2(a); S. REP. NO. 100-413, at 22 (1988); H.R. REP. NO. 100-274, at 30 (1987).

27. *See* § 2(b), 103 Stat. at 16 (codified at 5 U.S.C. § 1201 note (1994)).

28. *See* S. REP. NO. 100-413, at 7-8 (1988). As summarized in the House Report, "former Special Counsel K. William O'Connor denied any responsibility to assist wronged individuals. He maintained that his client was the merit system, and that he had no duty to help individuals. Indeed, Mr. O'Connor referred to the victims of retaliation as 'witnesses.' His views directly conflict with congressional intent." H.R. REP. NO. 100-274, at 22 (1987). Because the Whistleblower Protection Act of 1988 was passed in the closing days of the session and there was not time for a Conference Committee, the House and Senate reconciled their closely related versions of the legislation with a Joint Explanatory Statement [hereinafter JES]. 134 CONG. REC. 27,853 (1988) (remarks of Rep. Schroeder). The JES decisively resolves the debate about the Special Counsel's lawful role:

[T]he Special Counsel's view of the role of the Office — protecting the merit system — can and has led to instances in which the Special Counsel has acted to the actual detriment of employees seeking help from that Office. Such instances are at odds with our view of the very purpose of this Office. The purpose set out in section 2, as well as a number of operative provisions contained in the bill, is intended to foreclose the possibility that the Special Counsel will act to the detriment of an employee who comes to the Special Counsel for help.

Id.

prohibited personnel practices.[29] Disciplinary prosecutions of harassers —
which the OSC had emphasized at the expense of remedial litigation — are
only a subsidiary means by which to "help accomplish" that "paramount"
goal.[30]

The policy decision underlying all specific revisions of the OSC's
authority is "that the Office of Special Counsel shall act in the interests of
employees who seek assistance from the Office of Special Counsel . . . ."[31]
This is the foundation both for reducing the OSC's discretionary authority
to undercut complainants' rights, and increasing its power to seek relief for
prohibited personnel practice victims.[32] The Whistleblower Protection
Act's unstated but unequivocal premise is that the Special Counsel also
may not act *against* the interests of employees seeking assistance.[33] The
final language was a compromise that attempted to gain the benefits of the
1986 and 1987 House versions of the WPA, which created an attorney-

---

29. *See* § 2(b)(2)(A), 103 Stat. at 16 (codified at 5 U.S.C. § 1201 note (1994)). As noted in
the Senate Report, "[a]ssuring employees that the OSC's priority is to protect them from reprisal
rather than punishing someone else is an essential step in encouraging the whistle." S. REP. NO.
100-413, at 8 (1988).

30. *See* § 2(b)(2)(C), 103 Stat. at 16 (codified at 5 U.S.C. § 1201 note (1994)); S. REP. NO.
100-413, at 8 (1988).

31. *See* § 2(b)(2)(B), 103 Stat. at 16 (codified at 5 U.S.C. § 1201 note (1994)).

32. *See* 135 CONG. REC. 2653-54 (1989) (remarks of Sen. Metzenbaum); 135 CONG. REC.
4521-22 (1989) (remarks of Sen. Roth).

33. Originally the phrase "and not contrary to those interests" was in section 2(b) of the
Whistleblower Protection Act of 1988, Senate Bill 508, as reported out of the Senate Government Affairs Committee. S. REP. NO. 100-413, at 23 (1988). As clarified in the Joint Explanatory Statement, "[l]anguage in the Senate passed bill saying that the Special Counsel may not act
contrary to interests of employees was deleted as unnecessary." 135 CONG. REC. 5033 (1989).
Congress reasoned that WPA accomplished that goal by delineating strict limitations on the
OSC's lawful authority. Before final passage, Representative Sikorski explained that the Act
"clearly establishes the limits of the OSC's duties and responsibilities." The Office of Special
Counsel's powers are confined within boundaries which mandate that the OSC: "Protect employees, especially whistleblowers, from prohibited personnel practices," and "act in the interests of employees who seek assistance from the Office . . . . It puts substantive law behind the
notion that it is clearly inappropriate and absolutely contrary for the Special Counsel to act
against the interests of whistleblowers." 135 CONG. REC. 5032 (1989). Representative Schroeder's explanation of the limitation suggests that any future actions by OSC employees that violate complainants' constitutional rights could subject the offender to tort liability under *Bivens v.
Six Unknown Named Agents of Federal Bureau of Narcotics*, 403 U.S. 388 (1971).

> One key element . . . is the limitation on the powers of the Special Counsel. The
> statements in the purposes section that it is the job of the Special Counsel to protect
> employees and to act in their interests are meant to limit the Special Counsel's
> authority. That is, the Special Counsel would exceed its authority and act in contra-
> vention of the law if it were to act against the interests of an employee who comes to
> the Special Counsel for assistance.

135 CONG. REC. 5021 (1989) (remarks of Rep. Schroeder).

client relationship with the Special Counsel,[34] while satisfying OSC objections that formalizing such a relationship would make it a legal services agency powerless to turn away undeserving employees seeking a free lawyer.[35] The compromise allows employees to file an OSC complaint without lawful risk of undermining their case due to the Special Counsel's actions or ultimate judgment. But the Act retains the OSC's discretionary authority to deny a case, so it can strategically tailor a limited budget to unlimited demands for help.[36]

B. Giving Whistleblowers Control of Their Cases — the Individual Right of Action

Perhaps the most obvious change under the WPA is the reduction of dependence on the Special Counsel, by giving whistleblowers the right to defend themselves. Under the 1978 law, most victims of prohibited personnel practices had only one possibility of a hearing to challenge most forms of reprisal. Their chances rested solely on the Special Counsel's willingness to litigate before the Merit Systems Protection Board. That is because an alleged victim's only right was to seek OSC assistance. As evidenced by the vacuum of remedial litigation since 1979, the odds of the Special Counsel seeking a hearing on behalf of whistleblowers slipped from minuscule to nonexistent.

By contrast, the WPA includes the right to a due process hearing[37] for *any* alleged victim of a violation of 5 U.S.C. § 2302(b)(8) (1994).[38] Ini-

---

34. The purposes section of that legislation, House Bill 4033 and House Bill 25, respectively, provided that "the Office of Special Counsel represent employees, former employees, and applicants for employment with the Federal government who claim to have been subject to prohibited personnel practices." H.R. 25, § 2(b)(3), reprinted in H.R. REP. NO. 100-274, at 1 (1987).

35. *See 1986 House Hearings supra* note 24, at 7 (testimony of K. William O'Connor); *Hearings on the Whistleblower Protection Act of 1987 Before the House Subcomm. on Civil Service of the House Comm. on Post Office and Civil Service*, 100th Cong. 25-28, 36-40 (1987) (testimony of Mary Wieseman) [hereinafter *1987 House Hearings*].

36. In the Senate Report on Senate Bill 508, the Government Affairs Committee explained the dynamic of the compromise whose material elements survived in the final version of the legislation: "While S. 508 is not intended to establish such an attorney-client relationship between the OSC and complainants, several provisions in the bill would create specific protections for complainants similar to those in an attorney-client relationship." S. REP. NO. 100-413, at 10 (1988).

37. *See* 5 U.S.C. § 1221(a) (1994).

38. *See id.* The provisions of the Act also apply to appellants challenging adverse actions under 5 U.S.C. § 7513(d) and raising the whistleblower defense. *See id.* § 1221(i). An employee must choose between the traditional appeal under § 7513 and a WPA cause of action. Both are not available. H.R. REP. NO.100-274, at 39 (1987). As stated in section 13 of the Joint Explanatory Statement, while exceptions exist for decisions not based on the merits, "it is not

tially, the WPA expanded personal jurisdiction. Under the old law, only those employees qualifying for administrative appeals before the Board could litigate violations of the whistleblower statute, as an affirmative defense.[39] As a result, the general rule was that only competitive service employees were directly entitled to a Board hearing.[40] All others seeking to challenge prohibited personnel practices had to file a complaint with the Office of the Special Counsel, which had absolute discretion whether to proceed beyond an investigation.[41]

Under the WPA, any individual eligible to file an OSC complaint of whistleblower reprisal now can challenge the same personnel action through an MSPB hearing. This expands the pool of eligible litigants to include, inter alia, applicants, former employees, part-time and temporary employees, probationary workers, and Schedule C political appointees.[42]

Equally significant, the WPA expands subject matter jurisdiction of the MSPB. Under the old law hearings were only available for discipline more severe than a fourteen day suspension[43] and actions based on unacceptable performance.[44] Under the WPA any listed personnel action violating § 2302(b)(8) is subject to a Board hearing. Employees now have full due process rights against common forms of harassment such as reprimands, removal of duties, failure to provide necessary training and other forms of harassment.[45]

---

intended that the MSPB hear the same case twice. If an individual has pursued the matter before MSPB under one authority, the Board is expected to dismiss a case brought under the other authority concerning the same matter under the doctrine of stare decisis." 135 CONG. REC. 5035 (1989). Curiously, the Act does not specify that its provisions can be used as an affirmative defense under 5 U.S.C. § 4303 against actions based on unacceptable performance, leaving its coverage uncertain in that context.

39. *See* 5 U.S.C. § 7701(b)(2) (1976 & Supp. IV 1980).

40. *See* ROBERT G. VAUGHN, PRINCIPLES OF CIVIL SERVICE LAW, Ch. 2 (1976).

41. *See* 5 U.S.C. § 1206(c)(1)(B) (1976 & Supp. IV 1980).

42. *See* Maroldo, *supra* note 11; Borrell v. United States Int'l Communications Agency, 682 F.2d 981 (D.C. Cir. 1982); Cutts v. Fowler, 692 F.2d 138 (D.C. Cir. 1982); Braun v. United States, 707 F.2d 922 (6th Cir. 1983); Hallock v. Moses, 731 F.2d 754 (11th Cir. 1984); Poorsina v. MSPB, 726 F.2d 507 (9th Cir. 1984). The expanded options are neatly summarized in the Senate Report. "Under current law, there are a number of situations for which an alleged whistleblower's only route of appeal is the OSC; this provision is intended to allow whistleblowers who suffer reprisal the further right of appeal to the MSPB once the OSC route is exhausted." S. REP. NO. 100-413, at 32 (1988).

43. *See* 5 U.S.C. §§ 7503, 7512 (1976 & Supp. IV 1980). Jurisdiction also existed for denial of an in-grade pay increase. *See* Parker v. Defense Logistics Agency, 1 M.S.P.R. 505 (1980).

44. *See* 5 U.S.C. § 4303 (1976 & Supp. IV 1980).

45. *See* 5 U.S.C. § 2302(a)(2) (1994). As Representative Patricia Schroeder explained, "[c]ourts held that, where an employee went to the Special Counsel and the Special Counsel decided not to help, the employee was out of luck. We eliminate that problem by giving em-

The opportunity to nip harassment in the bud is highly significant. Through a hearing to challenge the first tangible manifestations of the reprisal cycle, a whistleblower can shrink the drawn out struggle for career survival by an earlier litigation victory. This can reduce the emotional drain from suffering through prolonged career threats without the ability to fight back with discovery and cross-examination. The stress maximizes opportunities for mistakes, errors of judgment, and weaker performance due to tension, pressure, and distractions. This can give the employer justification to complete the harassment cycle through termination.[46]

The legal advantage of preventing harassment is equally compelling. Even if the employee is not worn down or baited into a mistake, an employer can gain an edge merely by successfully accumulating a record of adverse personnel actions to justify the termination.[47] Not only does the early hearing opportunity allow the employee to curtail record building, it creates another cause of action for the whistleblower in subsequent disputes. Merely participating in the first hearing triggers an additional prohibited personnel practice — reprisal for exercise of appeal rights.[48]

The Individual Right of Action also extends to temporary relief. As soon as the employee has jurisdiction for a Board hearing, the employee also has jurisdiction to petition for a stay.[49] The affected agency may file comments on the stay petition,[50] which the MSPB must grant or deny within ten days[51] and remains in effect "for such period as the Board determines to be appropriate."[52] Although the statute is silent on the legal standards to prevail, the legislative history suggests reliance on the traditional standard for injunctive relief, such as a substantial likelihood the individual will prevail on the merits, and whether there would be extreme hardship for the agency subjected to the stay.[53]

---

ployees an individual right of action to take their cases to the Board." 134 CONG. REC. 27,853 (1988).

46. *See* DEVINE, *supra* note 3, at 3-39.

47. As one commentator observed, "[a]gencies often seek to justify adverse action on the basis of current charges coupled with reference to past discipline imposed against the employee." PETER B. BROIDA, A GUIDE TO MERIT SYSTEMS PROTECTION BOARD LAW & PRACTICE, 1979-1989, at 668 (1989). This is even the case for unrelated disputes while an adverse action is pending. *See* Meads v. Veterans Admin., 36 M.S.P.R. 574 (1988); *see generally* Douglas v. Veterans Admin., 5 M.S.P.R. 280 (1981).

48. *See* 5 U.S.C. § 2302(b)(9) (1994).

49. *See id.* § 1221(c)(1).

50. *See id.* § 1221(c)(3)(A).

51. *See id.* § 1221(c)(2).

52. *See id.* § 1221(c)(3)(B).

53. As explained in section 10 of the Joint Explanatory Statement, "In making these determinations of appropriateness, the Board shall primarily consider whether there is a substantial likelihood that the individual will prevail on the merits and whether the stay would result in ex-

The major qualifier for the larger pool of litigants is a built-in time lag before jurisdiction is available, either to seek permanent or temporary relief. Individuals whose eligibility for a Board hearing is based solely on an alleged violation of the WPA must first file a complaint with the OSC.[54] The employee has jurisdiction to file a complaint with the Board if the Special Counsel does not issue a corrective action complaint within 120 days or rules negatively, whichever comes first. The individual must file for an MSPB hearing within 60 days of an adverse OSC decision.[55] The option remains open as long as the complaint is still pending before the Special Counsel after 120 days.[56] Interestingly, there is no statute of limitations for initially filing an OSC complaint. This means whistleblowers also can start the process leading to a hearing anytime after the alleged prohibited personnel practice occurs, limited only by the practical consequences of delay.

While most of the enhanced due process reforms only benefit whistleblowers during the term of their employment, there are notable exceptions. Board jurisdiction was expanded generally to cover retired annuitants.[57] This allows senior employees to avoid the previous dilemma of choosing between retirement benefits and appeal rights. Formerly, a decision to retire as a means of escaping personnel harassment was final. Retirement cut off the option to return victoriously, by canceling jurisdiction for an appeal.[58]

---

treme hardship to the agency subject to the stay." 135 CONG. REC. 5035 (1989); *see* H.R. REP. NO. 100-274, at 38 (1987); S. REP. NO. 100-413, at 17 (1988) ("It is expected the Board will be fairly liberal in granting these stays, since they would be only temporary and would not significantly affect the agency's functioning.").

54. *See* 5 U.S.C. §§ 1214(a)(3), 1221(a)-(b) (1994); S. REP. NO. 100-413, at 17, 29, 32 (1988); H. REP. No. 100-274, at 23 (1987).

55. *See* 5 U.S.C. § 1214(a)(3)(A)(ii) (1994).

56. *See* S. REP. NO. 100-413, at 18 (1988). Section 6 of the Joint Explanatory Statement contains unambiguous instructions that the cause of action remain open as long as the OSC complaint is not formally resolved: "If the individual receives no notice of termination within 120 days of filing the complaint, he or she may file the individual right of action at any time after the 120 day period has elapsed." 135 CONG. REC. 5035 (1989).

57. *See* 5 U.S.C. § 1221(j) (1994). The provisions providing interim relief also apply to an appellant who prevails at the hearing level for an allegation of any prohibited personnel practice. *See infra* note 58.

58. Section 14 of the Joint Explanatory Statement makes reference to additional implications of this provision.

This section is not limited to individual right of action cases. If an individual who has retired or received a lump sum refund is subsequently reinstated pursuant to a MSPB or court decision with back pay, the [B]ack [P]ay [A]ct (5 U.S.C. 5596) provides that adjustments shall be made to provide that the individual is treated as if the unjustified personnel action had never occurred. This means that the individual receives back pay. If that happens, the money received from the retirement fund should be treated as if it were erroneously paid and the Office of Personnel Management

Section 1221 has a carrot for the bar to litigate more actively — more generous opportunities for attorney fees. Previously, fees were only available after prevailing due to a prohibited personnel practice or other circumstance serving "the interests of justice,"[59] and even then a significant portion of costs were not recoverable.[60] Without punitive damages, this meant that the triumphs even of successful appellants could be Pyrrhic victories financially — both for the employee and counsel.

Under § 1221(g)(1) of the WPA, an employee who prevails under any prohibited personnel practice is entitled to all reasonable costs.[61] The scope is even broader for successful court appeals of MSPB decisions. If an appellant prevails for any reason at the Federal Circuit Court of Appeals, which has exclusive jurisdiction for appellate judicial review, the agency must pay full attorney fees and costs.[62] This change is modestly significant, because since its 1982 creation the Federal Circuit has never ordered an employee's reinstatement due to whistleblower reprisal. Congress recognized that the potential for any relief is limited at the Federal Circuit.[63]

---

should recover the payment. The waiver provisions under sections 8346(b) and 8470(b) of title 5 should not be applicable.
135 CONG. REC. 5035 (1989).

59. 5 U.S.C. § 7701(g)(1) (1976 & Supp. IV 1980).

60. *See* Bennett v. Department of Navy, 699 F.2d 1140 (Fed. Cir. 1983) (holding that the statutory provision of "fee" awards did not include such expense portions of the litigation bill as deposition costs or witness fees). The MSPB further implemented the philosophy of denying payment by disallowing expenses for photocopying. *See* Koch v. Department of Commerce, 19 M.S.P.R. 219 (1984); *see generally* BROIDA, *supra* note 47, at 1263-1413.

61. Section 12 of the Joint Explanatory Statement neatly expresses Congress's intention to eliminate the reimbursement loopholes established through case law:
MSPB and the courts have established substantial case law on what constitutes reasonable attorneys fees. The additional phrase "and any other reasonable costs incurred" is meant to include costs directly related to the litigation, such as photocopying, long distance telephone calls, and production of evidence, but is not meant to include other extraneous costs such as job retraining.
135 CONG. REC. 5035 (1989).

62. *See* 5 U.S.C. § 1221(g)(2) (1994). *Compare* proposed § 1221(g) of Senate Bill 508, *and* 134 CONG. REC. 29,540 (1988), *with* sec. 3, § 1221(g) of Senate Bill 20, *and* Pub. L. No. 101-12, 103 Stat. 30 (1989) (showing that the Whistleblower Protection Act of 1988, Senate Bill 508, did not include attorney fee awards for all successful appellants at the Federal Circuit, regardless of the reason. Instead the expanded fee award was inserted at Congress's insistence after President Reagan's veto of the 1988 legislation). The Explanatory Statement on Senate Bill 20, which congressional leaders prepared for the 1989 legislation to supplement the core Joint Explanatory Statement, includes the legislative intent for the expanded attorney fee provision: "The amendment is intended to make the appellate process a more realistic option." 135 CONG. REC. 5033 (1989).

63. *See* H.R. REP. NO. 99-859, at 23-24 (1986).

From October 1982 to April 1987 the Federal Circuit reversed or remanded a mere six percent of decisions adverse to employees.[64]

C. Controlling the Office of the Special Counsel

While not necessarily the most significant problems, the Special Counsel's excesses were the most visible, politically potent reasons for passage of the Whistleblower Protection Act. Critics actively challenged the 120 day mandatory stop-off at the OSC for cases with newly-available IRA hearing rights.[65] Congress maintained the OSC pass-through as a mandatory cooling off period to resolve heated whistleblower disputes, and to provide a reality check for parties to frivolous litigation that otherwise could flood the Board.[66]

There was no intent, however, to continue risking prejudice of an employee's rights by permitting OSC involvement. In fact, the WPA prohibits use of the OSC's decision denying relief in any other judicial or adminis-

---

64. *See id.*; H.R. REP. No. 100-274, at 26 (1987).

65. Whistleblowers and their advocates testified in favor of abolishing the Office of the Special Counsel. *See Hearings on Whistleblower Protection Before the House Comm. on Post Office and Civil Service Subcomm. on Civil Service*, 99th Cong. 207 (1985) (testimony of William Tuesberg, Construction Analyst, U.S. Department of Housing and Urban Development) [hereinafter *1985 House Hearings*]; *1987 Senate Hearings, supra* note 24, at 234 (testimony of Edward Wright). Indeed, that was precisely the approach of the first post-CSRA legislative initiative, House Bill 6392, the Whistleblower Protection Act of 1982. Representative Schroeder introduced the bill in response to exposure of Special Counsel Alex Kozinski's abuses, including his training program in how agency managers could fire whistleblowers without violating the Civil Service Reform Act. After being forced to resign, Mr. Kozinski came back. He now sits as a member of the U.S. Court of Appeals for the Ninth Circuit. Controversy over his misconduct as Special Counsel sparked 43 Senators to oppose his confirmation in 1985. After significant oversight efforts, Senator Levin subsequently introduced and shared leadership of the Senate campaign for the Whistleblower Protection Act. The 43 opposition votes to a judicial appointment were the largest since President Nixon's attempt to place Judge Harold Carswell on the Supreme Court. The backlash also derailed plans for the Administration to nominate Kozinski for the Supreme Court. Under House Bill 6392 the OSC would have been abolished. Employees would have had their choice of appealing alleged prohibited personnel practices through the Merit Systems Protection Board, or in district court. *See* S. REP. No. 100-413, at 5 (1988).

66. There was no provision in either of the House-passed Whistleblower Protection Acts of 1986, or 1987, House Bills 4033 and 25, respectively, for appellants to exhaust any OSC administrative remedy. Without explanation on the record, the pass-through was increased from 90 days in proposed § 1214(a)(3)(B) of the Senate's 1987 WPA, Senate Bill 508, to 120 days in sec. 3, § 1214(a)(3)(B) of Senate Bill 20, the final version of the legislation. The origin was 1986 administration objections to House Bill 4033 that the Act would "clog the calendar of the [MSPB]" to the extent that the Board would not be able to function in the manner contemplated when it was created. Statement of Administration Policy, House Bill 4033 — Whistleblower Protection Act of 1986, Sept. 18, 1986.

trative proceeding without the complainant's consent.[67] Significantly, the changes apply to the OSC's handling of all prohibited personnel practice complaints, not just alleged violations of the whistleblower provision.[68]

1. Eliminating the Discretion to Abuse

The plan to make the OSC a risk-free and effective remedial agency has three parts: (1) better service to complainants, (2) employee control over information obtained by the Special Counsel, and (3) employee control over the OSC's procedural options. The enhanced duty to serve is specified at the beginning and end of the complaint cycle. Initially, within fifteen days of filing, the OSC must provide written receipt to the complainant and designate a contact person.[69] While the complaint is pending, the Special Counsel must follow through by giving the complainant a written progress report on the case's status and any actions taken within ninety days and at least every sixty days thereafter.[70] This provision responds to frustrated whistleblowers who complained to Congress that the OSC left them "slowly twisting in the wind" and ignorant of what, if anything, the OSC was doing on their cases.[71] At the end of the cycle the Special Counsel must comply with an enhanced "duty to explain."[72]

When the Office closes a case, the WPA beefs up the old law requiring an explanation[73] to also contain "a summary of relevant facts ascertained

---

67. *See* 5 U.S.C. § 1214(b)(2)(E) (1994). Senator Levin explained on the floor before the Senate's 1988 approval of Senate Bill 508 that the provision means employees "are protected from any use in any other proceeding of a decision by OSC to terminate an investigation." 134 CONG. REC. 19,981 (1988).

68. This is in contrast with the Individual Right of Action (IRA), which only applies to alleged violations of § 2302(b)(8), the whistleblower prohibited personnel practice. *See* 5 U.S.C. § 1221(a) (1994). In the original House-passed bill, employees would have had jurisdiction for an IRA when challenging any prohibited personnel practice. *See* H.R. REP. NO. 100-274, at 67 (1987).

69. *See* 5 U.S.C. § 1214(a)(1)(B) (1994).

70. *See id.* § 1214(a)(1)(C)(i)–(iii).

71. *See 1987 House Hearings, supra* note 35, at 100 (testimony of John M. Berter). The Senate Report includes a discussion of whistleblowers' bewilderment to explain the congressional intent for these status reports:

[E]mployees have made similar complaints about the infrequency of the OSC's contact with complainants and the confusion with which investigators handle some cases. In order to keep employees aware of the status of their cases and to promote confidence in the process, S. 508 requires the OSC to regularly inform complainants about developments with their cases.

S. REP. NO. 100-413, at 19 (1988).

72. *See infra* note 73 (defining "duty to explain").

73. *See* 5 U.S.C. § 1214(a)(2)(A)(i)–(iv) (1994) (explaining heightened requirements of OSC to give specific reasons for its decisions).

by the Special Counsel, including the facts that support, and the facts that do not support, the allegations of such person."[74] Perhaps the most common complaint of employees under the 1978 law was that the explanations were no more informative than form letters. They did not further understand why the OSC refused to help them after reading the often-standardized explanations. They further complained that explanations that were provided were one-sided, ignoring the victim's evidence.[75]

The complainant also gets a voice under some circumstances. Before settling a case in which it finds a prohibited personnel practice, the OSC must first consult with the complainant, then file its findings with the Board and include any comments the complainant wants to submit.[76] Formerly, if the Special Counsel decided that an agency ceased a prohibited personnel practice by satisfactorily implementing recommended corrective action, all the OSC had to do was declare victory. It did not have to defend its judgment, and the complainant's views were not formally relevant.[77] On occasion, whistleblowers bitterly attacked these settlements as institutionalizing substantive defeat under the banner of symbolic victory.[78]

Even when the OSC chooses to file a corrective action petition, the victim continues to have an independent, on-the-record role. The Board must provide for "written comments by any individual who alleges to be the subject of the prohibited personnel practice."[79] This allows complainants

---

74. *Id.* § 1214(a)(2)(A)(ii). The Senate Government Affairs Committee notes that even the most favorable assessments of OSC performance conceded that one-third of rejected OSC complainants did not receive a closeout letter that was straightforward and informative. "The provision of such [mandatory explanatory] information describing briefly the strong points and the weak points of an employee's case should prove particularly helpful to those employees who intend to appeal on their own to the MSPB." S. REP. NO. 100-413, at 20 (1988).

75. *See* Devine & Aplin *supra* note 14, at 30-31.

76. *See* 5 U.S.C. 1214(b)(2)(C). The contrast with the CSRA is explained in the Senate Report. "Current law does not require that the individual involved be provided an opportunity to comment." S. REP. NO. 100-413, at 30 (1988).

77. At 1985 House Hearings, Special Counsel O'Connor's testimony concisely expressed where the lack of OSC accountability left reprisal victims. "[H]e said we settled 'his' case. That is not right. We settled our case. His case is something else." *1985 House Hearings, supra* note 65, at 258.

78. The employee whose interests Mr. O'Connor deemed irrelevant was William Tuesberg, one of the earliest HUD whistleblowers. After challenging the loss of $2.5 million in a public housing audit, the agency attempted to fire him. His Pyrrhic OSC victory was a persuasive reason for other would-be HUD whistleblowers to keep quiet. The OSC found whistleblower reprisal and negotiated a settlement in which the agency withdrew the termination. Unfortunately, the OSC also allowed HUD to institutionalize enough other long-term retaliation, such as a demotion and transfer from his home in St. Louis to oversee public housing in rural Louisiana. Mr. Tuesberg resigned rather than endure the approved substitute retaliation. *Id.* at 206-08.

79. 5 U.S.C. § 1214(b)(3)(B) (1994).

to fill in the record if they feel the OSC is pulling its punches by withholding relevant information.

By far the most significant attempted shift was in § 1212(g)(1), which was intended to give the complainant nearly total gatekeeper authority over release of OSC information on the case. It provides that "[t]he Special Counsel may not respond to any inquiry or disclose any information from or about any person making an allegation" of prohibited personnel practice, except pursuant to the Privacy Act or as required by federal statutes.[80] Even those exceptions do not apply to whistleblower cases, where the complainant's control is substantially broader. Unless the individual consents, the Office "may not respond to *any* inquiry concerning an evaluation of the work performance" under § 2302(b)(8), the whistleblower provision.[81] The only exception involves investigations of security clearances

---

80. *Id.* § 1212(g)(1).

81. *Id.* § 1212(g)(2) (emphasis added). In the Joint Explanatory Statement, Congress tied this provision to the principles expressed in the Purposes section. *See supra* notes 33, 53 & 58. "Again, the policy behind this provision is that employees should be able to go to the Special Counsel without fear of information being used against them." 135 CONG. REC. 5034 (1989). The significance and sensitivity is clear from legislative history limiting the loophole permitting OSC releases of information required by statute. "The language 'as required by any other applicable Federal law' does not refer to any existing law. It is inserted in case some future statute specifically requires Special Counsel to provide information otherwise protected by this section." *Id.*

Congress expressed its determination through the lengths it went to avoid confusion. With respect to the OSC's limited option to intervene in Independent Right of Action appeals, the Joint Explanatory Statement contains the following reminder: "Moreover, under no circumstances may the Special Counsel engage in ex parte contacts with the agency or supply information to agency management which would serve as the basis for agency action against an employee. Once again, the Special Counsel should not act to the detriment of employees." *Id.*

Employee advocates were concerned that since that limitation was not similarly expressed in the JES section on release of information about investigations, the Special Counsel would interpret the unqualified prohibition against *ex parte* contacts as limited to interventions involving IRA appeals. To eliminate that possibility, Representative Schroeder, the House floor manager for the bill, sent an October 5, 1988 letter to her counterpart, Senator Levin. As she explained,

[s]pecifically, at the end of item 3 concerning Special Counsel intervention in adverse action and independent right of action cases, the Joint Explanatory Statement states that the Special Counsel may not engage in ex parte contacts. Obviously, this prohibition is applicable as well to item 4, concerning Special Counsel release of information about investigations.

134 CONG. REC. 31,760 (1989). Based on his agreement, Senator Levin inserted it into the Congressional Record. *See id.* The document was subsequently reaffirmed and cited in the legislative histories for both chambers when Congress passed the Whistleblower Protection Act of 1989. *See* 135 CONG. REC. 4510 (1989) (statement of Sen. Levin); 135 CONG. REC. 5032 (1989) (statement of Rep. Sikorski).

for access to information the unauthorized disclosure of which "could be expected to cause exceptionally grave damage to the national security."[82]

Control of information is the heart of the plan to stop the Special Counsel from being a threat to victims of prohibited personnel practices. While poor OSC service was frustrating and left the remedial process a waste of time, the Special Counsel became dangerous when it served as a free discovery vehicle — briefing employers about the evidence underlying a whistleblower's case, passing along further derogatory information gained about the complainant, coaching the employer on the legal strategy necessary to prevail, pursuing public relations attacks on whistleblowers with its adverse rulings, and using the closed case files as dossiers to permanently blacklist those whom it had refused to assist.[83]

Complainants also have a new right to control the Special Counsel's procedural options. If whistleblowers pursue an Individual Right of Action hearing under § 1221, the OSC cannot continue an investigation after 120 days without their consent.[84] Nor may the Special Counsel intervene in any MSPB appeal or IRA proceeding without the individual's consent.[85]

---

82. 5 U.S.C. § 1212(g)(2)(B) (1994). See the Joint Explanatory Statement, 135 CONG. REC. 5034 (1989) for further commentary limiting permissible circumstances for disclosures on a complainant to passive cooperation with particular leads involving high-level clearances.

83. The provision was adopted in response to the OSC's abuse of discretion in the Elaine Mittleman case, where the OSC used her closed case file as the basis to recommend a negative determination in a background security investigation by the Office of Personnel Management. In records obtained under the Privacy Act, Ms. Mittleman learned that after she gave up seeking return to her original job and sought a new government position, an OSC representative had recommended to OPM investigators "not [to] hire the subject to work in any sensitive position in the United States government." United States Office of Personnel Management, Report of Investigation: Elaine Mittleman 22 (1983). In part, he based his assessment upon "the belief of some Treasury Managers that Mittleman had leaked sensitive matters to the press or through a United States Congressman." Id. at 19. Ms. Mittleman's experience was specifically cited and summarized in S. REP. NO. 100-413, at 10-11 (1988).

84. See 5 U.S.C. §§ 1214(a)(4), (3)(B) (1994).

85. This is another area in which the OSC's authority was reduced after the 1988 Presidential veto. Senate Bill 508 permitted OSC intervention if the agency initiated the disciplinary action with the Special Counsel's approval during an OSC investigation, or if the appellant was charged with conduct constituting a prohibited personnel practice. See 134 CONG. REC. 29,537 (1988). The post-veto Explanatory Statement on Senate Bill 20 again tied in this new limitation to the Purposes section: "The inclusion of the provision represents a clear narrowing of the Special Counsel's authority and is intended to absolutely prohibit the Special Counsel from taking any action to vindicate other interests at the expense of the whistleblower." 135 CONG. REC. 5032 (1989). In his floor statement, Senator Levin candidly discussed the history of the OSC's shrinking right to intervene:

We had agreed to this provision only as part of our compromise with the last administration. When that compromise bill was vetoed, we sought and achieved this change to the bill as a part of the new compromise. . . . Under our amendment, the Special

2. *Strengthening Remedial Authority*

Congress's effort to restore the OSC as an effective remedial agency also included constructive initiatives. The first was to improve the quality of Special Counsels. Under § 1211, the Special Counsel must be an attorney "who, by demonstrated ability, background, training, or experience, is especially qualified to carry out the functions of the position."[86]

This provision may preclude future appointments of inexperienced lawyers who receive the post as a political prize. This happened with Alex Kozinski, an active campaigner in the 1980 election and protegé of Attorney General Edwin Meese, who had no litigation experience or background, either in merit system advocacy or personnel law. Kozinski nearly destroyed the Office by politicizing it, purging staff sympathetic to whistleblowers, and setting up training programs for managers to fire whistleblowers without getting caught.[87] His abuses of discretionary authority led to his forced resignation and sparked legislation to abolish the OSC a little more than a year after his appointment.[88]

Congress also sought to upgrade the OSC by granting it formal independence.[89] The OSC's previous status as an autonomous sub-unit of the MSPB had left it vulnerable to bureaucratic turf fights with the Board, which in 1981 unsuccessfully tried to assume administrative control of the Office.[90]

The Act significantly increases the scope of OSC litigation authority. To illustrate, the Special Counsel can file disciplinary complaints with the relevant government agency head against military and contract personnel engaging in prohibited personnel practices.[91] Within sixty days, the agency chief must report on resolution of the matter.[92] With mixed supervisory chains of command, this is a modest step toward closing an expanding loophole in prior accountability. Previously, officers or contractor employees could serve as reprisal shock troops with impunity.

Similarly, the Special Counsel has new authority for remedial litigation. Under the Civil Service Reform Act,[93] the OSC could investigate arbitrary

---

Counsel would be permitted to intervene in a case brought by a Federal employee to the MSPB only with the approval of that employee.
135 CONG. REC. 4510 (1989).
    86. 5 U.S.C. § 1211(b) (1994).
    87. *See supra* notes 65 & 66 and accompanying text.
    88. *See supra* notes 65 & 66 and accompanying text.
    89. *See* 5 U.S.C. § 1211(a) (1994).
    90. *See* H.R. REP. NO. 100-274, at 25, 30 (1987).
    91. *See* 5 U.S.C. § 1215(c)(1) (1994).
    92. *See id.* § 1215(c)(2).
    93. Pub. L. No. 95-454, 92 Stat. 1111 (1978).

and capricious violations of the Freedom of Information Act;[94] violations of civil service laws, rules, and regulations generally; and personnel actions involving prohibited discrimination already found by a court or administrative authority.[95] Unfortunately, the law provided no authority for the Special Counsel to act on its investigations. Under the WPA, the Special Counsel may pursue corrective action on these matters, as if they were prohibited personnel practices.[96] In effect, the Act transforms this type of misconduct into three new prohibited personnel practices under the old CSRA model, in which the OSC has total discretion whether to act on its investigation.[97] Because of the OSC monopoly, it is unlikely that these gestures will have much impact on the merit system. To date, there are no cases on record in which the OSC has used this authority.

The Act streamlines procedures for the Special Counsel to seek temporary relief through a stay. Under old law it was necessary to petition the MSPB separately for fifteen and thirty day relief; the Board could dissolve the stay at will.[98] The WPA permits the OSC to petition immediately for a forty-five day stay. Both complainants and the OSC are entitled to provide written comments before any Board action to lift the reprieve prematurely.[99]

Finally, the Act provides new authority for the Board, the Special Counsel, and employees to defend the integrity of administrative proceedings. The OSC can petition for Board protective orders to shield witnesses or others from harassment during any proceeding.[100] Individual employees gain jurisdiction to seek sanctions for contempt of Board orders, which the MSPB can enforce by cutting off the offender's paycheck.[101]

---

94. 5 U.S.C. § 552 (1994).

95. *See id.* § 1206(e) (Supp. III 1979).

96. *See id.* § 1216(c) (1994).

97. Consistent with previous lessons learned, Congress therefore placed an asterisk on this authority in the legislative history. In the Joint Explanatory Statement (JES), the lead sponsors indicated that they intended this as a vehicle to act against "major abuses of the civil service processes," such as the Watergate era civil service scandals of the 1970s. In item 6, the JES summarizes the limitations on OSC discretion. 135 CONG. REC. 5035 (1989). "This section is not intended as plenary authority or as a writ appointing the Special Counsel policeman of the merit system. Moreover, the Special Counsel should not use this authority to seek discipline against an individual who comes to the Special Counsel for assistance." *Id.*

98. *See* 5 U.S.C. § 1208 (Supp. III 1979).

99. *See* 5 U.S.C. § 1214(b)(1) (1994); *see also* H.R. REP. NO. 100-274, at 23 (1987); S. REP. NO. 100-413, at 29 (1988).

100. *See* 5 U.S.C. § 1204(e)(1)(B) (1994). Additionally, the Act allows the Board to grant a protective order after a request from "any other person, whether or not a party to the case, or on the Board's own motion." 135 CONG. REC. 5034 (1989) (Joint Explanatory Statement, item 2).

101. *See* 5 U.S.C. § 1204(e)(2)(A) (1994).

D. Expanding the Scope of Protection

One of the most concise but significant changes in the law attempts to definitionally solve the "Swiss cheese syndrome" that was a primary cause of failure. Under the CSRA, it was illegal to retaliate against whistleblowers for making "a" disclosure that evidenced illegality or specified misconduct. The Whistleblower Protection Act amends 5 U.S.C. § 2302(b)(8) by substituting "any" for "a,"[102] thereby making protection mandatory whenever justified by the evidence in a disclosure.

The Special Counsel, the Board, and the Federal Circuit had all interpreted the mandate to protect "a" significant whistleblowing disclosure as discretionary in any given case. Qualifying on the merits of the information's public policy value was necessary but not sufficient. Over a decade, so many loopholes opened that it became clear the number of eventual exceptions would be limited only by the imagination. The Federal Circuit carved out the boldest in *Fiorillo v. Department of Justice*.[103] Initially, the court restored the First Amendment balancing test that Congress had intended to replace with specified categories of speech in which protection is absolute. The court went on to specifically apply a "selfless motives" test that disqualifies dissent from protection, regardless of its public policy value, absent proof that "the *primary* motivation of the employee [was] to inform the public on matters of public concern, and not personal vindictiveness."[104] The *Fiorillo* court's strike three for whistleblowers was a requirement that the complainant be the first to expose a problem or challenge the same misconduct. The court explained that dissent against previously exposed, long-term abuses was "stale" and therefore unprotected.[105]

In *Stanek v. Department of Transportation*,[106] the Federal Circuit erased the most basic form of whistleblowing from the statute — dissent that contradicts agency policy. This type of disclosure was deemed "protected" but

---

102.   5 U.S.C. § 2302(b)(9) (1994).

103.   795 F.2d 1544 (Fed. Cir. 1986).

104.   *Id.* at 1549-50 (emphasis in original). As noted in S. REP. NO. 100-413, at 13 (1988), "[t]he court reached this conclusion despite the lack of any indication in CSRA that an employee's motives are supposed to be considered in determining whether a disclosure is protected." Senator Levin explained the impact unequivocally in an August 2, 1988 floor statement before the Senate unanimous vote. This provision is intended to preclude the Board from considering such factors as whether the employee was the first person to make the disclosure, whether the disclosure was made to someone other than the responsible agency official, what the motives of the employee may have been in making the disclosure, or other similar factors, in determining whether a disclosure is protected. 134 CONG. REC. 19,981 (1988).

105.   *See Fiorillo*, 795 F.2d at 1550.

106.   805 F.2d 1572 (Fed. Cir. 1986).

nonetheless "independent[ly] actionable grounds for removal because of the conflict" with agency policy.[107]

The Special Counsel invented the most creative, if contradictory, exceptions to the whistleblower statute. The OSC had disqualified disclosures from protected speech status when the disclosures were, inter alia, dissent phrased as a request for assistance; "casual," meaning to a co-worker or someone besides the "responsible agency official;" or "personal," meaning outside the scope of one's job description.[108]

By changing "a" to "any," Congress erased all this sophism. In legislative history the drafters specifically declared their intent to nullify the *Fiorillo* holdings,[109] and unequivocally explained that only content matters when evaluating whether speech qualifies for protection. If the disclosure is reasonable and significant to public policy, then time, manner, place, form, motives, audience, and anything else are irrelevant.[110]

In addition to closing the loopholes, Congress increased the scope of protected conduct to include activities analogous to but distinct from whistleblowing. The prohibited personnel practice protecting exercises of appeal rights[111] was expanded to include complaints or grievances,[112] testimony or assistance to anyone else exercising appeal rights,[113] cooperating with or disclosing information to the Special Counsel or an Inspector General,[114] or "for refusing to obey an order that would require an individual to

---

107. *Id.* at 1580.

108. *See, e.g.*, S. REP. NO. 100-413, at 12-13 (1988).

109. After summarizing OSC practices, Board precedents and the *Fiorillo* holding, the Government Affairs Committee concluded, "[t]he Committee intends that disclosures be encouraged. The OSC, the Board and the courts should not erect barriers to disclosures which will limit the necessary flow of information from employees who have knowledge of government wrongdoing." S. REP. NO. 100-413, at 13 (1988). Originally, the WPA would have eliminated the Federal Circuit's monopoly on MSPB appeals, substituting normal appellate jurisdiction in the D.C. Circuit or the circuit where the employee lives. *See id.* at 71. The expanded jurisdiction was removed as part of a compromise with the administration. *See infra* note 189.

110. The Senate Report, continues,

> For example, it is inappropriate for disclosures to be protected only if they are made for certain purposes or to certain employees or only if the employee is the first to raise the issue. S. 508 emphasizes this point by changing the phrase "a disclosure" to "any disclosure" in the statutory definition. This is simply to stress that *any* disclosure is protected (if it meets the requisite reasonable belief test and is not required to be kept confidential).

S. REP. NO. 100-413, at 13 (1988) (emphasis in original).

111. *See* 5 U.S.C. § 2302(b)(9) (1994).

112. *See id.* § 2302(b)(9)(A).

113. *See id.* § 2302(b)(9)(B).

114. *See id.* § 2302(b)(9).

violate a law."[115] The last provision provides a remedy for those who honor their duties under the Code of Ethics for Government Service,[116] and capped a twenty year campaign for public employees challenging their employment duty to act illegally upon command.[117]   Unfortunately, since these new categories of protection are codified under 5 U.S.C. § 2302(b)(9) instead of § 2302(b)(8), they do not trigger an Individual Right of Action unless the dispute is otherwise appealable to the Board.   That means reprisal victims will face the same handicap as pre-WPA whistleblowers: Their rights will be at the whim of the Special Counsel.

Congress expanded the scope of illegal employer activity under both §§ 2302(b)(8) and 2302(b)(9).   Under the CSRA, there was no jurisdiction until the agency formally proposed a personnel action.   The Whistleblower Protection Act only requires the employer to "threaten" a personnel action that would be illegal under those two subsections.[118]   The goal was to dissolve artificial legal distinctions that are irrelevant to the chilling effect of bureaucratic bullying.   "Mere harassment and threats, without any formally proposed personnel action, can constitute a prohibited personnel practice . . . ."[119]

E.   Easing the Burdens of Proof

Without better prospects for success at Merit Systems Protection Board hearings, all of the reforms summarized above would only realistically mean more whistleblowers could lose their cases in due process administrative hearings than before.   With only four successful exercises of the whistleblower defense out of some two thousand cases[120] before passage of the WPA, expanded hearing rights realistically only represented an opportunity for more expensive, formal endorsements of reprisal.

The heart of the Whistleblower Protection Act is the reduced burdens of proof to win relief.   There are three primary changes in the new legal standard — (1) eliminating the relevance of employer motives; (2) easing the standard to establish a prima facie case, which can be satisfied by proving that protected speech was a "contributing factor" in the challenged person-

---

115. *Id.* § 2302(b)(9). Senate Bill 508 did not contain any analogous protection. House Bill 25 had prohibited reprisal "for failing to follow orders to disobey a law." H.R. REP. NO. 100-274, at 69 (1987). In item 17 of the JES, Congress explained that the final language is the "narrower form of a provision that was in H.R. 25, as reported." 135 CONG. REC. 5035 (1989).

116. *See supra* note 2 and accompanying text.

117. *See generally,* Robert G. Vaughn, *Public Employees and the Right to Disobey,* 29 HASTINGS L.J. 261 (1977).

118. *See* 5 U.S.C. § 2302(b)(8)-(b)(9) (1994).

119. 135 CONG. REC. 5035 (1989) (Joint Explanatory Statement, S. 2784, item 16).

120. *See supra* note 16.

nel action;[121] and (3) reversing the burden of proof for agencies, who must then prove legitimate, independent justification for the personnel action by "clear and convincing evidence."[122]

1. Eliminating the Motives Test

Another concise, watershed modification of § 2302(b)(8) completed the policy shift for protected speech to be assessed primarily on the significance and merits of disclosures. Under the 1978 law an employer did not violate § 2302(b)(8) unless the challenged personnel decision was "in retaliation for" protected speech.[123] The Whistleblower Protection Act changes that phrase to "because of."[124] The Act makes the same substitution for the expanded scope of protected conduct at 5 U.S.C. § 2302(b)(9).[125]

This means that proof of the employer's punitive or vindictive intent no longer is necessary or even relevant. Decisions on personnel actions may not be based on whistleblowing disclosures, regardless of the presence or absence of animus. It eliminates the common employer defense that there are "no hard feelings," but a supervisor no longer can work with a dissenter after what was said.[126] In the legislative history Congress specifically overruled federal court decisions that required proof of an intent to punish as unduly restrictive.[127]

2. Easing the Burden to Establish a Prima Facie Case — the Contributing Factor Test

The most common reason whistleblowers lost under the 1978 statute was their inability to establish a prima facie case. In the absence of any statutory provision, the Board consistently adopted the test in *Mt. Healthy v. Doyle*,[128] for First Amendment relief, which over time has meant an employee must prove that protected speech played a "substantial" or "motivating" factor in the contested personnel decision.[129]

---

121. *See* 5 U.S.C. §§ 1214(b)(4)(B)(i), 1221(e)(1) (1994).

122. *Id.* §§ 1214(b)(4)(B)(ii), 1221(e)(2).

123. *See id.* § 2302(b)(8).

124. *Id.* § 2302(b)(8).

125. Pub. L. No. 101-12 § 4(a)(2), 103 Stat. 32 (1989).

126. *See, e.g.*, Harvey v. MSPB, 802 F.2d 537 (D.C. Cir. 1986).

127. *See* S. REP. NO. 100-413, at 15-16 (1988).

128. 429 U.S. 274 (1977).

129. *Id.* at 287; *see also* Warren v. Department of the Army, 804 F.2d 654 (Fed. Cir. 1986); H.R. REP. NO. 100-274, at 27 (1987); S. REP. NO. 100-413, at 13-14 (1988); 135 CONG. REC. 4509 (1989) (statement of Sen. Levin); 135 CONG. REC. 5035 (1989) (Joint Explanatory Statement, item 7). In the Explanatory Statement on Senate Bill 20, Congress left no doubt that it

New statutory provisions in the WPA[130] replace the former synonyms with a new test, both to establish a prima facie case and as a bottom line for the quantum of evidence necessary to prevail. Now the Board must order corrective action if the appellant "has demonstrated that a disclosure described under § 2302(b)(8) was a contributing factor in the personnel action which was taken or is to be taken against such employee, former employee, or applicant." Although there is no specific statutory definition of "contributing factor," Congress left no question about what it means the standard to entail. During floor speeches and consensus legislative histories submitted prior to several unanimous votes, the primary drafters defined the burden as follows — "any factor, which alone or in connection with other factors, tends to affect in any way the outcome . . . ."[131]

"specifically intended to overrule existing case law, which requires a whistleblower to prove his protected conduct was a 'significant,' 'motivating,' 'substantial,' or 'predominant' factor in a personnel action in order to overturn that action." 135 CONG. REC. 5033 (1989).

130. 5 U.S.C. §§ 1214(b)(4)(B)(i) (OSC litigation) and 1221(e)(1) (Individual Right of Action).

131. 135 CONG. REC. 4509 (1989). *See id.* at 4518 (statement of Sen. Grassley); *id.* at 4522 (statement of Sen. Pryor); *id.* at 5033 (explanatory statement of Senate Bill 20); *id.* at 4522 (statement of Rep. Schroeder). This is the same definition Senator Levin gave for a "material factor" in the original version of Senate Bill 508. 134 CONG. REC. 19,981 (1988). A concurring letter from Attorney General Thornburgh was consistent. "A 'contributing factor' need not be 'substantial.' The individual's burden is to prove that the whistleblowing contributed in some way to the agency's decision to take the personnel action." 135 CONG. REC. 5033 (1989).

Concerns about the standard for establishing a prima facie test were at the core of President Reagan's pocket veto of the 1988 bill. The only difference between Senate 508 and Senate Bill 20 on this issue was to insert the word "contributing" in front of "factor," which was unqualified initially in §§ 1214(b)(4)(B)(1) and 1221(e)(1).

Although the modification satisfied the concerns of Attorney General Thornburgh about possible abuses, all sides agreed that the final language merely stated more precisely what Congress had intended all along. "Contributing" refers to the relevance of evidence, not its significance. As pointed out in the Explanatory Statement on Senate Bill 20, "This is not meant to change or heighten, in any way, the standard in S. 20, which is that the disclosure must be 'a factor' in the action. The word 'contributing' is only intended to clarify that the factor must contribute in some way to the action against the whistleblower." 135 CONG. REC. 5033 (1989). In fact, when defining "contributing factor" Congress made a point that the definition applied equally to the term "factor." *Id.* See also the explanation of Senator Levin, the leading negotiator for the compromises added to Senate Bill 20: "I believe this was clear in the original statutory language. To me, there was no doubt that a factor in an action is something that contributes to that action. Indeed, my dictionary defines a 'factor' as 'one of the elements contributing to a particular result or situation.'" 135 CONG. REC. 4509 (1989).

3. Reversing the Burden of Proof Under the "Clear and Convincing Evidence" Standard

The final step in the *Mt. Healthy* standard is shifting the burden of proof to the employer, who must demonstrate by a preponderance of the evidence that the personnel action would have occurred anyway in the absence of protected speech.[132] While endorsing this standard,[133] the MSPB deviated from it in two significant respects. First, if a whistleblower established a prima facie case the Board only shifted the burden of production to the employer. The burden of proof always remained with the employee.[134] Second, in a 1987 decision, *Berube v. General Services Administration,*[135] the Board reversed eight years of administrative precedents and effectively substituted "could have" for "would have" in the examination of alternate explanations.[136] By allowing after-the-fact justifications, the Board invited investigative witch-hunts to rationalize prior reprisals and made it nearly impossible for whistleblowers to prevail. Nearly everyone has a skeleton in the closet, if the government looks hard enough.

Congress's final amendment to the legal standards cancelled *Berube* and completed codification of a modified *Mt. Healthy* standard more sympathetic to employees by raising the preponderance of evidence standard to a significantly tougher hurdle. Under 5 U.S.C. §§ 1214(b)(4)(B)(ii) and 1221(e)(2),[137] the Board may not order corrective action if the agency demonstrates through "clear and convincing evidence" that it "would have taken the same personnel action in the absence of such disclosure." By imposing this test Congress also created a clear and convincing mandate for its intention to reverse prior case law trends. "Clear and convincing evidence" is a far more difficult evidentiary standard to meet in civil law.[138]

---

132. *See Mt. Healthy,* 429 U.S. at 287.

133. *See* Gerlach v. FTC, 8 M.S.P.B. 599 (1981).

134. *See* In the Matter of Frazier, 1 M.S.P.B. 159 (1979), *aff'd,* Frazier v. MSPB, 672 F.2d 150 (D.C. Cir. 1982).

135. 30 M.S.P.R. 581 (1986), *remanded,* 820 F.2d 396 (Fed. Cir. 1987), 37 M.S.P.R. 448 (1988).

136. *See Berube,* 820 F.2d 396, 400-01 (Fed. Cir. 1987).

137. These provisions refer to OSC litigation and Individual Right of Action cases, respectively.

138. S. REP. NO. 100-413, at 15 (1988), puts the agency's net burden in perspective: "Under this modified *Mt. Healthy* test, if whistleblowing was a material factor in the personnel action, the agency would lose its defense." The Explanatory Statement on Senate Bill 20 explained the rationale.

"Clear and convincing evidence" is a high burden of proof for the Government to bear. It is intended as such for two reasons. First, this burden of proof comes into play only if the employee has established by a preponderance of the evidence that the whistleblowing was a contributing factor in the action — in other words, that the

MSPB case law has interpreted the standard to require consideration of the following factors: "(1) the strength of the evidence in support of the personnel action; (2) the existence and strength of any motive to retaliate on the part of the agency officials who were involved in the decision; and (3) any other evidence that the agency takes similar actions against employees who are not whistleblowers, but who are otherwise similarly situated."[139]

The package of modified standards leaves whistleblowing on a legal pedestal, at least in theory.[140] Speech protected under § 2302(b)(8) rises above the pack from other speech protected by the First Amendment, under which the employee's conduct must survive increasingly difficult balancing tests.[141] No other prohibited personnel practice, even the new witness protection and code of ethics provisions in § 2302(b)(9), enjoys the same modest burden to prevail. In this context, the Whistleblower Protection Act is

---

agency action was "tainted." Second, this heightened burden of proof required of the agency also recognizes that when it comes to proving the basis for an agency's decision, the agency controls most of the cards — the drafting of the documents supporting the decision, the testimony of witnesses who participated in the decision, and the records that could document whether similar personnel actions have been taken in other cases. In these circumstances, it is entirely appropriate that the agency bear a heavy burden to justify its actions.

135 CONG. REC. 5033 (1989).

139. Shaw v. Department of the Air Force, 80 M.S.P.R. 98, 115 (1998); *see also* Rutberg v. Occupational Safety and Health Review Comm'n, 78 M.S.P.R. 130, 141 (1998).

140. Congress left no doubt that it intended a significant break from prior law. After summarizing the changes in the prima facie test and *Mt. Healthy* affirmative defense, Senator Cohen emphasized, "Those are important changes. They mark significant changes in existing law." 135 CONG. REC. 4517 (1989). The Explanatory Statement on Senate Bill 20 again put the intent in perspective.

By reducing the excessively heavy burden imposed on the employee under current case law, the legislation will send a strong, clear signal to whistleblowers that Congress intends that they be protected from any retaliation related to their whistleblowing and an equally clear message to those who would discourage whistleblowers from coming forward that reprisals of any kind will not be tolerated. *Whistleblowing should never be a factor that contributes in any way to an adverse personnel action.*

135 CONG. REC. 5033 (1989) (emphasis added).

At the same time, Congress also made clear that it did not intend to provide self-described whistleblowers with employment immunity. "[T]his new test will not shield employees who engage in wrongful conduct merely because they have at some point 'blown the whistle' on some kind of purported misconduct." *Id.* Senator Cohen again put the changes in perspective. "We do not want to see a situation where individuals who are either mischievous, maladjusted, or have personal agendas try to hide behind this legislation. That is why I think this represents an appropriate balance . . . ." 135 CONG. REC. 4517 (1989).

141. *See generally* Devine & Aplin, *supra* note 14, at 16-18, 57-60.

becoming the precedent followed generally by Congress and state legislatures in fashioning similar protections for other workers.[142]

F. Other Modifications

1. Interim Relief

One disincentive for agencies to resolve whistleblower disputes was that the trier of fact's decision was not effective until the Board completed any review.[143] Since that could take over two years,[144] even the rare whistleblower who won at trial level could be finished off financially while waiting for the decision to become effective. Further, the chilling effect is reinforced on other workers the longer a whistleblower is off the job, particularly one who has prevailed initially. Finally, the odds were high that the Board would overturn the administrative judge.

With exceptions, the WPA definitionally solves this problem as well for all employees, whether the dispute involved whistleblowing, a different prohibited personnel practice, or merely a successful appeal. If the employee or applicant prevails, that person "shall be granted the relief provided in the decision effective upon the making of the decision, and remaining in effect pending the outcome of any petition for review . . . ."[145]

There are two broad exceptions to interim relief, which also does not include advance payment of costs or attorney fees:[146] (1) if the deciding offi-

---

142. An increasing number of federal and state statutes are applying the WPA burdens of proof to govern proceedings under analogous whistleblower statutes. *See, e.g.,* 42 U.S.C. § 5851 (concerning corporate nuclear power and weapons employees); National Institutes of Health Revitalization Act, Pub. L. No. 103-43, § 163, 107 Stat. 140, 142 (1993) (ordering HHS to issue whistleblower regulations with WPA burdens of proof for workers of federally-funded Public Health Service biomedical research); D.C. Code Ann. §§ 1-602.1 to 1-602.2, 1-616.1 to 1-616.3, 1-616.11 to 1-616.19, 1-1177.1 to 1-1177.7 (Supp. 1999) (protecting District of Columbia civil service and contractor employees).

143. *See* S. REP. NO. 100-413, at 22 (1988).

144. Normally, the Board issued its decisions expeditiously, but that pattern was unreliable for politically sensitive cases, where the public policy stakes are highest and whistleblowing is the most significant. For example, Bertrand Berube, the General Services Administration's regional administrator for the National Capitol Region — and a highly visible whistleblower whose dissent sparked exposure of the GSA corruption scandals during both the Carter and Reagan administrations — was fired on September 30, 1983. His ultimately successful appeal took nearly five years. *See generally Berube*, 820 F.2d 396, 400-01 (1987). Final resolution in another case, involving Air Force whistleblower John White, has been pending due to government appeals for seven years at publication time, despite three Board decisions backing him in the same case. *See infra* notes 245-48 and accompanying text.

145. 5 U.S.C. § 7701(b)(2)(A) (1994).

146. *See id.*

cial decides it is not appropriate,[147] or (2) if the employing agency decides "that the return or presence of such employee or applicant is unduly disruptive to the work environment."[148] In the latter instance, however, the agency must nevertheless provide the employee with all pay and benefits of the position.[149]

2. Transfer Preference

Through offering whistleblowers who win their cases a potential transfer preference, the WPA addressed a common phenomenon that can make legal success a Pyrrhic victory: the "you can't go home again" syndrome. It can be unrealistic to return to work under a vengeful supervisor after beating that official in litigation. The employee can not relax or make mistakes like others, or the agency predictably will try to fire the employee again. It has been hard enough to win once under the whistleblower defense, let alone twice. Two of the four employees who prevailed under § 2302(b)(8) from 1979-1988 were fired again after they returned, and the second time around the agency finished each one off.[150]

The new law allows whistleblowers who prevail to petition for a transfer. Agency heads can give preference either in response to the request or on their own initiative. Three conditions are that the employee is qualified for the job sought, is eligible for the position, and has prevailed under § 2302(b)(8).[151] The transfer must occur within eighteen months of the litigation success,[152] and there is a limit of one transfer preference per employee.[153]

This new provision is more an opportunity than a right. The agency's decision whether to grant the petition is discretionary. However, the whistleblower can compel the selecting official to explain within thirty days why a request was turned down[154] and may subsequently require further review by the agency head,[155] who within another thirty days must explain a final rejection both to the employee and the Board.[156] Further, since a

---

147.   *See id.* § 7701(b)(2)(A)(i).

148.   *Id.* § 7701(b)(2)(A)(ii)(II).

149.   *See id.* § 7701(b)(2)(B).

150.   *See, e.g.,* Devine & Aplin, *supra* note 14, at n.112 (detailing experience of plaintiff in *Anderson v. Department of Agriculture,* 9 M.S.P.R. 536 (1982), who won case but was later removed by agency after continued harassment).

151.   *See* 5 U.S.C. § 3352(a)(1)-(3) (1994).

152.   *See id.* § 3352(e)(3).

153.   *See id.* § 3352(e)(1).

154.   *See id.* § 3352(c).

155.   *See id.* § 3352(d).

156.   *See id.*

transfer is a listed personnel action,[157] failing to take it triggers jurisdiction for another whistleblower IRA, as well as for a complaint to the Special Counsel under 5 U.S.C. § 2302(b)(9) challenging the denial as retaliation for exercise of an appeal right. In short, the transfer preference offers prevailing whistleblowers an opportunity to make a fresh start, or at least to put any employer who denies it on the defensive.

3. Nonpreclusion

The significance of the Reform Act's failure to protect whistleblowers went far beyond MSPB defeats and dirty tricks by the Office of the Special Counsel. Under the *Bush v. Lucas*[158] doctrine, the Supreme Court reasoned that by creating a comprehensive administrative remedy Congress must have meant to cancel out jurisdiction for federal workers to file constitutional tort suits for damages when individual managers retaliated for exercise of the employee's First Amendment rights. Over time the courts extended the *Bush* doctrine to also cancel out alternative statutory remedies, such as the Privacy Act[159] and the Tucker Act.[160] The unmistakable trend was to deny federal workers any forum beyond the Board or Special Counsel, and any statutory relief besides the Civil Service Reform Act.[161] Due to the Board and OSC's bleak track record, loss of alternate causes of action and fora evolving into the Reform Act's most serious threat to employee rights.

The WPA restores all the endangered remedies except constitutional torts.[162] The subsection on "[a]vailability of other remedies" takes the guess work out of congressional intent[163] by declaring that "nothing in this chapter or chapter 23 shall be construed to limit any right or remedy available under a provision of statute which is outside of both this chapter and chapter 23."[164] Among the statutory remedies saved are those in the Back-

---

157. *See id.* § 2302(a)(2)(iv).
158. 462 U.S. 367 (1983).
159. *See generally* Henderson v. Social Sec. Admin., 716 F. Supp. 15 (D. Kan. 1989).
160. *See* United States v. Fausto, 484 U.S. 439 (1988).
161. *See generally Fausto*, 484 U.S. 439; Schweiker v. Chilicky, 487 U.S. 412 (1988); Carr v. United States, 864 F.2d 144 (Fed. Cir. 1989); Hambsch v. United States, 857 F.2d 763 (Fed. Cir. 1988); Witzkoske v. USPS, 848 F.2d 70 (5th Cir. 1988); Hubbard v. EPA, 809 F.2d 1 (D.C. Cir. 1986).
162. This rolls back the impact of *Bush* to its original boundaries. *See Bush*, 462 U.S. at 371-74.
163. 5 U.S.C. § 1222 (1994).
164. Initially the legislation did not have a specific provision protecting alternate remedies, although the House Committee Reports contained a generalized reassurance that Congress did not intend to cancel other causes of action by providing Board hearings. "The determination to provide an independent right of access is not intended to cut off any right that individuals now

pay Act,[165] Civil Rights Act of 1871,[166] Privacy Act,[167] Tucker Act,[168] Veterans Preference Act,[169] and a series of environmental protection whistleblower statutes adjudicated at the Department of Labor.[170]

The nonpreclusion clause is another generic reform. It restores access to Article III courts and alternative statutory remedies for all persons covered by the 1978 law, not just whistleblowers. The provision is most useful for employees whose disputes do not involve whistleblowing. The nonpreclusion clause may restore the most favorable forum and preferred remedy for causes of action not benefiting from more sympathetic burdens of proof.

4.   Strengthened Whistleblowing Disclosure Channels

The WPA has taken deference to the strategy that the best defense is a good offense, in this instance by slightly modifying the disclosure channels through which employees can dissent to gain an executive branch investigation into alleged misconduct.[171]   On balance, however, Congress bypassed the process of maximizing constructive potential from dissent, a curious omission since one of the WPA's objectives is to spark increased challenges of bureaucratic misconduct.

---

have to seek redress of wrongs in court." H.R. REP. No. 99-859, at 20 (1986); H. Rep. No. 100-274, at 23 (1987). Over time it became clear this approach would be insufficient. The lesson of *Schweiker* is that Congress must explicitly say so if it wants to preserve old remedies when it creates new reforms for the same problems. *See* 487 U.S. at 414-29.

165.   *See* 5 U.S.C. § 5596 (1994).

166.   *See* 42 U.S.C. § 1985 (1994).

167.   *See* 5 U.S.C. § 552(a) (1994 & Supp. III 1997).

168.   *See* 28 U.S.C. § 1491 (1994).

169.   *See* 5 U.S.C. § 2108 (1994).

170.   The list of specific whistleblower provisions includes, inter alia, the Comprehensive Environmental Response, Compensation and Liability ("Superfund") Act, 42 U.S.C. § 9610 (1994); Clean Air Act, 42 U.S.C. § 7622 (1994); Energy Reorganization Act, 42 U.S.C. § 5851 (1994); Safe Drinking Water Act, 42 U.S.C. § 300j-9 (1994); Solid Waste Disposal Act, 42 U.S.C. § 6971 (1994); Surface Transportation Act, 49 U.S.C. § 31,105 (1994); and the Water Pollution Control Act, 33 U.S.C. § 1367 (1994).

171.   Under 5 U.S.C. § 1206(b) (1976 & Supp. III 1979), an employee could make disclosures of illegality, mismanagement, abuse of authority, gross waste "or a substantial and specific danger to public health or safety." If the OSC determined there was a substantial likelihood the employee was correct, under § 1206(b)(3) the Special Counsel ordered the head of the agency to investigate and report back within 60 days with findings of fact and any appropriate corrective action. The reports went into a public file. The OSC also evaluated each report for reasonableness and completeness. If the OSC determined that the whistleblowing qualified merely as protected speech evidencing a reasonable belief, under § 1206(b)(7) the Special Counsel still referred the report for a mandatory agency response. Based on that more limited approval, however, the agency chief had complete discretion how to answer, and only had to respond within a reasonable period.

The new law contains some provisions to increase a whistleblower's impact. If an agency is tardy in meeting the Special Counsel's schedule to issue a report,[172] the OSC must transmit the whistleblower's unanswered charges to the President, congressional oversight committees and the Comptroller General, along with a statement noting the agency chief's default.[173] At the end of the cycle, the whistleblower receives a guaranteed opportunity to prepare comments evaluating the report.[174] The OSC must send the whistleblower's comments, along with its own evaluation and the final agency report, to the same audience — President, congressional oversight committees and Comptroller General.[175] The agency report and its underlying evidence also goes into a public file, along with the whistleblower's comments.[176]

This may be the most significant document in the process, since agencies seldom confess to wrongdoing after a self-investigation. However, the report forces disclosure of how an agency will deny whistleblower charges. By flushing out the agency's defenses, the whistleblower has an early opportunity to study and rebut denials that might not have been released until

---

172. *See* 5 U.S.C. § 1213(c) (1994).

173. *See id.* § 1213(e)(4) (1994 & Supp. III 1997).

174. *See id.* § 1213(e)(1) (1994). House Report 274 contains an explanation of the problem Congress sought to address through this provision:

When the head of the agency transmits the agency report back to the Special Counsel, the Special Counsel does not share the supporting exhibits and investigative basis for the report's conclusions with the whistleblower unless the agency consents. This is troubling because the whistleblower is often in a good position to evaluate whether the agency's response represents a good faith investigation.

H.R. REP. No. 100-274 at 25 (1987).

175. *See* 5 U.S.C. § 1213(e)(2) – (e)(3) (1994); *see also* 5 U.S.C. § 1213(e)(4) (1994 & Supp. III 1997). The former provisions require the OSC and whistleblowers' comments, respectively, to be included, and the latter specifies the audience.

176. *See* 5 U.S.C. § 1219 (1994). Although the statute only makes a general reference to the agency report, the Joint Explanatory Statement specifies that Congress meant the entire package of materials resolving the charges. "The Special Counsel should place in the public files the comments of the individual who discloses information under § 1213 on the agency report unless the individual does not consent to the public availability of such comments." 135 CONG. REC. 5035 (1989).

Similarly, the public file requirement will not be satisfied through cursory summaries signed by an agency chief. The report should contain the entire package, including investigative summaries and supporting evidence. The inadequacies of the previous system are explained in House Report 274.

The same restriction applies to the information going into the public file. The agency head's summary is available, but not the evidence underlying it unless the agency agrees. In certain cases this restriction has been significant because the agency head's report contradicted the evidence presented by the Inspector General who investigated the whistleblower's charges. H.R. REP. No. 100-274, at 25 (1987).

there was no chance to call the bureaucratic bluff, as at a congressional hearing or in the media. Overall, this reform provides whistleblowers an opportunity for the last analytical word in the opening round of public policy disputes. It immediately advances the debate to a level often not previously attained until the end of the process.

The WPA includes important provisions to make OSC whistleblowing disclosures less risky. It eliminates the frequently abused OSC practice of "informal referrals," in which the Special Counsel ruled that the dissent did not have enough merit to order an agency investigation but nonetheless forwarded it to the agency chief.[177] Now the Special Counsel may not forward the rejected disclosure to the agency unless the whistleblower consents. Additionally, the OSC must return the whistleblowing disclosure and supporting evidence to the employee.[178]

From any perspective, informal referrals had made affected disclosures counterproductive for employees. On a policy level, informal referrals meant that the charges had been formally rejected as worthy of response. More significantly, they gave the agency a sneak preview to review the charges and supporting information, and perfect its defenses or destroy evidence before the dissent reached third parties willing and able to seriously address it in good faith.

Informal referrals also were an invitation to retaliate. Since the standard for mandatory referrals was the same as for protected speech — a significant disclosure evidencing a "reasonable belief"[179] — an informal referral inherently meant the dissent was not protected — in effect an "all clear" sign for retaliation. The whistleblower was left exposed and legally defenseless.[180]

Similarly, the new law tightens confidentiality protections for allegers. Under the 1978 law the OSC could disclose an alleger's identity when nec-

---

177. As explained in House Report 274, "[i]n recent years, the Special Counsel has been making 'informal' referrals. In some cases, these referrals have included cover notes from the Special Counsel criticizing the whistleblowers' charges." H.R. REP. NO. 100-274, at 25 (1987).

178. *See* 5 U.S.C. § 1213(g) (1994).

179. *Compare* 5 U.S.C. § 2302(b)(8) (1976 & Supp. III 1979) (stating that employees are protected for disclosures that evidence a "reasonable belief" of significant misconduct), *with* 5 U.S.C. § 1206(b)(2) (1976 & Supp. III 1979) (noting that the OSC had to refer for agency investigation any allegations that evidenced a "reasonable belief" of significant misconduct).

180. As described in House Report 274, if the OSC does not order a response,

the Special Counsel must return the material to the individual who transmitted it to the Special Counsel and inform the individual of why the disclosure cannot be pursued and other recourse the individual might want to pursue. . . . The committee heard testimony of employee concern that such informal referrals led to reprisals against the employee who made the disclosure. By eliminating the possibility of informal referrals, the committee intends to foreclose the possibility of such reprisals.

H.R. REP. NO. 100-274, at 34 (1987).

essary to carry out the functions of the Office.[181]   Congress retained that exception when it passed the 1988 WPA.[182] After the veto, however, Congress decided not to take any chances and closed the more discretionary loophole. Under the final version of the WPA, the Special Counsel may not disclose the alleger's identity without consent unless first determining that exposure is necessary, "because of an imminent danger to public health or safety or imminent violation of any criminal law."[183]

In some respects, the law restricts whistleblowing disclosures. Congress no longer permits the Special Counsel to order investigations of agency "mismanagement."[184]   Now "gross mismanagement" is necessary.[185]

---

181.   *See* 5 U.S.C. § 1206(b)(1) (1976 & Supp. III 1979).

182.   Section 1213(h)(1) of Senate Bill 508 contained the prior loophole permitting the OSC to expose the whistleblower when "necessary in order to carry out the functions of the Special Counsel . . . ." 134 CONG. REC. 29,538 (1988). Analogizing to retaliation complaints, a wary Congress emphasized the exception should be read narrowly.

> Again, the overriding purpose of the bill is to protect individuals who seek the assistance of the Special Counsel; they should not be subject to harm because they sought help. These exceptions are to be defined narrowly. . . . For example, a decision by the Special Counsel to initiate an action before the MSPB may necessitate the disclosure of the identity of the individual on whose behalf the action is initiated. This provision is not intended to permit the [OSC] to disclose an individual's identity, without that individual's consent, merely because such disclosure could be helpful in an investigation.

134 CONG. REC. 27,854 (1988) (Joint Explanatory Statement, item 5).

183.   5 U.S.C. § 1213(h) (1994). The final version of the Joint Explanatory Statement defines this exception, which also had been included in Senate Bill 508. "This narrow exception recognizes the countervailing public interest in protecting health and safety. The exception is quite narrow; it might be used, for example, where the Special Counsel learns that the individual making the disclosure plans to take violent action against a supervisor." 135 CONG. REC. 5035 (1989).

Even in 1988, Congress had not been comfortable with retaining any broad OSC authority to turn a confidential whistleblower back in to his or her bosses. The Explanatory Statement on S.20 has a description of the lingering concern that is addressed in the 1989 Act.

> The deleted provision, if retained, could seriously undermine efforts to encourage whistleblowers to come forward with disclosures. It is unrealistic to expect whistleblowers to help in the struggle against waste if they risk the exposure of their names and possible retaliation. This provision was inserted last year only as a part of a compromise with the prior Administration. The current Administration has agreed to delete it in this new compromise. . . . This amendment will help assure that the Special Counsel will be on their side in the future and that information they give to the Special Counsel in confidence will not later be used against them.

135 CONG. REC. 5033 (1989); *see also* 135 CONG. REC. 4508-11(1989).

184.   5 U.S.C. § 1213(b) (1976 & Supp. III 1979).

185.   *See id.* § 1213(a)(1)(b) (1994). As explained in the Senate Report, the concern here was to guard against making a full federal case about "disclosures of trivial matters." S. REP. No. 100-413, at 13 (1988). *Compare* 5 U.S.C. § 2302(b)(8) (1976 & Supp. III 1979), *with* 5 U.S.C. § 2302(b)(8) (1988 & Supp. II 1990) (demonstrating that the new de minimus standard

Similarly, the previous mandatory duty to order an unstructured agency review of any disclosure evidencing a "reasonable belief" of significant misconduct is now discretionary.[186] This is balanced somewhat by expanded personal jurisdiction for any such discretionary referral. The law now clearly permits the OSC discretion to forward dissent from anyone for agency review, which restores the option for citizen whistleblowing disclosures.[187]

On balance, while the modifications to whistleblowing disclosure rules are sound, their only significant impact will be defensive because dissent through the Special Counsel is less likely to cause retaliation. None of the changes address the basic conflict of interest inherent in agencies investigating themselves. Until that occurs, whistleblowers are well-advised to continue dissenting outside the civil service system if they want an objective review of their charges.

II. PROVISIONS OF THE 1994 AMENDMENTS

Just after midnight, before Congress adjourned on October 8, 1994, lawmakers amended the Act by adding at least twenty new teeth for public servants to turn their paper rights under 5 U.S.C. § 2302(b)(8) into reality.[188] Congress overhauled the law for a basic reason: It had failed. As the House Post Office and Civil Service Committee concluded, "Unfortunately, while the Whistleblower Protection Act is the strongest free speech law that exists on paper, it has been a counterproductive disaster in prac-

---

for whistleblowing disclosures of mismanagement also shrinks the scope of protected speech so that it does not include challenges to "trivial" mismanagement).

186. Under 5 U.S.C. § 1213(g)(2) (1994), the OSC "may" refer a "reasonable belief" disclosure to the agency.

187. *See* 5 U.S.C. § 1213(g)(1) (1994). Even here, the OSC has no discretion to tip off the agency that is the target of the criticisms, unless the Special Counsel orders an agency investigation. *See id.* This provision restores an option the OSC had used effectively in 1980 to refer the charges of a private sector whistleblower that the Nuclear Regulatory Commission (NRC) was not enforcing quality assurance and general nuclear safety laws at the Zimmer nuclear power plant near Cincinnati, Ohio. The OSC referral sparked a more thorough NRC internal review, which eventually led to a $200,000 fine, orders for a comprehensive reinspection, revelation that the facility had been constructed since 1971 in systematic violation of quality assurance laws and its conversion to a coal-fired plant. *See* Devine & Aplin, *supra* note 14, at 53. Unfortunately, it also led to a Justice Department opinion that the OSC exceeded its authority and could not order any more investigations based on disclosures unless the whistleblower had the required civil service status. The WPA eliminates this technicality. If the information deserves to be investigated, the source can no longer be used as an excuse to avoid scrutiny. *See* S. REP. No. 100-413, at 27 (1988).

188. 140 CONG. REC. 29,048-49 (1994). *See also* 140 CONG. REC. 29,350-53 (1994).

tice. The WPA has created new reprisal victims at a far greater pace than it is protecting them."[189]

The amendments reinforced the four cornerstones of the 1989 Act. First, Congress converted labor management arbitrations into an even stronger option than IRAs for sixty-five percent of federal workers covered by collective bargaining agreements. As under prior law, employees can assert the whistleblower defense and have an equal voice in picking the arbitrator who decides their cases.[190] But now they can also seek temporary relief through stays,[191] and counterclaim directly for discipline against managers who attempt reprisals.[192] In the legislative history, Congress specified the WPA's sympathetic legal burdens of proof for the arbitrations.[193]

Congress added a more modest option for employees to seek personal liability through conventional IRAs. The Merit Systems Protection Board must refer managers for disciplinary investigations whenever there is a finding that reprisal was a contributing factor in a personnel action,[194] and an MSPB victory creates an inference that any responsible Senior Executive Service manager has failed the new performance element of merit system compliance.[195] For the first time, agency bullies realistically may have something to lose by doing the dirty work of retaliation.

The amendments continued to expand IRA access through increased personal jurisdiction. Congress gave IRA and merit systems jurisdiction to Department of Veterans Administration professionals covered by Title

---

189. H.R. REP. No. 103-769, at 12 (1994). House Report 769 referenced Merit Systems Protection Board (MSPB) survey findings "that, by a 60-23 margin, employees do not believe their rights will help them, and fear of reprisal remains as strong a reason why would-be whistleblowers remain silent as in 1983." *Id.* at 13, (citing MSPB: Office of Policy Evaluation, *Merit Systems Protection Board, Whistleblowing in the Federal Government: an Update,* (1993)). *See also* S. REP. No. 103-358, at 2-3 (1994). The Senate referenced an analogous General Accounting Office (GAO) study and emphasized the MSPB survey findings that only "[h]alf of the employees who witnessed such illegal or wasteful acts said they had reported it." *Id.* at 3.

190. *See* 5 U.S.C. § 7121(b)(1)(C)(iii) (1994).

191. *See id.* § 7121(b)(2)(A)(i).

192. *See id.* § 7121(b)(2)(ii).

193. 140 CONG. REC. 29,353 (1994) (statement of Rep. McCloskey). Due to lack of time for a conference committee, the House and Senate bills were reconciled through informal negotiations and passage of identical substitute legislation. Other than Senator Dorgan's explanation of a provision requiring OSC disclosure of proposed decisions for comment by complainants, *infra* note 211, Representative McCloskey's floor statement is the only legislative history for the eventual consensus.

194. *See infra* note 211.

195. *See infra* note 211.

38,[196] and created whistleblower protection for employees of government corporations like the Legal Services Corporation.[197]

The amendments also sustained the pattern of increasing subject matter jurisdiction for whistleblowers already eligible to file IRAs. It created a new prohibited personnel practice that flatly outlaws retaliatory orders to take psychiatric fitness for duty examinations.[198]

The most useful initiative to plug loopholes may be an expanded "catch-all" prohibited personnel practice against harassment in the form of hostile working conditions. Former law prohibited changes in duties or responsibilities inconsistent with an employee's grade or salary.[199]

The amendments added a catchall clause that effectively outlaws discrimination through "any other significant change in duties, responsibilities, or working conditions."[200] In legislative history Congress specifically instructed that this broad provision includes security clearance reprisals,[201] which, since a 1983 Supreme Court decision, *Navy v. Egan*,[202] has been the Achilles heel of the merit system.[203]

---

196. *See* 5 U.S.C. § 2105(f) (1994).

197. *See id.* §§ 2302(a)(2)(A), (a)(2)(C)(i).

198. *See id.* § 2302(a)(2)(A)(x).

199. *See id.* § 2302(a)(2)(A)(x) (1976 & Supp. III 1979).

200. *See id.* § 2302(a)(2)(A)(xi) (1994). As explained in the legislative history, "[t]his personnel action is intended to include any harassment or discrimination that could have a chilling effect on whistleblowing or otherwise undermine the merit system, and should be determined on a case-by-case basis." 140 CONG. REC. 29,353 (1994). Its origins are a more generalized provision outlawing discrimination in the original Senate Bill (S. 508). While the refined language establishes a boundary that harassment must be job related, nothing in the record retreats from the mandate in Senate Bill 508 to fill any materials gaps where coverage is excluded through a technicality. Senate Report 358 spells out the new "no-loopholes" rule.

> The intent of the Whistleblower Protection Act was to create a clear remedy for all cases of retaliation or discrimination against whistleblowers. The Committee believes that such retaliation must be prohibited, regardless of what form it may take. For this reason, Section 5(d) would amend the Act to cover any action taken to discriminate or retaliate against a whistleblower because of his/her protected conduct, regardless of the form that discrimination or retaliation may take.

S. REP. No. 103-358, at 10 (1994).

201. *See* 140 CONG. REC. 29,353 (1994) (statement of Rep. McCloskey). *See also* S. REP. NO. 103-358, at 9-10 (highlighting security clearance actions to illustrate the scope of § 2302(a)(2)(A)(xi)).

202. 484 U.S. 518 (1988).

203. The legislative history instructs that security clearance coverage includes "denial, revocation or suspension of a security clearance. . . ." 140 CONG. REC. 29,353 (1994)\(statement of Rep. McCloskey). The House committee report explained the basis for closing this coverage gap:

> Because security clearances are a precondition for nearly three million Federal and contract workers to hold their jobs, employers can de facto terminate an employee by removing his or her clearance for access to classified information. Unfortunately,

Congress also illustrated the scope through references to practices like "issuing, denying or removing an employee from specific assignments, changes in duty station, removal of support staff; and any analogous actions taken because of protected activity."[204]   Whistleblowers formerly could not challenge these type of common dirty tricks through an Individual Right of Action, because they were not listed personnel actions.

In introducing the final consensus bill, House Civil Service Subcommittee Chairman Frank McCloskey emphasized that "[t]he techniques to harass a whistleblower are limited only by the imagination."[205]   In that spirit, Congress also expanded the reach of prior statutory language to create comprehensive protection.   For example, the legislative history highlights "retaliatory investigations, threat of or referral for prosecution, defunding, reductions in force and denial [of] workers compensation benefits" to illustrate "threatened" personnel actions, because they are a prelude or create a precondition for more conventional reprisals.[206]   The primary criterion for a prohibited threat is that alleged harassment "is discriminatory, or could have a chilling effect on merit system duties and responsibilities."[207]

Congress strategically reinforced its efforts against OSC abuses of discretion.   Most significantly, the legislative history flatly prohibits OSC leaks of information about employee cases.   Even after the 1989 Act, this continued as the primary reason cited by whistleblowers who accused the Special Counsel of undermining their interests before they were eligible to file an IRA.[208]   Congress reinforced the specter of OSC personal liability

---

Federal workers have no functional due process rights to defend their clearances, leaving them defenseless against back door retaliation when a forthright attempt at firing could not succeed. Due to secrecy and the lack of procedural rights, commentators have analogized the legal system for security clearances to the system of justice in Kafka's *The Trial*. Through six hearings since 1987 jointly held with the House Judiciary Committee, this committee has developed a record detailing how rampant retaliation has filled the due process vacuum. Examples of security clearance abuses against whistleblowers in the Army's Strategic Defense Command, or Star Wars, program are illustrative.

H.R. REP. NO. 103-769, at 15 (1994)

204.   140 CONG. REC. 29,353 (1994) (statement of Rep. McCloskey). Senate Report 358, also emphasized that the point of its catchall clause is to eliminate the technicality permitting agencies to retaliate by removing whistleblowers from "high-profile assignments." S. REP. NO. 103-358, at 9-10 (1994).

205.   140 CONG. REC. 29,353 (1994) (statement of Rep. McCloskey).

206.   *See id.* at 29,353. *See also* H.R. REP. NO. 103-769, at 15.

207.   140 CONG. REC. 29,353 (1994) (statement of Rep. McCloskey).

208.   Congress noted that the Special Counsel has obeyed WPA confidentiality restrictions: as the exception, rather than the rule . . . 59 percent of OSC complainants reported to GAO that the special counsel undercut their rights by leaking information about their cases back to their employers. This can impose a fatal handicap on the employees in

by continuing the tradition of leaks, because "[w]ithout the complainant's consent, an OSC employee is acting outside the scope of his or her Government authority."[209]

A floor amendment by Senator Dorgan addresses another long term source of frustration. His amendment requires the Special Counsel to notify complainants of all significant proposed findings and wait ten days for a response before closing a case.[210] The point is to address the "lack of communication" between the Office and reprisal victims, one of the most persistent complaints by civil service employees in GAO and MSPB surveys.[211]

As in the 1989 Act, however, the bottom line for whistleblowers is the burden of proof to prevail on the merits. The amendments intensified the process of codifying realistic burdens of proof and neutralizing hostile case law. Most significant, they overturn a disastrous Federal Circuit Court of Appeals decision, *Clark v. Department of Army*,[212] that threatened to functionally cancel the WPA by legalizing any reprisal an agency "could have" taken for legitimate reasons. The Act now explicitly provides that employees can successfully prove the connection between whistleblowing and prohibited personnel practice through a time lag, when "the personnel action occurred within a period of time such that a reasonable person could conclude that the disclosure was a contributing factor in the personnel action."[213] The legislative history reaffirms that this standard has been met

---

a subsequent MSPB appeal or individual right of action. . . . [T]he decision on what risks to take is the complainant's alone. The complainant controls the information the same way [as] a client seeking private counsel . . . even if the lawyer chooses not to take the case. The restriction exists as soon as the OSC obtains the information, and lasts as long as it is in the special counsel's possession.

145 CONG. REC. 29,352 (1994) (statement of Rep. McCloskey); *see also* S. REP. NO. 103-358, at 5-6; H.R. REP. NO. 103-769, at 16, 21.

209.   145 CONG. REC. 29,352 (1994) (statement of Rep. McCloskey).

210.   *See* 5 U.S.C. § 1214(a)(1)(D) (1994).

211.   *See* 140 CONG. REC. S14,670 (daily ed. Oct. 7, 1994) (statement of Sen. Dorgan). As he further explained:

All too often cases are closed out by OSC well before critical witnesses have been interviewed or documents reviewed.

All the employee knows is that the fate of his or her career has entered a black box known as the OSC and that after an undetermined amount of time his or her case is spit out of the black box with a little note — called a closeout memo — that says, in effect, "Sorry, you're out of luck."

It should be noted that, in one survey, over a third of cases closed out by the OSC were later won by the employee on appeal. Obviously, the OSC is missing something.

Id.

212.   997 F.2d 1466 (Fed. Cir. 1993).

213.   5 U.S.C. § 1221(e)(1)(B) (1994).

when an action is taken after protected speech but before a new performance appraisal.[214]

In addition to overturning *Clark*, the legislative history rejects fourteen MSPB and Federal Circuit decisions as illegal under the new law.[215] The systematic legislative reversals were necessary, because "[t]he body of case law developed by the Board and Federal Circuit has represented a steady attack on achieving the legislative mandate for effective whistleblower protection."[216]

The outlawed doctrines[217] include decisions holding that the Whistleblower Protection Act: (1) does not protect employees challenging violations of "interpretive rules"; (2) excludes those who fail to cite specific laws when they disclose or allege illegality; (3) omits protection for an employee challenging illegality for which there is enforcement discretion; (4) limits relief in Board proceedings to the record and issues an employee previously made to the Office of Special Counsel in the informal complaint that is a prerequisite for filing an Individual Right of Action;[218] (5) requires employees to plead proposed findings of fact in their initial Board proceeding, before gaining the knowledge learned through pre-hearing discov-

---

214. *See* 145 CONG. REC. 29,353 (1994) (statement of Rep. McCloskey). In its detailed rejection of the *Clark* doctrines, the Senate Report "reaffirms that Congress intends for a[n] agency's evidence of reasons why it may have acted (other than retaliation) to be presented as part of the affirmative defense and subject to the higher [clear and convincing] burden of proof." S. REP. NO. 103-358, at 7-8.

215. *See infra* notes 218-21 and accompanying text (detailing the holdings of each of the 14 MSPB and Federal Circuit decisions rejected by Congress).

216. H.R. REP. NO. 103-769, at 17. The House noted that:
[s]ince FY 1991 [whistleblowers had only won five percent of decisions on the merits], far lower than analogous statutes with tougher burdens of proof administered by the Department of Labor. Instead of restoring balance, the U.S. Court of Appeals for the Federal Circuit [was] more hostile than the Board. Since its 1982 creation . . . employees have prevailed only twice on the merits with the whistleblower defense.
Id. (citations omitted).

217. The cases and doctrines that Congress rejected as erroneous are listed in H.R. REP. NO. 103-769, at 17-18 & n.15, and reaffirmed in 145 CONG. REC. 29,353 (1994) (statement of Rep. McCloskey).

218. 145 CONG. REC. 29,353 (1994) (statement of Rep. McCloskey), explains that this interpretation may have been the most significant violation of the Whistleblower Protection Act's mandate, in part because initial complaints to the OSC often are filed without help from an attorney. Representative McCloskey declared unequivocally,
There should not be any confusion. To exhaust the OSC administrative remedy and qualify for an individual right of action, an employee or applicant only must allege a violation of [§] 2302(b)(8). The examples of alleged reprisals listed in the OSC complaint, and the scope of the evidence that a whistleblower presents to the OSC, are completely irrelevant to establish jurisdiction for an IRA.
Id.

ery; (6) dilutes scrutiny of agency reasons to deny or restrict interim relief; (7) fails to provide back pay for employees suspended during investigations but who are subsequently cleared and returned to the job; (8) excludes relief when outside scrutiny from protected whistleblowers is upsetting to co-workers; (9) permits ex parte contacts between proposing and deciding officials for intra-agency appeals, or allows the two functions to be merged in the same person; (10) allows an agency to finalize a personnel action without waiting for the employee's answer to proposed charges; (11) flunks a one month time lag between protected activity and a challenged personnel action under the time lag doctrine for nexus in a prima facie case, due to the preexisting schedule for a performance appraisal; (12) denies consequential damages;[219] (13) excludes protection for whistleblowing initiated in the context of a grievance; (14) and screens out non-whistleblower prohibited personnel practices from being challenged in an Individual Right of Action for alleged violations of § 2302(b)(8).

Congress expressed frustration that one issue covered in legislative history could not be further cleared up through changes in statutory language. The House Report observed, "Perhaps the most troubling precedents involve the Board's inability to understand that 'any' means 'any.' The WPA protects 'any' disclosure evidencing a reasonable belief of specified misconduct, a cornerstone to which the MSPB remains blind."[220] The Floor Statement reaffirmed the sweeping, no exceptions scope of coverage for protected whistleblowing whose disclosure is not specifically prohibited by statute or classification law:

> It also is not possible to further clarify the clear statutory language in [§] 2302(b)(8)(A) that protection for "any" whistleblowing disclosure evidencing a reasonable belief of specified misconduct truly means "any." A protected disclosure may be made as part of an employee's job duties, may concern policy or individual misconduct, and may be oral or written and to any audience inside or outside the agency, without restriction to time, place, motive or context.[221]

The legislative history offers bread and butter help covering relief, settlements, attorney fees and costs. The amendments make victories more meaningful by giving consequential damages to employees who win,[222] paying medical expenses, and otherwise restoring them to the same posi-

---

219. As with *Clark*, the legislative rejection also is codified. *See* 5 U.S.C. § 1221(g)(1)(A)(ii) (1994) (codifying legislative approval of consequential damages).

220. H.R. REP. NO. 103-769, at 18. *See also* S. REP. NO. 103-358, at 10-11 (indicating that plain language of WPA extends to retaliation for "any disclosure").

221. 145 CONG. REC. 29,353 (1994) (statement of Rep. McCloskey).

222. *See* 5 U.S.C. § 1221(g)(1)(A)(ii) (1994).

tion as if no retaliation had occurred.[223] Similarly, employees do not have to wait until filing an MSPB complaint to receive back pay.[224] If they exercise civil service rights and subsequently the reprisal is canceled "independently," attorney fees may not be denied on the excuse that their legal action was irrelevant and the happy ending was a coincidence.[225] The legislative history clarifies that employees are entitled to reimbursement for all direct or indirect expenses incurred to win, whether the bill was paid by the attorney or the client.[226]

There was bad news from Congress as well. Most frustrating, the price for accomplishing anything in the adjournment rush was deferring to the Senate by abandoning House-passed reforms that would have given whistleblowers jury trials to fight reprisals,[227] and a provision that would have discarded the monopoly of the hostile Federal Circuit of Appeals for judicial review of MSPB decisions.[228] The House voted to free whistleblowers from the OSC entirely, providing direct access to Board due process hearings.[229] The House bill also would have expanded Individual Right of Action jurisdiction to provide a Board hearing challenging any prohibited personnel practice with significant consequences, instead of requiring alleged whistleblower reprisal as a prerequisite.[230] This would have empowered numerous merit system reprisal victims whose rights are dependent on the limited resources of the Office of Special Counsel. They include employees harassed for being non-whistleblower witnesses in Office of Inspector General (OIG) or other government investigations; refusing an order to violate the law; exercising their constitutional or civil service appeal rights;

---

223. *See id.* § 1221(g)(1)(A)(i). *See also* 145 CONG. REC. 29,352 (1994) (statement of Rep. McCloskey).

224. Employees who assert their civil service rights "under any available procedure" and subsequently obtain substantial relief are entitled to attorney fees, even "[if] unilateral agency action render[ed] the dispute moot." 145 CONG REC. 29,352 (1994) (statement of Rep. McCloskey). As a result, employees are entitled to reimbursements for attorney fee costs after prevailing in an intra-agency appeal or OSC complaint, through asserting or settling their claim. *See id.*

225. *See id.* "If an employee with a pending case wins substantial relief, the agency's motives for providing it are not relevant grounds to deny fees." H.R. REP. No. 103-769, at 25. "There is no requirement . . . to demonstrate a nexus between the relief and the proceeding." 145 CONG REC. 29,352 (1994) (statement of Rep. McCloskey).

226. *See* S. REP. NO. 103-358, at 8.

227. *See* H.R. 2970, 103d Cong. § 5(d) (1993); *see also* H.R. REP. No. 103-769, at 23-4.

228. *See* H.R. 2970, 103d Cong. § 5(b); *see also* H.R. REP. NO. 103-769, at 23.

229. *See* H.R. 2970, 103d Cong. § 5(c); *see also* H.R. REP. NO. 103-769, at 23.

230. *See* H.R. 2970, 103d Cong. § 5(a); *see also* H.R. REP. NO. 103-769, at 23. The House limited expanded jurisdiction to removals, suspension of more than 14 days, reduction in pay or grade, furlough of 30 days or less, detail, transfer, reassignment, or any performance-based action. *See* H.R. 2970, § 5(a).

participating in an environmental or other outside organization's activities challenging bureaucratic misconduct; and similar protected activities.[231]

There would not have been any new rights without extraordinary efforts by the staffs of the Senate Governmental Affairs Committee and the House Post Office and Civil Service Committee. Kim Weaver, staff director of the Senate Subcommittee on Federal Services, Post Office and Civil service, shepherded the bill in partnership with Deborah Kendall, staff director of the House Subcommittee on Civil Service. After the Senate vote, Weaver waited personally for the administrative paperwork to be signed and ran it to the House floor in the closing minutes before Congress shut down.

To date, the effort appears to be paying off, thanks to a fresh influx of decisionmakers who do not appear hostile to the Act. Since the 1996 arrival of new Merit Systems Protection Board member Beth Slavitz, Board case law has begun to reflect the congressional mandate. Prior to 1996 whistleblowers consistently lost decisions on the merits reviewed by the Board.[232] Since Slavitz's confirmation, however, the patterns have reversed and the trend has been increasingly been to support the employee in whistleblower cases.[233] To illustrate, in 1997 whistleblowers won half of the eight Board decisions on the merits.[234]

The Board also has been establishing a trend to strengthen employees' due process rights through victories on disputed procedural matters. Even the procedural victories have tangible consequences that can be dispositive for whether the statute is relevant. In *Russell v. Department of Justice*,[235] the Board upheld legislative history in the 1994 amendments that a new catchall provision protects employees from retaliatory investigations, the most common form of knee jerk reaction to dissenters. Equally valuable, in *Special Counsel v. Spears*,[236] the Board held that personnel actions taken against employees because of a mistaken perception they blew the whistle is just as illegal as reprisal based in reality.[237] In *Morrison v. Department of Army*,[238] the Board held that when the OSC reopens an investigation the

---

231. *See* 5 U.S.C. § 2302(b)(9)–(b)(11) (1994).

232. *See supra* notes 13-16 and accompanying text.

233. *See* DEVINE, *supra* note 3, at 131.

234. Favorable decisions on the merits include: *Brewer v. Department of the Interior*, 76 M.S.P.R. 363 (1997), *Russell v. Department of Justice*, 76 M.S.P.R. 317 (1997), *Special Counsel v. Costello*, 75 M.S.P.R. 562 (1997), and *Jones v. Department of the Interior*, 74 M.S.P.R. 666 (1997).

235. 76 M.S.P.R. 317, 323-24 (1997).

236. 75 M.S.P.R. 639, 652 (1997).

237. *See id.; see also* Juffer v. United States Info. Agency, 80 M.S.P.R. 81, 86 (1998) (citations omitted).

238. 77 M.S.P.R. 655 (1998).

employee also receives another opportunity to file an Individual Right of Action after 120 days or sooner if the Special Counsel again declines to provide requested relief. This can be an invaluable second bite of the apple for whistleblowers who fail to seek a due process IRA Board hearing after an OSC turndown, if they subsequently discover new evidence that convinces the Special Counsel to reconsider.

Even the harshest OSC critics must concede that the times are changing at that agency. Since passage of the 1994 amendments, complaints about unauthorized leaks have dropped off the radar screen for organizations monitoring the Office. The 1998 confirmation of new Special Counsel Elaine Kaplan may be another breakthrough, helping restoring the OSC to a remedial agency in substance, as well as form. As Deputy General Counsel of the National Treasury Employees Union, she helped pass the 1994 amendments that the OSC administers. To date, she has sponsored repeated public meetings with practitioners, agencies, and non profit organizations advocating merit system rights.

Ms. Kaplan has publicly announced her commitment to increase remedial litigation by the OSC; launch a campaign to prevent retaliation through ambitious agency outreach programs; introduce alternative disputes resolution as a thrifty way to increase the number of employees helped; and intensify disciplinary actions against managers who retaliate.[239] The latter initiative displays good government guts, coming on the heels of a decision making the Special Counsel liable for the attorney fees of managers who successfully defend themselves against disciplinary prosecutions.[240] Perhaps the most noteworthy initiative to date has been filing an amicus curiae brief before the Board to follow Congress's legislative history guidance for the 1994 catch-all amendment,[241] and fill the security clearance loophole in the Whistleblower Protection Act.[242]

There should be no delusions that the federal bureaucracy has found religion. The administration's Reinventing Government initiative has been conspicuously silent on whistleblower protection. Indeed, the Justice Department issued a binding interpretation that "reinventing government" reforms at the Federal Aviation Administration meant stripping agency em-

---

239. *See Interview: Q & A: Special Counsel Discusses Goals for Whistleblower Agency,* 37 Gov't Empl. Rel. Rep (BNA) No. 1804, at 301 (Mar. 15, 1999).

240. Santella v. Special Counsel, M.S.P.B. Nos. CE-1215-91-0007/0008-A-1 (Dec. 12, 1998).

241. *See generally* Amicus Curiae Brief of the United States Office of Special Counsel at 1, Roach v. Department of the Army (No. DC-1221-97-0251-W-1) and Hesse v. Department of State (No. DC-0752-97-1097-I-1).

242. *See id.*

ployees of MSPB and OSC remedies under the Whistleblower Protection Act.[243]

Similarly, the executive branch Office of Personnel Management[244] is waging a sustained legal counterattack on the scope of protected speech. A microcosm is the case of John White, an Air Force education specialist who lost his job in May 1992, a month after blowing the whistle on a suspect initiative that was subsequently withdrawn.[245] Although Mr. White has won three Board decisions upholding Whistleblower Protection Act violations in the same case, OPM is still appealing. One challenge was that his disclosures were unprotected, because he had feelings such as "fear" concerning the consequences of alleged government misconduct he was disclosing, and therefore could not objectively possess a reasonable belief.[246] The latest challenge is that the Board erred by ruling in Mr. White's favor on grounds that his concerns were supported by his own expertise, as well by the consensus of experts inside and outside the government.[247] OPM concluded that is an insufficient basis for disclosures to qualify as protected speech, because it merely demonstrates the disclosure is popular and does not include an independent Board analysis of "reasonableness."[248]

This type of surreal attack remains viable because the Federal Circuit has not ruled in favor of a whistleblower on the merits since passage of the 1994 amendments. Indeed, the Circuit continues to defy legislative history for the 1994 amendments. To illustrate, in *Willis v. Department of Agriculture*,[249] the Court held that the WPA does not protect employees who make otherwise protected disclosures that are part of their jobs. That not only defies plain statutory language and congressional intent that "any" means "any,"[250] but removes coverage for the most common type of whistleblowing.— when a government employee attempts to defend the public by enforcing the law against the politically powerful. It means whistle-

---

243. Both chambers of Congress approved 1998 legislation closing the loophole, but the solution was stymied due to irreconcilable differences on ancillary matters. *See generally* S. 100, 105th Cong. (1997).

244. *See* Civil Service Reform Act of 1978, Pub. L. No. 95-454, §§ 1101-1105, 92 Stat. 1121 (codified at 5 U.S.C. § 1101) (stating that OPM would assume management duties of abolished Civil Service Commission).

245. *See generally* White v. Department of the Air Force, 78 M.S.P.R. 38 (1998).

246. *See id.*

247. *See id.*

248. *See id.* at 42; *see generally* Amicus Curiae Brief for the Government Accountability Project, Lachance v. White (No. 98-3429) (1998).

249. 141 F. 3d 1139, 1144 (1998).

250. *See supra* notes 102-110, 221, and accompanying text. Similarly, in Serrao v. Merit Systems Protection Board, 95 F.3d 1569, 1576 (Fed. Cir. 1996), the court continued a pre-1994 trend of disqualifying protection for whistleblowing disclosures raised in the context of a personnel grievance.

blowing is only protected as an extracurricular activity. When employees attempt to perform their duties as public servants instead of bureaucrats playing it safe, they proceed at their own risk. The court's animus against the Act is not surprising, since the new Chief Judge is Robert Mayer, the Deputy Special Counsel, who in 1981-1982 helped then Special Counsel Alex Kozinski transform the OSC into a Trojan horse that became the executive's worst threat to whistleblowers.[251]

Nor has the Board's improved track record adjudicating administrative petitions for review necessarily trickled down to administrative judges who conduct WPA hearings. In October 1998 the Office of Special Counsel filed an amicus curiae brief with the Board challenging an administrative judge ruling that effectively required employees to file proposed findings of fact and conclusions of law in advance of an IRA hearing as a prerequisite for having their administrative day in court; excluded employees from protection for disclosing any information not presented to the Office of Special Counsel; disqualified employees from protection based on composite information evidencing a reasonable belief through multiple disclosures; and disqualified employees from protection unless their disclosures are sufficient to justify opening a formal government investigation, without coming back to ask further questions.[252]

The fragility of apparently unqualified rights on paper was illustrated by an administrative judge in another unpublished decision affirmed without comment through the Supreme Court.[253] In that case the administrative judge assumed the whistleblower's disclosure of illegality was correct to the extent that taxpayers would not receive land exchange appraisal income to which they were entitled by law. But the judge ruled that this evidenced neither a reasonable belief of illegality, abuse of authority or mismanagement, in part because it was merely an "error," and not the first of its kind. As a result the whistleblower's disclosure was unprotected, and his termination literally for making it was upheld.

III. RECOMMENDATIONS

The Whistleblower Protection Act is a work in progress. Freedom of employment dissent is continuing to evolve for federal employees, but they still would be foolhardy to rely on the law's promise of strengthened free

---

251. *See supra* notes 65, 66, 87, and accompanying text; Devine & Aplin, *supra* note 14, at 27-29.

252. *See* Amicus Curiae Brief for the U.S. Office of Special Counsel, Keefer v. United States Dept. of Agric., MSPB Docket No. SE-1221-96-0548-W-1 (1998).

253. Grijalva v. Department of Interior, Docket No. De-0752-95-0061-I-1 1, Initial Decision 25 (Apr. 21, 1995), *aff'd* 68 M.S.P.R. 690 (Nov. 9, 1995), *aff'd* 104 F.3d 374 (Fed. Cir. 1997), *cert. denied*, 520 U.S. 1251 (1997).

speech rights. That promise will be more realistic with amendments that address the most serious threats to its ongoing legitimacy. A list of the most significant reforms ranges from new definitions and linguistic fine-tuning that would overcome hostile precedents, to structural changes expanding jurisdiction and access to court.

1. Permanently pass a supremacy of law provision for the Act's protected whistleblowing. Each year since fiscal year 1988 Congress has passed an appropriations amendment known as the "anti-gag statute" that forbids spending for enforcement of nondisclosure agreements or policies that would cancel Whistleblower Protection Act rights.[254] The appropriations rider not only shields the WPA from gag orders that otherwise would override its free speech rights, but protects anonymous dissent and bans functional prior restraint due to the absence of prior notice. The anti-gag statute's catalyst was nondisclosure agreements known as Standard Forms (SFs) 189 and 312, which as a prerequisite for security clearances required to employees to seek advance permission before disclosures to learn whether virtually any information was classified. This was because SFs 189 and 312 disregarded the normal rule that information is not classified unless it is specifically designated as "secret" in advance.[255] The anti-gag statute must be adopted permanently.

2. Create a statutory definition of "reasonable belief" that is consistent with the Act's remedial purpose. As evidenced in the *White* case, the scope of legally protected dissent is too unstable to reliably predict whether it is even covered by the Act.[256] That creates an inherent chilling effect.

3. Create a statutory definition of "any" that is consistent with the Act's remedial purpose. The *Willis* decision illustrates the Federal Circuit's inability to resist the temptation of judicial activism by making exceptions based on the context of disclosures.[257] Congressional persistence is necessary to prevent more potholes that cover the road.

4. Close the Federal Aviation Administration loophole. Congress should not permit "reinventing government" to be a synonym for canceling the public's right to know. This aberration should be promptly reversed as a deterrent against analogous creativity.

---

254. The legislative pioneers of the successful campaign to defend whistleblower rights against this threat were Senators Charles Grassley and David Pryor. *See* Letter from Senators Charles Grassley and David Pryor to Senator Pete Domenici (August 1, 1989) (on file with the *Administrative Law Review*). The current version of the anti-gag statute is found in § 636 of the Treasury, Postal and General Government Appropriations Act of 1999, Pub. L. No. 105-277, § 636, 112 Stat. 2681 (1998).

255. *See, e.g.,* 50 U.S.C. 426. For an in-depth review of the roots for SFs 189, 312 and similar national security secrecy contracts, see H.R. REP. NO. 100-991, at 1 (1988).

256. *See generally White*, 78 M.S.P.R. 38 (1998).

257. *See generally* Willis v. Department of Agric., 141 F.3d 1139 (Fed. Cir. 1998).

5. Close the security clearance loophole. Even if the Merit Systems Protection Board agrees with the Special Counsel's recommendation to honor the legislative intent for expansive protection, the issue could remain uncertain for years during judicial review, in light of the Supreme Court's decision in *Navy v. Egan.*[258] In the absence of any legislative opposition or debate on this issue before passage of the 1994 amendments, Congress should end any possibility of confusion by adding it to the list of covered personnel actions in 5 U.S.C. § 2302(a)(2).

6. Permit Merit Systems Protection Board Individual Right of Action hearings for any prohibited personnel practice. Under current law, for any prohibited personnel practice besides 5 U.S.C. § 2302(b)(8), an employee does not have any options beyond asking the Office of Special Counsel for assistance. Again contrary to legislative history, an employee may not join any other prohibited personnel practice beyond alleged violations of § 2302(b)(8) in a pending IRA proceeding defending whistleblower rights.[259] This applies even against violations of 5 U.S.C. § 2302(b)(9)(D), retaliation against refusals to violate the law.

7. Shield Office of Special Counsel disciplinary proceedings: The threat that the Special Counsel may have to finance managers' attorney fee bill, *supra* note 240, could have a chilling effect disciplinary prosecutions, which are essential to deter retaliation. Motions to dismiss or for summary judgment are adequate to cut short any irresponsible prosecutions.

8. Relieve whistleblowers of the necessity to file complaints at the Office of Special Counsel. The prerequisite to first seek relief from the Special Counsel has become a vehicle to deny protection on technicalities that require whistleblowers to hire attorneys and flood the OSC with allegations and evidence during the "informal" stage of their cases.[260] The public policy goal to screen unrealistic or frivolous litigation can be achieved through mandatory mediation or an analogous alternative dispute resolution requirement.

9. Give whistleblowers the option for district court jury trials. As long as whistleblowers' rights are adjudicated at administrative tribunals by executive branch judges without independence, the protections will be suspect. Since whistleblowers allege they suffer retaliation for defending the

---

258.   484 U.S. 518 (1988).

259.   *See* Carolyn v. Department of Interior, 63 M.S.P.R. 684, 689 (1994), Costin v. HHS, 72 M.S.P.R. 525, 530 (1996), Thomas v. Department of Treasury, 77 M.S.P.R. 224 (1998).

260.   *See supra* note 241.

public, they should be able to seek juries of their peers as the most legitimate decisionmakers to resolve the conflicts.[261]

10. Restore "all circuits" judicial review. The ongoing necessity for Congress to legislatively overturn the pattern of disastrous decisions by the Federal Circuit Court of Appeals could continue indefinitely. Congress would create increased credibility for statutory language, and end this broken record syndrome, by removing the Federal Circuit's monopoly on judicial review since the Federal Courts Improvement Act of 1982,[262] and restoring normal Administrative Procedure Act judicial review in the regional circuit courts of appeal.

In short, the struggle to transcend whistleblower reprisal promises to be no easier than to overcome segregation or other forms of discrimination. The stakes are worth the persistence, however. Civil service employees will act as public servants instead of bureaucrats, to the extent that the Whistleblower Protection Act bridges the gap between paper and reality.

---

261. The campaign for jury trials is gaining increasing legitimacy. *See* Editorial, *Helping Whistle-Blowers Survive*, N.Y. TIMES, May 1, 1999, at A24. It is a cornerstone of the newly passed District of Columbia Whistleblower Reinforcement Act, *supra* note 142, § 1554(a), D.C. Code § 1-616.14. Further, a bipartisan legislative effort is in progress to extend protection enforced by jury trials to D.C. court employees who blow the whistle. On March 16, 1999, without dissent the House passed the expanded coverage in House Bill 858. 145 CONG. REC. H2179-81 (daily ed. March 16, 1999).

262. 5 U.S.C. § 7703(b)(1) (1994).

[8]

FREEDOM OF INFORMATION: WILL BLAIR BE ABLE TO BREAK THE WALLS OF SECRECY IN BRITAIN?

DEBRA L. SILVERMAN[*]

*   J.D. Candidate 1999, American University, Washington College of Law; B.A., 1996 University of Wisconsin–Madison. The author would like to thank Professor Robert G. Vaughn for his invaluable direction and advice, Stephanie R. Martz for her tireless guidance, and the ILR staff for their arduous assistance during the completion of this Comment. Special thanks also to her family and friends for their love and support. Finally, thanks to Jason Epstein for his patience, laughter, and encouragement.

INTRODUCTION

Britain is one of the most secretive democracies in the world to-day.[1] The results of health checks on cruise liners,[2] the length of the queue at the local post office,[3] and inspections of British pharmaceutical plants are all considered official secrets.[4] Since the 1970s, the

---

1. *See* 219 PARL. DEB., H.C. (6th ser.) 584 (1993) (statement of Mark Fisher) [hereinafter Fisher Arguments] ("Britain is still one of the most secretive societies in the western world and one of the few democracies not to have some form of freedom of information legislation."); *see also* Des Wilson, *1984 . . . and On-wards? The Level and Effects of Secrecy in Britain Today*, in THE SECRETS FILE: THE CASE FOR FREEDOM OF INFORMATION IN BRITAIN TODAY 1, 1-12 (Des Wilson ed., 1984) (stating that Britain is "probably the most secretive" of democracies while advocating for greater freedom of information in Britain today). *See generally* CLIVE PONTING, SECRECY IN BRITAIN (1990) (discussing the extent and nature of official secrecy in Britain).

2. *See* Richard Norton-Taylor, *Secret Society: Bill Would Open Whitehall Closet*, GUARDIAN, Feb. 19, 1993, at 9 (stating that reports of cockroaches found in the cruise ship QE2's kitchens in 1989 and 1991 were available in the United States under its Freedom of Information Act but were not available in Britain under its secrecy laws).

3. *See* 219 PARL. DEB., H.C. (6th ser.) 635 (1993) (statement of Kate Hoey) [hereinafter Hoey Arguments] (citing the length of the queue at her local post office as an example of an official secret).

4. *See* Norton-Taylor, *supra* note 2, at 9 (describing how Britons use the United States Freedom of Information Act to learn about inspections of British pharmaceutical and poultry plants). "By using the United States' Freedom of In-

United States,[5] Canada,[6] Australia[7] and many other countries[8] have introduced a freedom of information law[9] that grants statutory rights

formation Act, Britons can find more about British policy from the U.S. than from British archives." *Id.*

5. *See* OFFICE OF INFO. AND PRIVACY, U.S. DEP'T OF JUSTICE, FREEDOM OF INFORMATION ACT GUIDE & PRIVACY ACT OVERVIEW (Sept. ed. 1996) [hereinafter FOIA GUIDE] (noting that Congress enacted the Freedom of Information Act, 5 U.S.C. § 552, in 1966). Congress amended the act extensively in 1974 and 1996. *See id.*; *see also Congress Enacts FOIA Amendments*, FOIA UPDATE, (DOJ/Office of Info. and Privacy, D.C.) Fall 1996, at 1 [hereinafter FOIA UPDATE] (detailing "Electronic Freedom of Information Act Amendments of 1996"); *infra* note 351 and accompanying text (providing the United States' amended Freedom of Information Act's new definition of agency records).

6. *See generally* STANDING COMM. ON JUSTICE AND SOLICITOR GENERAL, 33RD PARL., 2D SESS., OPEN AND SHUT: ENHANCING THE RIGHT TO KNOW AND THE RIGHT TO PRIVACY, REPORT ON THE REVIEW OF THE ACCESS TO INFORMATION ACT AND THE PRIVACY ACT (March, 1987) [hereinafter OPEN & SHUT] (detailing the date of enactment of Canada's Access to Information Act and explaining the statute's roots in the late 1960s and 1970s). Specifically, Canada's Access to Information Act, R.S.C., ch. 111 (1980-1983) (Can.), was enacted by Parliament in June 1982 and came into force in July 1983. *See id.* at 2-3; *see also infra* note 335 and accompanying text (stating that Liberals enacted Canada's Access to Information Act as a result of pressure from the Conservative opposition party).

7. *See generally* AUSTRALIAN LAW REFORM COMM'N & ADMIN. REVIEW COUNCIL, FREEDOM OF INFORMATION, ISSUES PAPER NO. 12, at 3-8 (1994) [hereinafter ISSUES PAPER] (explaining how Australia's FOI legislation was finally passed in 1982 despite the fact that it was first considered in the 1960s, following the introduction of FOI legislation in the United States). Australia's Freedom of Information Act, 1982, ch. 3 (Cth), was specifically enacted in December 1982, and substantively amended in 1983, 1986, and 1991. *See id.* at 6. On July 8, 1994, Acting Attorney-General of Australia, Duncan Kerr MP, asked the Australian Law Reform Commission (ALRC) and the Administrative Review Council (ARC) to review the Commonwealth's freedom of information (FOI) legislation to determine if further reform was necessary. *See id.* at 1; *see also infra* note 343 and accompanying text (discussing the Acting Attorney General's Order to the ALRC to conduct its FOI inquiry).

8. *See* Tom Riley, *News From Canada and Abroad*, ACCESS REPORTS, June 9, 1993, at 9 (noting that Manitoba's Freedom of Information Act came into force in 1988); *see also* IAN EAGLES ET AL., FREEDOM OF INFORMATION IN NEW ZEALAND 1-3 (1992) (observing that freedom of information became a political issue in New Zealand in the mid-1970s, which led to a review of the country's Official Secrets Act and the enactment of the "Official Information Act" on December 17, 1982); *cf.* Tom Riley, *News From Canada and Abroad*, ACCESS REPORTS, Sept. 28, 1994, at 5 [hereinafter *September Report*] (affirming the news of a draft freedom of information bill in India). Tom Riley also reports that "[i]n early 1994 the European Commission brought into effect its Code of Conduct on Access to government information." *Id.* at 4. The Code applies to all European Commission Institutions, not to any member country. *See id.*

9. *See* PATRICK BIRKINSHAW, FREEDOM OF INFORMATION: THE LAW, THE

of access to the above information. Britain, however, has opted for new secrecy legislation instead.[10]

Pledging to curtail the excessive government secrecy that exists in Britain, Prime Minister Tony Blair included a Freedom of Information Act in the New Labour Party's 1997 election manifesto. He stated: "We are pledged to a Freedom of Information Act, leading to more open government . . . ."[11] On the first of May, 1997, the British electorate demonstrated its preference for Blair and freedom of information legislation at the polls, allowing Blair to capture a commanding majority in the Parliament.[12]

PRACTICE AND THE IDEAL 1 (2nd ed. 1996) (defining freedom of information as "having access to files, or to information in any form, in order to know what the government is up to"); *see also* Richard A. Chapman, *Introduction* to OPEN GOVERNMENT: A STUDY OF THE PROSPECTS OF OPEN GOVERNMENT WITHIN THE LIMITATIONS OF THE BRITISH POLITICAL SYSTEM 11 (Richard A. Chapman & Michael Hunt eds.,1987) (advancing basic principles underlying freedom of information legislation). Three basic principles are: (1) Disclosure of official information as a right; (2) Exemptions prohibiting the release of certain kinds of information deemed necessary to be kept secret in the nation's interests; and (3) Machinery for appeal against denials by administrators to supply information. *See id.* In general, freedom of information laws grant rights of access to government held documents, except for certain categories of information which are protected from disclosure by statutory exemptions. *See infra* Part III (detailing the access statutes of the United States, Canada and Australia).

10. In 1989, Britain's "Official Secrets Act" was amended yet again. *See* Official Secrets Act, 1989, ch. 6 (Eng.) [hereinafter OSA 1989]; *see also infra* notes 31-32 (discussing the Official Secrets Act amendments of 1989). *See generally* Michael Cassell, *Fears of Severe Curbs on Freedom of Expression; Official Secrets Act*, FIN. TIMES (London), Dec. 20, 1988, at A10 (discussing the severe curbs on freedom that the "Government's new official secrets laws" have in Britain).

11. New Labour, *Because Britain Deserves Better: The Manifesto* (visited Nov. 3, 1997) <http://www.labour.org.uk/views/manifesto/britain/politics%5F1.html> [hereinafter New Labour].

12. *See* Fawn Vrazo, *Britain's Historic 'Ta-Ta' to the Tories*, NEWS & OBSERVER (Raleigh, NC), May 4, 1997, at A25 (stating that the "Labor Party didn't just win the general election Thursday, it swallowed it whole . . . Labor leader Tony Blair and his party ended 18 years straight of Conservative rule"); *Toasting the Tories*, STAR TELEGRAM (Fort Worth, TX), May 6, 1997, at 10 (stating "[t]here is winning, and then there is kicking the tea and crumpets out of the opposition . . . . [T]he latter is what the Labor Party did to the Conservative Party in the recent British elections"); David S. Broder, *After Victory, The Job Begins Across the Ocean, Clinton's Record Shadows Blair*, REC. (Northern New Jersey), May 5, 1997, at A15 (comparing the electoral success of Tony Blair to United States President Clinton and emphasizing how Blair, like Clinton, competed successfully for "information-age" votes).

Blair promised a White Paper on proposals for a freedom of information bill during the Queen's Speech at the opening of Parliament.[13] The lack of an identifiable time table for a bill, however, has led many to question the New Labour Party's commitment.[14] Since 1974, a Freedom of Information Act has permeated Labour manifestos, only to be dropped once the Party was in power.[15] The govern-

---

13. *Queen's Speech on the Opening of Parliament, Wed. May 14, 1997* (visited Aug. 3, 1997) <http://www.open.gov.uk/coi/qs97/speech.html>. In general, a white paper is an official government report prepared on any subject.

14. *See* Ann Clwyd, *End Secrecy Before It's Too Late Again,* GUARDIAN, May 20, 1997, at 17 (lamenting that a Freedom of Information Act is not among the measures the Labor Party has brought forward in the first session of Parliament and arguing that "[i]f we wait two or three years before legislating, ministers will have slipped into the traditional, cosy, protected way of making decisions"); *Leader: Don't Keep us in the Dark,* INDEP., May 11, 1997, at 22 [hereinafter *Leader*] (stating that "the absence of a freedom of information Bill is disappointing" and asking whether the Government regards people's involvement in politics as being restricted to periodic elections). *But see* Nicholas Timmins, *Delay on Freedom of Information,* FIN. TIMES (London), May 15, 1997, at 10 (noting that Mr. David Clark, the Chanchellor of the Duchy of Lancaster, has assured that "the government was 'deadly serious' about enacting such a bill"); *infra* note 16.

15. *See* Clwyd, *supra* note 14, at 17 (reiterating that "[s]ince 1974, the Labour Party has committed itself to freedom of information in manifesto after manifesto"); Fiona Cairns, *Mandelson: Freedom of Information Bill Still On,* EVENING STANDARD, May 8, 1997, at A2 (detailing how "[i]n the past, under the leadership of Harold Wilson and Jim Callaghan, Labour promised Freedom of Information legislation—only to drop the idea once in government"); *see also* The Labour Party General Election Manifesto for 1974, *reprinted in* THE TIMES GUIDE TO THE HOUSE OF COMMONS OCTOBER 1974 309 (1974) (stating that "Labour believes that the process of government should be more open to the public . . . . We shall: Replace the Official Secrets Act by a measure to put the burden on the public authorities to justify withholding information."); The Labour Party General Election Manifesto for 1983, *reprinted in* THE TIMES GUIDE TO THE HOUSE OF COMMONS JUNE 1983 304, 325 (promising to "[i]ntroduce a Freedom of Information Bill, providing for a genuine system of open government and placing the onus on the authorities to justify withholding information"). *See generally* DAVID BUTLER, BRITISH GENERAL ELECTIONS SINCE 1945 (2d ed. 1995) (detailing the fourteen general elections that have occurred in Britain since 1945). General Parliamentary elections must be held at least every five years. *See id.* The Labour Party has won seven general elections since 1945 and the Conservative Party has won eight. *See id.* In order to clearly understand the pattern of the British Government's opposition to freedom of information and Labour's attempts, as demonstrated throughout the text it is necessary to have a detailed timeline of the Governments of Britain. The timeline is as follows: 1959-64— The Conservative Government of Harold MacMillan; 1964-66; The Labour Governments of Harold Wilson; 1966-74— The Conservative Government of Edward Heath; 1974-76— The Labour Government of Harold Wilson; 1976-79— The Labour Government

ment claimed that the delay was due to its desire to ensure full consultation on such a complex issue.[16]

This comment discusses what makes the enactment of freedom of information legislation so complex in the United Kingdom at the national level. Freedom of information and open government are considered part of an effective democracy. Secrecy breeds inefficiency, lack of accountability, and a general distrust for government. Freedom of information statutes are important because they dismantle governmental secrecy by granting individuals access to information. Part I provides an overview of the secret culture of Britain's government. Part II examines prior attempts to enact freedom of information legislation in Britain. Part III outlines the access statutes of the United States, Australia, and Canada as prototypes for Britain. Finally, Part IV recommends provisions that should be included in Blair's Freedom of Information Act.

---

of James Callaghan; 1979-92— The Conservative Governments of Margaret Thatcher; 1992-97— The Conservative Government of John Major; and 1997-present— The Labour Government of Tony Blair. *See* ALAN SKED & CHRIS COOK, POSTWAR BRITAIN: A POLITICAL HISTORY (2d ed. 1984) (tracing the Governments of Britain).

16. *Commitment to Freedom of Information Bill and More Open Government Reaffirmed (Cabinet Office Press Release of 14 May 1997)* (visited Nov. 8, 1997) <http://www.coi.gov.uk/coi> [hereinafter *Cabinet Office*]; *see Leader, supra* note 14 (providing Minister without Portfolio Peter Mandelson's argument as to the delay of a freedom of information bill which was that "Labour 'can't just pull some Bill from the shelf and implement it.'"); *see also Freedom of Information Unit* (visited Aug. 3, 1997) <http://www.open.gov.uk/m-of-g/foihome.html> [hereinafter FOI Unit] (setting forth the Government's freedom of information legislation schedule). "[T]he Government hopes to publish [a] White Paper this Summer [1997] and to publish a draft bill for consultation early next year [1998]." *Id.* The British Government failed to publish a White Paper during the Summer of 1997; however, to a certain extent, it has advanced its short term goal of "looking at ways in which the existing Code of Practice can best be used to extend openness in the short term." *Id.* Recently, the Lord Chancellor's Department published further information on Open Government, entitled "Open Government – Provision of Information." *See Open Government-Provision of Information* (visited Nov. 8, 1997) <http://www.open.gov.uk/lcd/open.html> (stating on Nov. 6, 1997 that [t]he Government is committed to a Freedom of Information Act . . . . Pending the introduction of such an act, the Lord Chancellor's Department is committed to providing information in line with the principles laid down in the Code of Practice on Access to Government Information").

I. BACKGROUND

A. THE SECRET CULTURE OF BRITAIN'S GOVERNMENT

Unlike many other parliamentary democracies,[17] Britain does not operate under a written constitution that sets forth the responsibilities and rights of the government and the people.[18] Instead, Britain's law is comprised of parliamentary statutes, common law and judicial decisions, and tradition.[19] In the nineteenth century, it was customary for ministers and civil servants to abide by an internal code of conduct for the dissemination of official information.[20] The pervasive underlying premise of this code was that a good government is a closed government. In other words, the public should know only what the government decides it should know.[21] This concept of gov-

---

17. *See* SYDNEY D. BAILEY, BRITISH PARLIAMENTARY DEMOCRACY at viii (1958) (defining "parliamentary democracy" as "that system of government in which the rulers are answerable to and dismissible by representatives elected by the people"); *cf.* David Winder, *Little Known British Tradition: Secrecy*, CHRISTIAN SCIENCE MONITOR, Dec. 17, 1986, at 1 (explaining that Britain, in addition to being the "'mother of Parliaments, . . . also laid the foundations for representative democracy and individual liberty with the signing of the Magna Carta in 1215").

18. *See* British Information Services, *Britain in the USA* (visited July 11, 1997) <http://www.britain.nyc.ny.us/> (differentiating Britain from most other countries because it does not have a written constitution set out in a single document); *cf.* Chapman, *supra* note 9, at 16 (explaining that Britain's unwritten constitution is the main difference between the United Kingdom and all other countries, as far as freedom of information legislation is concerned); *see, e.g.*, ROBERT PYPER, THE BRITISH CIVIL SERVICE 145 (1995) (advancing that the large expanses of the constitution which remain "unwritten" reinforce official secrecy by being "relatively easy to supplement with codes, rules and conventions"). In addition, Mr. Pyper asserts that the lack of any constitutional "right to know" hampers members of the public and their representatives when seeking access to official information. *See id.*

19. *See* British Information Services, *supra* note 18 (providing internet users with details as to how Britain is ruled); BAILEY, *supra* note 17, at 2 (detailing the "three sources from which the British Constitution is drawn").

20. *See* PONTING, *supra* note 1, at 1 ("For most of the nineteenth century Britain had no laws to enforce secrecy. Control of official information was exercised through an informal code of conduct among the elite group of politicians and administrators who had a strong interest in treating the conduct of public affairs as an essentially private matter.").

21. *See id.*; *see also* BIRKINSHAW *supra* note 9, at 25 (describing how, in Britain, political power and survival are inextricably bound with the control of information). Accordingly, if one takes away the government's control of information,

ernmental secrecy was later institutionalized[22] by the Official Secrets Act of 1911.[23]

1. The Official Secrets Act of 1911

Parliament passed the Official Secrets Act in 1911, with little debate, in response to fears of German espionage.[24] The Act combines espionage offense provisions with provisions on the disclosure of official information.[25] Although members of Parliament presented the bill as a necessary measure to combat espionage and preserve national security, many have argued that "the bill . . . was intended by the Government to have a wider scope."[26] Section two of the Official

---

of when and what to release, one takes away a bulwark of its power. *See id.*; *see, e.g.*, CLIVE PONTING, WHITEHALL: TRAGEDY AND FARCE 133 (1986) (characterizing the "information" that the government does disclose as "publicity material" or "public relations material" which masks the real level of secrecy and exposes the public to information that supports the government's activities). *See generally* DAVID LEIGH, FRONTIERS OF SECRECY: CLOSED GOVERNMENT IN BRITAIN at ix (1982) (maintaining that people with power have a vested interest not only in hanging on to as much power as possible, but also in obscuring the truth).

22. *See* Wilson, *supra* note 1, at 1 (stating that "[g]overnmental secrecy is institutionalized by the Official Secrets Act"); *see also* PYPER, *supra* note 18 (recognizing the Official Secrets Act of 1911 as the most sweeping secrecy statute in Britain). In addition, Pyper highlights the Thirty Year Rule which is an additional statute contributing to official secrecy by placing a blanket ban on publication of official documents for three decades. *See id.*

23. Official Secrets Act (OSA), 1911 (Eng.) [hereinafter OSA 1911]; *see also* 951 PARL. DEB., H.C. (5th ser.) 1256-61 (1978) (statement of Sir Michael Havers) [hereinafter Havers Statements] (tracing the history of the Official Secrets Act of 1911). The Official Secrets Act of 1911 was not the first Official Secrets Act to emerge; rather, Parliament passed the Breach of Official Trust Bill in 1889. *See id.* at 1256; *see also* BIRKINSHAW, *supra* note 9, at 82 (recounting the historical development of government's control of information and noting in particular that government control of information was not a problem when Parliament passed the first Official Secrets Act).

24. *See* PONTING, *supra* note 1, at 8 (noting that, at the turn of the century, fears of a German invasion and stories of German spies infiltrating Britain began to proliferate); *see also* Havers Statements, *supra* note 23, at 1257 (describing how on August 18, 1911, the Bill passed through "all of its stages" and the Attorney General said that there was "nothing novel in the principle of the Bill").

25. *See* PONTING, *supra* note 1, at 9 (asserting that the Government opted for additional protective cover by combining espionage and disclosure in the same act).

26. *See* BIRKINSHAW, *supra* note 9, at 97-98 (citing Frank Committee, Cmnd 5104, vol. 1 (1972), at 53). The Frank Committee Command Paper reported the circumstances surrounding the enactment of the OSA of 1911:

Secrets Act makes it a criminal offense to disclose official information without authority.[27] Under the Act, it is also an offense to receive such information.[28] "It is immaterial whether or not the recipient subsequently passes on the information."[29] As such, a presumption developed, and continues to exist, whereby all government information is presumed official and secret—not to be disclosed.[30] Although

---

The debates give a clear impression of crisis legislation, aimed mainly at espionage. Closer study, and reference to official sources, reveal a different story. This legislation had been long desired by governments. It had been carefully prepared over a period of years. One of its objects was to give greater protection against leakages of any kind of official information whether or not connected with defense or national security. This was clear enough from the text of the Bill alone. Although section two of the Act was much wider in a number of respects than section two of the 1889 Act, the files suggest that the Government in 1911 honestly believed that it introduced no new principle, but merely put into practice more effectually the principle of using criminal sanctions to protect official information. At all events, the Government elected not to volunteer complete explanations of their Bill in Parliament. And Parliament, in the special circumstances of that summer, did not look behind the explanations offered.

Id. at 97-98.

27. *See* 919 PARL. DEB., H.C. (5th ser.) 1878-81 (1976) (statement of the Secretary of State for the Home Department, Mr. Merlyn Rees) [hereinafter Rees Statements] (describing the criminal liability under Section two of the Official Secrets Act); Des Wilson, *Information is Power: The Causes of Secrecy, in* THE SECRETS FILE: THE CASE FOR FREEDOM OF INFORMATION IN BRITAIN TODAY 13, 13-15 (Des Wilson ed., 1984) (describing section two). *Compare id., with* OSA 1989, *supra* note 10, § 1 ("A person who is or has been a member of the security and intelligence services . . . is guilty of an offense if without lawful authority he discloses any information, document or other article relating to security or intelligence . . . ."), *and* OSA 1989, *supra* note 10, § 2 ("[A] person who is or has been a Crown Servant . . . is guilty of an offense if without lawful authority he makes a damaging disclosure of any information, document or other article relating to defense . . . .").

28. *See* Wilson, *supra* note 27, at 15 ("Not only does it [Section 2] make it an offence to disclose official information, but it also makes it an offence to receive it.")

29. *See id.* (clarifying the nature of an offense under the Official Secrets Act of 1911) Under the act, it had to be proved that the recipient knew at the time that he received the information that the information was communicated to him or her "in contravention of the Official Secrets Act." *Id.* If this is shown, what was done with the information subsequently is irrelevant. *See id.* An individual who receives such information can defend himself only by proving "that the information was communicated contrary to his or her desire." *Id.*

30. *See* PONTING, *supra* note 1, at 1; 219 PARL. DEB., H.C. (6th ser.) 598 (1993) (statement of The Chancellor of the Duchy of Lancaster in 1993, Mr. William Waldegrave) [hereinafterWaldegrave Statement] (conceding that the government "keep[s] too many secrets . . . . [W]e make secrets of matters that should not be secret").

the Official Secrets Act of 1911 was amended in 1989,[31] it still stands as a formidable barrier to the implementation of freedom of information legislation by maintaining Britain's traditional secretive culture and a norm of non-disclosure of information.[32]

2. Ministerial Accountability

Comprehending the principle of Ministerial Accountability is germane to understanding Britain's closed government.[33] This con-

---

31. *See* OSA 1989, *supra* note 10. *See generally* Patrick Birkinshaw, *Access, Disclosure and Regulation*, 140 NEW L.J. 1637 (1990) (describing the changes in provisions in the OSA that took place pursuant to the 1989 amendments, including the extensive 1920 amendments). In general, the 1989 legislation ends the broad criminalization of the "disclosure of 'official information without authority.'" *Id.* The OSA limits the application of the criminal law to the "unauthorized 'damaging' disclosures in six areas of protected information[:] security and intelligence; defense; prevention of crime; information obtained under security or interception warrants; information relating to international relationships; and that received from overseas Governments in confidence." *Id.*

32. *See* Birkinshaw, *supra* note 31, at 1637 (stating that although the legislation appears liberalising[,] . . . certain disclosures are automatically presumed damaging"); 219 PARL. DEB., H.C. (6th ser.) 641 (1993) (statement of Mr. Tony Wright) [hereinafter Wright Statement] (undercutting the reforms of the OSA which were eighty years in the making, while stating "the new legislation not only continued to allow ample scope for continued prosecutions . . . but was emphatically not intended to form part of a widening of access to official information"). *But see infra* notes 277-78 and accompanying text (setting forth the argument against a radical change of the OSA).

33. *See* LEIGH, *supra* note 21, at 19 ("Ministerial responsibility is stone dead as a justification for bureaucratic secrecy, but it is a pity it will not lie down."); Des Wilson, *The Struggle to Overcome Secrecy in Britain, in* THE SECRETS FILE: THE CASE FOR FREEDOM OF INFORMATION IN BRITAIN TODAY 125, 134-35 (Des Wilson, ed. 1984) (providing a copy of a letter written by Prime Minister Thatcher to the 1984 Campaign for Freedom of Information stating that Parliament is the reason why Britain does not need freedom of information legislation). The Prime Minister's letter states:

> Under our constitution, Ministers are accountable to Parliament for the work of their departments, and that includes the provision of information. A statutory right of public access would remove this enormously important area of decision-making from Ministers and parliament and transfer ultimate decision to the courts. No matter how carefully the rights were defined and circumscribed, that would be the essential constitutional result. The issues requiring interpretation would tend to be political rather than judicial, and the relationship between the judiciary and the legislature could be greatly damaged. But above all, Ministers' accountability to parliament would be reduced, and parliament itself diminished . . . . In our view the right place for Ministers to answer for their decisions in the essentially 'political' area of information is in parliament.

Id.

stitutional doctrine makes ministers, not civil servants, accountable to Parliament for their departments' policies and actions.[34] In effect, this doctrine makes ministers responsible for all decisions as to what information can be released to Parliament.[35] As such, the minister is

---

34. *See* GRANT JORDAN, THE BRITISH ADMINISTRATIVE SYSTEM 210 (1994) ("The basic idea of *individual* ministerial accountability is that it is a means of ensuring parliamentary control over individual ministers and departments."). In elaborating on this principle, Jordan notes that individual Ministers are accountable for not only their own actions and decisions, but also for those of civil servants under their authority. *See id.*; *see also* COLIN CAMPBELL & GRAHAM K. WILSON, THE END OF WHITEHALL: DEATH OF A PARADIGM? 11 (1995) (asserting that ministers are the "only legitimate representatives of their departments in public. . . [O]nly ministers could answer to Parliament. . . Civil servants were neither seen nor heard in public . . . "). Campbell and Wilson also compare the principle of individual ministerial responsibility to the principle of collective responsibility, which is generally represented as one of the major doctrines under the British constitution. *See id.* at 10-13. Collective responsibility is based upon the idea of collective decision making; that is, all ministers are responsible collectively for the government's policy. *See id.* at 12. For example, it is a requirement that the Minister of Agriculture be prepared to vote in the House of Commons or speak in the country in favor of the government's defense policy. *See id. See generally* Geoffrey Marshall, *Introduction* to MINISTERIAL RESPONSIBILITY 1, 1-11 (Geoffrey Marshall ed. 1989) (describing the doctrines of ministerial responsibility, the "most general principle of parliamentary government, and collective responsibility, "one of the major conventions of the constitution"). *But see* DAVID JUDGE, THE PARLIAMENTARY STATE 136-146 (1993) (characterizing individual ministerial responsibility as "an erroneous doctrine" and collective responsibility as "old wine in old bottles"); JORDAN, *supra* at 218 (discussing the "incompatibility" of collective and ministerial responsibility in that the delinquent Minister is able to "escape individual ministerial responsibility by sheltering under the probability that the House cannot selectively punish him"); TREVOR SMITH & ALISON YOUNG, THE FIXERS: CRISIS MANAGEMENT IN BRITISH POLITICS 3 (1996) (lambasting the concept of ministerial responsibility and describing it as "now accepted as almost totally inoperative"); *cf.* POLITICS UK 430 (Jones et al., 1991) [hereinafter POLITICS] (delineating the modern role of ministerial responsibility in the UK; whereby, ministers have to answer for their own conduct but are not deemed to be held responsible for that of their officials "unless this was in the name and cognizance of the minister").

35. *See* PONTING *supra* note 1, at 44-45 ("[A]lthough in this era of vastly expanded departmental responsibilities it is no longer feasible for a minister to exercise . . . control over . . . his civil servants, he can still control the flow of information provided to MPs through answers to parliamentary questions and the evidence presented to select Committees."). The Prime Minister must stand before Parliament bi-weekly and answer questions. *See id.* The procedure differs, however, for individual departments. *See* Harold Wilson, *Prime Minister Answerability, in* MINISTERIAL RESPONSIBILITY 95, 96 (Geoffrey Marshall ed., 1989). Most departmental ministers face questions only every three, four, or five weeks, and they can

482   AM. U. INT'L L. REV.   [13:471

able to control the flow of information pertaining to his department.[36] Moreover, under this doctrine, this information may never be placed in the public domain because media access to civil servants is restricted.[37] A freedom of information act will curtail a minister's ability to control the flow of information. Such a measure will make the minister more accountable to the public, as well as to Parliament, because the minister's activities will be open to wider scrutiny. In order for Blair to succeed in capturing Parliament's and his Cabinet's support, he must introduce a freedom of information bill that is in harmony with this principle. Particularly, he must focus on the greater accountability that will ensue under such legislation even if ultimate review rests with the courts.[38]

3. Crown Privilege

Another British tradition that aids in maintaining the culture of secrecy is the custom of using "public-interest certificates" under the doctrine of crown privilege.[39] "Crown privilege means that courts have no authority to disclose the workings of government if a minis-

---

divide the questions for answering among the members of the whole departmental team. *See id.; see also* POLITICS, *supra* note 34, at 336 (detailing Question Time). Ministers who oppose Freedom of Information legislation assert that Parliamentary Question Time provides sufficient openness and flow of information. *See id.* They characterize Question Time which occurs every day from Monday through Thursday for fifty-five minutes as an act of "scrutinizing government." *See id. But see* PONTING, *supra* note 1, at 45 (criticizing the ineffectiveness of Question Time).

36. *See* PONTING, *supra* note 1, at 45 (indicating that Ministers habitually reply to Parliamentary Questions with only a minimum of information and may decline to answer on the grounds that information is not readily available).

37. *See* CAMPBELL & WILSON *supra* note 34, at 11 (noting that journalists and academic researchers have been denied access to civil servants because of the doctrine of individual ministerial accountability).

38. *See* Wilson, *supra* note 33, at 134 (discussing Margaret Thatcher's strongly held views that any interference by the judiciary will damage the principle of ministerial responsibility).

39. *See* LEIGH, *supra* note 21, at 43 (stating in regard to informational control that "the final loophole stopped up by Whitehall is in the courts"). Specifically, Leigh explains that until 1968, a ministerial certificate was enough to prevent government documents from being disclosed in the courts. *See id. See generally* A.P. TANT, BRITISH GOVERNMENT: THE TRIUMPH OF ELITISM 25-27 (1993) (contrasting the role of British courts in bringing about Freedom of information legislation and going against the government with the roles of United States and Swedish courts in this area).

ter considers such disclosure to be against the public interest."[40] Under this doctrine, many categories of documents, including Cabinet minutes and diplomatic exchanges are barred from the courts.[41] Judges, in the past, did not draw on their official power to compel disclosure of documents or review ministers' reasons as to why the withholding of the documents is in the public interest. The implications of these withholdings are severe since British judges and juries are only required to review and evaluate the evidence placed before them.[42] Although the courts of England have narrowed the scope and application of this privilege since the 1970s by reviewing ministers' reasons for claiming such certificates,[43] the government continues to

---

40. *See* TANT, *supra* note 39, at 25 (defining Crown Privilege); E.R. HARDY IVAMY, MOZLEY & WHITELEY'S LAW DICTIONARY 216 (11th ed. 1993) (defining public interest immunity as "[t]he right of the Crown to withhold the disclosure and production of a document on the ground that its disclosure and production would be injurious to the public interest"). The Crown can decide either to waive or to claim such a right; however, the person to whom the document relates has no power to assert a claim. *See id.* Only the minister of the government department who seeks the certificate can claim that it should be withheld and/or disclosed on the basis of public interest. *See id.* The court can then either accept or deny the claim based on its discretion. *See id.*

41. *See* LEIGH *supra* note 21, at 44 (detailing the types of information that Ministers withheld under the doctrine including cabinet minutes, diplomatic exchanges, etc., and highlighting the extreme withholdings, such as an army doctor who was not allowed to testify on a report about a soldier's condition). The British crown privilege was picked up in the United States as a justification for the governmental "Executive Privilege" or the official information privilege now known as the "deliberative process privilege." *See generally* 26 CHARLES ALAN WRIGHT & KENNETH A. GRAHAM, JR., FEDERAL PRACTICE AND PROCEDURE, § 5663 (1992) (documenting the history of governmental privileges in the United States). Both the "executive privilege" and "deliberative process privilege" concern governmental information, the disclosure of which would chill the candor in policy making. *See infra* notes 415-17 and accompanying text (describing Exemption five of the United States' Freedom of Information Act which protects certain inter and intra agency documents pursuant to the deliberative process privilege).

42. *See* PONTING *supra* note 1, at 50 (emphasizing that official secrecy affects the process of civil law in Britain, particularly under the doctrine of Crown Privilege because the jury has no responsibility for ensuring that the evidence is complete).

43. *See* TANT, *supra* note 39, at 26 (describing the narrowing of the scope of Crown Privilege in the principle case of *Conway v. Rimmer*). Duncan v. Cammell Laird, 1 All E.R. 587 (H.L. 1939), established two public interest tests under British law: with regard to the content or with regard to the class of document. *See id.* The court held that the minister's decision was final where a signed affidavit held that the public interest was served by withholding a document falling into either of these categories. *See id.* In 1968, however, the House of Lords "revolutionized the

assert this privilege as a justification for withholding information, even when the disclosure of the information would be in the public interest.[44]

A freedom of information act would require ministers to disclose certain information and provide a more extensive mandatory system of review.[45] Ultimately, if Blair chooses the courts as the final review mechanism, the judicial system's power over the government will increase.[46] Accordingly, the British government fights freedom of information statutes and latches on to the traditional Crown Privilege, Official Secrets Act, and Ministerial Accountability as means of retaining control over its information and power.[47] The next section examines several scandals which have exposed the government's use of these three mechanisms to maintain its power through governmental secrecy.

B. RECENT SCANDALS EXPOSING BRITAIN'S SECRET CULTURE

Four main scandals have surfaced in the courts since the early 1980s that have revealed Britain's secretive culture.[48] These events

---

law on Crown Privilege" in Conway v. Rimmer, 1968 P.910 (Eng. C.A.). *See* T. MURRAY RANKIN, FREEDOM OF INFORMATION IN CANADA: WILL THE DOORS STAY SHUT? 19 (1977) (explaining how the Canadian judiciary continues to regard English Crown Privilege decisions as very persuasive, if not binding authority, citing celebrated English Crown Privilege cases). Specifically, Conway introduced two new principles: "first that courts did have the right to inspect documents for which Crown Privilege was being claimed, and secondly, that claims of Crown Privilege based upon the class of a document were more likely to be questioned." *Id.*; *see also infra* Part I.B.4 (discussing how five ministers signed public interest certificates under the doctrine of Crown Privilege preventing three British executives from proving their innocence in court in the Matrix Churchill affair).

44. *See infra* Part I.B.4 (describing the Matrix Churchill case).

45. *Cf.* BIRKINSHAW, *supra* note 9, at 138 (noting that the Local Government (Access to Information) Act of 1985 provides for access to local authorities' information).

46. *See id.* at 24 (suggesting that taking away the government's power to preserve information could establish new centers of power).

47. *See infra* Part II (detailing the strong ministerial reaction against several attempts to introduce freedom of information legislation).

48. Although the four scandals included in the text illustrate the excessive level of secrecy in Britain and the need for freedom of information legislation, another interesting court case and an incident that received public attention are *Regina v. Secretary of State for Defense, ex parte Sancto* and the "apple juice incident." *See* Roy Edey, *Minister's Outrageous Decision Not Unlawful*, 142 NEW L.J. 1748 (1992) (detailing the "absurdity" of the *Sancto* case); Adam Sage, *The Juice of*

are important because they have stimulated intense criticism over such secrecy, making it more likely that Prime Minister Blair's proposal for a freedom of information statute will reach fruition.

1. The Sarah Tisdall Case

Sarah Tisdall,[49] a 23 year old civil servant, working in the office of the Secretary of State for Foreign and Commonwealth affairs, plead guilty to communicating classified information in violation of Section two of the Official Secrets Act of 1911.[50] Tisdall sent photocopies of two "confidentially" marked documents pertaining to the arrival of cruise missiles in Britain to the local newspaper.[51] Affirming Tisdall's sentence of six months imprisonment, the appellate court held that such a sentence was unavoidable because "an element of deterrence was required."[52] Although Tisdall agreed to be prosecuted

---

This Apple is a British Secret, INDEP., Feb. 14, 1993, at 3 (revealing how the Ministry of Agriculture, Fisheries and Food kept secret their knowledge that "high levels of a carcinogenic chemical, patulin, had been found in some brands of apple juice" and stating that "In Britain, there is no Freedom of Information Act and no way of forcing the Government to disclose such details"). In *Sancto*, the Secretary of State denied Kirk Sancto's parents access to their dead son's Army Board of Inquiry Report, which contained wrongful allegations that their son died due to being the "worse for drink." Edey, *supra*, at 1748. Sancto's parents have no remedy because the "Minister can act as judge and jury in his own cause and protect the Army from embarrassment without impunity," even when there is a pathologist's report saying otherwise. *See id.*

49. *See* R v. Tisdall, 6 Crim. App. 155 (Eng. C.A.).

50. *See id.*; OSA 1911, *supra* note 23, at § 2; *see also* PONTING, *supra* note 1, at 63-64 (describing the trial); Wilson, *supra* note 33, at 146-47 (detailing the case). *See generally* DAVID CAUTE, THE ESPIONAGE OF THE SAINTS at ix (1986) (reporting on the punitive measures taken against a Zimbabwean writer, Dambudzo Marechera, and two British civil servants, Sarah Tisdall and Clive Ponting, who in 1984, committed "word-crime").

51. *See* R. v. Tisdall, 6 Crim. App. at 155 (recounting how on Oct. 21, 1983 Tisdall "took the opportunity of a lull in the busy affairs to read the contents of two minutes and she, having read them, decided to make an extra copy of each . . . and take them to the Guardian newspaper). The Guardian Newspaper was subsequently brought to Court by the British Crown in Secretary of State for Defense and another v. Guardian Newspapers Ltd., 3 All E.R. 601 (H.L. 1984) in order to compel the return of the documents. *See* 3 All E.R. 601 (H.L. 1984). At issue in the case was whether the Crown was entitled to order disclosure and whether disclosure was necessary in interests of national security. *See id.* The Court held that the Guardian must disclose the document because "a potential threat to national security was clearly revealed" but Lord Fraser dissented. *Id.*

52. *See Tisdall*, 6 Crim. App. at 155 ("It is of course impossible to run any concern, and certainly not possible to run a government department . . . if confi-

if she published any official information[53] when she signed the Official Secrets Act Declaration Form prior to her employment, many felt that her sentence was too severe.[54] Not only had national security not been compromised by the release of these documents, but Tisdall was not given the opportunity to make a defense on the grounds that she was acting in the public interest.[55] Furthermore, after her trial, Tisdall criticized her superior's "deliberate attempt to avoid accountability in Parliament" for her wrongful actions.[56] Interestingly, the Government used the Official Secrets Act to prosecute Tisdall, but it ignored the principle of ministerial accountability because its use would have caused further embarrassment and scandal among the higher echelons of the British government.[57]

2. The Clive Ponting Case

The second case to draw national attention to Britain's secretive

---

dential and secret memoranda are being divulged to outside bodies by members of the staff . . . . [T]hose who deliberately break the law in this way will not be treated with much sympathy . . . .").

53. *See id.* (citing the Official Secrets Declaration Form) In pertinent part, the form read: "I am aware that I should not divulge any information gained by me . .
[I] understand also that I am liable to be prosecuted if I publish without official sanction any information . . . ."

54. *See* PONTING, *supra* note 1, at 64 (stating that "the unexpected and disproportionate severity of the sentence provoked almost universal condemnation"); WILSON, *supra* note 33, at 147 (providing the arguments asserted by the 1984 Campaign for Freedom of Information about the Tisdall case); CAUTE, *supra* note 50, at 124 (noting that the Leader of the Opposition denounced Tisdall's prison sentence, MP's visited her in jail, and women demonstrated outside Holloway Gaol where she was imprisoned).

55. *See Tisdall,* 6 Crim. App. at 155 (stating that the Court did not allow the introduction of the argument that Tisdall was "incensed by political subterfuge" and that she had not realized that it was common knowledge that these missiles were due to be delivered from America); *see also* Wilson, *supra* note 33, at 147 (providing the Campaign for Freedom of Information's remarks about the Tisdall case and its argument that Tisdall should have been provided a public interest defense as it exists in the United States).

56. *See* PONTING, *supra* note 1, at 64 (describing how at trial Tisdall plead guilty but afterwards defended her actions and "spoke of the immorality of the Defense Secretary's deliberate attempt to avoid accountability in Parliament").

57. *See generally* JORDAN, *supra* note 34, at 210 (characterizing ministerial responsibility and the expectation that a minister step down for the actions of a civil servant as "fruitless" since, "this principle . . . runs into the party political factor that it would be politically embarrassing for the pro-Government majority party . . to criticize its own leading members").

culture, also for a breach of the Official Secrets Act of 1911, was the Clive Ponting case.[58] Ponting, as head of a section of the Defense Ministry, had the duty of preparing draft replies and answers on the sinking of the Argentinean battle cruiser "General Belgrano."[59] Ponting disagreed with his co-workers' interpretation of the event, and furthermore, how they planned to report this information to Parliament.[60] As a result, Ponting sent two documents to a member of Parliament who was trying to uncover the facts regarding the Belgrano.[61] He was subsequently prosecuted under Section two for communicating official information to a person with whom he was not authorized to share such information.[62] At Ponting's trial, the first full-scale public interest defense was aired,[63] and Ponting was ac-

---

58. *See* Godfrey Hodgson, *Why Section Two is Only the Tip of the Iceberg*, FIN. TIMES (London), Feb. 16, 1985, at 25 ("The Ponting case was not only about official secrecy. It was also about openness—or rather the lack of openness—in British Government."); *Official Cleared of Secrets Breach*, FACTS ON FILE WORLD NEWS DIGEST, Feb. 15, 1985, at 109 B1 (indicating that "the case's outcome was considered significant in the current debate over whether the secrets law should be strengthened or liberalized").

59. *See* BIRKINSHAW, *supra* note 9, at 101-03 (detailing the Ponting case); CAUTE, *supra* note 50, at 157 (providing a thorough discussion of the Ponting and Belgrano affair with the main focus being on the fact that the decision to prosecute Ponting was a political one). The General Belgrano, an Argentine battle cruiser, was torpedoed by a British submarine during the Falklands War with Argentina, and resulted in the death of 368 Argentine men. *See id.* at 153-55 (detailing Britain's role in the sinking of the Belgrano); *see also* Harvey Morris, *Secrets*, REUTERS, LTD., Feb. 17, 1985 (explaining why Ponting resigned).

60. *See* CAUTE, *supra* note 50, at 64 (illustrating the ways in which the Government was deceiving Parliament, for example, the different course and position that the Belgrano was in before the torpedoing and the fact that the HMS Conqueror had been shadowing the boat for thirty hours prior); *see also* Morris, *supra* note 59 (quoting Ponting who said that "his argument and that of the opposition is that the government deliberately misled parliament about the facts of the incident in order to save itself political embarrassment rather than to safeguard national security").

61. *See generally* CAUTE, *supra* note 50, at 145-211 (detailing the drafts and series of events that resulted in Ponting sending two documents to MP Tam Dalyell).

62. *See* BIRKINSHAW, *supra* note 9, at 101 (recounting how Ponting was prosecuted for breach of § 2(1)(a), which made it a crime to communicate official information to any person other than to whom is authorized to receive it, or "a person to whom it is his duty *in the interest of the state* to communicate it"). (emphasis added). Whether or not it was in the interest of the state was a key issue at trial. It resulted in Ponting's public interest defense.

63. *See* PONTING, *supra* note 1, at 64 (observing that "[t]he ten-day trial in

quitted, even though the crucial rulings in law went against him.[64] This trial was described by many as a "political prosecution brought by an embarrassed government,"[65] which marked the death for Section two of the Official Secrets Act of 1911.[66] Courts refused to allow the "catch-all," blanket prohibitions of Section two to ascertain criminal liability.[67] Although this case highlights the increasingly active role that British courts are taking to combat excessive secrecy by allowing a public interest defense, it was ultimately the jury who defied the law.[68]

A freedom of information act would further the courts' role in checking the government. Additionally, such an act would allow both the public and officials access to and freedom with information that is in the public interest, like the information in the Ponting case.

3. The Peter Wright Case

Commonly referred to as the Spycatcher Affair, this third case illustrating the government's desire to keep its activities secret, did not even take place in Britain.[69] Peter Wright, a former British Secret

---

February 1985 provided the first full-scale airing of a public interest defense"); Morris, *supra* note 59 (providing Ponting's justifications for disclosing the Belgrano information, particularly that the information stalled further questioning in Parliament was the most "blatant" and misleading cover-up that he had come across in his 14 years in the civil service).

64. *See* CAUTE, *supra* note 50, at 166, 173 (describing how part of the trial was held *in camera*, the "best interest of the state" was interpreted as the best interest of the government of the day, and lack of *mens rea* was not allowed as a defense).

65. PONTING, *supra* note 1, at 65.

66. *See* BIRKINSHAW, *supra* note 9, at 103 (stating that Ponting's acquittal was a death knell for Section two of the Official Secrets Act of 1911); *The Ponting Acquittal: Others May Still Be Caught In the Net*, ECONOMIST, Feb. 16, 1985, at 29 (stating in regard to the OSA that "Mr. Ponting's acquittal has been hailed as its death-knell"); *UK: David Hopper and Christopher Capro Look at the Planned Reform of the Official Secrets Act*, BROADCAST, Oct. 28, 1988 [hereinafter *Reform*] (advancing that "[t]he move to reform Section 2 arises because it has become unworkable since the acquittal of Clive Ponting in 1985").

67. *See infra* note 101 and accompanying text (discussing the "catch-all" quality of Section two).

68. *See Moles' Lib*, ECONOMIST, Feb. 16, 1985, at 13 (stating that "[e]verybody loves an independent jury . . . the eight men and four women . . . threw out the government's charges").

69. *See* PONTING *supra* note 1, at 65-66 (titling the excerpt in his book "the Spycatcher Affair" and describing the trial in Australia). Although the main case took place in Australia, the Thatcher Government brought suits in New Zealand,

Service agent published his memoirs in Australia in an attempt to avoid prosecution under the Official Secrets Act.[70] Accordingly, the British government brought suit in Australia seeking injunctions under the law of confidentiality[71] to prevent subsequent circulation of this information.[72] The Australian court held that it was not justified in restraining media reports concerning unauthorized disclosures unless there was a risk of further damage to Britain's national security.[73] Since this risk had become moot, due to the passage of time and the publication of the novel in the United States, the British government suffered a costly defeat.[74] The trial helped expose the illegal activities of Britain's Secret Service and "illustrated the government's resistance in allowing the public interest and freedom of the press to override the civil law of confidentiality." [75]

Hong Kong, and Britain to prevent the local papers from publishing Wright's allegations and details of all of the trials. *See id. See generally* THE SPYCATCHER CASES (Michael Fysh ed., 1989) (providing all of the Spycatcher Court Judgements that occurred in Australia, Britain, New Zealand, and Hong Kong).

70. *See* BIRKINSHAW *supra* note 9, at 103 (stating that "Wright sought to publish his memoirs in Australia—outside the criminal jurisdiction of [Section] 2").

71. *See* ALISON COLEMAN, THE LEGAL PROTECTION OF TRADE SECRETS 4 (1992) (detailing that in English law, three conditions must be satisfied for a civil action for breach of confidence: first, the information must be confidential, second, the information must have been disclosed in circumstances which give rise to an obligation of confidence, and third, there must be an actual or anticipated unauthorized use or disclosure of the information); Nicholas Rose, *Whistleblowing—Time for a Change?*, 145 NEW L.J. 6680 (1995) ("All civil servants owe the Crown, as their employer, a duty of confidentiality . . . . Whether or not the criminal law applies they must protect official information which is held in confidence because it has been communicated in confidence . . . ."). In response to the claim that Wright owed a duty to the Crown, his attorney argued that the government's case was an attempt to enforce the OSA in Australia, a separate sovereign entity, in contravention of the recognized principle of international law that "the courts of one country will not enforce the penal or public laws of another." MALCOLM TURNBULL, THE SPYCATCHER TRIAL: THE SCANDAL BEHIND THE #1 BEST SELLER 38 (1989).

72. *See* Attorney General v. Heinemann Publishers, Australia Pty. Ltd. and Wright (1987) N.S.W.S. Ct. Cas., *reprinted in* TURNBULL, *supra* note 71, at 352-53 (explaining that because there was no contract between the parties, the British Attorney General could only succeed by establishing that the disclosure of information would be detrimental to the public interest of the United Kingdom).

73. *See id.* (harmonizing the risk of national security with the public interest).

74. *See The Wright Case: Wrong Decision* 137 NEW L.J. 723 (expressing the absurdity of protecting information that has already been released in the United States). Spycatcher had been published in the United States and Canada prior to its release in Australia. *See id.*

75. *See* BIRKINSHAW *supra* note 9, at 103-04 (construing the Spycatcher as a

Although the British government suffered a defeat in this instance, the government might have prevailed in certain British courts. Had a freedom of information act been in place, the expensive trial could have been prevented since most of the information that Wright disclosed would have initially been deemed disclosable in the public interest.

4. The Matrix Churchill Case

Three company executives from the machine tools firm, Matrix Churchill, were prosecuted for the illegal export of arms to Iraq in violation of Export of Goods Control Orders.[76] The executives plead not guilty on the basis that the government was fully aware of these exports and was turning a blind eye to such exportation.[77] The executives made requests for internal memoranda which would prove their innocence; however, five ministers had signed public interest certificates to suppress the release of this information and the government's knowledge of the exportation.[78] Thus, these defendants were almost imprisoned because certain ministers thought that the

---

good example of the government's attempts to remain secret); *see also Reform, supra* note 66 (noting that "[f]ollowing the Spycatcher ruling, any intelligence officer seeking to emulate Wright would be held to be subject to a lifelong duty of confidentiality and could not publish his allegations without the consent of Government").

76. *See* PYPER *supra* note 18, at 161 (citing IAN LEIGH, MATRIX-CHURCHILL, SUPERGUN AND THE SCOTT INQUIRY (1993)).

77. *See* Richard Norton-Taylor, *The Scott Report: Punches are Pulled Over Blame But Ministers Feel Body Blow*, GUARDIAN, Feb. 16, 1996, at 12 (stating that three ministers secretly relaxed export controls to Iraq at the end of 1988 after the cease-fire in the Iran-Iraq war and failed to be forthcoming with this policy); *cf.* R v. Blackledge and Ors, 326 Crim. App. (1995) (using the documents and information discovered in the Matrix Churchill case, the defendants plead "not guilty" for the same reason and the court of appeals reversed the lower court's decision holding that the documents should have been made available to the defense before the trial to demonstrate their innocence).

78. *See* PYPER, *supra* note 18, at 161 (emphasizing the government's knowledge); Sally Weale, *The Scott Report: Sir Nicholas Lyell Should Have Told Prosecution of Heseltine's Reservations*, GUARDIAN, Feb. 16, 1996, at 15 (reporting on the criticism that Sir Nicholas, the Attorney General, received for preparing the Public Interest Immunity (PII) certificates which were more commonly known as "gag orders"). "The PIIs prevented disclosure to the court of documents which would have shown that guidelines on exports to Iraq had changed and thus that the Matrix Churchill directors were not in breach of government guidelines." *Id.*

withholding of this information was in the public interest.[79]

As illustrated in these four cases, the British Government goes to great lengths to conceal its inner-workings. Although the Official Secrets Act has lost some of its authority, as evidenced by the Ponting trial, the Act still makes it an offense to disclose or receive certain governmental information.[80] It is important to note that the Tisdall, Ponting, and Wright cases all focus on civil servants—not on the general public. In terms of the general public's comprehensive right of access to government information, little has changed.[81] These cases are important to the freedom of information campaign because they have prompted the public to distrust the government and to request statutory rights of access to information.[82] Britons fear more scandals. Hence, a freedom of information act is necessary to expose scandals and serve as a check on government officials so that scandals are less likely to occur in the first place.[83] Parliamentary debates as to why a freedom of information act is necessary in Britain further highlight this argument[84] and the Matrix Churchill case in particular.[85] The next section examines some of these debates.

---

79. *See* Maurice Frankel, *Implications of Government Secrecy Over Decisions on Exports to Iraq*, TIMES (London), Nov. 23, 1992, (Features) (charging that "[t]he implication is that ministers used their control of official information to protect themselves from embarrassment, regardless of the cost to the defendants"); Geoffrey Robertson, *Misleading By Example*, OBSERVER, May 25, 1997, at 18 (book review) (summarizing Scott's report and pointing out that "[t]he Matrix Churchill scandal occurred because Ministers and mandarins and lawyers employed by the Government chose to protect the State at the expense of their duty to justice"). According to Robertson, Scott's most important recommendation "is the urgent need for a freedom of information act." *Id.* "His report provides ample evidence that the decisions that were made about arming Saddam would have been better decisions had such legislation been in force." *Id.*

80. *See supra* notes 27, 31-32 (detailing the criminal liability under the Official Secrets Act, as amended in 1989).

81. *See supra* notes 11 & 14 (providing the Labour Government's promise to finally bring a freedom of information statute to Britain).

82. *See* New Labour, *supra* note 11.

83. *See* Timmins, *supra* note 14, at 10 (advocating the introduction of a freedom of information act).

84. 219 PARL. DEB., H.C. (6th Ser.) (1992-93).

85. *See* Frankel, *supra* note 79, (Features).

492   AM. U. INT'L L. REV.   [13:471

II. PRIOR ATTEMPTS AT CURTAILING THE SECRECY AND IMPLEMENTING FREEDOM OF INFORMATION LEGISLATION

Despite the scandals, Britain remains without a freedom of information act.[86] Over the years, however, the government has become more open.[87] Many argue that this increased openness, non-statutory rights of access,[88] and voluntary disclosure of official information, however, are not enough.[89] Before examining the access statutes of other countries and making recommendations as to the form of the United Kingdom's freedom of information act, it is necessary to examine prior acts,[90] initiatives,[91] and arguments[92] brought before Parliament.

---

86. *See* discussion *supra* Part I.B (detailing the Sarah Tisdall case, the Clive Ponting case, the Peter Wright case, and the Matrix Churchill case all of which expose Britain's secret culture).

87. *See infra* notes 269-76 and accompanying text (discussing five recently enacted statutes that British MPs point to as evidence of the government's increasing openness).

88. *See* discussion *infra* Part II.C.2 (explaining the non-statutory Code of Practice on Access to Official Information which currently controls information disclosure in Britain, on the national level).

89. *See* Clwyd, *supra* note 14 (quoting Tony Blair at the 1996 Campaign for Freedom of Information Awards Night). Blair said:

> A Freedom of Information Act would signal a culture change that would make a dramatic difference to the way that Britain is governed . . . It is part of bringing our politics up to date, of letting politics catch up with the aspirations of people *and delivering not just more open*, but more effective and efficient government for the future.

Id. (emphasis added).

90. *See* discussion *infra* Part II.B.2(discussing the Local Government (Access to Information) Act).

91. *See* discussion *infra* Parts II.A.1., II.C.2 (discussing Labour Prime Minister Harold Wilson's inquiry into governmental secrecy, the Croham Directive, and Conservative Prime Minister John Major's White Paper on open government).

92. *See* discussion *infra* Parts II.A., IIB., IIC (providing MPs arguments in favor of and in opposition to freedom of information legislation).

A. 1970-1980[93]

1. Wilson and Croham

Just prior to the 1970s, the Committee of the Civil Service, led by Lord Fulton, presented a report to Labour Prime Minister Harold Wilson.[94] The report argued that the government was excessively secret and that a full inquiry to put an end to this secrecy was necessary.[95] As a result of this report, Wilson conducted an inquiry and produced a White Paper entitled "Information and the Public Interest."[96] Many freedom of information advocates assert that Wilson's inquiry was incomplete and unsatisfactory because it was conducted without consulting other governmental departments and his deliberations were confidential.[97] Critics were also unhappy with the substance of the White Paper. The Paper reported that the government was already releasing more information to the public and that the Official Secrets Act was no barrier to greater openness.[98]

Two years later the Conservatives came to power pledging in their manifesto to curb secrecy and reform the Official Secrets Act.[99] An-

---

93. A chronological breakdown was chosen by the author as a means of evaluating the changes concerning access—or lack of it—to information in Britain, in the simplest way possible. This structure will allow the reader to easily match up the time periods with the government of the day.

94. *See* Wilson, *supra* note 33, at 124-25 (providing a thorough discussion of the Fulton Report).

95. *See id.* at 125. The Fulton report stated:

The increasingly wide range of problems handled by the government, and their far reaching effects upon the community as a whole, demand the widest possible consultation with its different parts and interests . . . It is healthy for a democracy increasingly to press to be consulted and informed. There are still too many occasions when information is unnecessarily withheld and consultation merely perfunctory . . . It is an abuse of consultation when it is turned into a belated attempt to prepare the ground for decisions that in reality have been taken already.

Id. (omissions in original).

96. PONTING, *supra* note 1, at 68.

97. *See id.* (stating, "[t]he Wilson Government's response was an internal inquiry with no outside consultation"); *see also* Wilson, *supra* note 33, at 125 (undercutting Wilson's inquiry into government secrecy because it was, somewhat ironically, "an internal inquiry, and its deliberations had been confidential").

98. *See* Wilson, *supra* note 33, at 125 (outlining the White Paper's conclusion that the OSA was no barrier because it "did not inhibit the 'authorised' release of information in any way").

99. *See generally* The Conservative Party General Election Manifesto for

other report, this time produced by Lord Frank and his committee, recommended that Section one of the Official Secrets Act be transformed into its own espionage act and Section two be "repealed and replaced by narrower and specific provisions"[100] due to its "catch all quality."[101] Specifically, the Frank Committee proposed an Official Information Act.[102] The Conservative government agreed with these recommendations but claimed that it needed more time to consider proposals and define the categories of protected information.[103]

Parliamentary debates in 1978 reflected the government's slow approach to implementing the Frank Committee's proposals.[104] Dur-

---

1970, *reprinted in* THE TIMES GUIDE TO THE HOUSE OF COMMONS JUNE 1970 (1970) (calling for less government secrecy).

100. Wilson, *supra* note 32, at 126 (quoting the Frank Committee's Report); *see also* 951 PARL. DEB., H.C. (5th ser.) 1264 (1978) (statement of Mr. John) [hereinafter John Statements] (reiterating that the government accepts the general thrust of the Frank Committee's argument that the section needs to be repealed and replaced by a narrower and more specific provision).

101. Havers Statements, *supra* note 23, at 1257-58 (quoting the Frank Committee's Report). The report reads as follows:

> The main offence which section 2 creates is the unauthorized communication of official information (including documents) by a Crown servant. The leading characteristic of this offence is its catch-all quality. It catches all official documents and information. It makes no distinction of kind, and no distinction of degree. All information which a Crown learns in the course of his duty is "official" for the purposes of section 2, whatever its nature, whatever its importance, whatever its original source. A blanket is thrown over everything; nothings escapes. The section catches all Crown servants as well as official information. Again, it makes no distinctions according to the nature or importance of a Crown servant's duties. All are covered. Every Minister of the Crown, every civil servant, every member of the Armed Forces, every police officer, performs his duties subject to Section 2.

Id.

102. *See* Wilson, *supra* note 33, at 126 (stating that the Franks Committee "proposed an Official Information Act making it an offence to disclose without authorization a more narrowly defined range of information"); *cf.* Rees Statements, *supra* note 27, at 1879 (voicing the government's conclusion that Section two of the OSA should be replaced by an Official Information Act encompassing the broad recommendations made by the Franks Committee).

103. *See* Wilson, *supra* note 33, at 126 (stating that the Heath government agreed); PONTING *supra* note 1, at 68 (stating that government cited the need to consider proposals as a reason for its delay in the production of a bill). The Franks Committee proposed that six categories of information should be protected. *See id. See, e.g.*, John Statements, *supra* note 100, at 1265 (detailing the proposed categories that should be protected as: "defence or internal security; foreign relations; the currency or the reserves; law and order; Cabinet documents; and information entrusted in confidence to the Government by a private individual or concern.")

104. *See* 951 PARL. DEB., H.C. (5th ser.) 1312 (1978) (statement of Mr.

ing a Parliamentary session in June of that year, MPs[105] debated the general implementation of any freedom of information bill in the United Kingdom, while examining reforms of Section two of the Official Secrets Act.[106] Most MPs referred to the freedom of information Acts of the United States and Sweden when determining if such an act could be implemented in the United Kingdom.[107] Generally, MPs opposed to the implementation of this bill argued that the constitutional frameworks of the United States, Sweden, and the United

---

Gardner) [hereinafter Gardner Statements] (complaining that that the government has "done virtually nothing" and that "ministers have been talking in their sleep" in regard to the recommendations of the Frank Committee).

105. MP stands for Member of Parliament. This term incorporates both Ministers and Private Members of the House of Commons. For the purposes of this paper, whenever a Minister is cited to, his or her title will be included in order to differentiate between the government and private members of Parliament.

106. *See generally* 951 PARL. DEB., H.C. (5th ser.) 1256-58 (1978) (debating how to narrow the provisions of the OSA so that criminal liability is limited to disclosure of specific confidential, official, and damaging information). Most MPs during this June 15th debate and a debate held one month later on July 19th regarding the OSA took the view that reform of Section 2 was a precursor to the implementation of a freedom of information act. *See* John Statements, *supra* note 100, at 1313 (suggesting that the modernization of Section 2 is an essential precursor to a freedom of information bill); Rees Statements, *supra* note 27, at 542 (voicing that "[r]eform of section 2 necessarily comes first").

107. *See* Havers Statements, *supra* note 23, at 1259 (referring to the Freedom of Information Acts of the United States and Sweden and noting their deficiencies). *See* 951 PARL. DEB., H.C. (5th ser.) 1276 (1978) (statement of Mr. Arthur Lewis) [hereinafter Lewis Statements] (welcoming the introduction of freedom of information legislation based on the United States and Sweden's models); 951 PARL. DEB., H.C. (5th ser) 1280 (1978) (statement of Mr. Emyln Hooson) [hereinafter Hooson Statements] (focusing on the United States FOIA in his rebuttal of Mr. Brittan's views on the benefits of that act); *cf.* 951 PARL. DEB., H.C.(5th ser.) 1289 (1978) (statement of Mr. Eric S. Heffer) [hereinafter Heffer Statements] (opining that Britain need not follow the freedom of information legislation in the United States and Sweden, but "should seek to lay down freedom of information legislation whose provisions are particular to this country"). Mr. Heffer, continued his speech, speaking on behalf of the Labour party and defending their commitment to freedom of information legislation. The text of his speech is as follows:

> The fact is that a committee of the Labour Party is on the point of publishing a freedom of information Bill-legislation on which we have worked at considerable length and which in our view is applicable to British conditions. That is a clear indication that, so far as is humanly possible within certain limits, we want the most open government that we can get. One recognises that there are limits because, for example, one cannot allow total freedom of information on defense, security or foreign diplomatic relations. However, no doubt we could go much further on the subject of foreign diplomatic relations than we do now . . . .

Id. at 1290.

Kingdom are dissimilar; thus, the United States and Swedish statutes would not work in the United Kingdom,[108] due to excessive costs,[109] administrative burden,[110] and the use of the legislation for business espionage.[111] At the conclusion of these 1978 debates, Parliament ta-

---

108. *See* Havers Statement, *supra* note 23, at 1259 (warning the House of Commons that it must remember that both the United States and Sweden have written constitutions "so that judicial intervention in establishing the rights of the citizen is much greater in the United Kingdom"). In addition, Havers noted that "[a]ny discussion of freedom of information must be in the context of the establishment of a system of administrative courts." *Id;. See also* John Statements, *supra* note 100, at 1266 (stating that the government is not hostile to the view of freedom of information legislation, but that it must be aware of "other countries with dissimilar constitutional arrangements . . . to see exactly how such a Bill . . . would fit into [Britain's] constitutional pattern").

109. *See* 951 PARL. DEB., H.C. (5th ser.) 1274 (1978) (statement of Mr. Brittan) [hereinafter Brittan Statements] (expressing his grave doubts about the desirability of a Freedom of Information Act like that of the United States because of its formidable costs, which he cites as 22 million dollars a year, and $146.67 per request). *But see* Hooson Statements, *supra* note 107, at 1281 (commenting that the 22 million dollar cost of the United States FOIA represents one-tenth of the original anticipated cost).

110. *See, e.g.*, Brittan Statements, *supra* note 109, at 1274 (describing how in the United States, the FBI assigned 400 agents to review 10 million pages of documents, and the United States Food and Drug Administration increased its staff from seven to 40 as a result of the passage of FOIA).

111. *See id.* at 1274 (criticizing the use of the United States FOIA by businesses for purposes amounting to "industrial espionage"). This MP's overall criticism was that the United States Act was not being used by its citizens for the purposes for which it was introduced. *See id.* Citizens were not using the FOIA to scrutinize government operations nor engage in a dialogue about reform. *See id.* Fear that this is how the FOIA would be used by Britons and the fact that once the United States passed the FOIA it had to pass the Privacy Act (access to person's files) and Sunshine Act (requiring Government agency meetings to be open to the public) led MP Brittan to change his views on the benefits of freedom of information legislation in the UK. *Id.* at 1275. *But see* 951 PARL. DEB., H.C. (5th ser.) 1258-1319 (1978) (describing the benefits of freedom of information legislation highlighted by various MPs). One MP argued that freedom of information legislation would provide certainty that information was not being deliberately fed to ministers. *See* Lewis Statements, *supra* note 107, at 1276 (noting that if the government had an official information act it would not have the daily errors and misleading information it receives from the Treasury and it would be able to ascertain whether information was being deliberately fed into the hands of ministers). In addition, Mr. Lewis argued that members of parliament and the electorate "ought to have the right to know" what the salary is of a chairman of a board. *Id.* at 1277. Mr. Lewis bases the electorate's right to know on the fact that each taxpayer pays the salary of the ministers and civil servants. *See id.* Another MP, Mr. Gardner, argued that freedom of information legislation would protect individuals against the misuse of

bled the enactment of freedom of information legislation.[112]

The Labour Government that followed the Conservative Government did even less to advance freedom of information.[113] The year ended, however, with a crucial directive entitled the Croham Directive.[114] This directive, which itself was confidential and leaked to the press,[115] directed ministers to make background material, both factual

---

power and position within a democracy. *See* Gardner Statements, *supra* note 104, at 1310-11 (detailing the positive effects such legislation will have). Furthermore, yet another MP stressed the positive change such legislation causes in the relationship between the government and the community. *See* 951 PARL. DEB., H.C. (5th ser.) 1297 (1978) (statement of Miss Jo Richardson) (implying that the need for a positive change in the relationship between the government and the governed, which would be fostered by freedom of information, is the reason why the House of Commons is having these debates). Another MP highlighted the amount the government pays now for the release of its information. *See* Hooson Statements, *supra* note 107, at 1282 (faulting other members for not considering the positive effects of the United States act and harmonizing the amount the United States pays for its FOIA to that which the United Kingdom allots for its federal information budget). Mr. Hooson's statement was as follows:

When one compares the cost of the Freedom of Information Act of 20 million dollars with, for example, the federal information budget— which gives the kind of information which the government wants fed out, as opposed to information that they do not— one can see that it is absolute chicken feed.

Id.

112. *See* Rees Statements, *supra* note 27, at 539 (explaining how the government does not yet have enough information to proceed in consideration of a freedom of information bill). One MP summed up a central issue concerning the debate of freedom of information that the government must consider when he stated that the proper public interest balance must be struck. *See* Havers Statement, *supra* note 23, at 1258. Havers stated:

The area where secrecy and confidentiality should be protected must clearly be defined and limited to the extent where it is generally acceptable and compatible with open government. A balance must be struck where the public interest is protected in both ways. I mean by that that the public interest requires that matters of defense, international security and Cabinet minutes . . . may need to be safeguarded against public disclosure. But the public interest also requires that there is no misuse of secrecy to cover up errors or bungling to avoid criticism.

Id.

113. *See* PONTING, supra note 1, at 68-71 (denouncing the method used by the Callaghan government to release government policy studies because the government retained discretion over what information was released and used the OSA to bring criminal charges against the press when unreleased information was made public).

114. *See* Wilson, *supra* note 33, at 128-29 (publishing most of the text of the Croham Directive due to its importance to the freedom of information debate).

115. *See* PONTING, *supra* note 1, at 69.

and analytical, available to the public.[116] Lord Croham, who initiated the directive, stated that it was time that ministers made more information available.[117] He also stated that those who longed for a freedom of information act would be disappointed by his directive since it did not require ministers to release information.[118] He chose the directive over an act mainly because of the alleged high costs and administrative burdens associated with such an act.[119]

2. Freud's Official Information Bill

The new year began with the second reading of Liberal MP Clement Freud's private member,[120] "Official Information Bill."[121] Since Labour was in power, Freud began his speech to Parliament noting that his bill was consistent with Labour's 1974 election manifesto calling for more open government.[122] Freud's bill consisted of three

---

116. *See* Wilson, *supra* note 33, at 128-29 (directing Ministers to have a more open attitude).

117. *See id.* (quoting Croham as arguing "it is intended to mark a real change of policy"). *But see* Michael Hunt, *Conclusion* to OPEN GOVERNMENT: A STUDY OF THE PROSPECTS OF OPEN GOVERNMENT WITHIN THE LIMITATIONS OF THE BRITISH POLITICAL SYSTEM 173, 178 (Richard A. Chapman & Michael Hunt eds., 1987) (alluding to the decision of Prime Minister Thatcher in 1979 to rescind the most active part of the Croham directive, putting an end to the experiment in open government).

118. *See* Wilson, *supra* note 33, at 129 ("[T]here are many who will have wanted the government to go much further on the lines of the formidably burdensome Freedom of Information Act in the USA.").

119. *See id.* (assessing Parliament's "prospects of being able to avoid such an expensive development"). *Compare id., with* Brittan Statements, *supra* note 109, at 1274 (arguing that a freedom of information act would be very expensive in Britain) *and infra* Part III.B (detailing the fees and costs associated with the access statutes of the United States, Canada, and Australia).

120. *See generally* DAVID MARSH & MELVYN READ, PRIVATE MEMBERS' BILLS 7-25 (providing a thorough discussion of the three types of Private Members' bills). Bills are either introduced by the Government or through Private Members of Parliament. *See id.* The Private Member's Bill procedure, however, "like cricket, would baffle the intelligent alien" because it is done by ballot, and there are only ten slots up for grabs. *See id.* at 7. Thus, it might take 30 years for a backbench member to introduce a private member bill. *See id.*

121. *See* 960 Parl. Deb, H.C. (5th Ser.) 2132 (1979) (statement of Mr. Clement Freud) [hereinafter Freud Arguments] (initiating the debate regarding the Official Information Bill).

122. *See* PONTING *supra* note 1, at 71 (describing how Clement Freud reminded the House of Commons that his proposals were consistent with Labour's declared policies for many years); Wilson *supra* note 33, at 129 (highlighting how Freud

main parts: (1) establishing access to official information, (2) repealing Section two of the Official Secrets Act, and (3) proposing legislation to replace the security and confidentiality of the Official Secrets Act.[123] Ideologically, Freud sought a total change of the government's attitude by advocating that "everything shall be open."[124]

Conceiving that civil servants would place one sentence containing information deemed exempt in a document to prevent the entire document from being disclosed, Freud included a provision mandating that only the exempt portions of that document be withheld.[125] Freud also included a provision calling for regular inspection of departments' information procedures, which prompted considerable discussion.[126] Most MPs advocated for a Parliamentary Ombudsman

began his speech reminding the House, and in particular Labour Ministers that what he proposed was consistent with Labour's policies over the years); *see also* Freud Arguments, *supra* note 121, at 2132 (tracing the Labour Party's commitment to openness in the 1974 party manifesto and 1977 and 1978 Queen's Speeches).

123. *See* Freud Arguments, *supra* note 121, at 2132 (ranking the three parts of his bill as stated in the text in order of importance). Specifically, Freud's bill contained twenty-three clauses. *See id.* at 2141. Clause one was designed to repeal the Official Secrets Act, while clause two sought to establish a general right of access to government documents. *See id.* Freud also defines an official document as "a document is not only a piece of paper but a record by whatever means." *Id. Compare id., with* discussion *infra* Part III.A (describing how Australia, Canada, and the United States define documents under their respective freedom of information acts). Clauses three, four, and five dealt with access to documents, and clauses six through ten dealt with the machinery of giving the public access. *See* Freud Arguments, *supra* note 121, at 2140 (detailing clauses of bill to Parliament). Clauses eleven and twelve detailed, respectively, refusals and exemptions, while clause sixteen limited fees to the costs of photocopying. *See id.* at 2141 (emphasizing that Parliament "do[es] not ask citizens to pay for the research that went into them").

124. *See* Freud Arguments, *supra* note 121, at 2131.

125. *See id.* at 2141 (describing how British civil servants put one exempt sentence in a document so that it will not be seen by the public and indicating that the idea to have a provision that mandates that only exempt material be withheld came from the United States' FOIA). *Compare id., with* 5 U.S.C. § 552(b) (1994), which is the United States FOIA provision stating "Any reasonably segregable portion of a record shall be provided to any person requesting such record after deletion of the portions which are exempt . . . ."

126. *See generally* 960 PARL. DEB., H.C. (5th ser.) 2185 (1979) (statement of Mr. Rees) [hereinafter Rees Arguments] (stating that one of the most important questions is that of independent review); 960 PARL. DEB., H.C. (5th ser.) 2186 (1979) (statement of Anthony Buck) [hereinafter Buck Arguments] (expressing his worries for this part of the bill and stating that "[s]ome of us share the misgivings" that Mr. Rees has stated). *But cf.* 960 PARL. DEB., H.C. (5th ser.) 2207 (1979)

to supervise the Act, rather than for judicial intervention.[127] An ombudsman, they argued, would be directly answerable to Parliament and would compliment the principle of Ministerial Accountability.[128]

Protection of Ministerial Accountability occupied a central role in the debate yet again.[129] Opponents of the bill claimed that such legislation was at odds with the principle of Ministerial Accountability[130] while advocates of the bill stated that "the democratic principle goes far beyond doctrines of ministerial responsibility and Parliamentary control."[131] MPs repeatedly highlighted the democratic interests involved in this legislation, such as the public's right to know how policy decisions are formulated and to have the opportunity to challenge them.[132] Furthermore, the idea that an informed populace

---

(statement of Christopher Price) [hereinafter Price Arguments] (deciding that he would prefer to have the courts, rather than ministers, make the final decisions about the effects of disclosure with regard to ministerial certificates and the safety and interests of the state).

127. *See* Rees Arguments, *supra* note 126, at 2185 (stating "[I]n my strong view, Ministers should be responsible to Parliament and to no one else for the exercise of their discretionary power"); Buck Arguments, *supra* note 126 (directing the Commissioner to see to it that when this bill is discussed in Committee, alternatives to a Parliamentary Ombudsman are raised).

128. *See* 960 PARL. DEB., H.C. (5th ser.) 2195 (1979) (statement of Mr. Percival) [hereinafter Percival Arguments] (noting that Parliament should not underestimate the current procedure of obtaining information from Ministers, and the Ombudsman and that "any new methods . . . must be dovetailed into that concept of ministerial responsibility").

129. *See id.*; Rees Arguments, *supra* note 126, at 2186 (stating "[w]e have to take into account our basic constitutional system, where Ministers are directly answerable to Parliament . . . [T]his is something that we must keep at the forefront of our minds"). *But see* 960 PARL. DEB., H.C. (5th ser.) 2201 (1979) (statement of Mr. Cook) [hereinafter Cook Arguments] (insisting that the different constitution argument "be thrown out of the window straight away").

130. *See, e.g.*, Rees Arguments, *supra* note 126, at 2186 (stating "[j]udicial review of the merits of decisions to deny documents would raise a profound constitutional issue . . . the major point I am making is that it is this House which should make the final decision . . . not the courts").

131. 960 PARL. DEB., H.C. (5th ser.) 2171 (1979) (statement of Mr. Heffer) [hereinafter Heffer Arguments].

132. *See* 960 PARL. DEB., H.C. (5th ser.) 2150 (1979) (statement of Arthur Lewis) [hereinafter Lewis Arguments] (questioning why a minister or member of the public does not have the right to know what information government civil servants base their decisions on); 960 PARL. DEB., H.C. (5th ser.) 2164 (1979) (statement of J.W. Rooker) [hereinafter Rooker Arguments] (stating that placing this statute on the books would be in the "interests of democracy"); Heffer Arguments, *supra* note 131, at 2170 (stating that democracy is all about an informed

makes the government more accountable, which in turn creates greater overall efficiency and economy, added another dimension to the debate.[133]

Unlike earlier debates, there was a strong consensus of support for the aims and exigency of the bill.[134] In addition to the argument that citizens are taxpayers and thus entitled to governmental information,[135] as heard in prior debates,[136] MPs offered new reasons for the bill, which included changes in technology[137] and the increase in the size of the government.[138]

---

public knowing what is happening, how policy is formed, and challenging the government's decisions).

133. *See, e.g.,* Freud Arguments, *supra* note 121, at 2144 (proffering that "greater disclosure of information prevents waste of public expenditure").

134. *See* 960 PARL. DEB., H.C. (5th ser.) 2197 (1979) (statement of Mr. Fraser) [hereinafter Fraser Arguments] (proclaiming that this is a considerable day for the advancement of human liberty and better government, to which honorable members of both sides of the house are committed); *see also* Heffer Arguments, *supra* note 131, at 2168 (stating that like many other members he welcomes the opportunity not only to debate the question but to support the bill); Lewis Arguments, *supra* note 132, at 2148 (listing all of the organizations and people who support such a bill, such as "[p]eople from the Right, the Left and the Centre of political thought"); Rees Arguments, *supra* note 126, at 2183 (describing how the aim is the same, the only thing lacking is a consensus on the right approach); *cf.* Rees Arguments, *supra* note 126, at 2181 (recognizing wide support for the measure and thus stating that "we must discuss not why people want a Bill, but what it will be like in practice"). In response, one MP highlighted that such a bill would enable Parliament to scrutinize the Executive. *See* Cook Arguments, *supra* note 129, at 2201 (comparing United Kingdom's Parliament with United States Congress and arguing that British are bad at controlling the Executive); *see also* Rooker Arguments, *supra* note 132, at 2162 (denying that the Executive is under constant scrutiny by Back-Bench members). Another MP commented that the bill would not be used as a means of finding fault with the government. *See* 960 PARL. DEB., H.C. (5th ser.) 2204 (1979) (statement of Mr. Warren) (concluding that the British want more information as an attitude of mind not as a means of finding out what is at fault in government).

135. *See* Freud Arguments, *supra* note 121, at 2138 (citing Mr. Herbert Morrison who argues that "it is in the national interest that the citizen and taxpayer should be adequately informed by the Government").

136. *See, e.g.,* Lewis Statements, *supra* note 107, at 1277 (stating [s]hould not the electorate have the right to know? Is not the electorate made up of taxpayers who pay the Minister's salary and who pay the salaries of all these top civil servants?").

137. *See* Fraser Arguments, *supra* note 134, at 2160 (arguing that the basic reason for the bill is a rapidly changing society).

138. *See* 960 PARL. DEB., H.C. (5th ser.) 2213 (1979) (statement of Mr. Litterick) (stating that the tradition of relying on the discretion of ministers and civil

One MP expressing grave doubts as to the benefits of legislation, offered an alternative approach.[139] The alternative was a Code of Practice. According to this MP, a Code is better than a statute because it offers more flexibility.[140] Ministers could effectively make changes, while experimenting with the access concept.[141] In all, it appeared that Parliament recognized that a democracy requires an "equilibrium between publicity, privacy and secrecy."[142] Freud's bill made it to the committee stage, but died with the fall of the Labour government.[143]

B. 1980-1990

Margaret Thatcher and the Conservative Party took control of Parliament in 1979, and shortly thereafter announced the "Protection of Information Bill."[144] This bill, unlike Freud's, provided no public rights of access,[145] proposed non-challengeable ministerial public interest certificates,[146] and increased the secrecy surrounding British intelligence agencies.[147] Amid controversy,[148] the bill was dropped

---

servants to decide what is good for the country can no longer work because of the "sheer size of the State mechanism").

139. *See* Perchival Arguments, *supra* note 128, at 2195 (explaining that there are two ways of tackling a matter such as this one, legislation and the introduction of a code, the first of which Perchival is not wholly committed to).

140. *See id.* (stating there are two ways of tackling this matter).

141. *See id.* at 2196 (arguing "that if we adopt a code of practice the Government will be under constant pressure to make changes to it . . . they would be able to accede to those pressures much more readily than if they were committed to legislation . . .").

142. Freud Arguments, *supra* note 121, at 2144.

143. *See* 55 PARL. DEB., H.C. (6th ser.) 738 (1984) (statement of David Steel) [hereinafter Steel] (attributing the death of Mr. Ely Freud's Official Information Bill to the General Election in 1979); *see also* PONTING, *supra* note 1, at 72 (stating that after the government fell, Freud's bill was automatically lost and a Conservative Government under Thatcher returned).

144. *See generally* Wilson, *supra* note 33, at 131 (reasoning that we should have seen a positive approach to freedom of information from Thatcher since she had earlier introduced a Private Members Bill to create access for citizens to meetings of their local authority; however, her administration announced a Protection of Information Bill).

145. *See id.* (detailing the provisions of Thatcher's Protection of Information Bill).

146. *See* PONTING, *supra* note 1, at 73 (stating that the bill included proposals for "conclusive ministerial certificates" that were not to be challenged in the courts).

147. *See* Wilson, *supra* note 33, at 132 (noting that this bill created even more

and freedom of information was "excluded altogether from the government agenda."[149] Thatcher expressed her opposition to freedom of information legislation describing such changes as "inappropriate and unnecessary."[150]

Despite the government's opposition, from 1980 onwards, private members of Parliament continued to introduce freedom of information legislation.[151] Labour MP Frank Hooley was the first to introduce such legislation, but the government ensured the bill's defeat at its second reading.[152] As the government mounted its offensive during the 1980s against freedom of information legislation, many campaigns developed in its support.[153] Although a comprehensive national freedom of information statute was not enacted, statutory rights of access to particular types of information were established,[154]

---

secrecy for the intelligence services, when it was designed to undo such secrecy).

148. *See id.* at 132 (asserting that had the Bill become law, "Andrew Boyle would not have been able to publish his book *The Climate of Treason*, which led to the disclosure by Ms. Thatcher . . . that Anthony Blunt (MP) had been a Russian spy").

149. PONTING, *supra* note 1, at 73.

150. Wilson, *supra* note 33, at 134 (quoting Mrs. Thatcher).

151. *See generally* Fisher Arguments, *supra* note 1, at 584 (saluting the members of Parliament who in the past introduced FOI bills, such as Mr. Smith, Mr. Kirkwood, Mr. Henderson and Mr. Shepard).

152. *See* PONTING, *supra* note 1, at 73 (placing responsibility on the government).

153. *See generally* Wilson, *supra* note 1, at preface (explaining that he is the Chairman of the 1984 Campaign for Freedom of Information in Britain). The 1984 Campaign for Freedom of Information [hereinafter the Campaign] was launched in January 1984. *See id.* One of its tactics has been to publish a series of "Secrets Files." *See id.* The Campaign has been influential in drafting bills, awarding individuals with Freedom of Information Act Awards who further the disclosure of information, and creating a movement which would make the demand for FOI irresistible. *See* TANT, *supra* note 39, at 200-46 (tracking the Campaign throughout the 1980s until 1993). In addition to the Campaign, an Outer Circle Policy Unit was formed and Charter 88 advocated for FOI. *See generally* MARK EVANS, CHARTER 88: A SUCCESSFUL CHALLENGE TO THE BRITISH POLITICAL TRADITION? (1995) (detailing Charter 88, which was created in 1988 as a protest to challenge the government's satisfaction with the conditions of Britian's democracy).

154. *See infra* notes 274-76 (discussing Britons' rights of access to health records and computerized and manual personal files information held by the government); TANT, *supra* note 39, at 202 (arguing that the Campaign's tactics for a "Freud-like single FOI Act" have been set aside "in favour of a new piecemeal strategy aimed at gaining a 'toehold', which would subsequently facilitate extension of the FOI principle").

and a Local Government Access to Information Act was passed.[155] Many Britons cannot understand why the Government believes that the public should have a right to information on the local level but not on the national level.[156] This section addresses that question. Specifically, this section examines the Private Member's bill that followed Hooley's bill.[157] Blair should pay close attention to the criticism that this minister received regarding the degree of detail in his speech before Parliament in order to avoid making the same error.[158] In addition, this section examines the Parliamentary debates surrounding the enactment of the local access statute and reviews the public's experience with the Act. Perhaps if Blair frames his statute along the lines of the local statute, his legislation will finally become a reality. Blair might refrain from this action since the local Act does not contain an extensive appellate procedure,[159] and local governments remain criticized for being "unduly closed." [160]

1. Steel's Ten Minute Rule

Given Hooley's unsuccessful attempt, David Steel decided to introduce his freedom of information bill in a unique fashion.[161] Using the Ten Minute Rule procedure,[162] Steel introduced a bill that was

---

155. *See infra* Part II.B.2 (detailing the Local Government (Access to Information) Act).

156. *See* BIRKINSHAW, *supra* note 9, at 138 (depicting the Local Government (Access to Information) Act as a "FOIA for local government" and stating that there "is an immediate irony in the fact that it was passed with the approval of the Government, which had steadfastly refused such legislation for itself").

157. *See infra* Part II.B.1 (reviewing MP David Steel's Ten Minute Rule on freedom of information).

158. *See infra* notes 172-74 (providing MP Dennis Skinner's criticism of the narrow definition Steel provided to Parliament as to the types of information Britons would have access to under his Bill).

159. *See infra* Part II.B.1 (describing how the Act leaves review to the "proper officer" and chairman of a meeting).

160. DAWN OLIVER, GOVERNMENT IN THE UNITED KINGDOM: THE SEARCH FOR ACCOUNTABILITY, EFFECTIVENESS AND CITIZENSHIP 178 (1991).

161. *See* Steel, *supra* note 143, at 738 (confirming that "it is unusual for a party leader to use the ten-minute rule procedure" and justifying his action on the basis that it was done "in order to draw maximum attention to the measure itself").

162. *See* MARSH & READ, *supra* note 120, at 12 (stating that Private Members take advantage of Standing Order Number 13, the Ten-Minute Rule, to introduce legislation). Each week, two Members are allowed to make a short speech, usually no more than ten minutes long, asking their colleagues to support the introduction

promoted by the 1984 Campaign for Freedom of Information[163] and modeled on Freud's defeated "Official Information Bill."[164] Ideologically Steel, like Freud, proposed a "total change of attitude" from his colleagues.[165]

Steel differentiated his bill from Freud's by excluding opinions or advice tendered to ministers for policy-making purposes.[166] He did include defense and security matters, relations with foreign governments, law enforcement and legal proceedings, commercial confidences, and individual privacy as exemptions.[167] Additionally, he assigned the role of final review regarding disputes about exemptions to a Parliamentary Commissioner.[168] Steel directed his peers to weigh the costs associated with the Commissioner against the current substantial costs of secrecy when considering this provision.[169]

In order to gain the government's support, Steel advanced four main reasons why it should favor freedom of information including the fact that "regardless of which party is in office, the processes of government and the power of the Government over the individual are increasing all the time."[170] Thus, a proper balance between openness and secrecy is necessary.[171]

Due to the procedural nature of this debate, only one MP re-

---

of a new measure. *See id.*

163. *See* Steel, *supra* note 143, at 738 (assigning the promotion of his Bill to the 1984 Campaign for FOI, "a body that is supported by Members of all parties").

164. *See id.* (informing Parliament that the "text of the Bill follows closely the attempt by my hon. Friend . . . Mr. Freud").

165. *See id.* (stating that "[m]y bill proposes a total change of attitude so that everything shall be open unless specific exemption is made").

166. *See id.* (stating that this provision is one important addition to the Bill Freud introduced).

167. *See id.* (listing the exemptions contained in the Bill).

168. *See id.* (accepting that judgment would fall under the Parliamentary Commissioner for Administration).

169. *See* Steel, *supra* note 143, at 738 (accepting that there would have to be an enlargement of the Parliamentary Commissioner for Administration's office but noting that "open government costs money, that must be measured against the wastefulness of closed government").

170. *See id.* at 740 (pointing out that in addition to this issue extending over party lines, government politics would be more fully considered, better understood, and more acceptable with a freedom of information act).

171. *See id.* (indicating the current imbalance in Great Britain where the Government's privilege to conceal is valued more highly than the people's right to know).

506   *AM. U. INT'L L. REV.*   [13:471

sponded to Steel. According to this MP, Steel failed to detail what information individuals would have access to under the Bill.[172] Additionally, he emphasized that Steel did not mention and "would never wish to mention" how such an act could be used to expose the slush fund of Steel's Liberal party.[173] According to this MP, a "pandora's box" opens and information such as the financial accounts of political parties must be revealed under the premise that the public has a right to know.[174] Ultimately, the debate ended with the MP criticizing Steel for his lack of support of Hooley's Bill.[175]

Parliament ultimately defeated Steel's bill, even though it had the support of the Labour, Social Democratic, and Liberal Parties, since the Conservative Party followed the lead of Thatcher.[176] Now that Blair controls the government and stands firmly committed to the enactment of such legislation[177] the time is ripe for its implementation.[178] Blair need only maintain the multi-party support for the ini-

---

172. *See* 55 PARL. DEB., H.C. (6th ser.) 740 (1984) (statement of Dennis Skinner) [hereinafter Skinner] (expressing his displeasure over the very narrow definition Steel has given of what is needed and what people will be able to get to know if the Bill is passed); *cf. id.* at 741 (arguing that the bill itself is too narrow and stating that "[m]any of us would wish to support a much broader bill, but the narrowly defined one that the leader of the Liberal party is trying to sneak through is a bit of propaganda and gimmickry").

173. *See id.* at 740 (exposing the existence of a Liberal Party slush fund).

174. *See id.* at 740-41 (explaining how he would use the FOI Bill to examine the Liberal Party's accounts because "[t]he public has a right to know what makes political parties tick").

175. *See id.* at 741 (condemning Steel, who was not on "sabbatical," for his absence from the House of Commons on the day that Hooley's Freedom of Information Bill was introduced).

176. *See* Wilson, *supra* note 33, at 135 (describing how the "Prime Minister has given her lead and the Party largely followed" thus failing to make this initiative and positive results an all party issue).

177. *See* FOI Unit, *supra* note 16 (using the term "The Government's Commitments" as the initial heading on its home page, and providing under this heading the pledges made in the Labour Election Manifesto and the Queen's Speech); *Cabinet Office, supra* note 16; Timmins, *supra* note 14, at 10 (providing the Chancellor of the Duchy of Lancaster's assertment that "the government was 'deadly serious' about enacting such a bill").

178. *See* Clwyd, *supra* note 14, at 17 (warning that the passage of time before legislating will be detrimental); *see also The Freedom Files*, TIMES (London), May 9, 1997 (indicating that moving such a bill up the "legislative queue" requires "a forceful champion"). *Compare id.*, *with* ANDY MCSMITH, FACES OF LABOUR: THE INSIDE STORY 293-362 (1996) (entitling chapter seven of his book "Calling Tony Blair" and describing him as a man "blessed with a sharp mind," who "applies

tiative.[179]

2. The Local Government (Access to Information) Act

Although local governments are not governed by the Official Secrets Act, the "legal regime of secrecy to which the 1911 Official Secrets Act gave rise infected local government too."[180] During parliamentary debates over the local act, one MP described local government as even more secretive than the national government because there is not the same level of pressure for information from the local media.[181]

Generally, the measure opens up subcommittees to the public, makes the minutes of all committees available, requires reports that are discussed at meetings to be made public, and provides the general public and officials with access to documents like background papers, interim reports, and research data.[182] Although the statute provides Britons with "access" to official information, as its name denotes, this statute primarily deals with the concept of government openness—making government meetings more open.[183] Nevertheless,

---

himself with a steady and determined intelligence" and "all the tasks that a modern politician is required to do Blair does well").

179. *See* Richard Norton-Taylor, *Labour Leaders May Sideline Freedom of Information Act*, GUARDIAN, Feb. 12, 1997, at 11 (detailing the Liberal Democrats backing of a Labour introduced Freedom of Information Act).

180. OLIVER, *supra* note 160, at 176; *cf.* 72 PARL. DEB., H.C. (6th ser.) 547 (1985) (statement of Sir Bernard Braine) [hereinafter Braine States] (stating "[i]f we suffer from the British disease of excessive secrecy at the top, it is not surprising to find it throughout the administrative structure and operating at local government level").

181. *See* 72 PARL. DEB., H.C. (6th ser.) 544 (1985) (statement of Mr. Austin Mitchell) [hereinafter Mitchell States] (comparing the level of competition among local newspapers long ago with today).

182. *See* 72 PARL. DEB., H.C. (6th ser.) 520 (1985) (statement of Robin Squire) [hereinafter Squire States] (stating the benefits of the Local Government (Access to Information) Bill). According to Squire, the Private Member responsible for the Bill, "[p]ublicity is the greatest and most effective check against action." *Id.* (quoting the words of Prime Minister Margaret Thatcher which she spoke in Parliament when she introduced her Public Bodies (Admission to Meetings) Act of 1960). Accordingly, Squire created this measure to address "the important issues which are unnecessarily taken in private" by local government authorities. *Id.* at 522.

183. *See* BIRKINSHAW, *supra* note 9, at 51-60. Accordingly, the Local Government (Access to Information) Act more closely resembles the United States Sunshine Act, 5 U.S.C. § 552(b) (1994) rather than the Freedom of Information Act.

examination of this statute and the debates leading to its enactment are important because many MPs view the act as a comprehensive freedom of information act.[184]

During the debates, MPs argued that such legislation would interfere with the need to retain confidentiality in certain areas,[185] that the measure was too costly, impractical, and unworkable,[186] and that it would have negative effects on the candor of opinion shared between officials.[187] One MP expressed his fear that officials would conduct

---

"The Sunshine Act . . . is an 'open meeting' law allowing access to the meetings of those agencies within its scope. Its aim is to open up to the public portions of the 'deliberative processes' of certain agencies." *Id.* at 59; *see also* 5 U.S.C. § 552(b) (1994) (stating that "[e]xcept as provided in subsection (c), every portion of every meeting of an agency shall be open to public observation"). In comparison, the Freedom of Information Act addresses public access to agency records, rather than meetings. *See* BIRKINSHAW, *supra* note 9, at 51.

184. *See* 72 PARL. DEB, H.C. (6th Ser.) 554 (1985) (statement of Piers Merchant) [hereinafter Merchant States] (stating that "freedom of information is not just in the interests of the press and the public . . . [i]t is also in the overriding interest of the councils"); *see also* Braine States, *supra* note 180, at 547 (stating "[h]ere is local government moving ahead of Parliament").

185. *See* 72 PARL. DEB., H.C. (6th Ser.) 558-59 (1985) (statement of Mr. Fairburn) [hereinafter Fairburn States] (stating that he is not in favor of secrecy but understands the benefits of confidentiality and trust). Mr. Fairbairn then advances particular examples and reasons why certain matters should be kept confidential. *See id.* The main reason he gives for confidentiality is the need to avoid hurting those members of the public involved. *See id.; see also* 72 PARL. DEB., H.C. (6th ser.) 522 (1985) (statement of Mr. Dafydd Wigley) [hereinafter Wigley States] (confirming with Mr. Squire that the Bill gets at the "completely unnecessary privacy" since "[t]here are matters small as well as great which may need to be kept private because of their content"). Specifically, Mr. Wigley indicates the need to keep private personal matters of confidentiality that arise in social services committees. *See id.*

186. *See* Squire States, *supra* note 182, at 526 (providing what he foresaw as the three main arguments against the enactment of such legislation); *see also* Fairburn States, *supra* note 185, at 558 (arguing that the Bill would have "massive manpower implications for local authorities" and the "financial implications . . . are incalculable but inevitably huge").

187. *See generally* Fairburn States, *supra* note 185, at 560 (quoting COSLA as to the negative effects such a measure would have on the interchanges between officials). COSLA stated the following:

It will mean the end of the officers engaging in frank and meaningful written exchanges of view if they are to be the subject of public scrutiny. No officer is going to give a completely open opinion on a matter if he knows he may be called upon to justify his view in public or even in court.

Id.

all business over the telephone, thus increasing secrecy.[188] Diametrical to these arguments were the calls for an extension of the reach of the Bill.[189]

As a whole, Parliament and the Government supported this measure, offering many reasons for its enactment.[190] As during the debates on the national level for freedom of information legislation, MPs argued that such a bill must be enacted as a matter of principle because open government is an essential right of all citizens.[191] One MP stated that it is generally accepted that information is the "fuel of democracy."[192] As such, legislation providing increased access to information and governmental accountability is central at the local level which "still represents the most immediate form of accountability."[193]

Additionally, MPs argued that because local authorities are the biggest employers, they should set an example of "industrial democracy" by providing employers, workers, and union trade representatives with all known information.[194] MPs argued that disclosure of

---

188. *See id.* (advising every English local authority if this Bill is passed to "never commit anything to writing—always do business on the telephone"); 72 PARL. DEB., H.C. (6th ser.) 542 (1985) (statement of Charles Irving) [hereinafter Irving States] (describing how one local councillor implemented this strategy in his town). This councillor made all decisions on the telephone, and the committees never met. *See id.* The phone deliberations were later reported to the council and approved. *See id.* Thus, the councillor effectively excluded his colleagues and the public from participation in the deliberations. *See id.*

189. *See* Merchant States, *supra* note 184, at 551 (complimenting Squires on the work he has done, but criticizing him because "in some areas the Bill does not go far enough"); 72 PARL. DEB., H.C. (6th ser.) 569 (1985) (statement of Mr. John Fraser) [hereinafter Fraser States] (stating that he would like the Bill's provisions to be extended).

190. *See* 72 PARL. DEB., H.C. (6th ser.) 576-77 (statement of Mr. William Waldegrave, Parliamentary Under-Secretary of State for the Environment) (noting that there has been near unanimity in the debate and urging that the "Government welcome the Bill").

191. *See* Mitchell States, *supra* note 181, at 543 (declaring that "[o]pen government—the right to know—is basic to democracy").

192. 72 PARL. DEB., H.C. (6th ser.) 548 (1985) (statement of Mr. Michael Hancock) [hereinafter Hancock States].

193. Squire States, *supra* note 182, at 520.

194. *See* 72 PARL. DEB., H.C. (6th ser.) 556 (1985) (statement of Mr. Ernie Roberts) [hereinafter Roberts States] (arguing that because local authorities are the biggest employers in the country, they should set an example in industrial democracy). Roberts added that he learned about industrial democracy from his trade

this information will benefit future government-business negotiations and influence the private sector to act in the same manner.[195] Stating this point on a more general level, one MP said, "We are not just tackling local government in the Bill, but taking on a wide aspect of our society which affects all kinds of relationships."[196]

Restructuring of relationships played a central role in the discussion of this measure. Specifically, one of the main reasons advanced for the Bill was the need to improve the local government's status and its relationship with the electorate.[197] According to most MPs, secrecy alienates the electorate, inevitably leading to suspicion and unease and ultimately to a lack of confidence on the part of the public.[198] This bill would remove this suspicion, which is harmful to a good and efficient democracy, and force authorities to be more responsible and clear with their decisions.[199] Local government officials could do a better job because they would have access to all information to which they are currently denied.[200]

Furthermore, MPs argued that a new, stronger partnership was necessary between the electorate and local government officials to tackle the national government's attack on local democracy.[201] Addi-

---

union. *See id.* "All of its members have the right to know everything. The rules provide that members can get any information and find out how anyone voted on any issue. They have real democratic control." *Id.*

195. *See id.* (asserting that both sides should have information on which a decision is being made).

196. 72 PARL. DEB., H.C. (6th ser.) 574 (1985) (statement of Mr. Michael Knowles) [hereinafter Knowles States].

197. 72 PARL. DEB., H.C. (6th ser.) 538-39 (1985) (statement of Mr. Simon Hughes) [hereinafter Hughes States] (charging that such secretive behavior exists in the Southwark Borough Council and does no good to local government, nor "to the status of local government anywhere").

198. Mitchell States, *supra* note 184, at 546 (stating additionally that "[s]ecrecy breeds uncertainty . . . [s]ecrecy breeds rumors, circulates trivia and leads to suspicion, which is harmful to good and efficient democracy").

199. *See, e.g., id.* (arguing that "[o]peness forces authorities to make better, more responsible and more clear-cut decisions").

200. *See, e.g.,* Hughes States, *supra* note 197, at 539 (discussing how his colleague, the leader of the Liberal group on Hackney Council, took the council to court because it denied him access to necessary information). After the court in the Hackney Council case found that the Council had "acted unlawfully" by denying the councillor access to information, the ensuing openness put government officials "in a better position to do [their] job[s] and to advise people." *Id.*

201. *See generally* Roberts States, *supra* note 194, at 527-28 (making the case for open government at the local level "when local democracy is under attack

tionally, highlighted in this debate was the economic relationship between the local and national government.[202] Thatcher indicated her concern over the expense of local government, providing insight as to the reasons why the government supported this measure when it is so against its implementation on the national level.[203] Simply, inefficiency on the lower level, stimulated by a lack of accountability, was proving too costly for the national Government.[204]

Unlike debates on the national level for freedom of information legislation, MPs here could draw support from experiences of certain local authorities who adopted open government policies prior to the enactment of this Bill. For example, the experience of Bradford, which was the first local authority in Britain to adopt an open government policy, dispelled fears of administrative burdens and excessively high costs.[205] "Bradford has been operating a freedom of information policy, and it has worked."[206]

Although MPs could have argued that such a bill was unnecessary

from central Government, with rate capping and threats of abolition"). Furthermore, Mr. Roberts stated, "democratically elected local government must gather strength unto itself to resist the efforts of central Government to interfere more and more in local affairs." *Id.*

202. *See* Squires States, *supra* note 182, at 520 (noting "the importance of the role that local government plays in the [national] economy").

203. *See id.* at 520 (beginning his speech with a discussion on how Thatcher "was worried about local government expenditure").

204. *See id.* ("underlin[ing], above all, the importance of the role that the local government plays in the economy."); *see also* THATCHER'S LAW 28 (Andrew Gamble & Celia Wells eds., 1989) (stating that "[I]n short, the Government entirely lost control over local government expenditure").

205. *See* 72 PARL. DEB., H.C. (6th ser.) 576 (1985) (statement of Mr. Jeremy Hanley) (declaring that "the costs are minimal"); *see also* 72 PARL. DEB., H.C. (6th ser.) 572 (1985) (statement of Mr. Geoff Lawler) [hereinafter Lawler States] (boasting about the openness of government that his constituency has achieved and negating the arguments of those who say that freedom of information policies are too costly). The cost of implementing the policy in regard to Lawler's constituency, he claims, is "estimated to be a mere £2,000." *Id.* Therefore, he argues, "Some of the fears of the Honorable members are therefore somewhat exaggerated." *Id.* In regard to the administrative burden such policies impose, Lawler stated, "[I]t is the council's view, and mine, that the time that is spent . . . is worth while." *Id.*

206. Lawler States, *supra* note 205, at 573. *See generally* Anthony Clipson, *Bradford's 'Open Government' Experience, in* OPEN GOVERNMENT: A STUDY OF THE PROSPECTS OF OPEN GOVERNMENT WITHIN THE LIMITATIONS OF THE BRITISH POLITICAL SYSTEM 123-133 (1987) (providing a thorough accounting of Bradford's "Open Government" experience).

because of cities like Bradford, which opened their governments voluntarily; most argued that, left to their own devices, many local governments would never voluntary accept the freedom of information proposals in Squire's bill.[207] Voluntary acceptance would not occur mainly because this "bill is designed to try to make authorities justify secrecy and confidentiality, and secrecy is endemic in our system."[208]

Despite opposition, Squire's Bill was passed and stands as law today.[209] More than ten years after its enactment, the act has improved public rights of access to local authority information and meetings.[210] Some contend, however, that councils are still "unduly closed"[211] and such statutory intervention has not been "pervasive or necessarily influential."[212] The bill was passed deliberately without containing a special appellate procedure to resolve certain matters inside the authority.[213] Since the bill leaves "important matters of judgment in the hands of the 'proper officer' and the chairman of a meeting," there is growing support for "a new statutory power of assistance for individuals wishing to challenge a decision by their local authority in the court"[214] Hence, a freedom of information act implemented on the national level might not wish to make the same mistake.

During the debates, one MP realized that, although this Bill probably would not prevent the abuses it was created to decrease, "it should be enacted in order to establish a benchmark of standards and [make] it clear what the criteria of local councils should be."[215] Blair

---

207. *See, e.g.,* Hancock States, *supra* note 192, at 548 (contrasting the Bradford experience with those of Portsmouth and Hampshire, two local authorities where there has been "a progressive decline" in information forthcoming to the public).

208. Knowles States, *supra* note 196, at 573.

209. *See* BIRKINSHAW, *supra* note 9, at 138 (noting the "irony in the fact that [the Bill] was passed with the approval of the Government, which had steadfastly refused such legislation for itself").

210. *See id.* (maintaining that the Act provides greater public access).

211. OLIVER, *supra* note 160.

212. BIRKINSHAW, *supra* note 9, at 194.

213. *See* BIRKINSHAW, *supra* note 9, at 140 (relating how the Widdicombe report of 1986 recommended "that a new statutory power of assistance for individuals wishing to challenge a decision by their local authority in the court should be made available").

214. *See id.*

215. 72 PARL. DEB., H.C. (6th ser.) 565 (1985) (statement of Mr. Norris) (arguing that the value of the Bill lies in establishing a benchmark of standards simi-

should use this argument to gain support for his measure, although it appears that the legislation succeeded because the national government wished to control the costs and affairs of the local government.[216]

C. 1990-1997

Succeeding Thatcher as Prime Minister, John Major began the 1990s committed to reform. Specifically, he promised to "sweep away many of the cobwebs of secrecy which needlessly veil too much of government business."[217]

Major latched on to Citizen's Charters as a means of attaining his goals. Citizen's Charters were intended to "secure better services to the public by giving 'the citizen a better deal through extending consumer choice and competition.'"[218] Such charters are now prevalent at all levels of British government.[219] Essentially, the Charters seek to ensure greater efficiency in service delivery from governmental departments by making officials more accountable.[220] Throughout Parliamentary debates in the 1990s for freedom of information, MPs cited the Citizen's Charters as evidence of the government's commitment to openness, efficiency, and accountability.[221] Many MPs

---

lar to other legislation such as the Race Relations Act of 1976 and the equal opportunities legislation).

216. *See supra* notes 202-04 (discussing the important role that the local government plays in the national economy).

217. Richard Norton-Taylor & Nikki Knewstub, *Code of Practice to Fight Secrecy*, GUARDIAN, July 16, 1993, at 1 (quoting John Major).

218. J.A. Chandler, *Introduction* to THE CITIZEN'S CHARTER 1, 2-3 (J.A. Chandler ed., 1996).

219. *See id.* (detailing the success of Citizen's Charters).

220. *See* Howard Elcock, *What Price Citizenship? Public Management and the Citizen's Charter, in* THE CITIZEN'S CHARTER *supra* note 218, at 24, 33-37 (distinguishing three types of accountability and arguing that "accountability downwards" is the main concern of the Citizen's Charter). Elcock defines "accountability downwards" as accountability "to those receiving goods and services, whether as citizens, clients, customers and consumers." *Id.* at 34. This is to be compared with "accountability upwards" to superiors and "accountability outwards" to professionals or colleagues. *Id.* at 33.

221. *See* 219 PARL. DEB., H.C. (6th ser.) 613-14 (1993) (statements of Mr. John Wheeler) [hereinafter Wheeler Comments] (commending the Government for changing the political culture of government in regards to the release of official information and focusing on the Citizen's Charter as evidence of a move in that direction); 219 PARL. DEB., H.C. (6th ser.) 601 (1993) (statement of the Chancellor of the Duchy of Lancaster, Mr. William Waldegrave) [hereinafter Waldegrave

asserted that a comprehensive freedom of information statute was not necessary because the Citizen's Charters and additional statutes provided access to and efficiency in government.[222] Other MPs, however, were quick with responses to rebuke this sentiment.[223]

Continuing the reform, Prime Minister Major ordered a White Paper on Open Government.[224] The White Paper led to the development of a Code of Practice on Access to Official Information. This code currently controls information disclosure in Britain. In short, the Code provides a non-statutory right of access to government information, except where exemptions apply.[225] Persons with complaints have access to an internal departmental review, with final recourse to an independent Parliamentary Ombudsman.[226]

Many argue that the Code was introduced to forestall demands for a freedom of information act and specifically to quell the public support for Mark Fisher's Right to Know Bill.[227] Mark Fisher, a private member of Parliament, brought a bill entitled the "Right to Know" before the House of Commons in 1992.[228] This section examines

---

Argues] (offering the Citizen's Charter as an example of a "comprehensive campaign for opening up information").

222. *See infra* notes 272-76 (discussing the Local Government (Access to Information) Act, the Citizen's Charter, the Data Protection Act, the Access to Personal Files Act, and the Access to Health Records Act).

223. *See infra* notes 265-68 (providing MPs arguments that a freedom of information act is necessary for Britain's democracy to reach adulthood, to improve other countries views of Britain and to allow Briton's access to daily information that would not endanger national security).

224. *See* Chris Moncrieff, *Ministers Take New Broom to Whitehall Secrecy*, PRESS ASS'N NEWSFILE, July 15, 1993, *available in* LEXIS, News Library, ARCNWS File (detailing the origins of the Government's White Paper on Open Government).

225. *See generally* Cabinet Office, *Code of Practice on Access to Government Information* (visited July 11, 1997) <http://www.open.gov.uk/m-of-g/codete.html> [hereinafter *Code*]; *infra* Part II.C.2 (detailing the Code of Practice on Access to Government Information); *see also* Cabinet Office, *Explaining the Code of Practice on Access to Government Information* (visited July 11, 1997) <http://www.open.gov.uk/m-of-g/code97.html> [hereinafter *Code Guide*].

226. *See infra* notes 306-09 and accompanying text (explaining the review process under the Code).

227. *See, e.g.*, Stephen Ward, *Slow Response to Code on Freedom of Information*, INDEP., Mar. 9, 1995, at 8 (stating "it was introduced to forestall demands for a freedom of information act similar to those in the United States and several Commonwealth Countries").

228. *See* 219 PARL. DEB., H.C. (6th Ser.) 583 (1993).

Fisher's Bill and the debates surrounding its failed enactment. Such review is necessary in order to make recommendations to Blair because this was the last major freedom of information bill to come before Parliament. After this analysis, part two of this section details the Government's White Paper on Open Government and the Code of Practice on Access to Official Information. Generally, this section demonstrates the pattern of Labour's attempt to enact freedom of information legislation and the Government's repeated rejection of such a measure.[229] As it stands in Britain today, ministers still decide what information is placed in the public domain.[230] Many fear that Blair might not be able to break this tradition. Even worse some fear that he or Parliament might merely codify the Code of Practice.[231] The disadvantages of such actions are highlighted below.

1. Fisher's Right to Know Bill

Fisher, unlike his predecessors, entitled his bill in a way that highlights the crux of the issue present in freedom of information debates.[232] According to Fisher, the Bill focuses on two key questions.[233] "The first is, who should know? Should it be the

---

229. *See supra* Part II.B.1 (detailing the Government's defeat of MP David Steel's Ten Minute Rule on freedom of information because the Conservative Party followed the lead of Margaret Thatcer).

230. *See Minister Hails Move to More Open Government*, PRESS ASS'N NEWSFILE, July 15, 1993, *available in* LEXIS, News Library, ARCNWS File (quoting Labour member Dr. Marjorie Mowlam's distaste for the White Paper on Open Government, mainly because "in the end, it will be the Government minister that decides what information is available to the public").

231. *See* Richard Norton-Taylor, *Commentary: Whatch* [sic] *Out: Secrecy's About (Again)*, GUARDIAN, May 9, 1997, at 21 (noting that "[i]t will be ironic indeed if the F.O.I. Bill which finally emerges amounts to little more than putting in statutory form the Conservatives' code of practice on open government, with its many exemptions").

232. *See* 219 PARL. DEB., H.C. (6th ser.) 607 (1993) (statement of Mr. Jeff Rooker) [hereinafter Rooker Comments] (stating "[o]ver the years, people who have campaigned for freedom of information have been asked by Ministers what they want to know . . . Turning the title 'round the other way and stating that people have a right to know . . . is a clever means of highlighting the crux of the issue"); *see also* 219 PARL. DEB., H.C. (6th ser.) 616 (1993) (statement of Mr. Don Foster) [hereinafter Foster Comments] (congratulating Fisher on the title of the Bill).

233. *See* Fisher Arguments, *supra* note 1, at 583 (stating that his Bill focuses on two key questions).

Government and civil servants, or all of us? The second is, who should decide what we know? Should it be Ministers or a form of independent arbitration?"[234]

Fisher answers these questions during the debates by detailing the clauses of his Bill, which had its origins in Freud's Official Information Bill.[235] Fisher leaned heavily on the experiences of Australia and Canada, both of which introduced freedom of information legislation in 1982 and have parliamentary and judicial systems similar to Britain.[236]

MPs criticized Fisher's Bill as too large, a "blockbuster Bill" with over 30 clauses.[237] Under the Bill, the public is granted statutory rights of access to "records held by public authorities" and a system for review of decisions denying the assertion of these rights.[238] In addition, the Official Secrets Act of 1989 is reformed and the Companies Act of 1985 is amended.[239] Accordingly, the answer to Fisher's first question is that everyone should know what information the government holds.

Specifically, the Bill requires departments to publish lists of information contained in their departments so that the public will know

---

234. *See id.*

235. *See id.* at 584 (stating that "[the Bill] has its origins in the Official Information Bill introduced by a former Liberal Member of Parliament, Sir Clement Freud, in 1979, and in several Bills introduced by other hon. Members").

236. *See id.* at 585 (stating that the Bill leans heavily on the experiences of Australia, Canada, and New Zealand for the reasons mentioned in the text); discussion *infra* Part III (discussing the access statutes of Canada and Australia).

237. *See* Waldegrave Argues, *supra* note 221, at 604 (characterizing Fisher's Right to Know Bill as a "blockbuster Bill" and a "Christmas tree of a Bill because it is equivalent to four or five Bills put together"). Mr. Waldegrave questioned whether this bill is the biggest Private Member's bill ever. *See id.*

238. *See* BIRKINSHAW, *supra* note 9, at 337 (quoting the text of the Right to Know Bill).

239. *See* Fisher Arguments, *supra* note 1, at 587 (detailing the provisions of the Right to Know Bill). This Bill would amend the Companies Act of 1985 by requiring companies to publish in their annual reports all instances in which they were found to be in violation of environmental protection laws, health and safety laws, discrimination laws, and other consumer protections. *See id.* The need for this provision was illustrated by Des Wilson and his Campaign for FOI. *See* Maurice Frankel, *How Secrecy Protects the Polluter, in* THE SECRETS FILE: THE CASE FOR FREEDOM OF INFORMATION IN BRITAIN TODAY 22-58 (Des Wilson ed., 1984) (looking at the denial of information by factories and companies in regard to the environment).

what information is available.[240] When bodies receive requests they have thirty days to produce the documents unless the documents fall within one of the exempted categories detailed in the statute.[241] The categories of exemptions include: national security, defense and international relations, the enforcement of law, personal privacy, and commercial confidentiality.[242] If the publication of the information requested would cause " significant damage" to the above categories, such information can be withheld.[243]

Review of decisions would initially take place internally by the department who ordered the withholding and next by an independent Parliamentary Information Commissioner.[244] The Commissioner would have to report annually to Parliament,[245] and would have the power of the court to call for documents and order disclosure.[246] If there is still a conflict, an independent Tribunal would make the final decision.[247] Such a mechanism was not present in prior bills.[248]

---

240. *See* Fisher Arguments, *supra* note 1, at 585 (summarizing the provisions of his Bill).

241. *See id.* (describing the obtaining of information under the Bill).

242. *See id.* (listing the categories of protected information contained in his Bill).

243. *See id.*

244. *See* Fisher Arguments, *supra* note 1, at 587-88 (detailing the review mechanism under the Right to Know Bill); *see also* BIRKINSHAW, *supra* note 9, at 340-341 (providing a thorough discussion of the Right to Know Bill's review mechanism).

245. *See* Fisher Arguments, *supra* note 1, at 587 (stating that the " commissioner will lay an annual report before Parliament").

246. *See id.* at 586 (stating that the " Commissioner and tribunal shall have powers of the court to call for information or records and their findings will have the same force as a court order").

247. *See id.* (describing the role of the tribunal). The Tribunal and Commissioner are appointed by Her Majesty, on the reccomendation of the Prime Minister, the Leader of the Opposition, and a Select Committee. *See id.* The tribunal has the same substantial powers as the Information Commissioner, in that its recommendations would have the same force as a court order. *See* BIRKINSHAW, *supra* note 9, at 340 (comparing the levels of power between the tribunal and commissioner). Compared with Canada's Information Commissioner, who can only request but not compel disclosure, the British Commissioner would have increased power. *See id.* (differentiating the review mechanism in Fisher's Right to Know Bill with that of Canada); *infra* notes 371-76 (explaining the review process under Canada's Access to Information Act).

248. *See supra* notes 126-28, 213 (discussing the creation of a Parliamentary Ombudsman to supervise information disclosure under Freud's Official Information Bill and the lack of a special appellate procedure under Squire's Local (Ac-

In order to appease the Government and bring this mechanism in line with the principle of Ministerial Accountability, Fisher argued that the workings of the Tribunal would be subject to the Select Committee, which appoints the Commissioner.[249] Fisher stated that an independent mechanism was necessary because "[i]nformation is too powerful and important to place in the hands of any politicians . . . . [W]hen Ministers make a mistake, whatever party is in office, there is always temptation to save their embarrassment."[250] Thus, the answer to Fisher's second question is that independent commissioners and tribunals decide what information is to be withheld, not ministers.

In order to win the support of civil service organizations, the Bill included an exemption for policy advice.[251] Unlike other countries where a distinction is drawn between the deliberative process of decision making and the post decision stage,[252] Fisher was forced to distinguish between "policy advice" and technical and expert advice that officials receive,[253] the latter of which would be disclosable.

In response to the trials of Tisdall, Ponting, and Wright, Fisher proposed reform to the Official Secrets Act and tailored his provisions according to these incidents.[254] Fisher sought to end the absolute offense of any disclosure and provided the possibility of a public

---

cess to Information) Bill).

249. *See* Fisher Arguments, *supra* note 1, at 587 (responding to Mr. John Bowis's concern that this Bill would be "taking from Parliament a power that he would not wish to take away—the power to assess, monitor and question the tribunal").

250. Fisher Arguments, *supra* note 1, at 586.

251. *See* BIRKINSHAW, *supra* note 9, at 344 (asserting that "[t]he Bill has many interesting and useful aspects . . . [b]ut it also has drawbacks which were forced upon the proponents by bodies representing officials in order to secure their support," such as civil service organizations).

252. *See id.* at 345 (comparing the Right to Know Bill's provisions for information containing policy advice with Canada's policy advice provisions); *see also infra* notes 415-25 and accompanying text (detailing the provisions in the United States' Freedom of Information Act that deal with policy advice).

253. *See* Fisher Arguments, *supra* note 1, at 586 (maintaining that under the Right to Know Bill, policy advice given by civil servants is exempt, but not technical and expert advice they receive).

254. *See generally id.* at 587 (harmonizing the reform of the Official Secrets Act and the defenses of public interest and prior disclosure to the trial of Clive Ponting).

interest defense and defense of prior publication.[255]

During the debates Fisher told Parliament: "We have everything to gain: better democracy, better debate, better decisions, better efficiency, better accountability, and even greater credibility."[256] He also noted that what impressed him most while campaigning for the Bill on the road was its ability to empower individuals.[257] Under the Bill, Britons would be able to have greater knowledge with which to make important choices in their lives.[258] Specifically, Fisher highlighted a tragic incident in Bradford, which he and many allege could have been prevented with a provision like the Right to Know Bill.[259]

Certain MPs repeated his arguments while other MPs offered new

---

255. *See id.* (stating that "[t]he Bill would also reform the Official Secrets Act [of] 1989 . . . by ending the absolute offence of any disclosure"). The Public Interest Defense that Fisher advocated was similar to the one allowed in the Ponting Trial, but not allowed in the Tisdall Trial. *See supra* notes 55, 63 (detailing the lack of a public interest defense at Tisdall's trial and the assertion of such a defense at Ponting's trial). In addition, the defense of prior publication had its origins in the Wright Trial. *See supra* note 74 (explaining how the Australian courts refused to enjoin the publication of Peter Wright's novel in Australia since it was previously published in the United States and Canada).

256. Fisher Arguments, *supra* note 1, at 596. Mr. Fisher stated that the Bill would lead to better public debate because it would be based on information and informed choices. *See id.* at 587. The Bill would lead to better decisions being taken by Ministers because their work would be open to the public for scrutiny. *See id.* at 588. Futhermore, Fisher used a "Thatcherite Argument," contending that freedom of information would help make a "better and more efficient use of whatever Government expenditure was available." *Id.* at 589.

257. *See id.* at 590 (stating that "[m]ore than anything else, the important point is that the Bill would empower the individuals").

258. *See id.* (describing the increased choice and knowledge the public would receive under the Right to Know Bill).

259. *See id.* (stating that choices do "not apply simply to matters of food and safety. . . [t]here are sometimes tragic consequences from not having information and from not making choices"). Fisher explained that the government had known for years that the combination of accumulated rubbish and wood stands was dangerous and had even predicted an accident like Bradford's. *See id.* Yet, they remained silent. *See id. See generally, Cigarette Probably Caused Bradfire Fire, Inquiry Told,* REUTERS, June 5, 1985 (explaining that a cigarette dropped below a seat onto rubbish which caused a fire that swept through the Bradford City Stadium killing 56 people); Alan Nixon, *I Still Find It Hard to Talk About What Happened . . . I Could See The Fire As I Looked For My Family But Didn't Realise What Was Happening; Stuart McCall; on The Bradford Tragedy of 1985,* PEOPLE, May 7, 1995, at 54 (leaving a "lasting scar" on the people of Bradford, this Rangers Star "opens his heart" to relate how that blaze "terrified the world").

arguments.[260] One MP argued that this measure would allow individuals access to the courts by providing them with the necessary information to prove their cases.[261] This MP, like other MPs, spoke of the Matrix Churchill scandal, and concluded that had the Bill been in place, that event might not have occurred.[262] Furthermore, an MP noted that Britain's policy of secrecy made things difficult for the men and women of the armed forces during the Gulf War.[263] This MP stated that for far too long the Government has hidden behind the defense of national security.[264]

MPs also discussed the fact that other countries look in disbelief at the way Britain carries out its affairs and how this Bill would help improve the government's image.[265] Additionally, an MP argued that

---

260. *See* 219 PARL. DEB., H.C. (6th ser.) 621 (1993) (statement of Mr. Shepherd) [hereinafter Shepherd Comments] (reiterating Blair's arguments for accountable government and better quality of decisions); 219 PARL. DEB., H.C. (6th ser.) 590-91 (1993) (statement of Mr. Bob Cryer) [hereinafter Cryer Comments] (telling of another fire in Bradford and emphasizing that "[i]t is wrong that our constituents should be ignorant of potentially lethal dangers in their communities").

261. *See* 219 PARL. DEB., H.C. (6th ser.) 626-627 (1993) (statement of Mrs. Barbara Roche) [hereinafter Roche Comments] (detailing the experience of one of her constituents who was unable to bring a suit against a dye company and a hospital that inserted dye into her, because the hospital was not required by law to release the ingredients of the dye).

262. *See id.* (stating that "the documents that might have entered the public domain under the Bill would have shown the great lengths to which Whitehall advisors were prepared to go to keep the secret shifts in defense-related trade policy"); Foster Comments, *supra* note 232, at 618 (stating "many of the Government's difficulties in relation to Matrix Churchill, the miners' debacle or, more recently, the problems with the social chapter, might not have occurred had the Bill been in place").

263. *See* Roche Comments, *supra* note 261, at 625 (expressing her dismay over the Iraqi invasion of Kuwait and commenting on the role Britain's secrecy played in this event). In addition, Roche said "The fact that there was that secrecy and what was clearly happening was an arms trade with Iraq meant that there was no public debate whatever on the issue and it led to the consequences that resulted." *Id.*

264. *See id.* at 626 (stating that "[f]or far too long, Governments have hidden behind the defense of national security"); *cf.* 219 PARL. DEB., H.C. (6th ser.) 649 (statement of Ms. Glenda Jackson) [hereinafter Jackson Comments] (noting that most of Britain's democratic neighbors "find it perfectly possible to protect their freedom and security without enveloping themselves and their political institutions in a cloak of impenetrable secrecy").

265. *See* Roche Comments, *supra* note 261, at 627 (quoting an article written by Richard Norton-Taylor which appeared in THE GUARDIAN, in which Britain is described as "Ostrich-like"); Hoey Arguments, *supra* note 3, at 636 (stating that

most Britons wish to use the act for common "daily matters," not to obtain information to endanger national security or find fault with the government.[266] MPs received a voluminous amount of postcards from constituents expressing support for the Bill and detailing how they would use the act to obtain general information.[267] Also, MPs argued that the Bill was necessary for Britain's democracy to reach adulthood.[268]

According to the MPs who opposed the Bill, however, Britain's government is doing just fine with its slow piece-meal approach.[269] These MPs argued that one of the benefits of having an unwritten constitution is the ability to target reform and not impart on wholesale change.[270] Additionally, they advanced the theme of "progressive openness" to demonstrate the extent to which the Government has already created a more open and informed society.[271] The MPs pointed to the Local Government (Access to Information) Act,[272] the

---

"[w]e are viewed by many people as being liars and cheats who are prepared to cover up all manner of things" and "[w]hen there is no right to know and no freedom of information, it is difficult to disprove that view").

266. Roche Comments, *supra* note 261, at 626.

267. *See* Hoey Arguments, *supra* note 3, at 636 (stating that "[t]he number of cards and letters shows that there is broad support for the Bill across the political party divide"); *see also* Foster Comments, *supra* note 232, at 618 (detailing a MORI poll that showed that "77 percent of the British people favored freedom of information legislation, and 74 percent of Conservative Voters favored it").

268. *See* Fisher Arguments, *supra* note 1, at 595 (noting the need for Britain's democracy to go from childhood to adulthood, where everyone has "the right to share the information which is paid for with taxpayers' money and collected in our name but withheld from us"); *see also* Rooker Comments, *supra* note 232, at 608 (describing Britain's machinery of government as archaic and analogizing it in the operation of secrecy to be "on par with that of the 19th century high-class whorehouse in terms of protection of its clients").

269. *See* Wheeler Comments, *supra* note 221, at 614 ("Much of the information that people need and desire, and which the bill is aimed at, is already publicly available . . . There is no doubt that the Government were more open . . . Those moves in specific and targeted areas are far more effective than the Bill's blanket provisions.").

270. *See id.* at 612 (stating the "answer is not wholesale change but targeted reform").

271. *See id.* at 613 (stating after responding to a question, "I return to the theme of progressive openness"); *see also* Waldegrave Argues, *supra* note 221(arguing that much more information is now available and listing the measures that give such access).

272. *See supra* Part II.B.2 (providing a thorough discussion of the Local Government (Access to Information) Act).

Citizen's Charter,[273] the Data Protection Act,[274] the Access to Personal Files Act,[275] and the Access to Health Records Act[276] as evidence of openness.

Paralleling the above argument concerning wholesale change was the argument that the Official Secrets Act should not be reformed in the manner in which Fisher envisions because it would be throwing away "years of practical experience" and putting the Nation "at risk."[277] Alternatively, MPs believed that the correct way to deal with the secretive culture is to develop it, building on its strengths.[278] It appears, however, that this is what has been done for many years, yet problems still exist.[279]

In addition, MPs argued that freedom of information acts in other countries have added nothing[280] and that the Bill would interfere with the public's right to privacy.[281] As in prior Parliamentary debates,

---

273. *See supra* notes 218-20 and accompanying text (discussing the Citizen's Charter).

274. *See generally* INFORMATION TECHNOLOGY & THE LAW 22 (Edwards et. al eds., 1990) [hereinafter IT LAW] (explaining how the Data Protection Act of 1984 introduced into UK law a statutory concept of privacy in relation to computerized personal information). Under the Act, individuals are entitled to access to personal data held by users, and are compensated if the data is inadvertently disclosed or incorrect. *See id. Compare id., with*, the U.S.'s *Privacy Act*, 5 U.S.C. § 552a (1994) (regulating the collection, maintaince, use, and dissemination of personal information by government agencies).

275. *See* BIRKINSHAW, *supra* note 9, at 259-263 (detailing the provisions of the Act and how it provides the public access to manual files which contain their personal information).

276. *See id.* at 264-65 (elaborating on the Access to Health Records Act 1990, which gives access rights to health records). Health records are defined broadly, covering information relating to the physical or mental health of an individual made by or on behalf of a health professional in connection with their care. *See id.* Health care professionals include dentists, midwives, and nurses. *See id.*

277. Wheeler Comments, *supra* note 221, at 612.

278. *See id.* (stating that he believed that Britain should "reform what already exists, examine the areas of information already kept confidential and redefine more of them for the public domain").

279. *See supra* notes 31, 32 (discussing the Official Secrets Act of 1989).

280. *See* 219 PARL. DEB., H.C. (6th ser.) 648 (1993) (statement of Mr. Trend) [hereinafter Trend Comments] (stating "experience from other countries suggests that freedom of information adds nothing to the political response that one might achieve by asking a direct question in the legislature").

281. *See* Waldegrave Argues, *supra* note 221, at 597 (arguing that "conflicting interests" must be resolved, in particular, "the right to privacy"). Waldegrade alludes to trade union rights and commercial confidentiality, and claims it is the duty

MPs expressed concern over the Bill's interference with the principle of Ministerial Accountability, especially in regard to the appellate mechanism included in the bill.[282] In light of the above arguments, this Bill reached the Committee stage but was eventually talked out. A total of eighty-six amendments were attached to the Bill, ensuring its defeat.[283] To Fisher's dismay, most of the amendments were "designed to probe the need for the existence of the commissioner and the tribunal."[284]

The Committee that reviewed the Bill offered a sole Ombudsman procedure as an alternative mechanism.[285] According to this Committee, such a mechanism would be more flexible and speedier and would engender "less of a siege mentality" in those whose attitudes they seek to alter.[286] The Committee basically believed that Fisher's Bill, particularly the review mechanism, would not create the right climate for enforcement. Since the Bill's "openness" would be mandatory rather than natural, it would not "foster the right attitude of openness."[287] Again, MPs argued that if such measures were forced upon ministers, the candidness of their discussions would decrease

---

of the government to protect those rights. *See id.*

282. *See id.* at 606 (voicing "one issue of high principle" as being the relationship between Parliament and the Commissioner and the tribunal and recommending against adopting the Bill's structure or approach); Trend Comments, *supra* note 280, at 649-50 (explaining that his "aim would be to find the best way to reconcile the Westminister principle of ministerial accountability to Parliament with greatly increased public rights of information" but arguing further that "the piecemeal approach can be just as profound — perhaps more so than the statutory route").

283. *See* 227 PARL. DEB., H.C. (6th ser.) 1270 (1993) (statement of Mr. Deputy Speaker) (announcing to Parliament some of the 86 amendments); *see also* Nikki Knewstub, *MPs Angry As Private Members' Bills Succumb to 'Serial Killing'*, GUARDIAN, July 3, 1993, at 8 (detailing how Fisher's Bill had completed 15 hours in committee but was doomed when 90 amendments were tabled by Tory MPs).

284. 227 PARL. DEB., H.C. (6th ser.) 1271 (1993) (statement of Mr. Peter Luff) [hereinafter Luff Remarks].

285. *See id.* at 1273 (suggesting that "an alternative mechanism would better be modeled on the ombudsman procedure").

286. *See id.* In addition, Luff asserts:

We should pass legislation only if we believe that it will assist to alter attitudes as well as the legal framework. If we believe that a particular part of a Bill may have an adverse effect on attitudes and the way in which people conduct themselves, we should pause and think long and hard before passing legislation. Its enactment may make us feel better but it may make things worse in the outside world.

Id. at 1272.

287. *See id.* at 1273.

and more secrecy would entail.[288]

Fisher objected to the sole Ombudsman, stating that he purposely included a tribunal like that of Australia. He noted that the proposed Ombudsman structure was more similar to the system used in Canada, which "has a much weaker form of enforcement through its Commissioner" under its access statute.[289] He then argued with an MP over the wording of two new clauses appended to the bill.[290] Fisher was outraged because these "new" clauses were identical to ones that were contained in the original bill.[291] Fisher accused the Government of deliberately wrecking his bill by attaching so many amendments and conducting such "time-wasting" activities.[292] Moreover, Fisher called attention to the Government's alleged actions to inform the public about the techniques the Government uses to kill bills it does not like—particularly bills like his which seek to take power out of the hands of ministers.[293] Fisher relentlessly concluded that it is "very sad and democratically wrong" that private member bills are defeated not on their merits, but by the Government attaching so many amendments.[294]

2. The White Paper on Open Government and The Code of Practice On Access to Government Information

In July of 1993, the Government presented its White Paper on

---

288. *See id.* (asserting that MPs might rely on nods and winks instead of spoken, and therefore transcribed, words).

289. 227 PARL. DEB., H.C. (6th ser.) 1282 (1993) (statement of Mark Fisher) [hereinafter Fisher at Tabling]. In addition, Fisher argues, based on his years in government, that the ability of the Ombudsmen to "deliver decisions that are constrained by the rules and criteria under which they must work, is not great . . . . If we leave enforcement . . . to an ombudsman and not to a tribunal or commissioner that enforcement will take 6 months, 9 months . . . ." *Id.* The tribunal and Commissioner can function more quickly and "sometimes the speed and accessibility of information . . . is as important as the information itself." *Id.*

290. *See generally* 227 PARL. DEB., H.C. (6th ser.) 1275-80 (1993).

291. *See* Fisher at Tabling, *supra* note 289, at 1275 (observing that the wording of the new clause was virtually identical to that of clause 57).

292. *See id.* at 1284.

293. *See id.* at 1276 (stating that "[I]t is no mystery to Members of Parliament . . . what goes on here when private Member's Bills are debated, but it is important for the public to understand the actions of this House").

294. *See id.* at 1283.

"Open Government" to Parliament.[295] The Paper begins by stating, "Open government is part of an effective democracy."[296] The Paper is then broken down into nine chapters detailing the government's record, providing reasons for confidentiality, advocating and describing a code of practice on government information, and proposing two new statutory rights of access to personal records and health and safety records.[297] Included in the appendix is a Draft Code of Practice on Government Information.[298]

When the government released the Paper, many were not pleased with the recommendation for a Code over statutory rights of access.[299] Senior civil servants even privately agreed that the White Paper was a weak document allowing ministers a wide measure of discretion.[300] One critic thought that the Paper presented a paradox.[301] "If statutory rights of access really undermine ministerial accountability, why has the government accepted them in two important areas?"[302]

In April of 1994, the Code of Practice outlined in the White Paper took effect.[303] The Code of Practice contains five main governmental commitments. Individual departments are directed to comply with these commitments while responding to requests within twenty

---

295. *See* OPEN GOVERNMENT, 1993, Cmnd. 2290 [hereinafter White Paper].

296. *See id.* at 1.

297. *See id.*

298. *See id.* at 72 (Annex A).

299. *See* Stephen Alderman, *Minister Hails Move to More Open Government*, PRESS ASS'N NEWSFILE, *available in* LEXIS, News Library, ARCNWS File (reporting how on the day of the unveiling, Marjorie Mowlam, a Labor MP, stated that there "had been a deep failure" to deliver an open government). *But cf.* PYPER, *supra* note 18, at 159 (reasoning that although the White Paper may not have represented "open government" when measured against the standards of the United States, it was a "progressive measure" by British standards).

300. *See* Norton-Taylor, *supra* note 231, at 21 (detailing senior civil servants views on the Government's White Paper on Open Government).

301. *See* Maurice Frankel, *Freedom to Know*, TIMES (London), Aug. 2, 1993, *available in* 1993 WL10594180.

302. *See id.* The areas to which Frankel referred were the people's right of access to personal files and to health and safety information. *See id.* He argued that if access to this type of information would not undermine ministerial accountability, access to other types of information would not undermine it either. *See id.*

303. *See* PYPER, *supra* note 18, at 159 (providing April 1994 as the time in which the Code of Practice on Government Information, outlined in the White Paper, "came into force").

days.[304] Under the Code, a great deal of information should also "be provided free of charge."[305]

Fifteen categories of information are exempt from disclosure under the Code.[306] If an individual has a complaint, he or she must first contact the body that refused the information for an internal review.[307] The next step would be to approach a Member of Parliament who will bring the case to the Parliamentary Commissioner for Administration, also called the Ombudsman.[308] The Ombudsman is an independent officer of Parliament who has the power to see the documents and the duty to inform Parliament when government

---

304. *See Code, supra* note 225, Part I § 3.5 (listing the five code commitments, to supply facts and analysis with major policy decisions, to open up internal guidelines about departments' dealings, to give reasons for administrative decisions, to provide information under the Citizen's Charter about public services; and to respond to requests for information).

305. *See Code Guide, supra* note 225. Information will especially be provided free of charge under certain circumstances:

> Where it is necessary to explain: benefits, grants, and entitlements; the standards and performances of services; the reasons for administrative decisions . . . the way in which you may exercise your rights to appeal or regulatory requirements bearing on your business.

Id.

However, "to ensure that the Code does not create extra burdens on the taxpayer, there may be a charge if the information does not come within one of these categories." *Id.* The costs vary by department, so one must contact the appropriate department to find out if there will be a charge for a given request. *See id.*

306. *See Code, supra* note 225, Part II (including the following as exemptions: defense, security, and international relations, internal discussion and advice, communications with the Royal Household, law enforcement and legal proceedings, immigration and nationality, effective management of the economy and tax collection, effective management and operations of the public service, public employment, public appointments and honors, voluminous or vexatious requests, publication and prematurity, research, statistics and analysis, privacy of individual, third parties' commercial confidences, information given in confidence, and statutory and other restrictions).

307. *See id.* Part I, § 11. *See generally* Tom Riley, *News From Canada and Abroad,* 21 ACCESS REPORTS, Apr. 12, 1995, at 8 (noting that the internal review process can be conducted under the Code prior to a complaint going to the Commissioner). In addition, Riley provides a summary of the Internal Review Process after one year of the Code. *See id.* The summary is as follows: "The most oft-cited exceptions quoted were: exemption 2 (internal discussion and advice); exemption 7 (effective management and operation of the public service); exemption 13 (third party's commercial confidence); and exemption 14 (information given in confidence)." *Id.*

308. *See Code Guide, supra* note 225 (explaining the complaint procedure).

agencies and departments are violating the code.[309] Final decisions rest with the Ombudsman, who determines whether the departments were justified in refusing to release the documents and the information contained therein. The Ombudsman, however, can only make recommendations; he or she cannot order disclosure.[310]

Since the implementation of the Code, many have complained about the high fees charged for information and their deterrent effect.[311] In addition, individuals have complained that one does not re-

---

309. *See id.* (explaining the Ombudsman's powers). In 1994, the Parliamentary Commissioner for Administration received twenty-eight complaints. *See* Riley, *supra* note 307, at 8 (reporting on the Parliamentary Commissioner's activities from the Code's beginning to the date of this source's publication). As of April 1995, the Commissioner had issued five reports and completed six investigations. *See id.* Out of the twenty-eight complaints, seven were ruled out of his jurisdiction. *See id.* Mr. Riley includes in his reports the results of the first three investigations reported to Parliament by the Commissioner. *See id.* They are as follows:

(i) Two complaints that the Department of Transport had refused to give details of the Inspector's report on the inquiry into the proposed Birmingham Northern Relief Road scheme in 1988. These complaints were upheld, and the Ombudsman recommended release of the Inspector's report;

(ii) A complaint that the Valuation Office Agency had refused to reveal the identity of a house purchaser. The Complaint was dismissed, on the grounds that the release of the information would breach the purchasor's personal privacy; and

(iii) A complaint that the Department of Health had refused to give details of contacts with the pharmaceutical industry. The complaint was upheld in part, but the Ombudsman accepted that the identities of representatives involved in the discussions could be legitimately withheld. The Department agreed to give further information about the dates of contacts and the form they had taken.

Id.

310. *See* Tom Riley, *News From Canada and Abroad,* 19 ACCESS REPORTS Aug. 4, 1993, at 11 (noting that the Parliamentary Commissioner for Administration has only recommendation powers and stating that "experience in other countries has shown that a Commissioner solely with recommendation powers experiences many problems in convincing officials to release information").

311. *See* Cal McCrystal, *Freedom Fighter Amid the In-trays; Right to Know Comes at a Price,* INDEP., Nov. 13, 1994, at 11 (reporting on the Campaign for Freedom of Information's report that showed that high fees charged under the Code were often a deterrent to the use of the Code); Peter Victor, *Freedom of Information: It Will Cost You; The Facts We Need To Know Have Turned Into 'Government-Held Tradable Information,'* INDEP., June 18, 1995, at 4 (providing examples of large fees certain agencies had charged for general information, sometimes as much as £2,000 or £3,000). The Meteorological Office, for example, has charged exorbitant fees for weather information. *See id.* Victor worries that "many people who ask questions under the code are intimidated by the threat of charges." *Id.* Specifically, Victor reported that in 1994, 9 out of 90 people who asked the Inland Review for information under the Code dropped their requests

ceive the actual "pre-existing" documents, but rather "access to information."[312] This policy allows the Government to publish information in a manner which it finds appealing, frustrating the very purpose of freedom of information.[313] Another significant problem is the fact that citizens often do not know what information is available, nor do they fully understand the role of the Ombudsman.[314] In fact, most individuals are not aware of the Code's existence due to sparse advertising by the Government.[315] The Government recently conceded this point and has increased its efforts to educate the public about the Code.[316]

Press releases issued by the Cabinet Office highlight the positive effects that the Code is having in Britain.[317] Yet, the campaign for freedom of information legislation continues, and Select Commit-

---

when they were told how much the requests would cost. *See id.*

312. *See* Riley, *supra* note 307, at 12 (relating the Campaign for Freedom of Information's poor marks for the Code's first year in practice and citing the "thorny problem that the Code does not require release of the actual documents containing the information, but only the information itself"). Riley does state that this weakness has not gone unnoticed by the Parliamentary Commissioner for Administrative Complaints, "who in his first case, commented on how onerous and misleading this was and that, in fact, it would be better if the document itself were released". *Id.*; *see also Code, supra* note 225, Part I, § 5 (describing access to information).

313. *See* BIRKINSHAW, *supra* note 9, at 202 (explaining that under the code "there would be access to information which would be selected, filleted and presented by officials").

314. J. Ross Harper, *Open Season on the Protection of Privacy,* SCOTSMAN, July 13, 1994, *available in* LEXIS, News Library, TXTNWS File.

315. *See* Stephen Ward, *Code of Openness Fails To Catch the Public Imagination,* INDEP., Mar. 15, 1995, at 4 (reporting that official government figures confirmed expectations that few people used the open government code in its first year, possibly because there is little public awareness of its existence).

316. *See* Cabinet Office (OPS) Press Office, *Improving Access To Government Information,* Jan. 17, 1996 (visited July 18, 1997) <http://www.open.gov.uk/coi/ops/5/96.html> (explaining how the Home Office is circulating over 30,000 copies of a new leaflet explaining the Code as a part of "an ongoing campaign aimed at raising people's awareness . . . ").

317. *See* Cabinet Office (0PS) Press Office, *Freeman Welcomes Open Government Momentum: 17,000 More Records Released Since May ,* Oct. 23, 1995 (visited July 18, 1997) <http://www.open.gov.uk/coi/ops/264/95.html> (relating the increase in amounts of records released under the Code along with a statement by Roger Freeman, the Chancellor of the Duchy of Lancaster, that "release of these files is a further step in our programme to make government more accessible to the public").

tees,[318] and Blair,[319] are calling for the implementation of such legislation.

In sum, the concept of freedom of information has gained support from current members of Parliament. The idea of freedom of information legislation went from being strongly criticized in 1970, with concerns over high costs and administrative burdens, to being widely accepted by the time Freud introduced his Official Information Bill in 1980.[320] These ten years are important because they demonstrate the government's hold on Parliament's agenda. Had the Labour Party not lost the election in 1979, Britain might have a freedom of information act today.[321]

From 1980-1990 one sees further evidence of the government's power over Parliament in the area of freedom of information. Steel's bill died even with multiparty support.[322] Although one saw freedom of information enacted on the local level, it happened because the government wanted it for economic reasons—not freedom of information reasons.[323]

Over the past few years, while the British government has done more to open government, the government remains largely closed.[324]

---

318. *See British MPs Urge Freedom of Information Act*, REUTERS, Mar. 27, 1996, *available in* LEXIS, News Library, ARCNWS File (reporting that the Select Committee on the Parliamentary Commissioner for Administration stated that "[w]e recommend that the government introduce a Freedom of Information Act").

319. *See* New Labour, *supra* note 11 (demonstrating Blair's commitment to FOI).

320. *See supra* Part II.A.2 (providing an overview of Parliament's response to freedom of information legislation since the 1970s).

321. *See supra* note 143 and accompanying text (discussing the death of Freud's Bill with the fall of the Labour Government).

322. *See supra* notes 176 and accompanying text (discussing the fact that Steel's Bill died even though it had the support of the Labour, Social Democratic, and Liberal Parties).

323. Concern on the part of conservative councillors about profligate spending by local constituencies led Prime Minister Thatcher to support local freedom of information acts without endorsing a national one. *See* Squire States, *supra* note 182, at 520 (noting Thatcher's general concerns about local inefficiency and hoping that greater scrutiny of expenditure would lead to less local spending).

324. *See supra* notes 2-4 (citing examples of "secrets," such as the length of the queue at the post office); *see also supra* note 316 (discussing Government realization of and efforts to increase public awareness of that information to which they actually have access); *Putting the Case For A Freedom of Information Act*, SCOTSMAN, Mar. 8, 1996, at 14 (arguing that the Code "falls short of a Freedom of

Mark Fisher was not able to break down the walls of secrecy, so a new champion is needed.[325] Blair is already one step ahead of Fisher given his position as Prime Minister. If Blair wishes to see a freedom of information act implemented, he must address the main issues that arose in the Parliamentary debates discussed above, issues specific to Britain, rather than relying solely on the access statutes of other countries.[326] Those main issues are: Ministerial Accountability, program costs, administrative burden, confidentiality, and protection of cabinet confidences.

III. ACCESS STATUTES OF THE UNITED STATES, CANADA, AND AUSTRALIA

Although some MPs refuse to look to other countries' Acts as prototypes for Britain, other MPs have recognized the value of these countries' experiences.[327] Accordingly, this section outlines the freedom of information statutes of the United States, Australia, and Canada in order to formulate an appropriate statute for Blair.

The United States has the oldest statute, enacted in 1966.[328] The statute, entitled the Freedom of Information Act (FOIA),[329] provides access to all persons, even the British, and is liberally construed in favor of disclosure.[330] President Clinton[331] and Janet Reno,[332] the At-

---

Information Act" because it only promises "information," not the actual documents, and because it is not enforceable in the courts).

325. *See Leader, supra* note 14, at 22 (describing Marc Fisher's Right to Know Bill).

326. *See supra* notes 107-08, 270, 280 and accompanying text (detailing MPs preferences to disregard the experiences of other countries under their access statutes).

327. *See supra* notes 107, 236 (providing MPs arguments that parliament should look to the United States, Australia, Canada, and New Zealand for guidance on freedom of information).

328. *See supra* note 5 (detailing the date of enactment of the United States' Freedom of Information Act).

329. 5 U.S.C. § 552, *as amended by* Electronic Freedom of Information Act Amendments of 1996, 5 U.S.C.A. § 552 (West Supp. 1997).

330. *See* Bristol-Meyers Co. v. FTC, 424 F.2d 935 (D.C. Cir. 1970) (reiterating that the legislative plan for the FOIA creates a liberal disclosure requirement).

331. *See* President's Memorandum for Heads of Departments and Agencies Regarding the Freedom of Information Act, 29 WEEKLY COMP. PRES. DOC. 1999 (Oct. 4, 1993), *reprinted in* FOIA UPDATE (DOJ/Office of Information and Privacy, D.C.), Summer/Fall 1993, at 3 (calling upon federal agencies to renew their commitment to the Act). President Clinton stated:

torney General of the United States, recently reiterated this pro-disclosure attitude. In Canada, as well, the Information Commissioner called for a more pro-disclosure attitude among government departments.[333] Liberals enacted the Canadian Access to Information Act (AIA)[334] in 1982 as a result of strong pressure from the Conservative opposition party.[335] Parliament hotly debated the statute due to

---

> For more than a century now, the Freedom of Information Act has played a unique role in strengthening our democratic form of government. The statute was enacted based upon the fundamental principle that an informed citizenry is essential to the democratic process and that the more the American people know about their government the better they will be governed. Openness in government is essential to accountability and the Act has become an integral part of that process.

Id.

332. *See Attorney General Reiterates FOIA Policy,* FOIA UPDATE (DOJ/Office of Information and Privacy, D.C.), Spring 1997, at 1 (detailing how Reno redistributed a memo that was issued by her and President Clinton in 1993 pertaining to the importance of the FOIA with the direction that they be given to recent appointees). The 1997 memorandum, which accompanied and detailed the 1993 memo, stated in pertinent part, " I urge you to be sure to continue our strong commitment to the openness-in-government principles . . . . These principles include . . . applying a presumption of disclosure in FOIA decision making." *Id.*

333. *See* NOTES FOR AN ADDRESS TO THE CANADIAN ACCESS AND PRIVACY ASSOCIATION, (last visited July 20, 1997) <http://fox.nstn.ca/~smulloy/capa-eng.html> [hereinafter NOTES] (asking members of the Canadian Access and Privacy association to remember that "attitudes towards access cannot be legislated . . . . The beginning of reform is a will to make this law work" and that will not be accomplished by " offer[ing] more opportunity to insulate records from the right of access"); *cf.* INFO. COMM'R OF CAN., ANNUAL REPORT INFORMATION COMMISSIONER 1995-1996 (1996) [hereinafter ANNUAL REPORT 1995-96] (denying the principle that "everything is secret unless specifically stated otherwise," the Information Commissioner of Canada states that "the truth is precisely the opposite"). Furthermore, he states:

> The onus is plainly upon the government to demonstrate why a record cannot be released, either in whole or in part. Individuals do not have to prove their case for the release of government-held information any more than they need to say why they want the information. Unless the government can demonstrate before an information commissioner or a court a right to withhold a record, it must be released. That's the law. The assumption of this remarkable law is that information belongs to the people. In the British system, that's revolutionary.

Id.

334. *See* Access to Information Act, R.S.C., ch. 111 (1980-1983) [hereinafter AIA].

335. *See* Anthony Johnson, *The Frustrating Hunt for Information,* OTTAWA CITIZEN, July 3, 1993, at B4 (reporting that Canada's statute was passed in 1983 by Liberals but that " [i]ronically, it was the opposition Conservatives who pushed the hardest for freedom of information legislation and were harshly critical of the Act's cabinet secrecy provisions").

Canada's Westminister style of government and concerns over Ministerial Accountability.[336] Reports from Canada's Information Commissioner, who is appointed by Parliament, indicate that the Act has
proven extremely powerful and effective[337] and that it is able to stand
alongside Canada's Official Secrets Act.[338]

Australia, like Canada and Britain, operates under a Westminister

---

336. *See* 21 PARL. DEB., H.C. 6725 (1980) (statement of Mr. Fox) (thanking all
of the members who participated in the debate and stating: "we have given a great
deal of thought to reasonable proposals in the area of ministerial responsibility").
Furthermore, Fox stated, "The government decided to take the route of judicial
review . . . . However, we felt that there was a possible conflict between the principle of ministerial accountability and the principle of judicial review." *Id.*; *see
also* INFO. COMM'R OF CAN., THE ACCESS TO INFORMATION ACT: 10 YEARS ON
(1994) [hereinafter 10 YEARS] (emphasizing that Canada has inherited parliamentary sovereignty and that government tradition holds each minister responsible for
the actions of his or her department and therefore, "broad access, it was feared,
could dilute that responsibility and make ministers less accountable to the public"). Furthermore, "[t]his subtle, yet important, difference [to America] has
deeply shaded the discussion of information in this country." *Id.*

337. *See* ANNUAL REPORT 1995-96, *supra* note 333, at 5 ("Each and every day,
in newspapers, on radio and television, we see and hear the power and effectiveness of the access law."). For example, Canada learned about golf trips to Florida
for military generals, contracting practices at Natural Resources Canada, and a ten
percent pay increase to the Deputy Governors of the Bank of Canada. *See id.*; *see
also* 10 YEARS, *supra* note 336, at 23 (conceding that "no one expected that the
most restrictive elements of parliamentary sovereignty and ministerial secrecy
would be overturned in a decade").

338. *See* Official Secrets Act, R.S.C., ch. O-3, § (1985). Chapter O-5, section 3,
"Offenses" reads as follows:

  3. 1) Every person who is guilty of an offence under this Act, who, for any purpose
  prejudicial to the safety or interests of the State, (a) approaches, inspects, passes over,
  is in the neighbourhood of or enters any prohibited place; (b) makes any sketch, plan,
  model or note that is calculated to be or might be or is intended to be directly or indirectly useful to a foreign power; or (c) obtains, collects, records or publishes, or com-
  municates to any other person, any secret official code word, password, sketch, plan,
  model, article, note, document or information that is calculated to be or might be or is
  intended to be directly or indirectly useful to a foreign power.

Id. at ch. 0-5, § 3. This statute, unlike Britain's Official Secrets Act, relates to espionage only. The statute is also rarely used. *See Reform, supra* note 66 (discussing how Canada has an Official Secrets Act "but has given up using it"). In addition, other countries have similar legislation but do not use it. *See id.* For example,
Australia has similar provisions in its Commonwealth Crimes Act 1914 but never
uses it. *See id.* The United States confines itself to "legislation that protects clearly
identified national secrets such as the National Defense Act 1911, the Espionage
Act 1917, and the Comint Act 1950." *Id.*

style of government.[339] Concern as to whether the United States FOIA could be implemented in Australia, as a result of the countries' dissimilar constitutional and administrative frameworks, permeated the enactment of Australia's Freedom of Information (FOI) Act.[340] Today, Australia's Act is lauded as playing an important role in Australia's democratic system and increasing the accountability of officials.[341] Yet, as in other countries, calls for change in agency cul-

---

339. *See* PATRICK WELLER, *Introduction* to MENZIES TO KEATING: THE DEVELOPMENT OF THE AUSTRIAN PRIME MINISTERSHIP 1 (1993) ("The language of the Westminister system, however poorly that concept defines the workings of the political system, remains intact.").

340. *See generally* ISSUES PAPER, *supra* note 7, at 4-7 (providing the background to the introduction of the FOI Act). In 1974, the first of two Interdepartmental Committees formed to examine freedom of information concluded that "should the Government decide to enact FOI legislation, it would be necessary to modify the United States legislation to take account of Australia's constitutional and administrative structure." *Id.* at 4. Specifically, the Committee recommended that certain exemptions be included and that conclusive certificates exist. *See id.*

Following this report, the Interdepartmental Committee Report of 1976 maintained that "a person should have a legally enforceable right of access to any document in the possession of a department" and that such a right is essential for and complimentary to Australia's democratic government. *See id.* at 5. The Committee stated as follows:

The basic premise from which consideration of the issue in Australia must begin is that in a parliamentary democracy the Executive Government is accountable to the Parliament and through the Parliament to the people. An informed electorate is able to exercise a more informed choice at the ballot box. But, more than that, openness of access to information, in the words of the Royal Commission on Australian Government Administration, 'promotes an aware and participatory democracy.'

Id.

341. *See* AUSTRALIAN LAW REFORM COMM'N, DISCUSSION PAPER 59, FREEDOM OF INFORMATION (1995) at 9 [hereinafter DISCUSSION PAPER] (stating that the Law Reform Commission considers that the "Act has had a marked impact on the way agencies make decisions and the way agencies . . . record information"). Furthermore, the Commission reported that:

[T]he FOI Act has focused decision-makers' minds on the need to base decisions on relevant factors. The knowledge that decisions and processes are subject to scrutiny . . imposes a constant discipline on the bureaucracy. The openness guaranteed by the FOI Act has improved the accountability of government.

Id.

They also noted that public servants' accountability to Ministers is complimented by the fact that their decisions are open to public scrutiny. *See id.; cf.* Robert Richards, *The Freedom of Information Act,* AUSTRALIAN ACCT., May 1995, *available in,* LEXIS, News Library, ARCNWS File (advocating the use of the FOI Act for information from the Tax office, as a means of obtaining information). *But see* G. TERILL, SUBMISSION 17 ("In some ways the Act actually undermines efforts towards increased openness. The seriousness with which it is taken by government

ture are prevalent.[342] The Australian Law Reform Commission (ALRC)[343] recommended that the Act be amended to contain a preamble, which would make clear that access to government information is a right, and, most importantly, that the Act has its origins in the present understanding of the Constitution and Australia's form of democracy.[344]

British MPs are correct that attitudes towards openness are difficult to legislate. Experiences in these countries, however, demonstrate that the statutes have played a crucial role in positively changing the mechanics of government.[345] This section explores those experiences in detail, focusing on the issues raised in Britain's debates over freedom of information.

A. FORMS OF ACCESS

Unlike Britain, Australia, Canada, and the United States provide individuals with actual physical documents.[346] Canadians have the broad legal right to information recorded in any form and controlled by most federal government institutions.[347] Recent publications re-

---

. . . is often used to suggest that openness is a rule; this is not so. There are innumerable other ways to achieve openness.")

342. *See, e.g.,* DISCUSSION PAPER, *supra* note 341, at 11 (concluding upon a study of the FOI Act that "the culture of some agencies is not supportive of the philosophy of open government and FOI" and recommending that agencies change this culture through the use of training sessions inculcating the importance of the Act).

343. *See* ISSUES PAPER, *supra* note 7, at viii (providing a copy of the Acting Attorney General's Order to the Australian Law Reform Commission (ALRC) to conduct an inquiry and report under the Law Reform Commission Act 1973, Section 6 on whether the basic purposes and principles of the freedom of information legislation in Australia have been satisfied and whether they require modification). The ARLC was also instructed to conduct this inquiry with the Administrative Review Council (ARC). *See id.* at 1.

344. *See* DISCUSSION PAPER, *supra* note 341, at 13 (recommending that the FOI Act be amended to include a preamble and delineating what that preamble should include).

345. *See id.* at 9 (" [T]he review considers that the Act has had a marked impact on the way agencies make decisions and the way they record information.").

346. *See supra* note 312 (explaining that the current Code of Practice on Access to Government Information does not require the release of actual documents).

347. *See* AIA, *supra* note 334, § 3 (defining record)
"Record" includes any correspondence, memorandum, book, plan, map, drawing, diagram, pictorial, or graphic work, photograph, film, microform sound recording videotape, machine readable record, and any other documentary material, regardless of

leased by Canada's Information Commissioner, however, illustrate the need to reform the Act to reflect changes that have occurred in the infrastructure of information technology.[348]

In Australia, individuals have access to "documents."[349] The concept of document is very broad, as in Canada, and "has served the Act well to date." A shift to the concept of information is being requested, however, in addition to provisions to bring the Act in line with new technology.[350]

---

physical form or characteristics, and any copy thereof.
Id.; see also ANNUAL REPORT 1995-96, *supra* note 333, at 1 (describing Canadian's rights under the AIA).

348. *See* INFO. COMM'R OF CAN., ANNUAL REPORT INFORMATION COMMISSIONER 1994-1995, (1995) at 3-5 [hereinafter ANNUAL REPORT 1994-95] (discussing the information superhighway, the Information Commissioner stated that "[p]raise it or doubt it, this tantalizing and powerful image cannot be ignored by gatherers and custodians of information or by those with legislative . . . or statutory . . . responsibility towards a law called the 'Access to Information Act'"); *Minister of Public Works and Government Services, Information Technology and Open Government* (visited July 23, 1997) <http://infoweb.magi.com/~accessca/ogov-e.html> (assessing the impact of new information technologies and new information management practices on open government and the principles and application of the Access to Information Act). This report was prepared for the Information Commissioner of Canada by Information Management & Economics, Inc. of Toronto. *See id; see also* INFO. COMM'R OF CAN., ANNUAL REPORT INFORMATION COMMISSIONER 1993-1994, (1994) at 5-9 [hereinafter ANNUAL REPORT 1993-94] (making the case for reform by highlighting that "ten years ago government records were primarily paper records" and that this is rapidly changing and thus, the "access law has some catching up to do if our access rights are to remain vibrant into the next century"). *See generally* Tom Riley, *News From Canada and Abroad* 20 ACCESS REPORTS, Dec., 7, 1994 (describing the climate of change in Canada pertaining to their access to information act and information technology).

349. *See* Freedom of Information Act, 1982, ch. 3 § 4 (Cth) [hereinafter FOI] (defining document). "Document" includes:
(a) any of, or any part of any of, the following things: (i) any paper or other material on which there is writing; (ii) a map, plan, drawing or photograph; (iii) any paper or other material on which there are marks, figures, symbols or perforations having a meaning for persons qualified to interpret them; (iv) any article or material from which sounds, images or writings are capable of being reproduced with or without the aid of any other article or device; (v) any article on which information has been stored or recorded, either mechanically or electronically; (vi) any other record or information; or (b) any copy, reproduction or duplicate of such a thing; or (c) any part of such a copy, reproduction duplicate; but does not include: (d) library material maintained for reference purposes; or (e) Cabinet notebooks.
Id.

350. *See* DISCUSSION PAPER, *supra* note 341, at 31; ISSUES PAPER, *supra* note 7, at 29 (emphasizing that under the act, agencies are under no obligation to create a

The United States recently amended its FOIA to address the subject of electronic records, thus expanding the definition of agency "records" that must be made available to the public.[351] Such reforms were introduced in order to correct lengthy processing delays and fulfill FOIA's mandate of providing all "agency records."[352] The finding, releasing, and disseminating of records should now be much easier. Blair has already contemplated and addressed reforms of Britain's information technology in the Labour manifesto, linking such reforms to freedom of information legislation.[353]

B. FEES AND COSTS

Under all three statutes, access to information is subject to fees and charges. The costs have often been criticized as contrary to the

---

document from information in the possession of an agency in order to satisfy a request).

351. *See* FOIA UPDATE *supra* note 5, at 3-9 (providing the text of the Freedom of Information Act as amended, including the new definition of agency records). Section (a)(2)(D) "create[s] a new category of records that will be required to receive 'reading-room treatment'— a category consisting of any records processed and disclosed in response to a FOIA request that 'the agency determines have become or are likely to become the subject of subsequent requests.'" *Id.* at 1. In short, if an agency receives a number of requests for a certain type of information, under this provision, they will have to make it available via electronic reading rooms. *Cf. Is FOIA About Records or Information*, ACCESS REPORTS, Apr. 16, 1997, at 3 (grappling with the new EFOIA amendments and questioning whether the FOIA is concerned with records or information). Moreover, he states that twenty years ago the world of FOIA was "beginning to move from 'record' to 'information.' From a legal and policy standpoint, the words had begun to be used interchangeably with no particular awareness that the legal distinctions might become important at some time." *Id.*

352. *See* Michael Tankersly, *Opening Drawers: A Requestors Guide to the Electronic Freedom of Information Act Amendments*, LEGAL TIMES, May 19, 1997, at 29-30 (describing how agencies resisted the application of FOIA to electronic data and violated the FOIA's promise of a "prompt release of records"); Jamie A. Gordsky, *The Freedom of Information Act in the Electronic Age: The Statute is not User Friendly*, 31 JURIMETRICS J. 1 (1990) (exploring the conceptual and practical problems in applying the unamended Freedom of Information Act to computerized government information); Nancy Ferris, *Virtual Records*, GOV'T EXECUTIVE, Aug. 1997, at 43 ("EFOIA . . . will force agencies to use contemporary technology, while it prods them to cut their backlogs."). The EFOIA amendments extends the amount of days that an agency has to respond from 10 to 20. *See id.*

353. *See* New Labour, *supra* note 11, at *Information Superhighway*, <http://www.labour.org.uk/views/info-highway/social.html> (stating that "the information society can help make our society more open and accessible").

aims of the Acts.[354] All three countries, however, realize the necessity of having requesters contribute financially in order to keep administrative costs to a minimum.[355] Both the Information Commissioner for Canada and the ALRC have asserted that the number of requests per year is lower than initially predicted and that the law is not expensive.[356] Experience in Australia highlights the fact that staff costs are the main expense; however, it attributes these costs to the absence of a sole independent monitor of the program.[357] Recent proposals suggest an independent monitor to oversee the administration of the Act or a Parliamentary Committee.[358]

All three countries charge for search and retrieval, inspection and photocopying, and decision making, subject to fee waivers.[359] In ad-

---

354. *See* DISCUSSION PAPER, *supra* note 341, at 82 (shaping the issues in regard to costs).

355. *See id.* (noting that requestors must be responsible financially); OFFICE OF THE INFO. COMM'R OF CAN., THE ACCESS TO INFORMATION ACT: A CRITICAL REVIEW 51 (1994) [hereinafter CRITICAL REVIEW] (stating that "anyone seeking information for the purpose of holding the government accountable or for their own personal interest should pay minimal fees for obtaining the information").

356. *Compare* ISSUES PAPER, *supra* note 7, at 9 (stating that "unlike the Australian FOI Act, the Act is used by a large number of professional brokers" in the United States), *with* NOTES, *supra* note 333 (scolding the Prime Minister Chretien for being misinformed and misstating that "every day hundreds and even thousands of information requests are made by journalists, academics and members of Parliament"). The Information Commissioner stated, "[T]he exaggeration here is so patent as to require no rebuttal." *Id.* In addition, he stated that in his view, "much of the complaining about the excessive cost of administering the access law is without foundation." *Id.*; *see also* ANNUAL REPORT 1995-96, *supra* note 333, at 5 (stating "[t]ake note ye skeptics who say the right to know is costing the taxpayer too much" and detailing examples of where money has been saved in Canada under the Act).

357. *See* ISSUES PAPER, *supra* note 7, § 9.7 (noting that non-staff costs, for such things as photocopying, printing, legal fees and computer time, represent less than ten percent of total costs).

358. *See generally* DISCUSSION PAPER, *supra* note 341, at 20-30 (recommending an independent person to oversee the administration of the FOI act and providing a number of options as to who should perform the role of independent monitor, including a parliamentary committee; quasi autonomous unit within the Attorney General's Department; Ombudsman; Australian Archives; AAT; Privacy Commissioner; and Chief Government Information Officer). The Commission believes, however, that given the nature of Parliamentary Committees, it is unlikely that a committee would be able to provide the constant review that is necessary and envisioned by the Review. *See id.*

359. *See* U.S. Dep't of Justice & U.S. General Services Administration, *Your Right To Federal Records: Questions and Answers on the Freedom of Information*

dition, both Canada[360] and Australia[361] charge an additional application fee for requests. On top of these fees, Australia levies a charge
for review of adverse decisions.[362] Current review of the fee system
in Australia has resulted in a recommendation that the fees remain
the same.[363] In Canada, however, pressure continues to decrease
costs, or at least prevent further increases, because of the deterrent
effect of the fees.[364] A report of the costs associated with the AIA recently suggested other opportunities to reduce the Act's administrative costs, including the reduction of exemptions available, improvement in records management, and the streamlining of internal
review and approval procedures.[365] All of these alternatives displace

---

Act, Dec. 1996, 3 [hereinafter *Federal Records*] (detailing the cost of obtaining
information for United States citizens who are non-commercial requestors). In the
United States, pursuant to the Freedom of Information Reform Act of 1986, Government agencies assess fees based upon the type of requestor. *See generally*
FOIA GUIDE, *supra* note 5, at 391 (stating "[a]s amended by the Freedom of Information Reform Act of 1986, the FOIA provides for three levels of fees that may
be assessed in response to FOIA requests according to categories of FOIA requestors"). The Freedom of Information Reform Act of 1986 also placed the Office of
Management and Budget (OMB) in charge of establishing a uniform fee schedule
and guidelines for individual government agencies as to the fees that requestors are
required to pay. *See id.* at 390. Accordingly, individuals should consult the OMB
Fee Guidelines, 52 Fed. Reg. 10,011 (1987). In general, in the United States,
search fees usually range from ten to thirty dollars per hour. *See Federal Records,*
supra, at 3. The charge for copying may be as low as ten cents per page, but could
be higher depending on the agency. *See id.* The first 100 copies are free and two
hours of search are free. *See id.*; 10 YEARS, *supra* note 336, at 21 (stating that in
Canada, "Everyone pays a five dollar application fee which pays for hours of
search time. Thereafter charges for searches, photocopies or computer time can be
applied."); ISSUES PAPER, *supra* note 7, § 9.2 (charging Australians thirty dollars
for an initial application fee and for photocopying and search time with rates
varying by agency).

360. *See* NOTES, *supra* note 333, at 4 (noting that Canada imposes a five dollar
fee per request).

361. *See* ISSUES PAPER, *supra* note 7, § 9.2 (noting that an initial request in
Australia costs thirty dollars).

362. *See id.* (noting that Australia charges forty dollars for an internal review
application).

363. *See generally*, DISCUSSION PAPER, *supra* note 341, at 90 (rejecting the need
to change the fee system and rephrasing the issue in terms of the need to reduce
the costs of providing information, offering improved technology as the means).

364. *See* NOTES, *supra* note 333, at 4 (arguing that no reform is better than any
increase in rates).

365. *See* TREASURY BD. OF CAN., MANAGING BETTER: REVIEW OF THE COSTS
ASSOCIATED WITH THE ADMINISTRATION OF THE ATIP LEGISLATION [hereinafter
MANAGING BETTER] (advocating that agencies actively work to make information

the costs from requesters.[366] Blair must decide who should bear the costs—the requester, the taxpayer, or the government.[367]

C. REVIEW MECHANISMS

If a United States government agency denies a request, an individual need only send a letter to that agency requesting a review.[368] If the agency denies the appeal, the matter can be taken to a federal court for *de novo* review.[369] United States courts have the power to review documents, compel agency disclosure, and/or affirm the agency's withholding of information.[370]

Unlike the United States, there is no internal departmental review in Canada.[371] Upon denial of a request the individual appeals to an independent Parliamentary Ombudsman called the Information Commissioner.[372] The Commissioner has the power to investigate

---

available to the public domain, introduce "integrity controls" to ensure that information is accurately reported, and change how exemptions are applied). Specifically, it is argued that agencies use an "injury test" to determine if exemptions apply, in order to provide for a more efficient and inherently less confrontational review process. *See id.* at 23.

366. *See id.* at 20 (noting that these reforms could reduce costs to the government without imposing higher fees on requestors).

367. *Compare* NOTES, *supra* note 333 (arguing that requestors should not be required to pay higher fees because costs to the government are not high, but in fact are exaggerated by opponents of open government) *with* MANAGING BETTER, *supra* note 365 (stating that both requestors and the government alike could benefit from reduced costs if government procedures were streamlined).

368. *See Federal Records*, *supra* note 359, at 5 (directing persons on how to appeal a FOIA decision).

369. *See id.* ("You can file a FOIA lawsuit in the U.S. District Court where you live, where you have your principal place of business, where the documents are kept, or in the District of Columbia.").

370. *See* 5 U.S.C. § 552 (a)(4)(B) (1994) ("The court shall determine the matter *de novo*, and may examine the contents of such agency records in camera . . .").

371. *See* ANNUAL REPORT 1995-96, *supra* note 333, at 1.

372. *See id.* (detailing the review process and defining the commissioner as an ombudsman who is "independent of the government"); INFO. COMM'R OF CAN., ANNUAL REPORT INFORMATION COMMISSIONER 1990-91, (1991) at 36 [hereinafter ANNUAL REPORT 1990-91] (detailing the two levels of independent review under the Access to Information Act).

The first level gives applicants the opportunity to ask the Information Commissioner to investigate their complaints that the government has not responded properly to their applications . . . . The second level provides the ground rules for asking the Federal Court to review two types of decisions: government proposals to disclose third-party information, and—once the Commissioner has completed his investigation—com-

complaints, including the power to compell the review of documents. He may not, however, order an agency to disclose documents.[373] Thus, he must rely on persuasion to solve disputes.[374] If the Commissioner believes that the government has wrongly denied access or the appeal involves disclosure of third party information, he may ask the Federal Court to review the denial.[375] While the Canadian Ombudsman approach is criticized for its lack of power, the virtues of the approach are its informal, non-adversarial style, and expertise in freedom of information.[376]

Australia currently has all four approaches with some modifications. Initial review in Australia, like in the United States, is internally handled by the agency that denied the documents.[377] Unlike the United States, however, the individual must pay forty dollars for the review.[378] This form of review is considered the quickest and cheap-

---

plaints about improper denial of access. *Id.*

373. *See* ANNUAL REPORT 1995-96, *supra* note 333, at 1 ("Since he is an ombudsman, the commissioner may not . . . order a complaint resolved in a particular way."); CRITICAL REVIEW, *supra* note 355, at 42 ("The federal commissioner has very strong investigative authority, but makes recommendations as to how to resolve differences over refusals of access."); 10 YEARS, *supra* note 336, at 11 (stating that the Commissioner's order powers "are not part of his repertoire . . . [w]hile he is able to compel public servants to hand over information for review, he can only make recommendations, not enforce decisions as to whether the information should be released").

374. *See* ANNUAL REPORT 1995-96, *supra* note 333, at 1.

375. *See id.* (noting that the Commissioner asks "for a federal court review only if he believes an individual has been improperly denied access"). Of the 1,530 complaints reported to the Information Commissioner for the FY 1995-96, 13 were filed in Federal Court. *See id.*

376. *See generally* 10 YEARS, *supra* note 336, at 10-12 (detailing the virtues and disadvantages of Canada's Information Commissioner). From time to time in the U.S., informal proposals have been made for an ombudsman based administrative structure, along with calls for an independent administrative tribunal model. *See generally* Mark H. Grunewald, *Freedom of Information Act Dispute Resolution*, 40 ADMIN. L. REV. 1, n.5 (1988) (noting that the "most detailed proposal was made by Robert L. Saloschin, former Director of the Office of Information Law and Policy, Dep't of Justice" and providing additional examples of the use of an information ombudsman).

377. *See generally* ISSUES PAPER, *supra* note 7, at 8.1 (detailing the existing review mechanisms in Australia).

378. *Compare id.*, § 8.3 (stating that Australia charges forty dollars), *with* Federal Records, *supra* note 359, at 5 (stating that a fee is not required for internal review).

est, and the ALRC has recommended it remain the same.[379] If the individual is still dissatisfied, he can either opt for a free Ombudsman review or appeal to the Administrative Appeals Tribunal (AAT) at a cost of three hundred dollars.[380] Australia's Ombudsman is similar to Canada's in that he can compel documents, but cannot overturn an agency decision. Unlike Canada's Ombudsman, however, he has discretion to investigate a matter and may refer the appeal directly to the AAT.[381] Many believe Australia's Ombudsman serves a valuable function in investigating government agencies; the ALRC recommends his role remain the same.[382] Any further powers, such as the ability to overturn agency decisions, may hinder the effectiveness of his investigatory powers.[383] According to the ALRC, another effective review mechanism in Australia is the Administrative Appeals Tribunal (AAT).[384] The AAT has jurisdiction for review under the FOI act and the Administrative Appeals Tribunal Act 1975.[385] Thus, the AAT handles more than just FOI appeals and is considered a general tribunal.[386] The AAT has the power to affirm, vary, or set aside an agency decision.[387] Additionally, it can review all agency documents, but only at the tribunal hearing, not during the two preliminary conferences that are required by law.[388] Many have criticized this aspect of the AAT, and the ALRC has recommended that

---

379. *See* DISCUSSION PAPER, *supra* note 341, at 98 (stating that a majority of submissions favor internal review as the first stage).

380. *See id.* at 98-101 (providing a thorough discussion of the review stages in Australia under the Freedom of Information Act).

381. *See id.* (describing the discretionary powers of the Ombudsman).

382. *See id.* at 101 (proposing that the Ombudsman's role remain unchanged).

383. *See* DISCUSSION PAPER, *supra* note 341, at 100 (stating that "[i]t is apparent from submissions that the Ombudsman is performing a valuable function in investigating agenc[ies] . . . and determinative review powers" may significantly affect the existing valuable role). The ALRC also bases its decision on the fact that the Ombudsman investigates a wide range of matters relating to an agency's handling of a FOI application, not just denied requests. *See id.*

384. *See id.* (reporting on the AAT).

385. *See id.*; *see also* Administrative Appeals Tribunal Amendment Act, 1993 [hereinafter AAT Amdnts] (amending the AAT 1975).

386. *See* ISSUES PAPER, *supra* note 7, at 101 (weighing the advantages of a general tribunal of diverse membership, flexibility to suit individual cases, and reduced costs versus the disadvantages of the lack of specialized FOI expertise and lack of consistency in decisions).

387. *See id.* (explaining that ATT must give reasons for its decisions as well).

388. *See* DISCUSSION PAPER, *supra* note 341, at 106 (detailing the power of the AAT to inspect documents).

the AAT be granted the power to review documents during all stages of appeal.[389] Additionally, many have criticized the AAT's lack of power over conclusive certificates.[390] Conclusive certificates are similar to Britain's "public interest certificates" because they provide blanket protection to certain categories of information deemed sensitive by ministers.[391] The AAT cannot review a decision to grant a conclusive certificate, but it can determine whether reasonable grounds existed for the issuance of such a certificate.[392] The ALRC considered whether certificates were legitimate and the role that the AAT should play in their review. The ALRC decided that the certificates are necessary and that the AAT may not revoke certificates, but it can continue to assess whether ministers had reasonable grounds for the certificate.[393] Additionally, if the AAT believes that a certificate should be revoked and the minister disagrees, the minister must advise Parliament by tabling a notice and then reading it in his or her House.[394] According to the ALRC, this "imposes a considerable and sufficient discipline on Ministers."[395] Overall, the AAT is considered to be flexible, inexpensive, faster, and less formal than other approaches; yet, many say that the mechanism is too formal and adversarial.[396] Australians may also appeal to the Federal Courts if their appeal is based on a "question of law."[397] This type of review is rare, and falls under the Administrative Decisions (Judicial Review) Act 1977 rather than the FOI Act.[398] Blair must decide which mecha-

---

389. *See id.* (requesting that section 64 of the Act be changed because "the Review agrees that the AAT should be able to inspect the documents in dispute at any stage"). This reform would allow the AAT to form its own view as to the substance of the claims for exemption at a very early point in the proceedings. *See id.*

390. *See* ISSUES PAPER, *supra* note 7, at 45 (asking "whether the provisions for conclusive certificates are necessary and whether the AAT should be given power to make determinative decisions?").

391. *See id.* (specifying that the Minister responsible for an agency has discretion to grant a conclusive certificate for certain documents).

392. *See id.* (indicating the current way the AAT handles certificates).

393. *See* DISCUSSION PAPER, *supra* note 341, at 55 (stating that there is a legitimate role for the certificates and noting that the expiration of the certificates after two years is sufficient).

394. *See id.* (recommending this procedure as an additional safeguard).

395. *Id.*

396. *See id.* at 101-05 (providing an analysis of AAT review).

397. *Id.* at 101.

398. *See* ISSUES PAPER, *supra* note 7, at 97-98 (listing it as one of four possible review mechanisms but not elaborating on it at length because it is not often used).

nisms will be accepted by UK's Parliament and which will provide the most access to government information.

D. EXEMPTIONS

As Canada's Information Commissioner stated in his 1993-1994 Annual Report: "Exemptions are difficult creatures to draft [and] [i]t is even more difficult to obtain a consensus on what they should be."[399] The United States Congress agreed upon nine FOIA exemptions,[400] while Canada's Parliament affirmed fourteen[401] and Australia's Parliament nineteen.[402] Of the three countries, Australia's exemptions have received the most general criticism for being too extensive and broad and containing complex statutory language.[403]

---

399. ANNUAL REPORT 1993-94, *supra* note 348, at 16.

400. *See* 5 U.S.C. § 552(b) (1994) (containing nine exemptions which protect classified national defense and foreign relations information, internal agency rules and practices, information prohibited from disclosure by another law, trade secrets and confidential business information, inter-agency or intra-agency communications protected by legal privileges, information covering personal privacy, information compiled for law enforcement purposes, information relating to the supervision of financial institutions and geological information).

401. *See* AIA, *supra* note 334, §§ 13-27 (providing 14 exemptions). These exemptions are:

> (13) information obtained in confidence; (14) federal provincial affairs; (15) international affairs and defense; (16) law enforcement and investigations; (17) safety of individuals; (18) economic interests of Canada; (19) personal information; (20) third party information; (21) Advice; (22) testing, audits (23) solicitor-client privilege; (24) statutory prohibitions; (25) severability; (26) if information is to be published; (27) notice to third parties.

Id.

402. *See* FOI, *supra* note 349, §§ 33-47A (providing 19 exemptions). The exemptions are:

> (33) national security, defence or international relations; (33A) relations with states; (34) cabinet documents; (36) internal working documents; (36A) periods for which certificates remain in force; (37) law enforcement and public safety; (38) secrecy provisions of enactment's apply; (39) documents affecting financial or property interests of the Commonwealth (40) certain operations of agencies; (41) personal privacy; (42) legal professional privilege; (43A) documents relating to business affairs; (43A) documents relating to research; (44) national economy; (45) material obtained in confidence; (46) disclosure of which would be in contempt of court or Parliament; (47) documents arising out of companies and securities legislation; (47A) electoral rolls and decisions.

Id.

403. *See* ISSUES PAPER, *supra* note 7, at 34 (stating that the provisions "span sixteen pages of the Act" and are "worded in such a way that they are neither accessible nor intelligible to most people").

The ALRC has recommended that the Australian Parliament simplify the language so that requesters and officials can better understand and apply the statute.[404]

An area of exemption shared by all three countries and highlighted in Britain's debates is the protection of business information provided by third parties.[405] Such an exemption is necessary in order to protect businesses from unfair business competition.[406] Exemption four[407] of the United States FOIA protects trade secrets and other confidential business information; however, in order to further protect business contractors, the United States Congress passed a new statute that contains provisions prohibiting agencies from releasing certain information.[408] Thus, this information now falls under the protection of Exemption three of the FOIA as well as Exemption four.[409]

In Australia, section forty-three protects business affairs. It is comprised of two sections, one protecting trade secrets and the other protecting information with a potentially diminishing commercial value.[410] The ALRC has recently recommended that the two exemptions comprising section forty-three be repealed and combined.[411]

---

404. *See* DISCUSSION PAPER, *supra* note 341, at 11 (agreeing that the language and number of exemptions should be simplified).

405. *See* Fisher Arguments, *supra* note 1, at 585 (noting the importance of protecting commercial information).

406. *See* Ferris, *supra* note 352, at 44 (stating that "[t]he FOIA is not supposed to release commercial secrets to the world").

407. *See* 5 U.S.C. § 552(b)(4) (1994) (protecting "trade secrets and commercial or financial material obtained from a person and privileged or confidential").

408. *See New Statute Protects Contractor Proposals*, FOIA UPDATE (DOJ/Office of Information and Privacy, D.C.), Winter 1997, at 2 (explaining that new provisions contained in the National Defense Authorization Act for Fiscal Year 1997, Pub. L. No. 104-210, 821, 110 Stat. 2422 provide even more protection for bid contractors under the FOIA).

409. *See* 5 U.S.C. § 552 (b) (3) (1994).

> (3) specifically exempted from disclosure by statute (other than section 552b of this title), provided that such statute (A) requires that the matters be withheld from the public in such a manner as to leave no discretion on the issue, or (B) establishes particular criteria for withholding or refers to particular types of matters.

Id.

410. *See* FOI, *supra* note 349, § 43 (protecting trade secrets, information with a commercial value that could be destroyed or diminished, and certain information the disclosure of which would reasonably affect a person).

411. *See* DISCUSSION PAPER, *supra* note 341, at 75 (stating that "[i]n accordance with the desire to rationalise the exemption provisions, the Review proposes that

Use of the access statue to monitor competitors is more prevalent in Canada, even though the Act provides mandatory rather than discretionary exemptions for trade secrets and commercial, scientific, and technical information submitted in confidence to a government agency.[412] According to Canada's Information Commissioner, many of the Act's delay problems concern requests for business information.[413] The Commissioner argues that the law should make details of government contracts public because that would "put more accountability in the government contracting process."[414]

Britain is also debating the protection of Cabinet confidences, an area of information exempted from the Freedom of Information Acts in the United States, Canada, and Australia. In the United States, Exemption five[415] is used to "prevent injury to the quality of agency decisions" by providing a "discretionary deliberative process privilege."[416] Generally, the exemption is used to encourage open discussions on policy matters between high level and low level governmental officials, protect against the disclosure of pre-decisional policies, and protect against the disclosure of officials' reasons for policies that were not, in fact, the reasons upon which final decisions were made.[417] Accordingly, post-decisional documents do not fall within Exemption five protection. Unlike the United States, Australia adopted a mandatory, broader, class-based exemption that covers specific types of Cabinet documents.[418] "Once a document is deter-

---

§ 43(1)(a) and (b) be repealed").

412. *See* Tom Riley, *U.S. Canadian Information Acts Differ*, J. OF COM., Aug. 30, 1985 (discussing how Canada's Information Act provides mandatory exemptions for trade secrets, as well as commercial, scientific, and technical information submitted to the government). "Mandatory" means that if the information falls within the exemption, it cannot be released; whereas, if the exemption is "discretionary", it is up to the agency to decide if it can be released although it satisfies an exemption. *See generally* Chrysler Corp. v. Brown, 441 U.S. 281, 293 (1979).

413. *See* ANNUAL REPORT 1993-94, *supra* note 348, at 24 (attributing delays to business requests).

414. *See id.* As of October 5, 1997, the Commissioner's reforms had not been adopted. *See id.*

415. *See* 5 U.S.C. § 552(b)(5) (1994) (exempting "inter-agency or intra-agency memorandums or letters which would not be available by law to a party other than an agency in litigation with the agency").

416. *See* NLRB v. Sears, Roebuck & Co., 421 U.S. 132, 151 (1975).

417. *See* FOIA GUIDE, *supra* note 5, at 180 (pointing to the "three policy purposes consistently . . . held to constitute the basis for this privilege").

418. *See* FOI, *supra* note 349, § 34; *see also* THE INFO. COMM'R OF CAN., THE

mined to be of the class described, it is exempt."[419] Much like under United States Exemption Five, material must be pre-decisional to qualify for exemption.[420]

Compared to the United States and Australia, Canada's approach to cabinet confidences is "very much behind the times."[421] As a result, the act continues to be viewed as a "secrecy law camouflaged in the language of openness."[422] Under the AIA, cabinet confidences that have been in existence for less than twenty years are excluded from coverage of the entire Act.[423] A decade ago, the Standing Committee on Justice and Solicitor General agreed that it was time to replace the exclusion with an exemption bringing cabinet confidences within the purview of the AIA.[424] Experiences at the provin-

---

ACCESS TO INFORMATION ACT AND CABINET CONFIDENCES: A DISCUSSION OF NEW APPROACHES 16 (1996) [hereinafter INFORMATION COMMISSIONER] (detailing Australia's Cabinet Confidence Exemption as a model for Canada). Specifically, the Report summarizes Australia's exemption 34:

> The Australian Freedom of Information Act provides that each of the following documents is an exempt document: a document brought into existence for the purpose of submission to the Cabinet which has been, or is proposed by a minister to be submitted to Cabinet; an official record of Cabinet; a copy or an extract from a document covered above; and a document, the discussion of which would involve the disclosure of many deliberation or decision of the Cabinet, other than a document by which a decision of the Cabinet was officially disclosed.

Id.

419. *See* INFORMATION COMMISSIONER, *supra* note 418, at 16.

420. *See id.*

421. *See id.* at 1.

422. *Id.* at 3.

423. *See id.* at 2 (detailing the information that is excluded under the Act). Subsection 69(1) of Canada's AIA provides that the Act does not apply to confidences of the Queen's Privy Council for Canada, including:

> (a) memoranda the purpose of which is to present proposals or recommendation to Council; (b) discussion papers the purpose of which is to present background explanations, analyses of problems or policy options to Council for consideration by Council in making decisions; (c) agenda of Council or records recording deliberations or decisions of Council; (d) records used for or reflecting communications or discussions between ministers of the Crown on matters relating to the making of government decisions or the formulation of government policy; (e) records the purpose of which is to brief ministers of the Crown in relation to matters that are brought before, or are proposed to be brought before, Council or that are the subject of communications or discussions referred to in paragraph (d); (f) draft legislation; and (g) records that contain information about the contents of any record within a class of records referred to in paragraphs (a) to (f).

Id. at 1-2.

424. *See* INFORMATION COMMISSIONER, *supra* note 418, at 40 (referring to the

cial level in Canada should support the calls for reform at the federal level, since mandatory exceptions for Cabinet confidences have been enacted provincially and have "not had any significant impact on the effectiveness of the collective decision-making of these Cabinets."[425] Although the United States provisions provide the greatest degree of access, they may not be appropriate in Britain, given its style of government.

IV. RECOMMENDATIONS

In providing recommendations to Blair on a freedom of information statute, it is imperative to remember the pervasive governmental secrecy that exists in Britain and the particular constitutional framework within which Blair must work.[426] Blair is fighting tradition by shifting access to information from the government to the people. As expressed throughout the Parliamentary debates, many are concerned that the tenets of Britain's Parliamentary democracy will be injured by an access statute.[427] Experiences in Canada and Australia dispel such notions, but in view of these concerns it will be necessary for Blair to include a preamble similar to that recommended by the ALRC.[428] This preamble will demonstrate to the government, Parliament, and the people that Britain is committed to providing its citizens with statutory rights of access to information while maintaining important British concepts like Ministerial Accountability, Crown Privilege, and Parliamentary Democracy. All provisions following this preamble should build upon this concept. A sample of the type of provisions that Blair's statute should contain are as follows.

Report entitled *Open and Shut: Enhancing the Right to Know and the Right to Privacy).*

425. *Id.* at 26.

426. *See supra* Part I.A (discussing Britain's unwritten constitution, Westminister style of government, and the Government's adherence to the doctrines of Ministerial Accountability and Crown Privilege).

427. *See supra* notes 33, 129, 282 (detailing Prime Minister Margaret Thatcher's and other MPs views that a freedom of information act would threaten Ministerial Accountability and Crown Privilege).

428. *See supra* note 344 and accompanying text (providing the ALRC's recommendation that Australia's FOI Act include a preamble).

A. FORMS OF ACCESS

In the interest of simplicity and comprehensibility, Blair should employ the term "records" rather than "information." "Records" should be defined broadly, as in the United States, to include various types of media and up-to-date technology.[429] By removing the term "information," it will be clear to British ministers that persons are entitled to actual physical documents rather than prepared summaries. Including a broad form of access will also prevent ministers from communicating in certain formats to avoid the law.[430]

B. FEES AND COSTS

In order to prevent the use of costs as a deterrent to access, as is currently the case under the Code, no fees should be charged for the request for information.[431] Although Canada and Australia believe that such fees are necessary,[432] the United States experience proves otherwise.[433] Similar to all three countries, fees should be charged for search and retrieval, inspection and photocopying, and decision-making, subject to fee waivers. An independent administrative monitor should be created to ensure the most efficient handling of requests.[434] The independent monitor should not be involved in the

---

429. *See* Cabinet Office (OPS) Press Office, *Clark Outlines Vision For Electronic Government*, June 18, 1997, (visited July 18, 1994) <http://www.open.gov.uk/coi/cab/34/97.html> (announcing the Government's commitment to "revitalise government by harnessing new technology to provide, simpler, efficient and responsive services"). David Clark, the Chancellor of the Duchy of Lancaster, announced that "clever use of Information Technology will reduce the traditional boundaries between government departments . . . Technology will provide a simple and efficient link to any Government Agency or function." *Id*. Thus, the implementation of a Freedom of Information Act along the lines of the U.S. seems perfectly reasonable.

430. *See supra* note 188 (explaining that MPs threaten to conduct all business over the telephone in order to avoid the reach of an access statute).

431. *See supra* note 311 (discussing the fact that high fees charged under the Code of Practice on Access to Government Office are a deterrent to the use of the Code).

432. *See* DISCUSSION PAPER, *supra* note 341, at 83-90; *see also* 10 YEARS, *supra* note 336, at 21.

433. *See supra* note 359 (explaining the United States' fee system which does not charge an initial application fee).

434. *See supra* note 358 (discussing the ALRC's recommendation that an independent person oversee the administration of its FOI Act).

appellate review process; rather, its role should be limited to ensuring that the proper technology is in place at all agencies so that information can be provided in its cheapest form. Additionally, this independent monitor should tour agencies and examine their administrative procedures and report to Parliament.[435] Blair might consider forming a freedom of information Parliamentary committee to work with the independent monitor to ensure that records are not destroyed and that agencies are complying with the letter and spirit of the law.[436] Moreover, this proposal would complement the principle of Ministerial Accountability, since ministers would be responsible to Parliament for their agencies' administrative procedures.

C. REVIEW MECHANISMS

As suggested by Fisher and employed in the United States, Australia, and the United Kingdom, internal review should be the first stage of review and a prerequisite to all other stages.[437] Internal review is inexpensive and quick, and it allows the government to review its policies.[438] The second stage should be an investigation by an independent Parliamentary Ombudsman. Unlike the Ombudsman used in Britain under the Code, and in Canada, this Ombudsman should have determinative powers and the power to compel disclosure of records. Experience at the local level shows that an Ombudsman with mere recommendatory powers will be ignored.[439] The Ombudsman should not be the current Parliamentary Commissioner for Administration because he is in charge of too many measures. An official Information Commissioner should be created whose role is limited to freedom of information.[440] Finally, and importantly, the

---

435. *See supra* note 358 (listing the creation of a Parliamentary Committee to supervise its FOI Act as one of the ALRC's proposals).

436. *See supra* note 250 and accompanying text (explaining that government officials regardless of their party will seek to withhold embarrassing information).

437. *See supra* notes 244, 368 (detailing the internal review mechanism proposed under Fisher's Right to Know Bill and the United States' initial internal departmental review procedure).

438. *See* ISSUES PAPER, *supra* note 7, at 69 (showing effectiveness of Australia's internal review mechanism).

439. *See supra* notes 213-14 and accompanying text (providing recent arguments that Parliament amend the Local Government (Access to Information) Act to include an apellate procedure) .

440. *See supra* note 376. The proposed Information Commissioner's expertise should resemble the level maintained by the Canadian Information Commissioner

last stage of review should take place in the courts. Freedom of information case law will further control the government's proper disclosure of official information. As evidenced in the Ponting trial, the judicial system is willing and ready to take on the role and serve as a further check on the Executive.[441] Judicial intervention should not be considered incompatible with Ministerial Accountability because Ministers will have had the opportunity to plead their cases and respond to Parliament at the lower stages.

D. EXEMPTIONS

In order to avoid confusion, the statutory language of the exemptions should be clear.[442] The number of exemptions should be kept to a minimum in order to reinforce that this is an access law—not a secrecy law. In order to win support for his measure, Blair should not adopt the business recommendations proposed in Canada; rather, he should protect businesses and at the same time provide limited access to certain types of information as in the United States. With respect to cabinet documents, Blair should follow the lead of Australia and make the exemption mandatory. Such a provision will allow the candor of policy discussion to remain.

One final policy issue that must be addressed is whether the Official Secrets Act ought to be repealed.[443] Such an action is necessary in order to demonstrate that the Government is committed to official openness rather than official secrecy. Because Canada has an Official Secrets Act in place along with its access statute, it can be argued that Britain could retain its statute as well.[444] If that is the case, the Official Secrets Act would have to be amended allowing officials to disclose certain information.[445] As a final recommendation, the name of the act should be as Fisher suggested, "The Right to Know." This

---

of Canada.

441. *See* Maurice Frankel, *Britain's Secret Society*, GUARDIAN, Jan. 26, 1993, at 18 (reiterating that "judges are becoming increasingly critical of official secrecy").

442. *See supra* notes 403-04 (explaining the criticism that Australia's FOI Act receives for its numerous exemptions and difficult language).

443. *See supra* note 22 (discussing the pivotal role of the Official Secrets Act in maintaing Britain's governmental secrecy).

444. *See supra* note 338 (noting Canada's Official Secrets Act).

445. *See id.* If Britain were to amend its Official Secrets Act it should use Canada's Official Secrets Act as a model, limiting it solely to espionage offense provisions. *See id.*

name helps inculcate the attitudes of openness that are so difficult to legislate.[446]

CONCLUSION

Governments have become the custodians of information which can profoundly affect the lives of individual citizens.[447] That is why "access to government information is essential by right, not by the grace and favor of Government officials."[448] History has shown in Britain that voluntary openness does not provide the necessary disclosure of information which often times leads to tragedies. A British "Right to Know Act" will provide greater access, make government more accountable, and enhance Britain's parliamentary democracy.

---

446. *See supra* notes 286-88 and accompanying text (providing MPs arguments that attitudes towards openness must occur naturally since mandating openess could lead to greater secrecy).

447. *See* Annual Report 1995-96, *supra* note 333, at 3 (justifying freedom of information and in particular statutory rights of access).

448. *Id.*

Name Index